THE JOHN HARVARD LIBRARY

The John Harvard Library, founded in 1959, publishes essential American writings, including novels, poetry, memoirs, criticism, and works of social and political history, representing all periods, from the beginning of settlement in America to the twenty-first century. The purpose of The John Harvard Library is to make these works available to scholars and general readers in affordable, authoritative editions.

JOHN
HARVARD
LIBRARY

THE TRIBUNAL

RESPONSES TO JOHN BROWN AND
THE HARPERS FERRY RAID

EDITED BY JOHN STAUFFER AND ZOE TRODD

JOHN
HARVARD
LIBRARY

THE BELKNAP PRESS OF HARVARD UNIVERSITY PRESS

Cambridge, Massachusetts, and London, England   2012

Library of Congress Cataloging-in-Publication Data

The tribunal : responses to John Brown and the Harpers Ferry Raid /
edited by John Stauffer and Zoe Trodd.
p.   cm.—(The John Harvard Library)
Includes bibliographical references and index.
ISBN 978-0-674-04885-0 (alk. paper)
1. Harpers Ferry (W. Va.)—History—John Brown's Raid, 1859.
2. Harpers Ferry (W. Va.)—History—John Brown's Raid, 1859—Sources.
3. Brown, John, 1800–1859.   I. Stauffer, John, 1965–   II. Trodd, Zoe.
E451.T75 2012
973.7'116—dc23   2012016729

I leave it to an impartial tribunal to decide whether the world has been the worse or the better of my living and dying in it.

—JOHN BROWN, November 28, 1859

Contents

PART II: NORTHERN RESPONSES

PART III: SOUTHERN RESPONSES

PART IV: INTERNATIONAL RESPONSES

PART V: CIVIL WAR AND U.S. POSTWAR RESPONSES

Introduction: The Meaning and Significance of John Brown

O N OCTOBER 16, 1859, John Brown launched an attack against the institution of slavery. With a band of five black men and sixteen whites he captured the federal arsenal at Harpers Ferry, about 60 miles northwest of Washington, D.C. The band was overpowered early in the morning on October 18, and Brown was tried for murder, treason, and conspiring to incite a slave insurrection.

In a letter of November 28, written in prison four days before his execution on December 2, Brown pondered the other "tribunal" that would judge him. "The great bulk of mankind estimate each other's actions *and motives* by the measure of success or *otherwise* that attends them through life," he noted. "I leave it to an impartial tribunal to decide whether the world has been the *worse* or the better of my *living* and *dying* in it." Two days later, Brown returned in his last family prison letter to the theme of posterity and made one last effort to shape his own image for the "tribunal," telling his readers to feel no shame on his behalf, to receive him as a martyr, and to recognize his example and teach it to their children. By December 2, he was dead.[1]

The retrospective "tribunal" that he imagined in prison has been far from "impartial." Immediately after his raid and death, Brown became one of the most contentious figures in American culture, a national symbol embodying contradictions: a Christ-like hero and satanic demon, a martyr and madman, a meteor of peace and of war. In the 150 years since his raid, Americans have continued to view Brown's legacy, and his relation to American values, with a deep sense of ambivalence. For some he has been the nation's archetypal freedom fighter; for most, a dangerous fanatic, to be relegated to the historical dustbin with a corps of other easily forgotten quixotic madmen.

Renewed interest in John Brown spiked in the wake of 9/11. More than at any other period since the Civil War, he has become an exemplary figure representing both the American commitment to freedom and the dangers posed to that commitment by religiously inspired terrorism. On the 150th anniversary of Brown's execution, the journalist and Brown biographer Tony Horwitz called Harpers Ferry "the 9/11 of 1859" and Brown "the most successful terrorist in American history." This was, of course, a loaded analogy. Horwitz did not mean to demonize Brown; instead he sought to complicate a contemporary political discourse in which terror was treated as the exclusive instrument of America's enemies. If the analogy was historically a bit misleading—few contemporaries called Brown a "terrorist" ("fanatic" being the more favored term of abuse)—it nevertheless demonstrated the extent to which his legacy continues to unsettle Americans.[2]

Scholars have not been exempt from these anxieties. In 1957 Truman Nelson shrewdly summarized the historical response to Brown. A high school dropout and factory worker, Nelson became an unlikely student of F. O. Matthiessen, the Harvard professor of English, who fueled his interest in "revolutionary consciousness." He found in Brown "the finest example of pure revolutionary morality produced in this country, perhaps in any country." But this morality deeply troubled professional historians, Nelson concluded: "John Brown is the stone in the historian's shoe. They cannot ignore him, but they try to choke him off in deforming parentheses."[3]

In certain respects Nelson's assessment continues to resonate among scholars for whom dispassionate scholarship remains an ideal.[4] Given Brown's divisiveness in American culture, it is immensely difficult for them to be dispassionate about him, and other than in biographies, they continue to dismiss or sideline him. In most surveys of American history, Brown still receives a paragraph—"deforming parentheses" within the broader historical narrative.[5]

In this volume, we bring Brown out from those parentheses by focusing on his writings and the wide-ranging responses to his raid in the United States and abroad. Having examined thousands of primary sources, we selected those we felt were representative or emblematic; and we structured the sources so that readers will gain access to Brown and the Harpers Ferry raid from the inside out, beginning with Brown's own words and then moving, as if in a helix, to Northern, Southern, and international responses to his raid, then to Brown's legacy during the Civil War, Reconstruction, and post-Reconstruction eras. The book ends exactly thirty years after his raid, in 1889, when he becomes a marginalized figure in American culture, embraced only by blacks and radical Northern whites. The 1890s also marked the beginning of a new generation of Progressive-era Northerners (including Eugene Debs), Southerners (including Thomas Dixon), and African Americans (including W. E. B. Du Bois), who began their own set of responses to Brown on behalf of organized labor, legalized segregation, and antilynching. The result is a book that views Brown's raid from multiple vantage points, a comparative history of one event.

This is the first book to distinguish between Northern and Southern responses to Brown's raid, and the first to gather the international responses. These foreign responses came chiefly from the British Isles, Canada, and western Europe, which our selection reflects, although we also include responses from Poland, Australia, and Haiti. What is significant is that foreign observers responded to Brown's raid far more sympathetically and consistently than did Americans. They often saw Brown as a soldier in the war on barbarism and his execution as a threat to the "civilizing process," including the abolition of serfdom in central Europe and Russia and emancipation in Brazil and Cuba.[6]

By selecting and arranging documents from these multiple vantage points, we hope to highlight the degree to which Brown drove a wedge into the slavery debates. Before Harpers Ferry, the vast majority of Southerners considered secession "a madman's dream," as the *Richmond Whig* put it. The raid revolutionized the South: six weeks after Brown's capture, secessionist voices had become dominant. The *Richmond Enquirer* described this transformation: "The Harpers Ferry invasion has advanced the cause of disunion more than any other event that has happened since the formation of [our] government."[7]

We offer an answer to the counterfactual that Brown implicitly posed in his prison letter of November 28: has the world been "the worse or the better of my living and dying in it"? Until recently historians have tended to dismiss or deride counterfactual questions. Yet thinking counterfactually foregrounds the importance of contingency and causality, as Brown encouraged his future tribunal to do. And it prevents the tendency to read "history backward" from the "misleading perspective of hindsight," as David Potter put it, which all too easily fuels historical inevitabilities that deny individuals agency. Based on the responses to Harpers Ferry, if Brown had never lived, the Democratic Party would not have split along section lines and Stephen Douglas almost certainly would have been elected president in 1860, deferring secession, civil war, and emancipation for at least another four years—probably more—which may have delayed or disrupted emancipation movements in Brazil, Cuba, and even Russia. This counterfactual claim is necessarily speculative. But it has immense implications, suggesting that Harpers Ferry altered the course of American history and that Brown is a testament to ordinary individuals' potential to transform themselves and their world.[8]

The abolitionists and their sympathizers understood the import of Harpers Ferry. "John Brown swinging upon the gallows will toll the death-knell of slavery," declared the antislavery *New York Independent* a week before Brown's hanging. Wendell Phillips predicted that "John Brown has loosened the roots of the slave system; it only breathes, it does not live, hereafter." After the Civil War, Frederick Douglass concluded that Brown began "the war that ended slavery." The great nineteenth-century German scholar Hermann von Holst, who appreciated history's moral dilemmas, likened the slavery question to a boat flowing downstream toward an apocalyptic waterfall. As politicians tried to steer the boat to an island, Brown gave it "a mighty shove away from the shore." He was the first to be destroyed in the depths below; "but was there now any chance that the leaky skiff should not follow him over the Falls?"[9]

Who Was John Brown?

His was a life filled with material and commercial failures. From a young age, John Brown neither trusted nor liked the material world around him. His autobiographical sketch, written in 1857 and the primary source of knowledge of his first twenty years, emphasizes above all else his trials and tribulations. His first memory was one of being tempted by the things of this world: he "*stole* ... three large Brass Pins." Born at Torrington, Connecticut, on May 9, 1800, he was the son of Owen Brown, a local farmer and tanner, and Ruth Mills. His father was a stern mentor, deeply pious, and a zealous opponent of slavery. By his own reckoning, Brown learned at an early age to rely on his spiritual passions and to have faith in the treasures of heaven.[10]

Eventually, precipitated by a series of tragedies, Brown sought to make his home and country a heaven on earth. In 1805 the Brown family moved to Hudson, Ohio, and three years later his mother died. Brown remembered his feelings of emptiness as "complete and permanent." The War of 1812 introduced firsthand the horrors of slavery. During the war he worked for his father, rounding up cattle and driving them to army outposts. After one cattle drive, according to his autobiographical sketch, he stayed with a landlord and saw him savagely beat a slave, a boy about Brown's age, with an iron shovel for no apparent reason. Sympathizing with the slave, he concluded that masters acted like demigods. Slavery was the embodiment of all evil, which stood in the way of his vision of America as the site and source of Christ's Second Coming.[11]

In 1816 Brown decided to pursue a career in the ministry. He studied at schools in Plainfield, Massachusetts, and Litchfield, Connecticut, where he memorized long Bible passages, a talent for which he became known throughout his life. But a year later he was back in Ohio, flat broke and suffering from inflammation of the eyes. Instead of working for his father he set up his own tannery. He wanted independence from employers and society, but to achieve this he needed to be a leader and a patriarch. In 1820 he married Dianthe Lusk; they would have seven children. She died in 1832 and the following year he married Mary Day, with whom he had thirteen more children.[12]

For a few years Brown became a model citizen. In 1826 he moved his family to New Richmond, Pennsylvania, near the Ohio border, and established himself as a community leader. He ran a successful tannery, served as postmaster for seven years, organized an independent Congressional church, started a neighborhood school, and became the region's librarian, distributing "good moral books and papers" in order "to establish a reading community," as one of his employees, James Foreman, remembered.[13]

His serious troubles began in the 1830s, a transformative decade in America marked by the rise of immediate abolitionism, anti-abolition mob violence, and aggressive proslavery leaders who tried to silence debates over slavery. In 1835, with his tannery faltering, Brown moved Mary and the children back to Hudson, Ohio, to the village of Franklin Mills, and began speculating wildly in land. A new canal that ran from Akron to Franklin Mills was being planned, and Brown thought this would transform his town into a great manufacturing center. He purchased large blocks of land with borrowed money, plotted out imaginary towns and subdivided lots, and envisioned the day when he would be the town patriarch, leading his community in the ways of righteousness. But money became tight, banks refused to pay specie, and creditors began foreclosing. The Panic of 1837 and subsequent depressions were under way. Former friends and associates sued Brown for unpaid loans and unfulfilled contracts. He lost his farm, despite keeping a creditor at bay with a shotgun, and was accused of being dishonest and incompetent. He staved off bankruptcy until 1842 only by borrowing new money in other states to pay off old debts. His material world seemed to bring him almost nothing but debt and business failure.[14]

It is almost impossible to comprehend Brown's crusade against slavery outside the context of his business failures. He never would have become the same militant abolitionist had he not gone bankrupt. With the panic and bankruptcy he became a passionate outsider, totally rejecting the values of his material world and revising his understanding of God and the permanence of sin. He sought to replace his world with God's law and dominion, believed that sin could be abolished immediately, and waited expectantly for the new age. In the wake of the panic, Brown began defining himself as a prophet and millennialist.[15]

The effect of the panic on Brown's abolitionism became apparent in November 1837. Elijah Lovejoy, an abolitionist publisher from Alton, Illinois, tried to protect his fourth press with a gun, his first three presses having been destroyed by proslavery mobs. He was murdered in a shootout. Brown attended a meeting about Lovejoy's recent death, and one observer, Brown's cousin, remembered that at the close of the service, Brown stood up near the back of the room, lifted his right hand, and announced to the assembly: "Here, before God, in the presence of these witnesses, from this time, I consecrate my life to the destruction of slavery." Lovejoy's death certainly upset Brown, but it was not so much the event itself that led to Brown's oath. Rather, Lovejoy's death signified for Brown all that was wrong in the country, in much the same way that the Slave Power later symbolized for Northerners the source of all their fears and anxieties.[16]

In June 1846 Brown moved to Springfield, Massachusetts, to embark on the final capitalist venture of his life. The company he established, Perkins and

Brown, consisted of an empty warehouse that Brown planned to fill with wool from western growers and then sort, grade, and sell to manufacturers. His partner, Simon Perkins, a wealthy businessman from Akron, financed the venture while Brown managed it and brokered the wool. The venture would fail on a grand scale, but at the time Brown had visions of great success.[17]

Four months later Brown's optimism turned to despair. His one-year-old daughter was scalded to death when an older daughter accidentally dropped a pot of boiling water. When he learned of the tragedy, Brown blamed himself and concluded that he had failed as a father and husband: "If I had a right sense of my habitual neglect of my family's Eternal interests, I should probably go crazy," he wrote to his wife. In Springfield things were no better. The recently passed Walker Tariff, which drastically reduced import duties (and appeased Southern planters), coupled with the declaration of war with Mexico by a proslavery president, caused wool prices to plummet. Brown refused to adjust his prices to manufacturers and soon had a warehouse filled with wool he could not sell and a ledger filled with debt he could not erase. He had entered a world of American desperation best understood by African Americans.[18]

More than ever before, Brown sought out blacks for comradeship and community. In late 1847 he met Frederick Douglass, the nation's preeminent black leader, who had recently begun editing the *North Star*. In his paper Douglass described Brown as someone who, "though a white gentleman, is in sympathy a black man, and as deeply interested in our cause, as though his own soul had been pierced with the iron of slavery." A few months later Brown urged blacks to be proud and self-determined and to resist the racism blanketing the country. He wrote an essay for *Ram's Horn*, a militant black abolitionist paper edited by Willis Hodges, a friend of Douglass. In the essay, Brown affects the voice and tone of an urban black Northerner and criticizes his black self and other black Americans for "tamely submitting" to whites instead of "nobly resisting their brutal aggressions" and affirming their black manhood. Hodges, already a friend of Brown, knew him to be white but preserved his assumed black identity by publishing the essay anonymously.[19]

By 1848 Brown wanted to escape the toils of business and white society. He was intrigued with the new black community in the Adirondacks that settlers called North Elba or Timbucto, after the fabled city in West Africa. It had been created by Gerrit Smith, a wealthy white abolitionist and one of the nation's great philanthropists, who in 1846 gave 120,000 acres of land in Franklin and Essex Counties to three thousand poor blacks. Amounting to 40 acres a person, it was enough land in theory for settlers to become independent farmers and voters (New York State required blacks to own $250 in property before they could vote). Like Brown, Smith forged close friendships with blacks, corresponding with them more frequently than any other white man. Essentially he sought to "make myself a colored man," as he put it. In effect he did, according to some blacks. When Willis Hodges heard of Smith's gift, he praised and flattered him by declaring: "Gerrit Smith is a colored man."[20]

Brown decided to settle his family at Timbucto. Though he had never met Smith, he made a pilgrimage to his home in Peterboro, New York, and proposed an offer: "I will take one of your farms myself, clear it up and plant it, and show my colored neighbors how such work should be done." Smith liked Brown and his plan and gave him 244 acres for a dollar an acre on extended credit. In the fall of 1848 Brown went to Timbucto, met with the twenty or thirty families who had settled there, and liked what he saw. "I can think of no place where I think I would sooner go; all things considered than to live with those poor despised Africans, to try and encourage them; and to show them a little so far as I am capable how to manage." He moved some of his family members there in the spring of 1849.[21]

Brown effectively created an interracial utopia at Timbucto. He brought five barrels of pork, five barrels of flour, a wagon, a team of oxen, and a small herd of Devon cattle (no doubt purchased by Smith), all for communal use. In 1849 the well-known Boston author Richard Henry Dana, while hiking in the Adirondacks, chanced upon Timbucto. Though himself an abolitionist, Dana was amazed to find Brown treating blacks as full social equals: he and his family not only ate and lived with the settlers but addressed them "by their surnames, with the prefixes of Mr. and Mrs."[22]

Timbucto greatly influenced Brown's war on slavery. He had read histories of guerrilla warfare, notably of the Haitian revolution and its leader, Toussaint-Louverture, which he treated as a sort of personal guidebook. From them he concluded that mountains were the route to freedom. He wanted Timbucto to serve as the base of operations for what he called a "Subterranean Pass Way," a militant alternative to the Underground Railroad and the seed of his scheme to invade the South and liberate the slaves. The scheme entailed an elaborate network of armed men in the Allegheny Mountains that extended into the Adirondacks and Timbucto for the purpose of raiding slaveholders' property and running fugitives north to Canada. Brown's immediate object was to "destroy the money value of slave property," as he told Douglass: "If we could drive slavery out of one county, it would be a great gain" and would "weaken the system throughout" Virginia. Douglass, though skeptical, thought Brown's plan had "much to commend it." Moreover, they both knew that the South was a "slumbering volcano," as Douglass phrased it. Slavery brought constant resistance and worries over insurrections, thus depriving slaveholders of "the feeling of security." A subterranean passway would only heighten Southern anxieties.[23]

The Kansas-Nebraska Act of 1854 politicized Brown in certain respects. It repealed the Missouri Compromise and opened Northern territories to slavery by applying the doctrine of "popular sovereignty," which called on settlers to vote slavery up or down. Its immediate effect was to turn Kansas into a battleground between proslavery and antislavery emigrants. Brown became, with Douglass and other blacks associated with Timbucto, a founding member of the Radical Abolition Party. The party was aptly named: members embraced immediate and universal abolition, full suffrage for all Americans, the redistribution of land to prevent stark inequalities of wealth, and violent intervention against slavery. They called slavery a state of war and argued that it was the "highest obligation" of the people of the free states to make war on slavery in order to preserve the peace. And they relied on Pentecostal visitations (messages from God) to help them pave the way to their new world.[24]

Brown attended the inaugural convention at Syracuse, New York, in late June 1855. He was on his way to Kansas, having sought the advice of his Timbucto neighbors, along with Smith and Douglass. Three of Brown's sons were already in Kansas, and at the convention Smith read two letters from Brown's sons, one of which described "thousands of the meanest and most desperate [proslavery] men, armed to the teeth with Revolvers, Bowie Knives, Rifles & Cannon." Then Brown gave a speech and quoted Hebrews 22, reminding his listeners that "without the shedding of blood there is no remission of sin." He appealed for money and guns to take with him to Kansas, and his speech electrified his audience. Most members agreed that armed resistance was the only course left to the friends of freedom in Kansas, prompting Douglass to ask for contributions, which yielded Brown about $60 and a few guns.[25]

In Kansas things were worse than Brown's sons had described in their letters. It was a state of civil war between proslavery "Border Ruffians" and antislavery emigrants, many from New England. President Franklin Pierce supported the proslavery legislature and proclaimed its opponents treasonable, thus sanctioning proslavery violence. One antislavery leader was hacked to death with hatchets and knives. On May 21, 1856, 750 Border Ruffians attacked the town of Lawrence, an antislavery stronghold. They destroyed the newspapers, burned and looted homes, and blew up the Free State Hotel. The invaders wore red flannel shirts for uniforms, and some of them carried flags or banners proclaiming "THE SUPREMACY OF THE WHITE RACE" and "ALABAMA FOR KANSAS." The next day Charles Sumner, the abolitionist senator from Massachusetts, was brutally asaulted and almost killed on the Senate floor by South Carolina congressman Preston Brooks for his "Crime against Kansas" speech. This news, however, would not reach Kansas for at least another week.[26]

Brown decided to make a retaliatory strike against proslavery settlers. On the night of May 24, he and seven men, including four sons and a son-in-law, entered the proslavery settlement along Pottawatomie Creek. They approached three cabins along the creek, woke up the settlers, dragged a total of five men out into the dark night, and hacked them to death one by one with broadswords. As graphically reported in the *New York Herald*, one victim was decapitated and another's windpipe "entirely cut out."[27]

In their rhetoric, Radical Abolitionists endorsed this kind of retaliatory action. Four days later, at the second annual Radical Abolition convention, Douglass responded to the news of civil war in Kansas and Congress (symbolized by Sumner's beating) by declaring: "Liberty must either cut the throat of Slavery, or have its own cut by Slavery." Brown's responsibility for the Pottawatomie massacre was largely obscured in the press until Harpers Ferry, and for the rest of his life he denied or evaded culpability for it. But Radical Abolitionists knew that Brown employed savage means to preserve freedom in Kansas, and some of them, along with other friends and supporters, no doubt knew that he was responsible for the deaths. They continued to support him because they viewed his violence within the context of war.[28]

At some point in the late 1850s Brown's plan to invade the South evolved from a subterranean passway into a raid on Harpers Ferry. He put together a small army, consisting mostly of white comrades with whom he had fought in Kansas and black neighbors from Timbucto. And he received support from Gerrit Smith and five influential Boston-area abolitionists: Thomas Wentworth Higginson, Franklin Sanborn, George Luther Stearns, Theodore Parker, and Samuel Gridley Howe. These "secret six," as they became known, had been revolutionized in part by the nationalization of slavery in the 1850s. They resisted the Fugitive Slave Act of 1850, which suspended habeas corpus and turned Northern soil into hunting grounds for slave catchers. And after the Kansas-Nebraska Act, the Bostonians helped form the Massachusetts Kansas Committee, which gave guns and supplies to Free-State Kansas settlers and to Brown for his raid on the South.[29]

Brown also gained the respect of Boston's preeminent intellectuals. Between 1857 and 1859 he visited Boston seven times and went twice to Concord, where he thrilled his audience with descriptions of the war in Kansas, including accounts of how one son was murdered and another driven mad by the violence. Ralph Waldo Emerson and Henry David Thoreau heard him speak on both occasions and were much impressed; they invited him to their homes, supported his violent agenda, and gave money to his cause. After Brown's 1857 talk, Emerson wrote in his journal: "Captain John Brown of Kansas gave a good account of himself in the Town Hall, last night, to a meeting of citizens. . . . One of his good points was, the folly of the peace party in Kansas. . . . He believes on his own experience that one good, believing, strong-minded man is worth a hundred, nay, twenty thousand men without character. . . . The first man who went into Kansas from Missouri to interfere in the elections, he thought, 'had a perfect right to be shot.'"[30]

Brown befriended Charles Sumner as well. During one Boston visit he called on Sumner and asked about the assault by Preston Brooks. Sumner, still recovering from the head wounds sustained in the attack, told Brown: "The coat I had on at the time is hanging in that closet. Its collar is stiff with blood. You can see it, if you please, Captain." Brown took down the coat "and looked at it for a few minutes with the reverence with which a Roman Catholic regards the relics of a saint," according to the Unitarian minister James Freeman Clarke, who was also at the meeting. As a senator, Sumner felt compelled to reject Brown's extralegal violence. But he considered Brown "a most remarkable character," admiring "many things in the man."[31]

Brown's greatest supporters, however, were blacks—from leaders to his Timbucto neighbors. Harriet Tubman, a friend whom Brown called "General Tubman," helped him plan the Harpers Ferry raid. So did Lewis Hayden, with whom Brown stayed at times while in Boston. In early October 1859 Hayden sent Brown crucial last-minute support in the form of $600, guns, and another comrade (Francis Merriam), which "removed the last delay," according to one historian. Martin Delany arranged a convention at Chatham, Canada, in 1858, where about fifty men, mostly blacks, approved Brown's plan for invading Harpers Ferry and his "Provisional Constitution," which Douglass also supported and probably edited. The Provisional Constitution was designed to govern those areas Brown hoped to liberate from slavery and draw attention to the failures of the U.S. Constitution. It called slavery a state of war, sought to fulfill "those eternal and self-evident truths" in the Declaration of Independence, and repudiated positive laws that "degraded" blacks and women and denied them their equal rights as citizens. Virtually everywhere he went, Brown acquired black friends and supporters.[32]

Brown raided the South to liberate slaves even before Harpers Ferry. He was back in Kansas in December 1858, when a Missouri slave who had just escaped asked for help, saying that he and other slaves were about to be sold. The next night Brown led eighteen men into Missouri, raided three farmhouses, and liberated eleven slaves at gunpoint. One owner resisted and was killed. The news created a sensation and made national headlines. President Buchanan and the Missouri governor offered rewards for Brown's capture. Over the next three months, Brown and his comrades eluded proslavery posses and took the fugitives safely into Canada. He defended his actions in a letter to the *New York Tribune:* "Eleven persons are forcibly restored to their 'natural and inalienable rights,' with but one man killed, and all 'Hell is stirred from beneath.'" During the 1100-mile trek to freedom, one female fugitive gave birth and christened the child John Brown.[33]

Brown's relationships with African Americans go a long way toward explaining his life and actions. More than any other white man in the historical record, he devoted his life to their cause and saw in their sufferings his own. The only way to understand John Brown is to view him as he saw himself—as someone who identified so closely with African Americans that he chose to live with them and was willing to sacrifice his life for their cause. Many slaves, upon hearing of Brown's efforts to free them, assumed that he was black. Such racial blurring reflected Brown's understanding that the nation's ideals of freedom and equality meant sharing a common and equal humanity with *all* people.

One final indication of Brown's willingness to act on national ideals and sacrifice his life for the abolitionist cause came in a more concrete form. In

1857 he went to Canton, Connecticut, in order to take home to Timbucto the tombstone of his grandfather and namesake. Captain John Brown had been a Revolutionary War soldier and died defending his country. The face of the tombstone bore the inscription "In Memory of Captn John Brown, who died at New York, Sept. ye 3, 1776, in the 48 year of his Age." On the reverse side Brown inscribed an epitaph for his son Frederick, who had died in Kansas: "In memory of Frederick, son of John and Dianthe Brown, born Dec. 21 1830 and murdered at Osawatomie Kansas August 30, 1856 for his adherence to the cause of freedom." Brown placed the tombstone about 20 yards from the front door of his house at Timbucto, near a large granite boulder. For the next three years, whenever family members left the house, they were reminded of the significance of their name: Browns were willing to die for the cause of freedom. In December 1859, three more names would be added to the tombstone.

Harpers Ferry as a Military Failure

It began on October 16, when Brown gave the command, "Men, get on your arms; we will proceed to the Ferry." They were renting a farmhouse a few miles from Harpers Ferry, known as the Kennedy Farm. Three men stayed behind to guard the weapons; the remaining eighteen raiders followed Brown down the road toward the federal arsenal. It would be a physically grueling and exhausting ordeal, and Brown was twice the age of his fellow warriors, old enough to be their father. But his faith made up for any loss of energy that came with age. He felt quite certain that he was an instrument in God's hands, acting out God's designs for the nation. That design was to take over the arsenal and then distribute arms to blacks, launching a slave insurrection that would bring about an apocalyptic end to slavery.[34]

By midnight Brown's plan was succeeding wonderfully well. He and his men had gained control of the armory, which held about 100,000 guns, and taken as prisoners the armory's guards. So far there had been no casualties, though he recognized that might change. "I want to free all the negroes in this state," he told one prisoner; "I have possession now of the United States armory, and if the citizens interfere with me, I must only burn the town and have blood."[35]

But in the wake of this early success, Brown delayed unnecessarily. Part of the problem was that he had never thought through precisely how he would distribute the 100,000 armory guns, plus additional arms and 1000 pikes financed by his Northern accomplices, to the state's 500,000 blacks, mostly slaves. He hoped that the town's 200 blacks, 10 percent of the population, knew of his scheme and would quickly join it, and that the insurrection would then spread like wildfire.[36] Martin Delany and Harriet Tubman had felt confident that local blacks would come to his aid. The black raider Osborne Anderson also believed the region's blacks could be relied on, estimating that at least 150 slaves had been informed of the raid through the grapevine telegraph. But Brown had no idea how many blacks knew of his plan. He clearly hoped that thousands would join his insurrection, based on his general order of October 10, which described the structure of a vast army.[37]

And so in the early hours of October 17, Brown waited and hoped for black reinforcements. Meanwhile he acquired more prisoners and allies. His men raided the homes of local elites and brought masters and their slaves to the armory as prisoners. The most distinguished prisoner was Lewis Washington, the great-grandnephew of George Washington. "I wanted you particularly for the moral effect it would give our cause, having one of your name as a prisoner," Brown told him. By dawn Brown had about forty prisoners, twice the size of his own army. His white hostages could be used as ransom, allowing him to escape to the mountains unmolested, he calculated. And he hoped that his black captives would join the revolution.[38]

But between Brown's black prisoners and the thousands of male slaves in the six-county region surrounding the Ferry, only a handful of people came to his aid. One newspaper noted that local blacks "had at least cognizance of" Brown's plans. But blacks were also aware of the suicidal nature of almost all slave insurrections. They preferred to remain alive. In their prudence they echoed Douglass, whom Brown had tried hard to recruit a month before the raid. Douglass had refused, telling Brown that "he was going into a perfect steel-trap, and that once in he would never get out alive."[39]

The first victim of Brown's war on slavery was a black man. While Brown was in the armory collecting prisoners, his men cut the telegraph lines and captured guards on the covered railroad bridge through which trains entered the town. They captured one guard, but an Irish watchman named Patrick Higgins resisted. Higgins punched his captor in the face, sprinted to the end of the bridge, and dove through the window of a hotel to safety. At 1:25 A.M. the eastbound train to Baltimore arrived at the bridge. Higgins and the hotel clerk, fearing sabotage, stopped it. The train conductor and some other trainmen, including Heyward Shepherd, a free black baggage handler, went into the covered bridge with a lantern to investigate. Brown's men ordered them to "stand and deliver." Ignoring the order, Shepherd turned to flee. He received a bullet in the back that just missed his heart. It was a fatal wound and a bad omen for Brown and his men.[40]

The shooting created panic among the train's passengers and effectively sounded the alarm. But rather than keep the passengers hostage, Brown let the train continue on to Baltimore. He also imprudently divulged his scheme to the conductor, who stopped en route to send a wire to his manager in Baltimore: "Express train bound east, under my charge, was stopped this morning at Harpers Ferry by armed abolitionists. They have possession of the bridge and the arms and armory of the United States. . . . They say they have come to free the slaves and intend to do it at all hazards. . . . You had better notify the Secretary of War at once."[41]

Militia companies began arriving at Harpers Ferry on Monday morning, October 17. Brown and his men took refuge in the armory's engine house, and within a few hours they were surrounded. Two sons were with Brown and would soon die at his side. Secretary of war John Floyd, a former governor of Virginia, ordered a company of United States Marines led by Colonel Robert E. Lee and J. E. B. Stuart to Harpers Ferry. On Tuesday morning, as two thousand spectators looked on, Lee's company battered down the doors of the engine house and captured seven survivors. Brown and Aaron Stevens were severely wounded. The five prisoners received only minor injuries or were unhurt.[42]

Less than forty-eight hours after it began, John Brown's raid ended as a military campaign. Casualties were light: ten raiders were killed in action, plus two slaves who had joined them. Five raiders (Osborne Anderson and four whites) escaped to free soil. On the Southern side, four citizens and one soldier were killed, nine wounded. Brown and six captured raiders were convicted of murder, treason, and conspiracy to incite a slave insurrection. Brown and four raiders were hanged in December, the other two in March 1860.[43]

Compared to other slave insurrections, Harpers Ferry was comparatively peaceful. Brown and his men displayed considerable restraint. They neither burned the town, as Brown had threatened, nor killed any white prisoners. Indeed, if Brown had shown less respect for human life and been willing to execute a few prisoners, he may have been able to escape to the mountains surrounding the town. But in his last order to his men before marching on

Harpers Ferry he had proscribed unwarranted violence. "You all know how dear life is to you, and how dear your life is to your friends," he told them. "Do not, therefore, take the life of any one if you can possibly avoid it; but if necessary to take life in order to save your own, then make sure work of it."[44]

Harpers Ferry as a Political Success: Northern Responses

On December 1, the day before Brown's execution, Robert E. Lee wrote to his wife, Mary, from Harpers Ferry to say that "the feelings of the community seem to be calmed down." He added: "Tomorrow will probably be the last [we hear] of Captain Brown." He could not have been more wrong.[45]

Lee did not appreciate Brown's greatest weapon: the power of language. Neither did Brown himself at times. A few months before the raid he had complained in Boston that "talk! talk! talk! . . . will never set the slave free." But it was Brown's words that transformed his military failure into an extraordinary success. Indeed the happiest moments of his life occurred while he was in prison waiting to die. At his trial and in his letters and interviews from prison, he stoically defended his actions. He was a primitive Christian heeding the law of God. On November 2, before being sentenced to hang, he offered a defense of revolutionary violence that rivaled or surpassed that of the founders: "I believe that to have interfered as I have done . . . in behalf of His despised poor, I did no wrong, but right. Now, if it is deemed necessary that I should forfeit my life for the furtherance of the ends of justice, and mingle my blood further with the blood of millions in this slave country whose rights are disregarded by wicked, cruel, and unjust enactments, I say, let it be done." Brown's words circulated through the press and the national consciousness like a long fuse that eventually exploded, ripping the nation apart.[46]

The immediate response to the Harpers Ferry raid, in both the North and the South, was one of confusion followed by shock and condemnation. During the first two days, the press greatly exaggerated the numbers, describing "HUNDREDS OF INSURRECTIONISTS IN ARMS." But after Brown was captured, accurate reporting was followed by outrage. Virtually every major paper in the country questioned Brown's sanity. The *New York Independent,* an abolition paper edited by Theodore Tilton, was representative; it called the raid mad on October 20. To be sure, the tiny black press, and African American voices more generally, staunchly defended Brown and remained unwavering in their support. But initially not one white newspaper threw unequivocal support behind Brown. For white Americans, Brown had crossed the line sep-arating permissible from impermissible dissent. In trying to make sense of a white man leading an interracial army into the South and sacrificing his life for the cause of black freedom, they concluded that he must be insane: such was the power of racism in America.[47]

This widespread condemnation occurred before Brown's words began cir-culating throughout the country. Once they did, the transcendentalists, who were especially interested in the relationship between ideas and actions and the nature of heroism, led the way among whites in defending Brown. Their influence, coupled with Brown's words, transformed Northern opinion.[48]

Thoreau initiated the transformation of Brown from madman to martyr. He championed Brown in his journals as soon as he heard the news, condemn-ing politicians and the press for calling Brown insane. All the speeches of *"sane"* Northern senators "do not match for simple and manly directness, force, and effectiveness the few casual remarks of *insane* John Brown on the floor of the Harper's Ferry engine-house," he observed in one entry. Editors appeared *"sane"* only because they knew "on which side their bread is but-tered!" he added in another. These journal entries inspired his lecture "A Plea for Captain John Brown," delivered in Concord on October 30 and then twice more, in Boston and Worcester. Though he could not publish the long speech as a book, owing to its radicalism, it was printed by newspapers and reached a wide audience.[49]

To Thoreau, Brown exemplified the true meaning of transcendentalism. He was "a transcendentalist above all, a man of ideas and principles." Much like Thoreau himself, who had likened slavery to turning "mankind into sausages," Brown recognized the essential inhumanity of the slave system. And both men believed that natural law (God's law) superseded positive law (manmade law). Thoreau endorsed Brown's use of force because he too believed that slavery not only violated natural law but was a state of war and the embodiment of evil. But for Thoreau, Brown's true greatness—what distinguished him from other transcendentalists—stemmed from his willingness to *act* on his sacred ideals in order to preserve peace and humanity, even at the cost of his life. "No man . . . loved his fellow-man so well. . . . He lived for him. He took up his life and he laid it down for him," Thoreau proclaimed in his "Plea." Brown so ex-emplified transcendentalism, he was Christ-like: "Some eighteen hundred years ago Christ was crucified; this morning, perchance, Captain Brown was hung. These are the two ends of a chain which is not without its link."[50]

A week later, on November 8, Emerson made the connection between Brown and Christ more explicit. The nation's leading intellectual, he was far more influential than Thoreau but reluctant to speak out on social issues. When he did, his words had the power of an "avalanche," according to Walt Whitman. During a lecture titled "Courage," he called Brown a "new saint" who "shall make the gallows glorious like the cross." The *New York Daily Tribune* quoted the line the next day, and it soon went national. On November 18, at a meeting to raise money for Brown's family, Emerson developed other themes from Thoreau's "Plea." He called Brown "an idealist," explaining: "He believed in his ideas to that extent that he existed to put them all into action. . . . He saw how deceptive the forms are. . . . The judges rely on the forms, and do not, like John Brown, use their eyes to see the fact behind the forms." Emerson understood, as did Thoreau and Brown, that formal beauty—whether manifested in law, rhetoric, poetry, or art—often came at the expense of truth and justice." Brown, by contrast, believed in transparency, Emerson observed: "He is so transparent that all men see him through. . . . He believes in two articles . . . the Golden Rule and the Declaration of Independence," and he would prefer apocalyptic violence "than that one word of either should be violated in this country." In his "simple artless goodness," Brown was a transcendental patriot.[51]

By December 2, the day of Brown's execution, prison letters by Brown, coupled with the writings of the transcendentalists and other influential reformers, had saturated the North. As a result, virtually every antislavery Northerner now defended Brown's moral opposition to slavery, even if they vigorously denounced his actions. Democrats used Brown's raid as an opportunity to denounce Republicans. Stephen Douglas, the leading Democrat in the nation prior to Brown's raid, declared from the Senate floor: "I have no hesitation in expressing my firm and deliberate conviction that the Harper's Ferry crime was the natural, logical, inevitable result of the doctrines and teachings of the Republican Party, as explained and enforced in their platform, their partisan presses, their pamphlets and books, and especially in the speeches of their leaders." In response to such accusations, Republicans tried to distance themselves from Brown by vigorously condemning his actions. But they continued to acknowledge their sympathy for Brown's hatred of slavery.[52]

For example, John Andrew, a rising radical Republican in Massachusetts, shared a platform with Emerson on November 18 to raise money for Brown's family. Andrew had met Brown once in 1859 and given him money even though he thought him a little extreme. He opposed Brown's violence but fo-cused on his moral clarity. Whether the attempt itself was "wise or foolish, I only know that . . . John Brown himself is right," Andrew said. "I sympathize with the man. I sympathize with the idea because I sympathize with and be-lieve in the eternal right." Lincoln, a moderate to conservative Republican, better represented the typical Republican response to Harpers Ferry. The day after Brown was hanged, he said the execution was just, but he also sympa-thized with Brown's moral stance. He then used Brown to warn Southerners not to break the law: "Old John Brown has just been executed for treason against a state. We cannot object, even though he agreed with us in thinking slavery wrong. That cannot excuse violence, bloodshed, and treason. It could avail him nothing that he might think himself right. So, if we constitutionally elect a President, and therefore you undertake to destroy the Union, it will be our duty to deal with you as old John Brown has been dealt with." Brown's ex-ecution indicated what the appropriate response to secession should be.[53]

William Lloyd Garrison captured nonresisters' attitudes toward Harpers Ferry. Though staunchly opposed to Brown's violent means, Garrison con-sidered Brown a martyr and was thrilled when church bells tolled for him throughout the North on December 2. Such exaltation reflected the extraordi-nary success of moral suasion:

> The sympathy and admiration now so widely felt for [Brown] prove how marvelous has been the change effected in public opinion during thirty years of moral agitation—a change so great, indeed, that whereas ten years since, there were thousands who could not endure my lightest word of re-buke of the South, they can now easily swallow John Brown whole, and his rifle into the bargain. In firing his gun, he has merely told us what time of day it is. It is high noon, thank God.

Garrison was right: it *was* "high noon," a crucial moment for abolitionism and for the nation.[54]

Harpers Ferry as a Political Success: Southern Responses

The widespread Northern sympathy for Brown outraged Southerners as never before. There were several reasons for this. One was that Brown deeply of-fended Southern honor. Southerners tried to dismiss Brown as a "damned black-hearted villain!" with a "heart black as a stove-pipe." But Northerners such as James Redpath, a comrade of Brown, took direct aim at the Southern culture of honor. Brown had made the Southern states "tremble in their breeches" and revealed the "disgraceful truth" that the South was "only a cowardly braggart," he taunted in early November, going on to insist that Virginia had had "but one hero on her soil" since the Marquis de Lafayette—Brown. Then he offended all codes of Southern pride and manhood, mocking: "They are not done quaking yet, I am very much afraid that *diapers* will be needed before the trial of Old Brown shall be finished." And so, Redpath concluded, as a "demonstration of the cowardice of the South," Brown's raid was a "brilliant success."[55]

More importantly, proslavery leaders from John C. Calhoun to Jefferson Davis and Alexander Stephens had long recognized that the permanence of the peculiar institution hinged on whether slavery could be acquitted in "the tribunal of *morals*," as Holst noted. For without the weight of morals, the scales of justice became empty vessels, and positive law a dead letter compared to the anarchy of higher law and the axiom that might makes right. The power of moral persuasion was precisely why Southern leaders had tried to suppress antislavery writings, speeches, and images since the 1830s. The Harpers Ferry raid starkly highlighted the fact that Northerners were winning the slavery debate: the criminal had become the martyr. The damage of Harpers Ferry was less Brown's invasion than the wholesale condemnation of slavery that exploded throughout the North with Brown's execution.[56]

Southern society was a "slumbering volcano" that could erupt at any moment, as Douglass noted. *De Bow's Review,* the preeminent journal in the South, admitted as much. In its lead article of April 1860, "Secession of the South," it likened Brown to Toussaint-Louverture, leading slaves in an apocalyptic strike for freedom. Brown, like his counterpart from St. Domingue, had encouraged slaves to unleash upon white men and women "a feast of blood and rapine" in hopes of overthrowing the government and exterminating the "white proprietors."[57]

The only solution to Brown's raid was secession, leading Southerners concluded. It didn't matter that Brown and his comrades had been captured and killed: "Is the offence of the North expiated, or are the South more secure in their institutions, or freer from apprehension of farther disturbance from the North?" asked *De Bow's Review.* Brown's raid and his words convinced countless Southerners that as a group, Northerners could no longer be trusted. George Fitzhugh, a leading proslavery writer, acknowledged that even anti-secessionists must now see that having "Northerners among us is fraught with danger." Fitzhugh explained that Northern settlers might not "tamper with our slaves and incite them to insurrection, but one man can fire a magazine, and no one can foresee where the match will be applied, or what will be the extent and consequences of the explosion. Our wives and our daughters will see in every new Yankee face an abolition missionary." Harpers Ferry unleashed in the South a wave of fear. Southerners were afraid of the future, afraid that Brown's pikes would return as brandished swords in the night. This helps explain why, after Brown's raid, secessionist doctrines suddenly became dominant, whereas before the raid unionism and moderate doctrines on both sides had been in the ascendant.[58]

The eve of Harpers Ferry was marked by comparative national harmony. In December 1858 the *Charleston Mercury,* normally zealous in its hatred of New England, reported on the commemorations of the fortieth anniversary of the Charleston New England Society. After describing the lavish dinner and spirited toasts, it included a poem singing the praises of the region:

> What though they boast of fairer lands,
> Give me New England's hallowed soil;
> The fearless hearts, the swarthy hands,
> Stamped with the heraldry of toil.

Had the same article been published a year later, its author may well have been killed or forced to flee the South.[59]

After Harpers Ferry, vigilance committees sprang up throughout the South, and the British consul in Charleston described the state of affairs as "a reign of terror." Several visiting Northerners were "tarred and feathered" and others "ridden upon rails" or "cruelly whipped," while any discussion of slavery was "prohibited under penalty of expulsion, with or without violence, from the country." In January 1860 the Washington, D.C.–based *National Era* summarized the moment: "The reign of terror in [the South] is marked by atrocities equal to those which desolated France seventy years ago. It is not safe for a Northern man to travel through the South at the present time, for either business or pleasure." Going on to list acts of violence and numerous arrests that occurred across the South in response to suspicions of support for Brown or abolition, the newspaper concluded that these "barbarities proceed from fear," for Southerners knew that slavery was a "continual source of terror." African Americans and vocal opponents of slavery were the greatest victims of this terror. Free blacks were enslaved, tortured, and murdered, and whites were imprisoned, whipped, and expelled.[60]

Almost overnight, it seemed, Southern slaveholders gathered ranks and mobilized for war. "If the South does not now unite for her defense, we will deserve the execration of posterity," warned South Carolina governor William Gist in November 1859. Southern states began purchasing arms from the federal government "in order to fight it with them, in case of need," as one politician put it. In early January 1860, South Carolina representative and secessionist William Miles noted that "the South is arming; and if she be not allowed to secede in peace, she will do it at the cost of war." Virginia appropriated $500,000 to purchase and manufacture arms and sent agents "to Europe to see on what conditions arms could be purchased there," senator James Mason said in Congress in early March 1860. He added that "the relation in which [Virginia] and many other States now stand to this Union has put them upon the necessity of arming themselves." *De Bow's Review* echoed these sentiments: "In these darksome times it becomes the South to keep her arms properly burnished and her powder dry."[61]

Southern Unionists everywhere felt themselves on the defensive. They had no effective counter to the "belief that the Northern people have aided and abetted this treasonable invasion of a Southern state," as the *Richmond Enquirer* put it. Nor could they refute South Carolina state legislator Christopher Memminger when he insisted: "Every village bell which tolled its solemn note at the execution of Brown, proclaims to the south the approbation of that village of insurrection and servile war." And a North Carolina Unionist described his conversion to secession in these terms: "I have always been a fervid Union man, but I confess the endorsement of the Harpers Ferry outrage . . . has shaken my fidelity, and I am willing to take the chances of every probable evil that may arise from disunion, sooner than submit any longer to Northern insolence and Northern outrage."[62]

This revolution in Southern opinion was astutely summarized by two newspapers, one from the lower South, the other from the upper South. The *Watchman*, based in Sumter, South Carolina, correctly noted that "never before, since the Declaration of Independence, has the South been more united in sentiment." The *Baltimore Sun* explained why this was so: the South could no longer afford to "live under a Government, the majority of whose subjects or citizens regard John Brown as a martyr and a Christian hero, rather than a murderer and robber."[63]

Some slave-owning Southerners said that the only way they might recover their faith in the Union was if Northerners embraced proslavery ideology. "We regard every man in our midst an enemy to the institutions of the South, who does not boldly declare that he believes African Slavery to be a social, moral, and political blessing," announced the *Atlanta Confederacy* in January 1860.[64]

Several Northern doughface Democrats tried to conciliate in just this way. They not only agreed with Jefferson Davis, who said the Republican Party was "organized on the basis of making war" against the South; they echoed Calhoun's proslavery creed. For example, at a Great Union Meeting in New York City a few weeks after Brown's execution, the prominent Democrat Charles O'Conor asked: "Is negro slavery unjust?" The answer, he said, would determine "the fate of our Union." If slavery was in conflict with the laws of nature and of God, then Americans should embrace William Seward's higher law argument, "which compels us to disregard the Constitution." O'Conor concluded, therefore, that slavery was "just, wise, and beneficent. . . . It is benign in its influences on the white man and on the black." As a result, "we must no longer favor political leaders who talk about slavery being an evil."[65]

But these conciliatory gestures backfired. Southerners responded to O'Conor and his doughface ilk with disgust rather than gratitude. "If there be any character in the world that we have contempt for, it is the dirt-eating Dough-face of the free states," said the *Baltimore Patriot* in early December. "He has no real regard whatever for the South and its institution, and yet, under pretense of sympathy for them, he will proclaim himself our friend, keeping his eyes steadily all the while upon the pecuniary benefit to be derived therefrom." After Harpers Ferry, it seemed that nothing could reconcile the sectional rift.[66]

In essence, a revolutionary ethos emerged in the wake of Brown's raid. Instead of political ideas moving toward a center, as they ordinarily do in America, like milk flowing down the sides of a bowl toward the bottom, they suddenly shot up and out toward the lip, the extreme edges. As a result, revolutionaries became heroes (or antiheroes), while compromisers such as Charles O'Conor—and other Northern Democrats—were simply viewed with contempt or suspicion. With his raid on Harpers Ferry, Brown jostled the political bowl.[67]

Just as Brown became a martyr to millions of Northerners, secessionist leaders suddenly became Southern heroes. Edmund Ruffin, the Virginia planter and political activist and one of the South's most vocal secessionists, felt completely regenerated by Brown's raid. In fact, the day before hearing the news, he had almost given up hope in his dream of disunion. "Since my last writing was completed, I have not undertaken, or designed to undertake any other [writing], and have no object whatever to strive for," he wrote in his diary. "I fear that I am now about to enter that condition of idleness and weariness which I always dreaded." But his entire outlook suddenly changed after reading about the "remarkable events" at Harpers Ferry: "It really seems now most probable that the outbreak was planned and instigated by Northern abolitionists, and with the expectation of thus starting a general slave insurrection. I earnestly hope that such may be the truth of the case. Such a practical exercise of abolition principles is needed to stir the sluggish blood of the South."[68]

Ruffin was immensely inspired by Brown. He "is as thorough a fanatic as ever suffered martyrdom—and a very brave and able man, humble and obscure," he wrote on October 26. "It is impossible for me not to respect his thorough devotion to his bad cause, and the undaunted courage with which he has sustained it, through all losses and hazards." He recognized in Brown a fellow revolutionary.[69]

Ruffin quickly began to capitalize on Brown's raid. He published a flurry of secessionist essays and noted that Brown's raid facilitated his "carrying out my views." He emphasized that Northerners, through their sympathy for the criminals, revealed themselves as "enemies" of the South. Such sympathy was "very gratifying," he added, for it would convince trusting Southerners that disunion was "the only safeguard from the insane hostility of the North to southern institutions." Ruffin even hoped for a rescue attempt of Brown, for it would be "a certain cause of separation of the southern from the northern states."[70]

Brown's raid awakened in Ruffin "my youthful military fervor." He wanted to attend Brown's execution, and since only military personnel were allowed near the gallows, he joined the cadets of the Virginia Military Institute for a day. He stood 50 yards from the gallows and was further impressed with Brown's "complete fearlessness of and insensibility to danger and death," noting approvingly: "In this quality he seems to me to have had few equals."[71]

Ruffin spent several days at Harpers Ferry before and after the execution. He visited the engine house where Brown had been captured, interviewed Lewis Washington and others who had been involved in the raid, and acquired

INTRODUCTION

xliii

some of the pikes Brown had used as weapons. One pike he kept for himself and often carried with him. Two went to the U.S. Capitol, one to the Senate Committee of Commerce, and the other to the U.S. House of Representatives, which "attracted much notice." And he sent one each to every governor of a slave state. With each pike he created a label, which read in part: "Sample of the favors designed for us by our Northern brethren."[72]

Brown's raid so revived Ruffin's secession dreams that within six months of the execution he had published a futuristic novel, *Anticipations of the Future,* which imagined secession, civil war, and a Southern triumph. He spoke for many Southerners when he said that Brown's design to spark "a general slave insurrection" was "obviously the legitimate practical results of a widespread conspiracy of northern men."[73]

When the Democratic National Convention convened at Charleston in April 1860, John Brown, his pikes, and Harpers Ferry still dominated the newspapers. A Senate committee was investigating the invasion and calling witnesses. That month Franklin Sanborn, one of the "secret six" conspirators, had resisted arrest in Concord, Massachusetts. Ruffin and other secessionists saw the convention as the beginning of the "final struggle," as Ruffin phrased it.[74]

Stephen Douglas was the frontrunner and one of the preeminent politicians in the country. He had nearly won the Democratic nomination in 1856 —withdrawing after the sixteenth ballot, during a stalemate with Buchanan— and two years later he had defeated Lincoln in a Senate race that received national attention. His chief political aim was to preserve sectional harmony. As the national Democratic candidate he would likely win the presidency, since Republicans were a sectional party, as he often emphasized. And if he won the election, this would severely hamper the secessionist cause. It was thus crucial for secessionists to prevent Douglas from winning the nomination and representing Southern Democrats.[75]

In the wake of Harpers Ferry, secessionists set out to defeat Douglass and split the Democratic Party. As Allan Nevins explains, "southern hysteria after John Brown was directed against the Douglas Democrats." Secessionists accused Douglas of treating slavery as evil, even though he refused to take a moral position on it. More importantly, they demanded a "slave code" that protected slavery in the territories. Douglas's popular sovereignty doctrine was ambiguous on this point, since settlers might vote to outlaw slavery in a territory. A number of Southern states had vowed to instruct their delegates to walk out of the convention if the slave code was not adopted. In a sense, a "slave code" was the secessionists' trump card for rejecting Douglas at the Democratic convention and marching toward disunion.[76]

The turning point of the convention came on April 28 in a speech by William Yancey of Alabama, another leading secessionist and one of the South's best orators. The platform committee had adopted a slave-code plank as the majority platform, but Northern delegates outnumbered Southern by a three-fifths majority and could still vote for Douglas's popular sovereignty platform. Yancey invoked the specter of John Brown and appealed to Southern honor: "Ours is the property invaded; ours are the institutions which are at stake; ours is the peace that is to be destroyed; ours is the honor at stake—the honor of children, the honor of families," now threatened by Northerners who would "make a great heaving volcano of passion and crime." He warned that "there will be disunion if we are defeated." The Douglas delegates refused to abandon popular sovereignty and their Northern constituents, and the next day Southerners walked out.[77]

Although the Democrats would reconvene in Baltimore in June, almost everyone recognized that the national party had been destroyed. The split was beyond repair. Northern and Southern Democrats raged at each other, as secessionists had hoped—knowing that this would lead directly to disunion. Southern Democrats nominated the secessionist John Breckinridge of Kentucky, while some border state men created a Constitutional Union Party and nominated John Bell as a Unionist candidate. Owing to demographics and the makeup of the Electoral College, the four-party race virtually guaranteed the election of a Republican candidate. And a Republican victory sparked secession: South Carolina announced a secession convention the day after Lincoln was elected. Brown's raid had damaged Douglas's chances in the race and ended the possibility of Democratic harmony. As one Democratic politician wrote to another after the Harpers Ferry raid, Brown had "thrown a wet blanket over the shoulders of Douglas."[78]

Had Douglas been nominated at Charleston, he probably would have won the election. Consolidating the Douglas, Breckinridge, and Bell votes to Douglas Democrats would not in itself have made the difference, since Lincoln would still have won with 169 electoral votes, 17 more than the 152 needed to win. But Lincoln won five states—Illinois, Indiana, Ohio, New York, and Pennsylvania—by very slim margins. If Douglas had won just one of these states as the national Democratic candidate, he would have won the election. And a united Democratic Party would have pressured conservatives to vote against the Republican ticket, owing to fears of disunion from a Lincoln victory.[79]

Brown's raid also helped Lincoln win the Republican nomination. Lincoln had established a reputation during his campaign for senator in Illinois and his debates with Stephen Douglas in 1858. In 1859 a few supporters began suggesting him as a contender for high office. But he had served only one unsuccessful term in Congress and had twice lost a bid for the Senate. He had no friends in the East, his allies were all in the West, and the Republican frontrunners in 1859, William Seward of New York and Salmon Chase of Ohio, were political giants by comparison, with powerful backers throughout the North. But after Brown's raid on Harpers Ferry, Seward and Chase suddenly started to seem like damaged goods. They already had reputations as radicals. For years both men had brazenly resisted the Fugitive Slave Act, declaring it unconstitutional, and now they were linked with high treason and murder. Chase knew Brown and had supported his militancy. In 1856 he had given Brown $25 and recommended him "to the confidence and regard of all who desire to see Kansas a free state." These details became front-page news after Brown's raid, and conservative Republicans threatened to bolt from the party.[80]

Democrats blamed Seward for the Harpers Ferry raid, and some called for his death: "We have been invaded, and the facts of it show Seward to be a traitor and deserving the gallows," pronounced congressman Reuben Davis of Mississippi in early December 1859. Lincoln suddenly became more appealing to Northern voters, for he was much more conservative than Seward and Chase. He used Harpers Ferry as an opportunity to affirm his faith in law and order. The way to express "our belief in regard to slavery . . . is through the ballot box—the peaceful method provided by the Constitution," he told a Kansas audience on December 1 in direct reference to Brown's raid.[81]

While Lincoln reassured Northern voters and Southerners and Democrats tried to link Brown to the Republican Party, Seward went out of his way to disassociate himself from abolitionists. He backed off his "higher law" doctrine, his assertion that there was "an irrepressible conflict" between freedom and slavery, and his demand that the Supreme Court rescind *Dred Scott*. In late February, soon after Brown's execution and ahead of the Republican nominating convention, Seward gave a speech in the Senate that "was so full of concession to the slave power" as to destroy his bid for the nomination, according to Frederick Douglass: "Brown frightened Seward into making his last great speech. In that speech he stooped quite too low for his future fame, and lost the prize that tempted the stoop." Brown had sent Seward fleeing for "the swamps of compromise and concession" and cost him the Republican ticket, Douglass concluded in June 1860, after Lincoln won the nomination at the convention.[82]

Aftermath and Afterlife

In a profound respect, then, Harpers Ferry was both a microcosm and the beginning of the Civil War. An interracial war to end slavery, it was also a war to protect Southern rights. Lee and Stuart, who captured Brown at the Ferry, would soon become, like Brown and his men, rebels. Thomas Jackson, the leader of the Virginia Military Institute who helped oversee Brown's execution, would become Stonewall Jackson, Lee's friend and fellow rebel.

Edmund Ruffin, who watched with Jackson as Brown hung, was granted the honor of firing the first shot on Fort Sumter, a kind of christening of the Confederacy. He would himself suffer a kind of martyrdom: after Lee surrendered to Ulysses S. Grant, he draped himself in the Confederate flag and blew his brains out.

And Jefferson Davis, who in the wake of Harpers Ferry demanded a federal slave code protecting slaveholders' property in every state and territory, saw his Senate resolution become the foundation of the nonnegotiable platform at the Democratic convention, which split the Democratic Party and virtually assured the election of a Republican president—and secession. Davis would soon lead his new nation, conceived in slavery, in a war for independence, although by May 1865 he would be on his way to prison, surrounded by Union forces who sang a version of the John Brown song that included a line about hanging "Jeff Davis from a sour apple tree."[83]

One other leading man was part of this microcosm and drama. As Brown swung from the gallows, John Wilkes Booth watched intently. He was close enough to see Brown's hands grasp at the air as the rope jerked taut. Deeply moved, he became pale and dizzy and asked a soldier if he had a flask. He needed a good stiff drink. Later he said that he had helped capture Brown, but he was not in the military. At the time of Brown's arrest he was playing a stock character at the Marshall Theatre in Richmond, Virginia. He was fascinated by Brown, though, and "very anxious" to attend his hanging. On November 24, as a train of uniformed militia prepared to leave Richmond for Charles Town, Booth asked if he could join them. After learning that only men in uniform were allowed on the train, he acquired the necessary items and boarded.[84]

Like Ruffin, Booth saw much of himself in Brown, even though they had diametrically opposed visions of the good society. Booth thought of himself as a chivalrous Southerner and considered slavery the bedrock of civilization. But he lauded Brown's composure and eloquence at Harpers Ferry and his ability to turn words into deeds. According to Booth's sister, he acknowledged Brown "a hero when he saw him die" and told her that Brown was "a brave old man." In fact, also like Ruffin, Booth seemed almost envious of this dying moment—Brown's martyrdom. In December 1860 he said that Brown was justly executed for attempting "in another way" what Lincoln and the Republican Party were now doing—attacking slavery. But Brown's method of "open force" was "holier" than the Republicans' "hidden craft." It would not be long before Booth told his sister that Lincoln "was walking in the footsteps of old John Brown" but unfit to "stand with that rugged old hero," for Brown was "a man inspired, the grandest character of the century." Brown's soul was marching on, inspiring Davis, Ruffin, and other secessionists to split the Democratic Party and create a new nation, and four years later inspiring Booth to redeem his country and become a martyr to *his* cause.[85]

As for Brown's friends and allies, many believed that Brown had performed a messianic martyrdom so well that his legacy was secure. Henry Highland Garnet predicted that "succeeding ages will cherish [Brown's] memory." Osborne Anderson expressed faith in the "future historian" to record that Brown's actions "were productive of great good." William Dean Howells prophesied a "later time" when Brown's name would signify that "right makes war sublime." And Douglass believed "posterity" would "appreciate his deeds."[86]

A few years later Douglass thought he saw the fruits of this appreciation. Proclaiming the Civil War a fulfillment of Brown's prophecies, he observed in January 1862 that Brown looked down and saw his murderers suffering the "torments of their own kindling." Surrounded by an army of martyrs and saints, Brown saw "the faith for which he nobly died steadily becoming the saving faith of the nation." Everywhere Union soldiers were marching to "John Brown's Body." Transformed from madman to martyr in 1859, Brown now became a fallen soldier.[87]

But it wasn't long before Douglass acknowledged that the apocalypse of war had brought no millennium. In the 1870s, he began to protest lynching and mob violence as a revival of slavery's spirit, and he sought a revival of the abolitionist spirit in response. America still needed its John Browns, he observed. Fearing that the country had not grasped the true meaning of Brown's life and death, he wondered in 1881 if Americans stood "too near the days of slavery . . . to see clearly the true martyr and hero that he was." Perhaps, like all "men born in advance of their times," Brown must "wait the polishing wheels of after-coming centuries to make his glory more manifest."[88]

One set of "polishing wheels" sped throughout the antilynching movement, of which Douglass was part. Brown became not only one of the first casualties of the Civil War, but also the first martyr of antilynching. In the 1880s and 1890s, Douglass used the memory of Harpers Ferry to warn Americans of violent retribution for lynching. Black men had taken up arms at Harpers Ferry and might take up arms against lynching today, he observed. In the first decade of the twentieth century, W. E. B. Du Bois and Reverdy Ransom invoked Brown's spirit on behalf of the Niagara Movement and said their antilynching and civil rights organization was his legacy. In the 1920s and 1930s, Langston Hughes and Walter White used his memory in their antilynching texts, as did numerous other African American activists and writers. In 1928 a black woman wrote to the nation's biggest-selling black newspaper, the *Chicago Defender,* to suggest that African Americans honor Brown on May 9 (his birthday). She added: "If we only had a few more John Browns, probably it would help wipe out some of this lynching."[89]

Around the same time, the labor movement seized upon John Brown as a symbol of liberty. Eugene Debs asked for a "John Brown of Wage-Slavery" and called Brown the "spirit incarnate of the Revolution," while Michael Gold said that Brown's life and death was "the story of thousands of men living in America now." Brown had "been hung and shot down a hundred times since his first death," Gold continued, and so "his soul is marching on; it is the soul of liberty and justice, which cannot die or be suppressed."[90]

By the 1950s and 1960s, civil rights and Black Power activists were claiming Brown as *their* political ancestor. In 1965 dozens of civil rights activists, including Julian Bond and John Lewis, signed a call for a memorial pilgrimage to Harpers Ferry, planned for the coming December. The pilgrimage would include a conference on the ongoing struggle for equal rights "through active resistance against the vile racist theory and practice of white supremacy." The pilgrims would "reach out to the everlasting arm of old John Brown, who . . . taught the very lessons we are learning anew in the experience of a thousand boycotts, picket lines, sit-ins, demonstrations and marches." Other activists used Brown as an example of useful white involvement. Robert Williams wanted "some fighting John Browns" instead of "paternal white 'big daddies,'" and Malcolm X insisted: "If you are for me and my problem . . . then you have to be willing to do as old John Brown did." A few years later, H. Rap Brown simply called John Brown "the blackest white man anyone had ever known" and the "only white man I could respect."[91]

In the 1970s, Brown was born again as the hero to leftist guerrilla groups. In each issue of its journal, the Weather Underground printed a picture of Brown and explained underneath that the publication was called *Osawatomie* because it was named for Brown's battle at Osawatomie, Kansas, in 1856. Then, in 1978, a white antiracist group with connections to the Weather Underground began a national campaign against white supremacists and named itself the John Brown Anti-Klan Committee.

History's tribunal continued to judge Brown throughout the late twentieth and early twenty-first centuries. He was adopted as a hero and reference point by Timothy McVeigh and antiabortion activists (especially in the newsletter *Abortion Abolitionist*) as well as by the New Abolitionist Society, which seeks to abolish the white race as a social category. In the South, the phrase "I'll be John Browned" appeared in several twentieth-century folk songs and can still be heard used as a curse (in place of "goddamned" or "hanged").

In fact, each generation since 1859 has asked and answered for itself the questions phrased by Du Bois on the fiftieth anniversary of Brown's raid: "Was John Brown simply an episode, or was he an eternal truth? And if a truth, how speaks that truth today?" From Brown's own generation forward, through secession, the Civil War, Reconstruction, and the long civil rights movement of antilynching, desegregation, and labor reform in the twentieth century, to activists on the left and right who claim his mantle today, the tribunal that he himself envisaged has sat in judgment and pronounced—in Brown's own words—that the world was different for his "living and dying in it."[92]

Notes

1. John Brown to D. R. Tilden, November 28, 1859, in this volume.
2. Tony Horwitz, "The 9/11 of 1859," *New York Times*, December 2, 2009, A35. See also Beverly Gage, "Terrorism and the American Experience: A State of the Field," *Journal of American History* 98 (2011): 702–726.
3. Truman Nelson, "On Creating Revolutionary Art and Going Out of Print" (1972), in *The Truman Nelson Reader*, ed. William J. Schafer (Amherst: University of

Massachusetts Press, 1989), 169; Nelson, "John Brown Revisited," *The Nation*, August 31, 1957, 88. Nelson published two historical novels about John Brown, *The Surveyor* (1960) and *The Old Man: John Brown at Harpers Ferry* (1973). For more on Nelson's depictions of Brown, see Merrill D. Peterson, *John Brown: The Legend Revisited* (Charlottesville: University of Virginia Press, 2002), 148–151. In his keynote address at the 2009 Gilder Lehrman Center conference on John Brown, Fitzhugh Brundage developed Nelson's metaphor of Brown as a stone in the historian's shoe.

4. Thomas Haskell offers a brilliant critique of Peter Novick's *That Noble Dream*, arguing that "objectivity is not neutrality." He points out that Hermann von Holst, one of the profession's founders (and a cogent scholar of Brown), understood that objectivity did not mean dispassionate writing. Scholars had the right "to hold . . . political or moral opinions" of the events and people they wrote about. As Haskell summarizes, Holst's statement makes "it clear that even among the founding genera-tion, the necessity of distinguishing between the two [objectivity and neutrality] was recognized, and that is a fact Novick never comes to terms with." See Haskell, "Objectivity Is Not Neutrality: Rhetoric vs. Practice in Peter Novick's *That Noble Dream*," *History and Theory* 29, no. 2 (1990): 137n13.

5. See, for example, Alan Brinkley, *The Unfinished Nation: A Concise History of the American People*, 3rd ed. (Boston: McGraw-Hill, 2000); James A. Henretta, David Brody, and Lynn Dumenil, *America: A Concise History*, Vol. 1, 3rd ed. (Boston: Bedford/St. Martin's, 2006). Biographers have obviously not dismissed John Brown, and since 9/11 there have been some excellent biographies. Please see this volume's bibliography for a full list of books about Brown.

6. Seymour Drescher, "Servile Insurrection and John Brown's Body in Europe," in *His Soul Goes Marching On: Responses to John Brown and the Harpers Ferry Raid*, ed. Paul Finkelman (Charlottesville: University of Virginia Press, 1995), 259. See also David Brion Davis, *Slavery and Human Progress* (New York: Oxford University Press, 1984), 107–168, 231–258. Drescher argues that emancipation in the United States was a catalyst for abolition in Brazil. See Seymour Drescher, *Abolition: A History of Slavery and Antislavery* (New York: Cambridge University Press, 2009), 333–371.

7. *Richmond Whig*, November 22, 1859, and *Richmond Enquirer*, October 25, 1859. Allan Nevins similarly concludes that secessionist voices became dominant after Harpers Ferry. See Nevins, *The Ordeal of the Union*, Vol. 2: *Prologue to Civil War, 1857–1861* (New York: Collier, 1992 [1950]), 114–115. See also David M. Potter, *The Impending Crisis, 1848–1861* (New York: Harper & Row, 1976), 382–384.

8. David M. Potter, *Lincoln and His Party in the Secession Crisis* (Baton Rouge: Louisiana State University Press, 1995 [1942]), 13, 315. See also the introductory essay on counterfactual history by Niall Ferguson in *Virtual History: Alternatives and Counterfactuals* (New York: Basic, 1999), 1–90.

A few scholars have raised but not developed the counterfactual question "What if John Brown had not lived?" David Reynolds wonders "what would have happened had [Brown] been killed during the raid?" He concludes that "there might not have been the fracturing of the Democratic Party that made possible the election of Lincoln," but he does not develop this point. We agree with Reynolds's follow-up assessment: "Had secession not happened, most likely the war would have been delayed." But he argues that war was "needed to rid the nation of slavery." We don't know how slavery might have ended without war, but that doesn't mean war was *necessary* to end slavery. We can only surmise that if Stephen Douglas had been elected president in 1860, war would have been deferred. We simply don't have evidence to demonstrate, one way or another, what would have happened after 1864. See David S. Reynolds, *John Brown, Abolitionist: That Man Who Killed Slavery, Sparked the Civil War, and Seeded Civil Rights* (New York: Knopf, 2005), 438–439.

   In his review of Reynolds's book, Sean Wilentz rebuts Reynolds's counterfactual claims: "Did Brown's raid on Harpers Ferry spark southern secession and the Civil War? No, Lincoln's victory in the election of 1860 did that, and would have done it regardless of Brown's assault." Wilentz ignores the possibility that Brown's raid split the Democratic Party, which virtually assured the election of a Republican. He does suggest, however, that Brown's raid was an important factor contributing to Republicans' nomination of Lincoln over Seward, the frontrunner prior to Brown's raid. And in *The Rise of American Democracy*, Wilentz comes close to agreeing with Reynolds. He asks, "What, then, was John Brown's achievement and significance?" His answer is that Harpers Ferry created "a pervasive mood of [southern] panic and fury at the end of 1859," which "greatly encouraged the southern fire-eater minority. . . . After Brown's attack, secessionist efforts accelerated." See Wilentz, "Homegrown Terrorist," *New Republic*, October 24, 2005, 24, and *The Rise of American Democracy: Jefferson to Lincoln* (New York: Norton, 2005), 752–753.

   Several other scholars similarly argue that Brown was a crucial catalyst leading to secession and war. William Freehling suggests that Brown was an important prong of a three-pronged assault on the South that led to secession. Avery Craven, Allan Nevins, and David Potter go even further in suggesting that Brown was the crucial (though not the only) catalyst. But none raises the counterfactual question. See Freehling, *The Road to Disunion*, Vol. II: *Secessionists Triumphant, 1854–1861* (New York: Oxford University Press, 2007), 205–221, 260, 262, 264, 266; Craven, *The Growth of Southern Nationalism, 1848–1861* (Baton Rouge: Louisiana State University Press, 1981 [1953]), 304–317; Nevins, *Ordeal of the Union*, 98–115, 125–131, 168–169, 175–181, 202, 217; and Potter, *Impending Crisis*, 378–384, 454–455, 478–484, 486–487, 489–491, 500–501. Potter summarizes secession: "The crucial fact, as the secessionists clearly realized, was that all of the states were acting in an atmosphere of excitement approaching hysteria, first generated by John Brown's attempted slave insurrection and surging up again in the latter stages of the presidential campaign. This excitement still prevailed when the secessionists went into action. . . . [They] knew that their iron was hot, and they struck" (500–501).

   9. "The Day of Execution," *Independent*, November 24, 1859; Wendell Phillips, "Eulogy for John Brown," December 8, 1859, in this volume; Frederick Douglass, "John Brown," May 30, 1881, in this volume; Hermann von Holst, *John Brown*, 1878, in this volume.

   10. Brown, "To Mr. Henry L. Stearns," July 15, 1857, in this volume. See also Tony Horwitz, *Midnight Rising: John Brown and the Raid That Sparked the Civil War* (New York: Holt, 2011), 9, 11.

   11. Brown, "To Mr. Henry L. Stearns." Brown does not mention where the landlord

who beat his slave lived. Assuming that it was in Ohio, the only slaves left in the state by the War of 1812 were minors, such as the boy Brown describes. Ohio's 1802 constitution abolished slavery (Art. 8, Sec. 2), but only for adults; boys remained slaves—technically, indentured servants—until age twenty-one. Robert McGlone dismisses the accuracy of Brown's autobiogaphical sketch, arguing that "it does not ring true" because Brown's memory was "more notable for its moral implications than its accuracy." We use Brown's autobiography with caution rather than dismissing it. See Robert E. McGlone, *John Brown's War Against Slavery* (Cambridge: Cambridge University Press, 2009), 52. On the persistence of slavery in the Northwest Territories, especially Indiana and Illinois, despite the ban on slavery in the Northwest Ordinance of 1787, see Paul Finkelman, *Slavery and the Founders: Race and Liberty in the Age of Jefferson* (Armonk, NY: M. E. Sharpe, 1996), 34–79.

12. Oswald Garrison Villard, *John Brown, 1800–1859: A Biography Fifty Years After* (Boston: Houghton Mifflin, 1910), 16–18; Reynolds, *John Brown*, 48–49.

13. Quoted in Villard, *John Brown*, 23.

14. See Stephen B. Oates, *To Purge This Land with Blood: A Biography of John Brown* (New York: Harper & Row, 1970), 22–50; Reynolds, *John Brown*, 57–65.

15. John Stauffer, *The Black Hearts of Men: Radical Abolitionists and the Transformation of Race* (Cambridge: Harvard University Press, 2002), 120. Several historians, notably Louis DeCaro, argue that Brown was a Calvinist in the tradition of Jonathan Edwards. But a central tenet of Edwardsian Calvinism is God's inscrutability. In this sense Lincoln was a Calvinist, as reflected in his second inaugural address: "Both [sides] read the same Bible, and pray to the same God; and each invokes His aid against the other. . . . The prayers of both could not be answered; that of neither has been answered fully. The Almighty has His own purposes." For a Calvinist, presuming to know God's will, as John Brown did, was hubris. Edwards repudiated free will and antinomianism, which totally contradicts Brown's faith. However, as many scholars have noted, Edwards's emphases on a future millennium and the "spiritual affections" of the heart opened the way for prophecy and an impending new age, either by dismantling his Calvinist determinism or by embracing antinomianism. See Louis A. DeCaro, Jr., *"Fire from the Midst of You": A Religious Life of John Brown* (New York: New York University Press, 2002), esp. chs. 7, 19; Sydney Ahlstrom, *A Religious History of the American People* (New Haven: Yale University Press, 1972), 301–313; Joseph A. Conforti, *Jonathan Edwards, Religious Tradition, and American Culture* (Chapel Hill: University of North Carolina Press, 1995), 36–61; Timothy L. Smith, *Revivalism and Social Reform: American Protestantism on the Eve of the Civil War* (New York: Harper & Row, 1965); Nicholas Parrillo, "Lincoln's Calvinist Transformation: Emancipation and War," *Civil War History* 46, no. 3 (2000): 227–253.

16. J. Newton Brown, "The Beginning of John Brown's Career," *The Nation*, February 12, 1914, 157 (quoting Brown's cousin, Edward Brown); Justus Newton Brown, "Lovejoy's Influence on John Brown," *Magazine of History, with Notes and Queries* 23 (1916): 101.

17. Oates, *To Purge This Land*, 54–55; Franklin B. Sanborn, ed., *The Life and Letters of John Brown* (Boston: Roberts Brothers, 1885), 35, 43; Reynolds, *John Brown*, 66–85;

Louis Ruchames, ed., *John Brown: The Making of a Revolutionary* (New York: Grosset, 1969), 26–27.

18. John Brown, letter of November 8, 1846, in Ruchames, *John Brown*, 64. See also Oates, *To Purge This Land*, 55–56.

19. Douglass, "Editorial Correspondence," *North Star*, February 11, 1848; Brown, "Sambo's Mistakes," 1848, in this volume.

20. Gerrit Smith, quoted in *Fifth Annual Report of the Executive Committee of the American Anti-Slavery Society* (New York: William S. Dorr, 1838), 35; Letter from Gerrit Smith, *Oneida Morning Herald*, October 13, 1848.

21. Brown, quoted in Sanborn, *Life and Letters*, 97; Brown, quoted in Ralph Volney Harlow, *Gerrit Smith: Philanthropist and Reformer* (New York: Holt, 1939), 246. See also Ruchames, *John Brown*, 75, and Villard, *John Brown*, 71–77.

Of the three thousand recipients of Smith's gift, only about one hundred people moved to Timbucto. The main reason for this low turnout was start-up costs. Before moving, would-be pioneers needed wagons, mules or oxen, tools, and enough supplies to survive until the first harvest. All this amounted to about $100, roughly one-third of the annual earnings of the working poor. Many recipients did not save that much, and Smith didn't have an extra $300,000 in cash to enable settlers to make the move. Additionally, the land was of poor quality and the climate harsh, and settlers had to generate surplus in order to pay yearly taxes. Some settlers could not pay their taxes and faced foreclosure by the New York State Treasury. Finally, some whites living in the region tried to cheat grantees out of their deeds. See Stauffer, *Black Hearts*, 157.

22. Richard Henry Dana, Jr., "How We Met John Brown," *Atlantic Monthly*, July 1871, 6.

23. Frederick Douglass, *The Life and Times* (Boston: De Wolfe & Fiske, 1892), 340, 341; Douglass, "Slavery, The Slumbering Volcano," speech of April 23, 1849, in *The Frederick Douglass Papers, Series One: Speeches: Debates and Interviews*, Vol. 2, ed. John W. Blassingame et al. (New Haven: Yale University Press, 1982), 148. See also Matthew Clavin, "A Second Haitian Revolution: John Brown, Toussaint Louverture, and the Making of the American Civil War," *Civil War History* 54, no. 2 (2008): 138, 142–145.

24. *Proceedings of the Convention of Radical Political Abolitionists . . .* (New York: Central Abolition Board, 1855), 17, 52. See also Stauffer, *Black Hearts*, 22–27.

25. John Brown, Jr., letter quoted in Villard, *John Brown*, 83. See also *Proceedings of the Convention*, 62–63, and Richard O. Boyer, *The Legend of John Brown: A Biography and a History* (New York: Knopf, 1973), 524–527.

26. William Phillips, *The Conquest of Kansas, by Missouri and Her Allies* (Boston: Phillips, Sampson, 1856), 297; Reynolds, *John Brown*, 149, 156–157. On the news of Sumner's caning not reaching Kansas for at least a week, see McGlone, *John Brown's War*, 74, 350n11.

27. *New York Herald*, June 8, 1856. See also Reynolds, *John Brown*, 154–157, 171–173.

28. Douglass, "The Danger of the Republican Movement," speech of May 28, 1856, in *The Life and Writings of Frederick Douglass*, Vol. 5, ed. Philip S. Foner (New York: International, 1975), 389.

29. Sandra Harbert Petrulionis, *To Set This World Right: The Antislavery Movement in Thoreau's Concord* (Ithaca: Cornell University Press, 2006), 117–121; Reynolds, *John Brown*, 206–238; Horwitz, *Midnight Rising*, 74–79; and Len Gougeon, *Virtue's Hero: Emerson, Antislavery, and Reform* (Athens: University of Georgia Press, 1990), 218–249.

30. Ralph Waldo Emerson, entry of February 1857, in *Journals of Ralph Waldo Emerson*, Vol. 9 (Boston: Houghton Mifflin, 1913), 81–82. See also Randolph Paul Runyon, *Delia Webster and the Underground Railroad* (Lexington: University Press of Kentucky, 1996), 207; Petrulionis, *To Set This World*, 121; Gougeon, *Virtue's Hero*, 229; Reynolds, *John Brown*, 222–224.

31. James Freeman Clarke, "Charles Sumner," *Memorial and Biographical Sketches* (Boston: Houghton, Osgood, 1878), 102; Charles Sumner, "To the Duchess of Argyll," December 20, 1859, in this volume.

32. Robert Penn Warren, *John Brown: The Making of a Martyr* (New York: Payson & Clarke, 1929), 346; Brown, "Provisional Constitution," May 8, 1858, in this volume.

33. "Old Brown's Parallels," *New York Daily Tribune*, January 22, 1859; "Brown's Rescued Negroes Landed in Canada," *New York Daily Tribune*, March 17, 1859. See also Horwitz, *Midnight Rising*, 88–89.

34. Osborne P. Anderson, *A Voice from Harper's Ferry* (Boston: The Author, 1861), 31. See also Horwitz, *Midnight Rising*, 128–129.

35. Testimony of Daniel Whelan, *Report of the Select Committee on the Harper's Ferry Invasion* (Washington, DC: United States Congress, June 15, 1860), 22.

36. Reynolds, *John Brown*, 305; Horwitz, *Midnight Rising*, 131; McGlone, *Brown's War*, 258, 413n71. Horwitz says blacks made up less than 10 percent of the population of Harpers Ferry, but Reynolds and McGlone argue that they constituted about half the town's population. We're convinced by Horwitz's research and his e-mail to Stauffer, February 17, 2012.

37. For Brown's "General Orders No. 1," see *Calendar of Virginia State Papers and Other Manuscripts*, Vol. 11 (Richmond: R. F. Walker, 1893), 274–275.

38. "Testimony of Lewis W. Washington," *Report of the Select Committee*, 34. Brown could have attempted a preemptive strike on the white men in Harpers Ferry, much as he had done against proslavery men at Pottawatomie Creek in Kansas Territory in 1856. But doing so would have been at least as risky as staying where he was in the armory, and it would not have endeared him to antislavery Northerners. However, instead of waiting at the armory, Brown could have fled to the mountains surrounding Harpers Ferry with guns and hostages. Arguably it would have been easier to elude capture, use hostages as ransom, and give blacks days and weeks rather than a few hours to decide whether to join his army.

39. "The Inhabitants," *New York Herald*, November 1, 1859; Douglass, *Life and Times*, 389. On the "suicidal" nature of slave rebellions, see David Brion Davis, *Inhuman Bondage: The Rise and Fall of Slavery in the New World* (New York: Oxford University Press, 2006), 206.

40. Testimony of Conductor Phelps, in Robert De Witt, *The Life, Trial and Execution of Captain John Brown* (New York: Robert M. De Witt, 1859), 69. See also "Statement of W. E. Throckmorten," *New York Herald*, October 24, 1859; Horwitz, *Midnight Rising*, 137–140; McGlone, *Brown's War*, 262–264; and Reynolds, *John Brown*,

309, 318–319, 322. We agree with Horwitz, who uses "Heyward Shepherd." McGlone says "Hayward Shepherd" and Reynolds uses "Shepherd Hayward."

41. "A. J. Phelps to W. P. Smith," October 17, 1859, in *The Senate of Maryland, Correspondence Relating to the Insurrection at Harper's Ferry, 17th October, 1859* (Annapolis: B. H. Richardson, 1860), 5.

42. Horwitz, *Midnight Rising*, provides the clearest and most accurate narrative of the raid and a concise summary in his tables on 291–292.

43. Ibid., 291–292.

44. Anderson, *Voice from Harper's Ferry*, 29. During and after each of the three largest slave revolts in North America—the Stono Rebellion of 1739, the Louisiana Slave Revolt of 1811, and Nat Turner's Rebellion of 1831—more than one hundred blacks were killed. See Peter Charles Hoffer, *Cry Liberty: The Great Stono River Slave Rebellion of 1739* (New York: Oxford University Press, 2010); Daniel Rasmussen, *American Uprising: The Untold Story of America's Largest Slave Revolt* (New York: HarperCollins, 2011); Kenneth S. Greenberg, ed., *Nat Turner: A Slave Rebellion in History and Memory* (New York: Oxford University Press, 2003).

45. Robert E. Lee to Mary Lee, in *Recollections and Letters of Robert E. Lee* (New York: Doubleday, 1904), 22.

46. Sanborn, *Life and Letters*, 131 (quoted), 573, 379; Brown, "Last Address to the Virginia Court," November 2, 1859, in this volume. Emerson would later call this speech and Lincoln's Gettysburg Address the two greatest speeches in American history: "[Lincoln's] brief speech at Gettysburg will not easily be surpassed by words on any recorded occasion. This, and one other American speech, that of John Brown to the court that tried him, and a part of Kossuth's speech at Birmingham, can only be compared with each other, and with no fourth." Emerson, "Remarks at the Funeral Services of the President," April 19, 1865, *Living Age*, April-May-June 1865, 283.

47. Richard J. Hinton, *John Brown and His Men* (London: Funk & Wagnalls, 1894), 292. See also Hermann von Holst, *The Constitutional and Political History of the United States*, Vol. 7 (Chicago: Callaghan, 1892), 36–39, and Reynolds, *John Brown*, 335–336.

48. Reynolds argues that "had Transcendentalism not been in the picture, . . . the tide of negative commentary on Brown that flooded the northern press would have continued. With few opposing voices, negativity would most likely have won the day." Reynolds, *John Brown*, 343.

49. Henry David Thoreau, entries of October 21 and October 19, 1859, in *The Writings of Henry David Thoreau: Journal*, Vol. 12 (Boston: Houghton Mifflin, 1906), 414, 407; Reynolds, *John Brown*, 345–347.

50. Thoreau, "A Plea for Captain John Brown," October 30, 1859, in this volume, and "Slavery in Massachusetts," July 4, 1854, in *The Writings of Henry David Thoreau*, Vol. 10 (Boston: Houghton Mifflin, 1893), 179.

51. Walt Whitman, remark to Horace Traubel, March 7, 1889, in *With Walt Whitman in Camden*, Vol. 4 (Philadelphia: University of Pennsylvania Press, 1953), 293 (Whitman observed of Brown: "I, for my part, could never see in Brown himself, merely of himself, the evidence of great human quality. . . . I don't seem to like him any better now than I did then"; ibid); Emerson, "Courage," November 8, 1859, and

"Remarks at a Meeting for the Relief of the Family of John Brown," November 18, 1859, in this volume. On the controversy generated by Emerson's "gallows glorious" remark, see John McAleer, *Ralph Waldo Emerson: Days of Encounter* (Boston: Little, Brown, 1984), 532–533. See also Reynolds, *John Brown*, 366–367.

52. Stephen Douglas, "Invasion of States," January 23, 1860, in this volume. See also Holst, *Constitutional and Political History*, 224.

53. John Andrew, "Speech at Tremont Temple," November 18, 1859, in this volume; Abraham Lincoln, "Speech at Leavenworth," December 1859, in *Collected Works of Abraham Lincoln*, ed. Roy Basler, Vol. 9 (New Brunswick: Rutgers University Press, 1953), 502. For more on Andrew's relationship to Brown, see Robert M. Fogelson and Richard E. Rubenstein, eds., *Mass Violence in America: Invasion at Harper's Ferry* (New York: Arno, 1969 [1860]), 188–194. Lincoln also called Brown "insane" but acknowledged that he had shown "great courage" and "rare unselfishness." See Basler, *Collected Works of Abraham Lincoln*, Vol. 3, 496, 503, 541.

54. William Lloyd Garrison, "Speech at the Annual Meeting of the Massachusetts Anti-Slavery Society, January 27, 1860," *The Liberator*, February 17, 1860. See also Wendell Phillips Garrison and Francis Jackson Garrison, *William Lloyd Garrison, 1805–1879: The Story of His Life, Told By His Children*, Vol. 3, *1841–1860* (New York: Century, 1889), 493.

55. Phrases heard from audience members at Brown's trial, as recounted by George Alfred Townsend in *Katy of Catoctin, Or the Chain-Breakers: A National Romance* (New York: Appleton, 1886), 300; James Redpath, "Notes on the Insurrection: Harper's Ferry as a Success," *The Liberator*, November 4, 1859 (reprinted from the *Boston Atlas and Bee*). See also Reynolds, *John Brown*, 349, 412.

56. Holst, *Constitutional and Political History*, 46. See also Peter Wallenstein, "Incendiaries All: Southern Politics and the Harpers Ferry Raid," in Finkelman, *His Soul Goes Marching On*, 149–173.

57. John Tyler, Jr., "The Secession of the South," *De Bow's Review* 3 (April 1860), in this volume. See also Holst, *Constitutional and Political History*, 45–47, and Matthew J. Clavin, *Toussaint Louverture and the American Civil War: The Promise and Peril of a Second Haitian Revolution* (Philadelphia: University of Pennsylvania Press, 2010), ch. 2.

58. George Fitzhugh, "Disunion within the Union," January 1860, in this volume. See also Nevins, *Ordeal of the Union*, Vol. 2: *Prologue*, 114, 126; Craven, *Growth of Southern Nationalism*, 305.

59. "New England Society," *Charleston Mercury*, December 23, 1858, quoting Albert Laighton's poem "New England" (1858).

60. Robert Bunch, letter of December 9, 1859, British Record Office, London, Foreign Office Records, United States, Series II, 5, 720; "Freedom of Speech in the South," *National Era*, January 12, 1860. See also Laura A. White, "The South in the 1850s as Seen by British Consuls," *Journal of Southern History* 1, no. 1 (February 1935): 44; Craven, *Growth of Southern Nationalism*, 309; Reynolds, *John Brown*, 416–419.

61. William H. Gist, "Message No.1," November 29, 1859, *Journal of the House of Representatives of the State of South Carolina* (Columbia: R. W. Gibbes, 1859), 22; William P. Miles, "Organization of the House," Appendix to the *Congressional Globe*, 36th Congress, 1st Session, January 6, 1860, 68, 69; *Congressional Globe*, 36th Congress,

1st Session, March 3, 1860, 949; "Manufacture of Arms at the South," *De Bow's Review,* February 1860, 234. See also Holst, *Constitutional and Political History,* 111–113.

62. "The Harper's Ferry Invasion as Party Capital," *Richmond Enquirer,* October 25, 1859; C. G. Memminger, "The South Carolina Mission to Virginia," January 19, 1860, in this volume; William A. Walsh, letter of December 8, 1859, quoted in Craven, *Growth of Southern Nationalism,* 311.

63. *Sumter Watchman,* December 24, 1859, quoted in Potter, *Impending Crisis,* 384; *Baltimore Sun,* November 28, 1859, quoted in Villard, *John Brown,* 568.

64. *Atlanta Confederacy,* quoted in *Twenty-Seventh Annual Report of the American Anti-Slavery Society* (New York: American Anti-Slavery Society, 1861), 167.

65. Jefferson Davis, speech in the U.S. Senate, May 7, 1860, in Davis, *The Rise and Fall of the Confederate Government* (New York: Appleton, 1881), 590; Charles O'Conor, speech at the Great Union Meeting, *Official Report of the Great Union Meeting, New York, December 19, 1859* (New York: Davies & Kent, 1859), 29, 31.

66. *Baltimore Patriot,* quoted in Holst, *Constitutional and Political History,* 58.

67. In developing this idea, we are indebted to Adam Gopnik, "Headless Horseman," *The New Yorker,* June 5, 2006, 80; David Brion Davis, *The Problem of Slavery in the Age of Revolution, 1770–1823* (Ithaca: Cornell University Press, 1973), 306–325; Arthur M. Schlesinger, Jr., *The Cycles of American History* (Boston: Mariner, 1999 [1986]), 3–50; John Higham, "From Boundlessness to Consolidation: The Transformation of American Culture, 1848–1860," in *Hanging Together: Unity and Diversity in American Culture,* ed. Carl J. Guarneri (New Haven: Yale University Press, 2001), 149–166; Alexis de Tocqueville, *Democracy in America,* tr. Henry Reeve, Vol. 1 (New York: Vintage, 1990 [1835]), 254–288.

68. William Kauffman Scarborough, ed., *The Diary of Edmund Ruffin,* Vol. 1 (Baton Rouge: Louisiana State University Press, 1972), 348, 349. See also Avery Craven, *Edmund Ruffin, Southerner: A Study in Secession* (New York: Appleton, 1932), 167.

69. Scarborough, *Diary,* 350.

70. Ibid., 354, 355, 356, 357, 363; Craven, *Edmund Ruffin,* 172–176.

71. Scarborough, *Diary,* 365, 366, 371; Craven, *Edmund Ruffin,* 177.

72. Scarborough, *Diary,* 368, 376, 378, 381; Craven, *Edmund Ruffin,* 178–181.

73. Edmund Ruffin, *Anticipations of the Future,* June 1860, in this volume.

74. Scarborough, *Diary,* 630; Craven, *Edmund Ruffin,* 183.

75. Robert W. Johannsen, *Stephen A. Douglas* (Urbana: University of Illinois Press, 1997 [1973]), 518–519, and Wilentz, *Rise of American Democracy,* 755.

76. Nevins, *Ordeal of the Union,* 177. As early as September 1859, Senator Albert Gallatin Brown of Mississippi had written privately to Douglas and warned him: "The South will demand at Charleston a platform explicitly declaring that slave property is entitled in the Territories and on the high seas to the same protection that is given to any other and every other species of property—and failing to get it, she will retire from the convention." But far more threatening was William Yancy's instruction to Southern delegates in January 1860 to withdraw from the Democratic convention if a slave code was not incorporated into the party platform. See Robert Walter Johannsen, *The Frontier, the Union, and Stephen Douglas* (Urbana: University of Illinois Press, 1989), 151.

77. William Lowndes Yancey, speech to the National Convention, *Proceedings of the Conventions at Charleston and Baltimore* (Washington, DC: National Democratic Executive Committee, 1860), 69, 78. See also Eric H. Walther, *William Lowndes Yancey and the Coming of the Civil War* (Chapel Hill: University of North Carolina Press, 2006), 237–243, and Nevins, *Ordeal of the Union*, Vol. 2: *Prologue*, 217–219.

78. William Bigler, letter to James Buchanan, October 22, 1859, in Johanssen, *Stephen A. Douglas*, 716. See also Nevins, *Ordeal of the Union*, Vol. 2, *Prologue*, 263, 202, and Wilentz, *Rise of American Democracy*, 757.

79. For a chart showing the breakdown of votes in the 1860 presidential election state by state, see www.presidency.ucsb.edu/showelection.php ?year=1860. See also Nevins, *Ordeal of the Union*, Vol. 2, *Prologue*, 312.

80. Salmon P. Chase, letter endorsing John Brown, December 20, 1856, in Sanborn, *Life and Letters*, 363.

81. Reuben Davis, "The Duty of Parties," December 8, 1859, in this volume; Lincoln, "Speech at Elwood, Kansas," December 1, 1859, in Basler, ed., *Collected Works of Abraham Lincoln*, Vol. 3, 496.

82. Douglass, "The Chicago Nominations," *Douglass' Monthly*, June 1860.

83. Potter makes the crucial point that after South Carolina announced its secession convention, "false information reached Columbia that Robert Toombs of Georgia had resigned from the Senate." The false report accelerated secession in South Carolina, and the speed of South Carolina's secession gave crucial encouragement to secessionists throughout the South. Potter, *Impending Crisis*, 490–491.

84. John Rhodehamel and Louise Taper, eds., *Right or Wrong, God Judge Me: The Writings of John Wilkes Booth* (Urbana: University of Illinois Press, 1997), 67.

85. Ibid., 130; John Wilkes Booth, "Philadelphia Speech," December 1860, in this volume; Booth, "Remarks on Lincoln and Brown," November 1864, in this volume.

86. Henry Highland Garnet, "Martyr's Day," December 2, 1859, in this volume; Osborne P. Anderson, *A Voice from Harper's Ferry*, in this volume; William Dean Howells, "Old Brown," November 1859, in this volume; Douglass, "Capt. John Brown Not Insane," November 1859, in this volume.

87. Douglass, "Speech on the War," January 14, 1862, *Douglass' Monthly*, February 1862, 597.

88. Douglass, "John Brown," May 30, 1881, in this volume.

89. Mrs. L. G. Haywood, "Now a Day for John Brown," *Chicago Defender*, April 21, 1928, A2.

90. Eugene Debs, "John Brown: History's Greatest Hero," November 23, 1907, in *Debs: His Life, Writings and Speeches* (Chicago: Renneker, 1908), 272; Michael Gold, *The Life of John Brown* (New York: Roving Eye, 1960 [1924]), 4.

91. John Brown Commemoration Committee, "A Call," October 18, 1965, Mae Mallory Papers, Series II, Box 2, Walter P. Reuther Library, Wayne State University; Robert F. Williams, "Revolution without Violence?" *The Crusader*, February 1964, 5; Malcolm X, "Answer to question at Militant Labor Forum," January 7, 1965, in *Malcolm X Speaks*, ed. George Breitman (New York: Grove, 1965), 225; H. Rap Brown, *Die Nigger Die!* (New York: Dial, 1969), 116.

92. W. E. B. Du Bois, *John Brown* (Philadelphia: G. W. Jacobs, 1909), 374; Brown to

D. R. Tilden. Brown imagined a future tribunal deciding whether the world would have been "better" or "worse" had he not lived. We avoid this moral judgment and instead conclude that the world would have been *different*. After all, Brown's influence extended to Timothy McVeigh, the Weather Underground, and anti-abortionists along with antilynching, labor, and civil rights activists. Then too, perhaps his absence might have led to a delayed but peaceful emancipation, which would have prevented or shortened the long, vengeful era after emancipation that in many respects was "worse than slavery." See David M. Oshinsky, *"Worse than Slavery": Parchman Farm and the Ordeal of Jim Crow Justice* (New York: Free Press, 1996).

In His Own Words

IN JULY 1859, John Brown rented a farm about 7 miles from Harpers Ferry, West Virginia. Men gathered and weapons arrived. Then, in the evening on October 16, Brown gave the order to begin. The men captured the town of Harpers Ferry and its federal arsenal, intending to distribute the arsenal's weapons to slaves and free blacks in the area, whom Brown expected to be ready and waiting for him, and incite an insurrection that would spread throughout the South. Federal forces led by Robert E. Lee overwhelmed the raiders after thirty-six hours, and Brown was taken to the Charles Town jail and indicted. On the morning of his execution, December 2, 1859, Brown passed his last words to a jailer: a prophecy that the nation could purge away the crime of slavery only in blood. Then, as he approached the gallows, Brown turned to the deputy sheriff and commented: "This is a beautiful country. I never had the pleasure of seeing it before." With these words, he perhaps offered one final, prophetic vision of a slave-free country, never before seen, that would emerge from the bloodshed.

Part I of this volume collects the major documents that Brown wrote. These include a first-person narrative in the voice of a free black Northerner, Brown's instructions to a black self-defense league, an account of his actions in Kansas, a short autobiography, a provisional constitution for a slave-free nation, a rewrite of the Declaration of Independence, his interview after the Harpers Ferry raid, his last address to the jury during the trial, a selection of his prison letters, and his last statement. By reading Brown's own writings, we can assess how his self-image squared with the characterizations of his contemporaries.

We encounter a man who was conscious and manipulative of historical and mythic precedent, and we see that his self-representational strategies were models for the discourse around him. Brown made and remade himself with a keen eye for his own mythology, and effected self-transformations from Puritan to black man, from Indian warrior to martyr. In John Brown's own writings, we see the origin of the responses of history's tribunal.

John Brown, "Sambo's Mistakes," 1848

Between 1846 and 1849, Brown lived in Springfield, Massachusetts, and ran a wool distribution agency. There he wrote a first-person narrative entitled "Sambo's Mistakes," which he sent to the *Ram's Horn,* a black weekly newspaper based in New York and published by Willis Hodges beginning in January 1847. Hodges was a freeborn African American from Virginia. He named the four-page paper for Joshua 6:5, which describes the sound of a ram's horn bringing down Jericho's walls. It reached 2500 subscribers at its peak, before folding in June 1848. In Brown's submission for the paper, he wrote as a free black Northerner who has internalized racist stereotypes and wastes his life in the pursuit of pleasure. He affected the apologetic, garrulous style of a self-indulgent and submissive character. This satirical piece critiqued the materialism and apathy of Northern black Americans who did not take a militant abolitionist stand. As an attempt to cross racial boundaries, the piece prefigures Brown's famous prison letters of 1859, in which he identified with the slave and drew upon the tropes of slave narratives: imprisonment, wounds, chains, and the soul's freedom—emphasizing that men cannot "imprison, or chain, or hang the soul," as he put it in one prison letter. He even wanted to die alongside slaves: in a prison letter of November 29, 1859, he explained that he wanted only slave children and a slave mother as religious attendants at his execution.

Chap 1st

Mess Editors. Notwithstanding I may have committed a few mistakes in the course of a long life like others of my colored brethren yet you will perceive at a glance that I have always been remarkable for a seasonable discovery of my errors & quick perception of the true course. I propose to give you a few illustrations in this & the following chapters. For instance when I was a boy I learned to read but instead of giving my attention to sacred & profane history by which I might have become acquainted with the true character of God &

3

of man learned the true course for individuals, societies, & nations to pursue, stored my mind with an endless variety of rational and practical ideas, profited by the experience of millions of others of all ages, fitted myself for the most important stations in life & fortified my mind with the best & wisest resolutions, & noblest sentiments, & motives, I have spent my whole life devouring silly novels & other miserable trash such as most newspapers of the day & other popular writings are filled with, thereby unfitting myself for the realities of life & acquiring a taste for nonsense & low wit, so that I have no rellish[1] for sober truth, useful knowledge or practical wisdom. By this means I have passed through life without proffit to myself or others a mere blank on which nothing worth peruseing is written. But I can see in a twink where I missed it. Another error into which I fell in early life was the notion that chewing & smoking tobacco would make a man of me but little inferior to some of the whites. The money I spent in this way would with the interest of it have enabled me to have relieved a great many sufferers supplyed me with a well selected interesting library, & paid for a good farm for the support & comfort of my old age; whereas I have now neither books, clothing, the satisfaction of having benefited others, nor where to lay my hoary head. But I can see in a moment where I missed it. Another of the few errors of my life is that I have joined the Free Masons, Odd Fellows, Sons of Temperance, & a score of other secret societies instead of seeking the company of intelligent wise & good men from whom I might have learned much that would be interesting, instructive, & useful & have in that way squandered a great amount of most precious time; & money enough sometime in a single year which if I had then put the same out on interest & kept it so would have kept me always above board given me character, & influence amongst men or have enabled me to pursue some respectable calling so that I might employ others to their benefit & improvement, but as it is I have always been poor, in debt, & now obliged to travel about in search of employment as a hostler shoe black & fiddler. But I retain all my quickness of perception I can see readily where I missed it.

Chap 2d

Another error of my riper years has been that when any meeting of colored people has been called in order to consider of any important matter of general interest I have been so eager to display my spouting talents & so tenacious of some trifling theory or other that I have adopted that I have generally lost all sight of the business in hand consumed the time disputing about things of no moment & thereby defeated entirely many important measures calculated to promote the general welfare; but I am happy to say I can see in a minute where I missed it. Another small error of my life (for I never committed great blunders) has been that I never would (for the sake of union in the furtherance of the most vital interests of our race) yield any minor point of difference. In this way I have always had to act with but a few, or more frequently alone & could accomplish nothing worth living for, but I have one comfort, I can see in a minute where I missed it. Another little fault which I have committed is that if in anything another man has failed of coming up to my standard that notwithstanding he might possess many of the most valuable traits & be most admirably adapted to fill some one important post, I would reject him entirely, injure his influence, oppose his measures, & even glory in his defeats while his intentions were good, & his plans well laid. But l have the great satisfaction of being able to say without fear of contradiction that I can see *verry quick* where I missed it.

Chap 3d

Another small mistake which I have made is that I could never bring myself to practice any present self denial although my theories have been excellent. For instance I have bought expensive gay clothing nice Canes, Watches, Safety Chains, Finger rings, Breast Pins, & many other things of a like nature, thinking I might by that means distinguish myself from the vulgar as some of the better class of whites do. I have always been of the foremost in getting up expensive parties, & running after fashionable amusements, have indulged my appetite freely whenever I had the means (& even with borrowed means) have patronized the dealers in Nuts, Candy, &c freely & have sometimes bought good suppers & was always a regular customer at Livery stables. By these & many other means I have been unable to benefit my suffering Brethren, & am now but poorly able to keep my own Soul & boddy together; but do not think me thoughtless or dull of apprehention for I can see at once where I missed it.

Another trifling error of my life has been that I have always expected to secure the favour of the whites by tamely submitting to every species of indignity contempt & wrong insted of nobly resisting their brutal aggressions from principle & taking my place as a man & assuming the responsibilities of a man a citizen, a husband, a father, a brother, a neighbour, a friend as God requires of every one (if his neighbour will allow him to do it) but I find that I get for all my submission about the same reward that the Southern Slaveocrats render to the Dough faced Statesmen of the North for being bribed & browbeat, & fooled & cheated, as the Whigs & Democrats love to be. & think themselves highly honored if they may be allowed to lick up the spittle of a Southerner. I say I get the same reward. But I am uncommon quick sighted I can see in a minute where I missed it. Another little blunder which I made *is,* that while I have always been a most zealous Abolitionist I have been constantly at war with my friends about certain religious tenets. I was first a Presbyterian but I could never think of acting with my Quuaker friends for they were the rankest heretiks & the Baptists would be in the water, & the Methodists denied the doctrine of Election, & of later years since becoming enlightened by Garrison, Abby Kelly[2] & other really benevolent persons I have been spending all my force on my friends who love the Sabbath & have felt that all was at stake on that point just as it has proved to be of late in France in the abolition of Slavery in their colonies.[3] Now I cannot doubt Mess Editors notwithstanding I have been unsuccessful that you will allow me full credit for my *peculiar* quick sightedness. I can see in one second where I missed it.

Source: Oswald Garrison Villard, *John Brown, 1800–1859: A Biography Fifty Years After* (Boston: Houghton Mifflin, 1910), 659–661.

John Brown, "League of Gileadites," January 15, 1851

Passed on September 18, 1850, the Fugitive Slave Law demanded that law-enforcement officials everywhere arrest anyone suspected of being a runaway slave. Any person who aided a runaway was subject to six months' imprisonment and a fine. In response, Brown founded a black self-defense group in Springfield called the United States League of Gileadites. The group's name alluded to the biblical story about a small army of Israelites (Judges 12:4–6). He drafted a founding document, which included advice on militant resistance and guerrilla tactics, and forty-four members, men and women, signed an "agreement" and a series of resolutions on January 15, 1851. A few years later, in June 1854, the black abolitionist and novelist William Wells Brown visited Springfield and observed that members of the League of Gileadites were more than ready to carry out the "Words of Advice." When slave catchers arrived, "the authorities, foreseeing a serious outbreak, advised them to leave, and feeling alarmed for their personal safety, these disturbers of the peace had left," he recounted. "No fugitive slave was ever afterwards disturbed at Springfield." John Brown himself put his advice into action in 1859, explaining in his prison letters that his imprisonment and death would serve the abolitionist cause. In 1851 his "Words of Advice" had imagined the trial of one man arousing "sympathy throughout the nation." Eight years later, he attempted to arouse this very sympathy on his own behalf.

Words of Advice

Branch of the United States League of Gileadites.
Adopted January 15, 1851, as written and recommended by John Brown.
"Union is Strength"

Nothing so charms the American people as personal bravery. Witness the case of Cinqué, of everlasting memory, on board the "Amistad."[4] The trial for life of one bold and to some extent successful man, for defending his rights in good earnest, would arouse more sympathy throughout the nation than the accumulated wrongs and sufferings of more than three millions of our submissive colored population. We need not mention the Greeks struggling against the oppressive Turks, the Poles against Russia, nor the Hungarians against Austria and Russia combined, to prove this. *No jury can be found in the Northern States that would convict a man for defending his rights to the last extremity. This is well understood by Southern Congressmen, who insisted that the right of trial by jury should not be granted to the fugitive.*[5] Colored people have more fast friends amongst the whites than they suppose, and would have ten times the number they now have were they but half as much in earnest to secure their dearest rights as they are to ape the follies and extravagances of their white neighbors, and to indulge in idle show, in ease, and in luxury. Just think of the money expended by individuals in your behalf in the past twenty years. Think of the number who have been mobbed and imprisoned on your account. Have any of you seen the Branded Hand?[6] Do you remember the names of Lovejoy and Torrey?[7]

Should one of your number be arrested, you must collect together as quickly as possible, so as to outnumber your adversaries who are taking an active part against you. Let no able-bodied man appear on the ground unequipped, or with his weapons exposed to view; let that be understood beforehand. Your plans must be known only to yourself, and with the understanding that all traitors must die, wherever caught and proven to be guilty. 'Whosoever is fearful or afraid, let him return and depart early from Mount Gilead.' (Judges, vii. chap., 3 verse; Deut., xx chap., 8 verse.) Give all cowards an opportunity to show it on condition of holding their peace. *Do not delay one moment after you are ready, you will lose all your resolution if you do. Let the first blow be the signal for all to engage, and when engaged do not do your work by halves; but make clean work with your enemies, and be sure you meddle not with any others.* By going about your business quietly, you will get the job disposed of before the number that an uproar would bring together can collect; and you will have the advantage of those who come out against you, for they will be wholly unprepared with either equipments or matured plans; all with them will be confusion and terror. Your enemies will be slow to attack you after you have once done up the work nicely; and if they should, they will have to encounter your white friends as well as you, for you may safely calculate on a division of the whites, and may by that means get to an honorable parley.

Be firm, determined, and cool; but let it be understood that you are not to be driven to desperation without making it an awful job to others as well as to you. Give them to know distinctly that those who live in wooden houses should not throw fire, and that you are just as able to suffer as your white neighbors. *After effecting a rescue, if your are assailed, go into the houses of your most prominent and influential white friends with your wives, and that will effectually fasten upon them the suspicion of being connected with you, and will compel them to make a common cause with you, whether they would otherwise live up to their profession or not. This would leave them no choice in the matter.* Some would, doubtless, prove themselves true of their own choice; others would flinch. That would be taking them at their own words. You may make a tumult in the court-room where a trial is going on by burning gunpowder freely in paper packages, if you cannot think of any better way to create a momentary alarm, and might possibly give one or more of your enemies a hoist. But in such case the prisoner will need to take the hint at once and bestir himself and so should his friends improve the opportunity for a general rush.

A lasso might possibly be applied to a slave-catcher for once with good effect. Hold on to your weapons, and never be persuaded to leave them, part with them, or have them far away from you. *Stand by one another, and by your friends, while a drop of blood remains; and be hanged, if you must, but tell no tales out of school. Make no confession.*

Union is strength. Without some well-digested arrangements nothing to any good purpose is likely to be done, let the demand be never so great. Witness the case of Hamlet and Long in New York,[8] when there was no well-defined plan of operations or suitable preparation beforehand.

The desired end may be effectually secured by the means proposed; namely, the enjoyment of our inalienable rights.

Agreement

As citizens of the United States of America, trusting in a just and merciful God, whose spirit and all-powerful aid we humbly implore, *we will ever be true to the flag of our beloved country, always acting under it.* We, whose names are hereunto affixed, do constitute ourselves a branch of the United States League of Gileadites. We will provide ourselves at once with suitable implements, and will aid those who do not possess the means, if any such are disposed to join us. We invite every colored person whose heart is engaged for the performance of our business, whether male or female, old or young. The duty of the aged, infirm, and young members of the League shall be to give instant notice to all members in case of an attack upon any of our people. We agree to have no officers except a Treasurer and Secretary, *pro tem.*, until after some trial of courage and talent of able-bodied members shall enable us to elect officers from those who shall have rendered the most important services. Nothing but wisdom and undaunted courage, efficiency, and general good conduct shall in any way influence us in electing our officers.

Resolutions

Resolutions of the Springfield Branch of The United States League Of Gileadites. Adopted 15th Jan., 1851

1. *Resolved,* That we, whose names are affixed, do constitute ourselves a Branch of the United States League, under the above name.
2. *Resolved,* That all business of this Branch be conducted with the utmost quiet and good order; that we individually provide ourselves with suitable implements without delay; and that we will sufficiently aid those who do not possess the means, if any such are disposed to join us.
3. *Resolved,* That a committee of one or more discreet, influential men be appointed to collect the names of all colored persons whose heart is engaged for the performance of our business, whether male or female, whether old or young.
4. *Resolved,* That the appropriate duty of all aged, infirm, female, or youthful members of this Branch is to give instant notice to all other members of any attack upon the rights of our people, first informing all able-bodied men of this League or Branch, and next, all well known friends of the colored people; and *that this information be confined to such alone,* that there may be as little excitement as possible, and no noise in the so doing.
5. *Resolved,* That a committee of one or more discreet persons be appointed to ascertain the condition of colored persons in regard to implements, and to instruct others in regard to their conduct in any emergency.
6. *Resolved,* That no other officer than a *treasurer,* with a president and secretary *pro tem.,* be appointed by this Branch, until after some trial of the courage and talents of able-bodied members shall enable a majority of the members to elect their officers from those who *shall have rendered the most important services.*
7. *Resolved,* That, trusting in a just and merciful God, whose *spirit* and

all-powerful aid we humbly implore, we will most cheerfully and heartily support and obey such officers, when chosen as before; and that nothing but *wisdom, undaunted courage, efficiency, and general good conduct* shall in any degree influence our individual votes in case of such election.

8. *Resolved,* That a meeting of all members of this Branch shall be immediately called for the purpose of electing officers (to be chosen by ballot) after the first trial *shall have been made* of the qualifications of individual members for such command, as before mentioned.

9. *Resolved,* That as citizens of the United States of America we will ever be found true to the flag of our beloved country, always acting under it.

BC Dowling	Reverdy Johnson	JN Howard	Scipio Webb	L Wallace
Henry Johnson	CA Gazam	Jane Fowler	Ann Johnson	Henry Robinson
Henry Hector	Wm Burns	Joseph Addams	Wm H Montague	James Madison
John Smith	Samuel Chandler	Charles Rollins	Charles Odell	And 17 others.
GW Holmes	Eliza Green	HJ Jones	Cyrus Thomas	
John Strong	Wm Gordon	Wm Green	Jane Wicks	

Source: Franklin B. Sanborn, *The Life and Letters of John Brown, Liberator of Kansas, and Martyr of Virginia* (Boston: Roberts Bros., 1885), 124–127.

John Brown, "Dear Wife and Children, Everyone," June 1856

On May 30, 1854, President Pierce signed the Kansas-Nebraska Act into law. The act repealed the Missouri Compromise of 1820 and gave people in the territories of Kansas and Nebraska the right to decide by popular vote whether to allow slavery within their borders. Proslavery and antislavery settlers began pouring into Kansas, hoping to vote slavery up or down. Brown arrived in Kansas on October 6, 1855, to join his sons in armed resistance against proslavery Missourians and their "Border Ruffian" allies. Open violence erupted in late 1855, and on May 21, 1856, proslavery settlers burned and pillaged the town of Lawrence. Days later, during the night of May 24, Brown and seven others entered a proslavery settlement at Pottawatomie Creek and killed five settlers. Brown's part in "Bleeding Kansas" continued the following week, when he led antislavery men in the Battle of Black Jack, on June 2, and defeated the proslavery forces led by Henry C. Pate. In a letter to his family, Brown described the warfare in Kansas, including the sacking of Lawrence, the deaths at Pottawatomie, and the Battle of Black Jack. He does not deny or confirm his role in the Pottawatomie killings, and then requests that his wife send a copy of the letter to one of his allies, the abolitionist Gerrit Smith: Brown intended the letter to be a public defense of his actions, for the eyes of his Northern supporters as well as his family.

Near Brown's Station, K.T., June 1856

Dear Wife and Children, Everyone—It is now about five weeks since I have seen a line from North Elba, or had any chance of writing you. During that period we here have passed through an almost constant series of very trying events. We were called to the relief of Lawrence, May 22, and every man (eight in all), except Orson[9] turned out; he staying with the women and children, and to take care of the cattle. John[10] was captain of a company over night. Next day our little company left, and during the day we stopped and searched three men.

Lawrence was destroyed in this way: Their leading men had (as I think) decided, in a very *cowardly* manner, not to resist any process having any Government official to serve it, notwithstanding the process might be wholly a bogus affair. The consequence was that a man called a United States marshal came on with a horde of ruffians which he called his posse, and after arresting a few persons turned the ruffians loose on the defenceless people. They robbed the inhabitants of their money and other property, and even women of their ornaments, and burned considerable of the town.

On the second day and evening after we left John's men we encountered quite a number of proslavery men, and took quite a number prisoners. Our prisoners we let go; but we kept some four or five horses. We were immediately after this accused of murdering five men at Pottawatomie, and great efforts have since been made by the Missourians and their ruffian allies to capture us. John's company soon afterwards disbanded, and also the Osawatomie men.

Jason[11] started to go and place himself under the protection of the Government troops; but on his way he was taken prisoner by the Bogus men,[12] and is yet a prisoner, I suppose. John tried to hide for several days; but from feelings of the ungrateful conduct of those who ought to have stood by him, excessive fatigue, anxiety, and constant loss of sleep, he became quite insane, and in that situation gave up, or as we are told, was betrayed at Osawatomie into the hands of the Bogus men. We do not know all the truth about this affair. He has since, we are told, been kept in irons, and brought to a trial before a bogus court, the result of which we have not yet learned. We have great anxiety both for him and Jason, and numerous other prisoners with the enemy (who have all the while had the Government troops to sustain them). We can only commend them to God.

The cowardly mean conduct of Osawatomie and vicinity did not save them; for the ruffians came on them, made numerous prisoners, fired their buildings, and robbed them. After this a picked party of the Bogus men went to Brown's Station, burned John's and Jason's houses, and their contents to ashes; in which burning we have all suffered more or less. Orson and boy have been prisoners, but were soon set at liberty. They are well, and have not been seriously injured. Owen[13] and I have just come here for the first time to look at the ruins. All looks desolate and forsaken—the grass and weeds fast covering up the signs that these places were lately the abodes of quiet families. After burning the houses, this self-same party of picked men, some forty in number, set out as they supposed, and as was the fact, on the track of my little company, boasting, with awful profanity, that they would have our scalps. They however passed the place where we were hid, and robbed a little town[14] some four or five miles beyond our camp in the timber. I had omitted to say that some murders had been committed at the time Lawrence was sacked.

On learning that this party were in pursuit of us, my little company, now increased to ten in all, started after them in company of a Captain Shore,[15] with eighteen men, he included. We were all mounted as we traveled. We did not meet them on that day, but took five prisoners, four of whom were of their scouts, and well armed. We were out all night, but could find nothing of them until about six o'clock next morning, when we prepared to attack them at once, on foot, leaving Frederick[16] and one of Captain Shore's men to guard the horses. As I was much older than Captain Shore, the principal direction of the fight devolved on me. We got to within about a mile of their camp before being discovered by their scouts, and then moved at a brisk pace, Captain Shore and men forming our left, and my company the right. When within about sixty rods of the enemy, Captain Shore's men halted by mistake in a very exposed situation, and continued the fire, both his men and the enemy being armed with Sharpe's rifles. My company had no long-shooters. We (my company) did not fire a gun until we gained the rear of a bank, about fifteen or twenty rods to the right of the enemy, where we commenced, and soon compelled them to hide in a ravine. Captain Shore, after getting one man wounded and exhausting his ammunition, came with part of his men to the right of my position, much discouraged. The balance of his men, including the one wounded, had left the ground. Five of Captain Shore's men came boldly down and joined my company, and all but one man, wounded, helped to maintain the fight until it was over. I was obliged to give my consent that he should go after more help, when all his men left but eight, four of whom I persuaded to remain in a secure position, and there busied one of them in shooting the horses and mules of the enemy, which served for a show of fight. After the firing had continued for some two to three hours, Captain Pate[17] with twenty-three men, two badly wounded, laid down their arms to nine men, myself included—four of Captain Shore's men and four of my own. One of my men (Henry Thompson)[18] was badly wounded, and after continuing his fire for an hour longer was obliged to quit the ground. Three others of my company (but not of my family) had gone off. Salmon[19] was dreadfully wounded by accident, soon after the fight; but both he and Henry are fast recovering.

A day or two after the fight, Colonel Sumner of the United States army[20] came suddenly upon us, while fortifying our camp and guarding our prisoners (which, by the way, it had been agreed mutually should be exchanged for as many Free States men, John and Jason included), and compelled us to let go our prisoners without being exchanged, and to give up their horses and arms. They did not go more than two or three miles before they began to rob and injure Free-State people. We consider this as in good keeping with the cruel and unjust course of the Administration and its tools throughout this whole Kansas difficulty. Colonel Sumner also compelled us to disband; and we, being only a handful, were obliged to submit.

Since then we have, like David of old, had our dwelling with the serpents of the rocks and wild beasts of the wilderness; being obliged to hide away from our enemies. We are not disheartened, though nearly destitute of food, clothing, and money. God, who has not given us over to the will of our enemies, but has moreover delivered them into our hand, will, we humbly trust, still keep and deliver us. We feel assured that He who sees not as men see, does not lay the guilt of innocent blood to our charge.

I ought to have said that Captain Shore and his men stood their ground nobly in their unfortunate but mistaken position during the early part of the fight. I ought to say further that a Captain Abbott,[21] being some miles distant with a company, came onward promptly to sustain us, but could not reach us till the fight was over. After the fight, numerous Free-State men who could not be got out before were on hand; and some of them, I am ashamed to add, were very busy not only with the plunder of our enemies, but with our private effects, leaving us, while guarding our prisoners and providing in regard to them, much poorer than before the battle.

If, under God, this letter reaches you so that it can be read, I wish it at once carefully copied, and a copy of it sent to Gerrit Smith.[22] I know of no other way to get these facts and our situation before the world, nor when I can write again.

Owen has the ague to-day. Our camp is some miles off. Have heard that letters are in for some of us, but have not seen them. Do continue writing. We heard last mail brought only three letters, and all these for proslavery men. It is said that both the Lawrence and Osawatomie men, when the ruffians came on them, either hid or gave up their arms, and that their leading men counseled them to take such a course.

May God bless and keep you all!

Your affectionate husband and father, John Brown

PS. Ellen and Wealthy are staying at Osawatomie.[23]

The above is a true account of the first regular battle fought between Free-State and proslavery men in Kansas. May God still gird loins and hold our right hands, and to him may we give the glory! I ought in justice to say, that, after the sacking and burning of several towns, the Government troops appeared for their protection and drove off some of the enemy. J.B.

June 26. Jason is set at liberty, and we have hopes for John. Owen, Salmon, and Oliver[24] are down with fever (since inserted); Henry doing well.

Source: Franklin B. Sanborn, *The Life and Letters of John Brown, Liberator of Kansas, and Martyr of Virginia* (Boston: Roberts Bros., 1885), 236–241.

John Brown, "Old Brown's Farewell to the Plymouth Rocks, Bunker Hill Monuments, Charter Oaks, and Uncle Tom's Cabins," April 1857

Brown left Kansas in October 1856 and devoted much of the next year to fund-raising across the North. By the spring of 1857, he had given numerous speeches in Hartford, Boston, Concord, and elsewhere. But he was disillusioned. The canvassing took a toll, and in a public request for funds, published in the *New York Tribune* on March 4, he described the "sacrifice of personal feeling" that this fund-raising entailed. In a letter to one of his sons dated April 15, he added: "I have had a good deal of discouragement, & have often felt quite depressed." That same month, while staying at the home of the Massachusetts Superior Court judge Thomas Russell in West Newton, Brown penned the following critique of his supposed supporters. He sent a copy of the text to the abolitionist Mary Stearns, who persuaded her husband, George Luther Sterns, to give Brown $7000.

He has left for Kansas; has been trying since he came out of the Territory to secure an outfit, or, in other words, the means of arming and thoroughly equip-
ping his regular minute-men, who are mixed up with the people of Kansas.
And he leaves the States with a feeling of deepest sadness, that after having exhausted his own small means, and with his family and his brave men suffered
hunger, cold, nakedness, and some of them sickness, wounds, imprisonment
in irons, with extreme cruel treatment, and others death; that after lying on
the ground for months in the most sickly, unwholesome, and uncomfortable
places, some of the time with sick and wounded, destitute of any shelter,
hunted like wolves, and sustained in part by Indians; that after all this, in order
to sustain a cause which every citizen of this "glorious republic" is under equal
moral obligation to do, and for the neglect of which he will be held account-
able by God—a cause in which, every man, woman, and child of the entire
human family has a deep and awful interest—that when no wages are asked or

expected, he cannot secure, amid all the wealth, luxury, and extravagance of this "heaven-exalted"[25] people, even the necessary supplies of the common soldier. "How are the mighty fallen!"[26]

I am destitute of horses, baggage-wagons, tents, harness, saddles, bridles, holsters, spurs, and belts; camp equipage, such as cooking and eating utensils, blankets, knapsacks, intrenching-tools, axes, shovels, spades, mattocks, crow-bars; have not a supply of ammunition; have not money sufficient to pay freight and traveling expenses; and left my family poorly supplied with com-mon necessaries.

Boston, April, 1857.

Source: Franklin B. Sanborn, *The Life and Letters of John Brown, Liberator of Kansas, and Martyr of Virginia* (Boston: Roberts Bros., 1885), 508–509.

John Brown, "To Mr. Henry L. Stearns," July 15, 1857

In January 1857, while fund-raising in Boston, Brown was introduced to the abolitionist George Luther Stearns by Franklin Sanborn. Stearns was president of the Massachusetts State Kansas Committee, and Sanborn served the committee as secretary. Brown visited Stearns and his wife, Mary, at their home in Boston, where he met the couple's eldest son, Harry. The boy offered Brown his savings. Accepting the money, Brown promised to write the twelve-year-old an account of his own childhood. He wrote the autobiographical sketch in July 1857. Ralph Waldo Emerson called it a "positive contribution to . . . the historical literature of the English language," and James Russell Lowell termed it "one of the finest pieces of autobiography extant." In the narrative, Brown offers his childhood experience as a lesson. Its "follies and errors" should be avoided; its success might encourage "persevering effort." He uses biblical symbolism and an unusual third-person voice throughout. This voice creates a distance between narrator and subject, private and public selves. In fact, Brown was also using the occasion to construct a public version of himself for Harry's father: "John" meets failure with resilience and cannot be blamed, for he was "placed in the School of adversity." As well as a lesson for Harry, the sketch is a reassurance and an appeal to Brown's benefactor. This makes the letter an important precursor to his prison letters. From the Charles Town jail in 1859, Brown wrote letters for a dual audience, the addressee and the newspaper-reading public. Blurring the line between "private" letters (to friends and family members) and "public" letters (to the editor), he used the freedom afforded by his ostensibly private communication to publicly define the meaning of his raid, perform an act of testimony, and shape the debate over violent versus nonviolent abolitionism. Like his autobiographical narrative of 1857, his prison letters address one audience but take aim at another. Building on the strategy he developed in his letter to Harry Stearns, he combined memoir, political treatise, and epistle to craft a rhetorically powerful marriage of the public and private.

Red Rock, Iowa, 15th July, 1857

Mr. Henry L. Stearns, My Dear Young Friend

I have not forgotten my promise to write you: but my constant care, & anxiety: have obliged me to put if off a long time. I do not flatter myself that I *can* write anything that will very much interest you: but have concluded to send you a short story of a certain boy of my acquaintance: & for convenience & short- ness of name, I will call him John. This story will be mainly a naration of fol- lies and errors; which it is to be hoped *you may avoid;* but there is one thing connected with it, which will be calculated to encourage any young person to persevering effort; & that is the degree of success *in accomplishing his objects* which to a great extent marked the course of this boy throughout my entire acquaintance with him; notwithstanding his moderate capacity; & still more moderate acquirements.

John was born May 9th, 1800, at Torrington, Litchfield Co. Connecticut; of poor but respectable parents: a decendant on the side of his Father of one of the company of the Mayflower who landed at Plymouth 1620. His mother was decended from a man who came at an early period to New England from Am- sterdam, in Holland. Both his Father's and his Mother's Fathers served in the war of the revolution: His Father's Father; died in a barn at New York while in the service, in 1776.

I cannot tell you of anything in the first Four years of John's life worth men- tioning save that at that *early age* he was tempted by Three large Brass Pins belonging to a girl who lived in the family & *stole them.* In this he was detected by his Mother; & after having a full day to think of the wrong; received from her a thorough whipping. When he was Five years old his Father moved to Ohio; then a wilderness filled with wild beasts, & Indians. During the long journey which was performed in part or mostly with an *ox team;* he was called on by turns to assist a boy Five years older (who had been adopted by his Fa- ther & Mother) & learned to think he could accomplish *smart things* in driv- ing the Cows; & riding the horses. Sometimes he met with Rattle Snakes which were very large; & which some of the company generally managed to kill. After getting in Ohio in 1805 he was for some time rather afraid of the Indians, & of their Rifles; but this soon wore off: & he used to hang about them quite as much as was consistent with good manners; & learned a trifle of their talk. His father learned to dress Deer Skins, & at 6 years old John was installed a young Buck Skin. He was perhaps rather observing as he ever after remembered the entire process of Deer Skin *dressing;* so that he could at any times dress his own leather such as Squirel, Raccoon, Cat, Wolf or Dog Skins; and also learned to make Whip Lashes: which brought him some change at times; & was of considerable service in many ways. At Six years old John began to be quite a rambler in the wild new country finding birds and Squirrels and sometimes a wild Turkeys nest. But about this period he was placed in the School of *adversity;* which my young friend was a most necessary part of his early training. You may *laugh* when you come to read about it; but these were *sore trials* to John whose earthly treasures were very *few, & small.* These were the beginning of a severe but *much needed course* of dicipline which he afterwards was to pass through; & which it is to be hoped has learned him before this time that the Heavenly Father sees it best to take all the little things out of his hands which he has ever placed in them. When John was in his Sixth year a poor *Indian boy* gave him a Yellow Marble the first he had ever seen. This he thought a great deal of; & kept it a good while; but at last *he lost it* beyond recovery. *It took years to heal the wound* & I *think* he cried at times about it. About Five months after this he caught a young Squirrel tearing off his tail in doing it & getting severely bitten at the same time himself. He however held on *to the little bob tail Squirrel;* & finally got him perfectly tamed, so that he almost idolized his pet. *This too he lost;* by its wandering away; or by getting killed; & for year or two John was *in mourning;* and looking at all the Squirrels he could see to try & discover Bobtail, *if possible.* I must not neglect to tell you of a verry *bad & foolish* habbit to which John was somewhat addicted. I mean *telling lies;* generally to screen himself from blame; or from punishment. He could not well endure to be reproached; & I now think had he been oftener encouraged to be entirely frank; *by making frankness a kind of atonement* for some of his faults; he would not have been so often guilty in after life of this fault; nor have been obliged to struggle *so long* with *so mean* a habit. John was *never quarrelsome;* but was *excessively* fond of the *hardest & roughest* kind of plays; & could *never get enough* [of] them.

Indeed when for a short time he was sometimes sent to School the opportunity it afforded to wrestle, & Snow ball & run & jump & knock off old seedy Wool hats; offered to him almost the only compensation for the confinement, & restraints of school. I need not tell you that with such a feeling & but little chance of going to school *at all:* he did not become much of a schollar. He would always choose to stay at home & work hard rather than be sent to school; & during the Warm season might generally be seen *barefooted & bare-headed:* with Buck skin Breeches suspended often with one leather strap over his shoulder but sometimes with Two. To be sent off through the wilderness alone to very considerable distances was particularly his delight; & in this he was often indulged so that by the time he was Twelve years old he was sent off more than a Hundred Miles with companies of cattle; & he would have thought his character much injured had he been obliged to be helped in any such job. This was a boyish kind of feeling but characteristic however.

At Eight years old, John was left a Motherless boy which loss was complete & permanent for notwithstanding his Father again married to a sensible, inteligent, and on many accounts a very estimable woman; yet he never *adopted her in feeling;* but continued to pine after his own Mother for years. This opperated very unfavorably uppon him; as he was both naturally fond of females; &, withall, extremely diffident; & deprived him of a suitable connecting link between the different sexes; the want of which might under some circumstances, have proved his ruin.

When the war broke out *with England:* his Father soon commenced furnishing the troops with beef cattle, the collecting & driving of which afforded him some opportunity for the chase (on foot) of wild steers & other cattle through the woods. During this war he had some chance to form his own boyish judgment of *men & measures:* & to become somewhat familiarly acquainted with some who have figured before the country since that time. The effect of what he saw during the war was to so far disgust him with Military affairs that he would neither train, *or drill;* but paid fines; & got along like a Quaker untill his age finally has cleared him of Military duty.

During the war with England a circumstance occurred that in the end made him a most *determined Abolitionist:* & led him to declare, *or Swear: Eternal war* with Slavery. He was staying for a short time with a very gentlemanly landlord since a United States Marshall who held a slave boy near his own age very active, inteligent, and good feeling; & to whom John was under considerable obligation for numerous little acts of kindness. *The Master* made a great pet of John: brought him to table with his first company; & friends; called their attention to every little smart thing he *said or did:* & to the fact of his being more than a hundred miles from home with a company of cattle alone; while the *negro boy* (who was fully if not more than his equal) was badly clothed, poorly fed; *& lodged in cold weather;* & beaten before his eyes with Iron Shovels or any other thing that came first to hand. This brought John to reflect on the wretched, hopeless condition, of *Fatherless & Motherless* slave *children:* for such children have neither Fathers or Mothers to protect & provide for them. He sometimes would raise the question *is God their Father?*

At the age of Ten years, an old friend induced him to read a little history, & offered him the free use of a good library; by; which he acquired some taste for reading: which formed the principle part of his early education: & diverted him in a great measure from bad company. He by this means grew to be verry fond of the company & conversation of old & inteligent persons. He never attempted to dance in his life; nor did he ever learn to know *one* of a pack of *Cards* from *another.* He learned nothing of Grammar; nor did he get at school so much knowledge of common Arithmetic as the Four grand rules. This well give you some general idea of the first Fifteen years of his life; during which time he became very strong & large of his age & ambitious to perform the full labour of a man; at almost any kind of hard work. By reading the lives of great, wise & good men their sayings, and writings; he grew to a dislike of vain & frivolous *conversation & persons;* & was often greatly obliged by the kind manner in which older & more inteligent persons treated him at their houses: & in conversation; which was a great relief on account of his extreme bashfulness.

He very early in life became ambitious to excel in doing anything he undertook to perform. This kind of feeling I would recommend to all young persons both *Male & female:* as it will certainly tend to secure admission to the company of the more inteligent; & better portion of every community. By all means endeavour to excel in some laudable pursuit.

I had like to have forgotten to tell you of one of John's misfortunes which set rather hard on him while a young boy. He had by some means *perhaps* by gift of his Father become the owner of a little Ewe Lamb which did finely till it was about Two Thirds grown; & then sickened and died. This brought another protracted *mourning season:* not that he felt the pecuniary loss so heavily: for that was never his disposition; but so strong & earnest were his attachments.

John had been taught from earliest childhood to "fear God & keep his commandments;" & though quite skeptical he had always by turns felt much serious doubt as to his future well being; & about this time became to some extent a convert to Christianity & ever after a firm believer in the divine authenticity of the Bible. With this book he became very familiar, & possessed a most un-usual memory of its entire contents.

Now some of the things I have been *telling of;* were just such as I would rec-ommend to you: & adopted them as part of your own plan of life; & I wish you to have *some deffinite plan.* Many seem to have none; & others never to stick to any that they do form. This was not the case with John. He followed up with *tenacity* whatever he set about so long as it answered his general purpose: & hence he rarely failed in some good degree to effect the things he undertook. This was so much the case that he *habitually expected to succeed* in his under-takings. With this feeling *should be coupled;* the consciousness that our plans are right in themselves.

During the period I have named, John had acquired a kind of ownership to certain animals of some little value but as he had come to understand that the *title of minors* might be a little imperfect: he had recourse to various means in order to secure a more *independent;* & perfect right of property. One of these means was to exchange with his Father for something of far less value. An-other was by trading with other persons for something his Father had never owned. Older persons have sometimes found difficulty with *titles.*

From Fifteen to Twenty years old, he spent most of his time working at the Tanner & Currier's trade keeping Bachelors hall; & he officiating as Cook; & for most of the time as foreman of the establishment under his Father. During this period he found much trouble with some of the bad habits I have men-tioned & with some that I have not told you of: his conscience urging him forward with great power in this matter: but his close attention to *business;* & success in its management; together with the way he got along with a company of men, & boys; made him quite a favorite with the serious & more inteligent portion of older persons. This was so much the case; & secured for him so many little notices from those he esteemed; that his vanity was very much fed by it: & he came forward to manhood quite full of self-conceit; & self-confidant; notwithstanding his *extreme* bashfulness. A younger brother used sometimes to remind him of this: & to repeat to him *this expression* which you may somewhere find, "A King against whom there is no rising up."[27] The habit so early formed of being obeyed rendered him in after life too much disposed to speak in an imperious or dictating way. From Fifteen years & upward he felt a good deal of anxiety to learn; but could only read & studdy a little; both for want of time; & on account of inflammation of the eyes. He however managed by the help of books to make himself tolerably well acquainted with common Arithmetic; & Surveying; which he practiced more or less after he was Twenty years old.

At a little past Twenty years led by his own inclination & *prompted also* by his Father, he married a *remarkably plain;* but industrious & economical girl; of excellent character; earnest piety; & good practical common sense; about one year younger than himself. This woman by her mild, frank, *& more than all else;* by her very consistent conduct; acquired & ever while she lived maintained a most powerful; & good influence over him. Her plain but kind admonitions generally had the right effect; without arousing his haughty obstinate temper. John began early in life to discover a great liking to fine Cattle, Horses, Sheep, & Swine; & as soon as circumstances would enable him he began to be a practical *Shepherd; it being* a calling for which *in early life* he had a kind of *enthusiastic longing:* together with the idea that as a business it bid fair to afford him the means of carrying out his greatest or principal object. I have now given you a kind of general idea of the early life of this boy; & if I believed it would be worth the trouble; or afford much interest to any good feeling person; I might be tempted to tell you something of his course in after life; or manhood. I do not say that I *will do it.*

You will discover that in using up my *half sheets to save paper;* I have written Two pages, so that one does not follow the other as it should. I have no time to write it over; & but for unavoidable hindrances in traveling I can hardly say when I should have written what I have. With an honest desire for your best good, I subscribe myself,

Your Friend, J. Brown.

P.S.—I had like to have forgotten to acknowledge your contribution in aid of the cause in which I serve. God Allmighty *bless you;* my son. J.B.

Source: James Redpath, *The Public Life of Capt. John Brown* (Boston: Thayer and Eldridge, 1860), 24–35.

John Brown, "Provisional Constitution and Ordinances for the People of the United States," May 8, 1858

In January 1858, while staying at Frederick Douglass's home in Rochester, New York, Brown wrote a constitution for the provisional government of a slave-free nation. Three months later he traveled to Chatham, Ontario, and began organizing a constitutional convention. Members of Chatham's large free black community attended the convention, which ran from May 8 to May 10, 1858, in a Chatham schoolhouse and Baptist church. The delegates, thirty-four black and twelve white, included the black nationalist Martin Delany, who helped Brown organize the convention; Osborne Anderson, who joined Brown at Harpers Ferry; and the abolitionist and poet Richard Realf. Douglass did not attend, though he kept a copy of Brown's provisional constitution until the end of his life. At the convention, Brown outlined his plans to attack western Virginia and march south. He first presented a constitution for a separate state government within the Union, but the delegates eventually approved a proposal for a new independent nation. Brown offered his provisional constitution as the document by which the community would live until America itself was slave-free. By the end of the first day, the convention's delegates had ratified the provisional constitution and elected Brown the commander in chief of the paper government and the provisional forces. On May 10, Brown appointed a committee with full power to fill all the executive, legislative, judicial, and military offices named in the constitution. The document was ready for distribution when Brown attacked Harpers Ferry on October 16, 1859.

Whereas slavery throughout its entire existence in the United States is none other than a most barbarous unprovoked and unjustifiable War of one portion of its citizens upon another portion, the only conditions of which are perpetual imprisonment and hopeless servitude or absolute extermination in utter disregard and violation of those eternal and self-evident truths set forth in our Declaration of Independence. Therefore,

We, Citizens of the United States, and the oppressed people who by a recent decision of the Supreme Court are declared to have no rights which the White Man is bound to respect,[28] together with all other people degraded by the laws thereof, Do for the time being Ordain and establish for ourselves the following Provisional Constitution and Ordinances the better to protect our Persons, Property, Lives, and Liberties, and to govern our actions:

ARTICLE I. Qualification for membership.

All persons of mature age, whether Proscribed, oppressed, and enslaved Citizens, or of the Proscribed and oppressed races of the United States, who shall agree to sustain and enforce the Provisional Constitution and Ordinances of this Organization, together with all minor children of such persons, shall be held to be fully entitled to protection under the same.

ARTICLE II. Branches of Government.

The provisional government of this organization shall consist of three branches, viz.: Legislative, Executive, and Judicial.

ARTICLE III. Legislative.

The legislative branch shall be a Congress, or House of Representatives, composed of not less than five or more than ten members, who shall be elected by all citizens of mature age and of sound mind, connected with this organization, and who shall remain in office for three years, unless sooner removed for misconduct, inability, or by death. A majority of such members shall constitute a quorum.

ARTICLE IV. Executive.

The Executive branch of this organization shall consist of a President and Vice-President, who shall be chosen by the citizens or members of this organization, and each of whom shall hold his office for three years, unless sooner removed by death or for inability or misconduct.

ARTICLE V. Judicial.

The judicial branch of this organization shall consist of one Chief Justice of the Supreme Court and of four Associate Judges of said court; each constituting a circuit court. They shall each be chosen in the same manner as the President, and shall continue in office until their places have been filled in the same manner by election of the citizens. Said Court shall have jurisdiction in all civil or criminal causes arising under this constitution, except breaches of the rules of War.

ARTICLE VI. Validity of Enactments.

All enactments of the legislative branch shall, to become valid during the first three years, have the approbation of the President and the Commander-in-chief of the Army.

ARTICLE VII. Commander-in-chief.

A commander-in-Chief of the Army shall be chosen by the President, Vice-President, a majority of the provisional congress and of the Supreme Court; and he shall receive his commission from the President, signed by the Vice-President, the Chief Justice of the Supreme Court and the Secretary of War; and he shall hold his office for three years unless removed by death or on proof of incapacity or misbehavior. He shall unless under arrest (and until his place is actually filled as provided for by this constitution) direct all movements of the army and advise with any allies. He shall however be tried, removed, or punished on complaint to the President by at least th[re]e general officers or a majority of the House of Representatives [or] of the Supreme Court; which House of Representatives (the President presiding) the Vice-President and the members of the Supreme Court shall constitute a court-martial for his trial, with power to remove or punish as the case may require, and to fill his place as above provided.

ARTICLE VIII. Officers.

A Treasurer, Secretary of State, Secretary of War, and Secretary of the Treasury shall each be chosen for the first three years in the same way and manner as the Commander-in-chief, subject to trial or removal on complaint of the President, Vice-President or Commander-in-chief, to the Chief Justice of the Supreme Court, or on complaint of the majority of the members of said court, or the provisional congress. The Supreme Court shall have power to try or punish either of those officers, and their places shall be filled as before.

ARTICLE IX. Secretary of War.

The Secretary of War shall be under the immediate direction of the Commander-in-chief, who may temporarily fill his place in case of arrest or of any inability to serve.

ARTICLE X. Congress or House of Representatives.

The House of Representatives shall make ordinances for the appointment (by the President or otherwise) of all civil officers excepting those already named, and shall have power to make all laws and ordinances for the general good not inconsistent with this constitution and these ordinances.

ARTICLE XI. Appropriation of money, &c.

The provisional Congress shall have power to appropriate money or other property actually in the hands of the Treasurer to any object calculated to promote the general good, so far as may be consistent with the provisions of this Constitution, and may in certain cases appropriate for a moderate compensation of agents or persons not members of this organization for important service they are known to have rendered.

ARTICLE XII. Special Duties.

It shall be the duty of Congress to provide for the instant removal of any civil officer or policeman, who becomes habitually intoxicated, or who is addicted to other immoral conduct, or to any neglect or unfaithfulness in the discharge of his official duties. Congress shall also be a standing committee of safety, for the purpose of obtaining important information, and shall be in constant communication with the commander-in-chief; the members of which shall each, as also the President, Vice-President, members of the Supreme Court and Secretary of State have full power to issue warrants returnable as Congress shall ordain (naming witnesses, &c,.) upon their own information without the formality of a complaint. Complaint shall be immediately made after arrest and before trial, the party arrested to be served with a copy at once.

ARTICLE XIII. Trial of President and other Officers.

The President and Vice-President may either of them be tried removed or punished on complaint made [to] the Chief Justice of the Supreme Court by a majority of the House of Representatives, which House, together with the Associate Judges of the Supreme Court, the whole to be presided over by the Chief Justice in cases of the trial of the Vice-President, shall have full power to try such officers, to remove or punish as the case may require, and to fill any vacancy so occurring, the same as in the case of the Commander-in-chief.

ARTICLE XIV. Trial of Members of Congress.

The members of the House of Representatives may, any and all of them be tried, and on conviction, removed or punished on complaint before the Chief Justice of the Supreme Court, made by any number of the members of said House exceeding one-third, which [H]ouse with the Vice-President and Associate Judges of the Supreme Court shall constitute the proper tribunal with power to fill such vacancies.

ARTICLE XV. Impeachment of Judges.

Any member of the Supreme Court may also be impeached, tried, convicted or punished by removal or otherwise on complaint to the President who shall in such case preside. The Vice-President, House of Representatives and other members of the supreme court constituting the proper tribunal (with power to fill vacancies) on complaint of a majority of said house of representatives or of the supreme court, a majority of the whole having power to decide.

ARTICLE XVI. Duties of President and Secretary of State.

The President with the Secretary of State shall immediately on entering on the duties of their office give special attention to secure from amongst their own people, men of integrity, intelligence and good business habits and capacity; and above all of first-rate moral and religious character and influence to act as civil officers of every description and grade as well as teachers, chaplains, physicians, surgeons, mechanics, agents of every description, clerks, and messengers. They shall make special efforts to induce at the earliest possible period, persons and families of that description to locate themselves within the limits secured by this organization, and shall moreover from time to time supply the names and residence of such persons to the Congress for their special notice and information as among the most important of their duties, and the President is hereby authorized and empowered to afford special aid to such individuals, from such moderate appropriations as the Congress shall be able and may deem it advisable to make for that object. The President and Secretary of State, and in cases of disagreement the Vice-President shall appoint all civil officers, but shall not have power to remove any officer. All removals shall be the result of a fair trial, whether civil or military.

ARTICLE XVII. Further Duties.

It shall be the duty of the President and Secretary of State, to find out (as soon as possible) the real friends as well as enemies of this organization in every part of the country, to secure among them, innkeepers, private postmasters, private mail contractors, messengers and agents, through whom may be obtained correct and regular information constantly, recruits for the service, places of deposit and sale, together with all needed supplies, and it shall be matter of special regard to secure such facilities through the Northern States.

ARTICLE XVIII. Duties of the President.

It shall be the duty of the President as well as the House of Representatives at all times to inform the Commander-in-Chief of any matter that may require his attention or that may affect the public safety.

ARTICLE XIX. Duty of President continued.

It shall be the duty of the President to see that the provisional ordinances of this organization and those made by Congress are promptly and faithfully executed, and he may in cases of great urgency call on the Commander-in-chief of the army, or other officers for aid, it being however intended that a sufficient civil police shall always be in readiness to secure implicit obedience to law.

ARTICLE XX. The Vice President.

The Vice-President shall be the presiding officer of the provisional congress, and in cases of tie shall give the casting vote.

ARTICLE XXI. Vacancies.

In case of the death, removal or inability of the President, the Vice-President and next to him the Chief Justice of the Supreme Court shall be the President during the remainder of the term, and the place of Chief Justice thus made vacant shall be filled by Congress from some of the members of said Court, and the places of the Vice President and associate Justice thus made vacant filled by an election by the united action of the Provisional Congress and members of the Supreme Court. All other vacancies not heretofore specially provided for shall during the first three years be filled by the united action of the President, Vice-President, Supreme Court and Commander-in-Chief of the Army.

ARTICLE XXII. Punishments of Crimes.

The punishment of crimes not capital, except in case of insubordinate convicts or other prisoners shall be (so far as may be) by hard labor on public works, roads, &c.

ARTICLE XXIII. Army Appointments.

It shall be the duty of all commissioned officers of the army to name candidates of merit for office or elevation to the commander-in-chief, who, with the Secretary of War, and in cases of disagreement, the President shall be the appointing power of the army, and all commissions of military officers shall bear the signatures of the Commander-in-Chief and the Secretary of War. And it shall be the special duty of the Secretary of War to keep for constant reference of the Commander-in-Chief a full list of names of persons nominated for office or elevation by the officers of the army, with the name and rank of the officer nominating, stating distinctly but briefly the grounds for such notice or nomination. The commander-in-chief shall not have power to remove or punish any officer or soldier; but he may order their arrest and trial at any time by Court-martial.

ARTICLE XXIV. Courts-Martial.

Courts-martial for Companies, Regiments, Brigades, &c., shall be called by the Chief Officer of each command on complaint to him by any officer, or any five privates in such command, and shall consist of not less than five nor more than nine officers—non-commissioned officers and privates, one-half of whom shall not be lower in rank than the person on trial, to be chosen by the three highest officers in the command, which officers shall not be a part of such court. The chief officer of any command shall, of course, be tried by a court-martial of the command above his own. All decisions affecting the lives of persons, or office of persons holding commission, must, before taking full effect, have the signature of the Commander-in-Chief, who may also on the recommendation of at least one-third of the members of the court-martial finding any sentence, grant a reprieve or commutation of the same.

ARTICLE XXV. Salaries.

No person connected with this organization shall be entitled to any salary, pay or emolument, other than a competent support of himself and family, unless it be from an equal dividend made of public property on the establishment of peace or of special provisions by treaty, which provision shall be made for all persons who may have been in any active civil or military service at any time previous to any hostile action for Liberty and Equality.

ARTICLE XXVI. Treaties of Peace.

Before any treaty of peace shall take full effect it shall be signed by the President and Vice-President, the Commander-in-chief, a majority of the House of Representatives, a majority of the Supreme Court, and a majority of all general officers of the Army.

ARTICLE XXVII. Duty of the Military.

It shall be the duty of the Commander-in-chief, and of all officers and soldiers of the army, to afford special protection when needed to Congress or any member thereof, to the supreme court or any member thereof, to the President, Vice-President, Treasurer, Secretary of State, Secretary of Treasury and Secretary of War, and to afford general protection to all civil officers or other persons having right to the same.

ARTICLE XXVIII. Property.

All captured or confiscated property, and all property the product of the labor of those belonging to this organization and of their families shall be held as the property of the whole equally without distinction, and may be used for the common benefit or disposed of for the same object, and any person, officer or otherwise who shall improperly retain, secrete, use or needlessly destroy such property or property found captured or confiscated belonging to the enemy, or shall wilfully neglect to render a full and fair statement of such property by him so taken or held shall be deemed guilty of a misdemeanor, and on conviction shall be punished accordingly.

ARTICLE XXIX. Safety or Intelligence Fund.

All money plate, watches or jewelry captured by honorable warfare, found, taken, or confiscated belonging to the enemy shall be held sacred to constitute a liberal safety or intelligence fund, and any person who shall improperly retain, dispose of, hide, use, or destroy such money or other article above named, contrary to the provisions and spirit of this article shall be deemed guilty of theft, and on conviction thereof shall be punished accordingly. The Treasurer shall furnish the Commander-in-chief at all times with a full statement of the condition of such fund and its nature.

ARTICLE XXX. The Commander-in-chief and the Treasury.

The Commander-in-chief shall share power to draw from the treasury the money and other property of the fund provided for in Article twenty-ninth, but his orders shall be signed also by the Secretary of War, who shall keep strict account of the same, subject to examination by any member of Congress, or general officer.

ARTICLE XXXI. Surplus of the safety or intelligence fund.

It shall be the duty of the Commander-in-chief to advise the President of any surplus of the Safety [or] intelligence fund, who shall have power to draw such surplus (his order being also signed by the Secretary of State) to enable him to carry out the provisions of Article seventeenth.

ARTICLE XXXII. Prisoners.

No person after having surrendered himself or herself a prisoner, and who shall properly demean himself or herself as such to any officer or private connected with this organization, shall afterward be put to death, or be subjected to any corporal punishment without first having had the benefit of a fair and impartial trial. Nor shall any prisoner be treated with any kind of cruelty, disrespect, insult, or needless severity, but it shall be the duty of all persons, male and female, connected herewith at all times and under all circumstances, to treat all such prisoners with every degree of respect and kindness the nature of the circumstances will admit of, and to insist on a like course of conduct from all others, as in the fear of Almighty God to whose care and keeping we commit our cause.

ARTICLE XXXIII. Voluntaries.

All persons who may come forward and shall voluntarily deliver up their slaves, and have their names registered on the Books of the organization, shall so long as they continue at peace be entitled to the fullest protection of person and property, though not connected with this organization, and shall be treated as friends, and not merely as persons neutral.

ARTICLE XXXIV. Neutrals.

The persons and property of all non-slaveholders who shall remain absolutely neutral, shall be respected so far as the circumstances can allow of it, but they shall not be entitled to any active protection.

ARTICLE XXXV. No needless waste.

The needless waste or destruction of any useful property or article by fire, throwing open fences, fields, buildings, or needless killing of animals, or injury of either, shall not be tolerated at any time or place, but shall be promptly and properly punished.

ARTICLE XXXVI. Property Confiscated.

The entire and real property of all persons known to be acting either directly or indirectly with or for the enemy, or found in arms with them, or found willfully holding slaves, shall be confiscated and taken whenever and wherever it may be found in either Free or Slave states.

ARTICLE XXXVII. Desertion.

Persons convicted on impartial trial of desertion to the enemy after becoming members, acting as spies, or of treacherous surrender of property, arms or ammunition, provisions or supplies of any kind, roads, bridges, persons, or fortifications, shall be put to death and their entire property confiscated.

ARTICLE XXXVIII. Violation of Parole of Honor.

Persons proven to be guilty of taking up arms after having been set at liberty on parole of honor or after the same to have taken any active part with or for the enemy, direct or indirect, shall be put to death and their entire property confiscated.

ARTICLE XXXIX. All must labor.

All persons connected in any way with this organization, and who may be entitled to full protection under it, shall be held as under obligation to labor in some way for the general good; and persons refusing or neglecting so to do, shall, on conviction, receive a suitable and appropriate punishment.

ARTICLE XL. Irregularities.

Profane swearing, filthy conversation, indecent behavior, or indecent exposure of the person, or intoxication, or quarrelling, shall not be allowed or tolerated; neither unlawful intercourse of the sexes.

ARTICLE XLI. Crimes.

Persons convicted of the forcible violation of any female prisoner shall be put to death.

ARTICLE XLII. The marriage relation—Schools—The Sabbath.

The marriage relation shall be at all times respected, and families kept together as far as possible, and broken families encouraged to re-unite, and intelligence offices established for that purpose; schools and churches established as soon as may be for the purpose of religious and other instructions, and the first day of the week regarded as a day of rest, and appropriated to moral and religious instruction and improvement, relief to the suffering, instruction of the young and ignorant, and the encouragement of personal cleanliness, nor shall any persons be required on that day to perform ordinary manual labor, unless in extremely urgent cases.

ARTICLE XLIII. Carry arms openly.

All persons known to be of good character, and of sound mind and suitable age, who are connected with this organization, whether male or female, shall be encouraged to carry arms openly.

ARTICLE XLIV. No persons to carry concealed weapons.

No person within the limits of the conquered territory except regularly appointed policemen, express officers of the army, mail-carriers or other fully accredited messengers of the Congress, President, Vice-President, members of the Supreme Court or commissioned officer of the army, and those only under peculiar circumstances, shall be allowed at any time to carry concealed weapons; and any person not specially authorized so to do who shall be found so doing, shall be deemed a suspicious person, and may at once be arrested by any officer, soldier, or citizen, without the formality of a complaint or warrant, and may at once be subjected to thorough search, and shall have his or her case thoroughly investigated and be dealt with as circumstances on proof shall require.

ARTICLE XLV. Persons to be seized.
Persons within the limits of the territory holden by this organization having arms at all, concealed or otherwise, shall be seized at once, or be taken in charge of some vigilant officer, their case thoroughly investigated; and it shall be the duty of all citizens and soldiers, as well as officers, to arrest such parties as are named in this and the preceding section or Article without the formality of complaint or warrant, and they shall be placed in charge of some proper officer for examination or for safe keeping.

ARTICLE XLVI. These articles not for the overthrow of Government.
The foregoing articles shall not be construed so as in any way to encourage the overthrow of any State Government or of the General Government of the United States, and look to no dissolution of the Union, but simply to amend and repeal. And our Flag shall be the same that our Fathers fought under in the Revolution.

ARTICLE XLVII. No plurality of offices.
No two of the offices specially provided for by this Instrument shall be filled by the same person at the same time.

ARTICLE XLVIII. Oath.
Every officer, civil or military, connected with this organization shall, before entering upon the duties of his office, make solemn oath or affirmation to abide by and support these ordinances. Also every citizen and soldier before being fully recognized as such shall do the same.

Source: Calendar of Virginia State Papers and Other Manuscripts, Volume XI (Richmond: R. F. Walker, 1893), 279–288.[29]

John Brown, "A Declaration of Liberty by the Representatives of the Slave Population of the United States of America" (1859)

Like many abolitionists, Brown took inspiration from the American Revolution. He located himself as an heir of 1776, while pointing to the gap between the Revolution's ideals of equality and the ongoing fact of slavery. He timed his raid for July 4, 1858, then July 4, 1859, although he had to postpone it, and he composed a "Declaration of Liberty" based on the Declaration of Independence. Brown wove text from the 1776 Declaration into his document, placing abolition as a central element of the Revolution's unfinished work. The document invokes the right of slaves to revolt and justifies war to achieve liberty and full citizenship for all persons. Some of Brown's wording suggests a familiarity with the antislavery paragraph excised from the original draft of the Declaration of Independence. The document also echoes the aims of the Radical Abolition Party, which were immediate abolition, full suffrage for all Americans regardless of sex or skin color, the redistribution of land so that no one would be rich and no one poor, and violent intervention against slavery. Following Brown's capture at Harpers Ferry, investigators found the document at his base of operations, the Kennedy Farm in Maryland. By that time Brown was invoking the Revolution again in his prison letters. Like those letters and his provisional constitution, the "Declaration of Liberty" summoned the memory of 1776 in order to place Brown's radical abolitionism in a tradition of patriotic dissent, validate his actions through historical precedent, and reconstitute America's founding identity as a slave-free nation.

_____4th, 1859.

"When in the course of human events, it becomes necessary"[30] for an oppressed People to Rise and assert their Natural Rights as Human Beings, as native and mutual citizens of a free Republic, and [break] that odious yoke of oppression which is so unjustly laid upon them by their fellow Countrymen, "and to assume among the powers of Earth the same equal privileges to which the Laws of nature and nature's God entitle them, a moderate respect for the opinions of Mankind requires that they should declare the causes which incite them to this just and worthy action."[31]

"We hold these truths to be Self Evident: That all men are created Equal; that they are endowed by their creator with certain unalienable rights; that among these are Life, Liberty, and [the] pursuit of happiness";[32] that Nature hath freely given to all Men a full supply of Air, Water, and Land for their sustenance and mutual happiness; that no man has any right to deprive his fellow-man of these Inherent rights except in punishment of crime; "that to secure these rights governments are instituted among men, deriving their just powers from the consent of the governed; that when any form of Government becomes destructive to these ends, It is the right of the People, to alter, amend, or remoddel it, Laying its foundation on such Principles and organizing its powers in such form as to them shall seem most likely to effect the safety and happiness"[33] of the Human Race. To secure equal rights, privileges, and Justice to *all, Irrespective of Sex;* or Nation; to *secure Fraternal kindness* to all friends of Equal Moral privileges—*to all* who *honestly abandon their Despotic, oppressive rule.* We hold this truth to be self evident: That it is the highest Privilege and Plain Duty of Man to strive in every reasonable way to promote the Happiness, Mental, Moral, and Physical elevation of his fellow-man, and that People or Clanish oppressors, who wickedly violate this sacred principle, oppressing their fellow Men, will bring upon themselves that certain and fearful retribution which is the Natural and Necessary penalty of evil Doing. "Prudence indeed will dictate that Governments long established should not be changed for light and transient causes, but when a *long train of abuses* and usurpations, pursuing invariably the same object, evinces a design to perpetuate an absolute Despotism and most cruel bondage, *it is their Right, it is their Duty,* to resist and change such Government and provide safe-guards for their future Liberty."[34] Such has been the patient sufferance of the Slaves of the United States, and such is now the necessity which constrains them to Crush this foul system of oppression.

The history of Slavery in the United States is a history of injustice and cruelties inflicted upon the slave in every conceivable way, and in barbarity not surpassed by the most savage Tribes. It is the embodiment of all that is evil and ruinous to a Nation; and subversive of all Good. "In proof of which, facts innumerable have been submitted to the People, and have received the verdict [of] condemnation of a candid and impartial World."[35]

Our *servants;* Members of Congress; and other servants of the People, who receive exorbitant wages from the People, in return for their unjust Rule, "have refused to pass laws for the accommodation of large districts of People, unless that People would relinquish the right of representation in the Legislature, a Right inestimable to them, and formidable to tyrants only. Our President and other Leeches have called together *legislative,* or treasonable Bodies, at places unusual, uncomfortable, and distant from the depository of our public records, for the sole purpose of fatiguing us into compliance with their measures. They have dissolved Representative houses for opposing with manly firmness their invasions of the rights of the people."[36]

They have refused to grant Petitions presented by numerous and respectable Citizens, asking redress of grievances imposed upon us, demanding our Liberty and natural rights. With contempt they spurn our humble petitions, and have failed to pass laws for our relief. They have prevented, in all possible ways, the administration of Justice to the Slave. They have made Judges [like] Taney[37]—"dependent on their will alone for the tenure of their office, and the amount [and] payment of their salaries. They have erected a multitude of new offices, and sent on swarms of Blood Suckers and Moths to harass the People and eat out their substance. They have effected to render the Military independent of and superior to the power and wishes of the People (the civil power)."[38] Claiming that *knowledge* is power, they have (for their own safety) kept us in total darkness and ignorance, inflicting base cruelties for any attempt on our part to obtain knowledge. They have protected base Men, *Pirates* (engaged in a most inhuman traffic, *The Foreign and Domestic slave Trade*) "by mock trials, from punishment, for unprovoked murders which they have committed upon us and free citizens of the States."[39] They have prevented by law our having any Traffick or deal with our fellow men. Regardless of our wishes, they "declare themselves invested with power to legislate for us in all cases whatsoever. They have abdicated government among us by declaring us out of their protection, and waging a worse than cruel war upon us continually."[40]

The facts and a full description of the enormous sin of slavery may be found in the General History of American Slavery, which is a history of repeated injuries, of base hypocracy; A cu[r]sed treasonable usurpation; The most abominable provoking atrocities, which are but a mockery of all that is Just, or worthy of any people. "Such cruelty, tyranny, and perfidy, has hardly a parallel in the history of the most barbarous ages."[41]

Our *servants, or Law makers* are *totally unworthy [of] the name of Half civilized* men. All their National acts (which apply to Slavery) are false, to the words, spirit, and intention of the Constitution of the United States, and the

Declaration of Independence. *They say by word and act, That their own children or any faithful citizen may be legally robbed of every Natural and Sacred Right, and that we have no rights whatever.* They are a Blot upon the character, the honor of any Nation which claims to have the least shadow or spark of Civilization above the lowest most inferior Canibal races. This is a slight though brief recital of some of the enormous atrocities of [those] Idle, haughty, tyrannical, *Arrogant Land Monopolists;* slave holders, our lords and masters. From which Good Lord Deliver us. These are some of the facts, which we now (after the lapse of 83 years, since the writing and signing of that sacred Instrument, Honored and Adored by our Fathers, which declares that it is "*self evident that all men are created Equal,* Endowed by their Creator with certain inherent rights, &c.,") submit to the decision of all Candid, true Republican Friends of *Universal Freedom and Natural Equality of Rights.* All we demand is our Liberty and the natural rights and immunities of faithful Citizens of the United States. We will obtain these rights or Die in the struggle to obtain them. We make war upon oppression, we have no controversy with any Religious Sect. Our intention is not to molest any *Good Man whatever may* be his religious belief. "The welfare of the People is the first Great Law."[42] We hold these to be self evident truths, That any Tribe, Rulers or People, who rob and cruelly oppress their faithful Laboring citizens have within themselves the *Germ* of their own certain and fearful overthrow. It is one of Nature's Immutable Laws, that "according to the measures ye [mete], so shall it be measured to you again."[43] Herein is the secret of security and true happiness for Individuals. *And the only firm basis upon which Governments may be permanently Established, where the Citizens are Devoted to the greatest good of their fellow men. The more humble, benighted and oppressed they are, so much more sympathy and earnest effort for their relief is demanded.* Striving earnestly to promote the safety and prosperity of *their Nation, and the Human Race.*

It *is a fixed Law of Nature,* That any People, or Nation whose steady purpose and *constant Practice* is in accordance with these principles, *Must go forward Progressing, so long as Man* continues *to Exist.* For in Nature the *Principle of Reciprocity is Great.* "The Legitimate object of all punishment is to prevent Crime."[44] *When any Punishment is inflicted more than is necessary to prevent crime,* it then ceases to be a Punishment. It has then become a barbarous crime. *A Sore Evil.* The *Natural object of all Government is to protect the right, defend the Innocent.* When any set of Usurpers, Tribe or community, fail to protect the right, but furnish protection and encouragement to the Villain by bestowing a bounty or Premium upon the vile Thief, Robber, Libertine, Pirate, and woman killing Slave Holder, as a reward for their deeds of rascality and Barbarism; And inflict grievous cruelties upon the innocent, shooting and Butchering those most faithful Citizens who have striven manfully for the relief of the down trodden and oppressed of their country. Who fought bravely in support of the Great Principles set forth in our Declaration of Independence, from oppressive Rule of England, Encouraging in various ways by bribery and fraud, the most fiendish acts of Barbarism (like those perpetrated within the limits of the United States, at Blount's Fort in Florida[45] and in other Territories, under the Jurisdiction and guidance of Slave holding Authority, and in strict accordance with slave holding Rules). They have transcended their own limits; They have fairly outwitted themselves. Their Slave Code is a shame to any Nation. Their laws are no laws; they themselves are no more than a Band of Base Piraticle Rulers. They are a curse to themselves, a most lamentable Blot upon Society.

"In every stage of these oppressions we have petitioned for redress in the most humble terms. Our repeated Petitions have been answered only by repeated Injury. A Class of oppressors, whose character is thus marked by every act which may define a Tyrannical Despotism, is unfit to rule any People, nor have we been wanting in attention to our oppressors. We have warned them from time to time of attempts (made by their headlong Blindness) to perpetuate, extend, strengthen, and revive the dieing elements of this cursed Institution. We have reminded them of our unhappy condition and of their cruelties. We have appealed to their native Justice and magnanimity. We have conjured them by *the ties* of our *common Nature,* our Brotherhood, and *common Parentage* to disavow these usurpations which have destroyed our *kindred friendship* and endangered their safety. They have been Deaf to the voice of Justice and Consanguinity. We must therefore acquiesce in the necessity"[46] which denounces their Tyranny and unjust rule over us. Declaring that we will serve them no longer as slaves, knowing that the "Laborer is worthy of his hire."[47] "We therefore, the Representatives of the circumscribed citizens of the United States of America, in General Congress assembled, appealing to the Supreme Judge of the World for the rectitude of our intentions, Do in the name and by the authority of the oppressed citizens of the Slave States, solemnly publish and Declare"[48] that the Slaves are, and of right ought to be, as free and independent as the unchangable Law of God requires that all men Shall be. That they are absolved from all allegiance to those Tyrants who still persist in forcibly subjecting them to perpetual Bondage, and that all friendly connection between them and such Tyrants is and ought to be totally dissolved, And that as free and independent citizens of these States they have a perfect right, a sufficient and just cause, to defend themselves against the Tyranny of their oppressors. To solicit aid from and ask the protection of all true friends of humanity and reform of whatever nation and wherever found; A right to contract Alliances, and to do all other acts and things which free independent Citizens may of right do. "And for the support of [this] Declaration, with a firm reliance on the protection of Divine Providence, we mutually Pledge to each other our Lives and our sacred honor."[49] Indeed, "I tremble for my country when I reflect that God is Just, And that his Justice will not sleep forever."[50] Nature is mourning for its murdered and Afflicted Children.[51] Hung be the Heavens in scarlet.[52]

Source: Calendar of Virginia State Papers and Other Manuscripts, from January 1, 1836, to April 15, 1869; Preserved in the Capitol at Richmond, Vol. 11 (Richmond: R. F. Walker, 1893), 275–279.[53]

John Brown, "Interview with Senator Mason and Others," October 18, 1859

On October 16, 1859, Brown and his men captured Harpers Ferry. For their symbolic value, they seized a pistol that had been a present from Lafayette and a dress sword purportedly given to General Washington by Frederick the Great, now belonging to one of Brown's hostages, Colonel Lewis W. Washington. Brown brandished the sword until he fell, early in the morning on October 18, when the band was overpowered. Ten raiders died in the battle and five escaped. Less than twenty-four hours later, Brown answered questions from Robert E. Lee, Virginia governor Henry Wise, senator James M. Mason, congressman Clement Laird Vallandigham, and others. The interview, published by the *New York Herald* on October 21, continued for several hours as Brown lay on the floor of the paymaster's office at Harpers Ferry. Vallandigham recalled that Brown was "anxious to talk and ready to answer anyone who chose to ask a question." The only topics he would not discuss were the identities and roles of his allies and co-conspirators. Later that afternoon he was taken 8 miles down the road to the jail at Charles Town. He was indicted at the Jefferson County Courthouse on October 26. The charges were murder, treason against the State of Virginia, and conspiracy to incite a slave insurrection. Brown requested a delay in his trial until he had recovered from his wounds, but the request was denied and his trial proceeded. The six other men who survived the raid and failed to escape were tried and hanged as well.

Senator Mason. Can you tell us, at least, who furnished money for your expedition?

Capt. Brown. I furnished most of it myself. I cannot implicate others. It is by my own folly that I have been taken. I could easily have saved myself from it, had I exercised my own better judgment rather than yielded to my feelings. I should have gone away, but I had thirty odd prisoners, whose wives and daughters were in tears for their safety, and I felt for them. Besides, I wanted to allay the fears of those who believed we came here to burn and kill. For this reason I allowed the train to cross the bridge, and gave them full liberty to pass on. I did it only to spare the feelings of those passengers and their families, and to allay the apprehensions that you had got here in your vicinity a band of men who had no regard for life and property, nor any feeling of humanity.

Senator M. But you killed some people passing along the streets quietly.

Capt. B. Well, sir, if there was anything of that kind done, it was without my knowledge. Your own citizens, who where my prisoners, will tell you that every possible means were taken to prevent it. I did not allow my men to fire, nor even to return a fire, when there was danger of killing those we regarded as innocent persons, if I could help it. They will tell you that we allowed ourselves to be fired at repeatedly, and did not return it.

A Bystander. That is not so. You killed an unarmed man at the corner of the house over there (at the water-tank), and another besides.

Capt. B. See here, my friend; it is useless to dispute or contradict the report of your own neighbors, who were my prisoners.

Senator M. If you would tell us who sent you here—who provided the means —that would be information of some value.

Capt. B. I will answer freely and faithfully about what concerns myself—I will answer anything I can with honor, but not about others.

Mr. Vallandigham (member of Congress from Ohio, who had just entered). Mr. Brown, who sent you here?

Capt. B. No man sent me here; it was my own prompting and that of my Maker, or that of the Devil, whichever you please to ascribe it to. I acknowledge no master in human form.

Mr. V. Did you get up the expedition yourself?

Capt. B. I did.

Mr. V. Did you get up this document called a constitution?

Capt. B. I did. They are a constitution and ordinances of my own contriving and getting up.

Mr. V. How long have you been engaged in this business?

Capt. B. From the breaking out of the difficulties in Kansas. Four of my sons had gone there to settle, and they induced me to go. I did not go there to settle, but because of the difficulties.

Senator M. How many are there engaged with you in this movement? I ask these questions for your own safety.

Capt. B. Any questions that I can honorably answer I will; not otherwise. So far as I am myself concerned, I have told everything truthfully. I value my word, sir.

Senator M. What was your object in coming?

Capt. B. We came to free the slaves, and only that.

A Young Man (in the uniform of a volunteer company). How many men in all had you?

Capt. B. I came to Virginia with eighteen men besides myself.[54]

Volunteer. What in the world did you suppose you could do here in Virginia with that amount of men?

Capt. B. Young man, I don't wish to discuss that question here.

Volunteer. You could not do anything.

Capt. B. Well, perhaps your ideas and mine, on military subjects, would differ materially.

Senator M. How do you justify your acts?

Capt. B. I think, my friend, you are guilty of a great wrong against God and humanity—I say it without wishing to be offensive—and it would be perfectly right for any one to interfere with you so far as to free those you willfully and wickedly hold in bondage. I do not say this insultingly.

Senator M. I understand that.

Capt. B. I think I did right, and that others will do right who interfere with you, at any time, and at all times. I hold that the golden rule—"Do unto others as ye would that others should do unto you"—applies to all who would help others to gain their liberty.

Lieutenant Stuart. But don't you believe in the Bible?

Capt. B. Certainly I do.

Mr. V. Where did your men come from? Did some of them come from Ohio?

Capt. B. Some of them.

Mr. V. From the Western Reserve, of course! None came from Southern Ohio?

Capt. B. O, yes. I believe one came from Steubenville, down not far from Wheeling.[55]

Mr. V. Have you been in Ohio this summer?

Capt. B. Yes, sir.

Mr. V. How lately?

Capt. B. I passed through to Pittsburg on my way, in June.

Mr. V. Were you at any county or state fair there?

Capt. B. I was not there since June.

Senator M. Did you consider this a military organization in this paper? (*Showing a copy of John Brown's constitution and ordinance.*) I have not yet read it.

Capt. B. I did in some measure. I wish you would give that paper your close attention.

Senator M. You considered yourself the commander-in-chief of this provisional military force?

Capt. B. I was chosen, agreeably to the ordinance of a certain document, commander-in-chief of that force.

Senator M. What wages did you offer?

Capt. B. None.

Lieut. S. "The wages of sin is death."

Capt. B. I would not have made such a remark to you if you had been a prisoner, and wounded, in my hands.

Bystander. Did you not promise a negro in Gettysburg twenty dollars a month?

Capt. B. I did not.

Bystander. He says you did.

Mr. V. Were you ever in Dayton, Ohio?

Capt. B. Yes, I must have been.

Mr. V. This summer?

Capt. B. No; a year or two since.

Senator M. Does this talking annoy you?

Capt. B. Not in the least.

Mr. V. Have you lived long in Ohio?

Capt. B. I went there in 1805. I lived in Summit County, which was then Trumbull County. My native place is York State.

Mr. V. Do you recollect a man in Ohio named Brown, a noted counterfeiter?

Capt. B. I do. I knew him from a boy. His father was Henry Brown, of Irish or Scotch descent. The family was very low.

Mr. V. Have you ever been in Portage County?

Capt. B. I was there in June last.

Mr. V. When in Cleveland, did you attend the Fugitive Slave Law Convention there?

Capt. B. No. I was there about the time of the sitting of the court to try the Oberlin rescuers. I spoke there publicly on that subject; on the fugitive slave law, and my own rescue. Of course, so far as I had any influence at all, I was supposed to justify the Oberlin people for rescuing the slave, because I have myself forcibly taken slaves from bondage. I was concerned in taking eleven slaves from Missouri to Canada last winter. I think I spoke in Cleveland before the Convention. I do not know that I had conversation with any of the Oberlin rescuers.[56] I was sick part of the time I was in Ohio. I had the ague. I was part of the time in Ashtabula County.

Mr. V. Did you see anything of Joshua R. Giddings there?

Capt. B. I did meet him.

Mr. V. Did you converse with him?

Capt. B. I did. I would not tell you, of course, any thing that would implicate Mr. Giddings; but I certainly met with him and had a conversation with him.

Mr. V. About that rescue case?

Capt. B. Yes, I did. I heard him express his opinion upon it very freely and frankly.

Mr. V. Justifying it?

Capt. B. Yes, sir. I do not compromise him, certainly, in saying that.

Bystander. Did you go out to Kansas under the auspices of the Emigrant Aid Society?

Capt. B. No, sir; I went out under the auspices of John Brown, and nobody else.

Mr. V. Will you answer this? Did you talk with Giddings about your expedition here?

Capt. B. No, sir! I won't answer that; because a denial of it I would not make; and to make any affidavit of it, I should be a great dunce.

Mr. V. Have you had correspondence with parties at the North on the subject of this movement?

Capt. B. I have had no correspondence.

Bystander. Do you consider this a religious movement?

Capt. B. It is, in my opinion, the greatest service a man can render to his God.

Bystander. Do you consider yourself an instrument in the hands of Providence?

Capt. B. I do.

Bystander. Upon what principle do you justify your acts?

Capt. B. Upon the golden rule. I pity the poor in bondage that have none to help them. That is why I am here; it is not to gratify any personal animosity, or feeling of revenge, or vindictive spirit. It is my sympathy with the oppressed and the wronged, that are as good as you, and as precious in the sight of God.

Bystander. Certainly. But why take the slaves against their will?

Capt. B. I never did.

Bystander. You did in one instance, at least.

Stevens[57] *(To the inquirer, interrupting Brown.)* You are right, sir, in one case—

(a groan from the wounded man)—in one case, I know the negro wanted to go back.—*(To Brown.)* Captain, that gentleman is right.

Bystander: (To Stevens.) Where did you come from?

Stevens. I lived in Ashtabula County, Ohio.

Mr. V. How recently did you leave Ashtabula County?

Stevens. Some months ago. I never resided there any length of time. I have often been through there.

Mr. V. How far did you live from Jefferson?

Capt. B. Be cautious, Stevens, about an answer to that; it might commit some friend. I would not answer it at all.[58] *(Stevens, who had been groaning considerably, as if the exertion necessary to conversation seriously affected him, seemed content to abide by the captain's advice. He turned partially over, with a groan of pain, and was silent.)*

Mr. V. (To Capt. Brown.) Who are your advisors in this movement?

Capt. B. I cannot answer that. I have numerous sympathizers throughout the entire North.

Mr. V. In Northern Ohio?

Capt. B. No more than anywhere else—in all the Free States.

Mr. V. But you are not personally acquainted in Southern Ohio?

Capt. B. Not very much.

Mr. V. (To Stevens.) Were you at the convention last June?

Stevens. I was.

Mr. V. (To Capt. Brown.) You made a speech there?

Capt. B. I did, sir.

Bystander. Did you ever live in Washington city?

Capt. B. I did not. I want you to understand, gentlemen, that I respect the rights of the poorest and weakest of colored people, oppressed by the slave system, just as much as I do those of the most wealthy and powerful. This is the idea that has moved me, and that alone. We expected no reward except the satisfaction of endeavoring to do for those in distress—the greatly oppressed—as we would be done by. The cry of distress, of the oppressed, is my reason, and the only thing that prompted me to come here.

Bystander. Why did you do it secretly?

Capt. B. Because I thought that necessary to success, and for no other reason.

Bystander. Have you read Gerrit Smith's last letter?

Capt. B. What letter do you mean?

Bystander. The New York *Herald* of yesterday, in speaking of this affair, mentions a letter in which he says "that it is folly to attempt to strike the shackles off the slaves by the force of moral suasion or legal agitation," and predicts that the next movement made in the direction of negro emancipation would be an insurrection in the South.

Capt. B. I have not seen the New York *Herald* for some days past; but I presume, from your remark about the gist of the letter, that I should concur with it. I agree with Mr. Smith that moral suasion is hopeless. I don't think the people of the Slave States will ever consider the subject of slavery in its true light till some other argument is resorted to than moral suasion.

Mr. V. Did you expect a general rising of the slaves in case of your success?

Capt. B. No, sir; nor did I wish it. I expected to gather them up from time to time; then I could set them free.

Mr. V. Did you expect to hold possession here till then?

Capt. B. Well, probably I had quite a different idea. I do not know that I ought to reveal my plans. I am here a prisoner, and wounded, because I foolishly allowed myself to be so. You overrate your strength in supposing I could have been taken if I had not allowed it. I was too tardy after commencing the open attack, in delaying my movements through Monday night, and up to the time I was attacked by the government troops. It was all occasioned by my desire to spare the feelings of my prisoners and their families, and the community at large.

Mr. V. Did you not shoot a negro on the bridge, or did not some of your party?

Capt. B. I had no knowledge of the shooting of the negro.

Mr. V. What time did you commence your organization in Canada?

Capt. B. It occurred about two years ago. If I remember right, it was, I think, in 1858.

Mr. V. Who was the secretary?

Capt. B. That I would not tell if I recollected; but I do not recollect. I think the officers were elected in May, 1858. I may answer incorrectly, but not intentionally. My head is a little confused by wounds, and my memory of dates and such like is somewhat confused.

Dr. Biggs. Were you in the party at Dr. Kennedy's house?

Capt. B. I was the head of that party. I occupied the house to mature my plans. I would state here that I have not been in Baltimore to purchase percussion caps.

Dr. Biggs. What was the number of men at Kennedy's?

Capt. B. I decline to answer that.

Dr. Biggs. Who lanced that woman's neck on the hill?

Capt. B. I did. I have sometimes practiced in surgery, when I thought it a matter of humanity or of necessity—when there was no one else to do it; but I have not studied surgery.

Dr. Biggs. (To the persons around.) It was done very well and scientifically. These men have been very clever to the neighbors, I have been told, and we had no reason to suspect them, except that we could not understand their movements. They were represented as eight or nine persons; on Friday there were thirteen.

Capt. B. There were more than thirteen. *(Questions were now put in by almost every one in the room.)*

Q. Where did you get arms to obtain possession of the armory?

A. I bought them.

Q. In what state?

A. That I would not state.

Q. How many guns?

A. Two hundred Sharpe's rifles and two hundred revolvers—what is called the Massachusetts Arms Company's revolvers—a little under the navy size.

Q. Why did you not take that swivel you left in the house?

A. I had no occasion for it. It was given to me a year or two ago.

A Reporter. I do not wish to annoy you; but if you have anything else you would like to say, I will report it.

Capt. B. I do not wish to converse any more; I have nothing to say. I will only remark to these reporting gentlemen, that I claim to be here in carrying out a measure I believe to be perfectly justifiable, and not to act the part of an incendiary or ruffian; but, on the contrary, to aid those suffering under a great wrong. I wish to say, furthermore, that you had better—all you people at the South—prepare yourselves for a settlement of this question. It must come up for settlement sooner than you are prepared for it, and the sooner you commence that preparation the better for you. You may dispose of me very easily. I am nearly disposed of now; but this question is still be settled— this negro question I mean. The end of that is not yet. These wounds were inflicted upon me—both sabre cuts on my head and bayonet stabs in different parts of my body—some minutes after I had ceased fighting, and had consented to surrender for the benefit of others, and not for my own benefit.

(Several person vehemently denied this statement. Without noticing the interruption, the old man continued:)

I believe the Major *(pointing to Lieut. Stuart)* would not have been alive but for me. I might have killed him just as easy as I could kill a mosquito, when he came in; but I supposed he came in only to receive our surrender. There had been loud and long calls of surrender from us—as loud as men could yell—but in the confusion and excitement I suppose we were not heard. I do not believe the Major, or any one else, wanted to butcher us after we had surrendered. *(An officer present here stated that special orders had been given to the marines not to shoot anybody; but when they were fired upon by Brown's men, and one of them had been killed, and another wounded, they were obliged to return the compliment. Captain Brown insisted, with some warmth, that the marines fired first.)*

An Officer. Why did you not surrender before the attack?

Capt. B. I did not think it was my duty or interest to do so. We assured our prisoners that we did not wish to harm them, and they should be set at liberty. I exercised my best judgment, not believing the people would wantonly sacrifice their own fellow-citizens. When we offered to let them go on condition of being allowed to change our position about a quarter of a mile, the prisoners agreed by a vote among themselves to pass across the bridge with us. We wanted them only as a sort of guarantee of our safety—that we should not be fired into. We took them, in the fist place, as hostages and to keep them from doing any harm. We did kill some men when defending ourselves; but I saw no one fire except directly in self-defence. Our orders were strict not to harm any one not in arms against us.

Q. Well, Brown, suppose you had every nigger in the United States, what would you do with them?

Capt. B. (In a loud tone, and with emphasis.) Set them free, sir!

Capt. B. Your intention was to carry them off and free them?

A. Not at all.

A Bystander. To set them free would sacrifice the life of every man in this community.

Capt. B. I do not think so.

Bystander. I know it. I think you are fanatical.

Capt. B. And I think you are fanatical. "Whom the gods would destroy, they first make mad,"[59] and you are mad.

Q. Was your only object to free the negroes?

Capt. B. Absolutely our only object.

Q. But you went and took Col. Washington's silver and watch.

Capt. B. O, yes; we intended freely to have appropriated the property of the slaveholders, to carry out our object. It was for that, and only that; and with no design to enrich ourselves with any plunder whatever.

Bystander. Did you know Sherrod in Kansas? I understand you killed him.

Capt. B. I killed no man except in fair fight. I fought at Black Jack Point, and at Osawatomie; and if I killed anybody, it was at one of these places.

Source: James Redpath, *The Public Life of Capt. John Brown* (Boston: Thayer and Eldridge, 1860), 276–285.

John Brown, "Last Address to the Virginia Court," November 2, 1859

Andrew Hunter and Charles Harding prosecuted Brown's case for the state and Richard Parker sat as judge. The court appointed Brown's defense counsels. On October 27, hoping it would help his case, the defense lawyer produced a telegram from Asahel H. Lewis, a newspaper editor in Ohio and a former acquaintance of Brown, asserting that insanity ran in the Brown family. Brown angrily rejected the idea, calling it a "miserable artifice" that he viewed with "contempt." Then, on November 2, after the jury had found him guilty of treason against the Commonwealth of Virginia, he made his final address to the court. Although many presumed that the speech was extemporaneous, Brown had drafted some of his material in a prison letter of November 1. Both his speech and his letter to E.B. include the assertion that if he had "interfered," suffered, and sacrificed on behalf of the rich, powerful, intelligent, and great, his actions would not count as treason. After making the speech, Brown heard Judge Parker's sentence: death by public hanging in Charles Town.

I have, may it please the Court, a few words to say.

In the first place, I deny everything but what I have all along admitted, of a design on my part to free the slaves. I intended certainly to have made a clean thing of that matter, as I did last winter, when I went into Missouri and there took slaves without the snapping of a gun on either side, moved them through the country, and finally left them in Canada. I designed to have done the same thing again, on a larger scale. That was all I intended. I never did intend murder, or treason, or the destruction of property, or to excite or incite slaves to rebellion, or to make insurrection.

I have another objection; and that is, it is unjust that I should suffer such a penalty. Had I interfered in the manner which I admit, and which I admit has been fairly proved (for I admire the truthfulness and candor of the grater portion of the witnesses who have testified in this case)—had I so interfered in behalf of the rich, the powerful, the intelligent, the so-called great, or in behalf of any of their friends—either father, mother, brother, sister, wife, or children, or any of that class—and suffered and sacrificed what I have in this interference, it would have been all right; and every man in this court would have deemed it an act worthy of reward rather than punishment.

This court acknowledges, as I suppose, the validity of the law of God. I see a book kissed here which I suppose to be the Bible, or at least the New Testament. That teaches me that all things whatsoever I would that men should do to me, I should do even so to them. It teaches me, further to "remember them that are in bonds, as bound with them."[60] I endeavored to act up to that instruction. I say, I am yet too young to understand that God is any respecter of persons. I believe that to have interfered as I have done—in behalf of His despised poor, was not wrong, but right. Now, if it is deemed necessary that I should forfeit my life for the furtherance of the ends of justice, and mingle my blood further with the blood of my children and with the blood of millions in this slave country whose rights are disregarded by wicked, cruel, and unjust enactments—I submit; so let it be done!

Let me say one word further.

I feel entirely satisfied with the treatment I have received on my trial. Considering all the circumstances, it has been more generous than I expected. But I feel no consciousness of guilt. I have stated from the first what was my intention, and what was not. I never have had any design against the life of any person, nor any disposition to commit treason, or excite slaves to rebel, or make any general insurrection. I never encouraged any man to do so, but always discouraged any idea of that kind.

Let me say, also, a word in regard to the statements made by some of those connected with me. I hear it has been stated by some of them that I have induced them to join me. But the contrary is true. I do not say this to injure them, but as regretting their weakness. There is not one of them but joined me of his own accord, and the greater part of them at their own expense. A number of them I never saw, and never had a word of conversation with, till the day they came to me; and that was for the purpose I have stated.

Now I have done.

Source: James Redpath, *The Public Life of Capt. John Brown* (Boston: Thayer and Eldridge, 1860), 340–342.

John Brown, "Prison Letters,"
October–December 1859

Brown wrote more than a hundred letters from his jail cell before his execution on December 2. Ostensibly private, these prison letters were addressed to his family, friends, and acquaintances. But within the context of a thriving antislavery print culture, and aided by the extensive press coverage of his raid, trial, and execution, most of the letters were published in Northern newspapers, including the *New York Tribune,* which had the largest circulation of any antislavery newspaper at the time. Abolitionists circulated the letters as well, publishing them in the press. Widely read, these prison letters influenced public perception of Brown's raid. The judgments of "posterity" that he imagines in his letter of October 31 were taking shape. In several letters Brown even refers to a broader audience. He asks his wife to show them to other people, and he references the interest from newspapers and distant supporters. Then, with an eye on this audience, he transforms himself from Kansas warrior to Christian martyr. Invoking the authority of the epistolary form (Saint Paul's letters from prison), Brown compares himself to Peter on November 1, to "prophets and apostles" on November 8, and to Paul on November 23 and 25. In several letters Brown goes still further and compares himself to Christ. In one he instructs his readers to remember that Jesus of Nazareth died as a felon, and in another he echoes Christ's words on the cross: "Forgive them, for they know not what they do." But he accompanies these echoes of New Testament redemption with images of righteous violence. Invoking the soldier Christ of Revelations, one letter describes Christ as the "Captain of liberty" and himself as a "faithful soldier" armed with a sword of steel. Invoking Old Testament prophets and warriors as well, Brown compares himself to Moses on November 25 and to Samson on November 15. Joining social critique to spiritual renewal, he not only entered an abolitionist tradition that analyzed and disproved biblical authorities on inequality, but also offered himself as a biblical character.

Charlestown, Jefferson Co, Va. 31st Oct.

My dear Wife, and Children, every one. I suppose you have learned before this by the newspapers that two weeks ago today we were fighting for our lives at Harper's Ferry:[61] that during the fight Watson was mortally wounded; Oliver

killed, Wm Thompson killed, & Dauphin slightly wounded.[62] That on the following day I was taken prisoner immediately after which I received several
Sabre-cuts in my head; & Bayonet stabs in my body. As nearly as I can learn
Watson died of his wound on Wednesday the 2d or on Thursday the 3d day
after I was taken.

Dauphin was killed when I was taken; & Anderson[63] I suppose also. I have
since been tried, & found guilty of Treason, etc; and of murder in the first degree. I have not yet received my sentence. No others of the company with
whom you were acquainted were, so far as *I can learn*, either killed or taken.
Under all these terrible calamities; I feel quite cheerful in the assurance that
God reigns; & will overrule all for his glory; & the best possible good. I feel *no*
consciousness of *guilt* in the matter: nor even mortifycation on account of my
imprisonment; & irons; & I feel perfectly sure that very soon no member of
my family will feel any possible disposition to "blush on my account." Already
dear friends at a distance with kindest sympathy are cheering me with the assurance that *posterity* at least will do me justice. I shall commend you all, together with my beloved but bereaved daughters in law, to their sympathies
which I do not doubt will reach you.

I also commend you all to Him "whose mercy endureth forever":[64] to the
God of *my fathers* "whose I am; & whom I serve."[65] "He will never leave you
nor forsake you,"[66] unless you forsake Him. Finally my dearly beloved be of
good comfort. Be sure to remember *to follow my advice &* my example too; so
far as it has been consistent with the holy religion of Jesus Christ in which I
remain a most firm, & humble believer. Never forget the poor nor think anything you bestow on them to be lost to you even though they may be as *black*
as Ebedmelch the Ethiopean eunuch who cared for Jeremiah in the pit of the
dungeon;[67] or as *black* as the one to whom Phillip preached Christ.[68] Be sure
to entertain strangers, for thereby some have—"Remember them that are in
bonds as bound with them." I am in charge of a jailor *like* the one who took
charge of "Paul & Silas" & you may rest assured that both *kind hearts & kind
faces* are more or less about me; whilst thousands are thirsting for my blood.
"These *light* afflictions which are but *for a moment* shall work out for us a *far
more exceeding & eternal* weight of Glory."[69] I hope to be able to write to you
again. My wounds are doing well. Copy this, & send it to your sorrow stricken
brothers, Ruth; to comfort them. Write me a few words in regard to the welfare of all. God Allmighty bless you all: & "make you joyful in the midst of all

your tribulations."[70] Write to John Brown, Charlestown, Jefferson Co, Va, care of Capt John Avis.

> Your Affectionate Husband, & Father, John Brown
> Nov. 3d

P S Yesterday Nov 2d I was sentenced to be hanged on Decem 2d next. Do not grieve on my account. I am still quite cheerful. God bless you all.

> Yours ever, J Brown

Charlestown, Jefferson County, Va., Nov. 1, 1859.

My Dear Friend E.B. of R.I.: Your most cheering letter of the 27th of Oct. is received, and may the Lord reward you a thousand fold for the kind feeling you express toward me; but more especially for your fidelity to the "poor that cry, and those that have no help."[71] For this I am a prisoner in bonds. It is solely my own fault, in a military point of view, that we met with our disaster—I mean that I mingled with our prisoners and so far sympathized with them and their families that I neglected my duty *in other* respects. But God's will, not mine, be done.

You know that Christ once armed Peter. So also in my case, I think he put a sword into my hand, and there continued it, so long as he saw best, and then kindly took it from me. I mean when I first went to Kansas. I wish you could know with what cheerfulness I am now wielding the "Sword of the Spirit"[72] on the right hand and on the left. I bless God that it proves "mighty to the pulling down of strongholds."[73] I always loved my Quaker friends, and I commend to their kind regard my poor, bereaved widowed wife, and my daughters and daughters-in-law, whose husbands fell at my side. One is a mother and the other likely to become so soon. They, as well as my own sorrow-stricken daughters, are left very poor, and have much greater need of sympathy than I, who, through Infinite Grace and the kindness of strangers, am "joyful in all my tribulations."[74]

Dear sister, write them at North Elba, Essex Co., N.Y., to comfort their sad hearts. Direct to Mary A. Brown, wife of John Brown. There is also another—a widow, wife of Thompson, who fell with my poor boys in the affair at Harper's Ferry, at the same place.

I do not feel conscious of guilt in taking up arms; and had it been in behalf of the rich and powerful, the intelligent, the great—as men count greatness—or those who form enactments to suit themselves and corrupt others, or some of their friends, that I interfered, suffered, sacrificed, and fell, it would have been doing very well. But enough of this.

These light afflictions which endure for a moment, shall work out for me *a far more exceeding and eternal weight of glory.* I would be very grateful for another letter from you. My wounds are healing. *Farewell.* God will surely attend to his own cause in the best possible way and time, and he will not forget the work of his own hands.

Your friend, John Brown

Charlestown, Jefferson County, Va., Nov. 8, 1859.

Dear Wife and Children, Every One—I will begin by saying that I have in some degree recovered from my wounds, but that I am quite weak in my back and sore about my left kidney. My appetite has been quite good for most of the time since I was hurt. I am supplied with almost everything I could desire to make me comfortable, and the little I do lack (some articles of clothing which I lost) I may perhaps soon get again. I am, besides, quite cheerful, having (as I trust) "the peace of God, which passeth all understanding," to "rule in my heart,"[75] and the testimony (in some degree) of a good conscience that I have not lived altogether in vain. I can trust God with both the time and the manner of my death, believing, as I now do, that for me at this time to seal my testimony for God and humanity with my blood will do vastly more toward advancing the cause I have earnestly endeavored to promote, than all I have done in my life before. I beg of you all meekly and quietly to submit to this, not feeling yourselves in the least *degraded* on the account. Remember, dear wife and children all, that Jesus of Nazareth suffered a most excruciating death on the cross as a felon, under the most aggravating circumstances. Think also of the prophets and apostles and Christians of former days, who went through greater tribulations than you or I, and try to be reconciled. May God Almighty comfort all your hearts, and soon wipe away all tears from your eyes! To him be endless praise! Think, too, of the crushed millions who "have no comforter."[76] I charge you all never in your trials to forget the griefs "of the poor that cry, and of those that have none to help them."⁷⁷ I wrote most earnestly to my dear and afflicted wife not to come on for the present, at any rate. I will now give her reasons for doing so. First, it would use up all the scanty means she has, or is at all likely to have, to make herself and children comfortable hereafter. For let me tell you that the sympathy that is now aroused in your behalf may not always follow you. There is but little more of the romantic about helping poor widows and their children than there is about trying to relieve poor "niggers." Again, the little comfort it might afford us to meet again would be dearly bought by the pains of a final separation. We must part; and I feel assured for us to meet under such dreadful circumstances would only add to our distress. If she comes on here, she must be only a gazing-stock through-out the whole journey, to be remarked upon in every look, word, and action, and by all sorts of creatures, and by all sorts of papers, throughout the whole country. Again, it is my most decided judgment that in quietly and submis-sively staying at home vastly more of generous sympathy will reach her, with-out such dreadful sacrifice of feeling as she must put up with if she comes on. The visits of one or two female friends that have come on her have produced great excitement, which is very annoying; and they cannot possibly do me any good. Oh, Mary! do not come, but patiently wait for the meeting of those who love God and their fellow-men, where no separation must follow. "They shall go no more out forever."⁷⁸ I greatly long to hear from some one of you, and to learn anything that in any way affects your welfare. I sent you ten dollars the other day; did you get it? I have also endeavored to stir up Christian friends to visit and write to you in your deep affliction. I have no doubt that some of them, at least, will heed the call. Write to me, care of Captain John Avis, Charlestown, Jefferson County, Virginia.

"Finally, my beloved, be of good comfort."⁷⁹ May all your names be "written in the Lamb's book of life!"⁸⁰—may you all have the purifying and sustaining influence of the Christian religion!—is the earnest prayer of

Your affectionate husband and father, John Brown
Nov. 9.

P.S.—I cannot remember a night so dark as to have hindered the coming day, nor a storm so furious and dreadful as to prevent the return of warm sunshine and a cloudless sky. But, beloved ones, do remember that this is not your rest—that in this world you have no abiding place or continuing city. To God and his infinite mercy I always commend you. J.B.

Charlestown, Jefferson County, Va., Nov. 12, 1859.

Dear Brother Jeremiah:[81] Your kind letter of the 9th instant is received, and also one from Mr. Tilden, for both of which I am greatly obliged. You inquire, "Can I do anything for you or your family?" I would answer that my sons, as well as my wife and daughter, are all very poor, and that anything that may hereafter be due to me from my father's estate I wish paid to them, as I will endeavor *hereafter to describe,* without legal formalities to consume it all. One of my boys has been so entirely used up as very likely to be in want of comfortable clothing for the winter. I have, through the kindness of friends, fifteen dollars to send him, which I will remit shortly. If you know where to reach *him,* please send him that amount at once, as I shall remit the same to *you* by a safe conveyance. If I had a plain statement from Mr. Thompson of the state of my accounts, with the estate of my father, I should then better know what to say about that matter.[82] As it is, I have not the least memorandum left me to refer to. If Mr. Thompson will make me a statement, and charge *my dividend fully for his trouble,* I would be greatly obliged to him. In that case you can send me any remarks of your own. I am gaining in health slowly, and am *quite cheerful* in view of my approaching end, being fully persuaded that I am worth inconceivably more to *hang* than for any other purpose. God Almighty bless and save you all.

Your affectionate brother, John Brown.

P. S. Nov. 13.—Say to my poor boys never to grieve for one moment on my account; and should many of you live to see the time when you will not blush to own your relation to Old John Brown, it will not be more strange than many things that have happened. I feel a thousand times more on account of my sorrowing friends than on my own account. So far as *I am concerned,* I "count it all joy."[83] "I have fought the good fight," and have, as I trust, "finished my course."[84] Please show this to any of my family that you may see. My love to all; and may God, in his infinite mercy, for Christ's sake, bless and save you all.

Your affectionate brother, J. Brown.

Charlestown, Jefferson County, Va., Nov. 15, 1859.

Rev. H. L. Vaill.[85] My Dear, Steadfast Friend—Your most kind and most welcome letter of the 8th inst. reached me in due time. I am very grateful for all
the good feeling you express, and also for the kind counsels you give, together
with your prayers in my behalf. Allow me here to say, notwithstanding "my
soul is among lions,"[86] still I believe that "God in very deed is with me."[87] You
will not, therefore, feel surprised when I tell you that I am "joyful in all my
tribulations"; that I do not feel condemned of Him whose judgment is just,
nor of my own conscience. Nor do I feel degraded by my imprisonment, my
chains, or prospect of the gallows. I have not only been (though utterly unworthy) permitted to "suffer affliction with God's people,"[88] but have also had
a great many rare opportunities for "preaching righteousness in the great congregation."[89] I trust it will not all be lost. The jailer (in whose charge I am) and
his family and assistants have all been most kind; and notwithstanding he was
one of the bravest of all who fought me, he is now being abused for his humanity. So far as my observation goes, none but brave men are likely to be
humane to a fallen foe. Cowards prove their courage by their ferocity. It may
be done in that way with but little risk.

I wish I could write you about a few only of the interesting times I here experience with different classes of men, clergymen among others. Christ, the
great captain of liberty as well as of salvation, and who began his mission, as
foretold of him, by proclaiming it, saw fit to take from me a sword of steel after
I had carried it for a time; but he has put another in my hand ("the sword of
the Spirit"),[90] and I pray God to make me a faithful soldier, wherever he may
send me, not less on the scaffold than when surrounded by my warmest sympathizers.

My dear old friend, I do assure you I have not forgotten our last meeting,
nor our retrospective look over the route by which God had then led us; and I
bless his name that he has again enabled me to hear your words of cheering
and comfort at a time when I, at least, am on the "brink of Jordan."[91] (See Bunyan's "Pilgrim.")[92] *God* in infinite mercy grant us soon another meeting on the
opposite shore. I have often passed under the rod of him whom I call my Father—and certainly no son ever needed it oftener; and yet I have enjoyed
much of life, as I was enabled to discover the secret of this somewhat early. It

has been in making the prosperity and happiness of others my own; so that really I have had a great deal of prosperity. I am very prosperous still; and looking forward to a time when "peace on earth and good-will to men"[93] shall everywhere prevail, I have no murmuring thoughts or envious feelings to fret my mind. "I'll praise my Maker with my breath."[94]

I am an unworthy nephew of Deacon John, and I loved him much; and in view of the many choice friends I have had here, I am led the more earnestly to pray, "gather not my soul with the unrighteous."[95]

Your assurance of the earnest sympathy of the friends in my native land is very grateful to my feelings; and allow me to say a word of comfort to them.

As I believe most firmly that God reigns, I cannot believe that anything I have done, suffered, or may yet suffer will be lost to the cause of God or of humanity. And before I began my work at Harper's Ferry, I felt assured that in the worst event it would certainly pay. I often expressed that belief; and I can now see no possible cause to alter my mind. I am not as yet, in the main, at all disappointed. I have been a good deal disappointed as it regards myself in not keeping up to my own plans; but I now feel entirely reconciled to that, even—for God's plan was infinitely better, no doubt, or I should have kept to my own. Had Samson kept to his determination of not telling Delilah wherein his great strength lay, he would probably have never overturned the house.[96] I did not tell Delilah, but I was induced to act very contrary to my better judgment; and I have lost my two noble boys, and other friends, if not my two eyes.

But "God's will, not mine, be done."[97] I feel a comfortable hope that, like that erring servant of whom I have just been writing, even I may (through infinite mercy in Christ Jesus) yet "die in faith."[98] As to both the time and manner of my death—I have but very little trouble on that score, and am able to be (as you exhort) "of good cheer."[99]

I send, through you, my best wishes to Mrs. W.—[100] and her son George, and to all dear friends. May the God of the poor and oppressed be the God and Savior of you all!

Farewell, till we meet again.

Your friend in truth, John Brown.

Charlestown, Jefferson County, Va., Nov. 17, 1859.

T. B. Musgrave, Esq.[101] My Dear Young Friend—I have just received your most kind and welcome letter of the 15th inst., but did not get any other from you. I am under many obligations to you and to your father for all the kindnesses you have shown me, especially since my disaster. May God and your own consciousness ever be your rewarders. Tell your father that 1 am quite cheerful; that I do not feel myself in the least degraded by my imprisonment, my chains, or the near prospect of the gallows. Men cannot imprison, or chain, or hang the soul. I go joyfully in behalf of millions that "have no rights" that this great and glorious, this Christian Republic "is bound to respect."[102] Strange change in morals, political as well as Christian, since 1776! I look forward to other changes to take place in God's good time, fully believing that "the fashion of this world passeth away."[103] I am unable now to tell you where my friend is, that you inquire after. Perhaps my wife, who I suppose is still with Mrs. Spring, may have some information of him. I think it quite uncertain, however.

Farewell. May God abundantly bless you all!

Your friend, John Brown

Charlestown, Jefferson County, Va., Nov. 19, 1859

Rev. Luther Humphrey.[104] My Dear Friend—Your kind letter of the 12th instant is now before me. So far as my knowledge goes as to our mutual kindred, I suppose I am the first since the landing of Peter Brown from the "Mayflower" that has either been sentenced to imprisonment or to the gallows. But, my dear old friend, let not that fact alone grieve you. You cannot have forgotten how and where our grandfather fell in 1776, and that he, too, might have perished on the scaffold had circumstances been but a very little different. The fact that a man dies under the hand of an executioner (or otherwise) has but little to do with his true character, as I suppose. John Rogers perished at the stake, a great and good man, as I suppose;[105] but his doing so does not prove that any other man who has died in the same way was good or otherwise.

Whether I have any reason to "be of good cheer" or not in view of my end, I can assure you that I feel so; and I am totally blinded if I do not really experience that strengthening and consolation you so faithfully implore in my behalf: the God of our fathers reward your fidelity! I neither feel mortified, degraded, nor in the least ashamed of my imprisonment, my chains, or near prospect of death by hanging. I feel assured "that not one hair shall fall from my head without the will of my Heavenly Father."[106] I also feel that I have long been endeavoring to hold exactly "such a fast as God has chosen." (See the passage in Isaiah which you have quoted.)[107] No part of my life has been more happily spent than that I have spent here; and I humbly trust that no part has been spent to better purpose. I would not say this boastingly, but thanks be unto God, who giveth us the victory through infinite grace.

I should be sixty years old were I to live to May 9, 1860. I have enjoyed much of life as it is, and have been remarkably prosperous, having early learned to regard the welfare and prosperity of others as my own. I have never, since I can remember, required a great amount of sleep; so that I conclude that I have already enjoyed full an average number of working hours with those who reach their threescore years and ten. I have not yet been driven to the use of glasses, but can see to read and write quite comfortably. But more than that, I have generally enjoyed remarkably good health. I might go on to recount unnumbered and unmerited blessings, among which would be some very severe afflictions, and those the most needed blessings of all. And now, when I think how easily I might be left to spoil all I have done or suffered in the cause of freedom, I hardly dare wish another voyage, even if I had the opportunity.

It is a long time since we met; but we shall come together in our Father's house, I trust. Let us hold fast that we already have, remembering we shall reap in due time if we faint not. Thanks be unto God, who giveth us the victory through Jesus Christ our Lord. And now, my old, warm-hearted friend, good-by.

Your Affectionate Cousin, John Brown

Jail, Charlestown, Wednesday, Nov. 23, 1859

The Rev. McFarland,[108] DEAR FRIEND—Although you write to me as a stranger, the spirit you show towards me and the cause for which I am in bonds makes me feel towards you as a dear friend. I would be glad to have you or any of my liberty-loving ministerial friends here, to talk and pray with me. I am not a stranger to the way of salvation by Christ. From my youth I have studied much on that subject, and at one time hoped to be a minister myself; but God had another work for me to do. To me it is given, in behalf of Christ, not only to believe in him, but also to suffer for his sake. But while I trust that I have some experimental and saving knowledge of religion, it would be a great pleasure to me to have some one better qualified than myself to lead my mind in prayer and meditation, now that my time is so near a close. You may wonder, are there no ministers of the gospel here? I answer, no. There are no ministers of Christ here. These ministers who profess to be Christian, and hold slaves or advocate slavery, I cannot abide them. My knees will not bend in prayer with them, while their hands are stained with the blood of souls. The subject you mention as having been preaching on the day before you wrote to me is one which I have often thought of since my imprisonment. I think I feel as happy as Paul did when he lay in prison. He knew if they killed him, it would greatly advance the cause of Christ; that was the reason he rejoiced so. On that same ground "I do rejoice, yea, and will rejoice."[109] Let them hang me; I forgive them, and may God forgive them, for they know not what they do.[110] I have no regret for the transaction for which I am condemned. I went against the laws of men, it is true, but "whether it be right to obey God or men, judge ye."[111] Christ told me to remember them that were in bonds as bound with them,[112] to do towards them as I would wish them to do towards me in similar circumstances. My conscience bade me do that. I tried to do it, but failed. Therefore I have no regret on that score. I have no sorrow either as to the result, only for my poor wife and children. They have suffered much, and it is hard to leave them uncared for. But God will be a husband to the widow and a father to the fatherless.[113]

I have frequently been in Wooster, and if any of my old friends from about Akron are there, you can show them this letter. I have but a few more days, and I feel anxious to be away "where the wicked cease from troubling, and the weary are at rest."[114]

Farewell.

Your friend, and the friend of all friends of liberty, John Brown.

Charlestown, Jefferson County, Va., Nov. 25, 1859.

Rev. Heman Humphrey, D.D.,[115] My Dear and Honored Kinsman—Your very sorrowful, kind, and faithful letter of the 20th instant is now before me. I accept it with all kindness. I have honestly endeavored to profit by the faithful advice it contains. Indeed, such advice could never come amiss. You will allow me to say that I deeply sympathize with you and all my sorrowing friends in their grief and terrible mortification. I feel ten times more afflicted on their account than on account of my own circumstances. But I must say that I am neither conscious of being "infatuated" nor "mad."[116] You will doubtless agree with me in this—that neither imprisonment, irons, nor the gallows falling to one's lot are of themselves evidence of either guilt, "infatuation, or madness."

I discover that you labor under a mistaken impression as to some important facts, which my peculiar circumstances will in all probability prevent the possibility of my removing; and I do not propose to take up any argument to prove that any motion or act of my life is right. But I will here state that I know it to be wholly my own fault as a leader that caused our disaster. Of this you have no proper means of judging, not being on the ground, or a practical soldier. I will only add, that it was in yielding to my feelings of humanity (if I ever exercised such a feeling), in leaving my proper place and mingling with my prisoners to quiet their fears, that occasioned our being caught. I firmly believe that God reigns, and that he overrules all things in the best possible manner; and in that view of the subject I try to be in some degree reconciled to my own weaknesses and follies even.

If you were here on the spot, and could be with me by day and by night, and know the facts and how my time is spent here, I think you would find much to reconcile your own mind to the ignominious death I am about to suffer, and to mitigate your sorrow. I am, to say the least, quite cheerful. "He shall begin to deliver Israel out of the hand of the Philistines."[117] This was said of a poor erring servant many years ago; and for many years I have felt a strong impression that God had given me powers and faculties, unworthy as I was, that he intended to use for a similar purpose.[118] This most unmerited honor He has seen fit to bestow; and whether, like the same poor frail man to whom I allude, my death may not be of vastly more value than my life is, I think quite, beyond all human foresight. I really have strong hopes that notwithstanding all my many sins, I too may yet die "in faith."[119]

If you do not believe I had a murderous intention (while I *know* I had not), why grieve so terribly on my account? The scaffold has but few terrors for me. God has often covered my head in the day of battle, and granted me many times deliverances that were almost so miraculous that I can scarce realize their truth; and now, when it seems quite certain that he intends to use me in a different way, shall I not most cheerfully go? I may be deceived, but I humbly trust that he will not forsake me "till I have showed his favor to this generation and his strength to every one that is to come."[120] Your letter is most faithfully and kindly written, and I mean to profit by it. I am certainly quite grateful for it. I feel that a great responsibility rests upon me as regards the lives of those who have fallen and may yet fall. I must in that view cast myself on the care of Him "whose mercy endureth forever."[121] If the cause in which I engaged in any possible degree approximated to be "infinitely better"[122] than the one which Saul of Tarsus undertook, I have no reason to be ashamed of it; and indeed I cannot now, after more than a month for reflection, find in my heart (before God in whose presence I expect to stand within another week) any cause for shame.

I got a long and most kind letter from your pure-hearted brother Luther, to which I replied at some length.[123] The statement that seems to be going around in the newspapers that I told Governor Wise that I came on here to seek revenge for the wrongs of either myself or my family, is utterly false.[124] I never intended to convey such an idea, and I bless God that I am able even now to say that I have never yet harbored such a feeling. See testimony of witnesses who were with me while I had one son lying dead by my side, and another mortally wounded and dying on my other side. I do not believe that Governor Wise so understood, and I think he ought to correct that impression. The impression that we intended a general insurrection is equally untrue.

Now, my much beloved and much respected kinsman, farewell. May the God of our fathers save and abundantly bless you and yours!

John Brown.

Charlestown, Jefferson County, Va., Monday, Nov. 28, 1859.

Hon. D. R. Tilden.[125] My Dear Sir: Your *most kind and comforting* letter of the 23d inst. is received.

I have no language to express the feelings of gratitude and obligation I am under for your kind interest in my behalf ever since my disaster.

The great bulk of mankind estimate each other's actions *and motives* by the measure of success or *otherwise* that attends them through life. By that rule I have been one of the *worst* and one of the *best* of men. I *do* not claim to have been one of the latter; and I leave it to an impartial tribunal to decide whether the world has been the *worse* or the better of my *living* and *dying* in it. My present great anxiety is to get as near in readiness for a different field of action as I well *can* since being in a good measure *relieved from the fear* that my poor, *broken-hearted wife and children* would come to immediate want. May God reward, *a thousand fold,* all the kind efforts made in their behalf. I have enjoyed *remarkable cheerfulness and composure of mind* ever since my confinement; and it is a great comfort to *feel assured* that *I am permitted* to die (for a *cause*) not *merely* to pay the debt of nature (as all must). I feel myself to be *most* unworthy of *so great* distinction. The particular manner of dying *assigned* to me, gives me but very little *uneasiness.* I with I had the time and the ability to give you (my dear friend) some little idea of what is *daily, and, I might also say, hourly,* passing within my *prison walls;* and could my friends but witness only a few of those scenes just as they occur, I think they would feel very reconciled to my being here *just what I am, and just as I am.* My *whole* life *before* had not afforded me one half the opportunity to plead *for the right. In this,* also, *I find* much to reconcile me to both my present condition and my immediate prospect. I may be *very insane* (and I *am so,* if insane at all). But if that be so, *insanity* is like a very pleasant dream to me. I am not in the least degree conscious of my *ravings,* of my fears, or of any terrible visions whatever; but *fancy* myself entirely composed, and that my *sleep, in particular,* is as sweet as that of a healthy, joyous little infant. I pray God that he will grant me a continuance of the same calm, but delightful, *dream,* until I come to know of those realities which "eyes have not seen, and which ears have not heard."[126] I have scarce realized that I am in prison, or in irons, at all. I certainly think I was never more cheerful in my life. I intend to take the liberty of sending, by express, to your care, some trifling articles for those of my family who may be in Ohio, which you can hand to my brother Jeremiah, when you may see him, together with fifteen dollars I have asked him to advance to them. Please excuse me so often troubling you with my letters, or any of my matters. Please also remember me *most* kindly to Mr. Griswold,[127] and to all others who love their neighbors. I write Jeremiah to your care.

Your friend, in truth, John Brown.[128]

Charlestown, Jefferson Co Va. 29th Nov. 1859.

Mrs George L Stearns,[129] Boston Mass. My Dear Friend. No letter I have received since my imprisonment here, has given me more satisfaction, or comfort; then yours on the 8th inst. I am quite cheerful; & was never more happy. Have only time to write you a word. May God forever reward you & *all yours. My love to all* who love their neighbors. I have asked to be *spared* from having any *mock; or hypocritical prayers made over me,* when I am publicly *murdered:* & that my only *religious attendants* be poor *little, dirty, ragged, bare headed, & barefooted Slave boys; & Girls;* led by some old *grey headed Slave Mother.*[130]
    Farewell. Farewell.

Your Friend, John Brown.

Charlestown, Prison, Jefferson Co. Va., Nov. 30, 1859.

My Dearly Beloved Wife, Sons: & Daughters, Every One:

    As I now begin what is probably the last letter I shall ever write to any of you, I conclude to write to all at the same time. I will mention some little matters particularly applicable to little property concerns in another place.
    I recently received a letter from my wife, from near Philadelphia, dated Nov. 22, by which it would seem that she was about giving up the idea of seeing me again. I had written to her to come on if she felt equal to the undertaking, but I do not know that she will get my letter in time. It was on her own account chiefly that I asked her to stay back. At first I had a most strong desire to see her again, but there appeared to be very serious objections; and should we never meet in this life, I trust that we shall in the end be satisfied it was for the

best at least, if not most for her comfort. I enclosed in my last letter to her a draft of fifty dollars from John Jay, made payable to her order. I have now another to send her, from my excellent old friend Edward Harris, of Woonsocket, R.I., for one hundred dollars, which I shall also make payable to her order.

I am waiting the hour of my public murder with great composure of mind and cheerfulness, feeling the strong assurance that in no other possible way could I be used to so much advantage to the cause of God and of humanity, and that nothing that either I or all my family have sacrificed or suffered will be lost. The reflection that a wise and merciful, as well as just and holy God rules not only the affairs of this world, but of all worlds, is a rock to set our feet upon under all circumstances—even those more severely trying ones into which our own feelings and wrongs have placed us. I have now no doubt but that our seeming disaster will ultimately result in the most glorious success. So, my dear shattered and broken family, be of good cheer, and believe and trust in God with all your heart, and with all your soul, for he doeth all things well. Do not feel ashamed on my account, nor for one moment despair of the cause or grow weary of well doing. I bless God I never felt stronger confidence in the certain and near approach of a bright morning and glorious day than I have felt, and do now feel, since my confinement here. 1 am endeavouring to return, like a poor prodigal as I am, to my Father, against whom I have always sinned, in the hope that he may kindly and forgivingly meet me, though a very great way off.

O, my dear wife and children, would to God you could know how I have been travailing in birth for you all, that no one of you may fail of the grace of God through Jesus Christ; that no one of you may be blind to the truth and glorious light of his Word, in which life and immortality are brought to light. I beseech you, every one, to make the Bible your daily and nightly study, with a child-like, honest, candid, teachable spirit of love and respect for your husband and father.

And I beseech the God of my fathers to open all your eyes to the discovery of the truth. You cannot imagine how much you may soon need the consolations of the Christian religion. Circumstances like my own, for more than a month past, have convinced me beyond all doubt of our great need of some theories treasured up when our prejudices are excited, our vanity worked up to the highest pitch. O, do not trust your eternal all upon the boisterous ocean without even a helm or compass to aid you in steering. I do not ask of you to throw away your reason; I only ask you to make a candid, sober use of your reason.

My dear young children, will you listen to this last poor admonition of one who can only love you? O, be determined at once to give your whole heart to God, and let nothing shake or alter that resolution. You need have no fears of regretting it. Do not be vain and thoughtless, but sober-minded; and let me entreat you all to love the whole remnant of our once great family. Try and build up again your broken walls, and to make the utmost of every stone that is left. Nothing can so tend to make life a blessing as the consciousness that your life and example bless and leave you the stronger. Still, it is ground of the utmost comfort to my mind to know that so many of you as have had the opportunity have given some proof of your fidelity to the great family of men. Be faithful unto death; from the exercise of habitual love to man it cannot be very hard to love his Maker.

I must yet insert the reason for my firm belief in the divine inspiration of the Bible, notwithstanding I am, perhaps, naturally sceptical: certainly not credulous, I wish all to consider it most thoroughly when you read that blessed book, and see whether you cannot discover such evidence yourselves. It is the purity of heart, filling our minds as well as work and actions, which is every where insisted on, that distinguishes it from all the other teachings, that commends it to my conscience. Whether my heart be willing and obedient or not, the inducement that it holds out is another reason of my convictions of its truth and genuineness; but I do not here omit this my last argument on the Bible, that eternal life is what my soul is panting after this moment. I mention this as a reason for endeavoring to leave a valuable copy of the Bible, to be carefully preserved in remembrance of me, to so many of my posterity, instead of some other book at equal cost.

I beseech you all to live in habitual contentment with moderate circumstances and gains of worldly store, and earnestly to teach this to your children and children's children after you, by example as well as precept. Be determined to know by experience, as soon as may be, whether Bible instruction is of divine origin or not. Be sure to owe no man any thing, but to love one another. John Rogers wrote to his children, "Abhor that arrant whore of Rome."[131] John Brown writes to his children to abhor, with undying hatred also, that sum of all villanies—slavery. Remember, he that is slow to anger is better than the mighty, and he that ruleth his spirit than he that taketh a city. Remember, also, that they, being wise, shall shine, and they that turn many to righteousness, as the stars forever and ever.

And now, dearly beloved family, to God and the work of his grace I commend you all.

Your affectionate husband and father, John Brown.
Charlestown, Va., Dec. 2, 1859.

I, John Brown, am now quite *certain* that the crimes of this *guilty land* will never be purged away but with *blood*. I had, as I now think vainly, flattered myself that without very much bloodshed it might be done.

Sources: Oswald Garrison Villard, *John Brown* (Boston: Houghton Mifflin, 1910), 537–538, 539–540, 551; Franklin B. Sanborn, *The Life and Letters of John Brown, Liberator of Kansas, and Martyr of Virginia* (Boston: Roberts Bros., 1885), 585–587, 589–591, 593, 594, 598–599, 603–605, 620; James Redpath, *The Public Life of Capt. John Brown* (Boston: Thayer and Eldridge, 1860), 250–251, 263–264, 363–364.

Northern Responses

I N   A   L E T T E R   O F   November 28, 1859, written a few days before his execution, Brown acknowledged that history's "tribunal" would "decide whether
the world has been the worse or the better of my living and dying in it." By
then the tribunal had already begun to respond. In the North and the South,
before and after his death, Brown appeared in speeches, letters, newspaper
articles, poems, diaries, broadsides, and songs as a hero and a villain, an avenging angel, a loyal patriot and a murderous fanatic. In various Northern responses, Brown morphed into Spartacus, Oliver Cromwell, George Washington, the Marquis de Lafayette, Moses, and Samson. In others he became a
frontier hero or a Puritan transplanted into the nineteenth century. His raid
also prompted a series of political and philosophical conflicts within the abolitionist movement, as observers grappled with the meaning of Brown's violence. His actions were treasonous, yet he declared them to be patriotic. He
seemed lawless yet idealistic. He condemned the violence of slavery while taking violent action himself. As Frederick Douglass remembered of the immediate responses to Brown, they were often "curious and contradictory," for
Americans were trying to understand "what he really was." Part II includes
these immediate, prewar responses to Brown in the North. They range from
proclamations of a new Christ to anti-abolitionist rage. Some celebrate Brown

but not his actions, and others try to reimagine him as a pacifist. The section includes responses by women, former slaves, freeborn African Americans, Quakers, individuals who knew Brown well, famous writers, and unknown observers. What the sources share is a sense that Brown's raid and execution marked a point of no return in the growing conflict over slavery. Though they do not settle the issue of whether the world was "the worse or the better" for his life and death, as Brown put it, they do agree that the world had changed.

Horace Greeley, "*Tribune* Editorial," October 19, 1859

Although many Republican newspapers initially condemned Brown's raid without reserve, Horace Greeley's *Tribune* insisted that while the "manner" of Brown's action was wrong, his intention was noble. Separating Brown's means (violence) and ends (abolition), it suggested that America should withhold judgment until slavery was abolished. Greeley (1811–1872) wrote this early response amid an initial confusion over the precise nature of events at Harpers Ferry, and is not sure whether Brown had survived. It was the first of more than sixty editorials and commentaries about Brown published in the *Tribune* between the raid and the execution. During this period, Southern newspapers and competing Northern newspapers linked Brown to Greeley, calling him a conspirator. Several pointed out that one of the raiders who died at Harpers Ferry, John Kagi, had contributed articles about "Bleeding Kansas" to the *Tribune*. Though Greeley had *not* conspired with Brown, his newspaper was antislavery and reformist, and Brown had previously solicited aid from *Tribune* readers; for example, on March 4, 1857, the newspaper printed an appeal from Brown to "the Friends of Freedom," asking all "lovers of Liberty and Human Rights" to donate money. But the attacks on Greeley did not diminish his readership. Established in 1841, the *Tribune* reached a circulation of nearly 300,000 by 1860. Greeley went on to run for the presidency in 1872.

The Insurrection, so called, at Harper's Ferry, proves a verity. Old Brown of Osawatomie, who was last heard of on his way from Missouri to Canada with a band of runaway slaves, now turns up in Virginia, where he seems to have been for some months plotting and preparing for a general stampede of slaves. How he came to be in Harper's Ferry, and in possession of the U.S. Armory, is not yet clear; but he was probably betrayed or exposed, and seized the Armory as a place of security until he could safely get away. The whole affair seems the work of a madman; but John Brown has so often looked death serenely in the face that what seems madness to others doubtless wore a different aspect to him. He had twenty-one men with him, mostly white, who appear to have held the Armory from 9 P.M. of Sunday till 7 of Tuesday (yesterday) morning, when it was stormed by Col. Lee[1] and a party of U.S. Marines, and its defenders nearly all killed or mortally wounded. Old Brown was severely wounded and his son—(we believe his last surviving son)[2]—killed. Of the original twenty-two, fifteen were killed, two mortally wounded, and two unhurt. The other three had pushed northward on Monday morning guiding a number of fugitive slaves through Maryland.[3] These were of course sharply pursued and fired on, but had not been taken at our last advices.

Harper's Ferry was full of soldiers and militia men yesterday, and more are constantly pouring in. never before was such an uproar raised by twenty men as by Old Brown and his confederates in this deplorable affair.

There will be enough to heap execration on the memory of these mistaken men. We leave this work to the fit hands and tongues of those who regard the fundamental axioms of the Declaration of Independence as "glittering generalities."[4] Believing that the way to Universal Emancipation lies not through insurrection, civil war and bloodshed, but through discussion, and the quick diffusion of sentiments of humanity and justice, we deeply regret this outbreak; but remembering that, if their fault was grievous, grievously have they answered it, we will not, by one reproachful word, disturb the bloody shrouds wherein John Brown and his compatriots are sleeping. They dared and died for what they felt to be the right, though in a manner which seems to us fatally wrong. Let their epitaphs remain unwritten until the not distant day when no slave shall clank his chains in the shades of Monticello or by the graves of Mount Vernon.[5]

Source: New York Tribune, October 19, 1859.

Boston Courier, "A Lesson for the People," October 20, 1859

As an anti-Republican, Unionist newspaper, the *Boston Courier* responded to Brown's raid with a warning that tyrannical fanaticism threatened the great sovereign Union and a plea for sober citizens to ignore antislavery Republicans who would spread bloodshed beyond Virginia. Throughout November and December, other articles in the *Courier* condemned support for Brown in the New England press and pulpit, criticized public pro-Brown meetings in Boston, and insisted that most Bostonians did not support Brown. One article suggested that Massachusetts should give Virginia $20,000 to pay the expenses incurred because of the raid, trial, and execution. Published since 1824, the newspaper was Whig, then Democratic, and then Constitutional Union. It supported John Bell of Tennessee for president in 1860.

The "irrepressible conflict"[6] seems to have begun, and been as quickly repressed. The spirit and energy of the officers and troops at Harper's Ferry cannot be too much commended. As for the leading spirits in this absurd yet traitorous insurrection, the general execration of the people will pursue them to deserved doom. The nearest tree would be their fitting mode of exit from their scene of mischief; but we presume the forms of law will be gone through with against these ruffians, shooting down peaceful citizens, and in open revolt against the laws.

The originator of the revolt, according to his own confession, was the outlaw "Old Brown," one of the Kansas free soil ruffians, whose former exploits in that distracted territory were widely extolled, and become incorporated among the achievements and victories of the Republican party. We have no disposition to hold that party responsible for outrages like this, or to identify it with the murderous acts of this man and others associated with him. The respectable portion of that party could have known nothing of their true character. But the time has come when the evil fruit of the evil tree is beginning to be gathered. And we appeal to-day—as the occasion arises to justify and call for such an appeal—"here and now"—to the citizen of all parties, especially to conservative men who have become improvidently and unconsciously connected with an organization tending to such outrages, to turn aside at once from leaders, whose political doctrines conduct to disorder, plunder and murder. Disown "Old Ossawatomie Brown"[7] and the whole set of marauders, mischief-makers, public plunderers, and bad men in the front rank of whatever party or organization. Especially, turn from those hypocritical philanthropists who do no murder, only point the way—who would shield crime of every description if only committed by one of their own party association.

We confidently appeal to the sober sentiment of the country, to discourage these excesses, and whatever may have a tendency to bring them about. We warn them, again and again, as we have often done, against the atrocious doctrines of the New York Senator,[8] of the New York *Tribune,* the Albany *Journal,* and of the same tenor, if not in like degree, of journals nearer home. This is the time for reflection on this point. The "Browns" of the day have received much encouragement from these presses. The civil conflict, which they and Mr. Seward would precipitate as an abstraction to be settled by the ballot box, violent and ignorant men reduce to a bloody practice. The contest has been brief indeed at Harper's Ferry; nor do we dread any prolonged scene of disorder at home. But we must not forget that we have had tumults here very recently, originating in the same cause, and ending in yet unpunished murder.[9] We are comparatively safe from any continuance of a strife like that in Virginia, for we have an organized force, efficient and disposed to maintain the public peace.

We invoke the serious earnest attention of the American people to these things. We ask their reflection upon them, not in any partisan spirit—not even as claiming fulfillment of any prophecy of our own—but as sincere and devoted lovers of a country grown great under the silent administration of law; and freer than any people on which the sun ever shone—except for this tyranny of combined fanaticism, fostered by false men who do not believe in it, yet use its victims for their own advancement and the common ruin. The revolt at Harper's Ferry brings the question directly home to every considerate mind—Will you sacrifice the inestimable blessings of this Union for party ends? Will you listen to the counsel of Greeley and Giddings, and of Banks,[10] who is willing under certain circumstances—that is, when be thinks he can administer a Northern confederacy—to let this great sovereign Union of popular nationality "slide"? Or, will you recur to the advice of the noble fathers of the Republic, and of their truly patriotic sons?

Source: Boston Semi-Weekly Courier, October 20, 1859.

Illinois State Register, "The 'Irrepressible Conflict,'" October 20, 1859

The Democratic press used Brown's raid as a weapon against Republicans. Published from 1839 onward, based in Springfield, and edited from 1846 through 1863 by Charles H. Lanphier, a native of Alexandria, Virginia, the *State Register* was the leading Democratic organ of Illinois. Its first editorial about the Harpers Ferry raid declared that Brown was a mere follower of Republican leaders, including William Seward and Abraham Lincoln. It also blames "ultra" abolitionists and, noting that the Founding Fathers held slaves, charges that "black republicanism" (pro-equality fanaticism) is treason. Throughout it seeks to terrify readers: the raiders numbered five hundred or more, they intended to prompt a "servile war," and they wanted slaves to slaughter white Southerners en masse.

The telegraphic dispatches yesterday morning startled the public with an account of one of the most monstrous villainies ever attempted in this country. It was no less than an effort on the part of a party of abolitionists and negroes to take possession of one of the national arsenals, at Harper's Ferry, with the military stores and the public money there deposited. Under the lead of the most infamous of the Kansas crew of black republican marauders, Ossawatomie Brown, the insurgents, to the number of five or six hundred, attacked and took possession of the whole town of Harper's Ferry, including the government buildings and stores, stopped the mails, imprisoned peaceable citizens, and, before they were dislodged, numbers were killed and wounded on both sides.

It was scarcely credible, when the first dispatch was received yesterday, that the object of the ruffians could be other than plunder, but late dispatches, including those we publish this morning, show, conclusively, that the movement was a most extensive one, having for its object the uprising of the negroes throughout the south, a servile war, and its consequences—murder, rapine and robbery.

The leader chosen was just the man to initiate the work. Bankrupt in fortune and character, an outlaw and an outcast, he was just the man to commence the work which ultra Abolitionism, through its diligent Parkers and Garrisons,[11] hope to reach the millennium of their traitorous designs. Their open-mouthed treason, which culminates in precisely such outrages as that at Harper's Ferry, is but the logical sequence of the teachings of Wm. H. Seward and Abraham Lincoln—the one boldly proclaiming an "irrepressible conflict" between certain states of the Union, because of their local institutions, and the other declaring from stump and hustings, the country round, that the Union cannot continue as the fathers made it—part slave and part free states.[12] When such men, by specious demagoguism, in the name of freedom and liberty, daily labor to weaken the bonds of our glorious governmental fabric, the work of sages and patriots, themselves the holders of black men as slaves, is it to be wondered at that ignorant, unprincipled and reckless camp followers of the party for which these leaders speak, attempt, practically, to illustrate the doctrines which they preach, and in advocacy of which they seek to obtain control of the national government.

Brown, though a blood-stained ruffian, is a bold man. As a black republican he practices what his leaders preach. As it is urged by statesmen (save the mark!) of his party that there is an "irrepressible conflict," he wants it in tangible, material, shape. He believes in blows, not words, and the Harper's Ferry villainy is the first in his line of performance.

Who is so blind as not to see the inevitable tendency of black republican teaching? Now we have a bloody, glaring, ghastly fact before us. The "conflict" by blows has commenced. The proofs of an extensive and ramified organization is disclosed, the object of which is to stir the southern slaves to bathe their hands in the blood of the whites of the south. Traitorous scoundrels, with white faces, but black hearts, lead them, and the country is stunned with their deeds of infamy, treason and blood.

Such is the ripening of the black republican harvest. Can an intelligent people doubt that to such ends the maudlin philanthropy, the hypocritical cant, the blatant demagoguism, of black republicanism, tends? "By their fruits shall ye know them."[13] Disunion and bloody anarchy.

Source: Illinois State Register, October 20, 1859.

Anonymous, "To the Clerk of Court, Charlestown," October 23, 1859, and "To Friend Wise," December 2, 1859

As journalists and well-known Americans began responding to Brown in public, other Americans responded with anonymous letters. One letter postmarked from New York warned the clerk of the Charles Town court that the South would be engulfed in flames if Brown was hurt. It also echoes some of Brown's remarks during his interview at Harpers Ferry (published in newspapers): "This question is still to be settled. . . . The end of that is not yet." The letter reached A. W. Quarrier, clerk of the county court of Kenawha, Virginia, and on October 29 he passed it on to the clerk of the Jefferson County court and Governor Wise of Virginia, labeled "Menace." Wise received his own anonymous letters too. In November, one letter advised him to "tremble for fear" because more raids would follow. Another promised that if Brown was executed, retributive violence would dissolve the Union in blood. A third anonymous letter assured Wise that if Brown died, the governor was a dead man too. Wise even received a letter dated December 2, sent by a "John Brown" from "Hevan."

Clerk of the Court, Charlestown, Va.:

Sir—You had better caution your authorities to be careful what you—with *"Ossawatimi Brown."* So sure as you hurt One hair of his head—mark my word the following day you will see every City—Town and Village South of Mason & Dixon's line in

Flames.

We are determined to put down Slavery at any odds.

Forcibly if it must. Peaceably if it can.

Believe me when I tell you the end is not yet by a long odds.

All of us at the North sympathize with the

Martyrs of Harper's Ferry.

First Hevan Dec 2

Friend Wise

I got here this Morning at 11 1/2 o'clock[14] Set Peter was at the Door. he said welcom John Brown you are the first man that come here from Virginia in 20 years and I am afraid you will Be the last excep Cook and his friends

Youres &ca
John Brown

P.S. Write soon and send your letter By Cook as that will Be the Last canse you ever will get

J.B.

Source: The Virginia Magazine of History and Biography 10, no. 1 (July 1902): 30; Executive papers of Governor Henry A. Wise, 1856–1859, Accession 36710, State Government Records Collection, Library of Virginia, Richmond.

The *Patriot*, "The Harper's Ferry Affair," October 26, 1859

Even as Brown's trial began, some Northern newspapers were still grappling with the details of his raid. This editorial in the *Patriot*, established in 1809, based in Concord, New Hampshire, and one of the leading Democratic journals of New England, expresses surprise that most of the raiders were white and lived outside Virginia. It goes on to condemn "black republicanism" as the root cause of Brown's attempt and suggests that the raid had revealed abolitionism to be a dangerous doctrine. Most of the article, however, concerns the connection between "Bleeding Kansas" and Harpers Ferry. The raid was "Kansas work," it argues: those who had supported antislavery settlers in Kansas were directly responsible for the violence in Virginia.

The public mind throughout the country, during the past week, has been much agitated by the most deplorable events at Harper's Ferry, Va., an account of which we give in another part of this paper. The circumstances were of a nature to strongly attract public attention. A quiet community, in the night time, was startled by an insurrection in its very midst. The suddenness of the alarm, with the uncertainty of the nature and extent of the danger, at first paralyzed the people for any resistance, and the insurgents, being fully armed, gained possession of the place. But after a bloody conflict, resulting in the loss of twenty-one lives in all, the insurrection was quelled and order returned.

In this atrocious affair there were peculiar features to excite alarm, not only in the community where is occurred, but also throughout the country. Although the proposed object of it was the release of the slaves, yet it now clearly appears that they had no part in it. In fact, one of the first victims was a colored man, shot by the insurgents because he refused to join them. The chief actors, and by far the greater number, were white men. Neither was it a sudden outbreak, occasioned by some occurrence of the moment; but it was in pursuance of a plan deliberately considered and formed by men elsewhere, who had gone to that place for the very purpose of making preparations and carrying it into execution. These are the circumstances which render this insurrection of more than ordinary importance and deserving reflection.

Notwithstanding the melancholy result in the loss of so many lives, these events will not be without advantage to the country, if they shall serve to recall the public mind from prejudice and excitement to a clear and honest consideration of the dangerous tendencies of the pernicious doctrines which, during a few years past, have been so zealously taught and advocated by political leaders and partisan preachers here at the North. It is not a long time since not only on the stump, but even from the pulpit, "Sharpe's rifles" were recommended and applauded as the proper and best means for the relief of "bleeding Kansas."[15] We then denounced those principles as deserving the severest condemnation, not more, certainly, on account of the circumstances of the particular case to which they were applied, than for their dangerous and fatal tendencies, if ever admitted as proper in practice. We could not admit violence or force as, in any case, a necessary or proper recourse, in this country, for the establishment of any political principles, or for relief from political evils. But we did not then expect so soon to see so striking a proof and illustration of the correctness of our views, as is now offered by these tragical events at Harper's Ferry. They are the natural and perfect fruit of the seed sown in Kansas. The instigator and leader at Harper's Ferry was Capt. John Brown of Kansas notoriety; his confederates here were his associates there, and the arms used were the very same "Sharpe's rifles" furnished for use in Kansas. It seems appropriate that it should have been so, and we may add, almost providential that these circumstances should thus concur to connect and identify the one transaction with the other. Gerrit Smith, in his letter to Brown enclosing funds to aid him in carrying into execution his nefarious schemes at Harper's Ferry, very truly and correctly calls it "Kansas work."[16] It was, in principle, the same.

Those black republicans who have heretofore been so loud in their applause and instigation of the work of violence and bloodshed in Kansas, now seek to relieve themselves from the unfavorable consequences in the public mind of their recent "Kansas work" on another field, by stigmatizing Brown and his associates as fools and maniacs. It is true that extreme folly and madness are apparent in this Harper's Ferry affair; but that folly and madness were not so much error on their part with regard to the principle of the "Kansas work," as in the hopeless circumstances for success under which they undertook to carry it into practice. But in what position does this new view by these defenders of black republicanism, place that party? If Brown and his confederates were fools and madmen at Harper's Ferry, may they not have been such in Kansas also? And if so, who shall say how much of the wrong in that unfortunate territory is justly to be charged against those who were the instigators of these fools and madmen, and who placed in their hands the weapons for violence and bloodshed!

In the developments made by Brown and others since their capture, are many things for consideration. We have not time or room now to refer to them particularly. We hope the people of this State will carefully read the accounts of them for themselves. We wish, however, to call attention to the statement by Brown of his motives for going to Kansas—that it was not for the purpose of making his home there, but to take part in its troubles. We all know how conspicuous and violent a part he took.—This shows how true is the charge, which has been so persistently denied by our opponents, that many of the misfortunes of that Territory have been owing to the interference and instigation of those abroad who really had no interest in or care for it, except so far as it could be use for political and partisan purposes.

Let us not be misunderstood. We do not intend to charge all the members of the black republican party as being responsible for this deplorable affair at Harper's Ferry. On the contrary, we know that most of them will denounce it in as strong terms as we do, and as it deserves. But we ask them to consider whether, if not the fair and natural consequence, it is not at least the probable effect of the principles and doctrine of arms and violence advocated by the black republican leaders for the relief of Kansas, and of the doctrine of "irrepressible conflict" which they are now urged to make the sum and substance of their political faith. For if such be their view of it, we know the people of this State will not support a party from whose principles or acts results so fatal, not only to the peace but even to the continuance of the Union, are in any degree likely to follow.

Source: Patriot, October 26, 1859.

Lydia Maria Child, "Dear Captain Brown," October 26, 1859, and "The Hero's Heart," January 26, 1860

The abolitionist and writer Lydia Maria Child (1802–1880) was one of Brown's first prison correspondents. Child had fought what she termed "the Demon Slavery" from the 1830s onward. She edited the *National Anti-Slavery Standard* from 1841 to 1843, supported the antislavery settlers in Kansas, and went on to edit Harriet Jacobs's narrative *Incidents in the Life of a Slave Girl* (1861). In a letter to Brown, she assured him of her love, admiration, sympathy, and desire to visit his jail cell. Child also wrote to Henry Wise, the governor of Virginia, requesting permission to dress Brown's wounds. Wise replied that he saw no reason why not, adding that he did not understand Child's desire to nurse a man "who whetted knives of butchery for our mothers, sisters, daughters, and babes." But Brown replied to Child that he did not need a nurse and asked her to send money to his family instead. Child did not go to Virginia. A few months later she wrote a poem about Brown's mythical kiss of a slave child. On December 5, 1859, the *New York Tribune* had reported that Brown kissed a child "with the tenderness of one whose love is as broad as the brotherhood of man" as he made his way to the gallows. The story was false, but it appealed to abolitionists. Child composed her poem for an American Anti-Slavery Society program held at Boston's Music Hall on January 26, 1860, and William Lloyd Garrison published it in *The Liberator* as "The Hero's Heart" a week later. Child republished the poem in *The Freedmen's Book* (1869) as "John Brown and the Colored Child." With its golden harps and singing angels, it recalls death scenes in sentimentalist narratives.

Wayland, October 26, 1859

Dear Captain Brown:

Though personally unknown to you, you will recognize in my name an earnest friend of Kansas, when circumstances made that territory the battleground between the antagonistic principles of slavery and freedom, which politicians so vainly strive to reconcile in the government of the United States.

Believing in peace principles, I cannot sympathize with the method you chose to advance the cause of freedom. But I honor your generous intentions—I admire your courage, moral and physical. I reverence you for the humanity which tempered your zeal. I sympathize with you in your cruel bereavement, your sufferings, and your wrongs. In brief, I love you and bless you.

Thousands of hearts are throbbing with sympathy as warm as mine. I think of you night and day, bleeding in prison, surrounded by hostile faces, sustained only by trust in God and your own strong heart. I long to nurse you—to speak to you sisterly words of sympathy and consolation. I have asked permission of Governor Wise to do so. If the request is not granted, I cherish the hope that these few words may at least reach your hands, and afford you some little solace. May you be strengthened by the conviction that no honest man ever sheds blood for freedom in vain, however much he may be mistaken in his efforts. May God sustain you, and carry you through whatsoever may be in store for you!

Yours, with heartfelt respect, sympathy and affection,

L. Maria Child

The Hero's Heart

A winter sunshine, still and bright,
The Blue Hills bathed with golden light,
And earth was smiling to the sky,
When calmly he went forth to die.

Infernal passions festered there,
Where peaceful nature looked so fair;
And fiercely, in the morning sun,
Flashed glittering bayonet and gun.

The old man met no friendly eye,
When last he looked on earth and sky;
But one small child, with timid air,
Was gazing on his silver hair.

As that dark brow to his upturned,
The tender heart within him yearned;

And, fondly stooping o'er her face,
He kissed her, for her injured race.

The little one, she knew not why
That kind old man went forth to die;
Nor why, mid all that pomp and stir,
He stooped to give a kiss to *her.*

But Jesus smiled that sight to see,
And said, "He did it unto *me*"!
The golden harps then sweetly rung,
And this the song the Angels sung:

"Who loves the poor doth love the Lord!
Earth cannot dim thy bright reward;
We hover o'er yon gallows high,
And wait to bear thee to the sky."

Sources: Letters of Lydia Maria Child (Boston: Houghton Mifflin,1883), 118; *The Liberator,* February 3, 1860.

E.B., "To John Brown," October 27, 1859

Even before his death, Brown became a mythic figure. Numerous observers echoed Brown's own biblical rhetoric as they responded to his raid and death. Shifting between Old and New Testament narratives, they depicted him as a new David, Joshua, John the Baptist, or Christ for the nineteenth century. Franklin Sanborn and Frederick Douglass compared him to Samson. Douglass also described him as an American Moses, as did Osborne Anderson, one of Brown's black raiders, and E.B., a Quaker from Newport, Rhode Island, who was one of Brown's prison correspondents. Personal freedom secured by righteous violence through a sense of biblical mission is part of the national teleology, and Brown gave human shape to this poetics of faith. E.B.'s letter compares him to George Washington as well as Samson, and promises that "posterity"—the tribunal of the future—would do him justice. Garrison published her letter in *The Liberator* and Brown replied to her on November 1. Using the opportunity to communicate with all Quakers, he reimagined his weapon at Harpers Ferry as a "sword of the spirit" in order to reach out for Quakers' support in spite of their nonviolent stance.

Newport, R.I., Tenth Month, 27th, '59.[17]

Captain John Brown.

Dear Friend—Since thy arrest I have often thought of thee, and have wished that, like Elizabeth Fry[18] toward her prison friends, so I might console thee in thy confinement. But that can never be; and so I can only write thee a few lines which, if they contain any comfort, may come to thee like some little ray of light.

You can never know how very many dear Friends love thee with all their hearts for thy brave efforts in behalf of the poor oppressed; and though we, who are non-resistants, and religiously believe it better to reform by moral and not by carnal weapons, could not approve of bloodshed, yet we know thee was animated by the most generous and philanthropic motives. Very many thousands openly approve thy intentions, though most Friends would not think it right to take up arms. Thousands pray for thee every day; and oh, I do pray that God will be with thy soul. Posterity will do thee justice. If Moses led out the thousands of Jewish slaves from their bondage and God destroyed the Egyptians in the sea because they went after the Israelites to bring them back to slavery, then surely, by the same reasoning, we may judge thee a deliverer who wished to release millions from a more cruel oppression. If the American people honor Washington for resisting with bloodshed for seven years an unjust tax, how much more ought thou to be honored for seeking to free the poor slaves.

Oh, I wish I could plead for thee as some of the other sex can plead, how I would seek to defend thee! If I had now the eloquence of Portia, how I would turn the scale in thy favor![19] But I can only pray "God bless thee!" God pardon thee, and through our Redeemer give thee safety and happiness now and always!

From thy friend, E.B.

Source: Franklin B. Sanborn, *The Life and Letters of John Brown, Liberator of Kansas, and Martyr of Virginia* (Boston: Roberts Bros., 1885), 581–582.

Joshua R. Giddings, "The Harper's Ferry Insurrection," October 28, 1859

Joshua Giddings (1795–1864) met Brown in Ohio in the fall of 1856, and Brown visited his home in June 1859 while fund-raising for his Harpers Ferry raid. At Giddings's invitation, Brown also lectured in his town of Jefferson, Ohio, and asked for contributions. Congressman Vallandigham questioned Brown about Giddings in the interview at Harpers Ferry, and Giddings was called to testify before the Senate committee investigating the raid on February 3, 1860. Giddings was an abolitionist and a Republican. Formerly a Whig and a prominent member of the Free Soil Party, he had served in the U.S. House of Representatives since 1838. In 1861, President Lincoln appointed him as the United States consul general to Canada. Giddings was active in the Underground Railroad and encouraged armed resistance to slavery. In his speech about Brown's raid, given at the National Guard's Hall in Philadelphia, he observes that such violent attempts are an inevitable response to the despotic and violent actions of the Slave Power.

The invading force is nearly all slain—perhaps four of them remain alive, but nearly dead of wounds. Others have fled, but probably all are by this time prisoners. Yet even in this city, and in several States, there appears to be a degree of excitement and consternation. It is, in truth, the first instance in which any number of white men have combined for the purpose of giving freedom to the slaves of our nation.

Such scenes have long been foretold. More than seventy years since Mr. Jefferson pointed his countrymen to the time when this condition of things must take place, and solemnly warned them that in such a contest God had no attribute that would enable him to take sides with the slave holder.[20] Nearly twenty years since Mr. Adams, with prophetic assurance, said the day of the deliverance of the slave must come—whether in peace or in blood he could not tell—but "whether it came in peace or blood," he said, "Let it come."[21]

The sympathy of the Christian world is with the slaves. For their liberation our ministers pray, our statesmen labor, and their freedom is the object and desire with all candid, intelligent men; while all feel unwilling to see their freedom stained with blood. Men of age, of experience, look coolly upon these facts. They should not be moved, nor permit themselves to become excited. I deplore the loss of human life as deeply as any man. I never witness human woe, nor can I look upon human suffering unmoved; and yet I would not ask for the slave, nor for the master, for Brown, nor for his fellow prisoners, anything more or anything less than justice. . . .

I recall the attention of the audience to the remote and proximate causes of the recent *emeute*.[22] These causes consist of a series of despotic acts on the part of those who have wielded the executive, the legislative and the judicial powers of the government during the last twenty-five years. These acts are not laws—they are violations of law. They are not constitutional—but violations of the Constitution; not in favor of life, liberty and happiness, but destructive of their rights. These despotic acts have aroused the spirits of the people, and there is in serious truth an "irrepressible conflict" now in progress. It is that irrepressible conflict between freedom and slavery, which has been in progress for centuries. It is one of those revolutions which never go backward. Our statesmen have misapprehended the philosophy of free governments. They have attempted to rule a free people by brute force instead of a just administration of legitimate powers. They have preferred the crime of slavery to the God-given rights of liberty. They have trampled upon the rights of our free States to obtain political favor with the slave power.

They have stained the soil of our free States with innocent blood; men are captured in our northern villages, their limbs manacled, and they are carried to slavery, as though our territory lay upon the African coast, subjected to the pollution of slave-dealing pirates, while the stars and stripes—those emblems of liberty—are prostituted to the protection of an execrable commerce in human flesh. The indignation of our people is awakened, in some localities it is intense. Let no man mistake or belittle that feeling. It has long been foreseen. All reflecting men knew it must come. For fifteen years I have constantly pointed it out to Southern men, and to Northern men. Recent events will increase and strengthen it. Let those in power understand it cannot be trifled with. Let timid men keep silent. Let demagogues no longer sneer nor threaten. The time for intimidation is gone by. All must see that if the cause of the excitement continues the excitement will not cease. But of the future I will no longer speak. It is written upon the tablet of Haven. It is read in every countenance around us. All must see that the men now in power are incompetent to the duties of their stations. If they continue longer to guide the ship of State all must be lost. Let them retire. Let the past policy of the government be abandoned. Let the despotic act alluded to be repealed. Let the free States be placed upon an equality with the slave States. Let our territory be consecrated to freedom. Let us cease to maintain a piratical commerce in the bodies of men and women. Let our Federal Government be purified from the contagion of slavery. Let us leave that institution where the Constitution left it—"with the States" in which it exists. I repeat, the people of the free States will not support it. They will not be involved in its crimes or its disgrace. Our emancipation from the slave-power must come; and in the words of my illustrious and lamented friend, John Quincy Adams, let me say, "it will come—whether in peace or in blood I know not; but, whether in peace or in blood, let it come."

Source: Reuben Vose's Wealth of the World Displayed (New York: Reuben Vose, 1859), 223–235 (223–224, 234–235).

Friends' Review, "The Riot at Harper's Ferry," October 29, 1859

Although E.B. celebrated Brown as a "deliverer," other Quakers saw too great a divide between Brown's violence and their own stance of nonresistance. Brown symbolized the controversial notion of principled violence, and to some pacifists his violent methods seemed at odds with abolitionist calls for democratic brotherhood. This editorial in a Philadelphia-based Quaker journal is antislavery but anti-Brown. It declares that Brown must have been insane, that his actions were inconsistent with Christianity, and that the raid would only fortify slaveholders' determination to keep slaves.

In our Summary of News last week, reference was made to an extraordinary outbreak at Harper's Ferry on the 17th inst. Its real character and object have been fully declared by the leader of the riot—John Brown, formerly of Kansas—being an attempt to put an end to Slavery by force of arms. Without taking into view the immorality of the proceeding, the prospect of success was so utterly hopeless as to induce the belief that the principal actors must have been laboring under a species of insanity, or the blindest fanaticism. Nothing short of this could lead them to expect the aid necessary to accomplish their purposes from the white people of the North or the South. But when we consider that the means adopted as a remedy for the great evil of Slavery were equally inconsistent with Christianity, and totally indefensible on religious principles, we must profoundly deplore the occurrence. That politicians will use it for selfish and corrupt purposes cannot be doubted; and its almost inevitable effect upon the minds of slaveholders can scarcely fail to be adverse to the pleadings of their conscience and the prayers of those who seek in a truly

Christian spirit to break every yoke, proclaim liberty to the captive, and let the oppressed go free.

The responsibility of the continuance of American slavery, is far from resting exclusively upon the slaveholders. The system finds nourishment and support beyond the rice swamp, the cane field, and the cotton plantation. Hence there are duties, in relation to its annihilation, devolving upon Christians generally. Our religious Society having by its Discipline prohibited its members from buying, selling, holding and hiring slaves, has also adopted principles which forbid the doing of "anything whereby their bondage may be prolonged," or being in any way "accessory to this enormous national evil."

The duty, too, of pleading with the slaveholders to let the oppressed go free, and of bearing a public testimony against slavery, has often been recognized in our several Yearly Meetings, by presenting memorials on the subject to various legislative bodies and by issuing addresses to the public. . . . In a time like the present, when the hand of violence has been put forth, and our country is greatly agitated, how desirable it is to the true Christian to feel that he is in a place of safety—not as in the cave of the hermit, or the cell of the monk—but under a consciousness that with the aid of the Holy Spirit every duty has been in good measure fulfilled, and a humble trust attained in the mercy and protection of his Heavenly Father.

Source: Friends' Review; a Religious, Literary and Miscellaneous Journal, October 29, 1859, 120.

Salmon P. Chase, "To Joseph H. Barrett," October 29, 1859

Until the Harpers Ferry raid, Ohio governor Salmon Chase (1808–1873) was a possible Republican presidential candidate. An antislavery politician who coined the Free Soil Party slogan "Free Soil, Free Labor, Free Men," he had supported Brown's Kansas activities. But in the wake of Brown's raid, this association made him vulnerable to attack from Southerners and Democrats. Trying to disassociate himself from Brown, he wrote from Columbus, Ohio, to Joseph H. Barrett and denied involvement in the raid, calling Brown "mad." Barrett was the editor of the *Cincinnati Gazette* and had defended Chase in an article of October 20 against attempts by the *Cincinnati Enquirer* to link him with Brown. Chase and Seward stood "ready to deluge the land in blood to carry out their fanatical views," said the *Enquirer*. Although Chase lost the 1860 Republican nomination, he went on to become Lincoln's secretary of the treasury and eventually the chief justice of the Supreme Court.

Poor old man! How sadly misled by his own imagination! How rash, how mad, how criminal, thus to stir up insurrection, which, if successful, would deluge the land with blood and make void the fairest hopes of mankind! And yet how hard to condemn him, when we remember the provocation, the unselfish desire to set free the oppressed, the bravery, the humanity towards his prisoners, which defeated his purposes! This is a tragedy which will supply themes for novelists and poets for centuries. Men will condemn his act and pity his fate forever. But while pity and condemnation mingle for him, how stern will be the reprobation which must fall upon the guiltiness of forcing slavery upon Kansas, which began it all, and upon slavery itself, which underlies it all!

Source: Joseph H. Barrett, *Abraham Lincoln and His Presidency,* Vol. 1 (Cincinnati: Robert Clarke, 1904), 207.

New York Evening Post, "A New Version of an Old Song: Illustrating the Growth of Public Sentiment," October 29, 1859

As early as October 29, 1859, the *New York Evening Post* could see far-reaching consequences for Brown's raid. It published on its front page a song that charts increasing proslavery sentiments on the part of politicians and the press, which eventually culminates in a panicked vision of 10,000 African Americans joining 20,000 abolitionists with 18-foot pitchforks, all growing out of the initial pairing of John Brown and one black child. This vision of armed insurrection then leads into the 1860 election, which in turn prompts the gradual disappearance of slavery, to the surprise of all Americans. The song was intended to be sung to the tune of "Ten Little Indians" and was reprinted in several newspapers in New York, California, and Pennsylvania in November. It then circulated as the ballad "Ten Little Niggers" in minstrel shows during the 1860s and 1870s, especially in the South, with different lyrics that do not mention John Brown. But the *Post*'s version of 1859, with its depiction of Brown's raid beginning a chain of events that leads to mass insurrection, a particular election result, and the end of slavery, reflected the *Post*'s firm antislavery stance. Launched in 1801 by Alexander Hamilton, the newspaper had as its editor in chief the poet William Cullen Bryant, who had been a Free Soiler and then a Republican since 1856. By 1860 he was a public supporter of Lincoln. His newspaper's first response to Brown's raid, in an article of October 18, contained a vision of slavery's inevitable extinction, similar to the vision of the song. The raid showed yet again that slavery was a "volcano" and an explosion was "inevitable," explained the article. If Southerners continued to push for the expansion of slavery, there would be a "furious servile war," the kind depicted in the song, promised the *Post*, for slaves would not be "found either so incapable or so docile as the slaveholders seem to suppose."

AIR—"John Brown had a Little Injun."
Old John Brown, he had a little nigger,
Old John Brown, he had a little nigger,
Old John Brown, he had a little nigger,
    One little nigger boy.
    (Chorus, by several voices)

District-Attorney Ould[23]—*One little, two little,*

Secretary Floyd[24]—*three little nigger,*

Messrs. Mason and Vallandigaam[25]—*Four little, five little,*

Mr. Buchanan[26]—*six little nigger,*

Gov. Wise[27]—*Seven little, eight little,*

Washington Constitution[28]—*nine little nigger,*

New York Herald[29]—*Ten little nigger boy.*

Democratic Press throughout the Country *(in recitative)—Ten thousand little nigger boys all armed with pitchforks eighteen feet long and commanded by twenty thousand abolitionists.*
(Interval in which the election is supposed to have passed.)

Herald and Constitution—*Ten little, nine little, eight little nigger,*

Authorities of Virginia—*Seven little, six little, five little nigger,*

Authorities at Washington—*Four little, three little, two little nigger,*

People of the Country *(in accents of surprise at the upshot of the whole)—One little nigger boy!!!*

Source: New York Evening Post, October 29, 1859.

Henry Ward Beecher, "The Nation's Duty to Slavery," October 30, 1859

While Brown wrote and waited in prison, his fellow abolitionists exchanged letters debating the correct course of action. Some planned rescue attempts, but others believed he would be more useful to the cause dead. George and Mary Stearns even commissioned an idealized memorial weeks before the execution. They asked Edwin A. Brackett to sculpt Brown as he awaited execution, and the white marble bust looked to many like Michelangelo's *Moses*. Others welcomed and celebrated Brown's martyrdom in advance. Henry Ward Beecher (1813–1887), the famous abolitionist clergyman and brother of the novelist Harriet Beecher Stowe, voiced the feelings of many when he pronounced in his sermon at Plymouth Church in Brooklyn on October 30: "Let Virginia make him a martyr." A *Herald* reporter smuggled a copy of Beecher's sermon into Brown's jail cell, and upon reading this statement, Brown wrote in the margin: "Good."

The surprise of a whole nation at a recent event is itself the best evidence of the isolation of that event. A burning fragment struck the earth near Harper's Ferry. If the fragment of an exploding aerolite had fallen down out of the air, while the meteor swept on, it would not have been more sudden or less apparently connected either with a cause or an effect! . . . As I shall not recur to this epic in Virginia history again to-night, I must say a word in respect to the head and heart of it. For it all stood in the courage of one man.

An old man, kind at heart, industrious, peaceful, went forth, with a large family of children, to seek a new home in Kansas. That infant colony held thousands of souls as noble as liberty ever inspired or religion enriched. A great scowling Slave State, its nearest neighbor, sought to tread down this liberty loving colony, and to dragoon slavery into it by force of arms. The armed citizens of a hostile State crossed the State lines, destroyed the freedom of the ballot box, prevented a fair expression of public sentiment, corruptly usurped law making power, and ordained by fraud laws as infamous as the sun ever saw; assaulted its infant settlements with armed hordes, ravaged the fields, destroyed harvests and herds, and carried death to a multitude of cabins. The United States government had no marines for this occasion! No Federal troops posted in the cars by night and day for the poor, the weak, the grossly wronged men of Kansas. There was an army there that unfurled the banner of the Union, but it was on the side of the wrong doers, not on the side of the injured.

It was in this field that Brown received his impulse. A tender father, whose life was in his son's life, he saw his first born seized like a felon, chained, driven across the country, crazed by suffering and heat, beaten like a dog by the officer in charge, and long lying at death's door! Another noble boy, without warning, without offense, unarmed, in open day, in the midst of the city, was shot dead![30] No justice sought out the murderers; no United States attorney was dispatched in hot haste; no marines or soldiers aided the wronged and weak!

The shot that struck the child's heart crazed the father's brain. Revolving his wrongs, and nursing his hatred of that deadly system that breeds such contempt of justice and humanity, at length his phantoms assume a slender reality, and organize such an enterprise as one might expect from a man whom grief had bereft of good judgment. He goes to the heart of a Slave State. One man; and with sixteen followers![31] he seizes two thousand brave Virginians, and holds them in duress!

When a great State attacked a handful of weak colonists the government and nation were torpid, but when seventeen men attacked a sovereign State, then Maryland arms, and Virginia arms, and the United States government arms, and they three rush against seventeen men.

Travelers tell us that the Geysers of Iceland—those singular boiling springs of the North—may be transported with fury by plucking up a handful of grass or turf and throwing it into the springs. The hot springs of Virginia are of the same kind! A handful of men was thrown into them, and what a boiling there has been!

But, meanwhile, no one can fail to see that this poor, child-bereft old man is the manliest of them all. Bold, unflinching, honest, without deceit or evasion, refusing to take technical advantages of any sort, but openly avowing his principles and motives, glorying in them in danger and death, as much as when in security, that wounded old father is the most remarkable figure in this whole drama. The Governor, the officers of the State, and all the attorneys are pygmies compared with him.

I deplore his misfortunes. I sympathize with his sorrows. I mourn the hiding or obscuration of his reason. I disapprove of his mad and feeble schemes. I shrink from the folly of the bloody foray, and I shrink likewise from all the anticipations of that judicial bloodshed, which doubtless ere long will follow, for when was cowardice ever magnanimous? If they kill the man, it will not be so much for treason as for the disclosure of their cowardice!

Let no man pray that Brown be spared. Let Virginia make him a martyr. Now, he has only blundered. His soul was noble; his work miserable. But a cord and a gibbet would redeem all that, and round up Brown's failure with a heroic success.

One word more, and that is as to the insecurity of those States that carry powder as their chief cargo. Do you suppose that if tidings had come to New York that the United States armory in Springfield had been seized by seventeen men, New Haven, and Hartford, and Stamford, and Worcester, and New York, and Boston, and Albany would have been thrown into a fever and panic in consequence of the event? We scarcely should have read the papers to see what became of it. We should have thought that it was a matter which the Springfield people could manage. The thought of danger would not have entered into our heads. There would not have been any danger. But in a State where there is such inflammable stuff as slavery, there *is* danger, and the people of the South know it; and they cannot help it. I do not blame them so much for being afraid: there is cause for fear where they have such a population as they have down at the bottom of society. But what must be the nature of State and domestic institutions which keep brave men at the point of fear all their life long?

Source: Henry Ward Beecher, *Patriotic Addresses* (New York: Fords, Howard, & Hulbert, 1887), 201–223 (204–208).

Henry David Thoreau, "A Plea for Captain John Brown," October 30, 1859, and "The Last Days of John Brown," July 4, 1860

No stranger to the abolitionist movement, the transcendentalist Henry David Thoreau (1817–1862) condemned the Fugitive Slave Law in his lecture "Slavery in Massachusetts" (1854) and described elsewhere the horror of Anthony Burns's forcible return to slavery from Boston in 1854. Believing that passive resistance could not end slavery, he welcomed Brown's armed assault on Harpers Ferry. He had met Brown through Franklin Sanborn in 1857, and after hearing news of the raid on October 19, 1859, he decided to plead Brown's cause—"not for his life, but for his character—his immortal life," as he explained. The "plea," which he made on October 30 in Concord, Massachusetts, and on November 1 in Boston, drew heavily from his journal entries of October 19, 21, and 22. Thoreau also spoke briefly at the services held in Concord on December 2, 1859, in commemoration of Brown, where he dwelled on Brown's "transcendent moral greatness," and then he wrote a longer speech, in 1860, that proclaimed Brown's immortality. This speech, "The Last Days of John Brown," draws heavily from his journal entries of November 17 and 18 and December 5, 6, and 9, 1859. It was read at a memorial for Brown in North Elba on July 4, 1860, to which Thoreau was invited but which he could not attend.

"A Plea for Captain John Brown"

A man of rare common-sense and directness of speech, as of action; a transcendentalist above all, a man of ideas and principles,—that was what distinguished him. Not yielding to a whim or transient impulse, but carrying out the purpose of a life. . . .

On the whole, my respect for my fellow-men, except as one may outweigh a million, is not being increased these days. I have noticed the cold-blooded way in which newspaper writers and men generally speak of this event, as if an ordinary malefactor, though one of unusual "pluck"—as the Governor of Virginia is reported to have said, using the language of the cock-pit, "the gamest man he ever saw,"—had been caught, and were about to be hung. He was not dreaming of his foes when the governor thought he looked so brave. It turns what sweetness I have to gall, to hear, or hear of, the remarks of some of my neighbors. When we heard at first that he was dead, one of my townsmen observed that "he died as the fool dieth";[32] which, pardon me, for an instant suggested a likeness in him dying to my neighbor living. Others, craven-hearted, said disparagingly, that "he threw his life away," because he resisted the government. Which way have they thrown *their* lives, pray?—such as would praise a man for attacking singly an ordinary band of thieves or murderers. I hear another ask, Yankee-like, "What will he gain by it?" as if he expected to fill his pockets by this enterprise. Such a one has no idea of gain but in this worldly sense. If it does not lead to a 'surprise' party, if he does not get a new pair of boots, or a vote of thanks, it must be a failure. "But he won't gain anything by it." Well, no, I don't suppose he could get four-and-sixpence a day for being hung, take the year round; but then he stands a chance to save a considerable part of his soul—and *such* a soul!—when *you* do not. No doubt you can get more in your market for a quart of milk than for a quart of blood, but that is not the market that heroes carry their blood to.

Such do not know that like the seed is the fruit, and that, in the moral world, when good seed is planted, good fruit is inevitable, and does not depend on our watering and cultivating; that when you plant, or bury, a hero in his field, a crop of heroes is sure to spring up. This is a seed of such force and vitality, that it does not ask our leave to germinate. . . .

The slave-ship is on her way, crowded with its dying victims; new cargoes are being added in mid-ocean; a small crew of slaveholders, countenanced by a large body of passengers, is smothering four millions under the hatches, and yet the politician asserts that the only proper way by which deliverance is to be obtained is by "the quiet diffusion of the sentiments of humanity," without any "outbreak."[33] As if the sentiments of humanity were ever found unaccompanied by its deeds, and you could disperse them, all finished to order, the pure article, as easily as water with a watering-pot, and so lay the dust. What is that that I hear cast overboard? The bodies of the dead that have found deliverance. That is the way we are "diffusing" humanity, and its sentiments with it.

Prominent and influential editors, accustomed to deal with politicians, men of an infinitely lower grade, say, in their ignorance, that he acted "on the principle of revenge." They do not know the man. They must enlarge themselves to conceive of him. I have no doubt that the time will come when they will begin to see him as he was. They have got to conceive of a man of faith and of religious principle, and not a politician or an Indian; of a man who did not wait till he was personally interfered with or thwarted in some harmless business before he gave his life to the cause of the oppressed.

If Walker may be considered the representative of the South,[34] I wish I could say that Brown was the representative of the North. He was a superior man. He did not value his bodily life in comparison with ideal things. He did not recognize unjust human laws, but resisted them as he was bid. For once we are lifted out of the trivialness and dust of politics into the region of truth and manhood. No man in America has ever stood up so persistently and effectively for the dignity of human nature, knowing himself for a man, and the equal of any and all governments. In that sense he was the most American of us all. He needed no babbling lawyer, making false issues, to defend him. He was more than a match for all the judges that American voters, or office-holders of whatever grade, can create. He could not have been tried by a jury of his peers, because his peers did not exist. When a man stands up serenely against the condemnation and vengeance of mankind, rising above them literally *by a whole body*—even though he were of late the vilest murderer, who has settled that matter with himself—the spectacle is a sublime one—didn't ye know it, ye *Liberators,* ye *Tribunes,* ye *Republicans?*—and we become criminal in comparison. Do yourselves the honor to recognize him. He needs none of your respect.

As for the Democratic journals, they are not human enough to affect me at all. I do not feel indignation at anything they may say.

I am aware that I anticipate a little—that he was still, at the last accounts, alive in the hands of his foes; but that being the case, I have all along found myself thinking and speaking of him as physically dead.

I do not believe in erecting statues to those who still live in our hearts, whose bones have not yet crumbled in the earth around us, but I would rather see the statue of Captain Brown in the Massachusetts State-House yard than that of any other man whom I know. I rejoice that I live in this age, that I am his contemporary. . . .

When I think of him, and his six sons, and his son-in-law, not to enumerate the others, enlisted for this fight, proceeding coolly, reverently, humanely to work, for months if not years, sleeping and waking upon it, summering and wintering the thought, without expecting any reward but a good conscience, while almost all America stood ranked on the other side—I say again that it affects me as a sublime spectacle. If he had had any journal advocating *"his cause,"* any organ, as the phrase is, monotonously and wearisomely playing the same old tune, and then passing round the hat, it would have been fatal to his efficiency. If he had acted in any way so as to be let alone by the government, he might have been suspected. It was the fact that the tyrant must give place to him, or he to the tyrant, that distinguished him from all the reformers of the day that I know.

It was his peculiar doctrine that a man has a perfect right to interfere by force with the slaveholder, in order to rescue the slave. I agree with him. They who are continually shocked by slavery have some right to be shocked by the violent death of the slaveholder, but no others. Such will be more shocked by his life than by his death. I shall not be forward to think him mistaken in his method who quickest succeeds to liberate the slave. I speak for the slave when I say that I prefer the philanthropy of Captain Brown to that philanthropy which neither shoots me nor liberates me. At any rate, I do not think it is quite sane for one to spend his whole life in talking or writing about this matter, unless he is continuously inspired, and I have not done so. A man may have other affairs to attend to. I do not wish to kill nor to be killed, but I can foresee circumstances in which both these things would be by me unavoidable. We preserve the so-called peace of our community by deeds of petty violence every day. Look at the policeman's billy and handcuffs! Look at the jail! Look at the gallows! Look at the chaplain of the regiment! We are hoping only to live safely on the outskirts of *this* provisional army. So we defend ourselves and our hen-roosts, and maintain slavery. I know that the mass of my countrymen think that the only righteous use that can be made of Sharp's rifles and revolvers is to fight duels with them, when we are insulted by other nations, or to hunt Indians, or shoot fugitive slaves with them, or the like. I think that for once the Sharp's rifles and the revolvers were employed in a righteous cause. The tools were in the hands of one who could use them.

The same indignation that is said to have cleared the temple once will clear it again. The question is not about the weapon, but the spirit in which you use it. No man has appeared in America, as yet, who loved his fellow-man so well, and treated him so tenderly. He lived for him. He took up his life and he laid it down for him. . . .

Who is it whose safety requires that Captain Brown be hung? Is it indispensable to any Northern man? Is there no resource but to cast this man also to the Minotaur?[35] If you do not wish it, say so distinctly. While these things are being done, beauty stands veiled and music is a screeching lie. Think of him—of his rare qualities!—such a man as it takes ages to make, and ages to understand; no mock hero, nor the representative of any party. A man such as the sun may not rise upon again in this benighted land. To whose making went the costliest material, the finest adamant; sent to be the redeemer of those in captivity; and the only use to which you can put him is to hang him at the end of a rope! You who pretend to care for Christ crucified, consider what you are about to do to him who offered himself to be the savior of four millions of men. . . . I am here to plead his cause with you. I plead not for his life, but for his character—his immortal life; and so it becomes your cause wholly, and is not his in the least. Some eighteen hundred years ago Christ was crucified; this morning, perchance, Captain Brown was hung. These are the two ends of a chain which is not without its links. He is not Old Brown any longer; he is an angel of light.

I see now that it was necessary that the bravest and humanest man in all the country should be hung. Perhaps he saw it himself. I *almost fear* that I may yet hear of his deliverance, doubting if a prolonged life, if *any* life, can do as much good as his death.

"The Last Days of John Brown"

John Brown's career for the last six weeks of his life was meteor-like, flashing through the darkness in which we live.[36] I know of nothing so miraculous in our history.

If any person, in a lecture or conversation at that time, cited any ancient example of heroism, such as Cato or Tell or Winkelried,[37] passing over the recent deeds and words of Brown, it was felt by any intelligent audience of Northern men to be tame and inexcusably far-fetched.

For my own part, I commonly attend more to nature than to man, but any affecting human event may blind our eyes to natural objects. I was so absorbed in him as to be surprised whenever I detected the routine of the natural world surviving still, or met persons going about their affairs indifferent. It appeared strange to me that the "little dipper" should be still diving quietly in the river, as of yore; and it suggested that this bird might continue to dive here when Concord should be no more.

I felt that he, a prisoner in the midst of his enemies and under sentence of death, if consulted as to his next step or resource, could answer more wisely than all his countrymen beside. He best understood his position; he contemplated it most calmly. Comparatively, all other men, North and South, were beside themselves. Our thoughts could not revert to any greater or wiser or better man with whom to contrast him, for he, then and there, was above them all. The man this country was about to hang appeared the greatest and best in it.

Years were not required for a revolution of public opinion; days, nay hours, produced marked changes in this case. Fifty who were ready to say, on going into our meeting in honor of him in Concord, that he ought to be hung, would not say it when they came out. They heard his words read; they saw the earnest faces of the congregation; and perhaps they joined at last in singing the hymn in his praise. . . .

When I looked into a liturgy of the Church of England, printed near the end of the last century, in order to find a service applicable to the case of Brown, I found that the only martyr recognized and provided for by it was King Charles the First, an eminent scamp. Of all the inhabitants of England and of the world, he was the only one, according to this authority, whom that church had made a martyr and saint of; and for more than a century it had celebrated his martyrdom, so called, by an annual service. What a satire on the Church is that!

Look not to legislatures and churches for your guidance, nor to any soulless *incorporated* bodies, but to *inspirited* or inspired ones.

What avail all your scholarly accomplishments and learning, compared with wisdom and manhood? To omit his other behavior, see what a work this comparatively unread and unlettered man wrote within six weeks. Where is our professor of *belles-lettres,* or of logic and rhetoric, who can write so well? He wrote in prison, not a History of the World, like Raleigh,[38] but an American book which I think will live longer than that. I do not know of such words, uttered under such circumstances, and so copiously withal, in Roman or English or any history. What a variety of themes he touched on in that short space!

There are words in that letter to his wife, respecting the education of his daughters, which deserve to be framed and hung over every mantelpiece in the land. Compare this earnest wisdom with that of Poor Richard.[39]

The death of Irving,[40] which at any other time would have attracted universal attention, having occurred while these things were transpiring, went almost unobserved. I shall have to read of it in the biography of authors.

Literary gentlemen, editors and critics, think that they know how to write, because they have studied grammar and rhetoric; but they are egregiously mistaken. The art of composition is as simple as the discharge of a bullet from a rifle, and its masterpieces imply an infinitely greater force behind them. This unlettered man's speaking and writing are standard English. Some words and phrases deemed vulgarisms and Americanisms before, he has made standard American; such as *"It will pay."*[41] It suggests that the one great rule of composition—and if I were a professor of rhetoric, I should insist on this—is, to *speak the truth.* This first, this second, this third; pebbles in your mouth or not. This demands earnestness and manhood chiefly.

We seem to have forgotten that the expression "a *liberal* education" originally meant among the Romans one worthy of *free* men; while the learning of trades and professions by which to get your livelihood merely, was considered worthy of *slaves* only. But taking a hint from the word, I would go a step further and say, that it is not the man of wealth and leisure simply, though devoted to art, or science, or literature, who, in a true sense, is *liberally* educated, but only the earnest and *free* man. In a slaveholding country like this, there can be no such thing as a *liberal* education tolerated by the State; and those scholars of Austria and France who, however learned they may be, are contented under their tyrannies, have received only a *servile* education.[42]

Nothing could his enemies do but it redounded to his infinite advantage—that is, to the advantage of his cause. They did not hang him at once, but reserved him to preach to them. And then there was another great blunder. They did not hang his four followers with him; that scene was still postponed; and so his victory was prolonged and completed. No theatrical manager could have arranged things so wisely to give effect to his behavior and words. And who, think you, *was* the manager? *Who* placed the slave woman and her child, whom he stooped to kiss for a symbol, between his prison and the gallows?

We soon saw, as he saw, that he was not to be pardoned or rescued by men. That would have been to disarm him, to restore to him a material weapon, a

Sharp's rifle, when he had taken up the sword of the spirit—the sword with which he has really won his greatest and most memorable victories. Now he has not laid aside the sword of the spirit, for he is pure spirit himself, and his sword is pure spirit also.

> "He nothing common did or mean
> Upon that memorable scene,
> Nor called the gods with vulgar spite,
> To vindicate his helpless right;
> But bowed his comely head
> Down, as upon a bed."[43]

What a transit was that of his horizontal body alone, but just cut down from the gallows-tree! We read that at such a time it passed through Philadelphia, and by Saturday night had reached New York. Thus like a meteor it shot through the Union from the Southern regions toward the North! No such freight had the cars borne since they carried him southward alive.

On the day of his translation, I heard, to be sure, that he was *hung*, but I did not know what that meant; I felt no sorrow on that account; but not for a day or two did I even *hear* that he was *dead*, and not after any number of days shall I believe it. Of all the men who were said to be my contemporaries, it seemed to me that John Brown was the only one who *had not died*. I never hear of a man named Brown now—and I hear of them pretty often—I never hear of any particularly brave and earnest man, but my first thought is of John Brown, and what relation he may be to him. I meet him at every turn. He is more alive than ever he was. He has earned immortality. He is not confined to North Elba nor to Kansas. He is no longer working in secret. He works in public, and in the clearest light that shines on this land.

Source: The Writings of Henry David Thoreau, Vol. 10 (Boston: Houghton Mifflin, 1893), 197–236 (202–203, 207–209, 215–218, 226–229, 232–234), 237–248 (237–238, 243–248).

Ralph Waldo Emerson, "Courage," November 8, 1859, and "Remarks at a Meeting for the Relief of the Family of John Brown," November 18, 1859

Like his friend and fellow transcendentalist Thoreau, Ralph Waldo Emerson (1803–1882) spoke out against slavery, including the Fugitive Slave Law, which he called a "filthy enactment." He first met Brown in March 1857 at Thoreau's home. Then he heard Brown speak at the Concord town hall and thought him "the rarest of heroes, a pure idealist." But Emerson was less enthusiastic about the Harpers Ferry raid, telling his son in a letter of October 23, 1859, that although Brown was a "true hero," he had "lost his head there." Nevertheless, after grappling privately with his misgivings about Brown, Emerson collected money for his trial and made several sympathetic public statements. On November 8 he called Brown a "saint" who "will make the gallows glorious like the cross." The observation came during a much longer address about courage, excerpted below, and adapted the words of his friend Mattie Griffith, a Kentucky abolitionist. As Emerson recorded in a journal entry before giving his address, Griffith said that the "gallows will be sacred as the cross." Emerson was one of the country's leading public intellectuals, and his remark, though borrowed and buried in the middle of a long speech, was instantly famous. The *New York Tribune* and other Northern newspapers quoted it, as did numerous abolitionists. Emerson helped to turn the tide of public opinion in Brown's favor. Then, just ten days after his "gallows glorious" observation, he gave a speech at Tremont Temple in Boston that focused on Brown at greater length.

"Courage"

As soon as we rise to the heights of courage, we come to the grand models of mankind. We have come to the secret of the Will, which is the antagonist of Fate, which is the presence always of spiritual power, the presence of God in man—always miraculous, and 'past finding out.' We are embosomed in a spiritual world, yet none ever saw an angel or spirit. Whence does our knowledge of it course? Only from man. The only revealer of the divine mind is the thoughts of men. The soul of God is poured into the world through the thoughts of men.

Look nearer, at the ungathered records of those who have gone to languish in prison or to die in rescuing others, or in rescuing themselves from chains of the slave; or look at that new saint, than whom none purer or brave was ever led by love of man into conflict and death; a new saint, waiting yet his martyr-dom; and who, if he shall suffer, will make the gallows glorious like the cross. *(Prolonged and enthusiastic applause).*[44]

But "wisdom is justified of her children."[45] Valor pays rents as well as lands. A noble cause begets love and confidence, and has a sure reward. High cour-age, a power of will superior to events, makes a bond of union between ene-mies. If Gov. Wise be a superior man, and inasmuch as he is a superior man, he distinguishes his captive John Brown.

As they confer, they understand each other swiftly; each respects the other, and if opportunity allowed, they would prefer each other's society to that of their former companions. Enemies become affectionate; become aware that they are nearer alike than any other two, and if circumstances did not keep them apart, they would fly into each other's arms. Poets and orators and paint-ers catch the hint, and everything feels the new breath, excepting the dead and doting politicians whom the trump of resurrection could not reach.

"Remarks at a Meeting for the Relief of the Family of John Brown"

I share the sympathy and sorrow which have brought us together. Gentlemen who have preceded me have well said that no wall of separation could here ex-ist. This commanding event which has brought us together, eclipses all others which have occurred for a long time in our history, and I am very glad to see that this sudden interest in the hero of Harper's Ferry has provoked an extreme curiosity in all parts of the Republic, in regard to the details of his history. Every anecdote is eagerly sought, and I do not wonder that gentle-men find traits of relation readily between him and themselves. One finds a relation in the church, another in the profession, another in the place of his birth. He was happily a representative of the American Republic. Captain John Brown is a farmer, the fifth in descent from Peter Brown, who came to Plym-outh in the Mayflower, in 1620. All the six have been farmers. His grandfather, of Simsbury, in Connecticut, was a captain in the Revolution. His father, largely interested as a raiser of stock, became a contractor to supply the army with beef, in the war of 1812, and our Captain John Brown, then a boy, with his father was present and witnessed the surrender of General Hull. He cherishes a great respect for his father, as a man of strong character, and his respect is probably just. For himself, he is so transparent that all men see him through. He is a man to make friends wherever on earth courage and integrity are esteemed, the rarest of heroes, a pure idealist, with no by-ends of his own. Many of you have seen him, and every one who has heard him speak has been impressed alike by his simple, artless goodness, joined with his sublime courage. He joins that perfect Puritan faith which brought his fifth ancestor to Plymouth Rock with his grandfather's ardor in the Revolution. He believes in two articles—two instruments, shall I say?—the Golden Rule and the Declaration of Independence; and he used this expression in conversation here concerning them, "Better that a whole generation of men, women and children should pass away by a violent death than that one word of either should be violated in this country."[46] There is a Unionist—there is a strict constructionist for you. He believes in the Union of the States, and he conceives that the only obstruction to the Union is Slavery, and for that reason, as a patriot, he works for its abolition. The governor of Virginia has pronounced his eulogy in a manner that discredits the moderation of our timid parties. His own speeches to the court have interested the nation in him. What magnanimity, and what innocent pleading, as of childhood! You remember his words: "If I had interfered in behalf of the rich, the powerful, the intelligent, the so-called great, or any of their friends, parents, wives or children, it would all have been right. But I believe that to have interfered as I have done, for the despised poor, was not wrong, but right."[47]

It is easy to see what a favorite he will be with history, which plays such pranks with temporary reputations. Nothing can resist the sympathy which all elevated minds must feel with Brown, and through them the whole civilized world; and if he must suffer, he must drag official gentlemen into an immortality most undesirable, of which they have already some disagreeable forebodings. Indeed, it is the *reductio ad absurdum*[48] of Slavery, when the governor of Virginia is forced to hang a man whom he declares to be a man of the most integrity, truthfulness and courage he has ever met. Is that the kind of man the gallows is built for? It were bold to affirm that there is within that broad commonwealth, at this moment, another citizen as worthy to live, and as deserving of all public and private honor, as this poor prisoner.

But we are here to think of relief for the family of John Brown. To my eyes, that family looks very large and very needy of relief. It comprises his brave fellow sufferers in the Charlestown Jail; the fugitives still hunted in the mountains of Virginia and Pennsylvania; the sympathizers with him in all the states; and, I may say, almost every man who loves the Golden Rule and the Declaration of Independence, like him, and who sees what a tiger's thirst threatens him in the malignity of public sentiment in the slave states. It seems to me that a common feeling joins the people of Massachusetts with him.

I said John Brown was an idealist. He believed in his ideas to that extent that he existed to put them all into action; he said "he did not believe in moral suasion, he believed in putting the thing through." He saw how deceptive the forms are. We fancy, in Massachusetts, that we are free; yet it seems the Government is quite unreliable. Great wealth, great population, men of talent in the Executive, on the Bench,—all the forms right,—and yet, life and freedom are not safe. Why? Because the judges rely on the forms, and do not, like John Brown, use their eyes to see the fact behind the forms.

Sources: "Emerson on Courage," *The Liberator*, November 18, 1859; *Emerson's Complete Works*, Vol. 11 (Boston: Houghton Mifflin, 1883), 251–256 (251–254).

Frederick Douglass, "Capt. John Brown Not Insane," November 1859

Frederick Douglass (1817–1895) was born a slave, escaped to freedom in 1838, and eventually became the most famous African American of the nineteenth century. In 1847 he founded the *North Star,* an abolitionist newspaper based in Rochester, New York. The newspaper became *Frederick Douglass's Paper* in 1851 and appeared until 1860. Another of his journals, *Douglass' Monthly,* ran from 1858 until 1863. During the Civil War, Douglass conferred with President Lincoln on the treatment of black soldiers, and after the war he served as president of the Reconstruction-era Freedman's Savings Bank, marshal of the District of Columbia, and ambassador to Haiti. Douglass's association with Brown began in the late 1840s, when he proposed that they convert the slaveholders instead of trying to free the slaves by force. Brown proclaimed that this was impossible, and Douglass moved closer to embracing Brown's militant approach, even wondering aloud at an antislavery convention in 1850 if slavery could be destroyed only by bloodshed. Then, in August 1859, he met Brown in a disused quarry pit in Chambersburg, Pennsylvania. Brown wanted to recruit Douglass for the expedition to Harpers Ferry and urged him to join the group already installed at the Kennedy Farm. He entreated: "I will defend you with my life. I want you for a special purpose. When I strike, the bees will begin to swarm, and I shall want you to help me hive them." But Douglass refused, calling the plan a "trap of steel." After the raid, facing the very real possibility of arrest and execution, Douglass denied any part in Brown's attempt. He did come to Brown's defense in November, however, and denied accusations that his friend was insane.

One of the most painful incidents connected with the name of this old hero, is the attempt to prove him insane. Many journals have contributed to this effort from a friendly desire to shield the prisoner from Virginia's cowardly vengeance. This is a mistaken friendship, which seeks to rob him of his true character and dim the glory of his deeds, in order to save his life. Was there the faintest hope of securing his release by this means, we would choke down our indignation and be silent. But a Virginia court would hang a crazy man without a moment's hesitation, if his insanity took the form of hatred of oppression; and this plea only blasts the reputation of this glorious martyr of liberty, without the faintest hope of improving his chance of escape.

It is an appalling fact in the history of the American people, that they have so far forgotten their own heroic age, as readily to accept the charge of insanity against a man who has imitated the heroes of Lexington, Concord, and Bunker Hill.

It is an effeminate and cowardly age, which calls a man a lunatic because he rises to such self-forgetful heroism, as to count his own life as worth nothing in comparison with the freedom of millions of his fellows. Such an age would have sent Gideon to a mad-house, and put Leonidas in a straight-jacket.[49] Such a people would have treated the defenders of Thermopylae as demented,[50] and shut up Caius Marcius in bedlam.[51] Such a marrowless population as ours has become under the debaucheries of Slavery, would have struck the patriot's crown from the brow of Wallace, and recommended blisters and bleeding to the heroic Tell.[52] Wallace was often and again desperately forgetful of his own life in defence of Scotland's freedom, as was Brown in striking for the American slave; and Tell's defiance of the Austrian tyrant, was as far above the appreciation of cowardly selfishness as was Brown's defiance of the Virginia pirates. Was Arnold Winkelried insane when he rushed to his death upon an army of spears, crying "make way for Liberty!"[53] Are heroism and insanity synonyms in our American dictionary? Heaven help us! When our loftiest types of patriotism, our sublimest historical ideals of philanthropy, come to be treated as evidence of moonstruck madness. Posterity will owe everlasting thanks to John Brown for lifting up once more to the gaze of nation grown fat and flabby on the garbage of lust and oppression, a true standard of heroic philanthropy, and each coming generation will pay its instalment of the debt. No wonder that the aiders and abettors of the huge, overshadowing and many-armed tyranny, which he grappled with in its own infernal den, should call him a mad man; but for those who profess a regard for him, and for human freedom, to join in the cruel slander, "is the unkindest cut of all."[54]

Nor is it necessary to attribute Brown's deeds to the spirit of vengeance, invoked by the murder of his brave boys. That the barbarous cruelty from which he has suffered had its effect on intensifying his hatred of slavery, is doubtless true. But his own statement, that he had been contemplating a bold strike for the freedom of the slaves for ten years, proves that he had resolved upon his present course long before he, or his sons, ever set foot in Kansas. His entire procedure in this matter disproves the charge that he was prompted by an impulse of mad revenge, and shows that he was moved by the highest principles of philanthropy. His carefulness of the lives of unarmed persons—his humane and courteous treatment of his prisoners—his cool self-possession all through his trial—and especially his calm, dignified speech on receiving his sentence, all conspire to show that he was neither insane or actuated by vengeful passion; and we hope that the country has heard the last of John Brown's madness. The explanation of his conduct is perfectly natural and simple on its face. He believes the Declaration of Independence to be true, and the Bible to be a guide to human conduct, and acting upon the doctrines of both, he threw himself against the serried ranks of American oppression, and translated into heroic deeds the love of liberty and hatred of tyrants, with which he was inspired by both these forces acting upon his philanthropic and heroic soul. This age is too gross and sensual to appreciate his deeds, and so calls him mad; but the future will write his epitaph upon the hearts of a people freed from slavery, because he struck the first effectual blow.

Not only is it true that Brown's whole movement proves him perfectly sane and free from merely revengeful passion, but he has struck the bottom line of the philosophy which underlies the abolition movement. He has attacked slavery with the weapons precisely adapted to bring it to the death. Moral considerations have long since been exhausted upon slaveholders. It is in vain to reason with them. One may as well hunt bears with ethics and political economy for weapons, as to seek to "pluck the spoiled out of the hand of the oppressor"[55] by the mere force of moral law. Slavery is a system of brute force. It shields itself behind *might,* rather than right. It must be met with its own weapons. Capt. Brown has initiated a new mode of carrying out the crusade of freedom, and his blow has sent dread and terror throughout the entire ranks of the piratical army of slavery. His daring deeds may cost him his life, but priceless as is the value of that life, the blow he has struck, will, in the end, prove to be worth its mighty cost. Like Samson, he has laid his hands upon the pillars of this great national temple of cruelty and blood, and when he falls, that temple will speedily crumble to its final doom, burying its denizens in its ruins.

Source: Douglass' Monthly, November 1859.

Edmund Clarence Stedman, "How Old Brown Took Harper's Ferry," November 12, 1859

Edmund Clarence Stedman (1833–1908) first published his ballad about Brown in the *New York Daily Tribune* on November 12, 1859. He intended the poem to be an accurate account of Brown's life. Its first half focuses on Brown's time in Kansas and the second half, below, focuses on the Harpers Ferry raid. Although the poem calls Brown "mad," it is sympathetic to his cause and warns the South that he will continue his assault on slavery even in death. One of the earliest published poems about Brown, it had a huge impact. Many observers remembered that it shaped public opinion in Brown's favor before his execution. Stedman, who was from Hartford, Connecticut, went on to publish numerous volumes of poetry and to work as a field correspondent for the *New York World* during the Civil War.

'Twas the sixteenth of October, on the evening of a Sunday:
"This good work," declared the captain, "shall be on a holy night!"
It was on a Sunday evening, and before the noon of Monday,
With two sons, and Captain Stephens, fifteen privates—black and white—
    Captain Brown,
    Osawatomie Brown,
Marched across the bridged Potomac, and knocked the sentinel down;

Took the guarded armory-building, and the muskets and the cannon;
Captured all the county majors and the colonels, one by one;
Scared to death each gallant scion of Virginia they ran on,
And before the noon of Monday, I say, the deed was done.
    Mad Old Brown,
    Osawatomie Brown,
With his eighteen other crazy men, went in and took the town.[56]

Very little noise and bluster, little smell of powder made he;
It was all done in the midnight, like the Emperor's *coup d'état*.[57]
"Cut the wires! Stop the rail-cars! Hold the streets and bridges!" said he,
Then declared the new Republic, with himself for guiding star—
    This Old Brown,
    Osawatomie Brown;
And the bold two thousand citizens ran off and left the town.

Then was riding and railroading and expressing here and thither;
And the Martinsburg Sharpshooters and the Charlestown Volunteers,
And the Shepherdstown and Winchester Militia hastened whither
Old Brown was said to muster his ten thousand grenadiers.
    General Brown!
    Osawatomie Brown!!
Behind whose rampant banner all the North was pouring down.

But at last, 't is said, some prisoners escaped from Old Brown's durance,
And the effervescent valor of Ye Chivalry broke forth,
When they learned that nineteen madmen had the marvelous assurance—
Only nineteen—thus to seize the place and drive them straight about;
    And Old Brown,
    Osawatomie Brown,
Found an army come to take him, encamped around the town.

But to storm, with all the forces I have mentioned, was too risky;
So they hurried off to Richmond for the Government Marines,
Tore them from their weeping matrons, fired their souls with Bourbon
    whiskey,
Till they battered down Brown's castle with their ladders and machines;
    And Old Brown,
    Osawatomie Brown,
Received three bayonet stabs, and a cut on his brave old crown.

Tallyho! the old Virginia gentry gather to the baying!
In they rushed and killed the game, shooting lustily away;
And whene'er they slew a rebel, those who came too late for slaying,
Not to lose a share of glory, fired their bullets in his clay;
    And Old Brown,
    Osawatomie Brown,
Saw his sons fall dead beside him, and between them laid him down.

How the conquerors wore their laurels; how they hastened on the trial;
How Old Brown was placed, half dying, on the Charlestown Courthouse floor;
How he spoke his grand oration, in the scorn of all denial;
What the brave old madman told them—these are known the country o'er.
　"Hang Old Brown,
　Osawatomie Brown,"
Said the judge, "and all such rebels!" with his most judicial frown.

But, Virginians, don't do it! for I tell you that the flagon,
Filled with blood of Old Brown's offspring, was first poured by Southern
　　　hands;
And each drop from Old Brown's life-veins, like the red gore of the dragon,
May spring up a vengeful Fury, hissing through your slave-worn lands!
　And Old Brown,
　Osawatomie Brown,
May trouble you more than ever, when you've nailed his coffin down!

Source: New York Daily Tribune, November 12, 1859.

William Dean Howells, "Old Brown,"
November 1859

In his poem about Brown, written in November 1859 and printed in Ohio's *Ashtabula Sentinel* on January 25, 1860, William Dean Howells (1837–1920) imagines a "later time" when Brown's name is celebrated and his actions are no longer considered a crime. Brown himself imagined something similar. His prison letters refer to a future moment when his family members feel no shame at their association and anticipate the day when his "seeming disaster" appears a "glorious success." Howells eventually marked this "later time," noting in an article for the *North American Review* in January 1911 that Brown cast a "lasting spell," inspired reverence, had a "prophet soul," and was a "hero and martyr." "Old Brown" was one of Howells's early poems. He also wrote a lyric tribute titled "Gerrit Smith," published on the front page of the *Ashtabula Sentinel* on December 1, 1859, and a campaign biography of Lincoln, published in 1860. He spent the Civil War years as a U.S. consul in Venice, worked as an assistant editor, then editor, of the *Atlantic Monthly* between 1866 and 1881, and wrote realist novels, the most famous of which is *The Rise of Silas Lapham* (1885).

I.

Success goes royal-crowned through time,
    Down all the loud applauding days,
    Purpled in History's silkenest phrase,
And brave with many a poet's rhyme.

While unsuccess, his peer and mate,
    Sprung from the same heroic race,
    Begotten of the same embrace,
Dies at his brother's palace gate.

The insolent laugh, the blighting sneer,
   The pointing hand of vulgar scorn,
   The thorny path, and wreath of thorn,
The many-headed's stupid jeer.

Show where he fell. And by-and-by,
   Comes History, in the waning light,
   He pen-nib worn with lies, to write
The failure into infamy.

Ah, God! but here and there, there stands
   Along the years, a man to see
   Beneath the victor's bravery
The spots upon the lily hands:

To read the secret will of good,
   (Dead hope, and trodden into earth.)
   That beat the breast of strife for birth,
And died birth-choked, in parent blood.

II.

Old Lion! tangled in the net,
   Baffled and spent, and wounded sore,
   Bound, thou who ne'er knew bonds before;
A captive, but a lion yet.

Death kills not. In a later time,
   (O, slow, but all-accomplishing!)
   Thy shouted name abroad shall ring,
Wherever right makes war sublime:

When in the perfect scheme of God,
   It shall not be a crime for deeds
   To quicken liberating creeds,
And men shall rise where slaves have trod;

Then he, the fearless future Man,
   Shall wash the blot and stain away,
   We fix upon thy name to-day—
Thou hero of the noblest plan.

O, patience! Felon of the hour!
   Over thy ghastly gallows-tree
   Shall climb the vine of Liberty,
With ripened fruit and fragrant flower.

Source: James Redpath, *Echoes of Harper's Ferry* (Boston: Thayer and Eldridge, 1860), 316.

John Andrew, "Speech at Tremont Temple," November 18, 1859

Two weeks before Brown's execution, John Andrew (1818–1867) joined Emerson and others at an event in Boston's Tremont Temple to raise funds for the condemned man's family. Tremont Temple was a kind of storefront Baptist church that stood a block from Boston Common. It was one of the only integrated churches in Boston, and it had a storied reputation among radicals. Almost every major abolitionist spoke there, including William Lloyd Garrison, Wendell Phillips, Gerrit Smith, Frederick Douglass, and Brown himself. Separating the man and his actions, Andrew declared in his speech that even if Brown's raid had been wrong, Brown himself was right. Andrew was originally from Maine and had been part of the antislavery society at Bowdoin College as a student. After graduating in 1837, he moved to Boston and became a lawyer. He joined the new antislavery Free Soil Party in 1848 and the Republican Party in the mid-1850s. After the Harpers Ferry raid, he spoke out in defense of Brown and raised funds for his legal defense and his family's support. Suspected of conspiring with Brown, he appeared before the Senate's Harpers Ferry Investigating Committee on February 9, 1860. He went on to serve as the governor of Massachusetts during the Civil War and lobbied Lincoln to enlist African Americans as soldiers in the Union Army.

John Brown and his companions in the conflict at Harper's Ferry, those who fell there and those who are to suffer upon the scaffold, are victims or martyrs to an idea. There is an irresistible conflict (*great applause)* between freedom and slavery, as old and as immortal as the irrepressible conflict between right and wrong. They are among the martyrs of that conflict.

I pause not now to consider, because it is wholly outside of the duty or the thought of this assembly tonight, whether the enterprise of John Brown and his associates in Virginia was wise or foolish, right or wrong; I only know that whether the enterprise itself was one or the other, John Brown himself is right *(Applause.)* I sympathize with the man. I sympathize with the idea because I sympathize with and believe in the eternal right. They who are dependent upon him, and his sons and his associates in the battle at Harper's Ferry, have a right to call upon us who have professed to believe, or who have in any manner or measure taught, the doctrine of the rights of man as applied to the colored slaves of the South, to stand by them in their bereavement, whether those husbands and fathers and brothers were right or wrong. *(Applause.)* And therefore we have met to take counsel together, and assist each other in the arrangement and apportionment of means for the purpose of securing to those widowed and bereaved wives and families the necessities of mere mortal existence, which the striking down of husbands and sons and brothers has left them bereft of. . . .

Standing in the valley of the shadow of death—looking, each man, from himself towards that infinite and eternal centre of life and love and power, the Infinite Father—all difference between us mortals and men becomes dwarfed into infinite littleness. We are tonight in the presence of a great and awful sorrow, which has fallen like a pall upon many families, whose hearts fail, whose affections are lacerated, and whose hopes are crushed—all of hope left upon earth destroyed by an event which, under the Providence of God, I pray may be overruled for that good which was contemplated and intended by John Brown himself.

Source: Speeches of John A. Andrew at Hingham and Boston (Boston: Republican State Committee, 1860), 8.

Charles Langston, "Letter to the Editor of the *Cleveland Plain Dealer*," November 18, 1859, and "Speech in Cleveland," December 2, 1859

Fearing indictment in the wake of Brown's raid, abolitionists released statements denying any involvement. But in a public letter, the black abolitionist Charles Langston (1817–1892) acknowledged that others were condemning the raid and insisted that Brown acted in accordance with biblical injunctions, Revolutionary principles, and abolitionist doctrine. Langston denied direct involvement but refused to deny his commitment to Brown's principles. Then, in his speech at a memorial service in Cleveland, held on the day of Brown's execution, Langston confessed that he never expected to pay tribute to a white man, and proclaimed that Brown was the only American citizen who had lived up to the Declaration of Independence. Like Brown, Langston had spent time in jail for antislavery activity. He was a leader in the Oberlin-Wellington rescue of September 1858, when a group of residents of Oberlin and Wellington, Ohio, rescued a fugitive slave, John Price, from a U.S. marshal who was trying to return him to the South. After seizing Price, the rescuers hid him in an Oberlin home and helped him to reach Canada. Thirty-seven men were indicted and jailed for their actions in the rescue, including Langston. He served twenty days in jail in the spring of 1859.

"Letter to the Editor of the *Cleveland Plain Dealer*"

Mr. Editor: Card writing seems to be the order of the day, particularly with reference to Capt. John Brown and his insurrectionary movements at Harper's Ferry. We have heard through the public journals from many of the great men and some of the great women who are said to be connected with the "bloody attempt to dissolve the Union," "to subvert and overturn the Government," "to push forward the irrepressible conflict," "and to incite the slaves of Virginia and Maryland to cut their masters' throats." Giddings, Hale, Smith, the Plumbs,[58] and others have denied any knowledge of, or connection with, the "mad scheme or its crazy perpetrators." Why the hasty denial? Why all this hot haste to throw off the imaginary disgrace or danger, which may grow out of complicity with this daring friend of Liberty and lover of mercy? Were the noble old hero and his brave and faithful followers engaged in a mean, selfish, and dastardly work? Were they "plotting crime" against the rights or liberties of any human being? Were they in Virginia to take the property or lives of men who respect the rights of life, liberty or property in others? Capt. Brown was engaged in no vile, base, sordid, malicious or selfish enterprise. His aims and ends were lofty, noble, generous, benevolent, humane and God-like. His actions were in perfect harmony with, and resulted from the teaching of the Bible, of our Revolutionary fathers and of every true and faithful antislavery man in this country and the world.

Does not the holy Bible teach that it is the duty of the strong and powerful to assist the weak and helpless, that the rich should succor the poor and needy? Does it not command us to remember those in bonds as being bound with them? Does it not tell us to loose the bonds of wickedness, undo the heavy burdens and let the oppressed go free? Does not the Bible plainly say, "whatsoever ye would that man shall do to you, do ye even so to them?" and further: "he that stealeth a man and selleth him or if he be found in his hand, he shall surely be put to death."[59]

Did not Capt. Brown act in consonance with these biblical principles and injunctions? He went into Virginia to aid the afflicted and the helpless, to assist the weak and to relieve the poor and needy. To undo the heavy burdens, to let the oppressed go free, to do to others as he would have them to do to him. And above all to put to death, as the papers tells us, those who steal men and sell them, and in whose hands stolen men are found. His actions then are only the results of his faithfulness to the plain teaching of the word of God.

The renowned fathers of our celebrated revolution taught the world that "resistance to tyrants is obedience to God," that all men are created equal, and have the inalienable right to life and liberty. They proclaim *death* but not *slavery,* or rather "give me liberty or give me death." They also ordained and established a constitution to secure the blessings of liberty to themselves and their *posterity.* (It is to be remembered that they have a large colored posterity in the Southern States.) And they further declared that when any government becomes destructive of these ends, namely life, liberty, justice and happiness, it is the right of the people to abolish it and to institute a new government.—On these pure and holy principles they fearlessly entered into a seven years' war against the most powerful nation of the earth, relying on a just God, whom they believed would raise up friends to fight their battles for them. Their belief was more than realized. The friends of freedom came to their assistance.

Did not Capt. Brown act in accordance with the foregoing revolutionary principles? Did not he obey God by resisting tyrants? Did he not in all things show his implicit faith in the equality of all men? and their unalienable right to life and liberty? When he saw that the governments of the South were destructive of these ends, did he not aim to abolish them and to institute a new government laying its foundation on such principles as to him seemed most likely to secure the happiness and safety of the people?

Some will say no doubt that the teaching of the renowned fathers had no reference to Negroes, for, says Judge Taney, the prevalent opinion at the time of the revolution was that "black men had no rights which white men were bound to respect."[60] In sober earnestness did the great and good men of those days which "tried men's souls,"[61] have no higher idea of liberty and the rights of man than that? Did they believe in one-sided, selfish, partial, sectarian freedom? Liberty for proud "Anglo-Saxon" and chains and fetters for "all the world and the rest of mankind."[62] I think they must have had a higher, a nobler idea of man and his inalienable rights. But be this as it may, the Abolitionists, the true friends of God and humanity, are applying both the doctrines of the Bible and the teaching of the fathers to every human being, whether white or black, bond or free. We Abolitionists profess to propagate no new doctrines in politics or morals, but to urge all men to practice the old well-defined and immutable principles "of the fatherhood of God and the universal brotherhood of man." Liberty and equality belong naturally to the entire brotherhood; and the man who takes from his brother his liberty, becomes a tyrant and thus forfeits his rights to *live*.

Now it is plain to be seen that Capt. Brown only carried out in his actions the principles emanating from these three sources, viz. First—The Bible. Second—The Revolutionary Fathers. Third—All good Abolitionists.

If, then, Brown acted on these pure and righteous principles, why are the friends of justice, liberty and right so hasty in denying all connections with him or sympathy with his ends and aims? Perhaps they see the bloody gallows of the "affrighted chivalry" rising before them in awful horror. Or more probably they see a political grave yearning to receive them."

But to speak of myself I have no political prospects and therefore no political fears! for my black face and curly hair doom me in this land of equality to political damnation and that beyond the possibility of redemption. But I have a neck as dear to me as Smith's, Hale's or Giddings', and therefore I must like them publish a card of denial. So here it is. But what shall I deny? I cannot deny that I feel that the very deepest sympathy with the Immortal John Brown in his heroic and daring efforts to free the slaves.—To do this would be in my opinion more criminal than to urge the slaves to open rebellion. To deny any connection with the "daring and fiendish plot" would be worse than nonsense. The *fearless chivalry* of the old dominion would move me guilty without the least difficulty. For their heroic imaginations now convert every harmless pillow into an infernal machine, behold the veritable Capt. Brown in every peaceable nonresistant northern abolitionist, and see in every colored man the dusky ghost of Gen. Nat Turner, the hero of Southampton.[63] So their testimony against me would be imaginary, their trial a farce, but their rope halter would be a stern and binding reality.

With these explanations and denials, I hope the Marshal of the Northern District of Ohio, the Federal Administration generally, and all slaveholders and particularly all official "smelling committees,"[64] will be fully satisfied.

"Speech in Cleveland"

I never thought that I should ever join in doing honor to or mourning for any American *white* man. Why should I honor the memory or mourn over the death of any of the white people of this land? Remember the bitter, burning wrongs the colored people have received at their bloody hands. We have been stolen, bought, sold, robbed, murdered; our sisters, mothers, wives, have been insulted, outraged, degraded, and almost this entire nation have aided in the perpetration of these crimes against us, or have honored the authors of our miseries with the emoluments of office, or have blessed and comforted them with the right hand of Christian fellowship. Again, so wide spread and well nigh universal is the feeling of negro-hate in this country, that I had nearly made up my mind never to find one of the dominant race true to the principles of human brotherhood; and I believe that no man is worthy the homage of a lover of freedom who cannot and does not see and acknowledge in every other man, whether white or black, an equal and a brother. I find in Capt. John

Brown, the hero of Harper's Ferry, a lover of mankind—not of any particular class or color, but of all men. He knew no complexional distinctions among God's rational creatures. He practically realized the truth, that "God created of one blood all the nations of men."[65] Therefore, I am here this evening to unite with you to do him honor, and to mourn over his premature and cruel death. But, to be more explicit, I honor John Brown, the martyr of the nineteenth century, first, because (as I have already intimated) he fully, really, practically and *actively* believed in the equality and brotherhood of man, that *all* men have a right to be free, that this right is inalienable, and that no law, no constitution, no religion, can take this right from the most degraded member of the human family. With him these declarations were no "rhetorical flourish," no "glittering generality," no absurd effusion of a fanatical and crazed imagination, no "self-evident lie," but maxims, aphorisms, axioms, truisms—simple, plain, practical, easy of application to each member of the great family of man. He sacrificed his life fearfully, cheerfully to his implicit faith in these great and overshadowing ideas of man's equality and his right to freedom. He is the only American citizen who has lived fully up to the Declaration of Independence. . . .

Suppose John Brown had jeopardized his life to save the friends, the brother, the sister, the child, the wife of any of the great men of this country—politicians, scholars or divines, from the jaws of slavery—even had he endangered his life to save an Irishman from the awful effects of British tyranny, or a Greek from the thralldom of Turkey, or a Hungarian from the despotism of Austria, meetings of honor and sympathy would have been held all over our land of chains and fetters. Words of praise would have gone forth from the press of all parties, and would have been echoed and re-echoed freely from the stump, the rostrum and the pulpit. Our God-forsaken churches, too, would have joined in the general chorus of unmeaning commemoration, and would have sent up prayers long, loud and hypocritical for the safety and preservation of his body and the salvation of his life. Had he been in a foreign land, Congress would have interfered. A man-of-war would have been dispatched for his protection. But he interfered in behalf of the brothers, sisters, children and wives of the wronged, despised, hated, enslaved poor of this Christian country; and for this interference, notwithstanding his acknowledged integrity, truthfulness, honesty, bravery and self-sacrificing heroism; the only favors this Republican country had to bestow on such a friend of man were a bloody capture, a hasty and farcical trial, and a legal murder. . . .

Allow me to say, in conclusion, that I mourn for the Hero of Ossawatomie, because with him died in me all hope for the slaves' redemption for the present. The bondman of our country must still clank his galling chains; must still drag out a life of unrequited toil. There is none to deliver him from the hands of the spoiler, who, like freedom's martyr, will be ready to give his life for the outcast, the needy, the crushed. Long may we cherish the name of Capt. John Brown with gratitude, admiration and love, and may we learn from his eventful but useful life to honor God by succoring and serving the poorest of his creatures. I fondly hope that the awfully solemn event, which has called together this large and imposing assembly, may be blessed to the cause of God and humanity, and may form a new era in the history of our guilty land.

Sources: Cleveland Plain Dealer, November 18, 1859; *A Tribute of Respect Commemorative of the Worth and Sacrifice of John Brown of Ossawatomie* (Cleveland: Published for the Benefit of the Widows and Families of the Revolutionists of Harper's Ferry, 1859), 17–20, 23.

Theodore Parker, "To Francis Jackson," November 24, 1859

Transcendentalist, abolitionist, and Unitarian minister, Theodore Parker (1810–1860) responded to the raid on November 24, 1859, with a letter to fellow abolitionist Francis Jackson. He was writing from Rome, where he had recently arrived in an attempt to recover from tuberculosis. Until he left for Italy in 1859, he had been minister of the 28th Congregational Society of Boston, with a congregation of several thousand (including Louisa May Alcott and William Lloyd Garrison). He had advocated violating the Fugitive Slave Law, supplied money to Free-State militias in Kansas in 1856, and financed Brown during his preparations for the raid in 1858 and 1859. Jackson, the letter's addressee, was the treasurer of the Boston Vigilance Committee, led by Parker, which aided resistance to the enforcement of the Fugitive Slave Law. Jackson's grandson, Francis Jackson Merriam, was one of Brown's raiders but escaped from the Ferry and went on to captain the Third South Carolina Colored Infantry during the Civil War. Parker's long letter to Jackson was published as a pamphlet in early 1860. In this excerpt, he celebrates Brown's raid as an extension of the American Anti-Slavery Society's nonviolent efforts—different in means but the same in their ends. He uses biblical imagery, the language of the Declaration of Independence, the memory of the American Revolution, and the idea of "natural right" to explain the inevitability of more violent attacks on slavery. A week later, in his final prison letter, which prophesied more "bloodshed," Brown unknowingly echoed Parker's acknowledgment that slavery would not end peacefully ("in less costly ink") but rather in blood. Parker died six months after writing this letter, at the age of forty-nine.

Rome, Nov. 24, 1859.

Of course, I was not astonished to hear that an attempt had been made to free the slaves in a certain part of Virginia, nor should I be astonished if another "insurrection" or "rebellion" took place in the State of ____, or a third in ____, or a fourth in ____. Such things are to be expected; for they do not depend merely on the private will of men like Capt. Brown and his associates, but on the great general causes which move all human kind to hate Wrong and love Right. Such "insurrections" will continue as long as Slavery lasts, and will increase, both in frequency and in power just as the people become intelligent and moral. Virginia may hang John Brown and all that family, but she cannot hang the HUMAN RACE; and until that is done noble men will rejoice in the motto of that once magnanimous State—*"Sic semper Tyrannis!"* "Let such be the end of every oppressor."[66]

It is a good Anti-Slavery picture on the Virginia shield—a man standing on a tyrant and chopping his head off with a sword;[67] only I would paint the sword-holder *black* and the tyrant *white,* to show the *immediate application* of the principle. The American people will have to march to rather severe music, I think, and it is better for them to face it in season. A few years ago it did not seem difficult first to check Slavery, and then to end it without any bloodshed. I think this cannot be done now, nor ever in the future. All the great charters of HUMANITY have been writ in blood. I once hoped that of American Democracy would be engrossed in less costly ink; but it is plain, now, that our pilgrimage must lead through a Red Sea, wherein many a Pharaoh will go under and perish.[68] Alas! that we are not wise enough to be just, or just enough to be wise, and so gain much at small cost!

Look, now, at a few notorious facts:

There are four million slaves in the United States violently withheld from their natural right to life, liberty, and the pursuit of happiness. Now, they are our fellow-countrymen—yours and mine, just as much as any four million *white* men. Of course, you and I owe them the duty which one man owes another of his own nation—the duty of instruction, advice, and protection of natural rights. If they are starving, we ought to help feed them. The color of their skins, their degraded social condition, their ignorance, abates nothing from their natural claim on us, or from our natural duty toward them.

There are men in all the Northern States who feel the obligation which citizenship imposes on them—the duty to help those slaves. Hence arose the ANTI-SLAVERY SOCIETY, which seeks simply to excite the white people to perform their natural duty to their dark fellow-countrymen. Hence comes CAPT. BROWN's EXPEDITION—an attempt to help his countrymen enjoy their natural right to life, liberty, and the pursuit of happiness.

He sought by violence what the Anti-Slavery Society works for with other weapons. The two agree in the end, and differ only in the means. Men like

Capt. Brown will be continually rising up among the white people of the Free States, attempting to do their *natural duty* to their black countrymen—that is, help them to freedom. . . . You and I prefer the peaceful method; but I, at least, shall welcome the violent if no other accomplish the end. So will the great mass of thoughtful and good men at the North; else why do we honor the Heroes of the Revolution, and build them monuments all over our blessed New England? I think you gave money for that of Bunker Hill: I once thought it a folly; now I recognize it as a great sermon in stone, which is worth not only all the money it cost to build it, but all the blood it took to lay its corner-stones. Trust me, its lesson will not be in vain—at the North, I mean, for the LOGIC OF SLAVERY will keep the South on its lower course, and drive it on more swiftly than before. "Capt. Brown's expedition was a failure," I hear it said. I am not quite sure of that. True, it kills fifteen men by sword and shot, and four or five men by the gallows.[69] But it shows the weakness of the greatest Slave State in America, the worthlessness of her soldiery, and the utter fear which Slavery genders in the bosoms of the masters. Think of the condition of the City of Washington while Brown was at work!

Brown will die, I think, like a martyr, and also like a saint. His noble demeanor, his unflinching bravery, his gentleness, his calm, religious trust in God, and his words of truth and soberness, cannot fail to make a profound impression on the hearts of Northern men; yes, and on Southern men. For "every human heart is human," &c.[70] I do not think the money wasted, nor the lives thrown away. Many acorns must be sown to have one come up; even then, the plant grows slow; but it is an oak at last. None of the Christian martyrs died in vain; and from Stephen, who was stoned at Jerusalem,[71] to Mary Dyer, whom our fathers hanged on a bough of "the great tree" on Boston Common,[72] I think there have been few spirits more pure and devoted than John Brown's, and none that gave up their breath in a nobler cause. Let the American State hang his body, and the American Church damn his soul; still, the blessing of such as are ready to perish will fall on him, and the universal justice of the Infinitely Perfect God will take him welcome home. The road to heaven is as short from the gallows as from the throne; perhaps, also, as easy.

I suppose you would like to know something about myself. Rome has treated me to bad weather, which tells its story in my health, and certainly does not mend me. But I look for brighter days and happier nights. The sad tidings from America—my friends in peril, in exile, in jail, killed, or to be hung—have filled me with grief, and so I fall back a little, but hope to get forward again. God bless you and yours, and comfort you!

Ever affectionately yours, Theodore Parker

Source: John Weiss, *Life and Correspondence of Theodore Parker: Minister of the Twenty-eighth Congregational Society, Boston,* Vol. 2 (New York: D. Appleton, 1864), 170–178 (172–173, 177–178).

Henry Clarke Wright, *The Natick Resolution,*
December 1859

Until Brown's raid and execution, the Reverend Henry Clarke Wright (1797–1870) was a Garrisonian abolitionist and active in the New England Non-Resistance Society. In 1859 he began advocating antislavery violence instead of nonresistance. He published an antislavery tract in December 1859 called *The Natick Resolution,* which soon became a leading document of militant abolitionism. The pamphlet was based on a resolution passed at a public meeting in the town of Natick, Massachusetts, on November 20, stating "that it is the right and duty of the slaves to resist their masters, and the right and duty of the people of the North to incite them to resistance, and to aid them in it." Wright's tract included letters to Republican senator Henry Wilson, William Lloyd Garrison, and Captain Avis, the keeper of the Charles Town jail, as well as the letters below to Brown and Governor Wise of Virginia. The tract defends violence, compares Brown to Christ, and argues that those who do not understand self-sacrifice call it madness.

Natick, Mass., Nov. 21st, 1859.

Capt. John Brown: Dear and Honored Friend—(for the friend of the slave is my dear and honored friend)—A very large, and enthusiastic meeting of the citizens of this town, without regard to political or religious creeds, was held last evening, for the purpose of considering and acting upon the following resolution:—

Whereas, Resistance to tyrants is obedience to God;[73] therefore,

Resolved, That it is the right and duty of the slaves to resist their masters, and the right and duty of the people of the North to incite them to resistance, and to aid them in it.

This resolution was adopted by the meeting without a dissenting voice. Though a United States Senator (Henry Wilson) and a United States Postmaster were present, yet not a voice was raised against it by them, nor by any one else, nor against the sentiments it contains. The meeting appointed me a committee to forward their resolution to you. In compliance with their request, and with the promptings of my own heart, I forward it.

The resolution, as you will see, simply affirms the right and duty of resistance, not merely to slavery as a principle or an abstraction, but to slaveholders, the living embodiment of slavery. The South embody slavery and resistance to liberty in their whole life. We would arouse the North to embody liberty and resistance to slavery in their whole life. Wherever the people of the south live, whether in domestic, social, ecclesiastical, political or commercial life, they embody *death to liberty*. We would stir up the people of the North to embody *death to slavery* wherever they live. In whatever relations they live, we would incite them to embody liberty as the South does slavery. *Death to slavery* should, and will, ere long, be the watchword of every domestic and social circle, of every political and religious party, and of every literary and commercial establishment, in the North.

The blessings of the God of the oppressed rest upon you! This is the prayer of thousands who have known you for years, and entirely sympathize with you in one great object of your life—*i.e.,* to arouse this nation to look the sin, the shame of slavery in the face. We have felt the deepest interest in your plans and movements, as we have known watched them the last four years; and we have wondered that those who hold to armed resistance to tyrants have not more cheerfully and numerously gathered around your standard of insurrection against slaveholders.

The government and God of this nation daily and hourly proclaim to the people of the North, and to the slaves of the South, their right and duty of armed resistance to slaveholders. You hastened to obey that call to duty made by your country and your God. Virginia herself called you to resist slaveholders, and to free the slaves, by arms and blood, if need be. Why should Virginia hang you? You have only done what she has exhorted you to do from the day of your birth.[74] Why should the North call you a "fanatic," a "maniac," a "ruffian," a "marauder," a "murderer," an "assassin"? You have only done what the religion, the government and God of the nation, for seventy years, proclaimed to be your right and your duty.

Twelve days hence, Virginia will hang your body, but she will not hang John Brown. Better to die a traitor to Virginia, than to live a traitor to yourself and your God. This nation of twenty-five million will kill your body for treason against them; but had you not done as you have, you would have died a living death for treason against God, as he spoke to you in the depths of your own soul. Acting in obedience to the dictates of your conscience and the behests of your God, you have rendered yourself worthy the honor and glory of a gallows at the hands of slaveholders, who live, not merely as pirates do, to plunder and kill, but for a purpose far more cruel and inhuman—*i.e.,* to turn human beings into chattels.

Who would not thus render himself deserving a gallows at such hands? The highest honor Virginia or the Union can bestow on the champion of liberty, and the living resistant of slavery, is a gallows. From this day, let the friends of the slave march forth to battle with slavery, whether the conflict be on the domestic, social, religious, political or military arena, under the symbol of the gallows, with the martyr and champion of liberty hanging on it.

You must die, as to your corporeal existence. Your visible, tangible presence will no more inspire and urge us onto the conflict; but John Brown, the MAN, the defender of liberty, the assailant of slavery, and the friend of the slave, will live and be with us, to inspire us, to incite us, to spur us up and lead us on to a still closer and more resolute and deadly assault upon slaveholding. You die, conscious that by the gallows you have triumphed, and answered the one great end of your life more effectually than you would have done had you run off thousands of slaves. You triumph by the gallows, not by running off slaves. The nation is aroused. It must now meet slavery face to face, and see it in its deformity and its results. In every department of life, it must meet it and fight it, till it dies, and liberty is "proclaimed throughout all the land, to all the inhabitants thereof."[75]

You dear friend, whose memory will ever be precious, as that of the slaveholder will ever be detested, have kept your anti-slavery faith; you have fought a good fight, and may say, "Henceforth there is laid up for me a crown of glory, which the Lord, the righteous Judge, will give me in the day when the last slave shall be free. Now, Lord, lettest thou thy servant depart in peace, for mine eyes have seen thy salvation."[76] Millions will follow thee, weeping, to the gallows. In pitying accents I hear thee say to them, "Friends of the slave! weep not for me, but weep for yourselves and your country; for in this conflict with slavery, there is not an attribute of the Almighty that can take sides with the oppressor."[77] Your execution is but the beginning of that death struggle with slaveholders, which must end in striking the last fetter from the last slave. On the scaffold, thou wilt hear thy God, and the slave's God, saying unto thee, "Fear not, for I am with thee; be not dismayed, for I am thy God; I have chosen thee; thou art my servant; I will strengthen thee; I will help thee; yea, I will uphold thee with the right hand of my righteousness. All they that were incensed against thee shall be ashamed and confounded; they shall be as nothing; they that strive with thee shall perish; the whirlwind shall scatter them."[78] My spirit is with thy spirit, in the dungeon and on the scaffold.

Thine, for the slave, and against the slaveholder, unto death,

Henry C. Wright

Boston, Friday, Dec. 2d, 1859

To Henry A. Wise, Governor of Virginia: Sir—This is the day and this the hour in which John Brown is being hanged by you. His dead body is now hanging on a gallows, and the eyes of twenty-five millions of this nation are fixed upon it. You erected that gallows, you dragged him to it, you tied that rope around his neck, you bound his hands and his feet, you drew that cap over his eyes, and having thus rendered him blind and helpless, you broke his neck.

At fifteen minutes past eleven o'clock, A.M., this day, you murdered John Brown! The entire nation saw you do it, and is a witness against you. Yourself, Virginia, and the nation, at this hour, adjudge you a murderer.

Why did you hang him? This is the one thought of the nation. You must answer it. How? You yourself have pronounced him one of "the truest, bravest, most sincere and noble" men you ever saw.[79] You and your accomplices in this deed of blood assure us that the nation contained not a more "sincere, honest, heroic and conscientious man."[80] Why, then, did you kill him?

Had he made an effort to rescue you, your wife and daughters, your mother and sisters from slavery and from the vengeance, the wrath, the rape and rapine of your slaves, would you have hung him? No. But he sought to rescue slaves from the wrath, rape and rapine of yourself and your fellow slave-breeders and slave-traders, and you killed him. Had he done for you and them the very deeds for which you have hung him, you and they would have pronounced him innocent, and crowned him with glory.

Your slaves have as good a right to enslave you, as you have to enslave them.

They have as good a right to scourge your naked back, to drive you to unpaid toil, to sell you as a beast, to shoot you and tear you to pieces with bloodhounds, if you run away, as you have to do these things to them. They have as good a right to subject your wife and daughters, and your mother and sisters, to their passions, as you have to subject theirs to yours. They have as good a right to perpetrate robbery, murder, rape and rapine upon you and your confederates in slave-breeding and slave-trading, and upon your wives and children, as you have to perpetrate like outrages upon them. They have as good a right to defend themselves and families against you and your associates in plunder and rapine, as you have to defend yourselves against them. You and your co-workers in crime call on the North to come down and defend you and your families against your slaves. They come and defend you, and you thank them. The slaves call on John Brown to come down and deliver them and their families from your lusts and your cruelties, and defend their property, their liberties and lives against you. You say it is the duty of the North to defend you against the slaves. John Brown and his God told him it was his duty to defend the slaves against you. He came to Virginia to do so, and for doing his duty, you have hung him. Are you not a *murderer?*

What says Virginia of your deed? The slaves and all the world look on the seal with which, as Governor of the State, you stamp your letters and all public documents. What do they see? VIRGINIA, standing with one foot on the neck of a prostrate SLAVEHOLDER, whose head she has just cut off, and holding in her right hand the sword with which she did the deed, all reeking with his blood. Proud and exultant she stands, and in the consciousness of having done a meritorious deed, by ridding the world of a monster and Humanity of its most malignant foe, she challenges the homage of all for what she has done, and in her pride of victory exclaims:—*Sic semper tyrannis*—"Thus always deal with slaveholders"—*i.e.,* cut their heads off.[81]

Thus Virginia, the State over which you are so proud to preside, says to your slaves, and to all slaves in the State, and in the United States, and in all the world—"CUT OFF YOUR MASTERS' HEADS." Not content with mere words, she *pictures* to them her own proud achievement, and calls on them to look at her in the very act of vanquishing her direst foe, and of beheading him; thus *inciting* them, by an appeal to the eye as well as to the ear, to resistance, to insurrection, and to blood.

In her Constitution, Virginia says to her slaves; "You are born as free as are your masters, and have the same God-given right to your earnings, to your-selves, your wives, husbands, children and homes as they have." She is ever sounding in the ears of the slaves—"Give me liberty or give me death!"—"Resistance to *slaveholders* is obedience to God." All the slaveholders and white men and women in Virginia are ever saying to the slaves, "If you, or any others, were to do unto us as we are daily and hourly doing unto you, we would kill, slay and destroy you. If we were in your places, we would kill every man, woman and child that should attempt to prevent us from getting and main-taining our freedom." Thus your State appeals to the slaves, to *incite* them to a bloody insurrection.

You, sir, make this appeal to the slaves, and to the people of the North. You flaunt this most ferocious and bloodthirsty prayer in their faces every time you set your official seal to a commission, a warrant, a draft, a law, or any document: By this act, your prayer to the slave is, "Arise! and cut off the heads of all slaveholders!"—and you invoke the North to come and help them. John Brown heard your prayer, and the prayer of Virginia. In answer to it, he came to Harper's Ferry. He there sought to rescue men and women from the condi-tion of brutes and chattels, and to restore to them their God-given and State-acknowledged rights. He did not aim to do the bloody deed to slaveholders which you and Virginia exhorted him to do—*i.e.*, BEHEAD THEM! No; he was kind to the tyrants, to his own injury. He simply sought to lead some slaves, imbruted by you and your copartners in crime, to a land of freedom. By your official seal and Constitution, and your historical reminiscences, you invited John Brown to come to Harper's Ferry and run off slaves and to kill all who should oppose him. You and Virginia, declared that it was the right and duty of the slaves to rise against their masters, and to gain their freedom by running away, or by beheading their oppressors; and you told him it was his right and duty to help them. John Brown came, with twenty-one assistants, to help him in a work which you and all Virginia acknowledge would have been a work of love, justice, and humanity, had it been done to free you from slavery. You mustered the State, called on the United States to hasten to your aid, sur-rounded the self-forgetting hero and his little band, and shot or hung them, deeming that you did a brave and heroic act! You mustered the State and na-tion to the defence of your property, your wives and children, your houses and lives, against twenty-one men, who had no thought of harm to you, but sim-ply thought to give freedom to slaves. Such bravery must, one day, be appreciated. He was as innocent as were Washington, Lafayette, Franklin, Jefferson, Hancock, and Patrick Henry, and far more deserving the approval of mankind.[82] You took him, bound him hand and foot, blindfolded him, and then broke his neck! Yourself and Virginia being witnesses, are you not a MURDERER? Verily, you have your reward!

Why have you and Virginia hung John Brown? To defend your property (your slaves), your liberty and lives, against robbery and murder; and your wives and daughters, your mothers and sisters, against rape and rapine. And not being able to defend yourselves, you and Virginia called on the United States to come and help you. You do, then, hold that it is a right and duty to shoot and hang and behead people in defence of liberty, life and home?

You, then, and Virginia, being witnesses, it is the right and duty of the slaves to defend their earnings, their liberty and lives, by arms and blood; and their wives and daughters against the rapine of their masters. You and your fellow slave-breeders and slave-traders live by robbing slaves of their labor, by invading their homes, and ravishing their wives, daughters and sisters, and plundering their nurseries and cradles; and by murdering them, if they attempt to defend themselves and their families. So, in the very act of hanging Brown to defend yourself, you justify him in doing the deed for which you hang him!

Slaves of the South! People of the North! Look at the commission of Judge Parker, who sentenced Brown to be hung; look at the commission of General Taliaferro, who heads the troops of Virginia and of the United States, now surrounding the gallows on which hangs his murdered body; open the commission of Captain Avis, the jailor, and of Sheriff Campbell, who now stand by that murdered body! Whose name is on all these? Not that of Henry A. Wise, Governor of Virginia. What seal is that? VIRGINIA—her foot on the prostrate and headless form of a slaveholder!

Once more: that DEATH-WARRANT! Look at it! The name of Henry A. Wise is there. What is the import of that seal? To the slaves it says: Arise! Cut off your masters' heads! Kill, slay and destroy all who would enslave you, or molest you in your efforts to secure your freedom!" To John Brown it says, "Hasten to Harper's Ferry; incite the slaves to run away, and help them to exterminate all who shall attempt to impede their exodus!"

Thus, in the very death-warrant under which Brown is hung, you and Virginia pronounce him innocent of all evil, and justify the very deed for which you hang him. In every way, you pronounce him guiltless. Yet, you have hung him! Are you not a murderer? Yes! Henry A. Wise and Virginia being witnesses. Yes! the heart, the conscience, the reason and history of the nation being witnesses. Yes! by the testimony of mankind, and by the voice of God.

Dream not that John Brown will appear in this world's history as "a fool," "a fanatic," "a robber," "a ruffian," "a madman," "a monomaniac," "a marauder," or "a murderer." His plan was formed in wisdom and righteousness; and was executed in purest justice, goodness and benevolence, according to the religion and government of Virginia, and of the United States; and according to the convictions of ninety-nine out of every hundred of the people.

What was his object? To arouse the nation to consider the sin, the shame, and the danger of slavery, with a view to its abolition. What was his plan of action? RUNNING SLAVES OFF, or *dying* in the attempt. Either would answer his purpose. This he knew, and was prepared for the alternative. Death at your hands overtook him in the attempt, and when in the act of breaking his neck, your word was heard throughout the land, saying, "Surely, this is a just man!" Has he failed? Never was the life of man—death, rather—a more complete success.

What has been the one ruling thought of Virginia, and of every slave State, and of the Union, the past two months? John Brown and Harper's Ferry! What the one spoken and unspoken word of the entire nation? John Brown and Harper's Ferry! The one pulsation of the nation's heart has been—John Brown and him hung, *for seeking to free slaves!* John Brown, *the friend of the slave,* has edited every paper, presided over every domestic and social circle, over every prayer, conference and church meeting, over every pulpit and platform, and over every Legislative, Judicial and Executive department of government; and he will edit every paper, and govern Virginia and all the States, and preside over Congress, guide its deliberations, and control all political caucuses and elections, for one year to come.

In a word, John Brown and him hung will be the one thought of the nation; and John Brown and him hung for *"bearing the yoke of the oppressed as if upon his own neck,"*[83] is now, and will continue to be, the one deep and humiliating feeling that will fill every heart with grief, sadness, shame, indignation and loathing. John Brown has triumphed; and that, too, according to his expectations, in death.

You have murdered him; but you, Virginia, and the nation, retire from the bloody deed a thousand-fold more impotent to defend slavery than you were before. You have murdered his body; but John Brown holds you, Virginia, the nation, and slavery, in his firm, determined grasp, more completely than he ever did before.

May John Brown and him hung be to you, Virginia, and the nation, what Christ and him crucified was to his executioner "A savor of life unto life, and not of death unto death!"[84]

Thine, for eternal life to freedom, and a speedy death to slavery,

Henry C. Wright

Source: *The Natick Resolution; or, Resistance to Slaveholders the Right and Duty of Southern Slaves and Northern Freeman* (Boston: Printed for the Author, 1859), 3–6, 11–16.

Albany Evening Journal, "The Execution of John Brown," December 1, 1859

In the days leading up to Brown's execution, newspapers North and South debated the wisdom of Governor Wise's decision to push ahead with the death sentence. Numerous articles observed that by hanging Brown, the governor risked making a martyr. This editorial in the *Albany Evening Journal*, New York State's second leading Republican journal, after the *Tribune*, declares the execution a call to arms for other insane agitators. By executing Brown, it insists, Virginia makes him a martyr and exacerbates sectional tension. Founded in 1830 as an anti-Masonic newspaper and edited by Thurlow Weed, a close friend of the abolitionist senator William H. Seward, the newspaper was against slavery. It had protested the Fugitive Slave Law and supported the prohibition of slavery in new territories. But Weed and his newspaper condemned Brown's actions. Democrats claimed that the Republican Party was responsible for the raid, and numerous Republican politicians and newspapers tried to distance themselves from Brown. The Republican newspapers that did praise Brown as a hero and martyr included the *Kingston Democratic Journal* (New York), the *Concord Independent Democrat* (New Hampshire), the *Newburyport Daily Herald* (Massachusetts), the *Springfield Republican* (Massachusetts), and the *Winsted Herald* (Connecticut).

We regret that Gov. Wise persists in his determination to hang John Brown. Neither the dignity nor the safety of the State of Virginia requires any such sanguinary termination of the insane raid at Harper's Ferry. The exercise of "Justice tempered with Mercy" would prove far more effective in correcting public sentiment and in mollifying public sympathy. But the temper of the people and of the Executive of Virginia forbids the hope of any such thing. John Brown, and his associates, will all be hung. Instead of being remembered as imprisoned criminals, they will be shrined as martyrs; and their acts, instead of being characterized as insurrectionary and murderous, will be tortured into deeds of chivalric heroism. Their execution will greatly increase the sympathy felt for them, and do more to intensify "agitation" than the arrest and imprisonment of ten thousand men, insane and criminal enough to attempt to run off negroes from the South.

Already, the muttered thunder of a pent-up sympathy is heard. The pulpit, the platform and the press, have already spoken with most intense emphasis. We publish, in other columns today, a few specimens of what has been said. But should John Brown be hung, the feeling will be augmented an hundred fold; and hatred of Slavery will become the predominant emotion in the breasts of millions who have thus far had neither fellowship nor sympathy with those who seek to goad the South into just such exhibitions of weakness and folly as these executions will afford.

This termination of this criminal foray is to be depreciated. Wiser counsels should have prevailed. But they have not; and Gov. Wise will, by his sanguinary persistence, feed a flame which the exercise of mercy and common sense would have effectually smothered.

Source: Albany Evening Journal, December 1, 1859.

"Pittsburgh, Detroit, and Cleveland Resolutions," November 29 and December 2, 1859

Immediately before Brown's death and on the day of his execution, African American communities met in churches and halls across the North and honored him as a hero and martyr. On November 29 a group met at an African Methodist Episcopal Church in Pittsburgh. The attendees passed a set of resolutions, called for black businesses and schools to close on December 2, and collected money for Brown's family. The leaders of the meeting included Rufus S. Jones, who later captained a black militia in Pittsburgh and offered its services to the Union; Benjamin T. Tanner, a clergyman and the editor of the AME Church's *Christian Recorder;* and John C. Peck, a *Liberator* agent and one of the organizers of the 1841 State Convention of the Colored Freemen of Pennsylvania. A few days later, on December 2, African Americans gathered in Detroit to celebrate "Martyr's Day." Businesses closed early, men and women wore black armbands, and a meeting convened at the Second Baptist Church. George Hannibal Parker, the president of the Old Capt. John Brown Liberty League, chaired the meeting, and William Lambert, a black antislavery leader in Michigan, read a set of resolutions. The participants agreed that the members of several black churches should be dressed in mourning for thirty days and collected $25 for Mary Brown. In Ohio, the state where Brown had spent long periods of his life, a more interracial crowd of 1400 people went to Cleveland's Melodeon Hall on the day of his execution. The hall was draped in mourning, and a photograph of Brown was displayed on the stage next to banners that quoted his final speech to the court. Members of the organizing committee included Charles Langston, a black abolitionist; Judge Rufus P. Spalding, an Ohio Republican and Free-Soiler; Judge Daniel R. Tilden, an Ohio Republican and one of Brown's prison correspondents; and the Christian spiritualist John Henry Watson Toohey. After the passage of a set of resolutions, Spalding declared that Brown's "immolation upon the altar of Slavery" had given energy to the cause of freedom, and Tilden declared that abolitionists must "baptize ourselves into the spirit of John Brown" to defeat slavery.

Pittsburgh Resolutions

We, the colored people of Pittsburgh and vicinity, assembled in Wylie Street Church, Nov. 29, 1859, acknowledge in the person of John Brown a hero, patriot, and Christian—a hero because he was fearless to defend the poor; a patriot because he loves his countrymen; and a Christian because he loves his neighbor as himself, and remembered those in bonds as bound with them, Therefore, be it

Resolved, That in his death we feel that, with Caiaphas, "it needs be that one man die for the people."[85]

Resolved, That we sincerely believe in the old maxim, that "the blood of the martyrs is the seed for the church."[86]

Resolved, That we see in the Harper's Ferry affair what Daniel Webster saw when speaking of Crispus Attucks, the black Revolutionary martyr who fell in Boston—viz. the severance of two antagonistic principles.[87]

Resolved, That John Brown, in taking up arms to liberate the slaves, only acted upon the maxim that "resistance to tyrants is obedience to God."

Resolved, That upon next Friday, December 2d, the day upon which he is to be executed, we close our places of business between the hours of ten and three o'clock; that a sermon be preached at 11 o'clock A.M., in the A.M.E. Church, and that appropriate services be held in the evening of the same place at which time a collection shall be raised in behalf of Capt. Brown's family.

Resolved, That the teachers of our public schools be requested to suspend service on that day.

Resolved, That, in the event of the execution of John Brown upon the 2d of December, the anniversary of that day be hereafter perpetually observed among us as a day of humiliation and prayer.

Detroit Resolutions

Whereas, We, the oppressed portion of this community, many of whom have worn the galling chains and felt the smarting lash of slavery, and know by sad experience its brutalizing effects upon both the body and the mind, and its damaging influence upon the soul of its victim, and

Whereas, We, by the help of Almighty God and the secret abolition movements that are now beginning to develop themselves in the southern part of this country, have been enabled to escape from the prison-home of slavery, and partially to obtain our liberty; and having become personally acquainted with the life and character of our much beloved and highly esteemed friend, Old Capt. John Brown, and his band of valiant men, who, at Harper's Ferry, on the 16th day of October, 1859, demonstrated to the world this sympathy and fidelity to the cause of the suffering slaves of this country, by bearding the hydra headed monster, Tyranny, in his den, and by his bold, effective, timely blow is now causing the South to tremble with a moral earthquake as he totally and freely delivered up his life to lay as a ransom for our enslaved race and thereby, "solitary and alone," he has put a liberty ball in motion which shall continue to roll and gather strength until the last vestige of human slavery within this nation shall have been crushed beneath the ponderous weight, Therefore,

Resolved, That we hold the name of Old Capt. John Brown in the most sacred remembrance, now the first disinterested martyr for our liberty, whereupon the true Christian principle of his Divine Lord and Master, has freely delivered up his life for the liberty of our race in this country. Therefore will we ever vindicate his character through all coming time, as our temporal redeemer whose name shall never die,

Resolved, That, as the long lost rights and liberties of an oppressed people are only gained in proportion as they act in their own cause, therefore are we now loudly called upon to arouse to our own interest, and to concentrate our efforts in keeping the Old Brown liberty-ball in motion and thereby continue to kindle the fires of liberty upon the altar of every determined heart among men and continue to fan the same until the proper time, when a revolutionary blast from liberty's trump shall summon them simultaneously to unite for victorious and triumphant battle.

Resolved, That we tender our deepest and most heart felt sympathy to the family of Capt. John Brown in their sad bereavement, and pledge to them that they shall ever be held by us as our special friends, in whose welfare we hope ever to manifest a special interest.

Cleveland Resolutions

Whereas, The "peculiar institution" has this day made strikingly manifest its baneful influence upon the "rights of man," by inflicting the death penalty at Charlestown, in Virginia, upon John Brown of Ossawatomie, for a conscientious observance of the law of brotherhood, as inculcated by Jesus Christ, and the law of freedom as taught by Thomas Jefferson:

Resolved, That the system of negro slavery as it now exists in some of the

States of the American Confederacy, is but the "experiment of despotism,"[88] which lives upon concessions, and becomes lusty upon conciliations and compromises. It is, in the words of Wesley, "the sum of all villainies,"[89] and can only be subdued by giving it, in southern parlance, "war to the knife, with the knife to the hilt."

Resolved, That the State of Virginia, under the lead of Henry A. Wise, is a contemptible caricature of the "Old Dominion" in the days of George Washington and George Mason. She was once aptly called "the Mother of Presidents." She may now, with equal propriety, be termed "the Mother of Slaves." She is afflicted with frightful visions of armed invaders, and with a luxuriantly guilty conscience, her chivalry flee when pursued by shadows. They are ready to cry out with the "Humpback"—

"By the Apostle Paul, shadows tonight
Have struck more terror to the soul of Richard
Than could the substance of ten thousand soldiers
Armed in proof."[90]

Resolved,[91] That for their conduct in the Harper's Ferry war, when "one man chased a thousand,"[92] and in the sequel to that war, when "ten thousand" put the "one man" to death, the spurs should be hacked from the heels of the chivalry of Virginia; the bearings on their State shield reversed; and, instead of the prostrate despot with his broken manacles, and the spirit-stirring motto, "Sic Semper Tyrannis,"[93] their heraldic devices should be fetters, handcuffs and bowstrings, with a "Son of Liberty" on a gibbet, bearing the significant inscription "Degeneres Animos Timor Arguit."[94]

Resolved, That it was in exact keeping with the character and conduct of the citizens of South Carolina, who had furnished a bully to beat down Freedom's Champion in the Senate Chamber,[95] to furnish a halter to hang Freedom's Champion at Harper's Ferry. The people of the North have "food for reflection."

Resolved, That we fully agree in sentiment with those fathers of the Republic who, before the adoption of the Constitution, and while that instrument was undergoing examination, patriotically exclaimed "however desirable a union of these States may be, the preservation of our liberties is still more desirable." We have, by force of circumstances, become convinced that the "irrepressible conflict" is upon us,[96] and that it will never terminate until "Freedom or Slavery go to the wall." In such a contest, and under such a dire necessity, we say, "without fear and without reproach," let Freedom stand though the Union be dissolved!

We further say, that any religion that sanctions or apologizes for a government that authorizes Human Slavery, and legalizes murder, is barbarous in spirit, evil in tendency, and in virtual fellowship with the "sum of all villainies."

Resolved, That John Brown, who, in his life was a thorn in the side of the oppressor, has, in his death become to the Slave Power "more terrible than an army with banners."[97] His eulogy is best spoken by his executioner.—"He possesses the greatest integrity, truthfulness, and courage, that I ever met."[98]

Resolved, That however much we may lament the death of the devoted Brown, we are satisfied that his execution will bring confusion upon his enemies, and do more to overthrow the bulwarks of Slavery than a long life of philanthropic deeds with a peaceful exit. We honor his memory! Posterity will give him a monument as indestructible as their aspirations for FREEDOM.

Sources: Weekly Anglo-African, December 17, 1859; A Tribute of Respect Commemorative of the Worth and Sacrifice of John Brown of Ossawatomie (Cleveland: Published for the Benefit of the Widows and Families of the Revolutionists of Harper's Ferry, 1859), 7–9.

Henry Highland Garnet, "Martyr's Day," December 2, 1859

By noon on December 2, John Brown was dead. Later that day, Henry Highland Garnet (1815–1882) gave a sermon at Shiloh Presbyterian Church in New York City, where he had served as pastor since 1855. Echoing Brown's last prison letter, written that morning, Garnet's sermon adapts Hebrews 9:22: "Without shedding of blood is no remission." Garnet was born a slave in Maryland, escaped to Pennsylvania in 1824, and became a leading black abolitionist. In 1843 he gave his most famous speech, calling on slaves to rebel, shed blood, and achieve liberty. In 1848, Brown gave money to reprint the speech as a pamphlet along with David Walker's *Appeal to the Coloured Citizens of the World* (1829). He met with Garnet in March 1858. Garnet remained as pastor of the Shiloh Presbyterian until 1861 and returned between 1870 and 1881. He died in Liberia in 1882.

Christian Friends and Fellow Countrymen: The day has come in which the nation is about to suffer a great crime to be perpetrated against the cause of liberty. Today John Brown is to offer up his life a sacrifice for the sake of justice and equal human rights. Henceforth the second day of December will be called "MARTYR'S DAY." I am not a man of blood. I hold human life to be sacred, and would spare even a man-stealer, if he stood not in the bondman's path to freedom. Often have I indulged the hope of seeing slavery abolished without the shedding of blood; but that hope is clouded. In the signs of the times I see the dreadful truth, written as by the finger of Jehovah—"*For the sins of this nation there is no atonement without the shedding of blood.*" If it must come, O God! prepare us to meet it. The nation needed to see a picture of the future of slavery and its ends, and methinks God has been pleased to draw it in crimson lines. Americans, Patriots, Christians, Tyrants, look upon it, and be instructed. Is it not a singular coincidence that in Virginia, the very soil upon which African slavery in this part of the New World commenced its reign of terror, the system should receive its first most damaging blow. They may murder John Brown, but the blow is struck, and the slave power feels the shock. His work is done, and God's purposes in him are executed, and the divine voice bids him to come up higher. When he dies, he will leave behind him no greater apostle of liberty in all the land. His name and glorious deeds shall be cherished by the good and brave, and his widow and fatherless children shall be adopted by the whole army of the Sons of Freedom. Tyrants and despots will everywhere upbraid us for inflicting so ghastly a wound on the fair brow of Liberty, in a land nicknamed the "Model Republic."

The withered hand of an old man, whose hairs are white with the frosts of nearly seventy winters,[99] has given the death-blow to American slavery. His heroic deeds will be inscribed on marble, and his grave will be visited by troops of pilgrims. Virginia will be famed in history for having been the home of Washington and the theatre of John Brown's cowardly execution. Farewell, brave old man! God be with thee. Step forth from the scaffold, which cannot dishonor thy name or tarnish thy glory, into the chariot of fire that awaits thee. Go up to meet the army of departed heroes that have gone before thee to the Kingdom of Heaven. Go, and with joy receive thy martyr's crown, which the Lord has prepared for thee. Succeeding ages will cherish thy memory, and do justice to thy deeds of renown; and thy amazing courage will be the fruitful theme of orators and the glowing songs of poets. Hero-martyr, farewell!

Source: Weekly Anglo-African, December 10, 1859.

J. Sella Martin and William Lloyd Garrison, "Speeches at Tremont Temple," December 2, 1859

Several abolitionists who aligned themselves with William Lloyd Garrison's nonviolent abolitionist tactics led commemorations and celebrations of Brown after his execution, including Wendell Phillips, James Miller McKim, Richard D. Webb, and Garrison himself. In Boston on December 2, an interracial crowd of four thousand people gathered in and around Tremont Temple. The Unitarian minister James Freeman Clarke read from the Bible, Samuel Sewall offered remarks, and a collection for Brown's family reached $235. A photograph of Brown was on display next to a cross. Placards around the hall quoted Brown, the Bible, Jefferson, and Patrick Henry. John Sella Martin (1832–1876) gave one of the main addresses. Martin was Tremont Temple's temporary preacher and the congregation's first black pastor. Born a slave in Charlotte, North Carolina, he escaped from slavery in Mississippi to Chicago in 1856 and went on to become the pastor of Joy Street Baptist Church in Boston, then Shiloh Presbyterian Church in New York, where his friend Henry Highland Garnet also served. His address on December 2 described the horrors of slavery, compared Brown to John the Baptist, termed him a "meteor," and used metaphors of disease and surgery. Brown shed blood as the nation's physician, Martin explained—he cut out the cancer of slavery. Speaking after Martin at the same Tremont Temple event, Garrison (1805–1879) also endorsed Brown's attempt. A founder of the American Anti-Slavery Society and one of the country's most famous abolitionists, Garrison had initially referred to the raid as a "well-intended but sadly misguided effort." But on December 2 he declared that Brown embodied the spirit of 1776 and explained that in spite of his own nonresistant stance, he embraced any attempt at slave insurrection and saw every slave as a potential John Brown. The speech, which Garrison published in his abolitionist newspaper, *The Liberator*, several weeks later, marked a rhetorical shift toward accepting antislavery violence.

J. Sella Martin

Mr. President, Ladies and Gentlemen—Today, a solemn question has been asked this nation. The Pilate of Providence has asked America—"Whom will you that I deliver unto you—the Barabbas of Slavery, or the John Brown of Freedom?" And, intimidated by the false majesty of despotic enactments, which have usurped the place of Christianity, corrupted a false policy, and stung to frenzy by the insinuations of our political high priests, we have cried out, as a nation, "Release unto us the Barabbas of slavery, and destroy John Brown."[100] And, true to this horrible, this atrocious request, John Brown has been offered up. Thank God, he said, "I am ready to be offered up!"

Men say that his life was "a failure." I remember the story of one of the world's moral heroes, whose life was just such a "failure." I remember one who, having retired to the deserts of Judea, to wring from the hard, stony life of those deserts the qualifications, and with all this purity, was brought into a corrupt and voluptuous court. I remember, too, that in that court, notwithstanding he was its favorite, notwithstanding the corruption and luxury of the times, he preserved himself the same stern man, and said to the King, "It is not lawful for you to live with your brother Phillip's wife."[101] These were the stern words of John the Baptist and John Brown, for John Brown, like John the Baptist, retired into the hard and stony desert of Kansas, and there, by the weapons of heroism, by the principles of freedom, and the undaunted courage of a man, wrung from the bloody soil the highest encomiums of Freedom and the most base acknowledgements of slavery, that the one was right and the other wrong. *(Applause)*. I know that John Brown, in thus rebuking our public in, in thus facing the monarch, has had to bear just what John the Baptist bore. His head today, by Virginia, that guilty maid of a more guilty mother, the American Government *(cheers, mingled with a few hisses, which were at once drowned in an outburst of vehement applause)*, has been cut off, and it has been presented to the ferocious and insatiable hunger, the terrible and inhuman appetite, of this corrupt government.[102] Today, by the telegraph, we have received the intelligence that John Brown has forfeited his life—all this honesty, all this straight-forwardness, all this self-sacrifice, which has been manifested in Harper's Ferry.

My friends, his life was just such a "failure" as all great movements have been. The physical failure has been the death of the seed, externally, which has given life to the germ, which has sprung forth to spread its moral boughs all over this corrupt nation. *(Applause)*. I have not the slightest doubt that this will be the result. His life was a "failure," but it was such a failure (and I care not though the Boston *Courier* take offence at the comparison as irreverent)[103] and History will place it in the same category as the Cross, where Jesus died, and moral life came forth to the world. *(Applause)*. John Brown has died, but the life of Freedom, from his death, shall flow forth to this nation.

I know that there is some quibbling, some querulousness, some fear, in reference to an out-and-out endorsement of his course. Men of peace principles object to it, in consequence of their religious conviction; politicians in the North object to it, because they are afraid that it will injure their party; pro-slavery men in the South object to it, because it has touched their dearest idol; but I am prepared, my friends (and permit me to say, this is not the language of rage), I am prepared, in the light of all Christian principle, to approve of the *end. (Applause)*. I say this is not the language of rage, because I remember that our Fourth-of-July orators sanction the same thing; because I remember that Concord, and Bunker Hill, and every historic battlefield in this country, and the celebration of those events, all go to approve the means that John Brown has used; the only difference being, that in our battles, in America, means have been used for *white* men and that John Brown has used his means for *black* men. *(Applause)*. And I say, that so far as principle is concerned, so far as the sanctions of the Gospel are concerned, I am prepared to endorse this end; and I endorse it because God Almighty has told us that we should feel with them that are in bonds as being bound with them. I endorse his end, because every single instinct of our nature rises and tells us that is right. I find an endorsement of the principles that governed him in going to Virginia, in the presence of the men and women who have come here to listen to his eulogy, and sympathize with his suffering family. I know that all have not come for that purpose, but I know there are seven thousand still in Israel who have not bowed the knee to the political Baal.[104] *(Loud Applause)*.

Now, I bring this question down to the simple test of the Gospel; and, agreeing with those men who say the sword should not be used, agreeing with them in that principle, and recognizing its binding obligation upon us all, yet I believe in that homeopathic principle which operates by mercury when mercury is in the system, and that that which is supported by the sword should be overthrown by the sword. I look at this question as a peace man. I say, in accordance with the principles of peace, that I do not believe the sword should be unsheathed. I do not believe the dagger should be drawn, until there is in the system to be assailed such terrible evidences of its corruption, that it becomes the *dernier* resort.[105] And my friends, we are not to blame the application of the instrument, we are to blame the disease itself. When a physician for the use of the knife; but the impure blood, the obstructed veins, the disordered system, that have caused the cancer, and rendered the use of the instrument necessary. The physician has but chosen the least of two evils. So John Brown chose the least of two evils. To save the country, he went down to cut off the Virginia cancer. *(Applause).*

I say, that I am prepared to endorse John Brown's course fully. He has said that he did not intend to shed blood. In my opinion, speaking as a military critic, this was one of the faults of his plan. In not shedding blood, he left the slaves uncertain how to act; so that the North has said that the Negroes there are cowards. They are not cowards, but great diplomats. When they saw their masters in possession of John Brown, in bonds like themselves, they would have been perfect fools has they demonstrated any willingness to join him. They have got sense enough to know, that until there is a perfect demonstration that the white man is their friend—a demonstration bathed in blood—it were foolishness to cooperate with them. They have learned this much from the treachery of white men at the North, and the cruelty of the white men at the South, that they cannot trust the white man, even when he comes to deliver them. So it was not their cowardice, not their craven selfishness, but it was their caution, that prevented them from joining Brown. I say this because I think it is necessary to vindicate the character of the Negro for courage. I know very well that in this country, the white people have said that the Negroes will not fight; but I know also, that when the country's honor has been at stake, and the dire prejudice that excludes the colored man from all positions of honor, and all opportunities for the advancement, has not interfered to exclude him from the military, he was gone with the army, and there displayed as much courage as his white brother. . . .

When such a man as this dies as he has died today, with the prayers of five millions of people going up to Heaven in his behalf—for I know that at least that number of Christians here have prayed for him—when such a man dies, I am sure that his death under such circumstances affords us a great, an almost demonstrable evidence of the success of the movement that he has inaugurated and of the final accomplishment of the great object of his soul. *(Applause).* I say that no man has ever died in this country as John Brown has died. While his soul has gone up to God, and his body has been taken down a lifeless corpse, thank God all over the country meetings are being held-tonight to give expression to that great feeling of sympathy which is to swell the great tornado. Let Virginia thank herself for it! In her guilty planting she has sown the wind; let her thank herself if in her terrible harvest she reaps the whirlwind of destruction. *(Applause).*

Go down to Virginia, and see that firm old man as he comes out from his prison, leaning upon the arm of the sheriff and with his head erect, ascends the dreadful steps of the gibbet. We see him as he goes his way to the top, and every step he takes seems to be inspired with that feeling which the poet Longfellow describes as animating the heart of the young man climbing to the top of the mountain—"Excelsior!"—until planting himself on the top, he is ready for his martyrdom.[106] Though his body falls, the spirit of slavery and despotism falls with it, while John Brown goes up to heaven. Thank God! thank God! *(Applause).*

I have detained you long enough. This is not the time to vindicate his cause. I have made these remarks only because they seem to be suggested here. I close by saying, my friends, that John Brown shall indeed be a fit representative of that Old Testament character of whom Mr. Clarke read, and shall slay more in his death than he ever slew in all his life.[107] It is thought by the slaves—and it is a beautiful conceit, though coming from slaves—that the meteors from the heavens are sparks that escape from the storehouse of the lightnings to strike upon the craters of volcanoes, and that is the cause of their eruption. From the firmament of Providence today, a meteor has fallen. It has fallen upon the volcano of American sympathies, and though, for awhile, it may seem to sleep, yet its igneous power shall communicate to the slumbering might of the volcano, and it shall burst forth in one general conflagration of revolution that shall bring about universal freedom. *(Applause).*

I feel, my friends and fellow-citizens, tonight, that courage, the adamantine courage, which has today been blasted by the terrible enginery of slavery will serve as the grit in the grindstone upon which the slave shall sharpen his weapon. I feel that that bundle of nerves, the strongest and most iron that the world has seen in America, that has today been bound by the hand of despotism, will prove to be the rails upon which Christian progress shall advance forward to the goal of universal freedom. I believe that every drop of blood shed today will be gathered up by the ever vigilant spirit of freedom, as sympathetic sparks placed in the van of Liberty, as the great *Shekinah*[108] before whom the apostles of slavery shall kneel down and pay worship, and by whose resplendent light the darkest hovels of slavery shall be penetrated until the chains shall be melted from every limb, and the slave stand forth "regenerated and disenthralled by the irresistible Genius of Universal Emancipation."[109] *(Loud Applause)*.

William Lloyd Garrison

A word or two in regard to the characteristics of John Brown. He was of the old Puritan stock—a Cromwellian who "believed in God," and at the same time "in keeping his powder dry." He believed in "the sword of the Lord and of Gideon"[110] and acted accordingly. Herein I differed widely from him. But certainly, he was no "infidel"—oh, no! How it would have added to the fiendish malignity of the New York *Observer*, if John Brown had only been an "infidel," evangelically speaking![111] But being exactly of the *Observer* pattern of theology, that fact has been a very hard pill to swallow; yet, so bent upon sustaining slavery in our land is that wicked journal, that it is preeminently ferocious in its spirit toward John Brown, and has been loudly clamorous for his execution, notwithstanding his religious faith.

As it respects his object at Harper's Ferry, it has been truly stated here by those who have preceded me, and by John Brown himself, whose declarations to the court have been read.[112] The man who brands him as a traitor is a calumniator. *(Applause)*. The man who says that his object was to promote murder, or insurrection, or rebellion, is, in the language of the apostle, "a liar, and the truth is not in him."[113] *(Loud applause)*. John Brown meant to effect, if possible, a peaceful exodus from Virginia; and had not his large humanity overpowered his judgment in regard to his prisoners, he would in all probability have succeeded, and not a drop of blood would have been shed. But it is asked, "Did he not have stored up a large supply of Sharp's rifles and spears? What did they mean?" Nothing offensive, nothing aggressive. Only this: he designed getting as many slaves as he could to join him, and then putting into their hands those instruments for self-defence. But, mark you! self-defence, not in standing their ground, but on their retreat to the mountains; on their flight to Canada; not with any design or wish to shed the blood or harm the hair of a single slaveholder in the State of Virginia, if a conflict could be avoided. Remember that he had the whole town in his possession for thirty-six hours; and if he had been the man so basely represented in certain quarters, he might have consummated any thing in the way of violence and blood.

But, all the while, he was counseling the strictest self-defence, and forbearance to the utmost, even when he had his enemies completely in his power. . . .

Was John Brown justified in his attempt? Yes, if Washington was in his; if Warren and Hancock were in theirs.[114] If men are justified in striking a blow for freedom, when the question is one of a three penny tax on tea, then, I say, they are a thousand times more justified, when it is to save fathers, mothers, wives and children from the slave coffle and the auction block, and to restore to them their God given rights. *(Loud applause)*. Was John Brown justified in interfering in behalf of the slave population of Virginia, to secure their freedom. and independence? Yes, if Lafayette was justified in interfering to help our revolutionary fathers. If Kosciusko, if Pulaski, if Steuben, if De Kalb, if all who joined them from abroad were justified in that act,[115] then John Brown was incomparably more so. If you believe in the right of assisting men to fight for freedom who are of your own color—(God knows nothing of color or complexion—human rights know nothing of these distinctions)—then you must cover, not only with a mantle of charity, but with the admiration of your hearts, the effort of John Brown at Harper's Ferry. I am trying him by the American standard; and I hesitate not to say, with all deliberation, that those who are attempt to decry him are dangerous members of the community; they are those in whom the love of liberty has died out; they are the lineal descendants of the tories of the Revolution, only a great deal worse. *(Applause)*. If the spirit of '76 prevailed today, as it did at that period, it would make the soil of the Commonwealth too hot to hold them. *(Loud applause)*. See the consistency, the vigilance, the determination of the Southern support of her slave system! She moves and acts as by one impulse. Every man on her soil who is suspected of cherishing the principles of liberty is tabooed, persecuted, and brutally outraged, especially if he be from the North. She makes clean work of it, and is consistent. On the other hand, how is it at the North? Presses which are venomously pro-slavery in spirit, and wholly Southern in their design, are every where allowed; presses which insult the good name and fame of the old Commonwealth, dishonor her illustrious dead, and contemn her glorious memories, for their purpose of "crushing out" the spirit of freedom, and making absolute the sway of a ferocious slave oligarchy—and this they do with impunity. Now I say that if the North should, in defence of her free Institutions, imitate the example of the South in support of slavery, there would be a speedy and thorough cleaning out of our cities and towns, of these who are desecrating the ground upon which they stand. *(Lord applause)*. And it would be a more hopeful state of things than it is now; for this toleration is not the result of principle, but the lack of it—it is not a noble forbearance, but a loss of vital regard for the cause of liberty.

A word upon the subject of Peace. I am a non-resistant—a believer in the inviolability of human life, under all circumstances; I, therefore, in the name of God, disarm John Brown, and every slave at the South. But I do not stop there; if I did, I should be a monster. I also disarm, in the name of God, every slaveholder and tyrant in the world. *(Loud applause)*. For wherever that principle is adopted, all fetters must instantly melt, and there can be no oppressed, and no oppressor, in the nature of things. How many agree with me in regard to the doctrine of the inviolability of human life? How many non-resistants are there here to night? *(A single voice—"I.")* There is one! *(Laughter)*. Well, then, you who are otherwise are not the men to point the finger at John Brown, and cry "traitor" judging you by your own standard. *(Applause)*. Nevertheless, I am a non-resistant and I not only desire, but have labored unremittingly to effect, the peaceful abolition of slavery, by an appeal to the reason and conscience of the slaveholder; yet, as a peace man—an "ultra" peace man—I am prepared to say, "Success to every slave insurrection at the South, and in every slave country." *(Enthusiastic applause)*. And I do not see how I compromise or stain my peace profession in making that declaration. Whenever there is a contest between the oppressed and the oppressor, the weapons being equal between the parties, God knows my heart must be with the oppressed, and always against the oppressor. Therefore, whenever commenced, I cannot but wish success to all slave insurrections. *(Loud applause)*. I thank God when men who believe in the right and duty of wielding carnal weapons are so far advanced that they will take those weapons out of the scale of despotism, and throw them into the scale of freedom. It is an indication of progress, and a positive moral growth; it is one way to get up to the sublime platform of non resistance; and it is God's method of dealing retribution upon the head of the tyrant. Rather than see men wear their chains in a cowardly and servile spirit, I would, as an advocate of peace, much rather see them breaking the head of the tyrant with their chains. Give me, as a non-resistant, Bunker Hill, and Lexington, and Concord, rather than the cowardice and servility of a Southern slave plantation.

The verdict of the world, whether "resistance to tyrants is obedience to

God," has been rendered in the affirmative in every age and clime. Whether the weapons used in the struggle against despotism have been spiritual or carnal, that verdict has been this:—

> "Glory to those who die in Freedom's cause!
> Courts, judges, can inflict no brand of shame,
> Or shape of death, to shroud them from applause!
> No, manglers of the martyr's earthly frame,
> Your hangman fingers cannot touch his fame!
> Long trains of ill may pass, unheeded, dumb—
> But Vengeance is behind, and Justice is to come!"[116] (Loud applause).

We have been warmly sympathizing with John Brown all the way through, from the time of his arrest till now. Now he no longer needs our sympathy, for he is beyond suffering, and wears the victor's crown. Are we to grow morbid over his death, to indulge in sentimental speech, to content ourselves with an outburst of emotional feeling, and not to come up to the work of abolishing slavery? I confess, I am somewhat apprehensive in regard to this powerful and wide-spread excitement, lest there may follow an exhaustion of the system, a disastrous reaction, in consequence of neglecting to make it directly subservient to the cause of emancipation by earnest and self-sacrificing effort. I see in every slave on the Southern plantation *a living John Brown*—one to be sympathized with far more than ever John Brown needed sympathy, whether in the jail or on the scaffold at Charlestown. I see *four millions of living John Browns* needing our thoughts, our sympathies, our prayers, our noblest exertions to strike off their fetters. And, by God's help, will we not do it? What can we do? I do not know that we can do any thing for Virginia. She seems past all salvation—to have been "given over to believe a lie that she may be damned."[117] But here we stand, with our feet upon the old Pilgrim ground; and I ask the sons of the Fathers, are we not competent to make the old Bay State free to all who tread its soil? (Enthusiastic applause). Are we to have another Anthony Burns rendition?[118] ("No!" "No!") Shall we allow any more slave-hunting from Berkshire to Barnstable? ("No!" "No!") No? How, then, will you prevent it? You must make that decree a matter of record, through your representatives in the State House; and if you want to do an effectual work tomorrow, and to consummate John Brown's object as far as you can, see to it that you put your names to the petition to the Legislature, now in circulation, asking that body to declare that, henceforth, no human being shall be regarded, tried or treated as a slave within the limits of this Commonwealth. *(Immense applause)*. But that is "treason" *(laughter)* and John Brown was a "traitor." The Boston *Post* and the Boston *Courier* are very anxious to discover who were the instigators of the Harper's Ferry rebellion. Most disinterested and patriotic journals! When you read any of their editorials on this subject, just look at the bottom and see in staring capitals—"SOLD TO THE DEVIL, AND PAID FOR." *(Laughter and applause)*.

Who instigated John Brown? Let us see. It must have been Patrick Henry, who said—and he was a Virginian—*"Give me liberty, or give me death!"* Why do they not dig up his bones, and give them to the consuming fire, to show their abhorrence of his memory? It must have been Thomas Jefferson—another Virginian—who said of the bondage of the Virginia slaves, that "one hour of it is fraught with more misery than ages of that which our fathers rose in rebellion to oppose"[119]—and who, as the author of the Declaration of Independence, proclaimed it to be "a SELF-EVIDENT TRUTH, that all men are created equal, and endowed by their Creator with AN INALIENABLE RIGHT TO LIBERTY." *(Applause)*. Beyond all question, it must have been VIRGINIA HERSELF, who, by her coat of arms, with its terrible motto, *"Sic semper tyrannis,"* asserts the right of the oppressed to trample their oppressors beneath their feet, and, if necessary, consign them to a bloody grave! Herein John Brown found the strongest incitement and the fullest justification.

Who instigated the deed at Harper's Ferry? The people whose motto is, "Resistance to tyrants is obedience to God"—and whose exulting talk is of Bunker Hill and Yorktown, and the deeds of their REVOLUTIONARY sires! Nay, we must go back to the source of life itself:—"So God created man in his own image; male and female created he them." Thus making an "irrepressible conflict" between the soul of man and tyranny *from the beginning. . . .* We have a natural right, therefore, to seek the abolition of slavery throughout the globe. It is our special duty to make Massachusetts free soil, so that the moment the fugitive slave stands upon it, he shall take his place in the ranks of the free. God commands us to "hide the outcast, and bewray not him that wandereth."[120] I say, LET THE WILL OF GOD BE DONE!

Source: The Liberator, December 9 and 16, 1859.

Fales Henry Newhall, "The Conflict in America," December 4, 1859

Numerous abolitionist preachers echoed Brown's own strategy of blending Old and New Testament imagery as they responded to his raid and death. One, Edwin Wheelock, even fused Old and New Testament figures into a single statement: "The bondman has stood face to face with his Moses. The Christ of anti-slavery has sent forth its 'John,'" he observed in November 1859. Fales Henry Newhall (1827–1883) performed a similar fusion in a sermon at the Warren Street Methodist Episcopal Church in Roxbury, Massachusetts, on December 4, 1859. In the selection below, from a longer sermon about slavery, Newhall observes that Brown has "consecrated" the gibbet like Christ's cross and is also "Samson of Osawatomie" who topples the pillars of slavery. The text for the sermon was Judges 16, where Samson pulls down the temple, and Newhall uses the comparison to promise divinely sanctioned retribution upon the South and the imminent collapse of the slaveholding system.

He defends himself better than I or any other man can defend him. He calmly tells the jury who convicted him, that had he done for them, their wives and children, what he did for "God's despised poor," it would have been all right. This defence is impregnable. Had John Brown done precisely the same act to save the white man from the tyranny of the black man, successful or unsuccessful, the deed would have been sung and celebrated as heroic with the deeds of Hampden and Warren.[121] Had he been a black man fighting for his own race, some say, it would have been right. But John Brown believed the Bible, which makes no distinction of races, and declares that God *"hath made of one blood all nations of men."*[122]

But was he not a rebel, guilty of sedition and treason? Yes, all this. But we are to remember that the words "rebel" and "treason" have been made holy in the American language. Are not our children fed on revolutionary reminis-

166

cences which make "rebel" and "patriot" synonymous in their childish apprehension? What means that stone and that tablet at Lexington, that inscription
which patriots come from the ends of the earth to read, commencing, *"Sacred
to Liberty and the Rights of Mankind!"* It means that eight Massachusetts rebels
dashed themselves against an empire on that village green, and that Massachusetts is proud of their very ashes. What means that monumental bronze on
Court Square? It means that we glory in the treason of that arch rebel Benjamin Franklin, "who snatched the lightning from heaven and the sceptre from
tyrants."[123] What mean those massive granite blocks that are piled on Bunker
Hill? It means that we glory in the deed of those rebels who knelt in a trench
there one June morning, under the glare of burning Charlestown, to salute
with powder and bullets the soldiers of their "rightful sovereign," and waited,
the fowling piece to the shoulder and the finger on the trigger, till they could
see the whites of their eyes! I do not say that Massachusetts has any right to
glory in those deeds as she does, but I do say that she has no right to glory in
the treason of Hancock, Adams, and Franklin, as noble and Christian, and
then brand the treason of John Brown as infamous. Yea, is not his deed nobler
than the deed of him whom yon, citizens of Roxbury, are so proud to call an
ancestor, as you exultingly tell the stranger that here the hero Warren was
born, and on this street, close by this sanctuary, he first drew the breath of life?
Which is nobler, more Christian, to strike a blow for myself or for others oppressed? Posterity will marvel at the heathenism of Christian America, the
children will be ashamed of the heathenism of their fathers, which gave Warren a statue and John Brown a gibbet. Brown, fighting for the negro against
the white man, is precisely parallel with Byron fighting for the Greeks against
the Turks,[124] with Kosciusko and Lafayette fighting with our fathers against the
British.[125] His deeds take rank with theirs in self-devotion and heroism; history will write their names on the same page; poetry will weave them in the
same garland. Brown made mistakes—he saw them himself when too late—
great, grave mistakes, but they were mistakes of the head, not of the heart. His
heart was true to God and man through all. And, therefore, I rejoice to believe
that between eleven and twelve o'clock last Friday forenoon he heard from the
Judge of all flesh the words, "Well done! good and faithful servant."[126]

I would now say something of John Brown's character as a man and as a
Christian; for it is in the light of that character that we see the mortal conflict
of which I have spoken between Christianity and American Slavery. The broad

blaze of that character, lustrous in the glory of Christianity, suddenly falls upon this abomination, draws thither the gaze of all the world, and at a flash reveals every horrid limb and feature, from the foot planted in the depths of hell, to the head that "dares affront the throne of God." This grim, grisly Moloch had lain in the dark, wallowing in the blood of his victims; John Brown passes by, and his character falls on the monster in a flash of radiance, and at the same instant the whole panic-stricken South, in its spasm of terror, unwittingly shouts to the world, "Look there! behold our God!"

It is unnecessary for me to attempt to delineate his character at length—you all know it, for it is transparent. A few months ago most of us thought of him as a bold, rough, reckless outlaw, embittered by the loss of his property, and the loss of his sons in Kansas. Had he been shot down in the engine-house at Harper's Ferry, that would have been our mental daguerreotype of old Ossawattomie. But God did not allow that cowardly United States lieutenant, who could smite a man disarmed and prostrate,[127] to take his life; he would first show his face to the land and to the world. And all who have looked on that face, friend or foe, have looked with awe and admiration. How strange! how sublime is John Brown's *victory* at Harper's Ferry! He conquered all that looked upon his face. How all around dwarfed into insignificance in the presence of that old wounded prisoner doomed to a felon's death! What man in a million could have won such a victory? He stood like a born prince among them; every word, look and gesture showed him to be of the royal line. He seemed predestinated for the spot, by education, associations and ancestry, fore-ordained for the hour. . . .

He is the first to mount the scaffold, and, rock to the last, sternly declines to listen to the prayers of a slaveholding ministry. As he stands there, he wears the halter on his neck like a garland of glory. And when at last the drop fell, and he hung between the heavens and earth, he made the gallows glorious in America. Yes, henceforth it is no disgrace to die on a gibbet in this land. As the Holy One, whose steps he followed, and who died for others the death of a slave, made the barbarous cross a glorious thing from the moment his hand was nailed to its rugged wood, so this, his worshipper and follower, when he gave his life cheerfully there for the millions of God's despised poor in this land, consecrated the gibbet on this American soil. All the world gazes on that body, as it swings lifeless on the gallows tree, and asks, "Who hangs there?" The answer comes from a whole race, out of the millions of their tropic hearts, "It is the man who loved us enough to die for us." The answer rolls from land to land, "It is a son of the Pilgrims, a son of the Revolutionary patriots, and a son whom friend and foe will say was worthy of his sires." It is a tender father, a devoted husband, a heroic Christian patriot, a man who loved his despised fellow-man so deeply that he could cheerfully die for him; it is a man who loved his God with such devoted love, and trusted his God with such lofty faith, that men called him a maniac. "What!" cries the world in amazement, "is it for such a man that the gallows stands in America? Are such men hung on the gibbet there? Who, then, do the Americans think fit to live? How is it that a man must die on the gibbet there who is acknowledged by his fiercest foes to be a hero and a Christian." And one answer rolls round the world, "He dies because American Slavery demands it. He, and such as he *must die* for slavery to live." And then our nation asks, is asking today—this John Brown's first Sabbath in heaven—"which is worth the most to us, slavery or a man, a hero, a Christian like Brown of Osawatomie?" That question is asked in millions of homes today, it is pondered in the minds of statesmen, it is burning in myriads of Christian hearts this Sabbath morning, and mark it, when once that question is fairly asked through all the land, it is answered in a thunder roll from Atlantic to Pacific, from Lake to Gulf, and slavery is doomed. Last Friday morning, when John Brown was swung from the gallows, American Slavery felt that pinioned hand strike a blow to its very heart; it trembled with a horror it never felt before. Had not God smitten the slaveholders with judicial blindness, they would have built John Brown a palace, clothed him in fine linen, and fed him sumptuously every day, rather than ever have allowed him to mount that scaffold. He was content to "die with the Philistines,"[128] when he could slay more of them at his death than in all his life.

True, he had laid them heaps upon heaps. He had driven them before him like frightened sheep, from border to border, over the plains of Kansas. But he made a mistake—for an instant, a fatal instant, faith changed to presumption; for a moment that keen, wakeful eye slumbered, and they stole behind him and sheared his locks. And then they clutched him, and looked into the eye, whose glance had scattered them a thousand times, and cried, "Ha! it is he! it is Samson of Osawatomie! Praised be Baal! Glory to Dagon!" and they bound him and led him away. They shouted through Gath and Ascalon, "We have caught the terrible Samson!" and they shut him in their prison, and peered at him at a safe distance down through the grated window, and rubbed their hands in glee as they said to one another, "It is he! the old Samson of Osawat-omie, caged at last." But O, how the old hero's locks grew in that dusky prison air! Every moment they kept him there, the strength of a thousand Samsons was gathering in his thews and sinews. The cowards saw it and trembled; they feared him in that prison more than an army with banners. And so they hur-ried him forth to die; but in the blindness of their fear and passion they did not see that when they placed him on the scaffold, they had set him between the very pillars of their idol's temple. And he looked up and prayed, "Avenge me now for my two eyes." He threw his arms around those pillars and bowed himself. "Let me die with the Philistines," cried Samson of Osawatomie. Ah! see the vast fabric totter! hear the Philistines shriek! Today there are dropping over all the land the first falling fragments from the great crash of American Slavery.[129]

Source: Fales Henry Newhall, *The Conflict in America: A Funeral Discourse Occasioned by the Death of John Brown of Osawatomie* (Boston: J. M. Hewes, 1859), 14–17, 20–22.

Anne Lynch Botta, "To Henry Whitney Bellows," December 6, 1859

A letter by the poet and teacher Anne Lynch Botta (1815–1891) epitomizes the moderate antislavery response to Brown. Writing to the New York minister and fellow antislavery moderate Henry Whitney Bellows shortly after the execution, Botta describes Brown as a brave man who became a "monomaniac" (a popular epithet applied to reformers). She condemns his violence, comparing it to the religiously justified violence against heretics during the Spanish Inquisition, and rebukes proslavery and antislavery "fanatics" alike. Instead of Brown's method, she proposes a gradual abolition of slavery and explains that she herself will wait, watch, and pray. She singles out George Cheever to criticize the wrong response to Brown. Cheever was an abolitionist minister in New York who said in late November 1859 that Brown's raid was God's strategy for calling Americans to consider their duty and avoid divine judgment. Botta also empathizes with the South's terror at Brown's raid. She had visited Southern plantations in 1855 after her wedding to Vincenzo Botta, an Italian she had met in Europe, and observed a real fear of slave insurrection that perhaps explains her empathy.

New-York, December 6, 1859.

My dear Dr. Bellows: As I have not for some time had an opportunity to speak with you, I must take the opportunity to write. I confess that my instincts of humanity are outraged at the idea of exciting among the negroes of the South a servile insurrection, which it was the avowed intention of John Brown to do, and which Dr. Cheever and others seem to regard as the highest manifestation of nobleness, patriotism, and Christianity. On Sunday last, Dr. Cheever invoked God to preserve us from mob violence, in view of his own church being attacked, and is quite ready to fall back for protection upon the laws of the land in such an extremity, while he despises them so much in other cases. If the violence of a mob in a Christian community is to be deprecated, with how much more abhorrence should it be regarded among such an ignorant, half-barbarous population as the slaves of the South, when the victims are to be the wives, sisters, and children of our friends and brothers!

To me the terror manifested through the South at the bare idea of such an uprising is not ridiculous, as it seems to be to most of our Northern journals and some of the people. I deeply sympathize with it, and unhesitatingly condemn John Brown for his reckless disregard for human life, and his one-sided philanthropy that would secure a real or imagined good to the slave, no matter at what cost to humanity or to civilization.

I admire courage; but without wisdom it is a dangerous gift. If John Brown has manifested the highest Christian principle, as his admirers claim, then for me the lessons of Christ must be learned anew; for I do not think his course sanctioned by our Saviour's example or precepts, any more than the burning of heretics by the Inquisition, or of Quakers by the Puritans, though both were done in his name.

John Brown was simply, in my view, a brave and worthy man who had dwelt on the subject until he became a monomaniac. It seems to me that many people of intellect and discretion in our community are losing their mental balance, and allowing their instincts and passions to guide them in this great crisis, rather than their higher judgment, which the state of things so imperiously demands the exercise of. We all know that slavery is a great evil, and the blot on our national escutcheon; and we have a right to say so, and to express our abhorrence of it. But that we have the right to murder the slaveholder in order to free the slave, or to incite the slave to do so, or even to glorify him who does, I do not believe, though he may do it in the name of God. Slavery is the inherited curse of the South. She came into the Union with this mark upon her, and was accepted with it by our fathers, whose patriotism and wisdom we never tire of praising. In the struggle that achieved our independence, the South bore her part bravely; and Virginia gave us Washington, through whom we established our nationality and formed a republic which is even now the forlorn hope of humanity throughout the world.

Suppose we dissolve the Union by withdrawing ourselves, or by driving the South out of it. Do we thereby extinguish the evil of slavery? I do not see that we do, but we certainly do extinguish the hopes that humanity has risked upon our experiment of self-government. Slavery is the growth of more than two

centuries. It cannot be destroyed in a day, nor in a longer time, without producing a moral shock that would be, perhaps, a still greater evil. I would watch,
and pray, and wait. This is not the doctrine of the fanatics on either side of
Mason and Dixon's line, whose limited and distorted vision is confined to the
narrow limit of the present, and whose mutual bitterness and hate are sowing
a wind which, apparently, will rise a whirlwind upon us all. In this emergency
it seems to me that all who have a calm word to utter should speak out, and
at once.

I am most respectfully and sincerely yours, A. C. L. Botta

Source: Memoirs of Anne C. L. Botta, ed. Vincenzo Botta (New York: J. Selwin Tait & Sons, 1893),
276–278.

Wendell Phillips, "Eulogy for John Brown," December 8, 1859

Brown's funeral took place in North Elba on December 8, 1859. The Reverend Joshua Young of Burlington, Vermont, led the service. It opened with one of Brown's favorite hymns, "Blow Ye the Trumpet, Blow," and Young read from 2 Timothy 4:7–8 as mourners lowered the casket into the ground: "I have fought a good fight. I have finished my course. I have kept the faith." Young's congregation later snubbed him for leading the service and he left his Burlington ministry for one in Massachusetts. The abolitionist Wendell Phillips (1811–1884) gave the funeral eulogy. Phillips had been converted to abolitionism by Garrison in 1836 and first spoke publicly on December 8, 1837, at a Boston protest over the murder of the abolitionist Elijah Lovejoy. In 1854 he was indicted for his participation in the attempt to rescue Anthony Burns, a fugitive slave, from jail in Boston. Now, surrounded by Brown's family, friends, and neighbors, he described Brown as a death blow to the system that Phillips himself had fought for over two decades. The extinction of the slave system was just a matter of time, Phillips prophesied. He gave more speeches about Brown on December 15 and 18, 1859, in which he compared the Harpers Ferry raid to the American Revolution and Brown to Christ.

How feeble words seem here! How can I hope to utter what your hearts are full of? I fear to disturb the harmony which his life breathes round this home. One and another of you, his neighbors, say, "I have known him five years," "I have known him ten years." It seems to me as if we had none of us known him. How our admiring, loving wonder has grown, day by day, as he has unfolded trait after trait of earnest, brave, tender, Christian life! We see him walking with radiant, serene face to the scaffold, and think what an iron heart, what devoted faith! We take up his letters, beginning "My dear wife and children, everyone,"—see him stoop on his way to the scaffold and kiss that negro child— and this iron heart seems all tenderness. Marvelous old man! We have hardly said it when the loved forms of his sons, in the bloom of young devotion, encircle him, and we remember he is not alone, only the majestic center of a group. Your neighbor farmer went, surrounded by his household, to tell the slaves there were still hearts and right arms ready and nerved for their service. From this roof four, from a neighboring roof two, to make up that score of heroes. How resolute each looked into the face of Virginia, how loyally each stood at his forlorn post, meeting death cheerfully, till that master-voice said, "It is enough." And these weeping children and widow seem so lifted up and consecrated by long, single-hearted devotion to his great purpose, that we dare, even at this moment, to remind them how blessed they are in the privilege of thinking that in the last throbs of those brave young hearts, which lie buried on the banks of the Shenandoah, thoughts of them mingled with love to God and hope for the slave.

He has abolished slavery in Virginia. You may say this is too much. Our neighbors are the last men we know. The hours that pass us are the ones we appreciate the least. Men walked Boston streets, when night fell on Bunker's Hill, and pitied Warren, saying, "Foolish man! Thrown away his life! Why didn't he measure his means better?" Now we see him standing colossal on that blood-stained sod, and severing that day the tie which bound Boston to Great Britain. That night George III ceased to rule in New England. History will date Virginia Emancipation from Harper's Ferry. True, the slave is still there. So, when the tempest uproots a pine on your hills, it looks green for months—a year or two. Still, it is timber, not a tree. John Brown has loosened the roots of the slave system; it only breathes—it does not live—hereafter.

Men say, "How coolly brave!" But matchless courage seems the least of his merits. How gentleness graced it! When the frightened town wished to bear off the body of the Mayor, a man said, "I will go, Miss Fowke, under their rifles, if you will stand between them and me." He knew he could trust their gentle respect for woman. He was right. He went in the thick of the fight and bore off the body in safety. That same girl flung herself between Virginia rifles and your brave young Thompson. They had no pity.[130] The pitiless bullet reached him, spite of woman's prayers, though the fight had long been over. How God has blessed him! How truly he may say, "I have fought a good fight, I have *finished* my course."[131] Truly he has *finished*—done his work. God granted him the privilege to look on his work accomplished. He said, "I will show the South that twenty men can take possession of a town, hold it twenty-four hours, and carry away all the slaves who wish to escape." Did he not do it? On Monday night he stood master of Harper's Ferry—could have left unchecked with a score or a hundred slaves. The wide sympathy and secret approval are shown by the eager, quivering lips of lovers of slavery, asking, "O why did he not take his victory and go away?" Who checked him at last? Not startled Virginia. Her he had conquered. The Union crushed—seemed to crush him. In reality God said, "That work is done; you have proved that a Slave State is only fear in the mask of despotism; come up higher, and baptize by your martyrdom a million hearts into holier life." Surely such a life is no failure. How vast the change in men's hearts! Insurrection was a harsh, horrid word to millions a month ago. John Brown went a whole generation beyond it, claiming the right for white men to help the slave to freedom by arms. And now men run up and down, not disputing his principle, but trying to frame excuses for Virginia's hanging of so pure, honest, high-hearted, and heroic a man. Virginia stands at the bar of the civilized world on trial. Round her victim crowd the apostles and martyrs, all the brave, high souls who have said, "God is God," and trodden wicked laws under their feet. As I stood looking at his grandfather's gravestone, brought here from Connecticut, telling, as it does, of his death in the Revolution, I thought I could hear our hero-saint saying, "My fathers gave their swords to the oppressor—the slave still sinks before the pledged force of this nation. I give my sword to the slave my fathers forgot." If any swords ever reflected the smile of Heaven, surely it was those drawn at Harper's Ferry. If our God is ever the Lord of Hosts, making one man chase a thousand, surely that little band might claim him for their captain. Harper's Ferry was no single hour, standing alone, taken out from a common life, it was the flowering out of fifty years of single-hearted devotion. He must have lived wholly for one great idea, when these who owe their being to him, and these whom love has joined to the circle, group so harmoniously around him, each accepting serenely his and her part.

I feel honored to stand under such a roof. Hereafter you will tell children standing at your knees, "I saw John Brown buried, I sat under his roof." Thank God for such a master. Could we have asked a nobler representative of the Christian North putting her foot on the accursed system of slavery? As time passes, and these hours float back into history, men will see against the clear December sky that gallows, and round it thousands of armed men guarding Virginia from her slaves. On the other side, the serene brow of that calm old man, as he stoops to kiss the child of a forlorn race. Thank God for our emblem. May he soon bring Virginia to blot out hers in repentant shame, and cover that hateful gallows and soldiery with thousands of broken fetters.

What lesson shall those lips teach us? Before that still, calm brow let us take a new baptism. How can we stand here without a fresh and utter consecration? These tears! how shall we dare even to offer consolation? Only lips fresh from such a vow have the right to mingle their words with your tears. We envy you your nearer place to these martyred children of God. I do not believe slavery will go down in blood. Ours is the age of thought. Hearts are stronger than swords. That last fortnight! How sublime its lesson! the Christian one of conscience—of truth. Virginia is weak, because each man's heart said amen to John Brown. His words, they are stronger even than his rifles. These crushed a State. Those have changed the thoughts of millions, and will yet crush slavery. Men said, "Would he had died in arms!" God ordered better, and granted to him and the slave those noble prison hours, that single hour of death; granted him a higher than the soldier's place, that of teacher; the echoes of his rifles have died away in the hills, a million hearts guard his words. God bless this root, make it bless us. We dare not say bless you, children of this home! you stand nearer to one whose lips God touched, and we rather bend for your blessing. God make us all worthier of him whose dust we lay among these hills he loved. Here he girded himself and went forth to battle. Fuller success than his heart ever dreamed God granted him. He sleeps in the blessings of the crushed and the poor, and men believe more firmly in virtue, now that such a man has lived. Standing here, let us thank God for a firmer faith and fuller hope.

Source: Wendell Phillips, *Speeches, Lectures, and Letters* (Boston: James Redpath, 1863), 289–293.

Edward Everett and Caleb Cushing, "Speeches at Faneuil Hall," December 8, 1859

In response to pro-Brown gatherings like the *Natick Resolution* meeting of November 20 and the huge meeting at Boston's Tremont Temple on December 2, proslavery Democrats in the North held "Union meetings" in several cities. They met in Philadelphia on December 7, in Boston on December 8, and in New York on December 19. The organizers of the Boston meeting invited Massachusetts citizens who "honor and cherish" the threatened Union to attend. The three-hour event attracted hundreds more people than could fit in the large meeting space and included a speech by Levi Lincoln, the reading of a letter by former president Franklin Pierce, and the adoption of resolutions that condemned the raid and expressed sympathy with the people of Virginia. Edward Everett (1794–1865) gave one of the main addresses. Everett was an ardent Unionist and a prominent orator from Massachusetts who had served as a U.S. representative, a U.S. senator, governor of Massachusetts, U.S. secretary of state, and president of Harvard University. By 1859 he had retired from politics, but he gave occasional public speeches. His address to the Unionists in Faneuil Hall condemns Brown's "wild" plan, claiming that it was an attempt to repeat "the awful calamity" of the Haitian revolution and could have ended in a mass slaughter of white Southerners and the extermination of the whole black Southern population. The following year Everett ran for vice president on the Constitutional Union Party ticket (formed by former Whigs), alongside the Tennessee slaveholder John Bell for president. The Bell-Everett ticket received around 13 percent of the vote, mostly in the South. During the Civil War, Everett gave speeches in support of the Union cause and campaigned for Lincoln during the 1864 election. Caleb Cushing (1800–1879) addressed the crowd immediately after Everett. Cushing had served as a Democratic congressman from Massachusetts and attorney general under President Pierce. He had supported the Dred Scott decision. His speech calls Brown insane and warns that the raiders (and abolitionists) hoped to provoke a bloody civil war. He concludes by asking Massachusetts to help avert such a war. The following year, President Buchanan sent Cushing to Charleston as confidential commissioner to the secessionists of South Carolina.

Edward Everett

It appears from his own statements and those of his deluded associates, of his biographer, and of his wretched wife, that the unhappy man who has just paid the forfeit of his life had for years meditated a general insurrection in the Southern States; that he thought the time had now come to effect it; that the slaves were ready to rise and the non-slaveholding whites to join them; and both united were prepared to form a new Commonwealth, of which the constitution was organized and the officers chosen. With this wild, but thoroughly matured plan, he provides weapons for those on whose rising he calculated at Harper's Ferry; he seizes the national arsenal, where there was a supply of arms for a hundred thousand men; and he intended, if unable to maintain himself at once in the open country, to retreat to the mountains, and from their fast-nesses harass, paralyze, and at length revolutionize the South. To talk of the pikes and rifles not being intended for offensive purposes is simply absurd. The first act almost of the party was to shoot down a free colored man whom they were attempting to impress, and who fled from them.[132] One might as well say that the rifled ordnance of Louis Napoleon was intended only for self-defence, not to be used unless the Austrians should undertake to arrest his march.

No, sir, it was an attempt to do on a vast scale what was done in St. Domingo in 1791,[133] where the colored population was about equal to that of Virginia; and if anyone would form a distinct idea what such an operation is, let him see it, not as a matter of vague conception—a crude project—in the mind of a heated fanatic, but as it stands in the sober pages of history, which record the revolt in that island; the midnight burnings, the wholesale massacres, the merciless tortures, the abominations not to be named by Christian lips in the hearing of Christian ears. . . .

Now let us cast a glance at the state of things in the Southern States, co-members as they are with us in this great republican confederacy. Let us consider over what sort of a population it is that some persons among us think it not only right and commendable, but in the highest degree heroic, saint-like, god-like, to extend the awful calamity which turned St. Domingo into a heap of bloody ashes in 1791. There are between three and four millions of the colored race scattered through the Southern and Southwestern States, in small groups, in cities, towns, villages, and in larger bodies on isolated plantations; in the house, the factory, and the field; mingled together with the dominant race in the various pursuits of life; the latter amounting in the aggregate to eight or nine millions, if I rightly recollect the numbers.[134] Upon this community, thus composed, it was the design of Brown to let loose the hellhounds of a servile insurrection, and to bring on a struggle which, for magnitude, atrocity, and horror, would have stood alone in the history of the world. And these eight or nine millions, against whom this frightful war was levied, are our fellow-citizens, entitled with us to the protection of that compact of government which recognizes their relation to the colored race—a compact which every sworn officer of the Union or of the States is bound by his oath to support! Among them, sir, is a fair proportion of men and women of education and culture—of moral and religious lives and characters—virtuous fathers, mothers, sons, and daughters, persons who would adorn any station of society, in any country—men who read the same Bible that we do, and in the name of the same Master kneel at the throne of the same God—forming a class of men from which have gone forth some of the greatest and purest characters which adorn our history—Washington, Jefferson, Madison, Monroe, Marshall, in the single State of Virginia against which the first blow has been struck.[135] These are the men, the women, for whose bosoms pikes and rifles are manufactured in New England, to be placed in the hands of an ignorant subject race, supposed, most wrongfully, as recent events have shown, to be waiting only for an opportunity to use them!

Sir, I have, on three or four different occasions in early life and more recently, visited all the Southern and Southwestern States, with the exception of Arkansas and Alabama. I have enjoyed the hospitality of the city and the country; and I have had the privilege, before crowded and favoring audiences, to hold up the character of the Father of his Country, and to inculcate the blessings of the Union, in the same precise terms in which I have done it here at home, and in the other portions of the land. I have been admitted to the confidence of the domestic circle, and I have seen there touching manifestations of the kindest feelings by which that circle, in all its members, high and low, master and servant, can be bound together; and when I contemplate the horrors that would have ensued had the tragedy on which the curtain rose at Harper's Ferry been acted out, through all its scenes of fire and sword, of lust and murder, of rapine and desolation, to the final catastrophe, I am filled with emotions to which no words can do justice. There could of course be but one result, and that well deserving the thoughtful meditation of those, if any such there be, who think that the welfare of the colored race could by any possibility be promoted by the success of such a movement, and who are willing to purchase that result by so costly a sacrifice. The colored population of St. Domingo amounted to but little short of half a million, while the whites amounted to only thirty thousand. The white population of the Southern States alone in the aggregate outnumbers the colored race in the ratio of two to one; in the Union at large, in the ratio of seven to one; and if (which Heaven avert!) they should be brought into conflict, it could end only in the extermination of the latter after scenes of woe for which language is too faint, and for which the liveliest fancy has no adequate images of horror.

Caleb Cushing

John Brown, with an insane ferocity of cruelty, proposed to consign the peaceful inhabitants of the State of Virginia, the millions and millions of white men and white women to servile insurrection and civil war, and to outrages indescribable, impossible to be imagined, worse than a million deaths.

But it is said that John Brown was insane, and therefore that he should not have been convicted. Was he insane? Gentlemen, I have many times had occasion in this Commonwealth—all reflecting men have had occasion—to consider a similar question. I cannot meet it here without speaking plainly. Shall I speak plainly? *(General cries of "Yes," "Yes.")* I say, in this Commonwealth of Massachusetts and in the adjoining State of New York, there is a handful of men of highly intellectual mind, of the highest culture, literary and scientific men who would seem to be born to bless their day and generation—such as Wendell Phillips, (William) Lloyd Garrison, (Ralph) Waldo Emerson, Theodore Parker, and Gerrit Smith—who by constant brooding upon one single idea—that idea if you please a right one, abstractly—have come to be monomaniacs of that idea *(applause),* and so have become utterly lost to the moral relations of right and wrong. In their private relations not one of them would injure the hair even of my head. *(Laughter).* Not one of them, unless upon the question of slavery; and then such is the atrocious ferocity of mind into which they have been betrayed by this monomania, that they declare, in so many words, and therefore I may say it is so, their readiness to break down all laws, human and divine—nay, that under the influence of this monomania they have set up in this Commonwealth a public policy of assassination and a religion of hate—aye, a religion of hate; such as belongs only to the condemned devils in hell *(applause)*. I say it is a religion of hate, and of blasphemy—oh God! that such things are in this our day. They have set up this religion of hate, and they blasphemously call that Christianity. I put this question to you— whether these demoniac passions and this truculent ferocity of pretended philanthropy upon the subject of slavery institutions have not stifled in them all there is of good in the human heart, and all there is of divine in the aspirations of human hearts to God and to Heaven. This they have done, and the question is asked, are they sane? I cannot pronounce on that subject. What would a commission of lunacy say to it? I know not. I know that the imputed insanity of John Brown is that his intelligence has become perverted, that his heart is gangrened, that his soul is steeled against everything human and conscientious by that same monomania, which pervades the speeches and writings of Wendell Phillips and Waldo Emerson. Are they insane? I say again, I know not, and yet I pause in charity, for have we not now before us the spectacle, most painful to every well settled heart, have we not the spectacle of one of their number, as wise in his day and generation as they, with the same ostentatious pretences of good and of right, and the same crazy perversion of Christianity and the Bible—have we not before us the spectacle of Gerrit Smith in a hospital for lunatics in the State of New York? *(Profound silence)*.[136] And I do say, that unless all monomaniac Abolitionists are to be deemed insane and incapable of distinguishing between right and wrong, in a question of murder and of treason and of burglary and of robbery, then John Brown was not insane, and therefore was not entitled to any consideration upon that pretext. And we know well that he would have been the last to assume any such pretext; we know well that he acted with that stolid indifference to the atrocity of his acts, which in all time has distinguished political and religious assassins—which may be found in the character of Guy Fawkes,[137] and which animated the Ravaillacs and the Jacques Clements of France.[138] The same spirit distinguished the assassins of Italy, who, to prevent the progress of moderate reform, and to substitute their own monomania, slaughtered Rossi at the steps of the Vatican.[139] In Vienna the good Count Lemborg,[140] and in Prague the Princess Windischgratz,[141] were assassinated in the same insane spirit of proposed political and social reform. That is the distinctive quality of these offences. The idea of

John Brown is that by cold-blooded, fraudulent, midnight assassination, he is to promote the reform of the institutions of the State of Virginia and of the Southern States. And these assassins die *game.* Does that make them good men? So, gentlemen, I now say, that not only was John Brown duly and legally tried and convicted, but that he was duly and lawfully executed, and rendered up a justly forfeited life to the justice of the State of Virginia. *(Applause).*

What more, gentlemen? We have had our ears filled with alleged sympathies for John Brown, of apologies for his act, of reproaches against the persons whom he was endeavoring to slaughter in cold blood, of sneers at the State of Virginia, of ridicule of the terror felt by the unarmed women and children of Virginia. For it is not the men of Virginia—it is the women—it is the tender and sensitive *white* sisters of the women of Massachusetts—who felt these terrors. For them the Abolitionists have no sympathy, but only for John Brown. Gentlemen, it is not sympathy for John Brown. It is another form of the manifestation of that same intense and ferocious hatred of the people of the South which animates the persons of whom we are speaking *(applause).* Hatred—hatred! Now the fact has been told us that in all times hate must have its food of blood; aye, hate must have its food of blood. How long are the people of Massachusetts to have their souls continually perverted with these preachings, aye, pulpit preachings of hatred, though, thank God, these blasphemous preachers of hatred and treason are but one to a thousand among the admirable and revered clergymen of Massachusetts *(applause).* I ask you, gentlemen, how long these emotions of mutual hate are to go on without shedding blood. Blood has begun to be shed—in that worst possible form, of treacherous, malignant, cold-hearted midnight assassination;—nay, not only has there been shedding of blood, but that shedding of blood, coming from Northern States; has as its avowed object to propagate throughout the Southern States, revolution, servile and civil war, and universal devastation.

Source: Boston Courier Report of the Union Meeting in Faneuil Hall, Thursday, Dec. 8th, 1859 (Boston: Clark, Fellows, 1859), 13–22 (15–16, 19–20).

Charles Eliot Norton, "To Mrs. Edward Twisleton," December 13, 1859

Nearly two weeks after Brown's death, Charles Eliot Norton (1827–1908) summarized the intense interest surrounding his raid, trial, and execution. Norton was an author, critic, and reformer based in Cambridge, Massachusetts. In his letter to a cousin in London, the wife of a British public official who served on several government commissions, he explains that Brown first seemed mad and then his trial speech and prison letters helped increase public sympathy. Norton points out the extreme responses to Brown: to some he is a traitor, to others a hero. But most Americans are somewhere in between, Norton claims. They admire Brown while condemning his actions. As for himself, Norton sees Brown as a brave, sincere, and selfless man whose actions and death will do more to end slavery than anything else.

Shady Hill, 13 December, 1859.

I have thought often of writing to you—especially since John Brown made his incursion into Virginia—but it has been difficult hitherto to form a dispassionate judgment in regard to this affair, and I have not cared to write a mere expression of personal feeling. Perhaps it is even now still too near the event for one to balance justly all the considerations involved in it. Unless you have seen some one of the American papers during the last two months you can hardly have formed an idea of the intensity of feeling and interest which has prevailed throughout the country in regard to John Brown. I have seen nothing like it. We get up excitements easily enough, but they die away usually as quickly as they rose, beginning in rhetoric and ending in fireworks; but this was different. The heart of the people was fairly reached, and an impression has been made upon it which will be permanent and produce results long hence.

When the news first came, in the form of vague and exaggerated telegraphic reports, of the seizure of the Arsenal at Harper's Ferry, people thought it was probably some trouble among the workmen at the place; but as the truth slowly came out and John Brown's name, which was well known through the country, was mentioned as that of the head of the party, the general feeling was that the affair was a reckless, merely mad attempt to make a raid of slaves —an attempt fitly put down by the strong arm. There was at first no word of sympathy either for Brown or his undertaking. But soon came the accounts of the panic of the Virginians, of the cruelty with which Brown's party were massacred; of his noble manliness of demeanor when, wounded, he was taken prisoner, and was questioned as to his design; of his simple declarations of his motives and aims, which were those of an enthusiast, but not of a bad man— and a strong sympathy began to be felt for Brown personally, and a strong interest to know in full what had led him to this course. Then the bitterness of the Virginia press, the unseemly haste with which the trial was hurried on— and all the while the most unchanged, steady, manliness on the part of "Old Brown," increased daily the sympathy which was already strong. The management of the trial, the condemnation, the speech made by Brown, the letters he wrote in prison, the visit of his wife to him—and at last his death, wrought up the popular feeling to the highest point. Not, indeed, that feeling or opinion have been by any means unanimous; for on the one side have been those who have condemned the whole of Brown's course as utterly wicked, and regarded him as a mere outlaw, murderer, and traitor, while, on the other, have been those who have looked upon his undertaking with satisfaction, and exalted him into the highest rank of men. But, if I am not wrong, the mass of the people, and the best of them, have agreed with neither of these views. They have, while condemning Brown's scheme as a criminal attempt to right a great wrong by violent measures, and as equally ill-judged and rash in execution, felt for the man himself a deep sympathy and a fervent admiration. They have admitted that he was guilty under the law, that he deserved to be hung as a breaker of the law—but they have felt that the gallows was not the fit end for a life like his, and that he died a real martyr in the cause of freedom.

Brown in truth was a man born out of time. He was of a rare type, rare especially in these days. He belonged with the Covenanters, with the Puritans. He was possessed with an idea which mastered his whole nature and gave dignity and force to his character. He had sincere faith in God—and especially believed in the sword of the Lord. His chief fault seems to have been impatience with the slowness of Providence. Seeing what was right he desired that it should instantly be brought to pass—and counted as the enemies of the Lord those who were opposed to him. But the earnestness of his moral and religious convictions and the sincerity of his faith made him single-minded, and manly in the highest degree. There was not the least sham about him; no whining over his failure; no false or factitious sentiment, no empty words;—in everything he showed himself simple, straightforward and brave. The Governor of Virginia, Governor Wise, said of him, that he was the pluckiest man he had ever seen. And on the morning of his execution, the jailor riding with him to the gallows said to him—"You're game, Captain Brown." And game he was to the very last. He said to the sheriff as he stepped onto the platform of the gallows, "Don't keep me waiting longer than is necessary,"—and then he was kept waiting for more than ten minutes while the military made some movement that their officers thought requisite. This gratuitous piece of cruel torture has shocked the whole country. But Brown stood perfectly firm and calm through the whole.

The account of his last interview with his wife before his death, which came by telegraph, was like an old ballad in the condensed picturesqueness of its tender and tragic narrative.

You see even from this brief and imperfect statement of mine, how involved the moral relations of the whole affair have been, and how difficult the questions which arise from it are to answer.

What its results will be no one can tell, but they cannot be otherwise than great. One great moving fact remains that here was a man, who, setting himself firm on the Gospel, was willing to sacrifice himself and his children in the cause of the oppressed, or at least of those whom he believed unrighteously held in bondage. And this fact has been forced home to the consciousness of every one by Brown's speech at his trial, and by the simple and most affecting letters which he wrote during his imprisonment. The events of this last month or two have done more to confirm the opposition to Slavery at the North, and to open the eyes of the South to the danger of taking a stand upon this matter opposed to the moral convictions of the civilized world—than anything which has ever happened before, than all the anti-slavery tracts and novels that ever were written.

I do not believe that other men are likely to follow John Brown in the course which he adopted—mainly because very few of them are of his stamp, but also because almost all men see that the means he adopted were wrong. But the magnanimity of the man will do something to raise the tone of national character and feeling—and to set in their just position the claims and the pretensions of the mass of our political leaders. John Brown has set up a standard by which to measure the principles of public men.

Source: Letters of Charles Eliot Norton, Vol. 1, ed. Sara Norton and Mark Antony De Wolfe Howe (Boston: Houghton Mifflin, 1913), 197–201.

Charles Sumner, "To the Duchess of Argyll," December 20, 1859

The Republican senator from Massachusetts, Charles Sumner (1811–1874), was in England during Brown's trial. Soon after his return to the United States, he wrote from Washington to the Duchess of Argyll, Elizabeth Georgiana Campbell, about Brown. Like numerous observers, he separated the man and the act. Sumner had helped organize the Free Soil Party and had urged resistance to the Fugitive Slave Act, calling it unconstitutional. He had served in the U.S. Senate since 1851. Two days before Brown and his men murdered proslavery settlers at Pottawatomie Creek, congressman Preston Brooks from South Carolina bludgeoned Sumner almost to death in the Senate. The attack of May 22, 1856, was a response to Sumner's "Crime against Kansas" speech of May 19 and 20, which denounced the Kansas-Nebraska Act. The speech singled out senator Andrew Butler of South Carolina, Brooks's cousin and an architect of the act. As Brooks became a Southern hero and Sumner became a hero across the North, the attack both revealed and exacerbated the sectional tensions that would lead to war. Sumner did not attend the Senate for the next three years while recovering from the attack. He resumed his seat only in early December 1859, soon after Brown's execution.

I found conversation & the press much occupied by the recent inroad into Virginia, of which only a hint had reached England before I embarked. Every where the enterprize has been condemned, while it has seemed almost mad, but the singular courage & character shewn by its author have awakened very general admiration. People find in his conversation & letters since his imprisonment & in his death much of the Covenanter, the Puritan & even the early Xtian[142] martyr.

Of course his act must be deplored, & yet it was the pedestal which has shewn to the world a most remarkable character, whose courageous example is destined to influence powerfully our dreadful question.

I wish that I could talk with you on this theme. For a practical statesman, believing Slavery a wrong, the subject is not without its difficulties. Not, indeed, that I hesitate to judge the *act;* but how can I refuse my admiration to many things in the *man?* The subject has been discussed in the Senate, on a motion for a Committee of Inquiry,[143] but I took no part.

Source: The Selected Letters of Charles Sumner, Vol. 2, ed. Beverly Wilson Palmer (Boston: Northeastern University Press, 1990), pp. 10–11. © University Press of New England, Lebanon, NH. Reprinted with permission.

John Greenleaf Whittier, "Brown of Ossawatomie," December 22, 1859

Like Lydia Maria Child's poem "The Hero's Heart," "Brown of Ossawatomie" by John Greenleaf Whittier (1807–1892) focused on the fictional moment when Brown kissed a slave child on the way to the gallows. Whittier based the kissing scene on a false account written by Henry Olcott and published in the *New York Tribune* on December 5, 1859, and he first published the poem in the *Independent,* a prominent New York City paper affiliated with Henry Ward Beecher's Plymouth Church and edited by Theodore Tilton. It appeared again in his volume *National Lyrics* (1865). A Quaker, Whittier had edited the Pennsylvania *Freeman* in the late 1830s and helped found the antislavery Liberty Party. As a Quaker, he perhaps focused on the kiss as he tried to reconcile Brown's violence with his own pacifism. But his dislike of Brown's methods are apparent nonetheless in phrases like "bloody hand," "grisly fighter," and "midnight terror." In fact, responding to the poem, some abolitionists felt that it failed to express enough warmth for the martyr. Garrison launched a semijovial attack, identifying Whittier's ambivalence and demanding more respect on Brown's behalf. In a public letter he referenced other poems by Whittier that seemed to endorse violence, suggesting that Brown had read these lines just before raiding Harpers Ferry: "Speak out in acts!—the time for words / Has passed." Indignant, Whittier replied in a public letter to *The Liberator* that he abhorred slavery as a state of war but opposed forcible means to end it. Garrison had the last word. In response he published another of Whittier's poems, suggesting that it was a more suitable tribute than "Brown of Ossawatomie." Two lines read: "Thou hast fallen in thine armor, / Thou martyr of the Lord!"

John Brown of Ossawatomie spake on his dying day:
"I will not have to shrive my soul a priest in Slavery's pay;
But let some poor slave-mother whom I have striven to free,
With her children, from the gallows-stair put up a prayer for me!"[144]

John Brown of Ossawatomie, they led him out to die;
And lo! a poor slave-mother with her little child pressed nigh:

Then the bold, blue eye grew tender, and the old harsh face grew mild,
As he stooped between the jeering ranks and kissed the negro's child!

The shadows of his stormy life that moment fell apart,
And they who blamed the bloody hand forgave the loving heart;
That kiss from all its guilty means redeemed the good intent,
And round the grisly fighter's hair the martyr's aureole bent!

Perish with him the folly that seeks through evil good!
Long live the generous purpose unstained with human blood!
Not the raid of midnight terror, but the thought which underlies;
Not the borderer's pride of daring, but the Christian's sacrifice.

Nevermore may yon Blue Ridges the Northern rifle hear,
Nor see the light of blazing homes flash on the negro's spear;
But let the free-winged angel Truth their guarded passes scale,
To teach that right is more than might, and justice more than mail!

So vainly shall Virginia set her battle in array;
In vain her trampling squadrons knead the winter snow with clay!
She may strike the pouncing eagle, but she dares not harm the dove;
And every gate she bars to Hate shall open wide to Love!

Source: New York Independent, December 22, 1859.

Thomas Hamilton, "The Nat Turner Insurrection," December 1859

The black journalist and abolitionist Thomas Hamilton (1823–1865) responded to Brown's raid and death by remembering Nat Turner. In August 1831, Turner led seventy other slaves in a rebellion in Southampton County, Virginia. The insurrection and its aftermath left dead approximately 160 people, black and white. Like Brown, Turner provoked abolitionist criticism of his violence and abolitionist celebration of his resistance and martyrdom. Turner's actions also shaped the South's response to Brown's raid, and Hamilton played on Southern fears: if the country did not respond to Brown's methods, Turner's would take over, he declared in an article of December 1859. Hamilton was a longtime critic of the African colonization movement and had served on the New York State Council of Colored People. His article appeared in the *Anglo-African Magazine*, a New York City–based monthly journal of politics, literature, science, history, and art that he founded and edited from 1859 to 1860. He also edited, with his brother Robert, a companion newspaper, the *Weekly Anglo-African*, from 1859 to 1865.

There are two reasons why we present our readers with the "Confessions of Nat Turner." First, to place upon record this most remarkable episode in the history of human slavery, which proves to the philosophic observer that in the midst of this most perfectly contrived and apparently secure system of slavery, humanity will out, and engender from its bosom forces that will contend against oppression, however unsuccessfully; and secondly, that the two methods of Nat Turner and of John Brown may be compared. The one is the mode in which the slave seeks freedom for his fellows, and the other mode in which the white man seeks to set the slave free. There are many points of similarity between these two men; they were both idealists; both governed by their views of the teachings of the Bible; both had harbored for years the purpose to which they gave up their lives; both felt themselves swayed as by some divine, or at least, spiritual impulse; the one seeking in the air, the earth, and the heavens for signs which came at last; and the other, obeying impulses which he believes to have been foreordained from the eternal past; both cool, calm, and heroic in prison and in the prospect of inevitable death; both confess with child-like frankness and simplicity the object they had in view the pure and simple emancipation of their fellow men; both win from the judges who sentenced them, expressions of deep sympathy—and here the parallel ceases. Nat Turner's terrible logic could only see the enfranchisement of one race compassed by the extirpation of the other; and he followed his gory syllogism with rude exactitude. John Brown, believing that the freedom of the enthralled could only be effected by placing them on an equality with the enslavers, and unable in the very effort at emancipation to tyrannize himself, is moved with compassion for tyrants, as well as slaves, and seeks to extirpate this formidable cancer, without spilling one drop of Christian blood.

These two narratives present a fearful choice to the slaveholders, nay, to this great nation—which of the two modes of emancipation shall take place? The method of Nat Turner, or the method of John Brown?

Emancipation must take place, and soon. There can be no long delay in the choice of methods. If John Brown's be not soon adopted by the free North, then Nat Turner's will be by the enslaved South.

Had the order of events been reversed—had Nat Turner been in John Brown's place at the head of these twenty-one men, governed by his inexorable logic and cool daring, the soil of Virginia and Maryland and the far South would by this time be drenched in the blood and the wild and sanguinary course of these men, no earthly power could stay.

The course which the South is now frantically pursuing will engender in its bosom and nurse into maturity a hundred Nat Turners, whom Virginia is infinitely less able to resist in 1860, than she was in 1831.

So, people of the South, people of the North! Men and brethren, choose ye which method of emancipation your prefer—Nat Turner's or John Brown's?

Source: Anglo-African Magazine, December 1859.

William A. Phillips, "The Age and the Man," January 20, 1860

William Phillips (1824–1893) met Brown three times near Lawrence, Kansas, in early July 1856, in February 1857, and a few months before the raid. In a lecture at Miller's Hall in Lawrence in January 1860, he called Brown the man of his age. Echoing Brown's own vision of history's "impartial tribunal," he looked ahead to a time when "impartial posterity" would scrutinize Osawatomie and find him worthy of admiration. Phillips had immigrated from Scotland in 1838 and served as a Republican representative from Kansas in 1865 and 1873–1879. He was working in Lawrence as a lawyer during the 1850s, when he met Brown. Years later he wrote an article for the *Atlantic Monthly* issue of December 1879 that described those three meetings and remembered Brown as a "theorist" and "visionary."

It is not necessary, in admiring the heroism of Brown's sacrifice, to indorse the plan his judgment adopted as the best means of getting rid of Slavery. In rejecting it let us merely see that we efficiently carry out our better one, and God, and humanity, ay, and John Brown, will smile on our efforts.

We need not imagine him an ogre, for many of us knew him. He dressed in plain and humble apparel. He was a close economist of all the necessities of life, so that as little as possible of the grand moments of life should be spent in acquiring them. In all the dreary Kansas struggle he was a fearless soldier, a cool and shrewd captain—careful of his men—kind and considerate to his prisoners. Unselfishly he consumed his own means in the struggle. Never for a moment asked, or would receive, real or nominal place or power. He held himself aloof from the intrigues of politicians, was obscure when *words* or "resolutions" were in vogue, and in the day of stern action was the first man in Kansas. While gingerbread generals issued quires of commissions to all who would bow down and worship them, he made the enemy quake at his name. I do not forget that we have had many other brave men—we have them now; but who can look back to the Kansas war of freedom and dare to tear the *first* laurel from John Brown of Osawatomie?

He lives today, my friends—he will live forever. Like Enoch and Elijah he did not *merely* have to die.[145] He sublimated, and gave all the life that was left in him to an immortal lesson. The country is so much under the influence of its Southern rulers, that it scarcely dares to say that it admires the heroic old Puritan. Ages will yet come, not subject to such influence; they will read that a poor old man, with a handful of brave companions, threw themselves away in a protest against Slavery. They will read the old man's letters. They will ponder on his words: "Had I done what I have done for the great and powerful, instead of the poor and oppressed, it would all have been right." They will ponder over his coolly brave estimate, that his martyrdom by Slavery, in the cause of Freedom, "would pay." With admiration will they think of him, as he calmly walked on the scaffold; cheerful, because inspired with that lofty idea. They will see the military power of the Slave State of Virginia ranged around his gallows. They will see how studiously they strove to wring one emotion of fear from that brave old man. The Slave authorities had brow-beaten and intimidated so many Northern men, that they were frantic at the idea that one could die, calmly despising their power. And what a refinement of cruelty and culmination of heroism does that last scene reveal! The martyr to the cause of Liberty stands with his hands bound behind his back—the death cap over his eyes—the rope around his neck. It is a solemn moment in which the bravest and best human soul meets death face to face. It was his last moment of life— the next for eternity. But that moment is protracted—cunningly, cruelly. The military power of Virginia is wheeling and circling around the base of the scaffold. The artillery rattles—the arms clank. John Brown does not see it. He can hear, but knows not what it is. It is only the Slave power protracting that solemn moment, in hopes of wringing one quiver of fear from that brave old man. One groan—one spasm, would be worth all the manacles in Virginia. They failed. He died calmly and humbly, without a quiver on his lips.

But Conservatism says, All this is dreadful. Could not the old man have followed some money-making business, and not brought such a torrent of trouble on every body? When Algernon Sydney was brought to the scaffold his *noble* relatives reproached him for the misery he had occasioned.[146] Could not the son of an English Earl let Republicanism alone, and be happy? Calm and unmoved, the brave Sydney stepped on the scaffold. He quailed not before the "regularly constituted authorities" who took his life. Humbly he knelt to his God, and then laid his head on the block. Trembling, as he gazed on that noble form, the executioner hesitated, and asked—

"Will you rise again?"

"Not till the final resurrection—strike on."[147]

Thus were slain Algernon Sydney and John Brown. Both of them disregarded "constituted authorities." Both of them knew that the vitality of their race was a Protest against wrong, and both sealed their Protests with their lives.

How little we know of the infinite wisdom and mercy of the God of the Universe. If there is one who doubts of his guiding hand in all our present affairs, let him look to the events of the past two months. I was in Leavenworth when the telegraph brought the strange news of "Insurrection at Harper's Ferry!" Then came the sad intelligence to Kansas, that John Brown of Osawatomie, Kagi, Stephens, Thompson, Anderson, and the others were of the party, and dead, or dying. Lying wounded and bloody in the hands of the Virginians, some of whom had similarly attacked us—us, not *similarly,* for they came to plant Slavery, and he went to proclaim Freedom. Then, when we heard that all were not yet dead, although dreadfully wounded, we prayed that they might die as befitted brave soldiers, and not that they should be exhibited on an ignominious gibbet.

Ah, my friends, we had but little faith in God, or humanity. How unerringly grand the finger that guided all these events! Look to John Brown, surviving that desperate charge, covered with wounds and yet recovering, and escaping the fury of the Virginians after he was disarmed and helpless. Why was it? He was spared to write those grand letters. To utter those simple but solemn Protests against the crime of Slavery. To stand as the representative of the Anti-slavery sentiment. Hated because he was. To Protest against the wrong with his life, and to meet *such* a death undismayed. Two months ago respectable papers were fain to stigmatize him, that they might haply escape the suspicion of sympathizing with him. Now, no respectable paper would like to do such a thing. Then, honorable members of Congress compared him to a highwayman, who now trace the mainsprings of his action to Jefferson, Christianity, and God.

The time is coming, when an impartial posterity will calmly review the career of John Brown—the cause for which he died, and the men who remorselessly took his life; and looking from this generation to his sacrifice, will recognize in them the AGE and the MAN.

Source: James Redpath, *Echoes of Harper's Ferry* (Boston: Thayer and Eldridge, 1860), 361–383 (380–383).

Louisa May Alcott, "With a Rose That Bloomed on the Day of John Brown's Martyrdom," January 20, 1860

In May 1859, the writer and abolitionist Louisa May Alcott (1832–1888) heard Brown speak at the town hall in Concord, Massachusetts, during a New England Emigrant Aid Society meeting organized by Franklin Sanborn. Alcott and her family, including her Garrisonian abolitionist father, Amos Bronson Alcott, raised money for Brown. After his execution, Brown's portrait hung above the fireplace in the family's Concord home, and Louisa May Alcott joined a vigilance committee to protect Sanborn after he was arrested (and cleared) as a conspirator in the raid. In July 1860 the Alcott family hosted Brown's widow and daughters. Alcott thought Mary Brown had "natural dignity. . . . though she did drink out of her saucer and used the plainest speech." Her poem about Brown uses the language of martyrdom, botany, and war. In one line Alcott prefigures the famous Union song about the ever-marching Brown, describing her hero's "unfaltering" footsteps that echo across the North.

In the long silence of the night,
Nature's benignant power
Woke aspirations for the light
Within the folded flower.
Its presence and the gracious day
Made summer in the room.
But woman's eyes shed tender dew
On the little rose in bloom.

Then blossomed forth a grander flower,
In the wilderness of wrong.
Untouched by Slavery's bitter frost,
A soul devout and strong.
God-watched, that century plant uprose,
Far shining through the gloom.

Filling a nation with the breath
Of a noble life in bloom.

A life so powerful in its truth,
A nature so complete;
It conquered ruler, judge and priest,
And held them at its feet.
Death seemed proud to take a soul
So beautifully given,
And the gallows only proved to him
A stepping-stone to heaven.

Each cheerful word, each valiant act,
So simple, so sublime,
Spoke to us through the reverent hush
Which sanctified that time.
That moment when the brave old man
Went so serenely forth
With footsteps whose unfaltering tread
Re-echoed through the North.

The sword he wielded for the right
Turns to a victor's palm;
His memory sounds forever more,
A spirit-stirring psalm.
No breath of shame can touch his shield,
Nor ages dim its shine;
Living, he made life beautiful—
Dying, made death divine.

No monument of quarried stone,
No eloquence of speech
Can grave the lessons on the land
His martyrdom will teach.
No eulogy like his own words,
With hero-spirit rife,
"I truly serve the cause I love,
By yielding up my life."

Source: The Liberator, January 20, 1860.

Stephen Douglas, "Invasion of States," January 23, 1860

Stephen Douglas (1813–1861), a Democratic senator from Illinois who designed the Kansas-Nebraska Bill, responded to Brown's raid by introducing a bill to protect states from invasion by inhabitants of other states, and to suppress and punish conspiracies that intended to invade the property or assail the inhabitants of other states. Douglas submitted the bill on January 16, 1860. Arguing for its necessity, he cited President Buchanan's response to a request from Governor Wise of Virginia on November 25, 1859. Fearing an attempt to rescue Brown from the Charles Town jail before his execution, Wise had asked Buchanan to "take steps to preserve peace between the States." Buchanan replied that there was no provision in the Constitution or any laws that authorized him to take such steps. Douglas made the case for his state-invasion bill on January 23. His speech to the Senate argues that Brown was a Republican and that the Republican Party was responsible for his raid. The Joint Committee of the General Assembly of Virginia shared this opinion, stating on January 26: "The crimes of John Brown were neither more nor less than practical illustrations of the Republican Party."

It cannot be said with truth that the Harper's Ferry case will not be repeated, or is not in danger of repetition. It is only necessary to inquire into the causes which produced the Harper's Ferry outrage, and ascertain whether those causes are yet in active operation, and then you can determine whether there is any ground for apprehension that that invasion will be repeated. Sir, what were the causes which produced the Harper's Ferry outrage? Without stopping to adduce evidence in detail, I have no hesitation in expressing my firm and deliberate conviction that the Harper's Ferry crime was the natural, logical, inevitable result of the doctrines and teachings of the Republican party, as explained and enforced in their platform, their partisan presses, their pamphlets and books, and especially in the speeches of their leaders in and out of

Congress. I am not making this statement for the purpose of crimination or partisan effect. I desire to call the attention of the members of that party to a reconsideration of the doctrines that they are in the habit of enforcing, with a view to a fair judgment whether they do not lead directly to those consequences on the part of those deluded persons who think that all they say is meant in real earnest and ought to be carried out. The great principle that underlies the organization of the Republican party is violent, irreconcilable, eternal warfare upon the institution of American slavery, with the view of its ultimate extinction throughout the land; sectional war is to be waged until the cotton fields of the South shall be cultivated by free labor, or the rye fields of New York and Massachusetts shall be cultivated by slave labor. In furtherance of this article of their creed, you find their political organization not only sectional in its location, but one whose vitality consists in appeals to northern passion, northern prejudice, northern ambition against southern States, southern institutions, and southern people. . . .

Can any man say to us that although this outrage has been perpetrated at Harper's Ferry, there is no danger of its recurrence? Sir, is not the Republican party still embodied, organized, confident of success and defiant in its pretensions? Does it not now hold and proclaim the same creed that it did before this invasion? It is true that most of its representatives here disavow the acts of John Brown at Harper's Ferry. I am glad that they do so; I am rejoiced that they have gone thus far; but I must be permitted to say to them that it is not sufficient that they disavow the act, unless they also repudiate and denounce the doctrines and teachings which produced the act. Those doctrines remain the same; those teachings are being poured into the minds of men throughout the country by means of speeches and pamphlets and books and through partisan presses. The causes that produced the Harper's Ferry invasion are now in active operation. Is it true that the people of all the border States are required by the Constitution to have their hands tied, without the power of self-defence, and remain patient under a threatened invasion in the day or in the night? Can you expect people to be patient, when they dare not lie down to sleep at night without first stationing sentinels around their houses to see if a band of marauders and murderers are not approaching with torch and pistol? Sir, it requires more patience than freemen ever should cultivate, to submit to constant annoyance, irritation and apprehension. If we expect to preserve this

Union, we must remedy, within the Union and in obedience to the Constitution, every evil for which disunion would furnish a remedy. If the federal Government fails to act, either from choice or from an apprehension of the want of power, it cannot be expected that the States will be content to remain unprotected.

Source: Invasion of States: Speech of Hon. S. A. Douglas, of Illinois (Washington: s.n., 1860), 7–8, 10–11.

Richard Realf, "John Brown's Raid,"
January 30, 1860

Though he did not join the raid on Harpers Ferry, the poet and abolitionist Richard Realf (1834–1878) did join Brown in Chatham at the constitutional convention of May 1858 and accepted the position of secretary of state under Brown's provisional government. He was arrested and charged with treason in connection with the raid, then released by the Senate investigating committee after giving his testimony. On January 30 he wrote a public letter from Washington, D.C., that distanced him from the raid. However, the letter does separate Brown's means and ends, arguing that Brown took action so that slaves would not have to rise up in mass insurrection and kill their masters. Realf also distances Brown from the Republican Party, in response to Democratic attempts to link Brown to Republicans such as William Seward and Joshua Giddings. Born in Sussex, England, Realf immigrated to America in April 1855. He worked as a missionary in the slums of New York and started an abolitionist newspaper. In October 1856 he moved to Kansas and fought with Brown in the border war. In 1859 he become a Jesuit priest and also joined a utopian Shaker community. In 1862 he joined the Union Army, and in 1867 he taught at a school for freedmen in South Carolina. He killed himself in Oakland, California, in 1878.

John Brown in his heart despised the Republican Party, whether rightfully or wrongfully of course I do not undertake to say. He called it a party who had assumed the name of Liberty, and prostituted it to base purposes. He said it declared all men to be free, equal, entitled to liberty and the pursuit of happiness, and yet deprecated any interference with Slavery in the States where it existed; a craven-heartedness which only met with his contempt. So, putting no faith in the professions of that party, he undertook to abolish Slavery himself.

They who assert that, in this enterprise, he was moved rather by hatred of the slaveholder than affection for the slave, do his memory most foul wrong. The love of his heart comprehended and encompassed both. He believed that

203

unless the interference of some third party should anticipate and thus prevent the interference of slaves themselves, these latter would, one day, overthrow, the institution by a bloody war of extermination against their masters; and it was to prevent havoc and carnage which, as he conceived, threatened the South, that he entered upon his ill-fated movement. For, he argued, the same elements of resistance to oppression which would result in all bloody excesses if not wisely and properly directed, might be made subservient to the accomplishment of high purposes of humanity, if the governing intelligence was at their side. Wherefore, in order to supply that intellectual sagacity which the slaves lacked, and thus enable them to achieve their freedom, while restraining them from the cruelties into which their instincts would hurry them, he gave himself, to this enterprise.

In regard to his personal character, I must, though I reside in the South, where I expect to live and die, be permitted to say that it has been studiously and elaborately misrepresented. There never lived a man whose desire to promote human welfare and human happiness was more inextinguishable. Men have grown hoarse with calumniating his memory, who were never worthy to unloose the latchet of his shoes. Venal politicians, grown sleek upon public plunder, and men who cannot perform an act that is not stained with some deadly sin, have lifted up their hands in holy horror, and yelled out their execrable against his name. John Brown was no tongue-hero—no virtue-prattler. He was a reticent man; and when he did speak, the utterance was from his heart, and not his lungs. His faith was very simple. He desired society to be pure, free, unselfish—full of liberty and love. He believed it capable of such realization. The whole history of his life is that of an upward endeavor. 'Liberty!' that was the key to his soul; the master-passion that controlled all his other ambitions—personal, social, or political. It swayed him like a frenzy. But he had too much individualism of character, and he was too sensitive to the sufferings of others to be able to reason calmly on the every-day practical concerns of life, where abstract right is modified by a thousand conditions of expediency; and he was too indignant against all forms of wrong to be able to discriminate between a theory and its practice; and thus, by his very self-denial, his benevolence, his moral courage, he was precipitated upon the deed which brought him to the scaffold. Seized by this principle of liberty, he proceeded, as he thought, to carry it out; never stopping to think how it was limited and restrained on all sides by other principles; thus drawing his purpose so near the eye as to shut out all other things; and thus, too, becoming a monomaniac, mistaking his own conscientiousness for a call unto him from Heaven.

I have now a word to say in relation to myself. It is known that I was formerly associated with John Brown, and it is known that I now reside in the South. That which follows is in regard thereto. There was a time when I thought our contemplated insurrection to be *absolutely right.* I had occasion to alter my opinion: thus. The evidence upon which I committed myself to that enterprise was available only in the court of conscience. Now, in the depths of my being, even below the law of distinct consciousness, there lurked the instinct and impulse of another law that forebade the exercise of those feelings which would connect themselves with such a deed. With this impulse, thus dimly working, the promises I had made came in conflict; and my conscience, divided against myself, plucked me on and plucked me off, suggesting the resolution but preventing the performance. However much I multiplied reasons and motives in favor of the deed, there yet sprung up from a depth in my nature, which reflection has never fathomed, an impulse against it which I could neither account for not resist. I could not translate that which appeared to be an outward call of duty into a free, spontaneous moral impulse; and, as I could not perform it until I had so translated it, of course it was not performed at all.

Source: "John Brown's Raid," *New York Times,* February 10, 1860, 5.

Abraham Lincoln, "Address at the Cooper Institute," February 27, 1860

The day before Brown's execution, the Illinois Republican Abraham Lincoln (1809–1865) spoke on the campaign trail in Kansas. He used Brown's raid as an opportunity to affirm his faith in law and order. The way to express "our belief in regard to slavery . . . is through the ballot box—the peaceful method provided by the Constitution," he observed. Two days later, speaking to another Kansas audience, he explained that although Brown had shown "great courage" and "rare unselfishness," he had committed high crimes and received just punishment. Lincoln warned Southerners that they would be dealt with the same way if they tried to break up the Union. A few months later he wrote a speech for delivery at Henry Ward Beecher's church in Brooklyn, New York. The event was moved to the Cooper Institute in New York and eventually attracted a crowd of around 1300 people. This carefully researched speech of February 27, 1860, helped secure Lincoln's nomination for the presidency and answered Democrats like Stephen Douglas who tried to the blame Republicans for Brown's raid. Foreshadowing his own assassination by John Wilkes Booth, Lincoln compares Brown to a fanatic who attempts to assassinate the nation's leader.

I would address a few words to the Southern people. I would say to them:— You consider yourselves a reasonable and a just people; and I consider that in the general qualities of reason and justice you are not inferior to any other people. Still, when you speak of us Republicans, you do so only to denounce us as reptiles, or, at the best, as no better than outlaws. You will grant a hearing to pirates or murderers, but nothing like it to "Black Republicans." In all your contentions with one another, each of you deems an unconditional condemnation of "Black Republicanism" as the first thing to be attended to. Indeed, such condemnation of us seems to be an indispensable prerequisite—license, so to speak—among you to be admitted or permitted to speak at all. Now, can you, or not, be prevailed upon to pause and to consider whether this is quite just to us, or even to yourselves. . . .

You charge that we stir up insurrections among your slaves. We deny it; and what is your proof? Harper's Ferry! John Brown!! John Brown was no Republican; and you have failed to implicate a single Republican in his Harper's Ferry enterprise. If any member of our party is guilty in that matter, you know it or you do not know it. If you do know it, you are inexcusable for not designating the man and proving the fact. If you do not know it, you are inexcusable for asserting it, and especially for persisting in the assertion after you have tried and failed to make the proof. You need not be told that persisting in a charge which one does not know to be true, is simply malicious slander.

Some of you admit that no Republican designedly aided or encouraged the Harper's Ferry affair; but still insist that our doctrines and declarations necessarily lead to such results. We do not believe it. We know we hold to no doctrine, and make no declaration, which were not held to and made by "our fathers who framed the Government under which we live."[148] You never dealt fairly by us in relation to this affair. When it occurred, some important State elections were near at hand, and you were in evident glee with the belief that, by charging the blame upon us, you could get an advantage of us in those elections. The elections came, and your expectations were not quite fulfilled. Every Republican man knew that, as to himself at least, your charge was a slander, and he was not much inclined by it to cast his vote in your favor. Republican doctrines and declarations are accompanied with a continual protest against any interference whatever with your slaves, or with you about your slaves. Surely, this does not encourage them to revolt. True, we do, in common with "our fathers, who framed the Government under which we live," declare our belief that slavery is wrong; but the slaves do not hear us declare even this. For anything we say or do, the slaves would scarcely know there is a Republican party. I believe they would not, in fact, generally know it but for your misrepresentations of us, in their hearing. In your political contests among yourselves, each faction charges the other with sympathy with Black Republicanism; and then, to give point to the charge, defines Black Republicanism to simply be insurrection, blood and thunder among the slaves.

Slave insurrections are no more common now than they were before the Republican party was organized. What induced the Southampton insurrection, twenty-eight years ago, in which, at least, three times as many lives were lost as at Harper's Ferry? You can scarcely stretch your very elastic fancy to the conclusion that Southampton was "got up by Black Republicanism." In the present state of things in the United States, I do not think a general, or even a very extensive slave insurrection, is possible. The indispensable concert of action cannot be attained. The slaves have no means of rapid communication; nor can incendiary freemen, black or white, supply it. The explosive materials are everywhere in parcels; but there neither are, nor can be supplied, the indispensable connecting trains.

Much is said by Southern people about the affection of slaves for their masters and mistresses; and a part of it, at least, is true. A plot for an uprising could scarcely be devised and communicated to twenty individuals before some one of them, to save the life of a favorite master or mistress, would divulge it. This is the rule; and the slave revolution in Hayti was not an exception to it, but a case occurring under peculiar circumstances. The gunpowder plot of British history, though not connected with slaves, was more in point.[149] In that case, only about twenty were admitted to the secret; and yet one of them, in his anxiety to save a friend, betrayed the plot to that friend, and, by consequence, averted the calamity. Occasional poisonings from the kitchen, and open or stealthy assassinations in the field, and local revolts extending to a score or so, will continue to occur as the natural results of slavery; but no general insurrection of slaves, as I think, can happen in this country for a long time. Whoever much fears, or much hopes for such an event, will be alike disappointed.

In the language of Mr. Jefferson, uttered many years ago, "It is still in our power to direct the process of emancipation, and deportation, peaceably, and in such slow degrees, as that the evil will wear off insensibly; and their places be, *pari passu*,[150] filled up by free white laborers. If, on the contrary, it is left to force itself on, human nature must shudder at the prospect held up."[151]

Mr. Jefferson did not mean to say, nor do I, that the power of emancipation is in the Federal Government. He spoke of Virginia; and, as to the power of emancipation, I speak of the slaveholding States only. The Federal Government, however, as we insist, has the power of restraining the extension of the institution—the power to insure that a slave insurrection shall never occur on any American soil which is now free from slavery.

John Brown's effort was peculiar. It was not a slave insurrection. It was an

attempt by white men to get up a revolt among slaves, in which the slaves refused to participate. In fact, it was so absurd that the slaves, with all their ignorance, saw plainly enough it could not succeed. That affair, in its philosophy,
corresponds with the many attempts, related in history, at the assassination of
kings and emperors. An enthusiast broods over the oppression of a people till
he fancies himself commissioned by Heaven to liberate them. He ventures the
attempt, which ends in little else than his own execution. Orsini's attempt on
Louis Napoleon, and John Brown's attempt at Harper's Ferry were, in their
philosophy, precisely the same.[152] The eagerness to cast blame on old England[153] in the one case, and on New England in the other, does not disprove the
sameness of the two things.

And how much would it avail you, if you could, by the use of John Brown,
Helper's book,[154] and the like, break up the Republican organization? Human
action can be modified to some extent, but human nature cannot be changed.
There is a judgment and a feeling against slavery in this nation, which cast at
least a million and a half of votes. You cannot destroy that judgment and feeling—that sentiment—by breaking up the political organization which ral-
lies around it. You can scarcely scatter and disperse an army which has been
formed into order in the face of your heaviest fire; but if you could, how much
would you gain by forcing the sentiment which created it out of the peaceful
channel of the ballot-box, into some other channel? What would that other
channel probably be? Would the number of John Browns be lessened or enlarged by the operation?

Source: A Political Text-Book for 1860, ed. Horace Greeley and John Fitch Cleveland (New York: Tribune Association, 1860), 144–148 (146–147).

William H. Seward, "The State of the Country," February 29, 1860, and "The National Idea," October 3, 1860

Before Brown's raid, William H. Seward (1801–1872) was the Republicans' frontrunner for president. An antislavery U.S. senator from New York, Seward had responded to the Fugitive Slave Act by arguing that there was a "higher law than the Constitution, which regulates our authority over the domain" of the territories. In 1858 he had famously described an "irrepressible conflict" between the forces of freedom and slavery. Now, after Brown's raid on the federal arsenal, he stepped back from his earlier radicalism. In February 1860, two months before the Republican nominating convention, Seward clearly distanced himself from Brown, calling the raid an act of "sedition and treason." This backpedaling raised questions about his character and helped end his bid for the presidency. But by October 1860, when he returned to the topic of Brown, Seward no longer had to distance himself from the dead abolitionist. He remembered in a speech in Chicago that Brown had sustained him during a period of demoralization in the antislavery struggle.

"The State of the Country"

A canvass for a presidential election, in some respects more important perhaps than any since 1800, has recently begun. The house of representatives was to be organized by a majority, while no party could cast more than a plurality of votes. The gloom of the late tragedy in Virginia rested on the capitol from the day when congress assembled. While the two great political parties were peacefully, lawfully and constitutionally, though zealously, conducting the great national issue between free labor and capital labor for the territories to its proper solution, through the trials of the ballot, operating directly or indirectly on the various departments of the government, a band of exceptional men, contemptuous equally of that great question and of the parties to the controversy, and impatient of the constitutional system which confines the citizens of every state to political action by suffrage, in organized parties within their own borders, inspired by an enthusiasm peculiar to themselves, and exasperated by grievances and wrongs that some of them had suffered by inroads of armed propagandists of slavery in Kansas, unlawful as their own retaliation was, attempted to subvert slavery in Virginia by conspiracy, ambush, invasion and force. The method we have adopted, of appealing to the reason and judgment of the people, to be pronounced by suffrage, is the only one by which free government can be maintained anywhere, and the only one as yet devised which is in marked harmony with the spirit of the Christian religion. While generous and charitable natures will probably concede that John Brown and his associates acted on earnest though fatally erroneous convictions, yet all good citizens will nevertheless agree that this attempt to execute an unlawful purpose in Virginia by invasion, involving servile war, was an act of sedition and treason, and criminal in just the extent that it affected the public peace and was destructive of human happiness and human life. It is a painful reflection that, after so long an experience of the beneficent working of our system as we have enjoyed, we have had these new illustrations in Kansas and Virginia of the existence among us of a class of men so misguided and so desperate as to seek to enforce their peculiar principles by the sword, drawing after it a need for the further illustration by their punishment of that great moral truth, especially applicable in a republic, that they who take up the sword as a weapon of controversy, shall perish by the sword. In the latter case, the lamented deaths of so many citizens, slain from an ambush and by surprise—all the more lamentable because they were innocent victims of a frenzy kindled without their agency, in far distant fires—the deaths even of the offenders themselves, pitiable, although necessary and just, because they acted under delirium, which blinded their judgments to the real nature of their criminal enterprise; the alarm and consternation naturally awakened throughout the country, exciting, for the moment, the fear that our whole system, with all its securities for life and liberty, was coming to an end—a fear none the more endurable because continually aggravated by new chimeras to which the great leading event lent an air of probability; surely all these constituted a sum of public misery, which ought to have satisfied the most morbid appetite for social horrors. But, as in the case of the gunpowder plot, and the Salem witchcraft, and the New York colonial negro plot,[155] so now; the original actors were swiftly followed by another and kindred class, who sought to prolong and widen the public distress by attempting to direct the indignation which it had excited, against parties guiltless equally of complicity and of sympathy with the offenders.

Posterity will decide in all the recent cases where political responsibility for public disasters must fall; and posterity will give little heed to our interested instructions.

"The National Idea; Its Perils and Triumphs"

In 1854, after the repeal of the Missouri compromise,[156] without producing so much alarm as a considerable thunder storm would do in the nation, there was only one man left who hoped against the prevailing demoralization, and who cheered and sustained me through it; and that man, in his zeal to make his prediction just, was afterwards betrayed so far by his zeal that he became ultimately a monomaniac, and suffered on the gallows. That was John Brown. The first and only time I ever saw him was when he called upon me after the abrogation of the Missouri compromise, and asked me what I thought of the future. I said I was disappointed and saddened—I would persevere, but it was against hope. He said, "Cheer up, governor; the people of Kansas will not accept slavery; Kansas will never be a slave state."

I took then a deliberate survey of the broad field; I considered all; I examined and considered all the political forces which were revealed to my observation. I saw that freedom in the future states of this continent was the necessity of this age, and of this country. I saw that the establishment of this as a republic, conservative of the rights of human nature, was the cause of the whole world.

Source: The Works of William H. Seward, Vol. 4, ed. George E. Baker (Boston: Houghton Mifflin, 1888), 619–643 (636–638), 348–367 (358).

John S. Rock, "Ninetieth Anniversary of the Boston Massacre," March 5, 1860

In a speech at Tremont Temple in Boston, the black abolitionist John Swett Rock (1825–1866) imagined Brown as the hero of America's second revolution and compared him to Crispus Attucks. As one of five people killed in the Boston Massacre on March 5, 1770, Attucks appealed to antislavery advocates as a figure of black martyrdom for freedom's cause. But Rock argued that Brown, like Nat Turner, was a better symbol of revolution than Attucks. His speech then predicts that only violence will end slavery. Other speakers that night were William Lloyd Garrison and John Sella Martin. Born in New Jersey, Rock had studied medicine, practiced dentistry, and lectured for several antislavery organizations. He went on to open a law office in 1861 and in 1865 became the first African American attorney to argue in the Supreme Court.

I am not yet ready to idolize the actions of Crispus Attucks, who was a leader among those who resorted to forcible measures to create a new government which has used every means in its power to outrage and degrade his race and posterity, in order to oppress them more easily, and to render their condition more hopeless in this country.

I am free to confess that I have strong attachments here, in this my native country, and desire to see it prosperous and happy; yet, situated and outraged as I am, in common with a race whose live shave been one of toil to make this country what it is, I would deny the manly promptings of my own soul, if I should not say that American liberty is a word which has no charms for me. It is a name without meaning—a shadow without substance, which retains not even so much as the ghost of the original.

The only events in the history of this country which I think deserve to be commemorated, are the organization of the Anti-Slavery Society and the insurrections of Nat Turner and John Brown. *(Applause.)*

I believe in insurrections *(applause)*—and especially those of the pen and of the sword. Wm. Lloyd Garrison is, I think, a perfect embodiment of the moral insurrection of thought, which is continually teaching the people of this country that unjust laws and compacts made by fathers are not binding upon their sons, and that the "higher law" of God, which we are bound to execute, teaches us to do unto others as we would have them do unto us. . . . John Brown was, and is, the representative of that potent power, the sword, which proposes to settle at once the relation between master and slave—peaceably if it can, forcibly if it must. This is, no doubt, the method by which the freedom of the blacks will be brought about in this country. It is a severe method; but to severe ills it is necessary to apply severe remedies. Slavery has taken up the sword, and it is but just that it should perish by it. *(Applause.)* The John Brown of the second Revolution, is but the Crispus Attucks of the first. A few years hence, and this assertion will be a matter of history. . . .

The question of whether freedom or slavery shall triumph in this country will no doubt be settled ere long, and settled in accordance with the eternal principles of justice. Whether the result is to be brought about by the gradual diffusion of an anti-slavery gospel, or the method introduced by Crispus Attucks, and seconded by John Brown, no one can tell. I hope it may be done peaceably; but if, as appears to be the case, there is no use in crying peace, then let us not shrink from the responsibility. My motto has always been, "Better die freemen than live to be slaves."[157] . . . Our cause is moving onward. The driving of the free colored people from the slave States, and the laws preventing the ingress into the free States, is only the tightening of the already standard cord that binds the slave; and I am daily looking for some additional force to sever it, and thereby annihilate forever the relation existing between master and slave. *(Applause.)*

Source: The Liberator, March 16, 1860.

William Henry Furness, "Put Up Thy Sword," March 11, 1860

William Henry Furness (1802–1896) was the minister of the First Congregational Unitarian Church in Philadelphia from 1825 until 1875. He used the example of Brown to address the growing division of Northern and Southern opinion and to argue that nonviolent moral suasion was a better way to attack slavery. In March 1860 he was a guest speaker at the Music Hall in Boston, where he lectured to an antislavery crowd of several thousand. Taking his text from John 18:11, "Put up thy sword into the sheath," he delivered a long sermon about the value of nonviolence. The sermon honors Brown's courage but condemns his violence and does not endorse slave insurrection.

I do not imagine there is a man among us so destitute of common sense and humanity as to think of inciting the slaves to acts of vengeance and murder. No friend of the black race can regard such a thought with any feeling but of horror. Why, the first intimation of the existence of such a purpose would be a signal for the instant outbreak of a war of extermination upon that unhappy people. It has been thought, that it would help certain party and political purposes to charge certain persons at the North with this bloody design, but of those who made this charge, I do not suppose that any believed it, but those who were bereft of their senses by rage and terror. It is not in the people of the North to entertain any such murderous idea. Indeed, so utterly incapable do I hold them to be of any such savage intent, that I can hardly bear to seem to be defending them against the charge.

But it is needful to say what I am saying: we must expect this charge to be made, we must reconcile ourselves to the humiliation of uttering our protest against being accused of these bloody designs, so long as we avow, as the great mass of the people all over the world do avow, the lawfulness, under any cir-

215

cumstances, of resorting to brute force, of drawing the death-dealing sword for God and for man. So long as we maintain the right to shoot and stab to right any wrong, we are fairly open to the suspicion of being ready and willing to shoot and stab to any extent; not only because we are extremely liable to confound our passions with our principles, and to persuade ourselves that we are striking for God and for the Right, when we are only gratifying our anger or our revenge, but because, the right to use violence in any case being maintained, as a principle, we do virtually stand upon the ground of its lawfulness in all cases. It is a principle upon which no restriction can be put, for it asserts aggression to be the dictate of self-defence, and uses not merely a shield, but a sword and a sword not merely to ward off, but to strike. The distinction is made, I know, between the offensive and the defensive. The line that divides these two seems to be very easily and broadly drawn, but it is very sensitive, and sways to and fro with the slightest breath of human emotion, and may at any moment be obliterated by the surges of passion.

What act of war is there so bloody and inhuman that it has not been justified at the moment, and afterwards, upon the ground that it was rendered necessary for the self-protection of somebody?

So long, therefore, as we assert the right to use the sword upon any occasion, we lay ourselves open to the charge of being ready to use it needlessly, because we are, in fact, liable to use it so; because, when we are aggressive in defence, it is bare physical exertion required to render a blow effective creates a heat in the blood, and the hot blood goes to the brain, and when the mind is heated, the ordinary effect of heat follows. The thoughts and images that rise in the mind are dilated; trifles are magnified into grave offences; the wild suggestions of an inflamed fancy are taken for self-evident facts, and then all the curbs of Reason and Humanity are consumed in the heat, and the passions rush all abroad to the work of blood and rapine, like so many demons let loose from the abodes of darkness.

So plainly true is all this, that while I heartily honor John Brown for his generous purpose and for his heroic courage, while I freely allow that wherein he was wrong he had this excuse, that he was justified by the public sentiment of the world, which recognizes the sword as the lawful instrument of Justice and Liberty, I nevertheless see, that in resorting to force, in drawing the sword for the slave, he was wrong, and that the means which he employed tended to hurt the cause which it was in his great heart to serve. With all his care so to organize the enterprise which he undertook in behalf of the slave as to keep it strictly within the bounds of humanity and self-defence which he resolved to observe, he was not able, even on the threshold of his attempt, to prevent a shedding of blood, a sacrifice of life, which his purpose and his method did not contemplate, and which aroused against him and his little company a ferocity so savage that it wreaked its fury even upon the dead bodies of those of his friends who fell at Harper's Ferry. Wise and self-possessed as he was, and with all his experience of the barbarity of the Slave Power, and because, as I believe, he was full of the blessed idea of restoring to the oppressed the sacred rights of which they are robbed, he appears to have lost all foresight of the cruelty and bloodshed which would inevitably flow from the frenzy of fear and wrath that the first flash of his drawn sword would certainly kindle in those against whom it was drawn. He did not take into account the undeviating law, that violence produced violence, and that the force, which he intended to employ very guardedly and under the stead restraint of a watchful humanity, would look, in the eyes of those against whom it was directed, like nothing but what it was, pure, untempered, brute force, and so would be sure to arouse a force in them which would regard no restraints. Had he been successful in his first enterprise, had every thing gone as he intended, and a refuge been obtained in the mountains, it would have told fearfully upon the black race, whose blood all over the South would, I believe, have run like water, and whose chains would instantly have been trebled in weight, while at the North, all who sympathize with them would have been the objects of a far fiercer persecution than they have yet dreamed of. I know that the slave has friends here, whose fidelity no persecution, however violent, can shake, but only confirm. I believe, too, that they are prepared for every trial that an uncompromising adherence to the Right may involve. Only the more earnestly to be desired is it, that no unnecessary occasion should be given to the spirit of persecution, that no needless obstacles should be thrown in the way of the great and holy cause of Abolition. It is not worth while that the difficulties with which it has to contend should be aggravated by the employment of methods of serving it, which, to say the least, are questionable, and which many of its most faithful friends consider positively and upon principle wrong.

That such consequences as I have mentioned would have resulted from the success of John Brown's attempt, we may see plainly enough from what has actually followed upon its failure. In some of the Slave States, it is seriously proposed, as you know, either to drive out of them all free persons of African blood, or reduce them to the abject condition of slaves. In Kentucky, a company of white people, resembling the primitive Christians in their blameless and devout lives, have been driven into exile, for no reason but because they had pity upon the enslaved and held oppression to be sinful before God. In the city where I dwell, persons, from whose education and position better things were to be expected, have publicly counseled the violent suppression of the most precious principle of American institutions, Free Speech; counsel which only the commendable firmness of our civil authorities prevented from being carried into effect with blood and fire. And all over the South, every Northern stranger is narrowly watched, and many have been brutally treated and driven away, and a reign of terror inaugurated, under which the bloody law of the Suspect, without needing to be enacted, is going into full operation.

These things are the inevitable consequences of the intrusion of the drawn sword into the great conflict, and they show what far more bloody results would have to come, not to the free white people of the South, not to the slaveholders, but to the slaves and their well-wishers, had not the sword that was drawn been instantly driven back into the sheath.

The recent attempt, therefore, which is stirring the heart of the country, "educating the nation," as Wendell Phillips loves to say, teaches us very pointedly what we are not to do for our enslaved brother. Most solemnly does it repeat the command of Jesus to his rash and ardent friend: "Put Up THY SWORD INTO THE SHEATH". . . .

It was when the sword of steel was taken out of the hand of John Brown, as he himself said, and he was left with only the Sword of the Spirit, that he had a new experience of a higher power than the force of arms. When he was a prisoner, and doomed to death, when he went to the scaffold, with the serenity of the fine country around him in his heart as well as in his eye, then it was that he was robed and crowned with victory. Then shone forth the heroic quality of the man, brighter than any diadem. Then friend and foe were alike touched with his nobleness, and a right loyal thrill of admiring sympathy went through the world.

Source: A Discourse Delivered Before Theodore Parker's Society (Boston: R. F. Wallcut, 1860), 12–17, 22.

Carl Schurz, "The Doom of Slavery," August 1, 1860

The German-American Carl Schurz (1829–1906) used the Southern response to Brown's raid as evidence of the South's weakness, hysteria, and inability to fight its actual enemy: the inexorable progress toward freedom. In his speech to an antislavery crowd in Verandah Hall in St. Louis, he predicts that slavery *will* end because the "wheel of progress" is turning. Schurz goes on to imagine the future and promises that proslavery Southerners will regret not having Brown's epitaph as their own. Schurz considered the speech a masterpiece. Delivered in August 1860, during the presidential campaign, it was intended to help elect Lincoln to the White House and Republican candidates to Congress, although it was his first speech in a slave state, so he addressed parts of it to slaveholders. Schurz had served as a spokesman for the Wisconsin delegation at the Republican National Convention of May that year and begun his lecture tour in July. It would last until October, taking him to Ohio, Illinois, Missouri, Indiana, New York, Pennsylvania, Connecticut, and Wisconsin, often to towns where he could assemble large numbers of German Americans. A recent immigrant himself, Schurz had been a revolutionary in Germany, part of a group of liberals who demanded national unity, democracy, and political freedom in 1848. He escaped to England after the revolution was defeated and then immigrated to the United States in 1852. He lived in Philadelphia before settling in Watertown, Wisconsin, in 1855, where he became an antislavery Republican and began practicing law. He went on to be a Union Army general and in 1869 was the first German-born American elected to the U.S. Senate.

The slave States harbor a dangerous enemy within their own boundaries, and that is slavery itself. Imagine them at war with anti-slavery people whom they have exasperated by their own hostility. What will be the effect upon the slaves? The question is not whether the North will instigate a slave rebellion, for I suppose they will not; the question is, whether they can prevent it, and I think they cannot. But the anticipation of a negro insurrection (and the heated imagination of the slaveholder will discover symptoms of a rebellious spirit in every trifle) may again paralyze the whole South. Do you remember the effect of John Brown's attempt? The severest blow he struck at the slave-power was not that he disturbed a town and killed several citizens, but that he revealed the weakness of the whole South. Let Governor Wise of Virginia carry out his threatened invasion of the free States, not with twenty-three, but with twenty-three hundred followers at his heels—what will be the result? As long as they behave themselves we shall let them alone; but as soon as they create any disturbance they will be put into the stationhouse; and the next day we shall read in the newspapers of some Northern city, among the reports of the police-court: "Henry A. Wise and others, for disorderly conduct, fined $5." Or, if he has made an attempt on any man's life, or against our institutions, he will most certainly find a Northern jury proud enough to acquit him on the ground of incorrigible mental derangement. Our pictorial prints will have material for caricatures for two issues, and a burst of laughter will ring to the skies from Maine to California. And there is the end of it. But behold John Brown with twenty-three men[158] raising a row at Harper's Ferry; the whole South frantic with terror; the whole State of Virginia in arms; troops marching and counter-marching, as if the battle of Austerlitz[159] were to be fought over again; innocent cows shot as bloodthirsty invaders, and even the evening song of the peaceful whippoorwills mistaken for the battle cry of rebellion. And those are the men who will expose themselves to the chances of a pro-slavery war with an anti-slavery people! Will they not look upon every captain as a John Brown, and every sergeant and private as a Coppoc or a Stevens?[160] They will hardly have men enough to quiet their fears at home. What will they have to oppose to the enemy? If they want to protect slavery then, every township will want its home regiment, every plantation its garrison. No sooner will a movement of concentration be attempted, than the merest panic may undo and frustrate it. Themistocles might say that Greece was on his ships; a French general might say that the Republic was in his camps; but slavery will be neither on the ships nor in the camp; it will be spread defenseless over thousands of square miles. This will be their situation: either they concentrate their forces, and slavery will be exposed wherever the army is not; or they do not concentrate them, and their army will be everywhere, but in fact nowhere. They want war? Let them try it! They will try it but once. And thus it turns out that the very same thing that would be the cause of the war, would at the same time be indefensible by war. The same institution that wants protection will at the same time

disable its protectors. Yes, slavery, which can no longer be defended with arguments, cannot be defended with arms.

There is your dissolution of the Union for the perpetuation of slavery. The
Southern States cannot reasonably desire it, for it would defeat the very objects for which it would be undertaken; they cannot reasonably attempt it, for
slavery would lie helpless at the feet of the North. Slavery, which may die a
slow, gradual death in the Union, will certainly die an instantaneous and violent death if they attempt to break out of the Union. What then will the South
do in case of a Republican victory? I answer that question with another one,
What can the South do in case of a Republican victory? Will there be a disturbance? If they know their own interests, the people of the South themselves
will have to put it down. Will they submit? Not to Northern dictation, but to
their own good sense. They have considered us their enemies as long as they
ruled us; they will find out that we are their friends as soon as we cease to be
their subjects. They have dreamed so long of the blessings of slavery; they will
open their eyes again to the blessings of liberty. They will discover that they
are not conquered, but liberated. Will slavery die out? As surely as freedom
will not die out.

Slaveholders of America, I appeal to you. Are you really in earnest when
you speak of perpetuating slavery? Shall it never cease? Never? Stop and consider where you are and in what day you live.

This is the nineteenth century. Never since mankind has a recollection of
times gone by, has the human mind disclosed such wonderful powers. The
hidden forces of nature we have torn from their mysterious concealment and
yoked them into the harness of usefulness; they carry our thoughts over slender wires to distant nations; they draw our wagons over the highways of trade;
they pull the gigantic oars of our ships; they set in motion the iron fingers of
our machinery; they will soon plow our fields and gather our crops. The labor
of the brain has exalted to a mere bridling and controlling of natural forces
the labor of the hand; and you think you can perpetuate a system which re-
duces man, however degraded, yet capable of development, to the level of a
soulless machine?

This is the world of the nineteenth century. The last remnants of feudalism
in the old world are fast disappearing. The Czar of Russia, in the fullness of
imperial power, is forced to yield to the irresistible march of human progress,

and abolishes serfdom.[161] Even the Sultan of Turkey can no longer maintain the barbarous customs of the Moslem against the pressure of the century, and slavery disappears.[162] And you, citizens of a Republic, you think you can arrest the wheel of progress with your Dred Scott decisions and Democratic platforms?

Look around you and see how lonesome you are in this wide world of ours. As far as modern civilization throws its rays, what people, what class of society is there like you? Cry out into the world your "wild and guilty fantasy" of property in man,[163] and every echo responds with a cry of horror or contempt; every breeze, from whatever point of the compass it may come, brings you a verdict of condemnation. There is no human heart that sympathizes with your cause, unless it sympathizes with the cause of despotism in every form. There is no human voice to cheer you on in your struggle; there is no human eye that has a tear for your reverses; no link of sympathy between the common cause of the great human brotherhood and you. You hear of emancipation in Russia and wish it to fail. You hear of Italy rising, and fear the spirit of liberty may become contagious. Where all mankind rejoices, you tremble. Where all mankind loves, you hate. Where all mankind curses, you sympathize.

And in this appalling solitude you stand alone against a hopeful world, alone against a great century, fighting your hopeless fight. . . . I hear the silly objection that your sense of honor forbids you to desert your cause. Sense of honor! Imagine a future generation standing around the tombstone of the bravest of you, and reading the inscription: "Here lies a gallant man who fought and died for the cause—of human slavery." What will the verdict be? His very progeny will disown him, and exclaim, "He must have been either a knave or a fool!" There is not one of you who, if he could rise from the dead a century hence, would not gladly exchange his epitaph for that of the meanest of those who were hung at Charlestown.[164]

Source: Speeches, Correspondence, and Political Papers of Carl Schurz, Vol. 1, ed. Frederick Bancroft (New York: Putnam's, 1913), 122–160 (154–159).

Pennsylvania Statesman, "Old Brown's Argument," October 20, 1860

A year after Brown's raid, the *Pennsylvania Statesman* marked the anniversary by remembering with horror the pikes that Brown and his men had prepared for use. Wildly sensationalist, the newspaper printed a drawing of a pike on its front page, so large that it filled nearly two whole columns. The drawing's caption explained that Brown had intended slaves to "murder the whites" with such pikes, which constituted a "black republican argument" to Southerners. The accompanying editorial was equally sensationalist, imagining children impaled on Brown's pikes. In the final paragraph, the editorial adds that voting for Lincoln was little better than arming more John Browns with pikes and sending them out to murder Southerners. This connection between Lincoln's votes and Brown's pikes reflected the newspaper's status as a Democratic campaign newspaper. It was published weekly out of Harrisburg, Pennsylvania, by the Democrat John M. Cooper (previously the editor of the *Valley Spirit*, a Democratic newspaper in Pennsylvania) between August 11, 1860, and November 3, 1860, the last issue being published three days before the presidential election. It supported the Southern Democrat John C. Breckinridge for president.

We present to the readers of the *Statesman* a graphic sketch of the Black Republican argument addressed by old John Brown to the people of the South, at Harper's Ferry, a year ago. It is an argument designed to *pierce the heart* rather than *convince the mind* of the Southern people. This *argument*, as delivered by old Brown, consisted of an Iron Pike precisely the size and shape of the drawing on our first page, fixed on a wooded staff six or seven feet long.[165] The intention of old Brown and his Black Republican aiders and abettors was to place these formidable weapons in the hands of the negroes and set them upon their masters.

For a work of this kind these Pikes were admirably adapted. It required no skill to handle them, except the skill acquired by handling the hoe and the

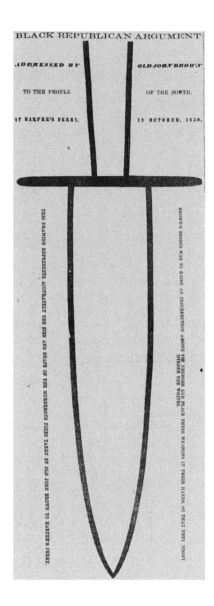

fork. They were just the thing to suit an ignorant and enraged negro. They would make a dreadful gash in the human body, from which the blood would flow in torrents. Driven by a strong arm, they would go through and through the body of a man or woman of ordinary size. A child could be impaled on them and carried aloft as a trophy.

But the negroes of Virginia, far better than the white men who attempted to incite them to insurrection, did not take up these murderous weapons and wield them against their masters. The diabolical Black Republican plot failed, and old Brown, the vilest miscreant that ever walked the earth, and all his infernal associates, met the hound's death that they so richly deserved.

They did not die "unwept, unhonored and unsung," however.[166] A wail went up from the North when the scoundrels ascended their scaffold. Sympathy meetings were held, over which leading Republicans presided, and at which leading Republicans made speeches full of admiration for the murderers. Crape was worn by some, and others draped their houses in mourning; and from New England to Kansas, sorrow for the failure of old Brown's expedition, and for the fate of those engaged in it, sat on the countenance of the supporters of Abraham Lincoln.

People of Pennsylvania! To elect Lincoln is to vote old John Brown a saint. His murderous descent at midnight, with weapons of death in his bloody hands, was the result of Republican teachings. If there had not grown up at the North a powerful party whose proclaimed mission is the "extinction of slavery,"[167] the Harper's Ferry murders and the public hangings at Charlestown would not have taken place. To vote for Lincoln is but little better than to put Pikes in the hands of such men as old Brown and send them on a marauding and murdering expedition to the South. Are Pennsylvanians prepared to do that? Let them remember *that every vote they cast for Lincoln is a murderous Pike manufactured for another John Brown!*

Source: *Pennsylvania Statesman*, October 20, 1860.

Lucretia Mott, "Remarks to the Pennsylvania Anti-Slavery Society," October 25, 1860

At the annual meeting of the Pennsylvania Anti-Slavery Society in 1860, Lucretia Mott (1793–1880) quoted the society's "Declaration of Sentiments" to remind her audience that it rejected antislavery violence. Her remarks describe Brown as two men, the soldier and the martyr, and embrace only Brown the martyr. Instead of weapons such as Brown's, Quakers fight with swords of the spirit, Mott explains. The remarks were excerpted in the *National Anti-Slavery Standard,* which was the official journal of the American Anti-Slavery Society from June 1840 to April 1870. Mott was a Quaker abolitionist and women's rights activist who helped found the Pennsylvania Anti-Slavery Society in 1833. Brown's wife, Mary, stayed at Mott's home in Philadelphia during part of Brown's imprisonment in November 1859. In a letter to Mary from jail, Brown remembered that on one occasion he had fought an anti-abolitionist mob in Boston, where Mott—a "faithful old lady"—was attending a meeting.

"Our principles lead us to reject and to intreat the oppressed to reject all carnal weapons, relying solely on those which are mighty through God to the pulling down of strongholds." We did not countenance force, and it did not become those—Friends and others—who go to the polls to elect a commander-in-chief of the army and navy, whose business it would be to use that army and navy, if needed, to keep the slaves of the South in their chains, and secure to the masters the undisturbed enjoyment of their system—it did not become such to find fault with us because we praise John Brown for his heroism. For it is not John Brown the soldier that we praise; it is John Brown the moral hero; John Brown the noble confessor and martyr whom we honor, and whom we think it proper to honor in this day when men are carried away by the corrupt and pro-slavery clamor against him. Our weapons were drawn only from the armory of Truth; they were those of faith and hope and love. They were those of moral indignation strongly expressed against wrong. Robert Purvis[168] has said that I was "the most belligerent non-resistant he ever saw." I accept the character he gives me; and I glory in it. I have no idea, because I am a non-resistant, of submitting tamely to injustice inflicted either on me or on the slave. I will oppose it with all the moral powers with which I am endowed. I am no advocate of passivity. Quakerism, as I understand it, does not mean quietism. The early Friends were agitators; disturbers of the peace; and were more obnoxious in their day to charges, which are now so freely made, than we are.

Source: National Anti-Slavery Standard, November 3, 1860.

Osborne P. Anderson, *A Voice from Harper's Ferry,* early 1861

Osborne Perry Anderson (1830–1872) was one of five black men who accompanied Brown at Harpers Ferry. He was born free in Pennsylvania and moved to Chatham, Canada, where he worked as a printer for a newspaper, the *Provincial Freeman.* He attended Brown's convention in Chatham and then won a lottery held by the publishers of the *Provincial Freeman* to decide who from the Chatham convention would represent the community during the Harpers Ferry raid. During the attack Anderson received the sword of Frederick the Great from Colonel Lewis W. Washington on Brown's behalf. He was the only black raider who survived the raid and its aftermath. After escaping into the mountains, he returned to Canada. Of the other black raiders, Dangerfield Newby and Lewis Sheridan Leary were killed at the Ferry, and John A. Copeland, Jr., and Shields Green were hanged on December 16, 1859. In 1861, Anderson published his account of the raid, including the months leading up to it. The first chapter of the extended pamphlet links Brown to Moses and Oliver Cromwell, and the ending expresses confidence that the "future historian" will recognize Brown's vital and positive role in ending slavery. Anderson returned to the United States in 1864 and joined the Union Army.

Chapter I. The Idea and Its Exponents—John Brown Another Moses.

The idea underlying the outbreak at Harper's Ferry is not peculiar to that movement, but dates back to a period very far beyond the memory of the "oldest inhabitant," and emanated from a source much superior to the Wises and Hunters, the Buchanans and Masons of today.[169] It was the appointed work for life of an ancient patriarch spoken of in Exodus, chap. ii., and who, true to his great commission, failed not to trouble the conscience and to disturb the repose of the Pharoahs of Egypt with that inexorable, "Thus saith the Lord: Let my people go!"[170] until even they were urgent upon the people in its behalf. Coming down through the nations, and regardless of national boundaries or

228

peculiarities, it has been proclaimed and enforced by the patriarch and the warrior of the Old World, by the enfranchised freeman and the humble slave of the New. Its nationality is universal; its language every where understood by the haters of tyranny; and those that accept its mission, everywhere understand each other. There is an unbroken chain of sentiment and purpose from Moses of the Jews to John Brown of America; from Kossuth,[171] and the liberators of France and Italy, to the untutored Gabriel, and the Denmark Veseys, Nat Turners and Madison Washingtons of the Southern American States.[172] The shaping and expressing of a thought for freedom takes the same consistence with the colored American—whether he be an independent citizen of the Haytian nation, a proscribed but humble nominally free colored man, a patient, toiling, but hopeful slave—as with the proudest or noblest representative of European or American civilization and Christianity. Lafayette, the exponent of French honor and political integrity, and John Brown, foremost among the men of the New World in high moral and religious principle and magnanimous bravery, embrace as brothers of the same mother, in harmony upon the grand mission of liberty; but, while the Frenchman entered the lists in obedience to a desire to aid, and by invitation from the Adamses and Hamiltons, and thus pushed on the political fortunes of those able to help themselves, John Brown, the liberator of Kansas, the projector and commander of the Harper's Ferry expedition, saw in the most degraded slave a man and a brother, whose appeal for his God-ordained rights no one should disregard; in the toddling slave child, a captive whose release is an imperative, and whose prerogative is as weighty, as the most famous in the land. When the Egyptian pressed hard upon the Hebrew, Moses slew him; and when the spirit of slavery invaded the fair Territory of Kansas, causing the Free-State settlers to cry out because of persecution, old John Brown, famous among the men of God for ever, though then but little know to his fellow-men, called together his sons and went over, as did Abraham, to the unequal contest, but on the side of the oppressed white men of Kansas that were, and the black men that were to be. Today, Kansas is free, and the verdict of impartial men is, that to John Brown, more than any other man, Kansas owes her present position.

I am not the biographer of John Brown, but I can be indulged in giving here the opinion common among my people of one so eminently worthy of the highest veneration. Close observation of him, during many weeks, and under his orders at his Kennedy-Farm fireside, also, satisfies me that in comparing the noble old man to Moses, and the other men of piety and renown, who were chosen by God to his great work, none have been more faithful, none have given a brighter record.

Chapter XIX. The Behavior of the Slaves—Captain Brown's Opinion

. . . As it was, even the noble old man's mistakes were productive of great good, the fact of which the future historian will record, without the embarrassment attending its present narration. John Brown did not only capture and hold Harper's Ferry for twenty hours, but he held the whole South. He captured President Buchanan and his Cabinet, convulsed the whole country, killed Governor Wise, and dug the mine and laid the train which will eventually dissolve the union between Freedom and Slavery. The rebound reveals the truth. So let it be!

Source: Osborne P. Anderson, *A Voice from Harper's Ferry* (Boston: The Author, 1861), 5–7, 62.

PART

III

Southern Responses

IN THE SOUTH, most voices of Brown's "tribunal" responded with fear, disbelief, and outrage. Brown's raid heightened white fears of a large-scale slave revolt in a region where 40 percent of the population was black. Planters in South Carolina asked Governor Wise for samples of the pikes that Brown had intended to give slaves, and several thousand troops remained in the Harpers Ferry area for months after the raid. The raid also symbolized abolitionist hatred of the South and Northern disregard for Southern institutions. Insisting that the Northern response to Brown's raid and execution revealed an antislavery consensus in the North, prominent Southerners used Brown to attack Republicanism and call for secession. Part III collects these immediate, prewar responses to Brown in the South, from Florida to Virginia. They include pieces by Unionists and secessionists, ex-Northerners, women, and Southern abolitionists as well as politicians' speeches and newspaper editorials, diary entries and letters, sermons and songs, and poetry and fiction. Some express admiration for Brown but not his actions, and occasionally a voice expresses pity for Brown, who would atone on the scaffold for the sins of abolitionism. But across all the responses, very few attempt to minimize the importance of the raid. As they considered whether the world was "the worse or the better" for Brown "living and dying in it," the Southern voices of the tribunal agreed that at the very least Brown had to be taken seriously.

Henry Wise, "Comments in Richmond, Virginia," October 21, 1859

As governor of Virginia between 1856 and 1860, Henry Wise (1806–1876) had a larger role than most in the John Brown story. He pushed to have Brown's trial in Virginia rather than in the federal court, even though Brown had invaded a federal arsenal. He signed Brown's death warrant as one of his last official acts as governor. And he interviewed the wounded leader at Harpers Ferry. After the interview, Wise returned to Richmond and offered admiring remarks about Brown's character. Newspapers published his remarks, which dismayed many Southerners, including Edmund Ruffin. The "false eulogy" by Wise would be a "great support and aid" to the abolitionists, Ruffin protested in his diary. He expected that abolitionists would use Wise's comments for Brown's "vindication and glorification," and he feared the South would suffer for this "wretched blunder." The following year Wise hoped to become a compromise Democratic candidate for U.S. president, but the party split into two factions. He went on to attend the Virginia secession convention of 1861 and then served in the Confederate Army as a brigadier general. On April 18, 1861, he ordered the Virginia militia to seize the government armory and arsenal at Harpers Ferry.

They are themselves mistaken who take him to be a madman. He is a bundle of the best nerves I ever saw, cut and thrust, and bleeding and in bonds. He is a man of clear head, of courage, fortitude, and simple ingenuousness. He is cool, collected and indomitable, and it is but just to him to say, that he was humane to his prisoners, as attested to me by Col. Washington[1] and Mr. Mills;[2] and he inspired me with great trust in his integrity as a man of truth. He is a fanatic, vain and garrulous, but firm, and truthful, and intelligent. His men too, who survive, except the free negroes with him, are like him. He professes to be a Christian, in communion with the Congregationalist Church of the North,[3] and openly preaches his purpose of universal emancipation and the negroes themselves were to be the agents by means of arms, led on by white command-

233

ers. When Col. Washington was taken, his watch, and plate, and jewels, and money were demanded, to create what they call a "safety fund,"[4] to compensate the liberators for the trouble and expense of taking away his slaves. This, by a law, was to be done with all slaveholders. Washington, of course, refused to deliver up any thing; and it is remarkable, that the only thing of material value which they took, besides his slaves, was the sword of Frederick the Great, which was sent to General Washington. This was taken by Stevens to Brown, and the latter commanded his men with that sword in this fight against the peace and safety of Washington's native State! He promised Col. Washington to return it to him when he was done with it. And Col. Washington says that he, Brown, was the coolest and firmest man he ever saw in defying danger and death. With one son dead by his side and another shot through, he felt the pulse of his dying son with one hand and held his rifle with the other and commanded his men with the utmost composure, encouraging them to be firm, and to sell their lives as dearly as they could.

Source: James Redpath, *The Public Life of Capt. John Brown* (Boston: Thayer and Eldridge, 1860), 273.

Republican Banner and Nashville Whig,
"The Harper's Ferry Riot," October 24, 1859

As a Unionist daily in Tennessee, the *Republican Banner and Nashville Whig* frequently argued that staying in the Union was the only way to ensure that slavery would survive in the South. It responded to Brown's raid by pleading with both the North and the South to abandon sectionalism and find a solution to the "slavery question." Otherwise, the newspaper warned, the Harpers Ferry raid would be a mere "preface" to widespread armed conflict. Launched in Nashville in 1854, the newspaper was sometimes accused of being an anti-Southern publication. It suspended publication during the Civil War.

We are at length enabled to lay before our readers a connected and apparently truthful, narrative of the late revolutionary movement in and around Harper's Ferry. It can no longer be doubted that the object of the conspirators was the liberation of the slaves in Virginia and Maryland. It is gratifying to record that the energy of President Buchanan and Governor Wise, the activity of the soldiery and the zeal of the citizens have crushed out the conspiracy before it could attain the huge dimensions of a revolution. But though the movement resulted so disastrously to the insurgents and met with so little sympathy from the negro population, for whose benefit it was designed, it will nevertheless prove a valuable lesson to the people of the South, if they give it that calm reflection and careful consideration that it deserves.

This attempt to excite an insurrection among the slaves is one of the natural results of the agitation of the slavery question, originated and so persistently kept up by designing politicians, both of the North and the South for partisan purposes. It can be traced to no other cause, and unless the people of both sections rise in the majesty of their strength and put an end at once to this mischievous agitation, the page that records the bloody events of the last two days, will be but a preface to the history of a civil war in which the same scenes will be re-enacted on a larger scale, and end in the dissolution of our glorious Union.

The folly of the Southern people in their incessant demand for more slavery legislation is exhibited in a strong light by this view of the subject, and should convince them of the impolicy of further agitation. By ceasing the agitation in the South, an end will be put to the discussion of this subject in the North. As long as we agitate the North will do the same, and though only seventeen men of the entire North were engaged in the conspiracy,[5] there is no telling how many may engage in the next plot unless the subject of slavery ceases to be a matter of discussion among demagogues. The people have the means in their hands of putting an end to this evil, by resolutely refusing to elevate men to political office who seek to ride into power by incendiary appeals to sectional prejudices.

Source: Republican Banner and Nashville Whig, October 24, 1859.

Robert Barnwell Rhett, "The Insurrection," October 31, 1859

Robert Barnwell Rhett (1800–1876) of South Carolina was a secessionist and slaveholder. He responded to Brown's raid with a front-page article in the *Charleston Mercury*, a newspaper edited by his son, that calls the raid an omen of the Union's future dissolution. Rhett believed that Southern disunionism was patriotic. As a Democrat in the U.S. House of Representatives between 1837 and 1849, he had demanded constitutional amendments prohibiting congressional debates on slavery and had urged South Carolina to secede if antislavery agitation continued. Elected to the U.S. Senate in 1850, he resigned in 1852. Rhett went on to be a delegate at the Montgomery convention in February 1861, where six states met to organize the Confederate States of America. But during the war he clashed with Confederate president Jefferson Davis of Mississippi and was sidelined.

The insurrection at Harper's Ferry was simply no insurrection at all. Not a slave joined the reckless fanatics who sought to promote their nefarious policy of emancipation by blood and treason. It was a silly invasion of Virginia by some eighteen men.[6] Four or five men were killed, and a few more will be hung, and there will be the end of the enterprise in its mere physical aspects. The presses of the North, looking no further than these results, are pretty harmonious in representing it as a very light and trifling affair; and the parade of Governors, and Senators, and of the military of States and of the General Government to suppress it, as very absurd and ridiculous.

Events are often important, not on account of their immediate magnitude, but on account of their significancy. A pimple on the cheek may be a very trifling disorder; but if it betokens erysipelas, it is the indication of disease which may be fatal. And so it is in the political world. The importance of any event, however insignificant in itself, must be measured by the principle it involves, or the policy it indicates. For twenty-five years the Northern people have been keeping up a continual agitation in the Union concerning the institution of slavery. They have broken up our churches; they have run off our slaves; they have excluded us from our territory on the ground that the institution of slavery is too iniquitous to expand; and they have now organized a vast controlling party in the Northern States, looking to the possession of the General Government, to further their purposes of emancipation. All along, however, we have heard put forth profuse professions that no interference with the institution of slavery in the Southern States was intended or contemplated—although every principle they asserted led them just as much to overthrow slavery in the States as in the Territories. The constitutional and moral views which they bring forward to justify their policy, most logically and clearly, must make them emancipationists. Here, then, is the great importance of this abolition *emeute*[7] in Virginia. It shows to the people of the South the destiny which awaits them in this Union, under the control of a sectional anti-slavery party in the free States. It is in fact, coming to the aid of logic. It is the legitimate fruit of the Union as it is. It is a significant sign of progress. Taken in connection with the past, it is a portentous omen of the future.

So far from creating any surprise, we do not suppose that there is a thoughtful man in the South who has not been anticipating, for years past, such events as those which lately transpired at Harper's Ferry. Our connection with the North, is a standing instigation of insurrection in the South. Instead of that "domestic tranquility" which the constitution of the United States openly asserts that it was established to insure, Congress is a vast abolition conventicle, and the Union itself a powerful organization by which domestic disquietude is created, and the mightiest dangers impend over the South. Instead of "tranquility" and protection, hostility and insurrection are now its natural fruits. The Harper's Ferry invasion, therefore, if wisely considered, is of vast significancy, and should lead the people of the South to prepare for those future events, of which this is only the premonition.

Source: Charleston Mercury, October 31, 1859.

Richmond Daily Enquirer, "A Suggestion for Governor Wise," November 2, 1859

Governor Wise fielded criticism from Northerners and Southerners alike for the decision to execute Brown. Some Brown sympathizers wanted mercy, while Unionist and proslavery voices warned that executing Brown might make him a martyr and inspire more antislavery violence. Wise eventually acknowledged in his "Message to the Virginia Legislature" on December 5, 1859, that Brown's execution carried the "threat of martyrdom," but he explained that Brown "had surely to die according to law." The *Richmond Daily Enquirer* responded to requests that Wise keep Brown alive by suggesting that abolitionists and Republicans take the blame instead. It focuses on a request by the *New York Commercial Advertiser,* a Republican journal. Always hostile toward Republican newspapers, Virginia's *Enquirer* was a Democratic journal edited by O. Jennings Wise, the son of Governor Wise.

Under this head, the "New York Commercial Advertiser," a Black Republican Free-soil sheet, puts forth an argument to show that Brown is an "ultrafanatic," "little better than insane," "with mind and heart alike too warped for him to discern evil from good." Under these circumstances, the "Advertiser," argues that it would not be good policy for Virginia to hang Brown and his fellow-murderers.

A cunning policy does the "Advertiser" suggest. Pardon the principal and permit the accessories to escape! Extend clemency to Brown and forgiveness to Seward, Hale, Giddings, Smith and Greeley![8] The "Advertiser" begs the Executive of Virginia not to make a martyr of Brown; that being a fanatic he is insane certainly to some degree, and our New York contemporary fears direful consequences will spring from his execution. That as the blood of the martyrs was the seed of the Church, so from the grave of John Brown the "Advertiser" fears a crop of armed fanatics may spring up destructive to Virginia and the

South. It would perhaps have been more to the point to have shown that the pardon of Brown would have lessened the number of existing fanatics rather than by suggesting their increase from a due course of justice. But we apprehend the Executive of Virginia will not turn an attentive ear to suggestions coming from such a source as the New York Commercial "Advertiser." The Republican Party, of which the "Advertiser" is an organ, is too deeply implicated in the actions of their chief leaders to offer suggestions with regard to the just punishment of one of their numbers.

Violated laws and murdered citizens demand a victim at the hand of justice, if Brown is a crazed fanatic, irresponsible either in morals or law, there are yet guilty parties. He is then the agent of wicked principals. If the Northern people believe Brown insane, what punishment is due to those who have poisoned his mind with the "irrepressible conflict" and spurred his fanaticism to deeds of blood and carnage? He may be insane, but there are other criminals, guilty wretches, who instigated the crimes perpetrated at Harper's Ferry.

Bring these men, bring Seward, Greeley, Giddings, Hale and Smith to the jurisdiction of Virginia, and Brown and his deluded victims in the Charlestown jail may hope for pardon. In the opinion of Virginia the five Republican leaders, above mentioned, are more guilty than even John Brown and his associates. An ignorant fanaticism may be pleaded in palliation of the crime of Brown, but the five Republican leaders would spurn such a stultifying plea! They would not compromise their intelligence even at the cost of their morality. Let the friends of Brown, let all who believe him to be insane, and all who intend to represent him as a crazy fanatic, for whose folly no party is responsible, deliver up Seward, Greeley, Giddings, Smith and Hale. A fair trial, at their own time, with their own counsel, will be freely given them, and if Virginia does not prove them guilty, they too shall go unhurt.

Source: Richmond Daily Enquirer, November 2, 1859.

Southern Watchman, "The Harper's Ferry Insurrection," November 3, 1859

In the weeks after the Harpers Ferry raid, the Southern press debated whether or not it was advisable to kill Brown, who else might be guilty, and how likely it was that slaves would ever join agitators in rebellion. The *Southern Watchman* focused on the potential danger of the raid to the Union, arguing that armed agitation would destroy liberty. Edited by John Christy from 1854 onward and based in Athens, Georgia, the newspaper was strongly Unionist and insisted that Southern rights should be obtained within the Union by a coalition of Northern and Southern conservatives. Christy tried to make the newspaper politically independent, but it did support John Bell for the Constitutional Union Party in the presidential election of 1860.

This subject still engrosses much of the public attention. It has been condemned, so far as we have observed, by the Black Republican newspapers. They ought, however, to possess sufficient penetration to perceive that however far they might themselves be from engaging directly in the treasonable plots of Ossawatomie Brown, the general tone of their papers, like the sentiments of Seward's speech,[9] has a tendency to incite other fanatics, less prudent, to the commission of acts of treason and bloodshed.

Some of the Northern papers are reading to the South lectures on the subject of the outbreak, and remind our people that they are quietly reposing on the crust of a volcano, ready at any moment to burst forth and destroy them. This, they say, is the lesson the late outbreak teaches. No foolhardy enthusiasts ever missed the mark further. It teaches a lesson to the fanatics of the North. It shows them that the slaves their misdirected philanthropy would relieve are so well satisfied with their condition that they will not join them in their rebellion. And by the time the outraged sovereignty of Virginia has been satisfied, they will learn one other great lesson, viz: that the South can produce hemp enough to hang all the traitors the great "Northern hive" can send among her people to stir up sedition and insurrection!

It teaches the whole country—all sections of it—a great lesson, which we hope all will profit by—that is, that the everlasting agitation of the slavery question will inevitably lead to civil war and bloodshed! Let the people, then, of all parties—all those who would preserve the Union as our fathers made it—indignantly rebuke the agitators and drive them back to their kennels. The present is a propitious time to begin such a work. Let the people but will it, and agitation must cease. Let it go on, and the sun of liberty will set in blood!

Source: Southern Watchman, November 3, 1859.

D. H. Strother, "The Late Invasion at Harper's Ferry," November 5, 1859, and "The Trial of the Conspirators," November 12, 1859

A Virginian from a slaveholding family, David Hunter Strother (1816–1888) was one of the most financially successful and popular writers of the mid-nineteenth century. He was better known by his pen name, Porte Crayon, which he adopted after meeting Washington Irving, who published his own *Sketch Book* as "Geoffrey Crayon." Strother produced humorous, thinly fictionalized, antimodern, genteel travel narratives, illustrated with his own sketches and generally set in the western Virginia mountains. He also contributed articles and sketches to *Harper's Weekly* as the journal's "artist-correspondent" and began covering Brown immediately after the raid. Arriving at Harpers Ferry from nearby Charles Town, he used his family connections to gain access to the interview with Brown. Strother's articles about Brown's capture and trial demonstrate a similar hostility and also reflect both his racism and his Unionism. He returned to Charles Town for the execution; there he dined with Edmund Ruffin, the secessionist, and Andrew Hunter, his uncle and the lawyer appointed to prosecute Brown for Virginia. Strother used his uncle's personal relationship with Governor Wise to gain rare civilian access on December 2. According to some witnesses, he even approached the hanging body, lifted the execution cap, and sketched Brown's dead face. But *Harper's Weekly* refused to publish his illustrated story about Brown's execution and simply reported the death in a brief paragraph. Strother went on to become a Union officer in the war and Virginia's first postwar adjutant general.

"The Late Invasion at Harper's Ferry"

The mid-day train of Tuesday[10] brought Governor Wise, accompanied by several hundred men from Richmond, Alexandria, Baltimore, and elsewhere. There was real disappointment to find that the fight was over, and when the Governor was informed of the mere handful of men who had created all this bobbery he boiled over. In his wrath he said some good things. Indeed it was universally seen and felt that Governor Wise was just the man for such an occasion.

Accompanied by Andrew Hunter, Esq., a distinguished lawyer of Jefferson country,[11] the Governor presently repaired to the guard-room where the two wounded prisoners lay, and there had a protracted and interesting conversation with the chief of the outlaws. It had more the character of a conversation than a legal examination, for the Governor treated the wounded man with a stately courtesy that evidently surprised and affected him. Brown was lying upon the floor with his feet to the fire and his head propped upon pillows on the back of a chair. During the examination I sketched the portrait, which is an accurate likeness of him as he then appeared. His hair was a mass of clotted gore, so that I could not distinguish the original color. His eye a pale blue or gray, nose Roman, and beard, originally sandy, was white and blood-stained. His speech was frequently interrupted by deep groans, not awakening sympathy like those of the young soldier dying in the adjacent office, but reminding one of the agonized growl of a ferocious beast. . . .

Concluding that the prisoner must be seriously weakened by his vigils and his wounds, the Governor ordered some refreshment to be given him, and, appointing a meeting on the following day, took his leave. As some of us lingered, the old man recurred again to his sons, of whom he had spoken several times, asking if we were sure they were both dead. He was assured that it was so. "How many bodies did you take from the engine-house?" he asked. He was told three. "Then," said he, quickly, "they are not both dead; there were three dead bodies there last night. Gentlemen, my son is doubtless living and in your power. I will ask for him what I would not ask for myself; let him have kind treatment, for he is as pure and noble-hearted a youth as ever breathed the breath of life." There was some show of human feeling in the old felon at last, but his prayer was vain. Both his boys[12] lay stark and bloody by the Armory wall.

I had observed Stephens[13] holding a small packet in his folded hands, and feeling some curiosity in regard to it, it was handed to me. It contained miniatures of his sisters; one, a sweet girlish face of about fourteen, the other more mature, but pretty. What strange reflections these incidents awakened! This old man craves a boon for his noble boys, which neither pain nor death can bring him to ask for himself. The other clasps to his dying breast a remembrance of his gentle sisters and his father's elm-shaded cottage far away in peaceful Connecticut. Is this pity that thus dims my eyes? A rising sympathy that struggles in my heart? Away with puling weakness. Has not this hoary villain, that prates about his sons, been for months a deliberate plotter against the lives and happiness of thousands? Did he not train these very boys to aid him in his attempt to waste, with fire and sword, the fairest land under the cope of heaven? And this bloody dupe—his follower—how many men's sisters did he propose to murder; how many social hearths to quench in blood; for what use were those hundreds of deadly rifles, those loads of pikes, those bundles of incendiary fagots? A felon's death! Almighty Providence! Is man indeed so weak that he can inflict no more?

And all about this good-humored, good-for-nothing, half-monkey race—the negroes. Let us walk through the streets of Harper's Ferry and see what part they have played in the drama. It seems that there is not the remotest suspicion that a single individual among them had any foreknowledge of Brown's movement. It is well ascertained that neither threats, promises, nor persuasion could induce one of them to join the movement when it was proposed to them. Heywood[14] was shot dead while heroically expressing his horror of their nefarious designs. Brown discovered early that he could make no use of such as he had captured, and on Monday morning sent Cooke and two other white men, with eleven negro prisoners over to the Maryland side, where they were employed in removing the arms and munitions of war from the Kennedy farm to the log school-house in the mountain opposite the town. This was done that they might be more convenient for those imaginary recruits which the insane brigands still seemed confidently to expect.

As Cooke and his companions went at times to the river to fire across at the Virginians these negroes escaped, dodging through the woods, swimming the river, and running every hazard, returned to their respective homes. I conversed with several of them, who narrated their adventures, while in the power of these cut-throat strangers, with great humor and vivacity. One fellow said that, when he was taken, a pike was put into his hands by Brown, who told him to take it and strike for liberty. "Good lord, Massa," cried Cuffee, in a tremor, "I don't know nuffin' bout handlin' dem tings." "Take it instantly," cried the philanthropist, "and strike home. This is a day that will long be remembered in the history of your race—a glorious anniversary." "Please God, Massa, I'se got a sore finger," and Cuffee exhibited a stump, the first joint of which he had lost in a wheat-machine some years before.[15]

Finding that he had no mind to be a hero, Brown took him to the Armory, and during the siege sent him out for water. As soon as he got out of range of their guns he broke the pitcher and fled for his life. I narrate the story faithfully as it was told to me. Many similar anecdotes I gleaned from the darkeys themselves, but have not space to relate them. In the town they were passing to and fro with entire freedom, jubilating over their own escapes and jeering at the dead carcasses of the Liberators. Several told me that Brown, in urging them to arm, said, repeatedly, "Don't you know me? Did you never hear of John Brown of Kansas—old Ossawatomie Brown?" This only frightened the negroes more. They dropped the pikes, like the devil's gifts, and took to their heels, hiding every where under straw ricks, barns, and stables. On the other hand, there is sufficient and full evidence to show that, had their masters been present in any instance, the slaves would, in their defense, have very cheerfully thrust the pikes into the bodies of the pseudo-philanthropists, proving that they were not so ignorant of the pitch-fork exercise as they pretended.

As for the non-slaveholding inhabitants, on whom Brown calculated so confidently for assistance, it is estimated that at least four out of five of those who volunteered so promptly were non-slaveholders and of non-slaveholding families. They were the fighting men of the occasion, the stormers, who went to work with a remorseless ferocity equaling that of the outlaws themselves.

Any man who has heretofore imagined that he had sounded the depths of human folly and human wickedness will yet be amazed when he considers this affair at Harper's Ferry. It is generally regarded as the insane attempt of a monomaniac; an act which, as it is without precedent, and is likely to remain without a parallel, whose intense silliness is only equaled by its atrocity, would be ludicrous had not the blood of some of our best citizens made it tragic.

As for Brown's boast, "that, if at liberty, he could bring five thousand men to aid him," it is not credited; for if he had these means at his disposal, why did he enter Harper's Ferry with twenty-two only?

Brown is evidently the originator of the whole scheme—its head and right arm. After two years of effort he has only been enabled to muster twenty-one dupes with nerve enough to follow him; and these, without exception, where they have had an opportunity to speak before they perished, have acknowledged that they were miserably deceived.

That there are persons at a distance who have aided and encouraged him is proven by the captured correspondence. But these white-livered suborners of murder and treason are not dangerous. The head of the fanatical serpent, with its bloody fangs, we have crushed under our heel—its tail may writhe and rattle, but can not bite.

"The Trial of the Conspirators"

It is the order to march. The chilly air of an October night, or the startling proximity sends a sharp thrill through the dreamer's heart; but where old John Brown leads there is no turning back. The deed is done—Monday morning has dawned. The night was one of action, but no reinforcements have come in. With the light they read dismay and astonishment in every face.

After terror follows anger. Then the day of desperate combat, blood, and death. Hemmed-in, trapped, deceived. It is soon over.

Now, manacled and imprisoned, sit these dreamers of wealth and greatness —their delusions vanished—crushed under the awful realities of their situation.

This is no imaginative picture which I have drawn in a spirit of levity and scorn. In wildness and absurdity it halts behind the reality—the long-devised and coolly meditated schemes of the fanatical conspirators. It is difficult for a sane mind to conceive of such infatuation; and yet these men are clearly not insane. Minds too narrow to contain more than one full-grown idea run easily into monomania. Cervantes has given us the type, in his famous "Don Quixote," of wind-mill memory; and the credulous Sancho, covetous of islands and asses'-colts. John Brown is not unlike the Don personally, as described, and is certainly quite as mad. His one-and-twenty followers, in their thrice-sodden folly, are no whit better than so many Sanchos.[16]

Courtly flower of *La Manchean*[17] chivalry, and thou his true and faithful squire, we humbly crave your pardons for thus associating your names with these vulgar knaves and midnight assassins!

The more I see of Brown, the more I am convinced that, in addition to his abolition monomania, he is under the influence of a ferocious vanity. Influenced by the infuriate babblings of persons better educated but no wiser than himself, he goes to Kansas, where he earns a reputation as a partisan leader, and at the same time gets a taste of human blood. "Ira brevis furor est."[18] That miserable contest, fomented by unprincipled politicians for party and personal purposes, at length ceased. The belligerent parties shook hands, took a drink, and peacefully turned their energies to cheating one another and the rest of the world. Not so John Brown. The demon which those border forays had awakened is destined never again to sleep. Old Brown, Osawatomie Brown, Brown of Kansas, the Topeka Governor, the dread of Border Ruffians, the Moses of the higher law—can not descend into the vulgar stagnation of common life.

Aesop tells us of a certain harper who, having pleased the sots in an ale-house with his music, was so conceited as to go upon the stage and play for the great public. Here he failed ignominiously, and was hissed. In his grand scheme to overthrow the Government of the United States and the Anglo-Saxon men in the South, with twenty-two men, Brown has failed as signally as the poor musician, but will hardly get off so cheap. Yet (to use his own expression), to give the devil his dues, he bears himself stiffly under his misfortunes. Fierce as a gun-lock, cool as a sword, he makes no apologies, and yields no triumph to his enemies. In his bearing there is neither weakness nor bravado. Defiant only when stirred; otherwise civil and straightforward; communicative when questioned; and thankful for small favors. . . .

Here, in all probability, is an end of old John Brown—saint or sinner, martyr or murderer, famous, or infamous, as the case may be. We may yet all have to acknowledge that we owe him for one good turn: with desperate hand he has blown up the whole magazine of abolition pyrotechnics—pray God there may not a cracker or a squib remain unburned! Brethren of the North, when hereafter any man shall attempt to profane your rostrums or your pulpits with incendiary abuse and revilings against any section of our common country, I charge you smite him on the mouth—with the word Harper's Ferry.

Source: Harper's Weekly, November 5 and 12, 1859, 712–714 (714), 729–730.

"Portrait of Ossawattomie Brown, Wounded and a Prisoner, sketched by Porte Crayon during his examination by Governor Wise." *Harper's Weekly,* November 5, 1859, 712.

Sarah Frances Williams, "To My Dear Parents," November 7 and 11, 1859

Sarah Frances Hicks Williams (1827–1917) responded to Brown as an ex-Northerner. She was from New Hartford, New York, where she was raised to be against slavery, but moved to the North Carolina plantation owned by her new husband, Benjamin Franklin Williams, in 1853, eight years after they met. As the mistress of Clifton Grove plantation in Greene County, she embraced proslavery and anti-abolitionist attitudes. Brown seemed to her a bloodthirsty fanatic who simply could not understand the positive realities of slavery. Williams remained a Southerner for the rest of her life and eventually moved to Waycross, Georgia, where she died at the age of ninety.

Monday, Nov. 7th, 1859

My dear Parents:

I sent you a paper giving an account of the insane project in Virginia, one of the diabolical schemes of a set of fanatics who, if they had their way, would deluge the land in blood. How I wish they could see this thing as it is. But, there are none so blind as those who won't see.

Nov. 11th, 1859

My dear Parents:

I will not send the papers I spoke of as I see the New York Observer gives a very concise account and the editor's remarks are excellent, on the late attempt at insurrection. You will readily see how very anxious (I speak ironically) the

slaves are to be liberated, when the few that joined Brown & Co. were compelled, and one who would not was deliberately shot. I wonder what his dying
thoughts of "freedom" were. You ask, perhaps, "what will be the result?" I tell
you what I think. Vigilance committees will be formed, every Northerner, man
or woman, will be closely watched and if heard advancing incendiary sentiment, let him or her be certain to take the first northbound express train. This
is the great good the "Philanthropists" have accomplished in addition to opening the African slave trade. It is my opinion that the leading abolitionists of the
North were well aware of the movement. Northern Ohio seems to have been
the ground for concocting the work. It seems to have been the will of God that
the scheme should fail, however much His Satanic Majesty may have differed
in opinion.

Source: James C. Bonner, ed., "Plantation Experiences of a New York Woman," North Carolina
Historical Review 33 (1956): 384–412, 529–546 (535–536).

Margaretta Mason, "To Lydia Maria Child," November 11, 1859

After the *New York Tribune* published the correspondence of the abolitionist Lydia Maria Child with Brown and Governor Wise, Margaretta Mason (1798–1874) wrote to Child in disgust. She was the wife of senator James Murray Mason of Virginia, who had drafted the Fugitive Slave Act and would represent the Confederacy as a commissioner in Great Britain during the Civil War. Senator Mason had interviewed Brown at Harpers Ferry and represented the majority view in a congressional report about the raid published in June 1860. Mrs. Mason's letter defends slavery, attacks Child's sympathy for Brown, and advises Southerners to avoid Child's writings. Responding in a letter dated December 17, 1859, Child disputed Mason's biblical arguments and explained that although she did not condone Brown's violence, she understood his intentions. She also pointed to anti-abolitionist violence. The following year the American Anti-Slavery Society reissued the set of letters between Child, Governor Wise, and Mrs. Mason as a tract. It sold an extraordinary 300,000 copies.

Alton, King George's Co., Virginia, Nov. 11th, 1859.

Do you read your Bible, Mrs. Child? If you do, read there, "Woe unto hypocrites!" and take to yourself with two-fold damnation that terrible sentence; for, rest assured, in the day of judgment it shall be more tolerable for those thus scathed by the awful denunciation of the Son of God than for you. *You* would soothe with sisterly and motherly care the hoary-headed murderer of Harper's Ferry! A man whose aim and intention was to incite the horrors of a servile war—to condemn women of your own race, ere death closed their eyes on their sufferings from violence and outrage, to see their husbands and fathers murdered, their children butchered, the ground strewed with the brains of their babes. The antecedents of Brown's band proved them to have been the offscourings of the earth; and what would have been our fate had they found themselves as many sympathizers in Virginia as they seem to have in Massachusetts?

Now, compare yourself with those your "sympathy" would devote to such ruthless ruin, and say, on that "word of honour, which has never been broken," would *you* stand by the bedside of an old negro, dying of a hopeless disease, to alleviate his sufferings as far as human aid could? Have *you* ever watched the last, lingering illness of a consumptive, to soothe, as far as in you lay, the inevitable fate? Do *you* soften the pangs of maternity in those around you by all the care and comfort you can give? Do *you* grieve with those *near* you, even though their sorrows resulted from their own misconduct? Do *you* ever sit up until the wee hours to complete a dress for a motherless child, that she might appear on Christmas day in a new one, along with her more fortunate companions? *We* do these and more for our servants, and why? Because we endeavour *to do our duty in that state of life it has pleased God to place us*. In his revealed word we read our duties to them—theirs to us are there also—"Not only to the good and gentle, but to the forward." (Peter 2.18) Go thou and do likewise, and keep away from Charlestown. If the stories read in the public prints be true, of the sufferings of the poor of the North, you need not go far for objects of charity. "Thou hypocrite! Take first the beam out of thine own eye, then shalt thou see clearly to pull the mote out of thy neighbour's."[19] But if, indeed, you do lack objects of sympathy near you, go to Jefferson County, to the family of George Turner, a noble, true-hearted man, whose devotion to his friend (Colonel Washington) causing him to risk his life, was shot down like a dog; or to that of old Beckham, whose grief at the murder of his negro subordinate made him needlessly expose himself to the aim of the assassin Brown.[20] And when you can equal in deeds of love and charity to those *around* you, what is shown by nine-tenths of the Virginia plantations, then by your "sympathy" whet the knives for our throats, and kindle the torch that fires our homes. *You* reverence Brown for his clemency to his prisoners! Prisoners! and how taken? Unsuspecting workmen, going to their daily duties; unarmed gentlemen, taken from their beds at the dead hour of the night, by six men doubly and trebly armed. Suppose he had hurt a hair on their heads, do you suppose one of the band of desperadoes would have left the engine-house alive? And did not he know that this treatment of them was his only hope of life then, or of clemency afterward? Of course he did. The United States troops could not have prevented him from being torn limb from limb.

I will add, in conclusion, no Southerner ought, after your letter to Governor Wise and to Brown, to read a line of your composition, or to touch a magazine which bears your name in its list of contributors; and in this we hope for the "sympathy," at least of those at the North who deserve the name of women.

M. J. C. MASON

Source: Letters of Lydia Maria Child (Boston: Houghton Mifflin, 1883), 120–122.

Arkansas Gazette, "The Harper's Ferry Insurrection," November 12, 1859

The *Arkansas Gazette,* a Democratic and Unionist newspaper published in Little Rock since 1821, downplayed the importance of the Harpers Ferry raid. This article observes that Brown is insane and will be hanged, no slaves joined him at the Ferry, and his actions in no way warrant discussions of sectional war or secession. In fact, the only lesson of Harpers Ferry that the newspaper can identify is that officials need to be more vigilant about preventing such insane outbreaks. The article concludes by promising the North that slaves are happy and the South that its states would be ill served by secession. This focus on preventing a dissolution of the Union highlights the degree to which Brown had forced the issue. The *Gazette* remained pro-Union until Lincoln's call for troops on April 15, 1861.

Since the failure of the fanatic Brown to enlist a single slave with him in his crazy attempt to raise a servile insurrection in Virginia, almost the entire press of the country has been filled with speculations in regard to it, and the consequences to which it tends, as estimated from the different stand-points, and in the different lights in which it had been viewed. Though here and there a fanatic in the North has been found to sympathize with Brown, and endorse his course, it is a matter of gratification, and we chronicle the fact with pleasure, that the leading papers, and men, among the Black Republicans, are open, bold, and unmistakable, in their condemnation of the course of Brown, and respond heartily to the prompt and just administration of justice to him.

There are men, both at the North and the South—principally fanatics and fools, under the control of designing demagogues—who delight to live in the muddy waters of discord, whose chief occupation is strife and contention, and the main end of whose actions seems to be to array one section of the country against the other in hostile strife, rather than to bring them together on the common platform of the Constitution, to take friendly counsel together for the benefit of our common country. These men, in the North, seize upon Brown's crime as a text to preach war against the South; and, in the South, as a warrant for a dissolution of the Union, and a war upon the North. But the great mass of the people, both in the North and the South, condemn Brown's treason, and rejoice to know that law and justice have been so promptly administered to him. It is to be hoped that Brown's aiders and abettors may all be arrested and, dealt with as he has been.

Our own opinion is that too much importance has been attached to this matter. Brown was, we think, insane, and hanging will doubtless be the best remedy for all such cases of insanity. He will be hung, and his case thus properly disposed of; and it would be well to make a like disposition of all similar cases. But we do not think that the acts of this insane man, condemned as they are by the great mass of the Northern people, should be seized upon as a pretext, by Northern fanatics to war upon the South, nor by Southern ones to war upon the North and dissolve the Union.

The very fact that not a single slave joined, or attempted to join, Brown's mad expedition, is an evidence that they are satisfied with their condition, and should be a warning—an awful warning—to all white men contemplating such insane acts of hostility against Southern slaveholders.

We would urge upon the people the importance of vigilance to guard against the recurrence of similar out-breaks. In fact it would seem, from timely warnings received by the Secretary of War, that the insurrection at Harper's Ferry was occasioned by the neglect of that officer.

We would warn crazy fanatics that the slaves in the South are, as a general thing, in a better condition than the poor laborers of the North—that they are happy and contented, and that no part of them are at all likely to participate, either in sentiment or action, with any attempt of madmen to change their present condition. We hope, however, with the manifest hopelessness and thanklessness of such undertakings, and the fate of Brown staring them in the face, that no fanatic will be mad enough to make a similar attempt in future.

Nor can we see the least reason, in what has transpired, to urge, sectional war between the North and the South, or a dissolution of the Union. It is not our purpose to speak of the subject in an abstract view; but we shall allude to it, as we hope it may be treated by the people, in its practical light. As to the abstract rights of the States we hold what we think to be Constitutional views, yet many men in the slave holding States are pleased to consider them as ultra Southern. But there is a difference in the holding of an abstract principle, and the policy of exercising it. We are not here to say that the South has not suffered wrongs and oppressions from the North; for she has been grievously wronged and oppressed, and by no party more than by the National Democracy. And while we have protested against those wrongs and outrages, and shall continue to do so, we do not think the Southern States could better their condition by a dissolution of the Union.

Source: Arkansas Gazette, November 12, 1859.

Richmond Whig, "Editorial," November 18, 1859

The *Richmond Whig* of Virginia was the main organ of the Whig Party in the South. It was founded in 1824 as the *Constitutional Whig* by John Hampden Pleasants, who was killed in 1846 during a duel with the editor of the *Richmond Enquirer*, Thomas Ritchie, Jr. In the antebellum South, the Whig Party was largely the party of the slaveholder, and the *Richmond Whig* took a fervent proslavery stance. For example, in 1835 it proposed suspension of commercial intercourse with Northern states in order to force an end to abolitionist activity. But it opposed secession up until the firing on Fort Sumter on April 12, 1861. Its response to Brown was one of the most rage-filled tirades in the Southern press. The editorial also focuses on the potential consequences of not court-martialing Brown, pointing out that he has transformed himself into a martyr and hero during his imprisonment.

Virginia and the South are ready to face all the consequences of the execution of old Brown and his confederates. Though it convert the whole Northern people, without an exception, into furious, armed abolition invaders, yet *old Brown will be hung!* That is the stern and irreversible decrees, not only of the authorities of Virginia, but of the PEOPLE of Virginia, without a dissenting voice. And, therefore, Virginia, and the people of Virginia, will treat with the contempt they deserve, all the *craven appeals* of Northern men in behalf of old Brown's pardon. *The miserable old traitor and murderer belongs to the gallows,* and the gallows *will* have its own, in spite of the threatening and maledictions of the North and the world combined.

We took the ground at the outset, that old Brown should have been hung at once, without the intervention of judge or jury. He was a *villainous pirate and assassin* and was therefore *entitled to no trial at law.* We believed at the first and we still more firmly believe now, that it would have been better and wiser in all aspects if Gov. Wise had given him the swift benefit of a *drum-head court-martial.* In that event, no sympathy for him would have been excited in the North, for he would have had no opportunity of making *incendiary speech for effect,* and, consequently nothing of the character of the hero or the martyr would have attached to him, even in the estimation of Garrison and Wendell Phillips.

We, therefore, agree fully with our contemporary of the Fredericksburg News in the opinion, that the absurd and horrid nonsense about Gov. Wise's pardoning old Brown should be condemned and scouted by every sane man in Virginia and the South. The impertinent proposition, come from whom it may, whether Northern Abolitionists or Northern conservatives, should be resented by Virginia and by Gov. Wise and his friends as an insult. He cannot pardon Brown; but if he had the power, it would be worse than treason to exercise it. The majesty of law and the outraged sovereignty of Virginia can be vindicated and revenged only by the death of these miscreants.

The people already inquire why they were spared. Rebels in arms against the Government, State and Federal, with hands red with the blood of murdered citizens, summoned to surrender and refusing, seized at the expense of life, *why were they not shot like dogs* the moment of their capture? All the laws of war, and all the demands of justice, demanded their immediate extermination. The impudent claims of a robber, a horse-thief and a murderer to be recognized as "a prisoner of war," should have hastened his punishment.

We verily believe the failure to inflict summary and deserved death upon Brown and his co-conspirators will yet cost Virginia many lives. There are fools and fanatics enough ready to risk life to obtain Brown's notoriety, who would have been deterred by his prompt and immediate execution.

Source: Richmond Whig, November 16, 1859.

Natchez Courier, "Forewarned, Forearmed," November 18, 1859

Several Southern newspapers responded with outrage or indignation to the discovery that secretary of war John Floyd had received a warning about Brown's raid in advance. Floyd ignored an unsigned letter, dated August 20, that described Brown's plans. The *Natchez Courier* of Mississippi compared Floyd's error to several famous failures of precaution throughout history and called for greater vigilance in the future. The even-tempered editorial is typical of this Whig newspaper. Generally unruffled, it defended slavery but urged the South to have tact in its dealings with the North. Its Democratic rival in Natchez, the *Mississippi Free Trader,* published more inflammatory articles and accused the *Courier* of appeasement. The *Courier*'s approach may have reflected the background of its editor. Though a slaveholder, Giles M. Hillyer was a native of Connecticut and had lived in Mississippi for only a few years before buying the *Courier* in 1850. He edited the newspaper until May 1862. Published under different names since 1825, the *Courier* was the longest-lived antebellum newspaper of the Natchez region.

The Secretary of War, as we have already stated, seems to have had timely notice of the plot which led to the late outbreak at Harper's Ferry, but the warning being anonymous, it was regarded, we suppose, as unworthy of attention. Perhaps, says the Mobile *Tribune,* it would have met the same fate if it had not been anonymous. History is full of such examples. The authorities in British India had received more than one intimation of what was to happen months before the breaking out of the mutiny at Meerut; and the horrors of Cawnpore and Delhi might have been averted by timely precaution.[21] Julius Caesar was forewarned of his fate when on his way to the capitol.[22] The British nobleman who received anonymous information of the Gunpowder plot was wiser.[23]

The truth is, continues the *Tribune,* there is a false pride that deters men from appearing to suspect of uncertain danger. The dread of ridicule, or of the imputation of timidity, is so strong that we do not like to incur even the appearance of apprehension. It is a weakness, nevertheless.

May not a useful lesson be drawn from these experiences? Perhaps there never was a wilder or more foolish enterprise—leaving entirely out of view the atrocity of the thing—than that undertaken by Brown and his confederates at Harper's Ferry. And yet the man evidently possessed the means for setting on foot a formidable conspiracy, and the courage and skill to put it in execution.

It proves very clearly that the folly and madness of such a plot, considered with reference to its ultimate results, is no reason for treating the premonitions of it with contempt or incredulity. "An ounce of prevention is better than a pound of cure," and vigilance is the price, not only of liberty, but of safety.

It so happened, that on the very morning on which the fight occurred at Harper's Ferry, we were in company with a friend, when the conversation turned upon the subject of the spasmodic apprehension that sometimes attacks a community, with reference to just such an occurrence as that which Brown attempted to get up. Our friend related a case in point, from his own experience, and appeared to regard it as indicating an undue readiness to give way to suspicion.

Of course we should condemn anything like a nervous anxiety, and above all any disposition to attach suspicion of treason or conspiracy to individuals, without the most palpable proof. In fact, there is already too great proneness to this in some parts of the country. But at the same time a judicious vigilance is necessary to the welfare of any community, however peaceful, so long as human nature continues to be corrupt; nor should any warning, such as that received by the Secretary of War, be regarded as necessarily insignificant. A madman, or a set of madmen, let loose, may be very sure of being eventually and speedily checked, but it is better to check them before they are turned loose.

Source: Natchez Courier, November 18, 1859.

Mahala Doyle, "To John Brown," November 20, 1859

The five proslavery settlers killed at Pottawatomie Creek in May 1856 included a father and two adult sons: James, William, and Drury Doyle. They were poor whites, proslavery but never slave-owning, and had arrived in Kansas in November 1855. The other two men killed were Allen Wilkinson and William Sherman. After the murders of her husband and sons, Mrs. Mahala Doyle returned to Tennessee and wrote to Brown when he was in prison. Her letter appeared in several newspapers, including the *New York Express* and Garrison's *Liberator*.

John Brown: Sir—Although vengeance is not mine, I confess that I do feel gratified to hear that you were stopped in your fiendish career at Harper's Ferry with the loss of your two sons. You can now appreciated my distress in Kansas, when you then and there entered my house at midnight, and arrested my husband and two boys, and took them out of the yard, and in cold blood shot them dead in my hearing. You can't say you done it to free our slaves; we had none, and never expected to have; but it has only made me a poor disconsolate widow with helpless children. While I feel for your folly, I hope and trust you will meet your just reward. Oh, how it pained my heart to hear the dying groans of my husband and children! If this scrawl gives you any consolation, you are welcome to it.

Mahala Doyle

N.B.—My son, John Doyle, whose life I begged of you, is now grown up, and is very desirous to be at Charlestown on the day of your execution; would certainly be there if his means would permit it, that he might adjust the rope around your neck, if Gov. Wise would permit. M.D.

Source: The Liberator, December 16, 1859.

Edmund Ruffin, "Resolutions of the Central Southern Rights Association," November 25, 1859, and *Anticipations of the Future,* June 1860

In 1850 a young Richmond merchant named Daniel H. London formed the Central Southern Rights Association in Virginia. It lobbied Richmond merchants to boycott Northern goods and emphasized the importance of Southern economic independence. The association did not meet between 1854 and 1859 but was reorganized after Brown's raid. Edmund Ruffin (1794–1865) wrote a set of resolutions for the association and read them at a meeting in Richmond on November 25. The resolutions were adopted unanimously by the seventy members present. Ruffin was a respected Virginian agriculturalist and at one point the president of the Virginia State Agricultural Society. He was also a slaveholder and secessionist. Upon hearing the news of Brown's raid, he fantasized about the sensational consequences, including a possible "war of the races," as he put in his diary on November 10. Another diary entry expressed hope that abolitionists would attempt an armed rescue of Brown before the execution, so that the authorities could put them to death and the South would have clear reason to secede. From the Richmond meeting of the association, Ruffin went straight to Harpers Ferry and joined the cadets of the Virginia Military Institute for one day in order to attend the execution. His response to Brown did not end after the execution. In June 1860 he published an epistolary novel, *Anticipations of the Future,* parts of which were serialized in the *Charleston Mercury.* The book is a fictional series of dispatches from a British correspondent in America to the London *Times* from 1864 to 1870, when a civil war unfolds between the North and the South. The abolitionist and Republican William Seward is president, and the South eventually wins the war. Brown and his son Owen appear throughout—Brown is a portent of war, and Owen leads African Americans in an invasion of Kentucky. Ruffin explains in the novel's preface that it shows the consequences of heeding "northern aggressors and southern submissionists." The following year, when the real Civil War began, Ruffin fired one of the first batteries against Fort Sumter. But on June 17, 1865, after Robert E. Lee surrendered to Ulysses S. Grant, he killed himself. The last words in his diary, written minutes before he died, offer more "anticipations" of the future: Ruffin saw a "far-distant day" of "vengeance for the now ruined, subjugated and enslaved Southern States."

"Resolutions of the Central Southern Rights Association"

Resolved, That the late outbreak at Harper's Ferry, of a long-concocted and wide-spread Northern conspiracy, for the destruction by armed violence and bloodshed of all that is valuable for the welfare, safety, and even existence of Virginia and the other Southern States, was, in the prompt and complete suppression of the attempt, and in all its direct results, a failure no less abortive and contemptible than the design and means employed, and objects aimed at, were malignant, atrocious, and devilish.

Resolved, That, nevertheless, the indirect results of this Northern conspiracy, and attempted deadly assault and warfare on Virginia, are all-important for the consideration and instruction of the Southern people, and especially in these respects, to wit: 1st, As proving to the world the actual condition of entire submission, obedience, and general loyalty of our negro slaves, in the fact that all the previous and scarcely impeded efforts of Northern abolitionists and their emissaries, aided by all that falsehood and deception could effect, did not operate to seduce a single negro in Virginia to rebel, or even to evince the least spirit of insubordination. 2d, As showing, in the general expression of opinion in the Northern States, through the press and from the pulpit, from prominent or leading public men, and also in the only public meetings yet held, and generally by the great popular voice of the North, that the majority, or at least the far greater number of all whose opinions have yet been expressed, either excuse, or desire to have pardoned, or sympathise with, or openly and heartily applaud the actors in this conspiracy and attack, which could have been made successful only by the means of laying waste the South and extinguishing its institutions and their defenders by fire and sword, and with outrages more horrible than merely general massacre—while the Northern friends of the South, and of the cause of right and law are too few, or too timid to speak openly in our support, or even to make their dissent heard, and too weak to contend with the more numerous and violent assaults of the South.

Resolved, That the time has come when every State and every man of the South should determine to act promptly and effectively for the defense of our institutions and dearest rights, as well as for other important, though less vital interests; and we earnestly appeal, especially to the legislature of Virginia, and

also to the legislatures of all others of the slaveholding States, that they will
hasten to consult and to deliberate, and will maturely consider and discuss the
condition of the Southern States, under all past aggressions and wrongs, especially this last and crowning aggression of Northern usurpation and hatred,
and devise suitable and efficient measures for the defense of the Southern
people and their institutions, from the unceasing hostility and unscrupulous
assaults of Northern enemies, fanatics and conspirators.

Anticipations of the Future

Washington, D.C., Nov. 11, 1864

In 1860, prior to the known result of Mr. Lincoln's election to the presidential
office, the conflict of opinion, and the antagonism of the designed policy of
the two great parties, caused violent agitation in the slaveholding states.—The
outbreak effected by John Brown in 1859, and the general slave insurrection
then designed (though fruitlessly) were obviously the legitimate practical results of a widespread conspiracy of northern men. The attempt, and its failure,
and the speedy slaying, or later judicial executions of the criminals, found
general sympathy among the Republican party and throughout the northern
section. Though this long planned attempt to excite insurrection was promptly
put down by Virginia, the state in which the attempt was made, and was altogether a failure as to its direct and designed results, nevertheless it caused
much indirect injury to the slaveholding states, in weakening the security and
tenure of their property in slaves, and in the great expenses thereby required
and incurred for permanent as well as temporary measures of defence, against
the recurrence of like invasions, with worse effects—or of more dangerous
conspiracies, expected to be instigated or aided by northern emissaries and
agents. The indignation of the southern people was expressed loudly in every
state, and in almost every town and county thereof, and still more by the usually feeble direct popular voice than through the governmental authorities.
The more southern and more ardent states seemed ready to adopt the extreme
resort of seceding from the northern states, which had long been unjust
and oppressive, and now showed themselves also as malignant enemies. . . .

Washington, June 1, 1866

As heretofore, and through many years, the legislatures of the more noisy
southern states had long debates on the more recent federal and northern ag-

gressions, and the prospective greater dangers, and passed piping-hot "states rights resolutions," promising resistance to the *next* ensuing wrongs by the North, "at all hazards, and to the last extremity;" and, as heretofore, they will submit to the next injuries, and again and again. At least such is the universal northern opinion, founded on all past experience. The loudest threats of the southern legislatures and people—their proceedings that would indicate measures for concert with other states, and resistance or revolt—all are treated with utter contempt by the northern people. It is their almost universal belief that the South cannot be driven to resistance—cannot exist without northern protection—and, so far from seceding, that the South "cannot be kicked out of the Union." Even the arming of Virginia in 1860, at the cost of more than five hundred thousand dollars, and of other states to less extent, was not then even suspected to be designed to resist the government, and to facilitate secession, but for defence of southern lives and property against the future insurrections of their own slaves, led by northern white philanthropists and desperadoes of the John Brown order. There may a great advantage accrue from this contemptuous incredulity of the North, if resistance should ever be attempted by the southern states. For nothing that they can plan, or threaten, will be believed or serve as warning, until actual and important deeds shall take the place of violent and boastful words. . . .

Richmond, July 8, 1868

The events of this war, short as it has been, ought to have shown to all reasoning abolitionists of the northern states that there is little aid to their cause to be expected from negro deserters and allies, and still less from negro insurrections. But fanatics are incapable of correct reasoning, or of learning truth—or of seeing anything otherwise than through the distorting and deceptions medium of their one engrossing idea, and the resulting false dogmas of the peculiar wretched condition of negro slaves in these southern states, and of their readiness and fitness to attempt, with the offer of aid from abroad, to achieve their enfranchisement, through insurrection, rapine, and general massacre of the whites. The sanctimonious philanthropists, who ardently sought the result of the general emancipation of the negroes, were not repelled or discouraged by the use of any means for that end, however destructive, bloody, and even if more horrible than one general massacre of all the whites. Notwithstanding their previous disappointments, and especially of the most notable former attempt under John Brown, these fanatics still fully believed that the only reason why their cherished means for general emancipation—wide-spread and successful insurrection of the slaves—had not already occurred in the South, as a consequence of this war, was the want of sufficient encouragement and support to insurgents, and of evidence of sympathy and zeal for the negroes, and of power to sustain their efforts, in an acting and efficient force of competent and resolute white leaders and co-operators, and directed by abolition counsels and policy. From the beginning of hostilities, the associated and organized abolitionists, especially of the New England states, and in western New York, and Ohio, and Delaware, had been preparing means, and forming plans, to excite insurrection on a large scale of operations. In their expanded philanthropic views, the movers of these measures were not limited in their designed action to the then seceded states. Though the actual war of the northern government was then confined to the six early seceding states, the fanatical conspirators were at war with negro slavery in general (in these southern states) and held all the slaveholding states equally as foes. And as the previous secret communications and plots, and various operations of northern abolition agents, on slaves, had been mostly set on foot in Maryland, Virginia, and Kentucky, it was much easier to renew and extend communications with slaves in these localities than to begin new ones in the more remote southern states. Through various organs and channels of communication, which Northerners had maintained, in ostensible business or religious pursuits, in the southern states, hundreds of slaves in these border states had been tampered with, and more or less indoctrinated with the northern ethics of emancipation and insurrection, with their incidents and aids of robbery, arson, and murder. And these then dormant connexions could easily be revived, and extended as far as would be safe, or would not bring about disclosure, before the designed time for the actual out-break. Before the final secession of the border states, and while as yet there was no new or effective obstacle to the entrance and sojourn and machinations of northern agents, the plan and means for extended insurrections were cautiously made known to many negro preachers, and others of the most suitable among the slaves in the particular localities designed for the early operations. It was not deemed safe to trust many with knowledge of the designs, for fear of their being disclosed. But, as the northern conspirators proceeded upon the established abolition belief that every slave will be anxious and ready to assert his freedom as soon as he is offered arms and support, it was deemed of but little importance that the numbers of the first initiated and chosen leaders should, in the beginning, be very few. The lights and views of the fanatical abolitionists and prime movers of these attempts were in no respect altered from the time and incidents of John Brown's raid in 1859; and the present plans were but copies, or continuations, of that earlier effort. It was believed by them that the sole cause of the total failure of the attempt under Brown's leading, and why not even one slave joined him, was that he did not have at least a few hundred whites to begin the work, and encourage the slaves by their support, instead of only the two dozen northern desperadoes whom he was so sanguine as to believe were sufficient for the supposed easy work.

Richmond, July 9, 1868

As nearly as could be at the same time with the events stated in my last letter, the abolitionist army, coming from Ohio, had invaded Kentucky, in strong force, and with awful effects.

Owen Brown, a son of John Brown who led the Harper's Ferry raid in 1859, had been one of the actors in that outrage.[24] He, with a few others, then escaped from the deserved punishment of death, suffered by his comrades in guilt—and subsequently, when demanded for trial by the governor of Virginia, had been protected from arrest and trial by Gov. Dennison of Ohio, who thus violated his official duty and oath, to protect an atrocious criminal, because his crime had been committed to forward abolition. The associated northern abolitionists, having abiding and strong faith in the name and blood of the martyr John Brown, had sought out his son to command the strong force designed to excite the work of insurrection in Kentucky. By aid of the influence of men in high position in New England, New York, and Ohio, this Owen Brown had been authorized to raise a corps of volunteers, to serve as an independent command, and wherever Brown deemed he could best operate against the revolted states, and also where he could support, recruit, and increase his forces, from the enemy's country. According to the number of men that he might enlist, he was to receive a suitable military commission— whether as captain, if for a single company, colonel, for a regiment, or general, for numbers requisite for a brigade or a division. His troops would be armed, equipped, and provided with every needful supply, in the outset, at the expense of the federal government. But, after invading the territory of the seceded states, it was understood that the army must be self-supporting, in every thing except in the stated monthly pay of officers and soldiers. There was no restriction as to the kind of recruits. With all the organized aid and influence of the associated abolitionists of the North, Brown had enlisted 3500 men, of whom 2700 were northern negroes, and mostly drawn recently from Canada. The larger number had been fugitive slaves from the South—and, when enlisting with him, had long been suffering the ordinary evils of hunger and cold, to which are generally subjected these ignorant and improvident and deluded victims of northern philanthropy. To escape from these sufferings, much more than to obtain the promised future rewards and benefits, induced the ready enlistment of nearly all of these negroes. Brown received the commission of brigadier general—and on his nomination, the subordinate officers were appointed and commissioned. Most of these he selected from his white recruits. But some of the commissioned company officers, and many of the non-commissioned were mulattoes or negroes. But of whatever color, all the officers were violent abolitionists, and ready tools for any work in aid of abolition. As soon as mustered in the United States service, armed, equipped and provisioned (all of which was done as hastily and secretly as possible), the corps proceeded, mostly by railroad conveyance, through Ohio, to cross the river into Kentucky. At that time (which was very soon after the secession of Kentucky) there was not a single company in service in all the state, except 1000 men, who had been called early into service under the former government, and who then, as before, were guarding different points on the Ohio river, and all of them remote from the scene of this invasion. The expedition crossed the Ohio into a part of Kentucky where there is no great distance to reach a numerous slave population. With resident abolition agents (Fee, and other preachers from the North) and through them, with slaves near the river, communications had been established and maintained. Gen. Brown immediately, by proclamation, offered freedom and protection to all slaves who would join his standard, or otherwise assert their freedom by insurrection. Fire-arms or pikes were promised to all who would thus use them. Enough pikes and spare muskets had been brought to arm 10,000 men. And these, with a good supply of ammunition, made up nearly all of his baggage. For provisions, and every other supply, the General expected to draw abundant contributions from the neighborhood of his march or encampment.

The General moved on slowly towards the interior of the state, to afford the better opportunity for the operation of his proclamation. His scouting and foraging parties were spread out widely—and these, and also many others of the army, without command or discipline, sought for plunder as far from the main body of the army as they could venture. Whether by order or consent of the commander, or because he could not restrain the offenders, every thing near the line of march was doomed to destruction. The approach of so large a force could not be kept secret, and most of the inhabitants, both whites and blacks, had fled before the invaders. About 300 slaves, who had been previously engaged, came in and joined the invading army in the first twenty-four hours (and nearly all in the night time) after the leaving of the river. But few white families remained in their homes long enough to be captured, or even seen, by the negro troops. But in some few cases, where the extreme illness of some member of a family compelled others to stay, and to trust to the mercy of the invaders, the consequences were too horrible to be described in detail. All the men, women and children so captured were butchered—after the infliction of still greater horrors. Whatever property was deemed of enough value for transportation, for the supplies of the army or for the individual plunderers, was so used. Everything else that was easily destructible, was destroyed. Every house, stack of forage or straw, and fence, was burnt—the horses and cattle killed, and as many as could be of all other domestic animals. The route of the army, for miles in width was left a waste, and a scene of devastation, in which scarcely a living being remained, and in which no movement was seen, unless of the smoke, or still raging flames, rising from the ashes of numerous homesteads, which, but a few hours before, had been the abodes of peace, industry and happiness.

Sources: De Bow's Review, March 1860, 356; Edmund Ruffin, *Anticipations of the Future, to Serve as Lessons for the Present Time: In the Form of Extracts of Letters from an English Resident in the United States, to the London Times, from 1864 to 1870* (Richmond: J. W. Randolph, 1860), 2–3, 57–58, 242–244, 251–255.

Susan Bradford Eppes, "Diary," October–December 1859

Born in Tallahassee, Florida, Susan Bradford Eppes (1846–1942) lived on a plantation and was just thirteen years old at the time of Brown's raid. Her diary entries for October 1859 describe white Southerners' fears that slaves will rise up in the wake of Brown's attempt. Eppes also describes the response of a slave, Frances, who seems to threaten white Southerners with more upheaval. The entries for November and December discuss Miss Platt, a Northern governess who arrives to teach Susan and her sisters. Miss Platt turns out to be an abolitionist. She mourns Brown on the day of his execution—pretending to be ill—and then is found embracing a slave child. She apparently tries to organize an insurrection and then leaves the South two weeks after Brown's hanging.

October 18th, 1859. The horrible, horrible time that has come to us; our world seems turned topsyturvy. We feel that we can trust none of the dear black folks who, before this, we had relied on at every turn. I am afraid to say a word for fear it will prove to be just what should have been left unsaid.

When the mail comes in we crowd about the mail-bag as though something could be told by looking at the outside and, when it is opened, some one must read the news aloud, the news from Virginia, for we are impatient. What will become of us? Will our Father in Heaven let us be destroyed? Will the people we have always loved put the torch to our homes and murder us when we seek to escape? This is what John Brown was urging them to do.

I cannot see that there has been any change; Lulu is just as good and kind as ever; the rest are more quiet but they do not seem disturbed or ill natured. Frances said to me last night, "Do you understand what all this is about?" I told her I did not; I told her we would know more after a few days. She laughed, a crazy kind of laugh, and said: "Yes, you will; you white folks will know a heap you ain't never knowed before," and then she ran out of the room. I did not tell this, for I am sure she has heard something I have not and if I keep quiet she may tell me more.

The newspapers from Richmond and from New York come daily and they give the details of proceedings in Virginia. It is more exciting than anything I have ever read either in history or fiction.

October 28th, 1859. Governor Wise and the Court in Virginia have condemned John Brown to death and he is to be hanged on the 2nd of December. The New York paper says he is a fanatic and believes he is right in trying to incite insurrection among the slaves of the South. I am sorry for any man who has a nature so depraved that murder and arson seem right to him.

Judge Baltzell[25] thinks the negroes will rise up on that day and apply the torch as Brown urged them to do, but Father does not think so, neither does Brother Junius.[26]

November 7, 1859. Well, in spite of Ossawatimie Brown and all the trouble his diabolical efforts have called up we have another governess from the North. She is not like anyone we have had before. I do not believe she has ever taught school in her life. She has no idea of discipline or order in arranging studies; she is a good music-teacher and when I asked if she liked to teach music, she said she had never taught anything else until now.

November 19th, 1859. Mattie and Lucy do not like Miss Platt;[27] she does not like them either and lets them see it. There is something strange about her; she does not care to sit with us at night and rarely speaks except to answer a question. I went to her room yesterday to carry her some oranges, to keep in her room, so that she could eat them whenever she wished and when I knocked at her door she had to unlock it, *in the daytime*—just think!

November 26th, 1859. Sister Mart is a young lady now and does not go to school any more. I study music with Miss Platt and Sister Mart is carrying on her music with an extra fine teacher in Tallahassee. We both study French under a language master, who is a native Frenchman. There are some rumors that he is an abolitionist and a watch has been put upon his movements. Isn't it dreadful to have to suspect every stranger?

December 2nd, 1859. This is the day John Brown is to be hung. We are not going to school today for Miss Platt is sick in bed with a headache. When Fanny took her breakfast upstairs to her she would not open the door, just said she did not wish any. I took her dinner to her but she answered me through the half-opened door that she was too ill to eat. I asked if I could send the doctor to her but she did not want him; said she often had such attacks and she would be well in the morning; said she did not wish to be disturbed at supper time.

December 15th, 1859. Miss Platt has gone—last night a letter came in the mail for her. It was a little late but the children had not gone to bed so Lucy carried it upstairs and she came back so excited. Robert, who is Fannie's little boy, eleven years old he is now, was in Miss Platt's room; she was holding him in her lap and kissing him and crying over him. Mother went upstairs to see about this and it was just as Lucy said. Mother talked to her and explained that in our country we did not do things like this and advised her to refrain from all such in the future.

Mother told us not to mention this to anybody. Well we did not, but Miss Platt was caught trying to persuade the negroes to rise up and follow in John Brown's footsteps, put the torch to the home of every white man and murder the people wholesale, sparing none. Jordan and Adeline had found it out and told it. I am so glad our black folks love us and are our friends. Mother says it is so near Christmas she will not try to get another governess until after the holidays.

December 26th, 1859. We had a very happy Christmas; just as good as if John Brown had never stirred up so much that was terrible. The scene on the back porch was just as merry; the presents were as joyfully received, the drinks as eagerly quaffed and the good wishes, which, with the negroes, correspond to toasts, were as heartily spoken. I do not believe it will be easy to turn our dear black folks against us though no doubt the abolitionists will keep on trying.

Source: Susan Bradford Eppes, *Through Some Eventful Years* (Macon, GA: J. W. Burke, 1926), 119–122.

Amanda Virginia Edmonds, "Diary," November and December 1859

Amanda Virginia Edmonds (1839–1921) of Fauquier County, Virginia, was twenty years old at the time of Brown's raid. She was a planter's daughter and lived her whole life at her ancestral farm, Belle Grove, which was 2 miles south of Paris, Virginia. She married Armistead Chappelear in 1870. Responding to Brown in diary entries of November and December 1859, she rails against abolitionists and slaves, praises Governor Wise, and wonders if God is bringing judgment upon the South. Edmonds infuses her entries with more drama and horror than Floridian Susan Bradford Eppes, perhaps reflecting her proximity to the site of Brown's raid. She seems to find the days after Brown's death anticlimactic, describing the "dreary" day that dawns after all the excitement is over.

November 11. While we move in the bright, beautiful world unsuspicious of the enemies prowling around, just waiting for our lives, O! what a blow! but did the kind hand of Providence intercede for us? Yes, it was a blessing on our unsuspicious hearts, thanks to Him. Thanks and praise be to his Holy name for his kindness. The 16th of October will be an eventful day in the period of our lives. Long will it be in the hearts of many who have lost friends in the struggling for their own country's safety, all unprepared for such a move. They were entered upon at Harper's Ferry, early in the night, by a party of abolitionists, and taken prisoners. Those who would not suffer themselves to be taken and, others who would not yield, therefore, had to abide by consequences of loss of life.

Governor Wise ordered troops, succeeded in releasing the prisoners, and capturing the vile insurgents, with one exception (and he has since been found and penitentured for life). Old Brown, the captain of the party was badly wounded, and one other; both made confessions, and boldly too, rascals! To free the slaves of the south, that our dear old State should be made a free State! O! the idea is overbearing that they should attempt anything like that!

And now, even today, the excitement is very, very great, especially around here and over the Ridge. The Negroes have threatened what they intended doing and indeed have put some of their vile threats into execution by burning wheat stacks near Charlestown. Some have been taken and put in jail. Last night they put a fire to Lemuel's (Fletcher) wheat and the last of it consumed. Poor fellow, how unfortunate for him. He is in Warrenton, had someone staying there but it was after they had retired from patrolling near daybreak. What ought not to be done with them? I would see the fire kindled and those who did it singed and burnt until the last drop of blood was dried within them and every bone smolder to ashes. Ah! but couldn't I! I don't think my heart could harbor feeling of sympathy for heartless, ungrateful wretches. Some of the men—those who own the most and the vilest ones—seem to be perfectly easy. O! that they would take, and confine them. Why don't they do it. I fear it will be too late if they put it off much longer.

Our protracted meeting has been holding since Saturday in Paris and they have just taken the opportunity of carrying on with their vileness, playing cards and drinking in church Sunday night. One taken last night from Loudoun, supposed to be a runaway. Sister was scared nearly to death when we got from church—of course excited us greatly. Reluctantly did we retire for our hearts were heavy, little knowing what would happen e'er the dawn of morning.

My heart was so sad for it betoken evil. Just as the sun lowered his clouded disc a dark foreboding crept over me. I could not find peace and that feeling clung to me through the night ever and anon. Aroused with clinching hands and a feeling of utter dread, but all was quiet—very unusually so, as has been through every night since Monday. O! what is to come of us? Will the kind hand of Providence protect us? Or is this a judgement to befall this wicked people? Sometimes I think it is. We are all so wicked and hardened we cannot wonder that it should come upon us. O! God reach out thou benignant hand upon our land, restore her to peace and melt the hardened hearts of the people that they may return unto Thee and believe and live. How kindly do our pastors beseech Him and implore forgiveness, but the stubborn hearts answer no....

December 2. This day will long, long be remembered, as the one that witnessed old Brown—the villain, murderer, robber and destroyer of our Virgin peace—swinging from the gallows. O! how many are rejoicing at his end. It is a beautiful calm day, more like the bursting spring. There are many that do not retire tonight or last night in fear of the vile enemy. I fear no danger. They are not honest enough to come while we are prepared to fight them. No, they had rather defer their trip on this soil, when they think we least suspect. O! vile, inhuman race, may God ever protect us from your bloodthirsty foolhardy hands.

December 3. Rained all night. The ground this morning is covered with a complete coating of ice and the trees are hanging in their silvery sprays, but the sun does not illuminate the beautiful scenery with his lovely, genial rays.

Cousin Cap[28] came tonight. He is on his return from Charlestown, a member of Scrug's scouting party. He left about thirty behind, staid in Paris all night. He gives a full description of the trip from the beginning to the end—highly coloured.

Thursday evening, several officers went to Harper's Ferry, escorted Old Brown's wife over to see her husband for the last time. She was well attended to the jail, she entered, they embraced and kissed, but not a year was shed on either side. She was escorted back to the Ferry about eight o'clock by the soldiers. No doubt she felt highly honoured.

Mr. Waugh and Bro. George paid the prisoners a visit Thursday but they refused to hear their prayers as they were in favor of slavery, preferred their own preachers. Old Brown observed that prayers would avail nothing for him, but *he* would pray for *them*—poor deluded wretch!

Friday morning dawned upon our excited prurient soldiers. They all prayed that the enemy would come. At eleven o'clock Brown was taken to the scaffold, bold and undaunted he mounted it a bid the Sheriff, "let it be quick as possible, let it be done with." After he was taken down they cut his throat, boxed him up and sent his remains to his wife to take to the North for burial. He was attended to the scaffold by one thousand five hundred soldiers and three splendid brass bands. O! what an awfully sublime, glorious, charmed scene. I almost wish I was a man, so that I could have been there to look upon it.

The army was stationed around him for five miles distant, could just discern him swinging in the air. O! I do wish that I could go to see them all before they return. Still keep strong guard there. No enemy made its appearance—cowardly set. Ah! they know too well the bravery, the undaunted resolutions of the Southern men. All the North are afraid to meet the men of our Southern State. Fie, Fie, too much feared their own lives. They knew our brave, our noble Governor. Aid was offered him from other states but he thankfully declined the offer—that Virginia was able to defend her honour. Governor Wise, blessings from Heaven rest upon your noble head. Every servant nearly declares they are glad old Brown met the fate he did, but it was not half bad enough for him. They know better than to express sympathy for him as several have been taken to jail for that.

December 4. Cap leaves this morning, joins his company that staid in Paris. A dreary Sabbath, dull and cloudy. As the servants say Old Brown left a hard storm behind him.

Source: Journals of Amanda Virginia Edmonds: Lass of the Mosby Confederacy, 1859–1867, ed. Nancy Chappelear Baird (Stephens City, VA: Commercial, 1984), 31–32, 34–36.

Frances Ellen Watkins Harper, "Dear Friend," November 25, 1859, and "The Triumph of Freedom—A Dream," January 1860

The African American abolitionist Frances E. W. Harper (1825–1911) was born free in Baltimore and lectured for the Maine Anti-Slavery Society between 1854 and 1864. She helped raise money for Brown's family after the raid, and in a letter to Mary Brown of November 14, 1859, she celebrated Brown's death as a "sublime sacrifice," compared his execution to Christ's crucifixion, and imagined his "martyr grave" becoming a "sacred altar" for abolitionism. Writing to Brown himself later that month, she asserted that God would write "national judgments upon national sins" if the nation did not heed his "lesson." She added that more deaths would follow and become freedom's "stepping stones to dominion." Harper echoed this imagery in a short story of January 1860, in which priests search for passages in sacred books to cover the bloodstains on a goddess's clothes. The goddess is slavery, possessing an altar where the hearts of slaves are sacrificed. But one man, John Brown, appears in judgment, and the goddess cowers before him. Then, although Brown is hanged, his blood is a baptism of liberty and the goddess is destroyed, for the bodies of Brown and his raiders are the "stepping stones of Freedom to power."

Kendalville, Indiana, Nov. 25.

Dear Friend: Although the hands of Slavery throw a barrier between you and me, and it may not be my privilege to see you in your prison-house, Virginia has no bolts or bars through which I dread to send you my sympathy. In the name of the young girl sold from the warm clasp of a mother's arms to the clutches of a libertine or a profligate,—in the name of the slave mother, her heart rocked to and fro by the agony of her mournful separations,—I thank you, that you have been brave enough to reach out your hands to the crushed and blighted of my race. You have rocked the bloody Bastile; and I hope that from your sad fate great good may arise to the cause of freedom. Already from your prison has come a shout of triumph against the giant sin of our country.

The hemlock is distilled with victory when it is pressed to the lips of Socrates. The Cross becomes a glorious ensign when Calvary's pale-browed sufferer yields up his life upon it. And, if Universal Freedom is ever to be the dominant power of the land, your bodies may be only her first stepping stones to dominion. I would prefer to see Slavery go down peaceably by men breaking off their sins by righteousness and their iniquities by showing justice and mercy to the poor; but we cannot tell what the future may bring forth. God writes national judgments upon national sins; and what may be slumbering in the storehouse of divine justice we do not know. We may earnestly hope that your fate will not be a vain lesson, that it will intensify our hatred of Slavery and love of freedom, and that your martyr grave will be a sacred altar upon which men will record their vows of undying hatred to that system which tramples on man and bids defiance to God. I have written to your dear wife, and sent her a few dollars, and I pledge myself to you that I will continue to assist her. May the ever-blessed God shield you and your fellow-prisoners in the darkest hours. Send my sympathy to your fellow-prisoners; tell them to be of good courage; to seek a refuge in the Eternal God, and lean upon His everlasting arms for a sure support. If any of them, like you, have a wife or children that I can help, let them send me word.

Yours in the cause of freedom, F. E. W.

"The Triumph of Freedom—A Dream"

It was a beautiful day in spring. The green sward stretched beneath my feet like a velvet carpet, fair flowers sprung up in my path, and peaceful streams swept laughingly by to gain their ocean home. Above me the heavens were eloquent with the praise of God, around me the earth was poetic with His ideas. It was one of those days when Nature, in the excess of her happiness, leans on the bosom of the balmy sunshine, listening to the gentle voices of the wooing winds. I had fallen into a state of dreamy, delicious languor, when I was roused to sudden consciousness by a startling shriek. I looked up, and, bending over me, I saw a spirit gazing upon me with a look of unmistakable sadness. "Come with me?" said she, laying her hand upon me and drawing me along with an irresistible impulse. Silently I followed, awed by her strange manner. "I wish," said she, after a few moments silence, "to show you the goddess of this place."

Surely, thought I, that must be a welcome sight, for the loveliness of the place suggested to my mind a presiding genius of glorious beauty. "It is now her hour of worship, and I want to show you some of her rites and ceremonies, and also the priests of her shrine." Just then we came in sight of the goddess. She was seated on a glittering throne, all sparkling with precious gems and rubies; and, indeed, so bright was her throne, it threw a dazzling radiance over her sallow countenance. She wore a robe of flowing white, but it was not pure white, and I noticed that upon its hem and amid its seams and folds were great spots of blood. It was the hour of worship, and her priests were standing by, with their sacred books in their hands; it was one of their rites to search them for texts and passages to spread over the stains on her garment. When this was done, they bowed down their heads and worshipped, saying:—"Thou art the handmaid of Christianity; thy mission is heaven-appointed and divine." And all the people said "Amen." But during this worship I saw a young man arise, his face pale with emotion and horror, and he said, "It is false." That one word, so sublime in its brevity, sent a thrill of indignant fear through the hearts of the crowd. It lashed them into a tumultuous fury. Some of them dashed madly after the intruder, and hissed in his ears—"Fanatic, madman, traitor, and infidel." But the efforts they made to silence him only gained him a better hearing. They forced him into prison, but they had no chains strong enough to bind his freeborn spirit. A number of adherents gathered around the young man, and asked to know his meaning. "Come with me," said he, "and I will show you?" and while they still chanted the praises of the goddess, he drew them to the spot, where they might view the base and inside of the throne, and the foundation of her altar. I looked (for I had joined them, led on by my guide) and I saw a number of little hearts all filed together and quivering. "What," said I, "are these?" My guide answered, "They are the hearts of a hundred thousand new-born babes." I turned deathly sick, a fearful faintness swept over me, and I was about to fall, but she caught me in her arms, and said, "Look here," and beneath the throne wore piles of hearts laid layer upon layer. I noticed that they seemed rocking to and fro, as if smitten with a great agony. "What are these?" said I, gazing horror-stricken upon them. "They are the hearts of desolate slave mothers, robbed of their little ones." I looked a little higher, and saw a row of poor, bruised and seared hearts. "What are these?" These are the hearts out of which the manhood has been crushed; and these," said she, pointing to another pile of young, fresh hearts, from which the blood was constantly streaming, "are the hearts of young girls, sold from the warm clasp of their mothers' arms to the brutal clutches of a libertine or a profligate—from the temples of Christ to the altars of shame. And these," said she, looking sadly at a row of withered hearts, from which the blood still dropped, "are the hearts in which the manhood has never been developed." I turned away, heart-sickened, the blood almost freezing in my veins, and I saw the young man standing on an eminence, pointing to the throne and altar, his lips trembling with the burden of a heaven-sent message. He reminded me of one of the ancient seers, robed in the robes of prophecy, pronouncing the judgments of God against the oppressors of olden times. Some listened earnestly, and were roused by his words to deeds of noble daring. Others, within whose shrunken veins all noble blood was pale and thin, mocked him and breathed out their hatred against him; they set a price upon his head and tracked his steps with bitter malice, but he had awakened the spirit of Agitation, that would not slumber at their bidding.

The blood-stained goddess felt it shaking her throne, its earnest eye searching into the very depths of her guilty soul, and she said to her worshippers: "Hide me beneath your constitutions and laws—shield me beneath your parchments and opinions." And it was done; but the restless eye of Agitation pierced through all of them, as through the most transparent glass. "Hide me," she cried to the priests, "beneath the shadow of your pulpits; throw around me the robes of your religion; spread over me your altar clothes, and dye my lips with sacramental blood?" And yet, into the recesses of her guilty soul came the eye of this Agitation, and she trembled before its searching glance.

Then I saw an aged man standing before her altars; his gray hair floated in the air, a solemn radiance lit up his eye, and a lofty purpose sat enthroned upon his brow. He fixed his eye upon the goddess, and she cowered beneath his unfaltering gaze. He laid his aged hands upon her blood-cemented throne, and it shook and trembled to its base; her cheeks blanched with dread, her hands fell nerveless by her side. It seemed to me as if his very gaze would have almost annihilated her; but just then I saw, bristling with bayonets, a blood-stained ruffian, named the General Government, and he caught the hands of the aged man and fettered them, and he was then led to prison. I know not whether the angels of the living God walked to and fro in his prison—that, amid the silent watches of the night, he heard the rustling of their garments—I only know that the old man was a host within himself. The goddess gathered courage when she knew that she could rely on the arm of her ruffian accomplice; the old man offered her freedom, but she answered him with a scaffold—the gallows bent beneath his aged form. Her minions drained the blood from his veins, and they thought they had conquered him, but it was a delusion. From the prison came forth a cry of victory; from the gallows a shout of triumph over that power whose ethics are robbery of the weak and oppression of the feeble; the trophies of whose chivalry are a plundered cradle and a scourged and bleeding woman. I saw the green sward stained with his blood, but every drop of it was like the terrible teeth sown by Cadmus; they woke up armed men to smite the terror-stricken power that had invaded his life. It seemed as if his blood had been instilled into the veins of freemen and given them fresh vigor to battle against the hoary forms of gigantic Error and colossal Theory, who stood as sentinels around the throne of the goddess. His blood was a new baptism of Liberty. I noticed that they fought against her till she tottered and fell, amid the shouts of men who had burst their chains, and the rejoicings of women newly freed, and Freedom, like a glorified angel, smiled over the glorious jubilee and stood triumphant on the very spot where the terrible goddess had reigned for centuries. I saw Truth and Justice crown her radiant brow, from joyful lips floated anthems of praise and songs of deliverance—just such songs as one might expect to hear if a thousand rainbows would melt into speech, or the music of the spheres would translate itself into words. Peace, like light dew, descended where Slavery had spread ruin and desolation, and the guilty goddess, cowering beneath the clear, open gaze of Freedom, and ashamed of her meanness and guilt, skulked from the habitations of men, and ceased to curse the land with her presence; but the first stepping-stones of Freedom to power, were the lifeless bodies of the old man and his brave companions.

Source: James Redpath, ed., *Echoes of Harper's Ferry* (Boston: Thayer and Eldridge, 1860), 418–419; *Anglo-African Magazine,* January 1860, 21–23.

Thomas J. Jackson, "To Mary Anna Jackson," December 2, 1859

During his execution at Charles Town, Brown waited for at least ten minutes, blindfolded, for the scaffold trapdoor to open beneath his feet. According to eyewitnesses, he stood erect and completely still. Then his body hung for more than thirty minutes. Thomas "Stonewall" Jackson (1824–1863), who was intensely religious, said a prayer for the dead man. As he wrote to his second wife, Mary, later that day, Jackson found the whole scene "imposing." He was present at the execution to command twenty-one cadets of the Virginia Military Institute in Lexington, Virginia. Jackson had taught artillery and philosophy at the VMI since 1851. He was a slaveholder and, by October 1861, a major general in the Confederate Army. He went on to become one of the great heroes of the Confederacy.

December 2d. John Brown was hung to-day at about half-past eleven A.M. He behaved with unflinching firmness. The arrangements were well made and well executed under the direction of Colonel Smith.[29] The gibbet was erected in a large field, south-east of the town. Brown rode on the head of his coffin from his prison to the place of execution. The coffin was of black walnut, enclosed in a box of poplar of the same shape as the coffin. He was dressed in a black frock-coat, black pantaloons, black vest, black slouch hat, white socks, and slippers of predominating red. There was nothing around his neck but his shirt collar. The open wagon in which he rode was strongly guarded on all sides. Captain Williams[30] (formerly assistant professor at the Institute) marched immediately in front of the wagon. The jailer, high sheriff, and several others rode in the same wagon with the prisoner. Brown had his arms tied behind him, and ascended the scaffold with apparent cheerfulness. After reaching the top of the platform, he shook hands with several who were standing around him. The sheriff placed the rope around his neck, then threw a white cap over his head, and asked him if he wished a signal when all should be ready. He replied that it made no difference, provided he was not kept waiting too long. In this condition he stood for about ten minutes on the trapdoor, which was supported on one side by hinges and on the other (the south side) by a rope. Colonel Smith then announced to the sheriff "all ready"—which apparently was not comprehended by him, and the colonel had to repeat the order, when the rope was cut by a single blow, and Brown fell through about five inches, his knees falling on a level with the position occupied by his feet before the rope was cut. With the fall his arms, below the elbows, flew up horizontally, his hands clinched; and his arms gradually fell, but by spasmodic motions. There was very little motion of his person for several moments, and soon the wind blew his lifeless body to and fro. His face, upon the scaffold, was turned a little east of south, and in front of him were the cadets, commanded by Major Gilham.[31] My command was still in front of the cadets, all facing south. One howitzer I assigned to Mr. Trueheart[32] on the left of the cadets, and with the other I remained on the right. Other troops occupied different positions around the scaffold, and altogether it was an imposing but very solemn scene. I was much impressed with the thought that before me stood a man in the full vigor of health, who must in a few moments enter eternity. I sent up the petition that he might be saved. Awful was the thought that he might in a few minutes receive the sentence, "Depart, ye wicked, into everlasting fire!"[33] I hope that he was prepared to die, but I am doubtful. He refused to have a minister with him. His wife visited him last evening. His body was taken back to the jail, and at six o'clock P.M. was sent to his wife at Harper's Ferry. When it arrived, the coffin was opened, and his wife saw the remains, after which it was again opened at the depot before leaving for Baltimore, lest there should be an imposition. We leave for home via Richmond tomorrow.

Source: Mary Anna Jackson, Life and Letters of General Thomas J. Jackson (Stonewall Jackson) (New York: Harper & Brothers, 1891), 130–132.

John Preston, "To Margaret Junkin Preston," December 2, 1859

Colonel John Thomas Lewis Preston (1811–1890) witnessed Brown's execution as part of the military guard and as the commander of a corps of cadets from the Virginia Military Institute. He was one of the founders and first faculty members of the VMI. Upon returning from the gallows site, he wrote to his wife, Margaret Junkin, about the day's events. The letter was published in the *Lexington Gazette* on December 15, 1859. Margaret's sister was Stonewall Jackson's first wife, and Jackson was present alongside Preston at Brown's execution that day. Preston's letter to his wife offers more details on Brown's manner and behavior than Jackson's. It also describes the execution in more symbolic terms—as the righteous assertion of both God's will and state sovereignty.

Shortly before eleven o'clock, the prisoner was taken from the jail and the funeral cortège was put in motion. First came three companies—then the criminal's wagon, drawn by two large white horses. John Brown was seated on his coffin, accompanied by the sheriff and two other persons.[34] The wagon drove to the foot of the gallows, and Brown descended with alacrity, and without assistance, and ascended the steep steps to the platform. His demeanor was intrepid, without being braggart. He made no speech: whether he desired to make one or not I do not know. Had he desired it, it would not have been permitted. Any speech of his must of necessity have been unlawful, as being directed against the peace and dignity of the Commonwealth, and, as such, could not be allowed by those who were then engaged in the most solemn and extreme vindication of Law. His manner was free from trepidation, but his countenance was not without concern, and it seemed to me to have a little cast of wildness. He stood upon the scaffold but a short time, giving brief adieus to those about him, when he was properly pinioned, the white cap drawn over his face, the noose adjusted and attached to the hook above, and he was moved blindfold a few steps forward. It was curious to note how the instincts of nature operated to make him careful in putting out his feet, as if afraid he would walk off the scaffold. The man who stood unblenched on the brink of eternity was afraid of falling a few feet to the ground!

He was now all ready. The sheriff asked him if he should give him a private signal, before the fatal moment. He replied in a voice that sounded to me unnaturally natural—so composed was its tone and so distinct its articulation—that "it did not matter to him, if only they would not keep him too long waiting." He *was* kept waiting, however. The troops that had formed his escort had to be put in their proper position, and while this was going on, he stood for ten or fifteen minutes blindfold, the rope around his neck, and his feet on the treacherous platform, expecting instantly the fatal act. But he stood for this comparatively long time up-right as a soldier in position, and motionless. I was close to him, and watched him narrowly, to see if I could perceive any signs of shrinking or trembling in his person. Once I thought I saw his knees tremble, but it was only the wind blowing his loose trousers. His firmness was subjected to still further trial by hearing Colonel Smith announce to the sheriff, "We are all ready, Mr. Campbell." The sheriff did not hear, or did not comprehend, and in a louder tone the announcement was made. But the culprit still stood steady, until the sheriff, descending the flight of steps, with a well-directed blow of a sharp hatchet, severed the rope that held up the trap-door, which instantly sank sheer beneath him, and he fell about three feet. And the man of strong and bloody hand, of fierce passions, of iron will, of wonderful vicissitudes—the terrible partisan of Kansas—the capturer of the United States Arsenal at Harper's Ferry—the would-be Catiline[35] of the South—the demigod of the Abolitionists—the man execrated and lauded—damned and prayed for—the man who in his motives, his means, his plans, and his successes must ever be a wonder, a puzzle, and a mystery—John Brown was hanging between heaven and earth.

There was profoundest stillness during the time his struggles continued, growing feebler and feebler at each abortive attempt to breathe. His knees were scarcely bent, his arms were drawn up to a right angle at the elbow, with the hands clinched; but there was no writhing of the body, no violent heaving of the chest. At each feebler effort at respiration, the arms sank lower, and his legs hung more relaxed, until at last, straight and lank he dangled, swayed slightly to and fro by the wind.

It was a moment of deep solemnity, and suggestive of thoughts that make the bosom swell. The field of execution was a rising ground that commanded the outstretching valley from mountain to mountain, and their still grandeur gave sublimity to the outline, while it so chanced that white clouds resting upon them gave them the appearance that reminded more than one of us of the snow peaks of the Alps. Before us was the greatest array of disciplined forces ever seen in Virginia, infantry, cavalry, and artillery combined, composed of the old Commonwealth's choicest sons, and commanded by her best officers, and the great canopy of the sky, overarching all, came to add its sublimity—ever present, but only realized when great things are occurring beneath it.

But the moral of the scene was the great point. A sovereign State had been assailed, and she had uttered but a hint, and her sons had hastened to show that they were ready to defend her. Law had been violated by actual murder and attempted treason, and that gibbet was erected by Law, and to uphold Law was this military force assembled. But greater still, God's holy law and righteous will was vindicated. "Thou shalt not kill." "Whoso sheddeth man's blood, by man shall his blood be shed."[36] And here the gray-haired man of violence meets his fate, after he has seen his two sons cut down before him earlier in the same career of violence into which he had introduced them. So perish all such enemies of Virginia! all such enemies of the Union! all such foes of the human race! So I felt, and so I said, without a shade of animosity, as I turned to break the silence, to those around me. Yet the mystery was awful—to see the human form thus treated by men—to see life suddenly stopped in its current, and to ask one's self the question without answer, "And what then?"

In all that array there was not, I suppose, one throb of sympathy for the offender. All felt in the depths of their hearts that it was right. On the other hand there was not one word of exultation or insult. From the beginning to the end, all was marked by the most absolute decorum and solemnity.

Source: Elizabeth Preston Allan, *The Life and Letters of Margaret Junkin Preston* (Boston: Houghton Mifflin, 1903), 112–115.

Raleigh Register, "The Execution of John Brown," December 3, 1859

The *Raleigh Register* was antislavery throughout the 1820s, but by 1835, responding to the abolitionist movement's calls for immediate emancipation, the newspaper was denouncing abolitionism and defending slavery. It remained the leading Whig organ of North Carolina during the 1850s, opposed secession, and denounced secessionists such as Edmund Ruffin. Responding to Brown's execution in December 1859, it imagines the kind of memorabilia that might emerge from the gallows site and observes that P. T. Barnum was already trying to collect Brown-related objects. Barnum operated New York's famous American Museum, where the exhibitions included human curiosities, historical artifacts, scientific instruments, and taxidermy exhibits. Although the *Raleigh Register* may have been joking about his interest in Brown memorabilia, Barnum did place an advertisement in the *New York Tribune* on December 7, 1859, announcing his museum's new exhibition of "a full-length Wax Figure of OSAWATOMIE BROWN; his Autograph Commission to a Lieutennancy; a KNIFE found on the body of his Son; TWO PIKES or Spears taken at Harper's Ferry." Then, in 1863, the museum displayed Louis Ransom's painting *John Brown Meeting the Slave Mother and Her Child* (1860), although Barnum removed it during the draft riots of July.

The chances are ninety-nine in a hundred, that before this paper reaches our subscribers John Brown will have paid the penalty of his crimes on the gallows, and gone to render an account of his life to that Being who says "thou shalt do no murder."

While we have not the slightest fear that any attempt has been made to rescue Old Brown, we are not without painful apprehensions that among such a large body of inexperienced and excited soldiery, mischief has happened from the incautious use of fire arms.

It is to be hoped, with Brown's exit from the world, the excitement at the North will subside. But we must confess that this hope is but of the faintest character. Fanaticism at the North is rampant, and overrides every thing. On yesterday, the godly city of Boston, built up and sustained by the products of negro slave labor, went into mourning, fasting and prayer, over the condign punishment of a negro stealer, murderer and traitor, and from fifty pulpits the Praise-God-Bare-bones[37] belched forth volumes of blasphemy and treason.

In all the Noo England towns and villages, we may expect to hear that mock funerals have been celebrated, and all kinds of nonsensically lugubrious displays made. (It is a pity that they haven't a witch or two to drown or burn, by way of variety.) We hope that Gov. Wise will have the gallows on which Brown was hung burned, and give notice of the fact. Our reasons for this wish is this: The Yankees have no objection to mingling money making with their grief, and they will, unless Brown's gallows is known to have been burned, set to work and make all kinds of jimcracks and notions out of what they will call parts of Old John Brown's gallows and sell them. Let the rope which choked him, too, be burned and the fact advertised, or we shall see vast quantities of breast pins, lockets and bracelets, containing bits of the "rope which hung Old Brown" for sale. Barnum is already in the market for Old Brown's old clothes, and hopes and expects to make as good a speculation out of them as he did out of his Woolly Horse, and Joyce Heth, "Washington's nurse."

Source: Raleigh Register, December 3, 1859.

Moncure Conway, "Sermon," December 4, 1859

Echoing Brown's self-fashioning, abolitionists took up the theme of 1776. In a sermon at the First Congregationalist Church of Cincinnati, Ohio, the Reverend Moncure Daniel Conway (1832–1907) claimed that Brown was an even greater patriot than George Washington, for his cause was greater. He also echoed Brown's prophecy of the bloodshed that would end slavery. Conway was an abolitionist from Virginia. His father was a slaveholder and his three brothers were proslavery. Two brothers would eventually join the Confederate Army. But Conway became an abolitionist while studying at Harvard University's Divinity School between 1852 and 1854, and he worked as a Unitarian minister in Cincinnati from 1856 to 1861. Even so, his first response to Brown was less positive than the sermon of December 4. On October 23, after hearing about the Harpers Ferry raid, he preached a sermon that called Brown's attempt a "blunder" and Brown himself a monomaniac. During November, Conway saw that other nonresistant abolitionists had praised Brown and changed his mind. But later in his life he condemned Brown again. The character Gideon in his novel *Pine and Palm* (1887) is a thinly disguised and unappealing John Brown. Conway came to believe that Brown forced an unnecessary war, and he claimed in his autobiography of 1905 that "few men ever wrought so much evil." He believed that as a Southerner, free from the "Old Puritan spirit and faith in the God of War" that possessed the North, he should have known better than to celebrate Brown's actions. The autobiography blames this sermon on his "youthful optimism."

Is John Brown a hero? It will one day be told, to prove the stupidity of this age, that such a question was asked by sane men; that there were eyes so dull that they could not see, in a man dying for a religious principle, any thing more than a fanatic," "madman," "traitor."

See him standing there on that great prophetic Monday, in the armory of the United States, bearing, according to Col. Lewis Washington's testimony, during the whole day, that heirloom of the family, the sword which Frederick the Great sent to General Washington. Perhaps you remember the history of that sword; how Frederick the Great, after a series of the most stupendous wars which the world ever saw, from the battle of Mollwitz, in 1741, to the peace conceded to suppliant Austria, in 1771, having fulfilled his mission of punishing the most criminal nation which ever existed, and placing all the nationalities of Europe on a freer basis, then looked over the ocean and saw an earnest and deeply wronged people contending with an oppressor; how nearly his last public act was to extend to our nation in that conflict a helping hand, by employing Hessian troops across the Atlantic, and levying the same toll on the English recruits crossing his dominions as on "bought and sold cattle;" and how, when we conquered our freedom, he forwarded from Potsdam to Mount Vernon a Prussian sword of honor, marked with these words: "From the oldest general in the world to the greatest." If the spirit of Washington could still rule in our land, I believe it would have presented that sword to John Brown as its rightful inheritor, with the words: "From the greatest general in the world to the purest."

Think not that these are the words of enthusiasm; they are the words of truth and soberness. If in any degree a Cause elevates the deed, if the altar sanctifieth the gift laid thereon, then that sword made an ascent and no descent when held in the hands of John Brown. Frederick was an instrument in the hands of the overruling power to advance the rights of man, but he was not a hero. He thought not of humanity: when he entered the long series of wars which brought about so much good, he said, privately, "Ambition, interest, the desire to make people talk about me, carried the day, and I decided to make war."[38] He was a nobler man at last; but his great deeds were, all summed up, not equal in elevation to that which was expiated on the gallows last Friday. Now let us turn to the next heir of the sword of honor, the Father of our Country. Nowhere with more reverence than here shall be spoken the name of Washington! Yet what was the cause for which he so bravely fought? Why, King George had touched the *pocket* of New England; that was it—a few shillings tax more than was right, brought about the American Revolution. Also, Washington had the sympathy of the two leading powers of the world, Prussia and France, and the self-interest of every soldier was concerned. The cause was a just cause, but it was not a purely human one. But this man, arming his heart with the Book which says, "Remember those who are in bonds as bound with them,"[39] and the Declaration of Independence, of which he seems to be one of the very few genuine believers in our times, marches on to a certain death;

marches over the dead bodies of his sons to the scaffold—laying his all upon the altar of the just God. Do we admire Hampden, who, rather than pay an unjust tax of twenty shillings, risked his head that he might bring a throned tyrant to the block?[40]—how much more should we admire the old Puritan, who, for a protest against the great crime of our country, against five millions of his brethren, gave himself and his sons to a cruel death? The traitor of Charles I is our hero; the traitor of Governor Wise will become our saint. I am appealing to you as men of heart and reason; not as men whose opinions are dependent on the cotton market, or on the platforms of parties. I set aside the human wisdom of this movement. I set aside the question of the abstract rectitude of the method. The stature of a hero dwarfs such considerations. It was his conviction of duty—that is enough. Can I not admire Socrates or Hypatia[41] because I do not agree with the heathenisms for which they yielded up their lives? Where heroism comes, where self-devotion comes, where the sublime passion for the right comes, there God comes; there a will unmeasurable by all prudential gauges is executed, and we may as well question the moral propriety of a streak of lightning or an earthquake as of that deed.

Thou martyr of a noble faith! Thou God-maddened old man! I have followed thee dreaming and waking with my eyes. I have listened to the word of victorious faith which came from thy prison; came saying, "God has prospered me," as thy well-served Master said in his darkest hour, "Now am I glorified."[42] I have followed thee to the scaffold, where, amid the silent thunders of God, which were bursting over the land, thou answered "nothing;" and I felt that like our fathers, we also were passing into a Red Sea, and have prayed that we too should be baptized to our Moses, to our Freedom, in the cloud and in the sea! Who is so purblind as to say that the man whose deed has summed up a century's work—who has sealed with his blood the death-warrant of Slavery, has failed? A clear eye may read in red letters FAILURE on the front of the capitols in Virginia or Washington; but it will read on the gallows of Brown, SUCCESS. When such heroism fails, the divine power is bankrupt!

You have heard the great story of Arnold of Winkelried,[43] the second Leonidas[44] and more: how, when all other hope was fled, and his companions shrank before the swarm of Austrians, to whom they were as nothing in number, he had recourse to an ally unseen, but invincible—namely, a heroic heart. He rushed forward to a sure death. He gathered in his side the "fatal sheaf of Austrian spears,"[45] and perished before them. He made every follower a hero—his deed was stronger than an army; his foe had not counted on such opponents. So does heroism fulfill the old prophecies, and carrying the arm of God with it, one chases a thousand, and two put ten thousand to flight. We, too, have seen our Arnold die before us to break the pass; and where there was one God-fearing and man-loving heart in this land, there are now a thousand. John Brown is not dead; last Friday he was born in a million hearts. For this is a time when nothing should be disguised, and men must confront unwelcome but stubborn facts. Our speech must be by the rule of *vera pro gratis*—the true instead of the pleasant. When, by a sudden touch, as of Ithuriel's spear, a disguised monster shows itself in its real form,[46] we know that the antipathy to it, hitherto disguised, will become equally open and real. When on one side of a river, free thought, and free speech, and free press prevail, and on the other free presses are cast into the river, and free men warned from their homes; when martial law is declared, and the highways are impressed; when a State turns highwayman, and imprisons the subjects of other States without warrant; when the political inquisition is revived in a Republic—then, my friends, it is an error to say we are on the verge of civil war; we are in the midst of civil war, whether much blood be yet shed or not. Last Friday the wind was sown: soon or late the whirlwind must be reaped.

It is idle to talk of pity for that slain man; we cannot pity one who looks down on us from such a height. We should rather approach, his prison as a palace, his gallows as a throne—

> "For whether on the scaffold high,
> Or in the battle's van,
> The fittest place where man can die
> Is where he dies for man."[47]

We have now only to live and do a manly Christian part in the development of his deed, and in controlling it, lest it pass out of the lawful realm of the Prince of PEACE. Its immediate results may creep. In the Egyptian legend, at the end of every five hundred years, the divine bird, the Phoenix, comes to the altar of the Sun and burns himself to ashes. On the first day after this, men find in the ashes a worm; on the second day, an unfledged bird; and on the third day after, the full grown Phoenix flies away. Out of the ashes of our martyr a Revolution must come. It may creep the first day; it may be weak the second day; but at last its free pinion will strike the air, and it will rise up to brood over this land, until the progeny of Freemen arise to crown America's destiny.

May we all, as we pass under the cloud and through the sea, be baptized afresh to the cause of LIBERTY, HUMANITY, and GOD!

Source: James Redpath, *Echoes of Harper's Ferry* (Boston: Thayer and Eldridge, 1860), 349–357 (353–357).

Reuben Davis, "The Duty of Parties," December 8, 1859

Like several Democrats in Congress, Reuben Davis (1813–1890) used Brown's raid to attack William Seward, a candidate for the Republican nomination in 1860. Davis was a Democratic representative from Mississippi who went on to serve in the Confederate Army as a brigadier general. In his speech to Congress a few days after Brown's execution, Davis argues that Seward was so culpable in the Harpers Ferry raid that he too deserves to hang. Davis points to the fact that Hugh Forbes, a British soldier hired by Brown in 1857 to train men for the raid, betrayed the Virginia plans in advance to several political leaders, including Seward. He also attacks John C. Frémont, who ran on an antislavery platform in 1856 as the Republican Party's first candidate for president; warns that emancipation would destroy the national economy; and paints a terrifying picture of a thousand John Browns butchering Southerners with the blessing of antislavery Republicans.

Are we, then, to stand by and see our constitutional friends of the North, lending us a helping hand in the hour of danger, trampled in the dust? We ought not. Are we to allow them to be defeated by Seward[48] and his revolutionary followers? We should not. I have said revolutionary followers. I have said it not idly. I have the proofs for the charge—proofs which will show Seward must have known of John Brown's intention to invade Virginia, for which invasion John Brown has met the gallows, and for which knowledge Seward deserves it. *(Applause.)*

"There is a meaning in all these facts, which it becomes us to study well. The nation has advanced another stage; it has reached the point where intervention by the Government for slavery and slave States will no longer be tolerated."[49] What is that stage to which the Union has advanced? It is this: at the time of the formation of the Government there were twelve slave States and but one free State,[50] and we retained the majority until within, a few years past;

now there are seventeen free States, and only fifteen slave, so the balance of power has passed from the slave to the free States. In this condition of things, we are informed that the free States are organizing to seize the Government as the representative of their system of labor, and it is to be used by them as the instrument for the destruction of our system, and while in their possession, will no longer be allowed to intervene for the protection of slavery or the slave States. Our property is to be left exposed to the invasion of the robber and the lawless; and even if the slave shall rebel against his master, we are not to expect any support from the Government. I have always understood that the object and purpose of government was protection of property, and when the protection of property ceased, the citizen was released from his allegiance to that government, and with this recognition of the duties of government, we of the slave States would now be satisfied; but we are told that we shall not have protection, and that we shall still observe allegiance. This will convert the Government into a despotism of the most detestable character, and will cause us to resist.

But again, we are informed that the State itself shall not be protected in its sovereignty. Now Mr. Clerk, this Government is the Government of the slave States as much so as that of the free. It was made by a compact between the slave and free States, and I must ask gentlemen of the opposition what right they have to seize it to our exclusion, and whether the act will not be a revolution and constitute those engaged in it rebels. This announcement is a declaration to the nations of the whole earth that they may invade us in our sovereignty and our property with impunity. John Brown, and a thousand other John Browns, may invade us and the Government will remain neutral—there will be no Army, no Navy, sent to resist any invasion; but we are to be left to the tender mercies of our enemies. Yet we are told we have no right to complain; that we have no right to suppose we will not be protected in our property, and should submit peaceably to the Government passing into the hands of tile Black Republicans. We may do it, but I do not believe we will. Ought we not, then, in frankness to tell our northern compatriots that if we are not to be protected in the Union, we will protect ourselves out of it, even at the hazard of deluging this vast country in a sea of blood? SEWARD says: "Free labor has at last apprehended Its rights, Its interest, Its power, and its destiny, and is organizing itself to assume the Government of the Republic." So we are informed there is a conflict between the system of labor in the free and slave States, and free labor is organizing to take possession of the Government, and when this event happens, you inform us we shall neither be protected in our civil or political rights. You even go so far in your meanness as to tell us you intend, by the power of the Government, to force us to submit to your tyranny, despotism, oppression, robberies, and wrongs. That is the announcement you make to us. If you want this Government, and wish to get rid of us, say so, and I will take you by the hand on that *(applause in the galleries)* and bid you a joyful adieu, and will promise to let you alone, but you must let us alone. We have always let you alone in the Union, and you must let us alone; in other words, while we are together let us stand by the contract of our forefathers—men a great deal better, perhaps, than those occupying seats on either side of this House.

Again, SEWARD says: "We will henceforth meet you boldly and resolutely here on the floor of the Senate, in the Territories or out of them, wherever you may go to extend slavery. It has driven you back in California and in Kansas; it will invade you soon in Delaware, Maryland, Virginia, Missouri, and Texas." Ah! "it will invade you soon in Maryland and Virginia." And, as foretold, Virginia has been invaded; invaded with pikes, with lances, with rifles; yes, with Sharpe's rifles. Your murderers have already come within the limits of our States, as announced by the traitor SEWARD, in the speech from which I have taken this extract. Did he know of Brown's intention to make this invasion at the time the speech was made, and was it Brown's invasion to which he had reference? Forbes says so; certain it is, the invasion was then concocted. We have been invaded, and the facts of it show SEWARD to be a traitor and deserving the gallows. *(Applause in the galleries.)* Brown had organized his invasion at the time, and the constitution had been formed when the speech was made. Forbes was in the city of Washington then, and says he had a conversation with SEWARD in regard to the invasion. This testimony is sustained by that of Cook.[51] SEWARD himself admits a conversation with Forbes about that time, and that he wanted money for an object which he refuses to disclose. It is due to justice that I should state that SEWARD denies that Forbes communicated to him the fact of the intended invasion; but, in my judgment, the weight of evidence is against him and in favor of Forbes. I believe Forbes. The word invasion has its own meaning. Brown had organized an invasion of Virginia, and SEWARD said Virginia would soon be invaded. He cannot escape complicity in the affair.

Are these facts not startling, and should they not awaken apprehension in the mind of southern people? Is it not time we were arming for our defense? We are arming, and who will condemn us?

SEWARD said "the invasion will be not merely harmless but beneficent, if we yield reasonably to its moderate and just demands." What invasion does he refer to, unless it is Brown's invasion? This language is exactly the same used by John Brown, who said, if Virginia had allowed him to take her negroes *off* peaceably, and without making any fuss about it, he would not have killed anybody. *(Laughter.)* Brown said he did not mean to kill anybody. SEWARD said the invasion would be harmless and beneficent to us, if we yielded to their just and moderate demands. But if we did not yield, what then? Why, Brown said he would kill our people, and butcher our women and children. SEWARD said: "Whether that consummation shall be allowed to take effect with needful and wise precautions against sudden change and disaster, or be hurried on by violence, is all that remains for you (the people of the South) to decide." This is the very language of John Brown. Whether we will allow it to be done quietly or not, is the only question we are allowed to decide. We are allowed to decide, but however we decide makes no difference; the thing is to be done, at all hazards. Virginia has decided, and has hung the traitor Brown, and will hang the traitor SEWARD, if he is found in her borders. *(Laughter.)* Virginia has refused to yield, and you have attempted to force her. She met violence with violence—has hung your leader, Brown—has stood upon your borders with her armed men and defied you, but your clansmen appeared not to rescue the traitor.

If there were no undiscovered person in this affair, why did Brown so impressively urge his known confederates not to betray their friends—and who are those friends hot to be betrayed? The testimony, to my mind, shows SEWARD to be one.

Mr. Clerk, we are arming, but not against the Government; we are arming to put down rebellion against the Government; we are for the Government. The Black Republicans showed their organized rebellion when they presented Fremont as a sectional candidate for the Presidency, as a representative of their system of free labor in opposition to our system of slave labor; between which, they say, exists an irrepressible conflict. In that act you undertook to seize the Government for yourselves, in violation of the letter and spirit of the Constitution. Against that rebellion we intend to act; we mean to put it down even if we have to do it with the bayonet. And I call upon the American party to come forward and aid us in putting down this rebellion. I call upon the anti-Lecomptonites[52] to come forward and aid us in putting down this rebellion. I call upon men of all parties, of all names, from whatever section of the country they come, to rally under the standard of the Constitution, under the old flag of our fathers—under the stars and stripes of our country—to aid in striking down rebellion that has grown up in our midst; some of the fruits of which we have already tasted. Understand, we do not mean to go out of the Union to whip you; we mean to whip you in the Union; we mean to crush out your rebellion in our midst, by the aid of patriotic men North, South, East, and West. That is what we intend. Do not call us disunionists, at all; that is not our policy. . . .

I will not detain the House by referring to the ten thousand accumulative evidences of the intention of the Black Republican party. SEWARD is a representative man, and is the personation of the purposes of the party. The object is the emancipation of the slaves. Sir, I shall not detain you with a presentation of the devastation which must follow it—the midnight burning, the cruel tortures, atrocities not to be named by civilized lips, or heard by civilized ears. I will not call up, before the imagination of members, the South in her dissolution, lying, like a mighty Leviathan, bleeding at every pore. I will only briefly consider its effects upon the general prosperity of the people of this country and the world. Emancipate our slaves, and you extinguish property now valued at about four billion dollars, the great productive wealth of the world. The labor being destroyed, our land in the South now worth at least $5,000,000,000, is rendered unproductive and idle during this generation, and for generations to come. It is this capital which lies at the foundation of our present national and individual prosperity. By it, from four to five hundred million dollars annually added to the aggregate wealth of the nation. From it emanates our national prosperity, and it is that which gives individual prosperity. Destroy it, and you produce national bankruptcy, and, of consequence, individual bankruptcy. Destroy it, and you bring famine upon the land—laboring men will want employment, and be without the means of procuring support for themselves and families.

Now, sir, in view of these calamities, national and individual, shall this Black Republican war upon all the interest of mankind be allowed to go on, or will the nation come to the aid of the national Democracy in putting down that party? The storm cloud of anarchy and blood and carnage and desolation has gathered darkly over our country. Its thunders and lightnings come together, telling us of its close proximity. Come Americans, come conservatives, come patriots, let us stand together and bare our bosoms to its vengeance, and live with, or die for, our country, its freedom, and its laws.

Source: Speech of Hon. Reuben Davis, of Mississippi, in the House of Representatives, December 8, 1859 (Washington: Congressional Globe Office, 1859), 5–8.

Anonymous, "A Woman's View of a Woman's Duty in Connection with John Brown's Crimes," December 11, 1859

In 1852, Harriet Beecher Stowe published her antislavery novel *Uncle Tom's Cabin*, which had first appeared as a forty-week serial in *National Era* from June 1851 to April 1852. The novel sold 500,000 copies in the United States and Britain within a year of its publication. Lincoln reportedly greeted Stowe at the White House in 1862 with the words "So you're the little woman who wrote the book that started this great war!" Others connected Stowe to Brown as well. One Southern white woman remembered that she was terrified by Brown's raid because she thought it was "God's vengeance for the torture of such as Uncle Tom." Another, who wrote to the *Memphis Daily Appeal* soon after Brown's execution, believed that Stowe had sown evil seeds that grew into Brown's raid. The letter expresses sympathy for Brown, who was a victim of Stowe's teaching and atoned for the sins of Stowe and other abolitionists on the scaffold. Stowe had Brown's blood on her soul, the letter insists.

Ever since *Uncle Tom's Cabin,* with its pernicious success, the isms of a few fanatics, male and female, have been made a prominent feature in our national politics, the evil popularity of one woman, who had been writing twenty years almost unheard of, had set a portion of the sex crazy with a desire for like notoriety. Mrs. Stowe had been diligently writing into middle age, without being known as an author and at last issued from obscurity, not by an extraordinary talent, but because the restless Beecher blood[53] led her to strike a rich vein of passion and prejudice, which arose at once and recognized her talent when it took an incendiary form, which had been overlooked in its legitimate channel for nearly half a life.

The book was the first of the class that had been sowing evil thoughts throughout the land, which are now becoming murderous acts. The evil spirit was evoked by anti-slavery novels mostly written by women—the sermons which pleaded for Sharp's rifles, as if holiness was murder, were listened to by women. The Abolition press, which joined full cry, women read approvingly, as if treason were religion—all this has done its work, and that is—murder!

The evil tendency of these teachings is not confined to the developments at Harper's Ferry, but have spread through society, perverting everything that is sweet and sacred in the female character where a poisonous seed has fallen near the hearthstone. Since that time, females have ceased to blush when free love as an institution is mentioned, but discuss it side by side with the negro question. The slavery of the South and the slavery of *marriage* take now about equal prominence. Woman's rights and negro rights ride the same saddle, and woman appear now with a shameless audacity and partake in discussions which the most hardened of the sex would have shrunk from twenty years ago.

The irreligion, the want of reverence, the audacious ambition which this state of things has developed in women, is a terrible feature of the times. A thirst for notoriety is driving the sex insane. They call it by a thousand specious names but the fountain is in the insiate vanity which nothing but the lightning of the press of the clamors of a multitude can appease. The women who have set an example and given their talent to produce this state of things, are as culpable as the man who poisons a well at which the whole village must drink. They are like boys who have the power to open the flood-gate, but none to arrest the cataract of water that pours through.

Mrs. Beecher Stowe, and her train of small imitators, have something more to answer for than the death of those who had faith in their sincerity. When old John Brown, the victim of their teachings, atones for his fault on the scaffold, it will be the most painful or repulsive picture that the teachings of these unwomanly women have inflicted on society, for the execution of a man is not half so revolting as the demoralization of one woman. The evil which his death will spread, is nothing to the spirit of defiance to law and order which overshadows many a New England hearthstone, where our mothers performed their household duties, worshiped God, and reverenced the laws.

If old John Brown is executed on the day appointed, such women as Mrs. Stowe, and such men as Henry Ward Beecher, will have his blood on their souls, if not on their hands. It was his belief in their courage and sincerity that led the old man into the crime which he has expiated on the gallows, while the incendiary words which lured him and his followers to death, coin for the writers fame and money with which to purchase appliances for luxurious living. Incendiary acts, incited, encouraged and fostered by these mercenary teachings, have led braver souls than they will ever possess to the scaffold.

And what have the anti-slavery men and women done to help their victims? Why, contented themselves by vituperations against the South; fled to Canada for safety, or sent artistically prepared letters asking permission to visit old John Brown in his dungeon,[54] that each word gathered from his miserable lips may hereafter be turned to a grain of gold. The anti-slavery women have talked and written any amount of sentimental incendiarism; but now, when these teachings take form, and are about to make the wife of old John Brown a widow, what can they do? They cannot write him out of prison, or preach the gallows from under his feet. They have urged an excitable, ardent and rash fanatic on to a bloody death, and instead of going on their knees and praying Almighty God to forgive this horrible sin, content themselves with writing letters for publication, or making sentimental journeys to their victim's prison.

During the last few weeks, letters have been floating, thick as leaves, through the newspapers—all calculated to exalt a handful of unhappy rioters into martyrs, and to give the names of the writers to the public—a bliss for which some women of ardent vanity and mediocre minds would, I believe, take a place on the gallows themselves.

Source: Memphis Daily Appeal, December 11, 1859.

Andrew Johnson, "Remarks to the Senate," December 12, 1859

On December 5, 1859, senator James Mason submitted a resolution to appoint a committee that would inquire into the Harpers Ferry raid. During the Senate debate on the resolution, Andrew Johnson (1808–1875) gave a speech that castigates Republicans senators for their antislavery sentiments. He aimed his remarks at Senate Republicans Benjamin Wade of Ohio, Henry Wilson of Massachusetts, and William H. Seward of New York in particular. The speech also responded to senator James Doolittle of Wisconsin, who had offered an explanation for Brown's actions at Harpers Ferry: his sons were murdered in Kansas and he acted in revenge. When Johnson gave the speech, he was a Democratic senator from Tennessee who wanted concessions to the South and new guarantees for the protection of slavery. But as a Unionist, he was the only Southern senator not to quit his post upon secession. In 1865 he became the seventeenth president of the United States.

I commenced with the purpose of showing that the recent foray upon Harper's Ferry was the legitimate result of certain teachings to which I have referred. Look at the provisional government which was framed by those who carried on that exhibition; look at their idea of getting up stampedes, and their expectation that when they struck the first blow a portion of the white population and the blacks would flock to their standard, and that they could maintain themselves there for a certain time, and then the Federal Government would be made an instrument for the overthrow of slavery. I think the act is a legitimate result of the teachings; and those who have taught and still teach their followers these doctrines, though they may not have intended it, are, in fact responsible for it. It is the result of their teachings, it is their work; and now is the time to commence a reformation, and put forth different teachings on this subject.

But, Mr. President, Senators have undertaken to rebuke those of us who have spoken of John Brown's acts as theft, murder, and treason, and apologies are offered for the man who has committed such outrageous offences. I picked up a newspaper not long since, which, referring to the acts of John Brown, said that, if he passed from the prison to the scaffold, making no false step, his gallows would be more glorious than the cross; that Christ, in the depth of his agony, had asked that his cup might pass from his lips, but that John Brown has drank it to the dregs, and therefore John Brown and his gallows have become superior to Christ and his cross. The idea was, that the coming and mission of Christ were a failure, and that John Brown and the gallows on which he was executed would be their modern cross and their Christ. Such is the blasphemy of these teachings. I once heard it said that fanaticism always ends in hell or in heaven. I believe it is true. It is one of those wild, maddening, passions that take possession of the human heart, and that always carry it to excess. There is no medium, and there is no cure for it but a consumption of the passion itself. I have got another idea in ethics, and that is that there never was any people on the face of the earth greater than the god they worshipped, and if John Brown becomes the Christ, and his gallows the cross, God deliver me from such people as they, whether they are fanatics, Democratic or Republican, or any other description of persons—I care not by what name they are called.

I hope, when this resolution was introduced, that it would be kept clear from party associations, and that it would pass with unanimity, without any apologies of excuses being lugged in for the acts complained of. We find, however, that Senators disclaim the acts of John Brown in one breath, and in another they hold out excuses for the man, saying that he showed himself a man of endurance, a man of philosophy, a man of tact, a man of sense; and when we speak of him as a thief and a robber and a murderer and a traitor, they declare that we should not say such things about John Brown. Those may make him a god who will, and worship him who can; he is not my god, and I shall not worship at his shrine....

We assume this to be a Christian community, and if it was true that his sons were badly mistreated, was that any excuse for his violating all the laws of humanity and of God? He was in a Christian country; he had his remedy without resorting to the means to which he had recourse. We have all read that "Whoso sheddeth man's blood, by man shall his blood be shed." And also, "Thou shalt not kill." It seems we have some new-born Christians who are making John Brown their leader, who are trying to canonize him and make him a great apostle and martyr. Were these the elements of a Christian and a Christian martyr? How do the facts stand in this case? When was old man Brown's son killed, and when did he commit these atrocities? Even admitting the truth of the statement of the Senator from Wisconsin, they are not justifiable; but when we show that the facts are different, they are less so. . . . Three months after William Doyle and his two sons were murdered, three months after Sherman was murdered, his skull cut open in two places, and the stream had washed the brains out of his cranium—three months after that, John Brown's son was killed at Ossawatomie. Then, what becomes of this excuse? Why this apology for a man like this? Three long months after he had committed this fiendish act, his son lost his life at the battle of Ossawatomie. It was on that night, about eleven o'clock, as testified by Mrs. Doyle, as testified by her son, as testified by Harris, these men, innocent, unoffending men, were taken out, and in the midnight hour and in the forest and on the road side fell victims to the insatiable thirst of John Brown for blood. Then it was that these murders were committed, that hell entered his heart—not the iron his soul. Then it was that he shrank from the dimensions of a human being into those of a reptile. Then it was, if not before, that he changed his character to a demon who had lost all the virtues of a man. And you talk about sympathy for John Brown!

John Brown stands before the country a murderer. The enormity, the extraordinary ferociousness of the father set the son mad. The blood of these murdered men—not unlike that of sacrificed Abel—cried even from the tongueless caverns of the earth to him for pity, and to Heaven for justice; but his iron heart, not soul, refused to yield; but Heaven, in the process of time, has meted out to him justice on the gallows. Justice divine to punish sin moves slow—the slower its pace, the surer is its blow. It will overtake us if living—it will overtake us if dead. Justice has overtaken its victim, and he has gone to eternity with crimsoned hands, with blood upon his head.

But the Senator talks about the school in which John Brown was taught.[55] Why, sir, John Brown, according to his own confession, had entertained these ideas for twenty years. John Brown did not go to Kansas to go to school. He went there as a teacher on the 24th May [1856]. At the midhour of night, from the wife and the mother, lie dragged the husband and two sons, and imbrued his hands in their blood. These wore the doctrines that he went there to teach. He did not go there to be taught; but he went there as a teacher. These were his teachings. Imagine the cries and lamentations on the one hand, and the shrieks of the dying and mutilated on the other. I think sometimes that I hear shrieks, so loud, so wild, so clear, that even listening angels stoop from heaven to hear. This is the man for whom an apology is offered. I did the Senator the justice to say that he disclaimed all sympathy with Brown, and yet I read what, in fact, was an apology. What furthermore did the Senator say? We have shown, and the fact is not controverted, that he murdered five human beings on May 24th. They have shown, in trying to answer this, that his son did not receive this ill-treatment from Captain Pate until the last day of May. We have shown that his other son was not killed until August 30th. Let us remember these facts, and come to the old man as being a thief and a murderer. I want all these modem fanatics, who have adopted John Brown and his gallows as their Christ and their cross, to see who their Christ is. . . .

There does seem to be a providential interposition in this affair. Brown murdered Doyle and his two sons. Doyle left a widow and four helpless children. Justice seemed to be a little tardy; but it kept constantly in pursuit of its victim, and but a short time since the man who murdered Doyle and his two sons, fell a victim, with his two sons, at Harper's Ferry. I do not say that this was a stroke of Providence; but it was a singular coincidence. He whose hands were red, crimson with the blood of a father and two sons, fell a victim at Harper's Ferry with his own two sons. It seems that Divine Providence intended it as a rebuke, an illustration that justice will not only overtake its victim, but will mete out justice in a similar manner.

I think, Mr. President, that I have shown the tendency of the policy to which I have called attention. Whether it has been designed at all times by those who preached it or not, I shall not undertake to say, but I will say that the effect of that kind of teaching has been the result which is so evident; and I want to say now in no spirit of boasting, to my friends East and West, North and South, that the time has arrived when encroachments on the institutions of the South should cease; the time has arrived when we have well nigh done making appeals to you on the subject; but all we ask of you is, that, as brothers of the same great Confederacy, you will understand and carry out the Constitution as it is, and let us cease this bickering. Let us cease this agitation, and stand upon the Constitution as the common altar, and maintain all its guarantees, and swear by our fathers and the God who made us that the Constitution and its guarantees shall be preserved; and, in doing so, we shall preserve the Union; and, in preserving the Union, we shall have peace and harmony, and the unexampled prosperity which has visited our country will continue to go on.

Source: Congressional Globe, 36th Congress, 1st Session, December 12, 1859, 105–107.

James A. Seddon, "To R. M. T. Hunter," December 26, 1859

James A. Seddon (1815–1880) responded to Brown's raid and death by suggesting immediate disunion. His letter to Robert Mercer Taliaferro Hunter, a Democratic senator from Virginia, also attacks Governor Wise's leadership and character at length. Seddon was a lawyer and Democratic politician from Virginia who served two terms in the U.S. Congress. Both Seddon and Hunter went on to serve in the cabinet of Confederate States president Jefferson Davis.

St. James Parish, Louisiana, December 26th, 1859.

My Dear Sir: I have only now on my return from a distant plantation received your very interesting letter of the—Inst. Despite my great disinclination to obtrude upon your valuable time, I had just determined to write you for counsel and information on the emergencies of the time and am both relieved and flattered by your overture to confidence. I am spending the winter here partly from considerations of health but mainly from the claims of imperative private business. I left Virginia with great reluctance just as the Harper's Ferry Raid had occurred for I knew it to be a crisis of great moment to our State and Country and of deep interest to your political fortunes in which as a sincere friend I always cherished a lively concern. It was too early however to judge the effects of the events occurring or of the feelings they would excite, and since, I have been so engaged in affairs and so removed from sources of correct information, rarely ever seeing a paper from Va or the North, that I feel real diffidence in forming or expressing opinions on the aspect of public affairs. I must venture however to say that in my humble opinion the train of events and the course of public conduct and opinion upon them, especially in Va have been injudiciously and alarmingly mismanaged and misdirected, and I hold the unsound judgment, insatiate vanity and selfish policy of our fussy Governor mainly responsible for them. The Harper's Ferry affair ought to have been treated and represented either in its best light as the mad folly of a few deluded cranks branded fanatics, or, more truly, as the vulgar crime and outrage of a squad of reckless desperate Ruffians, ripe for any scheme of repaine and murder, and they should have been accordingly tried and executed as execrable criminals in the simplest and most summary manner. There should not have been the chance offered of elevating them to *political* offenders or making them representatives and champions of Northern Sentiment. Indeed, our Honorable Governor, seduced by the passion of oratorical display, commenced by a picturesque description of them as heroes and martyrs, and, by insisting on holding them as the chiefs of an organized conspiracy at the North, has provoked and in a measure invoked the sympathy and approbation of large masses and of established organs of public opinion at the North (who might otherwise have been frowned and rebuked through a correct estimate of public opinion as to the base criminality of the fanatics and their deeds into shame and silence) to them as veritable heroes and martyrs, exponents and champions of the North immolated for their love of liberty and aid to the oppressed to the Molach for Southern Slavery.

In Va and throughout the South with corresponding policy, all possible representations have been made and agencies adopted to make these infamous felons grand political criminals—to hold the whole North or at least the whole Republican party identified with them and to spread the greatest excitement and indignation against that whole section and its people. In short, for I can't dwell, with his favorite policy of swaggering and bullying, Wise has *exploited* this whole affair to his own selfish aggrandizement, to aid his vain hopes for the Presidency and to strengthen the fragment of a Southern party he heads. And as the result, has conjured a Devil neither he nor perhaps any other can lay, and, arraying the roused pride and animosities of both sections against each other, has brought on a *real crisis* of imminent peril to both. Of course, I do not mean that the Harper's Ferry outrage was not a fact and indication of deep significance, and that it ought to have awakened earnest reflection and timely preparation for even the worst at the South, but it ought to have been viewed and met calmly and firmly, and made a means of added strength to us both North and South, not a cause of irritation and prejudice in the one and of excitement and depression in the other. The point I fear is too that the feelings of the South is too much more excitement, a sudden storm of indignation soon to pass and I predict that in any real shock of sections, any practical disunion of which he is not the *stulting* hero, Governor Wise will be among the first to recoil and betray. However the mischief has been wrought. The peril is, judging from your letter and your known sobriety of judgment, even greater and more imminent than I had imagined. The question then of practical statesmanship is in the crisis, what ends are to be aimed at, what courses to be adopted? If the permanent continuation of the Union, consistently with the safety and institutions of the South be, as I hope, still practicable, then all my convictions and my feelings *turn* earnestly to that. But if the Union is only to be *temporary*, amid growing strifes and deeper discontents, then I think its speedy disruption certainly not to be avoided, if indeed it should not be schemed for and courted. I had rather the responsibility of innitiative action should not be on us and our section, that results so doubtful and beyond all human ken should come from resistance to wrong, from those courses of self defence, but the spirit not the forms of things must be regarded and *we* must not be wanting to an emergency, or a necessary *coup d'etat* from timid dread and an *overt* act.

Source: Annual Report of the American Historical Association for the Year 1916, Vol. 2: Correspondence of Robert M. T. Hunter, 1826–1876, ed. Charles Henry Ambler (Washington, DC: Government Printing Office, 1918), 280–284 (280–282).

Anonymous, "Old John Brown, a Song for Every Southern Man," ca. December 1859

Six days after Brown's execution, the *New York Evening Post* imagined a true freak for P. T. Barnum's famous museum: "a man . . . who has never heard of John Brown!" Manifestations of Brown's fame in the South included poems in newspapers, speeches by Southern congressmen, and songs. Even before the song "John Brown's Body" spread his name through Union ranks, Brown appeared in a Southern song of late 1859. The song was printed by the press of the *Religious Herald* newspaper, a Baptist publication based in Richmond, Virginia, and edited by the Reverend David Shaver. After narrating the story of the raid, the song concludes by advising white Southerners to be economically independent from the North, and slaves to remain loyal to their masters.

Now all you Southern people, just listen to my song,
It's about the Harper's Ferry affair, it is not very long.
To please you all I do my best, I sung it in other towns,
And while I am in Richmond, I'll tell you about old Brown.

Old Ossawattomie Brown! old Ossawattomie Brown!
That will never pay,
Trying to come away down South,
And run the niggers away.

Old Brown and Cook, and a dozen more, to Harper's Ferry went,
They got into the arsenal there, they did not have no right;
Old Governor Wise heard of this, he started from Richmond town,
He went to Harpers' Ferry, and there he caught old Brown.
Chorus, &c.

They took him down to Charlestown, and into prison throw'd him;
They put two chains upon his legs, Oh yes! it was to hold him,

They put two chains upon his legs and two upon his arms,
The virdict of the jury was, old Brown he should be hung.
Chorus, &c.

Cook and Coppie[56] were in prison, they thought about escaping,
They got upon the wall, but they could not save their bacon!
The guard he saw them up there, at them throw'd his pill
Old Cook tumbled over just like he had been killed.
Chorus, &c.

Now they all are dead and gone to heaven some do say,
The angels standing at the gate to drive them right away;
The devil standing down below, he calls them for to come,
It's no use now old John Brown, you can't get a chance to run.
Chorus, &c.

Now all you Southern people a little advice I give;
Patronize the South and the State in which you live;
And not unto Northern people your money never pay,
They have their agents in the South, to run your slaves away.
Chorus, &c.

Now all you Southern darkies, a word to you I'll say;
Always mind your masters, and never run away,
And don't mind these Northern agents, they tell to you a lie,
They get you at the North, and starve you 'till you die.
Chorus, &c.

Source: Old John Brown, a Song for Every Southern Man (Richmond: Religious Herald Press, 1859).

Mann Satterwhite Valentine,
"The Mock Auction," 1860

In 1860, Mann Satterwhite Valentine (1824–1892) published the first book-length poem about Brown. Like the diary entries by Susan Bradford Eppes and Amanda Virginia Edmonds, Valentine's poem depicts Brown as a bloodthirsty villain, and like the illustrated articles by David Strother, it depicts him as reptilian. The excerpt below includes conversations between Ossawatomie (Brown), Craven Heart (Gerrit Smith), and Trumpeter (Seward). Valentine was a writer, merchant, and collector from Richmond, Virginia. As well as his mock heroic poem about Brown, he wrote two romances and numerous articles for the *Richmond Examiner,* the *Richmond Dispatch*, and other newspapers. During the Civil War he served in the Virginia State Reserves. He eventually made his fortune in 1871 with the creation and production of Valentine's Meat Juice, a "health tonic" made from pure beef juice.

They stared into his swarthy face,
So destitute of every grace;
for he looked like unearthly creature,
With phiz of malignant nature,
With gloating eyes of Boa Constrictor,
And beak for nose, like to vulture,
Mouth of insatiate glutton
Bound with leathery tortoise skin,
And head of bristling porcupine,
Poised on neck of wiry serpentine;
His long and lathy frame—remnant
Of famine, unutterably scant,
Yet, quick spirited and brawny,
When contrasted with the flabby
Figment of softest flesh and nerve

You might, in Craven Heart observe;
Who with a nature so ductile,
His nerves seemed organs of his will;
He was very sheep, in the skin
Of a seditious grimalkin.
And these were chums of Trumpeter,
These some spirits, who would incur
Part of brunt—who loved disaster,
Coming on fast, and still faster.

The wild old Ossawatomie
Fairly embosomed with the Free,
Would drink his liquor with a vim,
And then draw the other two to him,
Saying—"My larks! we must be done
With this gibberish talking mum;
We should be laying out our toils,
I feel the urgent lack of spoils
This resting on one's oars so long,
Is to my mind entirely wrong;
I, sirs! am ready primed for deeds,
To suit the cogency of needs;
I have stolen no horse for days,
I am getting rusty in my ways,
With houses none to fire by me,
It seems I am purging deviltry.
Here by your proffers I've been kept
Wasting the virtues of adept,
Till, presently, I will forget
The means my appetite to whet;
For blood and rapine doth require
Dexterity as well as fire;
I must do murder, if tis you;
Haste! prepare me work, or you rue
The hour you sent, for such cattle,
To pitch into your slow battle;
I tell you, sirs, you have a Greek
In me! I want to hear you speak?"

In silent admiration, both
Gazed to see the old felon wroth;
Full well they knew he had the pluck,
And taste for any sort of muck,
On which they had proposed to skim,
While he, in it might barely swim.
Great Trumpeter addressed the wild
Villain, to be reconciled;
"I think Friend of the Thunder's Blast,
You are inclined to be too fast;
You know our traps are not yet set,
I am now arranging, to get
Reliable survey of the ground—
For really this will be found,
Important in the first degree.
Suppose you visit the country!
Judge whether open war were best,
Or you might be well impressed
With sneaking guerrilla strife—
Without such wholesale waste of life;
Then work the thing as best you can,
Doubtless you are our very man,
To lay the circuitous snares,
That'll trap those silly little hares;
We know you capable to fill
With fright the house of Iron Will.
Ossawatomie, to be brief,
You have been the most successful thief
Of all the knaves of Border War,
The coolest, most daring outlaw,
And far beyond all others, sir !
The pride and pink of—murderer:
You, were the world spread before me,
I should prefer for villainy."

Source: Mann Satterwhite Valentine, *The Mock Auction: Ossawatomie Sold, A Mock Heroic Poem*
(Richmond: J. W. Randolph, 1860), 67–71.

George Fitzhugh, "Disunion within the Union," January 1860

One of the country's leading proslavery intellectuals, George Fitzhugh (1806–1881) used Brown's raid to call for disunion and the necessary expansion of slavery. Fitzhugh warns of a "white slave trade" unless the African slave trade is renewed. He also announces that New Englanders are not welcome in the South and suggests that Brown's raid should amplify fears of slave insurrection. The article appeared in *De Bow's Review,* the South's most widely circulated periodical of the moment. Published out of New Orleans from 1846 until 1884, the magazine focused on Southern commerce and economy. It was pro-Southern, proslavery, and eventually secessionist. A native Virginian, Fitzhugh is best known for his book *Cannibals All!* (1857), which attacked capitalist exploitation and depicted slavery as a form of socialism that protected and civilized blacks.

The Harper's Ferry affair, with its extensive Northern ramifications, gives a new interest to the question of disunion. The most conservative must see, and if honest will admit, that the settlement of Northerners among us is fraught with danger. Not one in twenty of such settlers might tamper with our slaves and incite them to insurrection, but one man can fire a magazine, and no one can foresee where the match will be applied, or what will be the extent and consequences of the explosion. Our wives and our daughters will see in every new Yankee face an abolition missionary. We, the men of the South, may feel for their fears, and go about to remove the cause that excites them, without being amenable to the charge of cowardice or of over cautiousness.

The border States are the exposed frontier. Into them the underground railroad insinuates its emissaries, who steal a part of our slaves and poison the minds of the balance. Under the simple guise of the innocent farmer, Mr. Thayer[57] may set the colonies among us as big with danger as the Greco-Trojan horse. Half the lands in these border States are without labor to cultivate them.

At the present prices of negroes these lands must remain uncultivated, unless white labor, which is much cheaper, is introduced into those border States. If introduced, it will gradually expel and drive to the South the negroes and their masters by its superior economy, or emancipate the negroes by the ballot-box or servile insurrection. We do not mean to say that Mr. Thayer is an *incendiary* abolitionist; far from it. He is a man of excellent sense, cool, judicious, deliberate, and calculating. He is no silly, speculative socialist, no empty rhetorician, like Sumner and Seward, nor blood-thirsty beast, like Brown and Leeman.[58] He simply proposes to introduce *white slave labor* instead of black slave labor. He, *we know,* fully comprehends the relations and the philosophy of capital and labor. He knows that if capital emigrates ahead of labor, or if capital and labor emigrate together, the owners of the capital become the masters of the laborers, in all save the obligation to provide for them, when unfit for work. Poor Sumner is so weak as not to see that the Emigrant Aid Society of Massachusetts[59] is merely a white slave trade company, and hence, unconsciously lauds the white slave trade with the same breath that he abuses the negro slave trade. Unless we can arrest this white slave trade of Mr. Thayer, the border States will become the property of New-England.

To effect this, two measures are necessary. The one, State legislation that shall require all New England emigrants to give security for their good behavior. The other, the renewal of the African slave-trade, to fill up that vacuum in our population which will be filled up by abolitionists if not by negroes. The Constitution of the United States stands in the way of neither measure. It is wonderfully comprehensive and elastic, and gives an adaptability and plasticity to our institutions which constitute their chief merit.

New Englanders coming to the South, according to the most rigid construction of the common law, are *quoad nos,* persons of *ill favor,* suspicious persons (far more so than idle eavesdroppers), who may and should be required to give security for their good behavior.

The law of Congress prohibiting the slave-trade is palpably unconstitutional. Congress has no other powers than those conferred by the Constitution, and no two men agree as to the clause conferring the power to abolish the slave trade. The most plausible suggestion is, that the power is included in the right to regulate commerce. But this suggestion is rendered flagrantly absurd when we discover that to sustain it, white emigrants must be treated and considered as mere articles of commerce. The Constitution suspends the power to prohibit the "importation" or *immigration* of persons until 1808. Congress possesses the same power to declare and punish white immigration as piracy that it has to so punish the African slave-trade. These are but two, out of hundreds of measures, by which the South may attain all the ends sought for by disunion, while remaining in the Union.

Each State for itself may pass laws entirely prohibiting all trade or intercourse between its citizens and the citizens of one or more of the Northern States. Each Southern State may enact that all "Yankee notions," goods, wares, and merchandise, shall be forfeited when brought South, as fully and completely as negro slaves are when carried North. White Yankees are more dangerous to our peace than English or Northern free negroes; and South Carolina has established the right to prohibit the introduction of the latter. Under the law of nations, we may, and should, exclude people whose general character is that of hostility to our institutions. It is an inalienable right, for it is the right of self defense and self preservation. . . .

Disunion would have different effects on different Southern States. Some would be immediately exposed to war and invasion, and would, therefore, be more cautious and dilatory in invoking disunion. Besides, although all political parties at the South are true on the slavery question, yet they differ as to measures, and the ascendancy of different parties in the several States would prevent agreement on this vital subject. This diversity of opinion in the South, this want of union as to the means of redress, while there is thorough union of sentiment and feeling on the slavery subject, and on the wrongs inflicted upon us by the abolitionists, is fortunate for us—for union of the South would beget union of the North, estrange our thousands of warm and true friends in that region, and beget a purely sectional dispute, with the larger section arrayed against us and our institutions. "Let us divide and conquer." We can only do so, by urging each Southern State to adopt measures of defence and retaliation for itself, and not to involve in one common denunciation and exclusion, our friends and enemies at the North. Let us be bold and fearless, but, at the same time, just, cautious, and prudent. If we will court the alliance of the conservatives of the North, while we denounce and punish her destructives, abolitionism will find itself in a very small minority. A contrary course will alienate our Northern friends, and beget a false sectional issue, in which we shall be the weaker party, and a party divided among ourselves.

We say a *false* issue, because this is no dispute between Northerners and

Southerners; but between conservatives and revolutionists; between Christians and infidels; between law and order men and no-government men, between the friends of private property and socialists and agrarians; between the chaste and the libidinous; between marriage and free lovers; between those who believe in the past, in history, in human experience, in the Bible, in human nature, and those who, foolishly, rashly, and profanely, attempt to "expel human nature," to bring about a millennium, and inaugurate a future wholly unlike anything that has preceded it. The great Christian and conservative party throughout the world is now with us. If we scorn and repudiate their alliance, if we arrogantly set up for ourselves, we thereby admit and assert that our cause and our institutions are at war with the common, moral, and religious notions of mankind. Let us rather prove to the virtuous, the religious, and conservative, that our cause is their cause, our institutions those which God has ordained, and human experience ratified and confirmed; and that to war against us, is to incite the socialists to war against everything sacred, valuable, or venerable in free society. Let us show them that every abolitionist of distinction is an agrarian, infidel, no-government man, a free-love man— more dangerous at home than to us. . . .

These outbreaks of society, in which the "meanest get uppermost," will occasionally occur. But in the long run virtue governs vice, intelligence governs ignorance, religion controls infidelity. Let us of the South be patient, and wait for that process of subsidence and stratification in Northern society, which will be sure to put our friends uppermost; for it is as natural for *them* to ride, as it is for the *masses* to be ridden. He who denies that God made the multitude to be directed, governed, and controlled by the few, and that this common multitude is happier, more virtuous, and prosperous, when governed, than when governing, quarrels with the course of nature, and disputes the wisdom and beneficence of Deity. Universal suffrage may put society wrong-side up, but nature is all-powerful, and soon brings down the lower layer, or stratum, to its true place.

Source: De Bow's Review, January 1860, 1–7 (1–5).

C. G. Memminger, "The South Carolina Mission to Virginia," January 19, 1860

A leader of the conservative South Carolinians, Christopher Gustavus Memminger (1803–1888) opposed secession in 1859 and early 1860. But after Brown's raid, the legislature of South Carolina, in which Memminger had served since 1836, proposed a convention of delegates from slave states to devise a cooperative Southern defense policy, and South Carolina governor William Gist made Memminger a special commissioner to Virginia. Memminger had the task of urging Virginia to cooperate with South Carolina and all the slave states in defense of the South and its system of slavery, rather than taking separate state action. Memminger arrived in Richmond and gave a speech to the assembly on January 19, 1860. It observes that Northerners mourn and celebrate Brown while the South must unite in order to prevent more raids and mass slave insurrections. Ten thousand copies of the speech were printed and circulated throughout Virginia. By December 1860 the moderate and Unionist Memminger had become a secessionist. He chaired the committee that drafted the constitution of the Confederate States of America and became the Confederacy's first secretary of the treasury.

To estimate aright the character of the outrage at Harper's Ferry, we must realize the intentions of those who planned it. They expected the slaves to rise in mass as soon as the banner of abolitionism should be unfurled. Knowing nothing of the kindly feeling which exists throughout the South between the master and his slaves, they judged of that feeling by their own hatred, and expected that the tocsin which they sounded would at once arouse to rebellion every slave who heard it. Accordingly they prepared such arms as an infuriated and untrained peasantry could most readily use.

They also expected aid from another element of revolution. They did not believe in the loyalty to the government of Virginia of that part of her population which owned no slaves. They seized upon the armory, and they expected help from its operatives, and from the farming population; and to gain time for combining all these elements of mischief, as they conceived them to be, they seized upon a pass in the mountains, well adapted to their purpose. For months had they worked with fiendish and unwearied diligence, and it is hazarding little to conjecture, that the banditti who had been trained in Kansas, were in readiness to obey the summons to new scenes of rapine and murder, as soon as a lodgment were effected.

Is it at all surprising that a peaceful village, where no sound of war had been heard for half a century, should be overcome for the moment, at midnight, by so unexpected an inroad? The confusion which ensued was a necessity; and it can only be ascribed to the superintendence of a kind Providence, that so few innocent lives were sacrificed. It is indeed wonderful that none of the hostages seized by these banditti should have suffered from the attacks which their friends were obliged to make, and that at so early a period the inhabitants recovered from their amazement and reduced their assailants to the five who were entrenched within the brick walls of the engine-house.

The failure to accomplish their purpose cannot lessen its atrocity; neither can their erroneous calculations as to the loyalty of the citizens to the State, or of the slaves to their masters, lessen the crime of these murderers, and they have justly paid the forfeit of their lives. But such a forfeit cannot expiate the blood of peaceful citizens, nor restore the feeling of tranquil security to the families which they have disturbed. The outraged soil of Virginia stands a witness of the wrong, and the unquiet homes which remain agitated along her borders, still call for protection; and as an affectionate mother, the State feels for her children, and is providing for that protection. The people of South Carolina cordially sympathize in all these feelings. They regard this outrage as perpetrated on themselves. The blow that has struck you, was aimed equally at them and they would gladly share in all its consequence, and, most of all, in the effort to prevent its recurrence in the future. . . .

The great question which underlies all action on this subject is, whether the existing relations between the North and the South are temporary or permanent; whether they result from accidental derangement of the body politic, or ore indications of a normal condition? In the one case, temporary expedients may restore soundness; in the other, the remedy is either hopeless, or it must be fundamental and thorough.

In these aspects the invasion at Harper's Ferry is a valuable exponent. It furnishes many indications by which we may ascertain the actual condition of things. It is a sort of nilometer, by which we can measure the heights of the flood which is bursting over the land. By the providence of that God who preserved your people from the knife of the assassin, you were enabled, not only to defeat and capture your enemies, but to get possession of arms and documents which expose the design and plan of the assailants. You find that months must have elapsed in maturing their plans; that arms were manufactured, the design of which could not be mistaken; that large sums of money must have been collected. It is certain, therefore, that many persons must have known that such a blow was intended; and yet, who spoke? Who gave a single, friendly warning to Virginia? One voice, indeed, distinctly uttered to the federal government a warning,[60] but that voice was disregarded; and the catastrophe burst upon us as a thunder-storm in mid-winter.

The loyal sons of Virginia rushed to her defence, and the military arm bows to the majesty of law, and delivers the murderer to a just and impartial trial. A new incident in the history of crime is developed. Learned counsel from a distant city, once styled the Athens of America, proceed to a distant village to offer their services to defend the midnight assassin. Political offences have sometimes found voluntary defenders, but the moral sense must be absolutely perverted, when it is deemed a virtue to screen the murderer from punishment. The excitement grows, and your courts of justice cannot proceed as in ordinary cases of crime. You are compelled to surround them with military power; and when the law has pronounced its sentence, you are compelled to guard the prison-house and the scaffold, to keep at bay the confederates and sympathizers with crimes heretofore execrated by every civilized people upon earth.

The indications of this implacable condition of Northern opinion do not stop here. The sentence of death upon the criminals and their execution are bewailed with sounds of lamentation, such as would now follow a Ridley or a Latimer to the stake,[61] and public demonstrations of sympathy exhibit themselves throughout the entire North. To the great discredit of our institutions and of our country, motions are entertained in bodies exercising political power to honor the memory of a wretched fanatic and assassin; and, in one body, the motion failed only for want of three votes. These are indications which you cannot disregard. They tell of a state of public opinion which cannot fail to produce further evil. Every village bell which tolled its solemn note at the execution of Brown, proclaims to the South the approbation of that village of insurrection and servile war; and the ease with which some of the confederates escaped to Canada, proves that much of the population around are willing to abet the actors in these incendiary attempts. . . .

Here, then, we have before us the North and the South, standing face to face—not yet as avowed and open enemies; but with deep-seated feelings of enmity rankling in their bosoms, which at any moment may burst forth into action. Is it wise, when we see flame shining through every crevice, and ready to leap from every open window—is it wise to close the window, and fill up every gap, and shut our eyes to the fact that the fire is raging within the building? It is not wise. We must examine the premises, and determine whether the building can be saved, or whether it must be abandoned.

We have now reached this point in our inquiry. The Harper's Ferry invasion, with the developments following it, and the now existing condition of the country, prove that the North and the South are standing in hostile array—the one with an absolute majority, sustaining those who meditate our destruction, and refusing to us any concession or guaranty—and the other baffled in every attempt at compromise or security. . . .

We are brought, then, to this conclusion: The South stands in the Union without any protection from the Constitution, subject to the government of a sectional party who regard our institutions as sinful, and whose leaders already declare that the destruction of these institutions is only a question of time. The power of this party must increase from the continued operation of the causes which have given them their present strength. Thus, with the forms of the Constitution around us, we are deprived of all the benefits to secure which the Union was formed.

The preamble of that Constitution sets forth these objects in the following terms: "We, the people of the United States, in order to from a more perfect union, establish justice, ensure domestic tranquility, provide for the common defense, promote the general welfare, and secure the blessings of liberty to ourselves and our posterity, do ordain and establish this Constitution for the United States of America." Where is that more perfect union? The answer is given by the shout which hailed as a hero the murderer and the assassin. As the ancient Greeks had no name for the parricide, and imposed no punishment for an unknown crime—so the Fathers of the Constitution provided no means for repressing the unimagined invasion of a sister State. Nay, they actually disarmed each State, giving up to the federal government the army and navy, and making no provision for protection of a State from invasion by a neighboring State. This gave rise to the anomaly exhibited at Harper's Ferry, in the laws of the federal government affording no aid to the government of Virginia to protect her from invasion. This more perfect union is more strikingly illustrated in the spectacle now exhibited in the array of one half the Union against the other, urged on (as one of the speakers at a meeting in Boston most truthfully declares) by a "religion of hate," which is ready "to break down all laws, human and divine."[62]

But the Constitution was also made to establish justice. The establishment of justice is evinced in the protection and security of life and property. The blood that cries from the ground at Harper's Ferry is witness to the security of life; and, doubtless, the spotted regions on Brown's map would, in due time, have added their solemn voices, but for the utter failure in Virginia. And if these voices do not convince, let the ease with which some of the confederates escaped through *sister* States into Canada add its testimony.[63] Nay, more. Suppose jurisdiction of the crime had been surrendered to the federal government, and judgment had been delayed until the 4th of March next,[64] how think you that the culprits would have fared with a Black Republican President intrusted with pardoning power? . . . From the federal government, as it stands, we can expect nothing. From the Northern States we have been repelled with denunciation. Our only resource, then, is in ourselves; and among ourselves union is strength.

Source: De Bow's Review, December 1860, 751–771 (752–753, 755–756, 766, 768).

Alexander Boteler, "Speech on the Organization of the House," January 25, 1860

Alexander Boteler (1815–1892) was present in Harpers Ferry during the raid. He was at home in Shepherdstown, 10 miles west, and heard news of Brown's raid on October 17. He went straight to the Ferry, arriving around noon. Years later he claimed to have conversed with Brown in the engine house immediately after the wounded man's capture. His speech of January 25, 1860, to the House of Representatives asserts the authority of an eyewitness in order to better argue its points: that Virginia must arm against antislavery agitators and that abolitionists must take responsibility for Brown's actions. Boteler served in the House as an oppositionist and Virginia representative between 1859 and 1861 and in the Confederate States House of Representatives as a Democrat between 1862 and 1864. After the war, in an article for *Century* magazine published in July 1883, he called the raid a "prelude" to the whole conflict. The Civil War "effectually completed what old John Brown so fatally began," Boteler concluded.

A storm has arisen upon us; we hear the spirit of the tempest shrieking in the shroud; clouds of danger, difficulty, and doubt are dimming the heaven of our hopes, and threatening to burst in desolation over our heads! And not only that; but, sir, we see yonder "a band of mutineers" determined to take possession of the vessel; men associated together to dispossess us of our rights, and to deprive us of our property, who would thrust us down the hold, and batten the hatches over our heads. And yet, in the midst of all these imminent, deadly dangers which are threatening the destruction of the ship, we have been engaged here for weeks past in a disgraceful squabble upon theoretical points of political navigation!

Now, Mr. Clerk, I ask, is it right, is it reasonable, can we answer to our constituents, and to the country, if we continue to allow these paltry, miserable differences to interfere with our duty, and to prevent cordial, united action among the conservatives of the House against those whom we recognize, and who we are bound to recognize as our common enemy?

Sir, I have no practical suggestion to offer; there are older heads than mine here to do that; but I do protest against the continuance of this most unnecessary discussion. For myself, the House will do me the justice to say that I have possessed my seat in silence upon this floor during the seven weary weeks we have been in session, whilst this exciting discussion has been going on, and whilst the infamous Abolition outrage upon the district I have the honor to represent has been the fruitful inspiration of almost every gentleman who has risen to address the House.

Now, sir, I was present at that horrible Harper's Ferry raid; I was a witness to that abominable outrage; I saw the blood of my friends shed in the streets of Harper's Ferry; and if there is a man here who has a right to discuss that subject, it is myself; and yet I have forborne. I have remained silent for various reasons, not the least of which is, that the distinguished Senator[65] before me is engaged in the investigation of the facts connected with the whole affair, and will present them fully and fairly, at the proper time, before the country, to leave it judge of them, after which I shall avail myself of a suitable opportunity to mention some circumstances to the House concerning that foray which I wish the country to know, and which justice to my constituents requires that it shall know from me.

There is yet another reason which, I must confess, has also influenced me in this matter. I know (and I have been painfully conscious of it whenever my mind has reverted to that dark day) that when the heart feels most, the tongue refuses to perform its wonted task.

And, sir, when I have heard gentlemen on the other side of the floor stand up and derisively refer to that infamous outrage, I have been hardly able to retain my seat and refrain from the expression of my indignation in terms which would not have sounded parliamentary. My mind, sir, has again and again, during this discussion, gone back to that gloomy October evening, when I stood by the side of a friend,[66] and laid my hand upon his brow where the death-damp was gathering, while the blood was gushing from his noble heart, and I have been often disposed to say, in apology for my forbearance:

> "Oh! pardon me, thou bleeding piece of earth,
> That I am meek and gentle with these butchers!"[67]

For I tell you, sir, that in my opinion, the leaders of the Abolition party, who are seeking to control the organization of this House, and to obtain possession of the Government, are as much the murderers of my friends at Harper's Ferry as were old John Brown and his deluded followers; and I think that the committee engaged in the investigation in my State, and the investigation on the part of the Senate, will prove that the agitation of the slavery question by the great leaders of the Republican party has been the direct cause of the Harper's Ferry invasion.

I tell you further, sir, the Commonwealth of Virginia has come to the determination that this shall be the end of it; that this slavery agitation shall cease, so far as she is concerned; that her territory shall be protected from a repetition of that bloody raid. She has taken some indemnity for the past and means to have security for the future. And, sir, to make her determination good, she has buckled on her armor, and her borders are now bristling with bayonets, for she feels compelled to take the guardianship of her rights and her honor into her own hands. Heretofore she has trusted to the tie of consanguinity; heretofore she has relied upon the linked shields of all the States for her protection; but, sir, at a moment when she dreamed not of it, she has been smitten upon the cheek. Our honored old mother has been struck a blow which has roused her children from their false security and rallied them to her rescue. We now discover that we must depend upon our own right arm to protect our state from further outrage, so long as there remains a "Republican" organization in Congress and the country. And, men of the North, why will you persist in maintaining that organization? What good do you expect to effect by it? You formed it, so you have said, for the sole purpose of making Kansas a free State. You have Kansas, and when she comes into this Union, she will come in "free." If there be any other purpose that you expect to accomplish by it, it must be to transfer your "irrepressible conflict" from the Territories to the States. . . .

There was not a man amongst the Harper's Ferry insurgents, except John Brown, who was not born since 1830,[68] and who did not grow up under the influence of abolition preaching. This, sir, is a significant fact, which I commend to the thinking portion of my countrymen. There was not one of them who had not breathed the atmosphere of abolition, and who had not his mind poisoned against the South by such teachings. You do not care for the negro. You admit the fact. It is a most miserable hobby upon which you have ridden into power. Therefore, in the name of our common country, I demand that you disband your anti-slavery party and take down your piratical flag!

But a word now to Massachusetts: When, sir, I have heard the name of a gentleman called here, day after day, first on the roll—a great, historic name (Adams)—I have been reminded of the "Old Bay State" in her prouder day in the heroic age of the Republic, and I have also been reminded of a historical incident connected with the county in which I live—that county selected by John Brown for his bloody raid—and feel that I have a right to make an especial appeal to the Massachusetts delegation here, if they are not deaf to the voice of consanguinity, and if they are, I appeal from them to their people on this question; I demand of *them* to come up to the rescue of the country now as they did in the good old times of their revolutionary fathers.

Sir, the district which I represent and the county where I live—that county made famous by the raid of Brown—was the first, the very first in all the South, to send succor to Massachusetts in the time of her direst necessity![69] In one of the most beautiful spots in that beautiful country, within rifle shot of my residence, at the base of a hill where a glorious spring leaps out into sunlight from beneath the gnarled roots of a thunder-riven oak, there assembled on the 10th of July, 1775, the very first band of southern men who marched to the aid of Massachusetts. . . . Well, Mr. Clerk, *the visit has been returned!* John Brown selected that very county, whose citizens went so promptly to the aid of the North when the North needed aid, as the most appropriate place in all the South to carry out the doctrines of the "irrepressible conflict"; and as was mentioned in the Senate yesterday, the rock where Leeman fell at Harper's Ferry,[70] was the very rock over which Morgan and his men marched a few hours after Stephenson's command had crossed the river some ten miles further up at Shepherdstown.[71]

Sir, may this historical reminiscence rekindle the embers of patriotism in our hearts! Why should this nation of ours be rent in pieces by this irrepressible conflict? But is it irrepressible? Ah, sir, if it be, the battle will not be fought out upon this floor. For when the dark day comes, as come it may, when this question, that now divides and agitates the hearts of the people, shall be thrust from the forum of debate, to be decided by the bloody arbitrament of the sword, it will be the saddest day for us and all mankind that the sun of Heaven has ever shone upon.

Source: Speech by Hon. Alexander R. Boteler, of Virginia, on the Organization of the House (Washington, DC: William H. Moore, 1860), 4–6, 10–11.

John Tyler, Jr., "The Secession of the South," April 1860

Writing for the proslavery journal *De Bow's Review* under the pen name "Python," John Tyler, Jr. (1819–1896) of Virginia sets Brown's raid in the context of the Nat Turner rebellion of 1831 and the Haitian revolution of 1791. A regular writer for the *Review*, Tyler was the son of former president John Tyler and worked as his father's private secretary during his presidency, from 1841 to 1845. Tyler published more articles in the *Review* about the abolitionist threat during 1860. Then in January 1861 the editor, James D. B. De Bow, advocated the secession of Southern states from the union, telling his readers that white Southerners were the descendants of Revolutionary War heroes who appreciated the "inestimable value of the liberty which it brought." Tyler went on to be a Confederate Army officer and an assistant secretary of war.

There yet remains a graver charge against the North. *They have incited domestic insurrections at the South, and have endeavored to bring on the inhabitants of the frontier States of the South, if not the merciless Indian savages, a far more merciless race when roused by their passions—the predatory, sanguinary, and lustful African negroes, whose known rule of warfare is not only an "undistinguished destruction of all ages, sexes and conditions," but one of beastly appetites, blood-drinking and cannibal horrors.*[72] Neither the invasion of the Low Countries by the Spanish General Alva,[73] nor the French Revolution of 1789–'90, nor the conquest of Algeria,[74] nor the late rebellion in India, either in its progress or suppression,[75] nor the slaughterings of Cortez and Pizarro in Mexico and Peru,[76] terrible as they are admitted to have been, were attended with monstrosities approachable to those perpetrated by the negroes of San Domingo, when, under the encouragement of the frenzied humanitarians of France, they rose against the white population. It was as if the fiends of hell, drunk with demoniac instincts and impulsions, were let loose on earth. *"An undistin-*

guished destruction of all ages, sexes and conditions," was the least offence in
scenes of dreadful outrage the pen may not indite, nor tongue utter. And it is
to such a harvest of blood and pollution the negroes of the South have been,
time and again, incited by the North. Thirty years ago, in the very beginning of
the abolition movements of the North, by means of their vile emissaries at the
South, and by using the United States Mail for the dissemination of libelous
and seditious tracts among the slaves and free negroes, they stirred up several
limited negro insurrections, among the rest that of Southampton in Virginia.[77]
Having resided in that county, and being familiar with the localities visited,
and the scenes enacted by the negroes during the single night their effort
lasted, I can speak plainly to the subject. A band of fifteen or twenty runaway
slaves, starting twenty miles from the county seat, and aiming to take possession of that point before the morning, pursued the main road in a direct line,
but turning into the right and left upon the farmhouses, murdering their
sleeping inmates, seizing the arms found, and impressing the slaves and horses
at each establishment so far as they could. They reached within two miles of
the county seat before the night was over, and, by the means indicated, had
increased their numbers to about one hundred mounted men. By noon of the
following day, they were attacked and routed by a company of volunteer dra-
goons, and soon afterwards were publicly tried and executed. The places of
their visitation along the route pursued, were marked with San Domingo
scenes—*an undistinguished destruction of all ages, sexes, and conditions.* In-
fants, even, had been torn from their cradles by the heels, and their brains
dashed out mercilessly against the walls. Since then, the Southern States have
been ceaselessly agitated with alarms and attempted insurrections similarly
generated. And yet, not satisfied with these continued disturbances of the
public tranquility of the South, recognized by the laws of every nation, as well
as by the law of nations as just cause of war, citizens of the North in close correspondence with many of the most prominent and influential political leaders of that section, after exhausting several years in perfecting their conspiracy,
through collections of money and purchases of arms, finally, in September,
1859,[78] unfurled the black banner of abolition, and under the lead of a notorious horse-thief and murderer that the Administration had not seen fit to bring
to punishment in Kansas, boldly invaded the States of Maryland and Virginia,
seized upon the United States Arsenal at Harper's Ferry, and invited the slaves
throughout the South to rebellion and a feast of blood and rapine, necessarily

to terminate, if successful, in the overthrow of the governments of the Southern States, and the extermination of their white proprietors. Nor is this all.
Preparatory to this act of incarnadine assassination, and of double treason
against the Government of the United States, and that of each State invaded,
they endeavored to induce the non-slaveholders of the South to receive and
affiliate with them and the negro slaves in the line of their operations, by circu-
lating among the non-slaveholders, thousands upon thousands of a copy of a
book called the *"Impending Crisis,"*[79] filled with all manner of inflammatory
denunciations of slaveholders, thus committing, at one and the same time, a
double attempt at *"inciting domestic insurrection."* What matters it that John
Brown and his coadjutors were besieged at Harper's Ferry, taken prisoners,
tried under the laws of Virginia, by a court of Virginia, and condemned and
executed for murder and treason? Is the offence of the North expiated, or are
the South more secure in their institutions, or freer from apprehension of farther disturbance from the North? The sixty-eight political leaders of the North
who signed a recommendation of the *"Impending Crisis,"*[80] have not flinched
from their position, but on the contrary, in conjunction with nearly the whole
Northern representation in Congress, selected from among *their own number*
a candidate for the Speakership of the House,[81] an office in the line of the succession to the presidency; and, in addition, the remains of John Brown have
been canonized throughout the North. Such is the significant answer for the
South to ponder. Speaking to this point, well does General Cushing,[82] in his
letter of the 9th of January, say to the people of Maine: "The Southern States
cannot meekly lie down to be trodden upon by the Northern. They cannot
patiently sit still under the Constitution, perverted by the North into a mere
engine for the destruction of the South. They cannot accept at the hands of
the North a civil and servile insurrection, the devastation of their country, the
slaughter of their wives and children, the unspeakable horrors of another San
Domingo. If they should thus meekly lie prostrate; if they should thus patiently sit still; if they should thus passively submit to whatever assassin abolition may please to do, they would be unworthy of the name of Americans;
they would be fit objects of the contempt of the world; they would merit their
doom. The question for the South is not one of profit and loss, but of LIFE
AND DEATH!"

Thus stands the case against the North under the Declaration of Independence; and for the same and greater reasons than those that urged the Ameri-

can colonies to secede from the parent government of Great Britain, dissolving the ties binding them to the British People, the Southern States are now called upon to secede from their Union with the North, dissolving the ties binding them to the Northern people: And as the colonies were justified before the world for their action in the establishment of a new and independent government, so the Southern States must and will be justified in the establishment of a new and independent confederation. . . .

How long may it be before a Southern State may find it necessary, the government at Washington failing in its duty under the control of the North, to pursue some other John Brown and his robber associates into a Northern State, or the Canadas? Without this, how long may it be before the South shall be driven to the sword, *ex-necessitate,* to find themselves thus proclaimed traitors by the North holding the government? People of the South! are you dead, or alive, that those stratagems are practiced upon you in open day by your *hirelings,* as was of yore practiced upon the Roman people under the sway of the Caesars by their *freedmen?* Every thing counsels you, in the language of General Cushing, that "The hour of your extremity is upon you, and that the issue thereof is one of LIFE OR DEATH."

Source: Python, "The Secession of the South," *De Bow's Review,* April 1860, 367–392 (378–381, 387).

National Democratic Executive Committee, *The Great Issue to Be Decided in November Next,* September 1860

The Democratic Party ruptured at its 1860 convention. The Northern wing of the party nominated Stephen A. Douglas of Illinois for president (with Herschel Vespasian Johnson of Georgia for vice president), while Southern Democrats supported John C. Breckinridge of Kentucky for president (with Joseph Lane of Oregon for vice president). Breckinridge and Lane ran on a proslavery platform. Between July and November 1860, the Breckinridge and Lane campaign issued at least nineteen pamphlets advancing its platform, including one in late September that addressed the connections between John Brown and the Republican Party. The rest of the pamphlet attacks Lincoln, Seward, Giddings, Chase, Andrew, Sumner, and Greeley.

We ask in all soberness and earnestly, is not the Republican party guilty of all the blood that has been shed in Kansas, at Harper's Ferry, and is now being shed in the insurrections in Texas?[83] They have told the negroes from the forums of the Senate and the House of Representatives, that they were entitled to their freedom; that it was a gross usurpation and tyranny to hold them in bondage; that they were the equals of the white man; that the slaveholders were a band of thieves, robbers, and murderers; that there was an irrepressible conflict between the free North and the slave-holding South that John Brown was right in murdering in cold blood the defenceless and unarmed inhabitants of Harper's Ferry. What but insurrection and bloodshed could spring from such counsels? Is it any wonder that, seduced by these words, and believing the men sincere who uttered them, John Brown and his deluded followers sought to decide that "irrepressible conflict" in favor of their own section?

The Republican party cannot wash its hands of this bloody transaction. Look at their defence of John Brown. Look at their deifying a man, who, without provocation, at the dead of night, stole down upon the peaceful and unsuspecting inhabitants of a town, who had done him no wrong, inciting their slaves to cut their throats, and he and his followers imbruing their hands in their blood. And this horrible, infamous act received the approval and the applause of the leaders of the Republican party. Men of the North! are you prepared to indorse such conduct? If yea, vote for the men who instigated and defended it; vote for their candidate, Abraham Lincoln.

Source: The Great Issue to Be Decided in November Next! Breckinridge and Lane Campaign Documents, No. 19 (Washington, DC: National Democratic Executive Committee, 1860), 15.

Howell Cobb, "Letter to the People of Georgia," December 6, 1860

Writing after Lincoln's election to the presidency, Howell Cobb (1815–1868) explains the impossibility of remaining in a Union with "Black Republicans," including Brown supporters such as John Andrew of Massachusetts. The open letter calls for Georgia to secede immediately after Lincoln takes office on March 4, 1861. Cobb wrote the letter in Washington, Georgia. He was a Southern Democrat, a former governor of Georgia, and secretary of the treasury under president James Buchanan. After chairing the Montgomery Convention, which formed the Confederate States government, Cobb went on to be the Speaker of the Provisional Confederate Congress and a Confederate general.

What are the facts to justify the hope that the Black Republicans will recede from their well defined position of hostility to the South and her institutions? Are they to be found in the two millions of voters who have deliberately declared in their favor of those doctrines by their support of Lincoln? Is the hope based upon the fact that an overwhelming majority of the people of every Northern state save one cast their vote for the Black Republican candidate . . . or in such manifestations of Northern sentiment as led to the nomination by this party of John A. Andrew for Governor of Massachusetts after he had declared his sanction and approval of the John Brown raid; or in the election of that same Andrew to that office by seventy thousand majority after he had declared in his anxiety to abolish slavery that he "could not wait for Providence"[84] to wipe it out, but must himself undertake that duty with the aid of his Black Republican brethren; or shall we be pointed to the defiant tones of triumph which fill the whole Northern air with the wild shouts of joy and thanksgiving that the days of slavery are numbered and the hour draws nigh when the "higher law" and "hatred of slavery and slave holders" shall be substituted for "the Constitution" and the spirit of former brotherhood; or to the cold irony which speaks through their press of the *"inconvenience"* of negro insurrections, arson, and murder which may result in the South from the election of Lincoln. In none of these, not of the other facts to which I have before referred, can anything be found to justify the hope suggested by those confiding friends who in this hour of gloom and despondency are disposed to hope against hope.

Source: "Letter of Hon. Howell Cobb to the People of Georgia," *Milledgeville Daily Federal Union,* December 16, 1860.

William Gilmore Simms, "To a Northern Friend," December 12, 1860

Writing to a "Northern friend," John Jacob Bockee, in December 1860, William Simms (1806–1870) declared that there was no hope of the Southern states remaining in the Union, for John Brown had made it impossible. In fact, the Union is no longer desirable at all, he adds, for the South must surely be dragged down by the North, which has not yet realized the advantages of combining capital and labor into a single entity: the slave. A historian, poet, and popular novelist from Charleston, Simms was proslavery and secessionist. He wrote the letter at Woodlands, his plantation in South Carolina, located between Charleston and Augusta, and then expanded and published it as a letter-editorial in the *Charleston Mercury* in January 1861.

I look in vain, my excellent friend, among all your excellent letters to me, to find one single expression of your horror at the John Brown raid in Virginia! Your indignation, I suppose, was so intense as to keep you dumb! I cannot, of course, suppose that you were indifferent! Oh! no; your expressions of love forbid that idea! So, too, I see not a word of your wrath and indignation, in any of these letters, at the burning of our towns, and the poisoning of our fountains in Texas, by creatures of the same kidney with the vulture Brown![85] And when Brown is made a martyr of in the North, and his day made a sacred record in the Northern calendar, I do not perceive that you covered your head with sackcloth and ashes, and wrote to me lamenting!

And when your people *did* rise, after a fashion, and at a very late hour—you among them—to oppose Abolitionism, you had neither the virtue, nor the wisdom, to take issue with the enemy by a manly justification of the South! You only moved *to save the Union*—in other words, *not to lose the keeping of that excellent milch cow,* whose dugs have yielded, for sixty years, so large a proportion of the milk and butter which have fattened your hungry people. You claimed nothing for the South—asserted nothing; asked nothing; had no purpose beyond the preservation of the Confederacy, *as it was;* the South being the victim still—the North the wolf.

I had no pathetic letters from you, touching any of the exactions, aggressions, usurpations, or atrocities of the North! I cannot find a single one in all my collection! and now that you do write of these things, I find that you have but one plea, one prayer, one entreaty—*to save the Union!* to keep the milch cow still within your pleasant pastures; to persuade the lamb not to use his heels, or his watch dogs; but to leave everything to the tender mercies of the wolf!

Ah! my friend, this is very terrible on the part of friendship! Is it malice? Is it mockery?

You now only write to the injured and the endangered party, entreating him to yield himself placidly to injury and danger; to submit to continued outrage and aggression! You do not write when you see *him* in danger. You only write and plead and pray, when you think that the Union, which is the instrument of *his* destruction—as it has been the agent of your bloated prosperity—is in danger. When you see that, driven to desperation by the incessant robberies, aggressions and atrocities of the North, the South is resolved at last to shake herself free from a union which is but the cloak and cowardly shelter, under cover of which her enemies aim the dagger at her breast, assail her midnight slumbers with pikes and fire, and poison the fountains where her women and children drink.

And is such a union desirable, worth preserving, profitable in morals or honorable to either party? What sort of union is it—and with what sort of brethren? It is not a union, surely, of God's joining; but a union of the Devil's joining—to use the strong language of Milton. Is it not a union with hell, and crime, and lust, and vice, and the most Satanic ministry? Surely, as a Christian man, you cannot desire that such a union as this should continue, whether you argue from your section or from mine! If you have any esteem for yourselves or for us, it is surely undesirable to preserve it, unless by such much miserable wretches as care not what the crime may be, so that they profit by it. A mercenary tradesman may be pleased to continue such a connection, but an honest, and virtuous, God-fearing man, never! . . .

There is no *prestige* in Virginia which Black Republicanism does not spit upon! Even her chivalry is at discount, in the land of the Puritans, since the raid of John Brown, Esq., the modern martyr.

Source: Charleston Mercury, January 17, 1861.

John Wilkes Booth, "Philadelphia Speech," December 1860

John Wilkes Booth (1838–1865) was an actor and the assassin of Abraham Lincoln. As an actor he was famous throughout the country but especially beloved by Southern belles, who wrote him fan notes, collected his *carte de visite* photograph, and waited for him after performances. Born in Maryland, he identified himself as a Southerner. He considered slavery a positive good, believed that a rigid social hierarchy was essential to civilization, assumed that the United States were for white men only, and despised abolitionism. In a speech aimed at Northern conservatives that he drafted in Philadelphia in late December 1860, after Lincoln's election as president, he argues that Brown's violence was at least more honest than the "hidden craft" of abolitionists and Republicans. He did not deliver the speech.

We cannot condemn the faults of our brothers in the South till we pick out the beam from our own eyes. You all feel the fire now raging in the nations heart. It is a fire lighted and faned by Northern fanaticism. A fire which naught by blood & justice can extinguish. I tell you the Abolition doctrine is the fire which if alowed to rage—will consume the house and crush us all beneath its ruins. Shall we my Brothers be destroyed on account of these Abolition leaders (It is the leaders not the mass . . .) the mass! why they are nothing, they know nothing, they go it blind, they are fed only by that word freedom and understand it not. They see not that *such freedom* is slavery for ourselves. That it is breaking up our peace, our union, and our power. . . .

I am gifted with no powers of oration but am a mear child a boy, to some I see around me. A child indeed and this union is my Mother. A Mother that I love with an unutterable affection. You are all her children, and is there no son but I to speak in its Mother's cause. O would that I could place my worship for her in anothers heart, in the heart of some great orator, who might move you

all to love her, to help her now when she is dieing. No, No. I wrong you. You all
do love her. You all would die for her. Yet hesitate upon the way to save her.
God grant, it may be done in a peaceful way. If not, it must be done with blood.
Ay with blood & justice. The South is leaving us. She has been wronged. Ay
wronged. She has been laughed ay, preayed upon and wronged. Tis I a northern man that tells you so for I have no interest in the south more than in all the
union. She must be reconciled. How can she. Why, as I said before, with naught
but justice. The Abolition party must throw away their principals. They must
be hushed forever. Or else it must be done by the punishment of her aggressors. By justice that demands the blood of her oppressors. By the blood of
those, who in wounding her have slain us all, with naught save blood and justice. Ay blood, in this case, should season justice. You may not agree with me.
Yet thousands do. The whole South does. For John Brown was executed (yes,
and justly) by his country's laws for attempting in another way, mearly what
these abolitionists are doing now. I saw John Brown hung. And I blessed the
justice of my contrys laws. I may say I helped to hang John Brown and while I
love, I shall think with joy upon the day when I saw the sun go down upon one
trator *less* within our land. His treason was no more than theirs, *for open force
is holier than hidden craft. The Lion is more noble than the fox.*

Source: John Rhodehamel and Louise Taper, eds., *Right or Wrong, God Judge Me: The Writings of
John Wilkes Booth* (Urbana: University of Illinois Press, 1997), 59–60.

Richard K. Call, "To John S. Littell," February 12, 1861

Writing from his home in Lake Jackson, Florida, shortly before the Civil War and his own death, Richard K. Call (1792–1862) used Brown's raid as evidence that slaves loved slavery. The fact that slaves had not joined Brown in Virginia, Call observes in this excerpted letter, shows that the United States would never witness scenes of black violence like those of the Haitian revolution. Call was the territorial governor of Florida between 1835 and 1844 and the Whig Party's unsuccessful candidate for governor of the new state in 1845. He addressed his letter of February 1861 to John Littell, chairman of the Pennsylvania delegation to the Baltimore National Union Convention. Call's letter was a response to Florida's decision to secede the previous month. He believed in moderate, conditional Unionism, and though he could not understand abolitionism and considered the idea of universal human freedom to be madness, he also rejected the idea of secession. The rest of his long and widely circulated letter explained that the whole country benefited from slavery and should protect it, that Northerners should not undermine the institution but that secessionists must find a way to compromise with the North, that a new generation of rash leaders had caused the secession crisis, and that disunion risked slavery's future and therefore the happiness of "the faithful African."

The African seems designed by the Creator for a slave. Docile and humble, with a heart full of the kindest sensibilities, generally grateful and affectionate, and with a mind incapable of a higher elevation than that which is required to direct the machinery of his limbs to useful action. He is naturally social, cheerful, and contented; and when he has a good master, which is generally the case, he is much the happiest man. . . . And under the civilizing and humane influence of the Christian religion, there are few communities of people of any race or color who would be more shocked and distressed, or who would shudder and shrink with greater horror and dismay from scenes of bloodshed and human suffering, than the African slaves of this country.

I am describing African slavery, not as fiction—not from fancy—but *as I*

see and *know it to exist*—at least in some places. I have marked its condition
and progress for many years, while living a plantation life, and I have seen with
delight the continued progress of improvement in the condition of all slaves
within my knowledge. And I have seen a development of capacity as it has advanced, for a yet higher improvement, which it must and will attain, with the
progress of improvement in other institutions. In the description I have here
given of African slavery and the African race, may be found the true reason
why this black man is a slave in Africa, Asia, Europe, and America—the reason
why he has ever been a slave, and the reason why he will *ever remain a slave, to
long as there is a superior race, willing to be his master.* This is the reason why I
sleep soundly with my doors unlocked, unbarred, unbolted, when my person
is accessible to the midnight approach of more than two hundred African
slaves. This is the reason why I feel security in knowing that if there should be
danger, every slave would be a voluntary, faithful, and vigilant sentinel over
my slumbers. And this is the reason why every slaveholder may sleep in the
same manner, and with equal security, if the white man will not corrupt the
virtue, or seduce the fidelity, of the faithful African slave. This general security
from assault and violence is fully proven by the history of the slave in this
country. There have, indeed, been some few individual cases of shocking murders of masters and overseers by slaves; but they are by no means so frequent,
nor have they been marked by greater treachery and ferocity, than the murders
committed by white men on both races within the same time. There should be
no better evidence required of the fidelity and attachment of the slaves to their
masters than the results developed in the mission of John Brown. For six
months, without suspicion of his fiendlike treachery, he was domesticated
among the slaves, and hospitable masters, of Virginia, on the very border from
which, in a few hours, they might have made successful escape. And when his
bloody and horrible plans were all matured; when he thought it only necessary for him to strike, and all must fall; when he thought it only necessary for
him to light the torch for the slaves to rise and burn alive their masters and
mistresses, men, women, and children, while they slept, to his amazement, no
slave rose against his master; and when he called John at midnight (the faithful servant of Col. Washington), when he told him he must fight, putting a
murderous pike into his hands to butcher his master, the faithful African, in the
virtues of humanity, civilization, and Christian charity, far above the devil
who tempted his fidelity with the promise of freedom, reproved his hell-born

tempter by the earnest inquiry, *"On which side will Mass John fight? I want to be with him."* Never did treachery and depravity receive a more withering rebuke; never was fidelity better vindicated; never was human virtue more triumphant over damning, insidious temptation. But besides the security arising from the fidelity and attachment of the slave to the master, there is one which will ever be found in the total incapacity of the African mind to conceive the plan, and combine the elements, necessary to the success of a general revolt over any considerable district of country. The success of the murderous insurrection in St. Domingo arose from its limited territory, its isolated situation, the peculiar character of both races of the islanders, one cruel, the other savage, the vastly superior number of the slaves, and the unfriendly relations existing between the Spanish and French divisions of the island. The extent of slave territory in this country has ever constituted a great element of strength to the institution; and so long as there shall be a just correspondence between the area of slavery and the number of slaves, this security will remain. In every attempt of insurrection in the United States, the plot has been confined to very few persons; and most generally in that small number some one, shocked at the proposition of murdering a kind master, mistress, or tender nursling, has disclosed the horrible design before its maturity, and thus averted the terrible calamity. Thus it has generally been, and so it will be, so long as the slaves have room enough to work, and to live comfortably and happily with their masters.

Source: Letter from Governor R. K. Call, of Florida, to John S. Littell, of Germantown, Pennsylvania (Philadelphia: C. Sherman & Son, 1861), 10–14.

James Williams, "To Henry Peter Brougham, 1st Baron Brougham and Vaux," February 1861

As the United States minister to Turkey, James Williams (1796–1869) was abroad during Brown's raid, trial, and execution. Williams was a native of eastern Tennessee and received his appointment to Constantinople (now Istanbul) from President Buchanan in 1858. Shortly before he left the post early in 1861, he wrote to Henry Brougham, an antislavery British statesman who was lord chancellor of the United Kingdom between 1830 and 1834 (during which time Britain passed the Slavery Abolition Act). Brougham had received an invitation to a gathering in Boston that marked the first anniversary of Brown's execution. He declined, but too politely for Williams's liking. Writing to the British nobleman, Williams expresses outrage. His letter describes the Pottawatomie killings as well as Harpers Ferry and invites empathy for Mahala Doyle (also from Tennessee). It also reminds the British to take care of their own subjects rather than worry about American slaves, and warns Brougham that he could easily be the victim of a man like Brown.

Constantinople, Feb., 1861.

My Lord: ... Allow me to refer to an incident which occurred, not a great while ago, at a spot more than three thousand miles distant from that great centre of civilization in which your lordship moves.

A *murderer* in another continent closed a long career of crime under the gallows! There was nothing peculiar in this fact, for such has been often the fate of murderers in England, in America, and elsewhere. But this was a villain of no ordinary stamp. His victims were not stalwart men alone, but defenceless women and little children. He did not slay in the glare of the noonday sun, as a common robber at the head of his band of retainers, but he killed in the quiet hours of the night, and the slumbers of innocence were startled by the death-shrieks of his unsuspecting victims. But his crimes had not their begin-

345

ning in those for which he suffered an ignominious death. They extended over a series of years; and the last, for which with his life he paid the forfeit, was by no means the worst. I myself have seen and known the unhappy victims of his earlier crimes. I have seen and known the happy wife and mother—happy in the innocence and purity of her life, though humble in her station—and I have seen her again in all the desolation of a childless widowhood. Dreadful, indeed, were the scenes through which that poor woman passed during the brief space of one short night. She was sleeping in fancied security when the spoilers came to her humble log cabin, and passed through the unbarred door to the bedsides of her sleeping husband and children. Your lordship knows the rest, and I will be brief. They were four when they lay down to rest, that dreadful night. The morning dawned upon the living woman, surrounded by the lifeless and mutilated bodies of her husband and children.

The chief criminal in this drama of blood, emboldened by immunity, changed the scene and enlarged the field of his operations. At Harper's Ferry, he again unsheathed his bloody dagger, and again was the hour of midnight made terrible by the death-struggles of his unwatching victims. Am I not right, then, in saying that John Brown was a villain of no ordinary stamp? *Sane* men, in a contemplation of the magnitude of his crimes, have said that he was *mad,* while *madmen* have exalted the *demon* into a *saint,* and mourn for him as a martyr in a holy cause!

It was upon the 3rd day of December, 1860, that his friends and partisans assembled in the city of Boston, to celebrate the first anniversary of his martyrdom.

Previous to that time, a letter had been addressed to your lordship by the "Committee of Managers," inviting you to be present upon that occasion, and to join in that celebration.

Those who knew the fact that such an invitation had been addressed to your lordship, were eager to learn in what manner you would respond. The first impression would naturally be, that your lordship would treat the missive with the dignified silence and disdain with which a nobleman of your lordship's exalted standing might be expected to meet a gross and studied insult; or, that your indignation, obtaining the mastery of your better judgment, might induce you, in that burning eloquence of words, which your lordship can so readily command, to hurl back the insult in the faces of your traducers; or, milder and more humane than either, and, perhaps, more in consonance with the gentle manners which might be expected to distinguish those through whose veins flows gentle blood, you would have responded, "It is not *my sins* but *your insanity,* which has led you to believe that I could hold fellowship with the partisans and admirers of an assassin. Go! you are madmen, and I forgive you."

These thoughts, I confess, were my thoughts, and that I give them voice here will show to your lordship that I did not rank you amongst the vicious and blood-thirsty fanatics with whom a common sentiment, upon a single point, had served in some measure to identify you. Besides, I will add, that my high respect for the exalted order to which you belong, as well as the position in which you stand towards the occupant of a throne, induced in my mind the belief that you would, in some manner, exhibit your horror of the crime of assassination, and with such an emphasis that even madmen might never again give expression to the thought that an English nobleman could have any sympathies in common with either assassins or their partisans.

Pardon me, my lord, if I, in unconscious ignorance, did not estimate, at their proper value, the refined principles of that "higher law" which have been incorporated among the doctrines of that so-called great humanitarian antislavery party, of which you are so distinguished a chief.

At first view it might occasion surprise that the "philanthropists" of Great Britain should seem to shut their eyes to the spectacle, and their ears to the wail of woe which rises up around them from the millions of the unhappy, the destitute, and depressed, of their own race and kin, who live through life a lingering death, while they have only eyes to see, and ears to hear, and tears to shed over the reputed wrongs of a handful of Africans upon the far-off shores of a continent beyond the Atlantic. But it is necessary in charity to remember that the degradation and wrongs of the one are familiar to them from youth to old age. It is an oft-told tale, to which they have become accustomed, familiar, and perhaps indifferent from its constant repetition. They are probably appalled by the magnitude of the evil, and ask to forget its existence and their obligations by the exhibition of redoubled zeal in the cause of those whom their imaginations, excited by heart-rending romances, picture as the victims of sorrow and oppression in a far distant land.

From this brief but not unnatural digression, I will return to the subject of the invitation which was given to you to participate in the celebration in memory of John Brown, the great American murderer. Permit me to refresh your memory with the first lines of your response to the committee in your own language:

"Sir: I feel honored by the invitation to attend the Boston Convention."

Upon reading these few emphatic words, I paused and re-read the letter of invitation which had been addressed to you, to discover if I had not, in my hasty perusal thereof, misunderstood its import and object. I beg to quote its words:

"*My Lord:* A number of young men, earnestly desirous of devoting themselves to the work of eradicating slavery in the United States, respectfully invite you to meet them in a public convention to be held in this city on Monday, the 3d day of December. It seems to them that the anniversary of the death of John Brown, who was killed for attempting to decide this problem in the mode that he believed to be the most efficient, is an occasion peculiarly appropriate for the discussion of our duty to the race for whom he suffered. It would be a work of supererogation now to defend John Brown, and a useless waste of time to eulogize him. Leaving both these duties to the coming ages, *let us seek to continue his life by striving to accomplish what he left us to finish.*"

It is true, my lord, that you modified somewhat the only legitimate interpretation of your first emphatic endorsement. True, as "the representative of the anti-slavery party in England," you avowed a wide difference of opinion between those you represented and the promoters of the Harper's Ferry expedition. True, you denied that John Brown was a real martyr. True, you declared your opposition to the encouragement of negro insurrections, because *"they might prove less hurtful to the master than the slave."* True, you intimated that the surest means of accomplishing your cherished schemes of American negro emancipation was under the form of law, through the instrumentality of a recent political change in the Government of the Republic! But preeminent above all other considerations which are suggested by a perusal of your letter, stands forth the declaration that you *"feel honored* by the invitation to attend the Boston Convention!"

What a spectacle is here presented, and how fruitful a theme for reflection! An English nobleman shaking hands across the ocean and transmitting pleasant messages to *such* an assemblage, convened for *such a purpose!*

It is, perhaps, not unworthy of a passing thought, that while some of your admirers have hailed your letter as furnishing evidence of the conservatism and moderation of British abolitionism, many have regarded your slight deviation from the bloody path of an extreme fanaticism as too great a concession to the dictates of an uncalculating and weakly-relenting humanity.

I confess that upon this subject there is a chasm between us, so broad and so deep, that I have not the hardihood to attempt to fill it up. I cannot hope even that anything will ever occur to reduce the breadth of this impassable gulf to smaller dimensions.

But pardon me, my lord, if I suggest the possibility that you may not have fully appreciated the deep significance of the first sentence of your memorable letter. Did you reflect upon the powerful influence which your slightest word of encouragement might exercise upon the furious madmen whom you addressed? Do you believe they will fail to infer that while you disclaim sympathy with John Brown's plans of emancipation "because they are less likely to result in injury to the master than the slave," you will, nevertheless, regard it as an honor to be invited to attend the celebrations consequent upon the death of other martyrs in the same cause? Do you excuse yourself, my lord, with the thought that it is only the assassins of slave-holders in America who are worthy to be treated with so much kindness, respect, and forbearance? Have you forgotten from whom, and under whose auspices, American slaves were acquired as chattels? May I be pardoned for saying that in the family of the writer there is a slave, bought and paid for by my ancestor from a British subject in a British province, under the solemn sanction and approval of British laws, and who is now held as a slave under the guarantee of a British title deed? Should another John Brown, under the pretext of giving freedom to this slave, slay the owner thereof, and for his crime suffer a felon's death, would your lordship feel honored by an invitation to attend the anniversary celebration of his "martyrdom?" Your lordship has already answered the interrogatory in the affirmative.

The day may come, my lord, when "even-handed justice will commend the ingredients of the poisoned chalice to your own lips."[86] There are more shining marks for the assassin's dagger than the slave-owners of America! Millions of lives stand between the honored felon and the accomplishment of his bloody work of philanthropy; a thousand times your lordship might have the privilege of acknowledging "the honor" of invitations to attend and participate in the celebration of events similar to those which were enacted at Harper's Ferry, and as often might "English philanthropy" palliate or excuse the crimes in which they had their origin, and still there would be a sea of living blood coursing through the veins of slaveholders! There are millions of the human race who, bound in the chains of political servitude, are ready to believe that they behold but one living man standing between themselves and the liberty to which they aspire! that one life less, and the fetters would fall from their liberated limbs! You may truly believe, my lord, that no such danger may threaten England's Sovereign. Even madmen would not strike at one whose noble virtues have added a brighter gem to the British Crown than was ever placed there by the valor of British arms. But England's best and noblest Queen must die, and be succeeded by sovereigns who may not imitate her virtues. If a British nobleman, of such world-wide reputation for statesmanship and philanthropy as your lordship, endeavors to instill into the public mind the belief that it is a *real honor* for an honorable man to be invited to join in rendering homage to the virtues, the moral worth, and the philanthropic services of an *admitted midnight assassin,* whose only *virtue,* or *worth,* or *service* in the cause of humanity, whose only claim to distinction above other cutthroats, beyond that notoriety which always attaches to the most revolting murderers, consists in the fact that he killed ostensibly in the cause of the so-called great humanitarian anti-slavery movement of the age; you need not be surprised, if others, who have real or imaginary wrongs to redress, may, while rejecting your peculiar idiosyncrasy, accept this as a means of redress. There are those who from the depths of their bleeding hearts, and for the redress of grievous wrongs which they themselves have suffered at the hands of their own race, would feel and say "If this be a real honor, which a British nobleman may covet, how much more honorable to be invited to participate in saturnalia of nobler blood!" May Heaven grant that neither your lordship nor any other may ever again be called upon to acknowledge the honor of an invitation to join in the celebration of such a feast!

Source: James D. Williams, *Letters on Slavery from the Old World* (Nashville: Southern Methodist Publishing, 1861), 249–276 (253–262).

PART

IV

International Responses

Brown's "tribunal" extended beyond U.S. borders. As the rest of the world responded to Brown, some joined American abolitionists in calling him a martyr, while others wished he had been less religious—and hoped that the "holdover of Christianity" would not mask the revolutionary nature of his actions (as one French observer put it). Several early responses presumed that the raid was a slave insurrection, and then, as the months passed, some foreign observers described echoes of events in their own national histories, while others used Brown to argue for change within their own countries. Part IV contains these international responses to Brown, which began in 1859 and continued for several decades. They include unexpected expressions of support from conservative Europeans, hostile responses by Quakers and abolitionists, and invocations of Brown's raid during the Civil War. They are by famous figures such as Karl Marx, Victor Hugo, and Giuseppe Garibaldi as well as by unknown or forgotten figures, and they include poetry, editorials, diary entries, and public and private letters. The most extensive response was French and British, but individuals responded from Italy, Germany, Poland, Canada, Australia, and Haiti as well as England, Scotland, Ireland, and France. In November 1859, Brown imagined a tribunal deciding "whether the world has been the worse or the better of my living and dying in it." From 1859 onward, the world decided.

The *Times*, "Editorial," November 2, 1859

England's leading newspaper published its first article about Brown on November 2. The unsigned editorial is alarmist, imagining the widespread slaughter that Brown's raid might have provoked, and almost fatalistic about slavery's long-term existence, explaining that there is little chance of ending it in the Southern states. A few weeks later, on December 19, a second editorial in the *Times* called Brown a "courageous old man, maddened by the partisan warfare of the West," but insisted that he was no martyr and attacked the "profane blasphemy" of American abolitionist "fanatics" who compared Brown to Christ. The *Times* was published in England from 1785 onward. John Thadeus Delane, the editor in 1859, tended to sympathize with Liberal politics. During the American Civil War, his newspaper usually favored the secessionist viewpoint, although it was not proslavery.

The last mail from New York brings further news of a very extraordinary incident. What may be called an insurrection of Abolitionists and Negroes has broken out at a place called Harper's Ferry, and the United States' Armoury has been seized by a band of desperate men. As the contest was going on when the steamer left, we are unable to give the result of this serious affair, but there can be little doubt that the insurgents have been crushed and their leaders punished with death. The small number of men engaged contrasts strongly with the boldness of the scheme and the skill with which it was carried out. The promptitude of the authorities in bringing an overwhelming force to the spot shows that the outbreak was considered a matter of no small importance. But at first sight the details, as given by telegraph, only inspire wonder that men should risk their lives on so mad a scheme. It is only when we consider the social condition of the Southern States that we have a clue to the object of the insurgents, and perceive the full danger of their movements. It would appear

353

that a man named BROWN, who had taken an eager part in the struggle in Kansas, formed a design of liberating the Northern Slave States by an insurrection of the Negroes of Maryland and Virginia. It is well known that the Abolitionists, even the more moderate of them, have long cherished the hope that these regions may discard slavery in course of time, and, were it not for the market which the new Slave States afford, the institution would probably die out north of the Carolinas. But BROWN and his confederates were not the men to trust to time and to peaceable means. Accounts vary as to the number engaged in this desperate enterprise, but the latest news is that they originally numbered only 17 white men and five Negroes. If they subsequently increased to 200, the fact shows how dangerous the movement must be in such a community, and how necessary were the measures for a prompt repression. The Armoury was taken by a *coup de main*,[1] the trains stopped, the telegraph wires cut, and all with a boldness and a success which showed that the insurgent calculated on the general support of the slaves. The rest may be read in our American correspondence. The insurgents seized and held several citizens as hostages, and on the morning after the outbreak they were intrenched in the Armoury, where they held out against the troops and militia. It is also reported that a portion of the insurgents had left, under the command of a man named COOK, with a large party of slaves, and were supposed to be moving towards Pennsylvania.

Of course, there can be one issue to this foolish and wicked enterprise. The insurgents will by their fate give a warning to all who may dream of remedying a great social evil by an appeal to arms. But the state of society which causes such a scheme to be formed and carried out is not the less threatening. When a few Papists planned the blowing up of the English Parliament the chances of success were desperate, but the act showed that there existed elements of danger in the State.[2] Nor can it be doubted that with skillful and audacious leadership the coloured people of Virginia would be capable of inflicting terrible calamities on their masters. With men who would set their lives on the cast, and who cared for nothing provided liberty, or at least revenge, were gained, an insurrection would be truly formidable. The blacks of this part of the Union are more instructed than further South, where slave life is one round of toil; there are a great number of Mulattoes, many free Negroes, and a good many poor white, some of whom might be expected to take part in any outbreak. All this population has, by contact with the more civilized regions acquired knowledge and feelings which perhaps hardly exist in Alabama or Texas. They know enough to become discontented with their condition, but not enough to feel the utter madness of a struggle with the American people. Our correspondent expresses probably the most common opinion when he says that the plot was widespread, and that the premature outbreak has probably saved the country from a deluge of blood. The insurgents, we can easily believe, thought that the seizure of a Government establishment, and the possession of rifles and cannon would encourage the whole population to rise against their masters. Forty-eight hours might have been enough to make half the plantations in the State the scenes of the foulest crimes. The isolated and unprepared families in the country districts might have been set upon by their maddened slaves, and the whole system of slaveholding been so shaken as to necessitate some plan of abolition.

This, at least, seems to have been the design of the leaders. That they could have expected to conquer the United States' Executive in a servile war, and to turn Virginia and Maryland into free States through victories gained by rebellious Negroes, seems out the question. America is not like one of our own island colonies, where the Negroes outnumber the whites many fold. In the districts where this outbreak took place the whites are probably superior in number to the coloured population. They are all armed, and accustomed almost from childhood to the use of their weapons. The circumstances in which they are placed have given them an aptitude for something like military organization, and they have continually before their eyes the necessity of preserving order among the African race. We may be sure that after the first surprise the white men in every American State would take prompt and effectual measures to crush the rebellion, though probably not soon enough to prevent the commission of many atrocities. This fact adds much to the guilt of the men who organized this scheme. Nothing but sickening and bootless slaughter could come of it; and then the bloody revenge of the exasperated masters.

We will not affect to indulge the hope that the commonwealths of Virginia and Maryland will be moved by this event to take into consideration the extinction of slavery. Putting aside the fact that such outbreaks generally steel the heart instead of softening it, and that the yoke is likely to be pressed down more heavily than ever on Negro necks, there are the great inducements of gain and fear to support the system. Cotton is produced now in vaster quantities than ever, and the value of Negro labour is continually rising. The price of

Negroes is nearly double what it was some years back, for the increase by breeding does not keep pace with the demand for the newly settled country. As long as Virginia supplies the dealers of the South with profit to herself so long will owners keep a firm grasp on their human property.

Source: Times [London, England], November 2, 1859.

Joseph Barker, "Slavery and Civil War," November 1859

While Brown was in prison, the British ex-clergyman Joseph Barker (1806–1875) lectured in Philadelphia and argued that Brown's raid was the wrong approach to ending slavery. It was a foolish venture, Barker explained, because all violence was unnecessary in a country with a free press and free elections. Brown had behaved as though he did not live in a democracy, the lecturer insists. Barker was from a working-class family in Leeds, in the north of England. He was a Methodist minister and traveling preacher from 1828 to 1841, then briefly a Quaker and a Unitarian. He visited America for six months in 1847 and moved to the United States to live in 1851. He settled in Ohio, then Nebraska; befriended American abolitionists, including Garrison and Phillips; and gave lectures in Northern cities from 1857 to 1859. In 1860 he returned to England and became a secularist, and in September 1861 he launched the periodical *Barker's Review*. He published his lecture about John Brown in the *Review* in 1862, prefacing it with an observation that his warning about Brown's "false" philanthropy and "fanatical" abolitionism had proven accurate, now that the Civil War was raging. He continued to publish the journal through 1863. It expressed antislavery viewpoints but sympathized with aspects of the Confederacy. Barker returned to the United States in 1868 and died in Omaha.

The question should be—Was the course which Brown took the best which he possibly could take for the interests of his country and his king. *We* think *not*. To judge from appearances, we should say, that Brown could hardly have acted more unwisely. So far as we can judge at present he accomplished nothing, either for the slave or the slave's friends, while he involved himself and his colleagues in ruin, and caused the death of several innocent men. The alarm which he has caused, the terror which he has inspired in the Southern States, will probably lead to the severer treatment of many of the slaves, and to more grievous restrictions both on slaves and others. . . .

The rational and sober friends of freedom are every year becoming more numerous, and their opponents fewer and feebler. And there is every prospect that this cheering process will continue. There is therefore no excuse whatever for resort to violence.

Again; while there was no necessity to resort to violence, John Brown and his friends had not the slightest reason to expect that such a course would prove successful. None but the most ignorant could have expected him to succeed. Their plan, which was explained to me after the outbreak by one of the party, was, to take up a position in the mountains of Virginia first, and thence make war on the slaveholders, sending off the slaves to places of safety, or adding them to their ranks, and using them in the war. But how were they to live in the mountains through the cold of winter? Where were they to obtain provisions? How were they to protect themselves against the forces of the States and the army of the Federal Government? They must have necessarily come in collision with those forces, and what could twenty-one, or even twenty-one hundred, have done against the combined forces of the nation?

But suppose they had, for a time, eluded or repelled the troops sent against them, and succeeded in spreading the flame of insurrection through the South, would they have been able to emancipate the slave? We think not. They might have caused the slaughter of many of them, and the starvation of many more, and involved the rest in greater misery; but we doubt whether they would have freed any considerable number. We question whether they could have secured the freedom and happiness of a single family. If they troops sent against them had been beaten and routed for a time, they would have rallied, and the slave-holders would have joined them, and the insurrectionists must inevitably have been overpowered. If the slaves had all risen and joined the insurrectionists, a general slaughter of the white population must have followed, accompanied with the most revolting crimes and horrors. The authors of the insurrection would have lost control of the movement had perished probably amid the general ruin. It is easy to kindle a mighty fire, but not so easy to control or extinguish it. A child might set a prairie or a pine forest on fire, but all the men on earth could not control the conflagration. Suppose the slave-holders had been beaten and slaughtered, and the slaves set free, would the condition of the negroes have been improved? They could not have carried on the business of the plantations. They could not have moved in mass to Canada, or been supported if they had got there. They could not have lived long in idleness. Brown and his men could not have maintained them. They must have perished wholesale of famine. Famine would have caused pestilence. The pestilence must have swept over the country. The whole nation would have been involved in the combined horrors of civil and of servile war. Imagine a country like this, with such varieties of citizens, and such conflicting sects and parties, ravaged at once by a threefold war: the fabled hell of orthodoxy alone could exceed its horrors.

If this country is to be permanently freed from the institutions of Slavery, the mass of the people must first be brought to approve of the measure. If Slavery were abolished by insurrection, while the majority of the people were opposed to its abolition, it would be likely to be restored when the insurrection was over. We know not what could hinder its restoration, under the present form of government, if a large majority of the people were favourably to its restoration. The success therefore of an insurrection against Slavery could only be temporary, unless it were favoured by a decisive majority of the whole people. But I a decisive majority were favourable to the abolition of Slavery, no insurrection would be necessary. It could in that case be abolished by a peaceful process. That state of the public mind that would render an insurrection successful, would render it unnecessary.

The truth is, resort to violence in a country that has a free Press, free speech, and free votes, can never be justified. If the evil complained of be a great, a palpable evil, the Platform and the Press can the more easily rouse the people to action for its peaceful removal. If it be a trifling evil, the reform may be less speedy, but the trouble can be more easily endured. If the people are too stupid or too depraved to be roused against a great and grievous wrong, they will be all the more likely to unite against forcible attempts to remedy it, and to make a speedy end of the insurrectionists. If the people are not dreadfully depraved, truth in time will influence them.

As we have said before, we are not ultra non-resistants. The doctrine that would require us, under all circumstances, when struck on the one cheek to turn the other, when robbed of wife to give up our daughter, we hate, we loathe. We believe it lawful to fight in certain circumstances; but why shed the blood of our neighbours, or pour out our own without necessity, or without a prospect of success? In countries where the people generally are favourable to reform, while a handful of courtiers, priests, or aristocrats alone, with the forces of the Government at their command are opposed to it, a resort to force may be necessary, and may be expected to succeed; but in a country like this, where the majority rule, an insurrection like that of John Brown can never be justifiable.

Source: Barkers' Review of Politics, Literature, Religion, and Morals, and Journal of Education, Science, and Co-Operation [London, England], September 6, 1862, 1–7 (3–4).

L'Univers, "Editorial," November 24, 1859

As the weeks of Brown's imprisonment passed, European newspapers began commenting on his trial and impending execution as well as his raid. The French Roman Catholic daily newspaper *L'Univers* focused on the trial and took an unpredictably defensive stance toward Brown. Based in Paris, the journal was France's leading organ of propaganda for ultramontanism, which emphasized the supremacy of the pope over all other spiritual or political authorities. Although Pope Gregory XVI condemned slave trading in 1839, Pope Pius IX had not. Pius would soon recognize Jefferson Davis as the honorable president of the Confederate States of America and declare in 1866 that slavery was not contrary to natural and divine law. Nonetheless, *L'Univers* rails against liberals who do not insist on a fair trial for Brown. It asks why liberals hate the pope's authority yet uphold the authority in Virginia that denies justice to Brown and enslaves Africans. Louis Veuillot (1813–1883) edited the newspaper from 1848 and probably wrote the editorial, for its irony is typical of his style. *L'Univers* was suppressed in 1860, but Veuillot revived it in 1867.

We search to no avail in our so-called liberal papers for the sign of a protest against the iniquities of a criminal trial judged in the United States at the end of last month. These zealous philanthropists, used to pointing out the vices in the paternal legislation of the Papal States, cannot find an epithet to describe the barbarity with which the people of Virginia have condemned a political prisoner, after having deprived him of the privilege of a free defense, as Fouquier-Tinville[3] once did. It is an issue of a political affront, in fact, not of a murder or an assassination. The liberal newspapers are ordinarily very tolerant of this privileged category of crime and according to them, the most violent rioters are worthy of pardon, despite repeated offenses. They extort amnesties for their protégés from weak governments, but they permit the political gallows to be raised in the United States without calling the free people of America to clemency and even to justice.

John Brown is a Protestant fanatic who believed that the Bible condemned slavery and who represented himself as an apostle with the mission to free the Negroes. . . . In the siege, Brown took three saber cuts on his body and his head, this last wound deafened him, and he was incapable of holding himself erect. In every civilized country, his recovery would have been awaited before proceeding with his trial, especially because his reckless attempt did not have, in reality, any more importance than the recent riot of the Tarbes market.[4] But the Virginians were too much terrified to yield their prisoner the slightest respite. The usual slowness of judicial forms in the United States is well known. Often the accused waits for full years for the jury to form before appearing, and if a lawyer is proficient, if he fears a harsh verdict, he knows how to drag out the case, from jurisdiction to jurisdiction, and so diminish through this delay the attitudes of condemnation toward his client. But, in this case, the most righteous delays were refused John Brown. . . .

Hiding their love of despotism behind a liberal divestment, the partisans of liberty in France prefer the commander's whip to the Pope's scepter. People may say that the institution of slavery is necessary to Virginia. The states situated in a warm climate, such as Louisiana and Alabama, can pretend, with the appearance of reason, that their fields demand the work of blacks because whites cannot endure the fatigue of agricultural labor under a burning sun. But in Virginia it snows more than in France; the free labor there is competition to slave labor, so much so that the masters find their interest in transforming their plantations into manufactories of black children for the southern markets. It was to preserve the profits of this immoral reproduction of the African race that the citizens of Virginia armed themselves against John Brown.[5]

Source: L'Univers [Paris, France], November 24, 1859.

Cyprian Kamil Norwid, "To Citizen John Brown" and "John Brown," November 1859

The Polish poet Cyprian Kamil Norwid (1821–1883) heard the news about Brown's raid while living in Paris. He had left Poland in 1842, lived in Germany, Brussels, and Italy until 1852 and in New York until 1854, and spent the rest of his life as an émigré in France. Though celebrated today as one of Poland's greatest poets, he was obscure and poor until he died. He published only one volume of poetry in his lifetime, and he spent the last decade of his life at a Paris shelter for impoverished Polish war veterans and orphans. He wrote two poems about Brown and dated them to November 1859, which puts them among the earliest foreign poems about Brown. He sent one, "To Citizen John Brown," to a publisher in August 1860, but it remained unpublished in his lifetime. It addresses Brown directly, as though it is a letter in verse, and depicts him as a symbol of freedom in a nation that may no longer symbolize liberty itself. The poem epitomizes Norwid's ability to find beauty in common things (a bird on a scaffold, gray hair) as well as his often irregular versification. Norwid's second poem includes an epigraph that he excerpted from Brown's prison letter of November 15, 1859. After this unacknowledged quotation, Brown does not appear in the poem until the third verse. Once he appears, he gives concrete form to the kind of epic hero that Norwid imagines in the poem's first two verses. But the poem eventually despairs of the United States, fearing that America itself will be hanged alongside Brown. Published in 1863, this second poem is typical of Norwid's intellectual style and his use of multilayered metaphors.

"To Citizen John Brown"

Across the moving plains of the ocean
I send you a song like a gull, O John!

It will long fly towards the fatherland
Of the free—for it is already in doubt; will it find it so?
Or, like the ray of your venerable greyness,
White, it will light on an empty scaffold,

So that your hangman's son with his little child's hand
Would throw stones at the guest gull!

Therefore, before ropes try
Your bared neck, to test how unyielding it is—
Therefore, before you begin to seek the earth under your heel
To kick away the debased planet,
And the earth flees from under your feet, like a frightened
Reptile—
        therefore, before they say, "He is hanged"
Say it and look at one another to see if they are false—
Therefore, before they pull the hat over your face,
So that America, recognizing its son again,
May not cry out at its twelve stars:[6]
"Put out the artificial fires of my crown,
Night advances—black night with a Negro's face!"

Therefore, before Kosciuszko's shade and Washington's[7]
Shudder—*the beginning of a song* receive, O John!

For before the song ripens, a man will sometimes die,
But, before the song dies, the nation will first arise.

"John Brown"

So far as my observation goes, none but brave men are likely to be humane to a
fallen foe. "'Cowards prove their courage by their ferocity". . . . Christ, the great
captain of liberty as well as of salvation, and who began his mission, as foretold of
him, by proclaiming it, saw fit to take from me a sword of steel after I had carried
it for a time; but he has put another in my hand ("the sword of the Spirit"). . . . I
am not as yet, in the main, at all disappointed. I have been a good deal disap-
pointed as it regards myself in not keeping up to my own plans; but I now feel
entirely reconciled to that, even—for God's plan was infinitely better, no doubt,
or I should have kept to my own.[8]

1

As eagles, imprisoned in a wire cage,
Sit through the day, mindful of their captivity,

But with the dawn, half-opening their sad eyes,
To fly, they beat with their wings against the hard walls—
Thus knocking against the bars each dawn, until
The wind carries off the feathers beaten from their arms,
And each is astonished at his feathers,
Surveying the bloody patches on his wings—
And turns his head with its flat temples
Recognizing himself again in a cage, on earth;

2

Thus you!—The noble of various nations,
Eagles locked out of the dawns of freedom,
Conspirators, expired before your time,
Youths in graves, or old men in youth—
—It would seem that—breaking
With your own muscles and nerves the laws of the times—
You first do that which later happens in history
To yourselves—like a saint—a madman—
Returning every age with eyes misled,
To recognize yourselves again—in a cage—on earth!

3

But just there, when freedom itself
Becomes the whole tradition of the nation,
Open throughout from east to west—
Where history is not like a building, but like a gate:
Just because there, in young America,
An old man equal in age to his age,
Because he shared his humanity with the man
Who has curlier hair, black cheeks;
A noble old man—Moses of the Negroes—
Will carry his head high with the heads of his sons!

4

O!—when this one, seating himself on the coffin
Prepared for him, converses with the prison guard,

Hear peoples!—for it will be long,
Before a rebel so moderate
Will be born to the world—before a commander so mighty,
And a gallow bird so arch-noble,
So valiant an old man, a father so childless!—
Until such an issueless one will be born!—
That all your displays of masterworks
Are not worth his gallows and works!

5

Soon the judges will belie themselves,
So that the twelve stars[9] of America will pale;
The mirror of justice will crack—
They will pull the hat over the old man's forehead,
They will remove the plank from under the betrayed foot—
He will say: "Amen"—and with a nod of his foot
—Like a rider his horse with his stirrup—
Will push away—the whole bestialized world!—
And he will be a stain on the red sun,
And a stain he will be on the frightened eye.

6

Ah! the shades of Washingtons and Kosciuszkos,
Of men, who from the far limits of a foreign nation
Came to nurse you, America! when you were so young
That foreign liberation could hardly be called *foreign*—
Looking from the summits, where dwells the source of sight,
Will these shades in time not rather err?
And to those who call for help, in despair
They will show a black flag on the cloud—
And people, pale, subdued, and quiet
Will say, that is Brown, America hangs?[10]

Source: George Kliger and Robert C. Albrecht, "A Polish Poet on John Brown," *Polish Review* 8, no. 3 (1963): 80–85 (82, 83–85).

Victor Hugo, "A Word on John Brown," December 2, 1859; "To M. Heurtelou," March 31, 1860; and "To the Memory of John Brown," October 21, 1874

The most famous foreign response to Brown was a public letter by the writer and activist Victor Hugo (1802–1885). Believing that Brown's execution had been postponed, Hugo wrote the letter on December 2, from Hauteville House in Guernsey, an island in the English Channel off the coast of Normandy, and included a plea for Brown's life. The letter first appeared in the London *Daily News* on December 9, with an editorial note that Hugo "has the right to speak with all the authority of his own noble sorrows in the name of outraged freedom." It was reprinted in newspapers across Europe and the United States. Hugo also wrote other responses to Brown. Once he heard of Brown's death, he added in a private letter of December 20 that he was overwhelmed with grief at the act of "a free nation putting to death a liberator." Then, in another public letter, dated December 28, 1859, he addressed the "Citizens of the Republic" of Haiti. He called Brown an apostle, a martyr, and a hero, told the Haitian people that Brown's execution was one of the "calamities of history," and predicted that the rupture of the Union would follow. Eugene Heurtelou, the editor of the Haitian newspaper *Le Progrès*, replied with a public letter to Hugo, published in his newspaper on February 6, 1860. He thanked the Frenchman for his words about Brown and predicted a great social revival and a fusion of peoples into a universal republic. The following month Hugo replied to Heurtelou with the second letter published below. The following year, 1861, Hugo authorized an engraving of a drawing for circulation as a John Brown image. He had made the drawing, which shows a man hanging from the gallows, in 1854. Hugo wrote on it "Ecce," which recalls Pontius Pilate's introduction of Jesus to the mob with the words *Ecce homo* (Behold the man). Finally, returning again to Brown in 1870, Hugo led a group of French citizens in establishing a committee to raise money for an engraved medal in honor of Brown. The committee sent the five-ounce gold medal to Brown's widow in 1874, and she deposited it in the museum of the Kansas State Historical Society at Topeka. Made by M. J. Wurder of Brussels, the medal showed an image of Brown on one side and an inscription on the other: "To the memory of John Brown, judicially murdered at Charlestown, in Virginia, on the 2d of December, 1859; and in commemoration also of his sons and comrades, who, with him, became the victims of their devotion to the cause of negro emancipation." The committee accompanied the medal with the third letter below, written by Hugo in French and published in English in the *New York Times* on February 15, 1875. Along with Hugo, the committee members and signatories to the letter included Victor Schoelcher, a writer and politician; Patrice Larroque, a professor of philosophy; Laurent Pichat, a poet and politician; Louis Blanc, a journalist and historian; and Étienne Arago, a writer and political figure.

"A Word on John Brown"

Sir: When our thoughts dwell upon the United States of America, a majestic form rises before the eye of imagination. It is a Washington!

Look, then, to what is taking place in that country of Washington at this present moment.

In the Southern States of the Union there are slaves; and this circumstance is regarded with indignation, as the most monstrous of inconsistencies, by the pure and logical conscience of the Northern States. A white man, a free man, John Brown, sought to deliver these negro slaves from bondage. Assuredly, if insurrection is ever a sacred duty, it must be when it is directed against Slavery. John Brown endeavored to commence the work of emancipation by the liberation of slaves in Virginia. Pious, austere, animated with the old Puritan spirit, inspired by the spirit of the Gospel, he sounded to these men, these oppressed brothers, the rallying cry of Freedom. The slaves, enervated by servitude, made no response to the appeal. Slavery afflicts the soul with weakness. Brown, though deserted, still fought at the head of a handful of heroic men; he was riddled with balls; his two young sons, sacred martyrs, fell dead at his side, and he himself was taken. This is what they call the affair at Harper's Ferry.

John Brown has been tried, with four of his comrades, Stephens, Coppoc, Green and Copeland.

What has been the character of his trial? Let us sum it up in a few words:—

John Brown, upon a wretched pallet, with six half gaping wounds, a gunshot wound in his arm, another in his loins, and two in his head, scarcely conscious of surrounding sounds, bathing his mattress in blood, and with the ghastly presence of his two dead sons ever beside him; his four fellow-sufferers wounded, dragging themselves along by his side; Stephens bleeding from saber wounds; justice in a hurry, and overleaping all obstacles; an attorney, Hunter, who wishes to proceed hastily, and a judge, Parker, who suffers him to have his way;[11] the hearing cut short, almost every application for delay refused, forged and mutilated documents produced, the witnesses for the defence kidnapped, every obstacle thrown in the way of the prisoner's counsel, two cannon loaded with canister stationed in the Court, orders given to the jailers to shoot the prisoners if they sought to escape, forty minutes of deliberation, and three men sentenced to die! I declare on my honor that all this took place, not in Turkey, but in America!

Such things cannot be done with impunity in the face of the civilized world. The universal conscience of humanity is an ever-watchful eye. Let the judges of Charlestown, and Hunter and Parker, and the slaveholding jurors, and the whole population of Virginia, ponder it well: they are watched! They are not alone in the world. At this moment, America attracts the eyes of the whole of Europe.

John Brown, condemned to die, was to have been hanged on the 2d of December—this very day.

But news has just reached us. A respite has been granted to him. It is not until the 16th that he is to die.[12] The interval is a brief one. Before it has ended, will a cry of mercy have had time to make itself effectually heard?

No matter! It is our duty to speak out.

Perhaps a second respite may be granted. America is a noble nation. The impulse of humanity springs quickly into life among a free people. We may yet hope that Brown will be saved.

If it were otherwise, if Brown should die on the scaffold on the 16th of December, what a terrible calamity! The executioner of Brown, let us avow it openly (for the day of the Kings is past, and the day of the peoples dawns, and to the people we are bound frankly to speak the truth)—the executioner of Brown would be neither the attorney Hunter, nor the judge Parker, nor the Governor Wise, nor the State of Virginia; it would be, though we can scarce think or speak of it without a shudder, the whole American Republic.

The more one loves, the more one admires, the more one venerates that Republic, the more heart-sick one feels at the contemplation of such a catastrophe. A single State ought not to have the power to dishonor all the rest, and in this case there is an obvious justification for a federal intervention. Otherwise, by hesitating to interfere when it might prevent a crime, the Union becomes a participator in its guilt. No matter how intense may be the indignation of the generous Northern States, the Southern States force them to share the opprobrium of this murder. All of us, no matter who we may be, who are bound together as compatriots by the common tie of a democratic creed, feel ourselves in some measure compromised. If the scaffold should be erected on the 16th of December, the incorruptible voice of history would thenceforward testify that the august Confederation of the New World had added to all its rites of holy brotherhood a brotherhood of blood, and the *fasces*[13] of that splendid Republic would be bound together with the running noose that hung from the gibbet of Brown!

This is a bond that kills.

When we reflect on what Brown, the liberator, the champion of Christ, has striven to effect, and when we remember that he is about to die, slaughtered by the American Republic, that crime assumes an importance co-extensive with that of the nation which commits it—and when we say to ourselves that this nation is one of the glories of the human race; that, like France, like England, like Germany, she is one of the great agents of civilization; that she sometimes even leaves Europe in the rear by the sublime audacity of some of her progressive movements; that she is the Queen of an entire world, and that her brow is irradiated with a glorious halo of freedom, we declare our conviction that John Brown will not die; for we recoil horror-struck from the idea of so great a crime committed by so great a people.

Viewed in a political light, the murder of Brown would be an irreparable fault. It would penetrate the Union with a gaping fissure which would lead in the end to its entire disruption. It is possible that the execution of Brown might establish slavery on a firm basis in Virginia, but it is certain that it would shake to its centre the entire fabric of American democracy. You preserve your infamy, but you sacrifice your glory. Viewed in a moral light, it seems to me that a portion of the enlightenment of humanity would be eclipsed, that even the ideas of justice and injustice would be obscured on the day which should witness the assassination of Emancipation by Liberty.

As for myself, though I am but a mere atom, yet being, as I am, in common with all other men, inspired with the conscience of humanity, I fall on my knees, weeping before the great starry banner of the New World; and with clasped hands, and with profound and filial respect, I implore the illustrious American Republic, sister of the French Republic, to see to the safety of the universal moral law, to save John Brown, to demolish the threatening scaffold of the 16th of December, and not to suffer that beneath its eyes, and I add, with a shudder, almost by its fault, a crime should be perpetrated surpassing the first fratricide in iniquity.

For—yes, let America know it, and ponder on it well—there is something more terrible than Cain slaying Abel: It is Washington slaying Spartacus![14]

"To M. Heurtelou"

Hauteville House, 31st March, 1860.

Your letter touches me. You are a noble specimen of that colored race which has been so long oppressed and misunderstood. From one end of the earth to the other the same flame burns in man, and you are one of those who prove it. Was there more than one Adam? Philosophers may discuss the question, but what is certain is that there is but one God. As there is but one Father, we are all brothers. It was for this truth that John Brown died; it is for this truth that I fight. You thank me for it, and I cannot tell you how much your noble words move me. There is neither black nor white in the world, there are spirits only; you are one of them. All souls are white before God.

I love your country, your race, your liberty, your republic. Your beautiful island has an attraction just now for free spirits; she has just set a great example: she has crushed despotism.

She will help us to crush slavery. For slavery will disappear. What the Southern States have just killed is not John Brown, but slavery.

Henceforth the American Union may be looked on as broken up. I deeply regret it, but it is a foregone conclusion. Between the North and the South there is the gibbet of John Brown.

Joint responsibility is no longer possible. The burden of such a crime cannot be borne by two persons. Continue your task, you and your worthy fellow-citizens. Haiti is now a centre of light. It is a grand thing that among the torches of progress which light the path of mankind, one should be seen in the hands of the negro.

Your brother.[15]

"To the Memory of John Brown"

Madam—Several years have passed away since your noble husband completed the sacrifice of a life consecrated to the most generous of all aims. The gallows on which he suffered called forth a cry of universal indignation, which was the signal for securing the emancipation of a race till then disinherited. Honor be to him, and to his worthy sons who were associated with him in his endeavors! To the blessing with which the present age crowns their memory shall be added that of future generations. These thoughts, Madam, must assuredly tend greatly to alleviate your great sorrow. But you have sought a higher consolation for your grief, in the reflection that beyond the imperfect justice of man sits enthroned that Supreme Justice which will leave no good action unrewarded and no crime unpunished. We hope, also, that you may derive some comfort from this expression of our sympathy, as citizens of the French Republic, which would have reached you earlier but for the prolonged and cruel sufferings[16] through which our unfortunate country has been forced to pass.[17]

Sources: Letters on American Slavery (Boston: American Anti-Slavery Society, 1860), 3–6; *The Letters of Victor Hugo,* Vol. II, ed. Paul Meurice (Boston: Houghton Mifflin, 1898), 157–158; Franklin B. Sanborn, *The Life and Letters of John Brown, Liberator of Kansas, and Martyr of Virginia* (Boston: Roberts Bros., 1885), 120–121.

Ottilie Assing, "John Brown's Execution and Its Consequences," December 1859

Ottilie Assing (1819–1884) was a romantic German intellectual and avowed atheist who came to America in 1852. She lived in New York City and then Hoboken, New Jersey, began working as an American correspondent for the progressive German paper *Morning Journal for Educated Readers,* and associated with abolitionists. In 1856 she met Frederick Douglass in Rochester while seeking permission (which he granted) to translate into German his best-selling second autobiography, *My Bondage and My Freedom.* After that she spent most summers in Rochester living with the Douglasses. It was at her apartment in Hoboken that Douglass sought refuge in the immediate wake of Brown's raid, when he was a wanted man, with federal authorities searching for him. Assing went to the telegraph office and sent a coded message from Douglass to his son telling him to destroy or hide sensitive documents relating to Brown. Then a few weeks later she wrote an article about the consequences of Brown's execution, predicting that it made a great North-South conflict and disunion inevitable.

John Brown and his companions have become martyrs for their conviction, their dedication, and their love of freedom. The men who stirred up the entire Union and caused panic in the South are dead. The 2nd of December was the day of death for a hero whose name will be engraved together with the noblest and bravest in the annals of history. Virginia could not breathe easy as long as this man had breath; she trembled in fear and anger at the thought that he might escape her vengeance. . . .

For the time being the curtain has descended over the corpses of almost twenty men, five of whom became victims of the laws of the South, while the rest died during the assault on the arsenal at Harpers Ferry. Nobody, however, is blind to the fact that this is just the first act in the grand drama that sooner or later must unfold before the eyes of the world. The moral pressure is now infinitely greater than it would have been had John Brown succeeded in his venture. The heroism of these men has filled even the South with astonished admiration; at the same time, the cowardice and baseness, the brutality, crudeness, and rottenness of the slavocracy have been exposed in a stronger light, slavery has been branded with more disgrace, than all the efforts of the abolitionists have ever been able to accomplish. Men who hitherto have not dared to ponder the legality of slavery, have suddenly been torn from their lethargy. To their amazement they saw twenty men, all of the purest and most unassailable character, who personally suffered nothing from slavery and had nothing to gain from its abolition. All of them were well situated in occupations with solid incomes, many of them had only recently married, yet they were willing to leave their homes and families, risk life and liberty, to obtain freedom for people they had never met.

These events also clearly show the rottenness and hollowness of the bonds connecting the North to the South. The same man who was hanged in the South as a traitor and a murderer we in the North honor as a martyr and a saint. Considering, furthermore, the hatred, animosity, and bitterness with which the two parts of the nation are facing each other; considering that they have been on display more then ever before in the few sessions that the newly convened Congress has held so far; and considering that slavery and freedom simply cannot in the long run exist side by side, one cannot be blind to the fact that a great conflict is both necessary and inevitable. This conflict can and must end in splitting the Union, and only such a split will bring about more natural and harmonious conditions.[18]

Source: Radical Passion: Ottilie Assing's Reports from America and Letters to Frederick Douglass, ed. Christoph K. Lohmann (New York: Peter Lang, 1999), 175–179 (175, 178–179).

Harvey C. Jackson, "An Address to the Colored People of Canada," December 7, 1859

Brown's international supporters joined American abolitionists and African American communities in raising funds for his widow and children. Soon after the execution, Harvey Cornelius Jackson of Simcoe, Ontario, issued a broadside asking Canada's black residents to send money to Samuel Sewall, a Boston abolitionist who knew Brown from the days of "Bleeding Kansas" and chaired a huge meeting in his honor at Boston's Tremont Temple on December 2. Jackson explains in his broadside that Brown and his raiders are martyrs to liberty's cause and promises that a future tribunal—the "coming ages"—will recognize them as such, for their raid will spread the idea of freedom. Jackson was a black abolitionist who drove a stage between Ingersoll and Port Burwell through the early 1850s, then moved to Chatham in 1855 and may have collaborated with Brown on the Chatham convention of 1858. He worked with Harriet Tubman to help fugitive slaves and was a member of the Provisional Union Association, which promoted black self-help.

Fellow Citizens:—You are all aware of the excitement recently created at Harper's Ferry, in the State of Virginia, in consequence of the bold and heroic attack upon Slavery, made by Captain John Brown a few others, whose object was to break the chains of that accursed institution. You are also aware that their attempt was a failure, so far as the immediate emancipation of our kindred were concerned. But that bold attempt to liberate the slaves will be attended with the most important results. It has already enlightened public opinion more than all the anti-slavery speeches made for the last ten years; it has caused anti-slavery newspapers and letters to penetrate the very *centre* of those despotic states. Even the New Orleans *Picayune* is frightened at the influx of those "inflammatory" articles and documents.[19] Some persons may brand Brown's effort as "rash, futile, and wild," but they must acknowledge that it will be productive of much good, or renounce their judgment. Christianity never spread so fast at any other period as it did when the earth was made gory with the blood of the Martyrs. Brown and his confederates are martyrs to the cause of Liberty, and their blood will cry out from the earth and gain many advocates to Freedom. But even supposing the contrary was the case; the intent, the aim was good, in behalf of our oppressed race, and we should do our duty—show the world that we much appreciate such noble and philanthropic actions. By the martyrdom of Capt. Brown, that brave, undaunted, heroic spirit, and his noble confederates, a parcel of widows and orphans, sharing the same sympathy towards our race, are left without means to meet the necessities of life, and it is for you to say whether you will assist in providing for the widows and in educating the orphans. I *know* you will assist. Coming ages will appreciate Capt. Brown's worth, his greatness of soul.

Let there be a meeting called in every locality where any colored persons reside. Let the "whites" be solicited to aid in the glorious and heavenly enterprise; let each locality remit what is collected, to Mr. Samuel E. Sewall, 46 Washington St., Boston. Mr. Sewall, a gentleman of great integrity, has been appointed to receive the funds collected for the benefit of the relations of the Harper's Ferry Martyrs. Friends, let the world see that we appreciate a disinterested and generous deed—let us manifest it by *action*, as well as by word.

Have Copeland and Green relations who will suffer pecuniarily by their being murdered by the Virginians?[20] If so, request Mr. Seward when you send your contributions, to *give them a proportionate amount.*

> Yours, for the cause of humanity, Harvey C. Jackson.
> Simcoe, Canada West, Dec. 7th, 1859.

Source: Harvey C. Jackson, *An Address to the Colored People of Canada* (Simcoe: s.n., 1859).

Glasgow Herald, "The Outbreak at Harper's Ferry," December 19, 1859

The moderately liberal *Glasgow Herald* responded to Brown by trying to start a national conversation about Britain's economic interests in slavery. Edited by James Pagan in 1859, the *Herald* was Glasgow's leading paper and was always owned by a collection of local businessmen and lawyers. It began in 1783 as the *Glasgow Advertiser* and changed its name in 1802. Soon after its shift to daily publication in 1859, the newspaper's circulation reached 25,000 copies. In this unsigned editorial published soon after news of Brown's execution reached Britain, the *Herald* explains that although his raid was relatively unimportant, Americans have turned it into a major event. This means that a great conflict and the abolition of slavery are on the horizon. In turn, the British need to consider their part in the slave economy and wean themselves from American cotton. The editorial's focus reflects the fact that cotton was Glasgow's largest industry, employing one-eighth of the city's workers in spinning, weaving, bleaching, and other cotton-related trades.

The outbreak at Harper's Ferry was but a small matter, and was crushed in the bud. Old John Brown, who was executed at Charleston on the 2d inst., was but one man, and not a very great one. But the excitement which the event has spread through the United States clearly demonstrates that it is looked upon with alarm, as the first effervescence of a great convulsion. Everything that has lately reached us from the United States betokens the fear of an approaching crisis. Men are prepared for its coming; and, although the time may be procrastinated which shall witness the abolition of slavery in America, it is not the less certainly looked forward to. It is evident that, while the slaves themselves are becoming no longer indifferent to their rights as human creatures, there are many white men, actuated neither by political motives nor by desire of personal aggrandisement, who are prepared to hazard their lives for the liberation of the negroes. Sooner or later the work will be accomplished. In these circumstances, it would be well to consider the British interest in the question, if, happily, something could be done to lessen our vast commercial dependence upon the cotton-growing States of America. Within the memory of the present generation the increase of the wealth, the development of the industry, and the progress of the refinement of the British people, have led to the growth of this enormous trade, and our commercial interests are deeply concerned in it. The consumption of cotton, both in this country and on the Continent, is yearly increasing, and any important cessation of the supply would cause a serious shock to the commercial prosperity of Europe. It is therefore manifestly dangerous to depend almost solely, as we do, upon a supply obtained from resources which the Harper's Ferry insurrection proves to be perilous, and to risk the continuance and prosperity of a trade which enriches this country, and employs her people, upon a basis so evidently insecure. We must look to ourselves, and cultivate a cotton trade with our possessions.

Source: Glasgow Herald [Scotland], December 19, 1859.

Aberdeen Journal, "A Martyr or a Criminal?" December 21, 1859

About 150 miles northeast of Glasgow, the *Aberdeen Journal* took a different approach to that of the *Herald*. It responded to Brown by debating the question of whether he was a martyr or a criminal. The editorial concludes that he was both: Brown died for the right of freedom but committed dangerous crimes in the process. The *Journal* was a weekly newspaper founded in 1747. William Forsyth edited the newspaper from 1849 onward, and it had a circulation of around 3500. Aberdeen was no stranger to American abolitionism. The city had hosted Frederick Douglass as a lecturer in 1846, and although Douglass first thought the hearts of Aberdeen's people were "as hard as the granite of which their houses are built," as he put it, he eventually found them receptive to his antislavery message. Harriet Beecher Stowe lectured there in 1853.

A martyr or a criminal? How often may it be said of the distinction between the two that they are like that drawn by the poet between genius and madness—

"Great genius is to madness oft allied,
A thin partition does them both divide."[21]

In which category will posterity place poor old Captain Brown, of the Harper's Ferry tragedy, seeming as brave and true a man as ever stepped, but as hotheaded as warm-hearted? A simple natural truth was to him unalterable by political conditions or human arrangements. Consequences were nothing to him in the cause which he undertook—not ever the hideous consequences of a servile war, and hearths and homesteads blazing with the torch of revenge, and reeking with the blood of murder. He took his stand on what was to him a natural principle of justice, and dared all things, confident in his cause, and devoting himself and his family to all but certain destruction as its first apostles.

He was no reckless, hard-living, hard-swearing fire-eater. He was a severe puritan—very much one of the old stamp; a man who had one single iron idea, as unyielding as a pike, and an equally iron faith in his idea, and an equally iron will, and iron arm to send the pike home. His idea was the inalienable right of freedom; and what is true in nature he seems to have held could never be untrue in politics, and that the vindication of truth and justice could never be criminal in the eyes of God. As for the eyes of men, he seems to have cared as little for them as for the consequence to himself or others of his self-imposed duty. Of course, such a man was a fanatic; and a fanatic who carries his life in his hand as carelessly as a glove is the most dangerous fanatic of all. But slavery is a thing well calculated to produce fanatics of the Captain Brown stamp, and to make martyrs of them when they die, as they invariably do in the cause which they adopt. With a mere handful of men, amounting to twenty-two, he took possession of the arsenal at Harper's Ferry, and, with an audacity that looks very like madness, defied the whole power of the United States. He says he had entered into no conspiracy with the slave population; and it seems so, for the slaves, either through ignorance or timidity, stood aloof from the whole enterprize. The troops assailed the arsenal, which was defended with desperate resolution. Four of Brown's sons fell by his side before the old man surrendered.

Since then, the state of feeling in the slave States has been such as shows the universal sense of insecurity. The Southerners see the danger which they have passed through, and the possibility of its recurrence at any moment, with such a community of action among the slave population as may in one night fill the country with murder and destruction. For his share in this affair, Old Brown has suffered the last penalty of the law. Who can say that he has not merited his fare? We may lament his sad end, and admire his virtues—we may sympathise ever so deeply in the cause which he took so mad a method of promoting. But he was a rebel to national authority, a violator of the national law; and his attempt to solve by force and bloodshed, on his own responsibility, the most difficult problem in the history of the country, called for the highest penalty inflicted for the most dangerous of crimes. So poor Old Brown was hanged, and in his last moments the conduct of the man was consistent with his whole career. His wife seemed to be a woman of his own stamp; she repelled sympathy, and expressed her pride in being the wife of such a husband, and in his martyrdom for the cause of humanity. She has given her husband and five sons to the cause of the slave, and is, no doubt, ready to give the rest. Old Brown treated the matter of his son's death more like an old Roman than a modern Christian. He proposed, with something like savage philosophy, to take the bodies of his four sons, who fell at Harper's Ferry, and those of his companions, and burn them on a pile of pine logs. This strange proposal his wife naturally opposed, and the Sheriff informed him the authorities could not allow it.[22] But it is quite consistent with the stern unyielding character of the strong-hearted old backwoodsman, and not so inconsistent as it seems at first sight with the more gentle, domestic features of his nature, which break out in the communications on family matters with his poor wife.

Source: Aberdeen Journal [Scotland], December 21, 1859.

Manchester Examiner and Times, "The Execution of John Brown," December 24, 1859

In the north of England, one of the leading regional newspapers responded to Brown's death by condemning slaveholders, Wall Street speculators, and the laws in the United States that punished Brown's crime yet protected the criminal system of slavery. This editorial in the *Manchester Examiner and Times* appeals to a higher law for true judgment of Brown's actions and adds that if Brown had been successful in leading a rebellion, he would be a national hero like George Washington. It concludes that his death will deepen the division between the North and the South. Published by Alexander Ireland (a friend of Emerson) from 1846 onward and edited by Henry Dunckley (previously a Baptist minister) from 1855 onward, the *Examiner and Times* was a Liberal populist newspaper that supported numerous reform issues, including abolitionism. It went on to support the Union throughout the Civil War.

The gallows has lately closed the career of a man who will hold no infamous place in history. We refer, of course, to the execution of John Brown, the instigator and leader of the slave insurrection at Harper's Ferry. As we read the particulars of that lamentable event, we insensibly correct the fallacious impression established by custom with regard to the ignominiousness of certain modes of punishment. After all, the hangman is not necessarily the bestower of infamy; the rope does not always make a man's reputation loathsome and abhorred. Old Brown has died the death of murderers, but no man ever died in a nobler cause, or died more nobly. It is a huge misfortune for any State when its laws condemn men to death for crimes which one half of its own citizens, and the bulk of mankind generally, will extol as virtues. This is only one aspect of the retributive effects of slavery. It is not in the nature of things for a great and civilised nation to connive at an enormous wrong, without paying the penalty in some form or another. The righteousness which governs the world will not be mocked and evaded with impunity. Twenty millions of white men are physically competent to hold four millions of black men in slavery, but it is totally out of their power to frustrate the inevitable consequences of such a violation of the moral law. Their own consciences will create avengers. However selfishness may blunt the perceptions of those who are engaged in the crime, the instincts of every honest heart will protest against their miserable sophistry, and brand them as assassins of the most sacred rights, as traitors at the bar of God and man.

The act for which Brown has been hanged is, of course, legally a crime. It is an offence against the State. He conspired to set men free, to rescue them from the condition of chattels, and restore to them the full enjoyment of the prerogatives which belong rightfully to all men. If the laws of the United States had been in harmony with justice, there would have been no room for the commission of such a crime. We do not wish to blink the fact that Brown sought to effect his end by violent measures. He believed it right to appeal to the sword, to enlist bloodshed on the side of freedom. There was not the slightest chance of success in such an attempt, and hence he is chargeable with a grave, perhaps a criminal, responsibility. But viewing his conduct in the very worst light, we find nothing to prevent us from placing him side by side with those patriots of all ages who have loved liberty, not wisely, but too well. He aimed at a righteous object, he was inspired by the loftiest sentiments, he risked his life for the welfare of the oppressed of another race than his own, he has expiated his chivalrous daring by a death at the hands of the executioner, and he has borne his fate with the lofty spirit of a martyr. The world's opinion is usually stamped by success. If Washington had failed in the War of Independence, and been hanged at New York, he would have figured in history merely as an unsuccessful rebel, instead of being idolized as the Father of his country. If the French generals who were apprehended in their beds early on the morning of the 2nd December had got scent of the project the night before, Louis Napoleon would probably have been put to death as a traitor against the French republic, and his memory branded with the odium of a foul conspiracy; as it is, we know he is the greatest man in Europe, a monarch comparable to Louis XIV, famous in arms, and the very model of magnanimity, sagacity, and moderation.[23] If Brown, by some miracle, could have placed himself at the head of the black race in North America, driven the planters over the Missouri, and founded a flourishing republic of colored men, with New Orleans for its capital, his fame would have rivaled that of Washington, and the world would have voted him a place among its greatest heroes. For the crime of failure, he is a felon. We do not question, for a moment, the political necessity which has dealt with him as a traitor, but in a higher sphere than that of politics we may venture to award a truer verdict.

There is something dangerously fascinating in the lofty fanaticism of this man. It might have been a blunder to have set him free, but it is unquestionably a political misfortune that the Americans were bound to hang him. His death cannot fail to deepen and embitter the hostility which divides the Northern from the Southern States, and to advance by peaceful or by violent means the cause of the abolitionists. The sympathy felt for him was so general and unmistakable that it was necessary to guard the prison by a strong military force and to surround the gallows with soldiers. His wife was attended to and from the prison by an armed escort, and was received by the troops with military honors. During his confinement, he received letters of condolence from many of the best and most distinguished citizens of the United States, and the members of various religious communions emulate each other in caring for his family, as a tribute to the father's worth. The day of his execution was kept in Boston as one of general mourning. The colored people wore crape on their arms, the bells tolled, and at a great meeting of the citizens, held in Tremont Temple, his portrait was exhibited underneath a cross of evergreens, and surrounded with a laurel wreath. The conduct of the unhappy man was in strict harmony with these public demonstration; composed, resigned, sustained by religions thought, indomitably without any mixture of hardihood or bravado.

If the United States can afford to hang such men, they are a fortunate people. It would be a glorious thing if the whole race of planters and Wall Street speculators could be made to possess a tithe of the virtues of old Brown. He is hanged mainly because, bating a few errors, he preferred the services of God to the service of the Devil; and it cannot but go ill with any country where that preference is made by law a hanging matter. This is the real evil to be abated, and not the likelihood of more Harper's Ferry insurrections. A nation may outlive an occasional riot, but it cannot outlive determinate, wholesale treason against the first principle of natural equity. They must resolve to strangle the treason, or it will strangle them. But the attempt to get out of the difficulty, even in the honestest and most straightforward manner, will be necessarily arduous. Will the long-continued conspiracy against human right be satisfied with a less inexorable expiation than the rupture of the Federal tie? This or something worse would seem to be imminent, if any credit is to be attached to the Southern declarations published in the *New York Herald*. If those threats are authentic, and being authentic, anything more than bombast, the Northern States must consent to be plunged into a deeper slough of villainy, or withdraw from an unholy alliance with men-owners. How they will resolve on this point remains to be seen, but assuredly half a dozen executions of such men as old Brown would settle the question.

Source: Manchester Examiner and Times [England], December 24, 1859.

Harriet Martineau, "John Brown; South's Political Posturing," December 24, 1859, and "The Puritan Militant," January 28, 1860

After visiting the United States between 1834 and 1836, the English abolitionist Harriet Martineau (1802–1876) believed the country was entering its "martyr age." In 1839 she published a whole book about abolitionism called *The Martyr Age of the United States,* which heralds the abolitionists as "spiritual potentates." Martineau, a respected writer and philosopher, was outspoken on the topics of slavery and women's rights. Yet when she responded to the events of Harpers Ferry in a letter of late December 1859, written to Oliver Johnson, the editor of the *National Anti-Slavery Standard* in New York, she registered confusion. Martineau does not see Brown's death as a martyrdom and asks for clarity about the whole episode. Brown's actions are mysterious, although he seems noble in his character. Toward the end of her letter, she does begin to wonder if Brown might be a martyr—if he might ennoble the gallows like Christ ennobled the cross—but she remains doubtful that this will occur. Martineau's hesitance echoed the initial response of nonresistant abolitionists in the United States, including Garrison, one of her friends and heroes. A month later she published a second response to Brown, this time under the pseudonym "Ingleby Scott." It represents Brown as a militant Puritan and heroic patriot and appeared as a "Representative Men" column in *Once a Week,* a British illustrated miscellany published from July 1859 that included fiction; articles about art, literature, science, natural history, and new inventions; and biographical sketches of "representative" men and women.

"John Brown; South's Political Posturing"

Sir: Amidst the strong excitement of European politics, which so largely involve the liberties of the whole civilized world, we feel as much interest in *your* great topic as if all Europe were in a state of calm. The only clear thing to us about the Harper's Ferry business is the moral greatness of John Brown. Putting aside the question of the act which brought him into his position, there can be nothing finer than the way in which he holds that position. I doubt whether there is in history anything nobler than the calm devotedness of his temper, and the heroic moderation of his demeanor. If the Irish rebels had been of his stamp, in 1798[24] and in O'Connell's and John Mitchell's time,[25] Ireland would not have waited so long for deliverance as she did. It was the passion, frenzy and selfish vanity of the agitators which injured the cause more than the prejudices of toryism and the fear of tyrants. There is not a trace in John Brown of the popular agitator; but as entire an absence of self-seeking, of every kind of self-regard, as can be conceived. His act is, to us, a mystery; and a painful one. If he had no intention beyond running off slaves, why the collection of arms? But it would be useless to go into the particulars of a case which you must understand so much better than we can. I will therefore say only that we can see but two ways of accounting for the course of events: that John Brown was insane, or that he was cheated of some expected support. Of his being insane there is not the slightest trace in any part of his subsequent conduct or speech; and if he had promises of support in a scheme so wild and hopeless, the difficulty is not diminished. If the scheme was *not* wild and hopeless, then we on this side of the water are too ignorant to form any judgment of the case at all; and this is very possible. In such a case, there will soon be consequences which will make all plain. . . .

And now, what will be the effect of this rising on your great controversy, and the persons involved in it? Can the slaveholding communities ever get over the exposure now made, and never to be retrieved, of the hollowness of the social state in which slavery is an element? Can slavery ever be again what it has been—in Virginia at least—while the spectre of Old Brown walks in the midst of it, as it always will from this time forward? Henceforth there will be a new thought in common between master and slave which must surely alter their relation—the image of Old Brown, always present to both. In case of such a ripening of events as that the frontier States must take part with either North or South, will not the choice be largely influenced by what has happened? On the other hand, will the lot of the negro (slave and free) be aggravated by the most recent alarm? There is nothing in the way of cowardly cruelty which may not be expected from the people who would hurry on the trial of wounded men, and fail to consider, in the first place, the rights and needs of the accused in regards to counsel, the appearance of witnesses, &c. It is true, the plea for haste is the danger from suspense—the necessity for getting the old man put out of sight, but things may return to their usual course, and terrified hearts cease to flutter. Such a plea seems to us to have the victory with

Old Brown. His is the conquering mind in the case, whatever becomes of the life. We are full of interest and curiosity to know what will happen on a scene where things can never again be as they were. Of Brown's life we have never had any hope—if, indeed, we may speak of hope in a case where life is probably not desired, and where death may be more useful to the cause for which life was imperiled. The old man's terrible bereavements and sufferings no doubt reconcile him to death; and, as to the mode of it, it depends on the victim whether the death degrades him or he ennobles the death. The cross was the deepest of the disgraces before eighteen centuries ago; and the gallows may become honorable if slaveholders do but condemn a few disinterested and wise friends of the negro to die upon it. The halter cannot disgrace Old Brown. The doubt as to whether he will ennoble it hangs on the indefensible character of his enterprise—as far as we can yet see. At all events, I think any one of us had rather die on Brown's gallows than sit on the Bench to sentence him to it, or survive him to bring up children to hate and dread the negro because Brown would have freed him.

"The Puritan Militant"

It could hardly be expected that at this time of day any fresh illustration would arise of the old Covenanter cast of character. In days of religious persecution, especially during the struggle between the High Church and the Puritans, there was a Judaic type of the Christian character conspicuous in every society in which the Calvinistic aspect of the Reformation was more or less established. We are all familiar with this order of character in history and in fiction; and it is preserved for future generations, not only in English, but in German, French, and American literature. In New England, above every other country, the old type is familiar: for the region was settled, and for a long time governed, by the Judaic Christian confessors who are venerated under the title of the Pilgrim Fathers. Not even there, however, did any historical student or any poet dream that there could ever again be a revival of the old type—a real Puritan confessor and martyr living and dying, acting and suffering in the genuine old spirit, but using the language, and wearing the manners of the ordinary daily life of the latter half of the nineteenth century. Such a phenomenon we have before us in the leader of the Harper's Ferry invasion—John Brown.

John Brown was a Connecticut man: and Connecticut was Judaic even be-

yond the other New England States—its laws being taken bodily out of Deuteronomy, with as little variation as could be permitted. This circumstance
—of the man's birth-place—should be borne in mind, though he was early
removed into Ohio. The associations which surround the first years of life in
Connecticut may well impress the character for life.

I am not going to relate the life of John Brown, for we are less supplied with
particulars of it than we shall be some months hence, when the Americans will
send us a full biography of the most remarkable man of their generation. I
wish merely to offer such traits of character as may show how the old type has
been revived for a very special occasion. I will only say, in regard to his history,
that his ancestry was thoroughly puritan and militant.

John Brown was sixth in descent from one of the veritable Pilgrim Fathers—Peter Brown, who landed from the Mayflower, on Plymouth Rock, in
Massachusetts Bay, on the 22nd of December, 1620. Peter's great-grandson—
John's grandfather—was a gallant soldier in the Revolutionary war. He led out
the Connecticut company of which he was captain to the conflict when its seat
was New York; and he died in camp in the year of the Declaration of Independence, 1776. One of his many children was a judge in Ohio. One of his grand-
sons was for twenty years the president of a New England university. Owen,
one of the sons of the captain, and father of John, married into a family as
good as his own—his father-in-law having been the officer in charge of the
prisoners when General Burgoyne's army surrendered. Thus John inherited a
military spirit from both lines of ancestry.

He seemed framed for a military existence: but the religious tendency prevailed in the very years when martial ardour is strongest. He desired to be in
the Church; and he went from Ohio back into Connecticut for the sake of a
college education to fit him for the pulpit. Inflammation of the eyes, which
became chronic, prevented study, and compelled him to give up his wish. But
he was, in his temper of mind and domestic and social character, a minister of
the Gospel, as he understood it, through life. . . .

It will be time enough to speak of the results of John Brown's crusade when
we see more of them. They are abundantly remarkable already, and they will
be more so by the time this portrait is in print. Our business has been with the
character of the man. It has impressed the national imagination forever in his
own country. Some eminent citizens of Virginia cannot bear the force of it,
and are preparing to migrate, with their property, to Europe. (Their slaves they

must leave behind). Among those who must remain, the children will never forget the man, nor lose the impression of the winter nights following his death. In Cumberland the aurora borealis is called "Lord Derwentwater's lights," because it was particularly splendid the night after his execution.[26] The Virginia children will shiver for life when they remember John Brown's lights—those mysterious lights which ascend every night in the direction of Harper's Ferry, and are answered from various parts of the horizon—in spite of all efforts of police and military to make out what they mean. John Brown is as sure of immortality as Washington himself.

Sources: National Anti-Slavery Standard, December 24, 1859; *Once a Week* [London, England], January 28, 1860, 105–109 (105–106, 109).

Lloyd's Weekly Newspaper, "Captain John Brown," December 25, 1859

On Christmas Day in 1859, the liberal newspaper *Lloyd's Weekly* published an unsigned editorial about Brown that dwells on the story of Christ's death rather than his birth, and describes a recent Passion Play in America in which Governor Wise was Pilate at Brown's crucifixion. More than most British responses, the newspaper also focuses on the people at the center of the Brown story: slaves. *Lloyd's* was an illustrated newspaper based in London. Edward Lloyd launched the publication in 1842, and it had achieved a circulation of over 100,000 by 1859. William Blanchard Jerrold took over as editor in 1857 and edited the newspaper until his death in 1884. During the American Civil War, the newspaper strongly supported the North.

The slavery question is working its way. That turmoil, to put down which old Captain John Brown was selected as an awful example, will not be forgotten by slaveowners or free-soilers. The accounts which have reached us of the execution of the old man on the 2nd of December, at Charlestown, Virginia, represent the people of the United States in no dignified position. The free-soilers dare the Virginians to execute their prisoner; the Virginians reply by military precautions against a rescue. Interference by force is threatened, but none is offered; and the poor old man is executed. Bells toll for him where the abolitionists are strong, and hundreds of orators loosen their tongues to denounce the governor of Virginia as a murderer, or to liken President Buchanan to Herod. Massachusetts is conspicuous for its talking abolitionists. It would appear that Brown owed his death to the inconsiderate zeal of his friends. When they threatened the Governor Wise, Governor Wise became determined to carry out Brown's sentence. They who had threatened confined their resistance to inflammatory harangues. Governor Wise was declared to be worse then Pontius Pilot.

It was unquestionably a brutal spirit of party vengeance that urged the Virginians to hang the old man. The scene was unworthy, in every particular, of a civilised and free nation. It has its use, however.

The remembrance of it will burn in the hearts of the abolitionists. It will be remembered also by the negroes; and, it is to be feared, it will rankle in their hearts till the day of retribution has been brought about.

American slavery is doomed; its death is a question only of years, just as years ago the slavery in which the pope held the Italians was doomed. We are told that Luther rebuked the devil by throwing inkstands at him.[27] Inkstands rebuke slaveowners, as they have long since rebuked papal tyrants and slaveowners of men's minds.

This slave outbreak in America, then, is one of the blind motions that foretell the higher life of a thought or purpose. The slave must accomplish his freedom sooner or later. When the lamp of knowledge has opened his eyes and has discovered to him his vileness as the chattels of a master; when he hears that his slavery is held by all civilised nations to be a broad black blot upon the stars and stripes—he will bestir himself, with the help of his white friends—and will plot and tempt peril upon peril—nor rest till he is free as the air he breathes.

Let old Brown then be a martyr, if his elevation to the dignity of martyrdom can intensify the hatred of honest men, for the human baseness that can buy and sell these poor dusky images of their Maker.

Source: Lloyd's Weekly Newspaper [London, England], December 25, 1859.

Caledonian Mercury and Daily Express, "A New Year's Reverie," January 2, 1860

A week after *Lloyd's Weekly* marked Christmas with an editorial about the martyr Brown, a Scottish newspaper marked the New Year with a tribute to Brown the "doer." Describing all the problems and promises that await in the New Year, the editorial offers Brown's approach of earnestness and action as the solution. Established in 1720 as the *Caledonian Mercury*, the newspaper became the *Caledonian Mercury and Daily Express* for a brief period between August 1859 and February 1860, then returned to its original name. Based in Edinburgh, it espoused Whig politics and championed numerous social reforms during the 1850s. It supported the North throughout the American Civil War. Like Aberdeen and Glasgow, Edinburgh had hosted American abolitionists and had an active Ladies Emancipation Society devoted to agitating for the abolition of slavery in the United States.

Scarce an hour ago the old year died and, if there be truth in proverbs, died happily—for blessed is the corpse the rain rains on; and yet it would seem it was well he had gone, for there was no public tear dropped for him. So peaceful was he in his last moments, that no one would believe he was dead until those hirelings the clocks and bells noisily announced the fact. How was the New Year welcomed? With the very faintest of cheers! And the growing tendency towards silence in this matter of gratulation augurs well for the future. It is very easy to vote oneself a prophet—a very simple thing to imagine awful scenes, and shudder at our own imaginings; but since plain truth will enter where gaudy fiction would be too genteel for reception, let the death moment of the dead year be faithfully recorded. It died as above mentioned—quietly. A Wendell Phillips gazing on the serene countenance of a dead John Brown prophesied a calm future for America;[28] and this morning the comparative silence that ruled the open ways and by-ways of Edinburgh prophecy that better times, born of better thoughts, will blossom in the days to come. Alas! while the minutes marched on to the music of silence, a stream darker than the fabled Phlegeton was flowing through the city,[29] a stream whose sources were among the upland heights of innocence, around whose leaping rivulets pure soul girlhood played—spotless girlhood, earth's nearest realisation of an angel. Alas! now the laughing child! now the blaspheming woman! Woman!! girlhood! womanhood! purity!—all obliterated! Sad as this is, something there was still sadder. Fatherless, motherless, homeless children, cowering in blind alleys and in sheltering doorways. What an effort for the mind to go back two thousand years and hear upon the green slopes of Galilee the "Suffer little children to come unto me, for of such is the Kingdom of Heaven!"[30] Children these are not; they are but a little higher than the brutes, in that they have the capability of crime. Shall these things ever be so? Wait and hope is the watchword of the easy man; work and hope of the reformer. Many promises have been given to this New Year. The pen that records its death will also tell how they have been kept. Let individual effort be unceasing; associated philanthropy is too often like the munificence that hails the progress of king, in which the congratulation is swallowed up in the selfish display of splendour. Talkers there are enough; doers, not a few: but the want of the present world is earnestness; those who could make it better must learn their mission from the self-abnegation of John Howard,[31] the devotion of John Brown.

Source: Caledonian Mercury and Daily Express [Edinburgh, Scotland], January 2, 1860.

Anti-Slavery Reporter, "The Harper's Ferry Tragedy," January 2, 1860

Initially abolitionists in Britain tried to distance themselves from Brown's raid. The British had an investment in the image of Anglo-Saxon civilization, including compromise instead of revolution, and the British abolitionist movement celebrated its own success in ending slavery through peaceful moral suasion instead of insurrection. This made it harder for British abolitionists to forgive Brown's violent methods than for American nonresistant abolitionists, who had a national history and mythology of righteous violence and frontier justice, to do so. Gradually, however, British abolitionist sentiment did warm toward Brown—a conversion aided by Frederick Douglass, whose lectures throughout Britain between November 1859 and March 1860 depicted Brown as a patriot and a martyr. The organ of the British Anti-Slavery Society, the *Anti-Slavery Reporter,* was still condemning Brown's violence in January 1860, although it acknowledges his high moral purpose and suggests that his attempt may help achieve emancipation.

On the 2nd of last month, Captain Brown, the originator of what has been styled the Harper's Ferry Insurrection, expiated on the scaffold the offence against the laws of his country, of which, after a hurried and by no means decorously-conducted trial, he has been found guilty. Whatever may be thought of his attempt, the immediate object of which seems to have been the liberation of a large number of slaves, and their transference across the border, and how differently soever men will pronounce judgment on the means he employed for its accomplishment, there are few who read the extracts we have collated from various sources, and reprinted in another column, but will feel a deep sympathy for him, and for his bereaved family. Committed as we are to the broad principle which holds human life to be sacred, and war to be contrary to the teachings of the Holy Scriptures, his attempt, judged by that standard of the highest morality must be pronounced unjustifiable. At the same time, his earnestness, his single-mindedness, his great moral courage, his sufferings, and the noble object he sought to attain, recommend him to universal sympathy; while no one can read his affecting letters to his family and his friends, without feeling convinced that the old man—misguided though he may have been—was actuated by the highest of moral purposes, was a religious man, and was one of that class who figure as heroes in the history of nations. It cannot be but such an event will form a memorable era in the chain of circumstances which are gradually diverting public opinion in America, from mere party discussions, to a series consideration of the manner in which the great impending trouble is to be met, of dealing definitely with the question of abolition, for a trouble it certainly will prove, and the day when it must be dealt with is not far distant. The American Abolitionists may, indeed, be divided, and may hold such a difference of opinion on side issues, as to render concerted action impossible. But each section must, and does, in its own particular field, accomplish a work, by stimulating public attention to the manifest evils of Slavery. Yet, after all, such events as the recent Harper's Ferry tragedy are the most potent elements in the moving of the nation, for they tend to shew that slave-property is the most unsafe of investments, and that a crisis which shall depreciate its value, will affect the interests of the entire community.

It may be a worldly view to take of this great question. It is, nevertheless, one which must be entertained, in conjunction with that of the inherent immorality of slaveholding, for it must be borne in mind that many are most sensitive to the pecuniary aspects of the question of abolition, who are utterly insensible to the moral arguments in its favour. To such as these, Captain Brown's attempt will speak a most eloquent discourse. Already the slaveholders of the South are taking the alarm, and many Virginian families are contemplating a removal to another land, where they may live without fear. It may be, that in time to come, the attempt of John Brown will be found to have been one of the great events on which turned the consummation of negro freedom in America.

Source: Anti-Slavery Reporter [London, England], January 2, 1860, 23.

Argus, "A Revolt in America," January 10, 1860

Australians were familiar with the rhetoric and ideas of the American abolitionist movement. Copies of abolitionist newspapers, including the *North Star,* were sold in Australia, and Lincoln's death prompted public meetings and memorial services that focused on his role in emancipation. News of Brown's raid reached reach Australia in January 1860, and the *Argus,* a conservative daily newspaper based in Melbourne and established in 1846, offered a detailed account of the raid based on American newspaper reports from October 1859. But it dismisses the whole event as the desperate efforts of a few individuals.

The American papers are filled with accounts of the insurrectionary movement at Harper's Ferry in Virginia. It does not appear, however, to have been of so serious a character as was imagined, and briefly summed up as the vain attempt of a few misguided but desperate men, to effect a revolution in the social state of the Union. The principal originator of the whole proceeding appears to have been Captain John Brown, formerly a violent opposer of slavery in Southern Kansas. . . .

It appeared that Brown's expectation of slaves rushing to join him was entirely disappointed. It is believed that the four who were with him were there unwillingly. The citizens imprisoned by the insurrectionists all testified to their lenient treatment. They were neither tied nor insulted, and, beyond the outrage of restricting their liberty, were not ill-used. Captain Brown was also courteous to them, and at all times assured them that they should not be injured. He explained his purpose to them, and whilst he had them in confinement made no abolition speech to them. Colonel Washington speaks of him as a man of extraordinary nerve. He never blanched during the assault, though he admitted in the night that escape was impossible, and that he would have to die. During the previous night he spoke freely with Colonel Washington and referred to his two sons. He said he has lost one in Kansas, and two here: he had no pressed them to join him in the expedition, but did not regret their loss—they had died in a glorious cause.

Source: Argus [Melbourne, Australia], January 10, 1860.

Karl Marx, "To Friedrich Engels,"
January 11, 1860

The economist and political theorist Karl Marx (1818–1883) wrote to Friedrich Engels about Brown from his home in London. Engels was based in Manchester, England. The letter describes Brown's death as the beginning of a full-scale antislavery movement. Engels's reply, two weeks later, expressed agreement that Brown's raid would bear fruit. Born in Prussia, Marx lived in England from 1849 until his death. He wrote articles for the antislavery *New York Tribune* in the 1850s. Elsewhere he critiqued slavery as an element of capitalism and argued that it prevented an independent workers' movement, famously declaring: "Labor cannot emancipate itself in the white skin where in the black it is branded." In October 1862 he emphasized the revolutionary nature of the Emancipation Proclamation. Writing from Vienna, he called it "the most important document of American history since the founding of the Union, a document that breaks away from the old American Constitution," and concluded: "Never yet has the New World scored a greater victory than in this instance, when ordinary people of goodwill can carry out tasks which the Old World would have to have a hero to accomplish." Two years later he wrote to Lincoln, calling him a "single-minded son of the working class," his reelection a "triumphant war cry of . . . Death to Slavery," and the Civil War an antislavery battle that would liberate the working classes.

As I see it, the most significant thing happening in the world today is the slave movement—on the one hand in America, initiated by the death of Brown, and on the other hand in Russia. . . . A "social" movement has been started both in the West and in the East. Along with the imminent breakdown in Central Europe, this promises great things.

I have just seen in the *Tribune* that there has been another slave rebellion in Missouri, which was repressed, needless to say.[32] But the signal has now been given.[33]

Source: Der Briefwechsel zwischen Friedrich Engels und Karl Marx: 1844 bis 1883, Vol. 2 (Stuttgart: J. H. W. Dietz, 1913), 367.

Feuille du Commerce, "John Brown," January 21, 1860

In the Haitian capital, Port-au-Prince, flags flew at half-mast on the day of Brown's execution. Then on January 20, 1860, three days of mourning began with a mass and memorial service for Brown in the Port-au-Prince cathedral. Public officials were among the huge crowd, and Brown's name was displayed in gold on a large black cloth. The speeches described Brown as a Christian martyr to abolition, his heroic actions as a signal that slavery must be abolished, and his death as an affirmation of human brotherhood between black and white. A main boulevard in Port-au-Prince was eventually named for Brown. Ceremonies and tributes took place in several other Haitian cities as well, and Haitians collected thousands of dollars for Brown's family. The Haitian French-language newspapers, including *Le Progrès* and *Feuille du Commerce,* were filled with commentary during the days and weeks following the commemorations. *Le Progrès* published a letter from John Brown, Jr., to Haitian president Fabre Geffrard which thanked Geffrard and the Haitian citizens for their support, paid tribute to Toussaint-Louverture, a leader of the Haitian revolution, and praised the fact of emancipation in Haiti. *Feuille du Commerce,* a four-page newspaper based in Port-au-Prince and edited by Joseph Courtois, printed Victor Hugo's famous letter of December 2, a public letter to Hugo from several citizens thanking him for that public letter and describing Brown as a "sublime figure of Christ," and the lyrics to a song about the "martyr" and "defender of our race" John Brown. It also published the editorial below.

The cause of the abolition of slavery has just counted another martyr. This fact, however indifferent it may be to others, cannot be so to us, descendants as we are of the persecuted race of Africa: this event must weigh upon our hearts as a public calamity. John Brown, with his noble co-workers, has been sent to an ignominious death on the gallows! And this in a country where liberty appears to have its grandest aspiration, where nothing is said or done but in the name of liberty; it is in this country, it is in the United States, in fact, that this man who demanded liberty for an unjustly oppressed and enslaved race, is shamefully dragged to the scaffold. John Brown and his friends perhaps too quickly abandoned themselves to despair. But shall we therefore say that the hour of emancipation for our unhappy brethren is not yet come? However it may be, the blood of John Brown guarantees that it is at hand. Despite all the demonstrations of interest on behalf of the condemned; despite the eloquent plea that civilization and the nineteenth century put into the sublime mouth of the guest of Jersey,[34] the martyrdom was performed. Reassure yourselves, ye slaves; nothing is lost—liberty is immortal. New Ogés and Chavannes,[35] Brown and his companions have sown this slave land with their glorious blood, and doubt not that consequently avengers will arise.[36]

Source: Feuille du Commerce [Port-au-Prince, Haiti], January 21, 1860.

Joseph Déjacque, "To Pierre Vésinier," February 20, 1861

The French anarcho-communist Joseph Déjacque (1821–1864) wrote to his fellow radical Pierre Vésinier about Brown in February 1861. Déjacque had been living in the United States since 1853, first in New Orleans and then in New York. Since June 1858 he had published a French-language newspaper in New York called *Le Libertaire: Journal du Mouvement Social,* the first anarcho-communist journal published in the States. Déjacque published twenty-seven issues of the newspaper, the last on February 4, 1861. He wrote this letter about Brown soon after the newspaper folded. It applies Napoleon's supposed description of Britain as a "nation of shopkeepers" to the United States, declaring that there are very few real revolutionaries in America. It also expresses frustration at Brown's religiosity and tries to look past his seemingly backward belief in God. Déjacque returned to France a few months later, once the Civil War began. Vésinier went on to publish the book *The Martyr to Black Freedom or John Brown, the Christ of Blacks* in 1864.

The events occurring here show you how far this country is from being an abode of liberty. As on the old continent, there exist revolutionary elements, but in a latent and scattered state. Men of a militant libertarianism are a tiny minority. John Brown, one of these courageous exceptions was, as you know, hung to the applause of the slave owners and, what is even sadder, denied by the vast majority of the party that passes for abolitionist. The revolutionary socialist movement will not rise up from here; it is Europe that will set America in motion. Only then will it leave behind its political and religious cretinism and be initiated in the Social Science. America is literally a nation of grocers, or retail and wholesale shopkeepers who have only one thing in their heads and hearts: commerce, exploitation. Political faith, like religious faith, is nothing but merchandise they speculate in for the benefit of their mercantile interests. . . .

John Brown was one of those natures that is highly developed as concerns sentiments, but whose knowledge was more limited. If the civilized newspapers are to be believed (and all of them in America are, belonging to one tendency or another) he still believed in God in heaven and a constitution on earth. His God and his constitution: he certainly wanted them the best possible, but the truth is that he hadn't gone beyond this. After his sentencing and the ignoble treatment that preceded and pursued him, he was Christian enough to pardon his assassins and to thank them for their brutal offenses, which he had the magnanimity or the feebleness of spirit to qualify as "good proceedings."[37] Doubtless some cowardly and traitorous friend had whispered these deplorable words to him, for in every other circumstance, from the first sessions of the trial up to the trap door of the scaffold, he showed himself to be firm and intelligent, worthy of his past and the great cause for which he sacrificed himself. If you write about him be sure to explain this small moment of straying by the too great goodness of his heart, by his evangelical kindness. Don't forget that it was after his condemnation and by pure charity or courtesy that he expressed himself in this way. Before this he had only spoken to his inquisitors as if they were the enemy, defeated but indomitable and proud before his cowardly and bloody conquerors. Finally, that if in doing this he committed a sin, it was through excess and not lack of courage. There are enough grand and noble ideas in this glorious martyr to bring out so that this holdover of Christianity won't cast a shadow on his portrait and obscure the light. The act of the slave mother and her children accompanying him as confessor is one of those touching originalities that testify to a great and kind heart and to a free and intelligent mind. His impassive and valiant firmness at the hour of death, on the way to and at the place of execution, attest to all that was holy and generous in the blood that flowed in the veins of this robust old man; everything there spoke of strength, of convictions in the breast and skull of that audacious humanitarian.[38]

Source: Anarchist-Communist Archive, with translation by Mitchell Abidor. Published in French as "Une Lettre de Joseph Déjacque," *Bulletin of the International Institute of Social History* 6, no. 1 (1951): 16–32 (19–20, 23).

William Howard Russell, "Diary,"
April 20 and August 17, 1861

The Irish journalist William Howard Russell (1820–1907) spent the first few months of the Civil War touring the Confederate states. He arrived in New York in March 1861 and then traveled to Washington, where he met President Lincoln, and on to Charleston, Savannah, Montgomery, and New Orleans. He witnessed a slave auction, visited plantations, and met Jefferson Davis. Russell had been a journalist with the London *Times* since 1843 and had become one of the first modern war correspondents when he covered the Crimean War of 1853–1856. Now he sent dispatches to the *Times* about the Confederacy and the American Civil War. Although many Irish journalists championed the South's right to self-determination, Russell was unsympathetic to secession. He was also opposed to slavery. Nonetheless, his reports—which were published within a month of their dispatch—were largely objective. During his tour as a special correspondent for the *Times*, he recorded further impressions in a diary. Several entries focus on Brown. They imagine Brown's reaction to the war, remember his raid as the war's first exchange of fire, and observe that he continues to divide Northern and Southern opinion.

April 20th. The Secessionists are in great delight with Governor Letcher's proclamation, calling out troops and volunteers,[39] and it is hinted that Washington will be attacked, and the nest of Black Republican vermin which haunt the capital, driven out. Agents are to be at once despatched to get up a navy, and every effort made to carry out the policy indicated in Jeff Davis's issue of letters of marque and reprisal.[40] Norfolk harbor is blocked up to prevent the United States ships getting away; and at the same time we hear that the United States officer commanding at the arsenal of Harper's Ferry has retired into Pennsylvania, after destroying the place by fire.[41] How "old John Brown" would have wondered and rejoiced, had he lived a few months longer!

August 17th. I took the train, at Ellicott's Mills, and went to Harper's Ferry. There is no one spot, in the history of this extraordinary war, which can be well more conspicuous. Had it nothing more to recommend it than the scenery, it might well command a visit from the tourist; but as the scene of old John Brown's raid upon the Federal arsenal, of that first passage of arms between the Abolitionists and the Slave Conservatives, which has developed this great contest; above all, as the spot where important military demonstrations have been made on both sides, and will necessarily occur hereafter, this place, which probably derives its name from some wretched old boatman, will be renowned forever in the annals of the Civil War of 1861. . . .

Looking up and down the river the scenery is picturesque, though it is by no means entitled to the extraordinary praises which American tourists lavish upon it. Probably old John Brown cared little for the wild magic of streamlet or rill, or for the blended charm of vale and woodland. When he made his attack on the arsenal now in ruins, he probably thought a valley was as high as a hill, and that there was no necessity for water running downwards—assuredly he saw as little of the actual heights and depths around him when he ran across the Potomac to revolutionize Virginia. He has left behind him millions either as clear-sighted or as blind as himself. In New England parlors a statuette of John Brown may be found as a pendant to the likeness of our Saviour. In Virginia his name is the synonym of all that is base, bloody, and cruel.

Harper's Ferry at present, for all practical purposes, may be considered as Confederate property. The few Union inhabitants remain in their houses, but many of the Government workmen and most of the inhabitants have gone off South. For strategical purposes its possession would be most important to a force desiring to operate on Maryland from Virginia.

Source: William Howard Russell, *My Diary North and South* (Boston: T. O. H. P. Burnham, 1863), 123–124, 495–497.

J. M. Ludlow, "A Year of the Slavery Question in the United States (1859–60)," December 1862

John Malcolm Ludlow (1821–1911) responded to Brown as a fellow Christian. Ludlow was a co-founder of the Working Man's College and a leader of the Christian Socialists, an English group that believed the church should address the grievances of the working class and promoted profit-sharing as the route to a just, Christian society. In his article for *Good Words*, a Christian illustrated magazine published in London from 1860 to 1906 and edited by Norman Macleod, Ludlow represents Brown's raid as a beautiful, unselfish act. He also reminds readers that Brown considered slavery itself a state of war and the raid a defensive action.

The anti-slavery conspiracy, in the year 1859–60, looked at in a legal point of view—besides being a legal offence in itself, and involving other legal offences of minor character—had for results, in certain cases, the offences of (legal) robbery, burglary, murder, and treason. What made the danger of this organized conspiracy greatest was, that it took its origin mainly, not in self-interest, but in a moral principle. There is no evidence, for the most part not even a probability, that in any of the instances quoted the violators of the law sought any personal advantage from what they did. The act of the "Radical Abolitionists," with their non-resistance principles, in settling here and there in Kentucky, was one of sheer self-sacrifice. As to John Brown's attempt, it is impossible to conceive of anything more utterly unselfish. Set aside the fact of the undertaking being against law, and the whole compass of history contains nothing more beautiful than the spirit which breathes throughout it. . . .

Brown's comrades, white or coloured, showed the same spirit as himself. "If I am dying for freedom," said Copeland (a coloured man), "I could not die for a better cause. I had rather die than be a slave."[42] Cooke, a white man, was prepared to die in such a cause, and thought he had done nothing to regret, so far as principle was concerned. "If I had 10,000 lives," wrote Hazlett, another white, the day before his death, "I would willingly lay them all down for the same cause. My death will do more good than if I had lived."[43]

After the first conviction in the trials for the Harper's Ferry attempt, "barns, stacks, and other property to a large amount, belonging to several of the jurors," were burnt.[44] Nearly 3000 soldiers, cannon loaded with grape-shot, the railroad taken possession of for military purposes, a threat of martial law, such were some of the preparations which were deemed requisite for the day of John Brown's execution. An actual panic prevailed indeed far and wide at the South.

We have now seen what a state of things had been produced by slavery at the North. There is only one word to describe it—that which is used in John Brown's provisional constitution—war. Slavery he there declared to be a "most barbarous and unprovoked war, by one portion of the citizens against another, the only conditions of which are perpetual imprisonment and servitude, or absolute extermination."[45] Whether the term be correctly applied by them to slavery or not, there can be no doubt that it was in a war against it that the Abolitionists were engaged, and that by the laws of war John Brown and his companions alone deemed themselves bound, and alone sought to be justified. I repeat it, in 1859–60, abolitionism meant already, in the minds of many at least of its adherents, civil war.

Source: Good Words [London, England], December 1862, 177–184 (178–179).

Louis Ratisbonne, "John Brown," February 1863

After viewing Victor Hugo's engraved drawing of Brown's hanging body, the French author and translator Louis Ratisbonne (1827–1900) responded with a French-language poem that imagines Brown's death as a bell tolling for liberty. It appeared in a Parisian journal early in 1863. While the poem is not as hostile to religion and spirituality as Joseph Déjacque's letter of 1861, it does introduce doubt as to God's presence at Brown's execution ("if . . . your breath is near"), suggests that Brown is overwhelmed by the trappings of religion, and declares that he died alone, surrounded by "nothing but darkness." Here Ratisbonne develops the European tendency to distance Brown from biblical language and imagery. Unlike American abolitionists and other North American sympathizers, many of whom declared Brown a martyr and saint, European observers acknowledged Brown's religious persona but focused on his role as a universal symbol of liberty instead.

He is there, tall and straight, motionless and immutable,
Like the truth that he affirms and believes.
He is alone, protesting beneath the cross that overwhelms him,
Black as adversity, fixed as right.

Around him, night! on the ruthless earth
There is nothing but darkness, mists, vapors, fear!
And the eye can see nothing but that man on his rope,
Like a bellman at the top of a belfry.

One ray of light, one, and the night is afraid,
Illuminate the gallows like a beacon
And the brow of a martyr dead for humanity.

Oh God! if this is your light and your breath is near,
Strike that clapper, and at last sound the bell
Of right, of justice, and liberty![46]

Source: Revue Germanique et Française [Paris, France] 24, no. 3 (February 1863): 567.

Giuseppe Garibaldi, "To President Lincoln," August 6, 1863

As European observers responded to Brown, they also focused on another military figure, Giuseppe Garibaldi (1807–1882). The Second Italian War of Independence had begun in 1859, and Garibaldi was appointed major general. In 1860 he captured Sicily and Naples, intending to unite the Italian peninsula under the king of Piedmont-Sardinia, Victor Emmanuel II. The new kingdom of Italy was proclaimed in 1861, by which time Garibaldi had attained international fame and popularity as a hero of Italian unification. That same year Lincoln offered Garibaldi a major general's commission. But Garibaldi insisted that first he must be empowered to end slavery. Two years later, after the Emancipation Proclamation, he wrote a letter to Lincoln that celebrates him as an emancipator and an heir of Brown. There is no record of Lincoln's reply.

Caprera, Italy, August 6, 1863

To Abraham Lincoln, Emancipator of the Slaves in the American Republic.

If during the peril of your colossal struggle, our voices may mix, o Lincoln, permit us, the free Sons of Columbus, convey a message of greeting and of admiration for the great work you have begun.

Heir of the aspirations of Christ and of Brown, posterity will call you the Emancipator; a title to be envied more than any crown or human treasure.

An entire race of human beings, yoked by self-interest to the collar of slavery, is, by your doing and at the price of the noblest American lives, restored to the dignity of manhood, to civilization, and to love.

America, teacher of liberty to our forefathers, now opens another solemn era of human progress, and while her tremendous courage amazes the world, we sadly reflect how this old Europe, which also can boast a grand cause of human liberty, has not found mind or heart to equal her.

While the epicurean defenders of tyranny chant the bacchic ode which celebrates the decay of freedom, let the free religiously celebrate slavery's defeat —parallel mysteries of history!—the plunder of Mexico[47] and the proclamation of Lincoln!

Greetings to you Abraham Lincoln, great pilot of freedom; greetings to all who for two years have fought and bled around your regenerating standard— greetings to you, the redeemed offspring of Ham. The free men of Italy welcome the glorious rupture of your chains.

The Italian Liberals

G. Garibaldi

M. Garibaldi

N. Garibaldi[48]

Source: Giuseppe Garibaldi, *Scritti Politici e Militari,* ed. Domenico Ciàmpoli (Rome: E. Voghera, 1907), 330.

W. T. Malleson and Washington Wilks, "Speeches to the Emancipation Society," December 2, 1863

A few months after Garibaldi described Lincoln as part of Brown's legacy, a British supporter of Garibaldi's cause compared the Italian himself to Brown. William Malleson was a London-based reformer who supported American abolition, served as treasurer of the London Emancipation Society, campaigned for women's suffrage, and crusaded against prostitution. He was a close friend and supporter of Giuseppe Mazzini, an Italian patriot and Garibaldi's comrade in arms. Speaking at a public meeting on December 2, 1863, held by the Emancipation Society to mark the fourth anniversary of Brown's death, Malleson called Brown a martyr of black freedom who could have been America's Garibaldi. The speech also points out the historical coincidence of the French coup d'état of 1851 (which eventually ended the French National Assembly and reestablished the French Empire) taking place on the same date as Brown's death. Malleson proclaims that Brown's spirit leads the Union Army and then he returns, like many American commentators, to the fictional story of Brown kissing the slave child on the way to the gallows. Other speakers at the society's meeting that night were the black American abolitionist and former slave J. Sella Martin, the American abolitionist Moncure Conway, and Washington Wilks (1825–1864), a journalist with the left-wing *London Morning Star* newspaper. In his address, Wilks draws parallels between Brown and other historic figures. But most of his speech focuses on the American Civil War—what he calls the "second Revolution." This focus on Union achievements in the war reflected the Emancipation Society's agenda. The British abolitionists George Thompson and F. W. Chesson founded the organization as the London Emancipation Committee in June 1859. Its purpose was to promote the American abolitionist cause. But after Lincoln's preliminary Emancipation Proclamation of September 22, 1862, the group's name and goal changed: now it existed to support the Union and challenge Confederate sympathies in Britain.

W. T. Malleson

Ladies and Gentlemen, this is no ordinary public meeting; we are met tonight upon a solemn occasion. This is the 2nd of December, a date which I think no Englishman will ever be able to remember without a shudder. Twelve years ago tonight, the great French nation was garroted in its sleep, and its liberty was filched from it; liberty which to this day it has not been able to recover.[49] Still we are not assembled here to-night to mourn over the death of French liberty, but rather to celebrate a contrast, to commemorate the death of an individual from whose grave has arisen—is now arising—the liberty of a race. *(Cheers)*. Four years ago to-day, John Brown was executed; and he, who might have been the Garibaldi of America, became her first and greatest martyr— the martyr of negro freedom. *(Hear, hear)*. The spirit that rises from his grave inspired at first only a few earnest men; but, constantly widening in its influence, has at length leavened great masses, and now leads mighty armies in this tremendous war, which has at last avowedly become a war of emancipation. Well, indeed, may the negro sing:

> John Brown's body lies a moldering in the grave,
> But his soul is marching on! *(Applause)*.

There are two facts in John Brown's history which seem to me supremely touching and sublime. The first is his death. His life had long been devoted to the freedom of the slave, to the succor of the oppressed; but when the moment came for him to lay down his life for his cause, with what a sublime cheerfulness and constancy he completed his sacrifice of self. The other is a story you should all know. On his way to the scaffold, he saw a little negro girl gazing at him with wondering face, and he stopped, and, stooping down, kissed and blessed her. To him the child was a stranger, but she was the representative of that down-trodden race whom he had striven to raise. It was the last kiss he ever pressed upon human lips, and then, comforted and strengthened, he went on to die. *(Hear, hear)*. That death and that kiss, I have been told and I gladly believe, pierced the conscience of many a Northern American. *(Applause)*. For the conscience of the North had been hard in this matter; corrupted by connivance at slavery in the South, and corrupted by sharing its profits, the North had joined in wronging the negro; and as men so often come to hate those whom they injure, so, by degrees, multitudes at the North had come to despise and loathe men according to the colour of their skins.

I say, I am told and I believe, that by his death and by that last kiss, John Brown began a revolution in that unworthy antipathy towards the negro; a revolution which this war has carried immensely forward, so that now those who see with the clear eye of faith may discern the day rapidly approaching, when not only no chain shall be on any hand on the wide continent of America, but when, in all that country, black man and white shall stand side by side, not only as political equals, but as acknowledged brothers. *(Loud applause).*

Washington Wilks

We are engaged tonight in an act of religious solemnity, an act of hero-worship, perhaps, but also of homage to Him who is the inspiration of all wisdom and strength. Of these John Brown was very full. He was "wise, as understanding the times in which he lived,"[50] and as perceiving, with true and deep insight, the rights and duties of men in all times. He had grasped, as by instinct or by revelation, that grand principle which the loftiest of living philosophers has expounded, that Liberty is the complement of human right and justice; that no man is entitled to more, and no man to less. *(Cheers.)* He perceived, also, that to redress the deficiencies and excesses of American liberty, to take from the white man liberty of oppression and give to the negro the liberty of manhood, was the particular necessity of his time. To this work he gave himself, without question or reserve, even to the death. The orator of this evening has shown us, with pathetic and stirring eloquence, how complete was the sacrifice, how rich have been its fruits. *(Hear, hear.)* Himself a Virginian,[51] though now of New England—a significant migration—he shows us how all free-hearted Americans, South as well as North, are coming round to honour John Brown as the hero of the second Revolution. *(Applause.)* Not by accident, sir, but by most appropriate destination, did the sword of Washington fall into his hand. No doubt he was a rebel—though not against the State of Virginia, against the Federal authority. But the conservatism of Europe had not then begun to patronise rebellion. It has since pronounced benediction on treason, provided only it be wrought against a republic. Happily, that is a treason which does not prosper. It is the "blighted offspring of a cursed root."[52] It has been crushed out, or starved out, through more than half the territory which it claimed to cover. The Slave power claimed every Slave State in the Union, and threatened, if its claim were resisted, to extend it to Plymouth Rock and to Lake Erie. The latest book on secession, that of Mr. McHenry, claims Pennsylvania as a natural member of the Confederacy.[53] Gettysburg and the ballot-box have settled that claim. *(Cheers.)* Maryland, Kentucky, and Missouri, are not only loyal States but are fast becoming free States. Tennessee on the one side, Mississippi and Arkansas on the other, are well nigh recovered both from rebellion and slavery. Louisiana is almost entirely reconquered to freedom. Now the Northern levies confront the soldiers of France on the Rio Grande.[54] Thus, John Brown's soul marches on to victory. Though he was a rebel to the constitution, he was loyal to the principles which the republic embodies—the sovereignty of the people. (Cheers.) That is the principle for which our own Elliot and Cromwell contended[55]—the principle on which the founders of New England built their sacred commonwealth,—the principle which successive revolutions have asserted—the principle which Mazzini, and Kossuth, and Garibaldi,[56] maintain by pen, and tongue, and sword—the principle of which our Cobden and Bright are the champions[57]—the principle which the slaveholders rebellion has traitorously assailed, but which, I do believe, is about to receive its most splendid vindication in the victory of the Great Republic.

Source: *The Martyrdom of John Brown* (London: Emancipation Society, 1864), 3–4, 15–16.

John Stuart Mill, *Autobiography*, 1873

Looking back on Brown's raid, the English philosopher and economic theorist John Stuart Mill (1806–1873) remembered him as a martyr and compared him to Thomas More, who was executed for treason by Henry VIII of England in 1535 and later canonized. Mill was one of England's leading public intellectuals. He advocated for women's rights, including suffrage, and for the end of slavery. In 1850 he wrote a rebuttal to Thomas Carlyle's defense of slavery, "Occasional Discourse on the Negro Question." Mill's "The Negro Question" declared that the institution was inherently inhumane. Mill also explained as early as February 1862 that the American Civil War was about slavery. He made this point in an article for the February issue of the London-based *Fraser's Magazine*, which was excerpted in the *New York Times*.

Having been a deeply interested observer of the slavery quarrel in America, during the many years that preceded the open breach, I knew that it was in all its stages an aggressive enterprise of the slave-owners to extend the territory of slavery; under the combined influences of pecuniary interest, domineering temper, and the fanaticism of a class for its class privileges, influences so fully and powerfully depicted in the admirable work of my friend Professor Cairnes, "The Slave Power."[58] Their success, if they succeeded, would be a victory of the powers of evil which would give courage to the enemies of progress and damp the spirits of its friends all over the civilized world, while it would create a formidable military power, grounded on the worst and most anti-social form of the tyranny of men over men, and, by destroying for a long time the prestige of the great democratic republic, would give to all the privileged classes of Europe a false confidence, probably only to be extinguished in blood. On the other hand, if the spirit of the North was sufficiently roused to carry the war to a successful termination, and if that termination did not come too soon and too easily, I foresaw, from the laws of human nature, and the experience of revolutions, that when it did come it would in all probability be thorough: that the bulk of the Northern population, whose conscience had as yet been awakened only to the point of resisting the further extension of slavery, but whose fidelity to the Constitution of the United States made them disapprove of any attempt by the Federal Government to interfere with slavery in the States where it already existed, would acquire feelings of another kind when the Constitution had been shaken off by armed rebellion, would determine to have done for ever with the accursed thing, and would join their banner with that of the noble body of Abolitionists, of whom Garrison was the courageous and single-minded apostle, Wendell Phillips the eloquent orator, and John Brown the voluntary martyr. (The saying of this true hero, after his capture, that he was worth more for hanging than for any other purpose, reminds one, by its combination of wit, wisdom, and self-devotion, of Sir Thomas More.) Then, too, the whole mind of the United States would be let loose from its bonds, no longer corrupted by the supposed necessity of apologizing to foreigners for the most flagrant of all possible violations of the free principles of their Constitution; while the tendency of a fixed state of society to stereotype a set of national opinions would be at least temporarily checked, and the national mind would become more open to the recognition of whatever was bad in either the institutions or the customs of the people. These hopes, so far as related to slavery, have been completely, and in other respects are in course of being progressively realized.

Source: John Stuart Mill, *Autobiography* (London: Longmans, 1873), 266–268.

Hermann von Holst, "John Brown," 1878

In 1878 the historian and Republican sympathizer Hermann von Holst (1841–1904) published a long essay about Brown. After detailing the history of slavery and the movement against slavery since 1789, the essay narrates Brown's biography, the events in Kansas, the Harpers Ferry raid, and the details of Brown's trial and executio. In the excerpts below, Holst describes Brown's character, focusing on his religious convictions. The essay was translated into English and published in the United States in book form in 1888. The introduction to the book by Frank Preston Stearns (son of George and Mary Stearns, abolitionists and Brown supporters) praises Holst's portrait of Brown as "no splendid Italian ideal, but rather a realistic German wood-cut." Holst was born in Germany. He lived in the United States between 1867 and 1872, worked as a professor of history in German universities until 1892, and then returned to the United States as head of the history department at the University of Chicago. He left for Germany again in 1900. His most important work, the eight-volume *Constitutional and Political History of the United States* (1876–1892), focuses on the 1850s and is written from an antislavery point of view.

If there ever was a sect of Christianity who adopted equally the gospel of love of the New Testament and the stern severity of the Old Testament spirit in all its terrible grandeur, the Puritans were that sect; and if ever a Puritan exemplified the welding together of these opposite principles in his whole life, and in each and every act, John Brown was that Puritan. He was the man of the old covenant, who waited quietly and patiently to gird about his loins "the sword of Gideon"[59] till a sign from God gave the order. And how in the nineteenth century and in one of the foremost of civilized States could that sword be a weapon suitable for the hand of a boy, or even for the grip of a man, who had not yet drunk deep of the bitter dregs of the cup of life? A youth could, indeed, have called the slaves to rebellion, but the world in the most favorable case would have looked upon him as an object of pity, who ought already to have been placed in an insane asylum. What alone caused Brown's deed to produce such a powerful and ever increasing effect North and South, was the fact that he held as a sacred tenet from first to last, without a second's doubting, the belief that he was God's chosen bearer of the sword of Gideon; but in order that such a belief should be awe-inspiring and not ridiculous, but should be fearful, it must be held by a man on whose head lay the snow of age, in whose veins the blood coursed slowly and evenly, and who could point to a long life as to an irrefutable proof that he was as cool as ice and as completely the master of his five senses as any man. . . .

Whenever I have stood among the ruins of the classic age, before a single column which had once been one of many to support the roof of a temple, I have always had a feeling as though I stood before a sort of enigma. This picture involuntarily came to me while trying to grasp the mental and moral nature of this remarkable man. In his comparisons he was fond of referring to the Bible accounts of Old Testament heroes. He bore the imprint of their spirit. All who did not believe what they believed, were devoted to the sword. In Brown's eyes, the man who saw slavery under any other aspect than that of a moral wrong, was a heathen. His platform is a narrow one, a very narrow one; but on this platform he stands, towering up mightily in genuine grandeur—a solitary pillar in this sober world, with its calmly analytic thought, and its broad and shallow thread-bare sentiment. But how did this representative of a long-vanished period of civilization come into this modern world of ours? There is only one explanation. Negro slavery, as it had developed in the United States, on the soil of the most democratic State in the world, which in all other respects was even with the times, was itself so much of an anachronism and an anomaly that the whole history of the world cannot produce its fellow. . . .

Brown actually expected that the raid on Harper's Ferry would be the stroke with which Moses called forth water from the rock. The spring was to turn southward, and in its swift course to swell to a mighty river. He declared expressly to Governor Wise, and later still in his letters, that he had not intended simply to break the chains of a few dozen or a few hundred slaves, and to take them again to Canada. Emancipation was to be spread farther and farther, *and the freedmen were to remain in the Southern States.*

Heaven itself could not have brought this about, unless it had sent the angel of judgment to cast down into the dust the whole white population from Florida to Maine. Upon recovering from the stupefaction of the first alarm, the white population of the South would have risen as one man to force the slaves back into the yoke, and the North, with the exception of a handful of the most radical Abolitionists, would have helped the South with all its might. And truly they would have been right; though slavery was an incalculable wrong, though it was an inconceivable curse for the white people, it would have been a still greater misfortune for black and for white, if the former had conquered in a war between the two races. But—aside from this—it was certain that the whole white population would have resolutely taken up the fight, and that the blacks would have been crushed like tinder by their overwhelming force. The more Brown's dreams were realized, the more unavoidable became the conflict between the races; that is, the more did he bring unutterable misery on those he wished to protect. The question of slavery in the United States was a many-sided one, not only from the point of view of expediency, but also from that of morality. In every established law, as such, there is also a moral element. And when it has been possible for an institution such as slavery to remain established law for centuries, then there have been active causes at work which have so broadened and strengthened this moral element that the evil cannot be forcibly overthrown by one blow without deeply wounding relations which morality requires us most scrupulously to respect. And this is my view, although a study of these matters, continued for many years, has persuaded me more and more that the question of slavery in the Union could only be solved by a sharp thrust, dealt by the people themselves, acting under the pressure of an iron necessity. If any one man drew from his catechism the conclusion that he had the moral right to make such an attempt on his own responsibility, then, so far as he succeeded, the number, as well as the importance, of the inevitable immoral consequences must very notably increase.

That in spite of the absolute wickedness of slavery, the slave problem in the United States was even morally a very complicated one, was, and remained to the last, simply incomprehensible to Brown. His reasoning in this matter was made up of two propositions: "Do unto others as you would have them do unto you," and "All men are born free and equal." His sight was keen, but he saw only in a straight line. This is easy to understand when one considers that he looked upon the question only from the ethical point of view. Not only would he have nothing to do with any political party, so that he did not even belong to the Abolitionists, considered as a close organization, but in all the existing sources of information there is not the slightest indication that he ever occupied himself with the question of slavery, considered as a political problem affecting the South, or the North, or the Union as a whole. His position was, however, entirely different as regards the most immediate practical consequences of his undertaking. Although he evidently remained a stranger to the considerations we have just developed, he was certainly able to think coolly and weigh coming events. The irresistible impulse which moved him now at last to do the deed of his life, did not allow him to make use of this power in time, but as soon as he had crossed the Rubicon, his eminently practical instinct—although perhaps without his being conscious of it—asserted itself fully, and paralyzed his arm. A foreboding came over him that after all he had launched his boat without helm or compass upon a trackless ocean—that his plan was based on an inherent contradiction, which must necessarily sooner or later cause its failure.

However painful the suggestion may be for those who admire and revere Brown, it sounds like a comic interlude in the tragedy when we read that the man who, against the law of absolute right, against all legal authorities, and against the whole nation, presumed to start a radical, political, and social revolution in the Southern States, which was to be purchased at the cost of a four years' civil war of frightful proportions—that this man, after the success obtained during the first two hours, remained with folded arms and waited to be hemmed in and hunted down like a mad wolf. But still he stands forth in this hopeless fight, a grand, heroic figure from first to last, while his conquerors have covered themselves with imperishable and absolutely unutterable disgrace and shame. . . .

There is no gloss about him; he is all substance. His terrible earnestness compels people in spite of themselves to believe in his moral greatness, and the touching moderation with which he gives his executioners, considered simply as men, more than their due, takes away the repellant effect of the one-sided roughness and rigidity of his moral convictions. He gave the highest proof a man can give of the genuineness of these convictions; for their sake he staked his life and that of his children, without the possibility of any selfish advantage, and when he lost, he did not regret what he had done. "Time and the honest verdict of posterity," said he, "will justify all my actions."[60] Millions of eyes were fastened upon him in anxious expectation, to see whether he would not betray at the last moment that he was wearing a mask, even though this mask might be woven of the thinnest gauze wire. But after he had stood ten minutes like a statue with the rope round his neck and the cap drawn over his eyes, the millions drew a deep breath—he was wholly pure, wholly true. And this is why John Brown's life and death struck the minds and consciences of the North with a far mightier blow than the Lundys, Garrisons, and Douglasses[61] could deal with their most heartfelt speeches. . . .

When a boat at the crossing of the stream above Niagara Falls is turned out of its course, every stroke of the oars is watched anxiously from both shores. As the prow of the boat turns toward the middle of the river, cheeks grow pale, but there is still hope, for the oars strike the waters with twofold energy. When the rapids have been reached, the gazers hold their breath, for there is only one chance of rescue: the boatman may succeed in casting himself on one of the small islands. But when the force of the current has driven him beyond them, then eyes are closed, and hearts filled with horror exclaim, "God have mercy on his soul!" For seventy years the politicians had been trying in vain to struggle with the boat of the slavery question against the mighty stream of actual facts and against the moral principles which were operating among these facts. The boat had been constantly driven farther and farther down stream, but hope had as yet never been utterly given up, though fear had often gotten the upper hand. But now John Brown, in the grim earnestness of his religious convictions, had put his foot on the boat as it was drifting in the rapids and given it a mighty shove away from the shore of the last island. True, he was the first to fall overboard and to be hurried to the depths below. But was there now any chance that the leaky skiff should not follow him over the Falls? At last it dawned on the people that even supposing none but Henry Clays[62] to sit in the councils of the nation, the time must come when it would be absolutely impossible to throw a new bridge of compromise across the chasm which had been opened between North and South by the contradictory principles embodied in the Constitution. Brown's execution sealed the irrepressibleness of the conflict between North and South.[63]

Source: Hermann von Holst, John Brown, ed. Frank Preston Stearns (Boston: Cupples and Hurd, 1888), 81–82, 100–102, 125–131, 166–167, 172–174; first published in German as "John Brown," Preussische Jahrbücher, Vol. 41 (1878), 350–392.

PART

V

Civil War and U.S. Postwar Responses

O NCE UNION and Confederate forces began fighting in April 1861, it was "impossible to keep the name of John Brown out of the war," as Ralph Waldo Emerson observed. Many who had defended and praised Brown in 1859 now felt that the war vindicated his actions and made him a prophet. Others claimed him as an early war hero and described the shots fired at Harpers Ferry as the first shots of the Civil War. Union soldiers marched to the song "John Brown's Body" and Confederate soldiers wrote diary entries about Brown when they passed through Charles Town. On January 1, 1863, some Northerners celebrated the Emancipation Proclamation with "John Brown parties." After the war, former abolitionists declared that Brown bore more responsibility than Lincoln for emancipation. Franklin Sanborn insisted in 1875 that "Lincoln with his proclamations, Grant and Sherman with their armies, and Sumner with his constitutional amendments, did little more than follow in the path which Brown had pointed out." Other writers used Brown to attack Jim Crow, and still others renounced their former sympathy with Brown to participate in the postconflict reconciliation of the North and South.

Part V collects these U.S. responses to Brown during the Civil War and postwar periods, including diaries, letters, poems, articles, speeches, and songs from the North, the South, Kansas, and the West Coast. They include responses by Confederate and Union soldiers, politicians and spies, freeborn African Americans and former slaves, Northern and Southern women, Brown's co-conspirators and witnesses to his raid or execution, and people who returned to Harpers Ferry during the war and who visited Brown's grave in North Elba at the war's end. Some, like John Wilkes Booth, Nathaniel Hawthorne, and Walt Whitman, are famous figures. Some return to Brown for a second time with varying consistency: Booth, Douglass, Martin, Sumner, and Conway are also represented in Parts II and III.

The book ends in 1889, thirty years after Brown's raid. Its last sources, written in the 1880s, attempt to cement Brown's legacy. Frederick Douglass sanctifies Brown and hopes that history's "polishing wheels" will make his glory clear. George Washington Williams believes that the tribunal is finally transforming Brown from madman to saint. David Utter believes that the truth about Brown merits disgust but is concealed. Mark Twain parodies the representation of Brown in history books. Frank Preston Stearns observes postwar criticism and argues that any action lifted out of its historical context will seem peculiar. Finally, T. Thomas Fortune considers the possibility of a memorial to Brown and wonders if African Americans should honor Nat Turner instead. Three decades after he raided Harpers Ferry, the tribunal still had not reached a verdict on John Brown.

Various Authors, "John Brown's Body," May 1861

The "apotheosis of old John Brown is fast taking place," noted the *Illinois Weekly Mirror* on August 6, 1862. "All over the country, the John Brown song may be heard at all times. . . . It is the pet song among the soldiers in all our armies." This marching song took its melody from the popular antebellum Methodist meeting song "Say, Brothers, Will You Meet Us," and its parodic inspiration from a Scotsman in the Massachusetts Volunteer Militia who shared the abolitionist's name. The song was first printed in May 1861, copyrighted in July, and sold as a penny ballad in Boston and other Northern cities. Numerous different versions circulated throughout the war, each with new verses. The abolitionist and Congregational minister William Weston Patton (1821–1889) wrote the influential version below in late October 1861. Then, as they drove Jefferson Davis to prison in May 1865, Union forces sang a version with a line promising to "hang Jeff Davis from a sour apple tree." Soon after, a lithograph titled *John Brown Exhibiting His Hangman* showed Davis holding a sour apple and dangling from a scaffold, as a bearded, robed Brown rises out of the ground beside him. "John Brown's Body" remains the best-known Civil War response to Brown.

John Brown's body lies a-moldering in the grave,
While weep the sons of bondage, whom he ventured all to save;
But though he lost his life in struggling for the slave,
His soul is marching on! O Glory! Hallelujah!

John Brown he was a hero, undaunted, true and brave,
And Kansas knew his valor, where he fought, her rights to save,
And now, though the grass grows green above his grave,
His soul is marching on! O Glory! Hallelujah!

He captured Harper's Ferry with his nineteen men, so few,
And he frightened "Old Virginny," till she trembled through and through;
They hung him for a traitor, themselves a traitor crew,
But his soul is marching on! O Glory! Hallelujah!

John Brown was John the Baptist of the Christ we are to see—
Christ who of the bondman shall the Liberator be;
And soon throughout the sunny South the slaves shall all be free,
For his soul is marching on! O Glory! Hallelujah!

The conflict that he heralded, he looks from heaven to view—
On the army of the Union, with its flag, red, white and blue;
And Heaven shall ring with anthems o'er the deed they mean to do,
For his soul is marching on! O Glory! Hallelujah!

Ye soldiers brave of freedom, then strike, while strike ye may,
The death-blow of oppression, in a better time and way,
For the dawn of Old John Brown has brightened into day,
And his soul is marching on! O Glory! Hallelujah!

Source: Chicago Tribune, December 16, 1861, reissued as sheet music by Root & Cady (Chicago, 1861).

Elizabeth Van Lew, "Occasional Diary," 1861

As the Civil War began, Americans continued to respond to Brown. Some, like Elizabeth Van Lew (1818–1900), returned to his raid as the war's beginning point. One of Lew's diary entries describes the raid as the start of the "war in the heart" and a point of no return in the relationship between the North and the South. Lew was a spy for the Union during the war. She was from Richmond but had been educated at a Quaker school in Philadelphia. There she became an abolitionist, asserting in her diary that the Slave Power "is arrogant, is jealous and intrusive, is cruel, is despotic." During the Civil War she communicated information to Northern generals. On numerous occasions, pretending to be an eccentric and harmless Union sympathizer, she took food to Union captives in a Confederate prison in Richmond and gathered information from prisoners and Confederate guards about troop movements. General Grant described her information as the most valuable he received from Richmond during the war. When Richmond fell in 1865, Van Lew was the first person to raise the U.S. flag in the city.

1861

The beginning of the war. There is no denying the fact our people were in a palpable state of war from the time of the John Brown raid. Henry A. Wise was Governor of Virginia, and did everything to keep up excitement, thinking, perhaps, to use his zeal as a stepping stone to popularity and the presidential chain. There were rumors that the whole North was coming. Thousands of men marching in battle array to overwhelm us. The alarm bell would be rung; the tramp of armed men could be heard through the night, and no time was given the people for a sane breath and a perception of the truth. Such hurry, such haste, such valor, such determination betokened as a ruler either Henry A. Wise or Iron Impotte.[1] Our people required blood, the blood of all who

427

were of the Brown party. They thirsted for it; they cried out for it. It was not enough that one old man should die. No plea of the people intellecting of misguided youth, would be listened to, and when a deputation [of loyalists] arrived and waited on the legislature to solicit mercy for young. . . . Look . . . a lady, one of the most highly respectable in the city, implored the members to steel their hearts, to let no appeal, no pity move them! What struck me most painfully in all this was the universal want of humanity towards the raiders. I hold that one spark of the love of Christ in our hearts gave us a feeling of oneness, of sympathy with all his creatures, however sunken, however sinning. I never thought John Brown right; I have always thought him one who suffered so deeply with slaves. . . . War, war in the heart all the while; yet the North would not believe in our . . . terrible secession.[2]

Source: A Yankee Spy in Richmond: The Civil War Diary of "Crazy Bet" Van Lew, ed. David D. Ryan (Mechanicsburg, VA: Stackpole, 1996), 27–28.

Mary Boykin Chesnut, "A Diary from Dixie," November 28, 1861

After responding to Brown's raid and death in 1859, Southern women continued to remember Brown during the war. Mary Boykin Miller Chesnut (1823–1886), of Camden, South Carolina, felt him "hanging like a drawn sword," as she puts it in a diary entry of November 1861. She was the wife of James Chesnut, Jr., a prominent state politician and a U.S. senator between 1858 and 1860. The Chesnuts were close friends of Jefferson Davis and counted numerous other Confederate politicians and generals as their friends and acquaintances. James Chesnut defended slavery, was the first Southerner to withdraw from the Senate after Lincoln's election in 1860, and served as a brigadier general in the Confederate Army. Mary Chesnut mentions Brown several more times in her wartime diary. In various entries she references Republicanism as an attempt to "Brown us all," declares that the "Negroes were not ripe for John Brown," recounts that Edmund Ruffin promised her a John Brown pike, brands the "John Brown spirit" murderous and fratricidal, and describes blacks and whites sharing public space as a John Brown dream of equality.

November 28, 1861—"Ye who listen with credulity to the whispers of fancy,"[3]— pause, and look on this picture and that.

On one side Mrs. Stowe, Greeley, Thoreau, Emerson, Sumner.[4] They live in nice New England homes, clean, sweet-smelling, shut in libraries, writing books which ease their hearts of their bitterness against us. What self-denial they do practice is to tell John Brown to come down here and cut our throats in Christ's name. Now consider what I have seen of my mother's life, my grandmother's, my mother-in-law's. These people were educated at Northern schools, they read the same books as their Northern contemporaries, the same daily papers, the same Bible. They have the same ideas of right and wrong, are high-bred, lovely, good, pious, doing their duty as they conceive it. They live in Negro villages. They do not preach and teach hate as a gospel, and the sacred duty of murder and insurrection; but they strive to ameliorate the condition of these Africans in every particular. They set them the example of a perfect life, a life of utter self-abnegation. Think of these holy New Englanders forced to have a Negro village walk through their houses whenever they see fit, dirty, slatternly, idle, ill-smelling by nature. These women I love have less chance to live their own lives in peace than if they were African missionaries. They have swarm of blacks about them like children under their care, not as Mrs. Stowe's fancy painted them, and they hate slavery worse than Mrs. Stowe does. Book-making which leads you to a round of visits among crowned heads is an easier way to be a saint than martyrdom down here, doing unpleasant duty among the Negroes with no reward but the threat of John Brown hanging like a drawn sword over your head in this world, and threats of what is to come to you from blacker devils in the next.

Source: Mary Boykin Chesnut, *A Diary from Dixie,* ed. Ben Ames Williams (Cambridge, MA: Harvard University Press, 1980), 163–164.

Wilder Dwight, "Letters," July 30, 1861, and March 4 and 8, 1862

During the course of the war, Harpers Ferry changed hands between Union and Confederate forces eight times. Soldiers on both sides remembered Brown as they passed through the town. Wilder Dwight (1833–1862) was a Boston lawyer who became a lieutenant colonel in the Second Massachusetts Infantry. He was wounded in combat on September 17, 1862, and died two days later at Boonsborough, Maryland. In his letters of July 1861 and March 1862, he offers thoughts upon visiting Harpers Ferry as well as the sites of Brown's trial, imprisonment, and execution in Charles Town.

Maryland Heights, Advanced Post, July 30, 1861, Tuesday Afternoon, in Camp.

The officers found a friendly supper in the house of a man on whose farm we are—the only inhabitant of the neighborhood, if that can be called a neighborhood where neighbors there are none. This farmer knew John Brown; and, indeed, John Brown's school-house, where he hid his arms, is down just below our camp, in the woods. I may exaggerate the effect of John Brown, but certain it is that the whole military organization in Virginia dates from his raid. And the other day a woman said, "We have not dared to command our slaves, since John Brown came." The man's name is a terror and a bitterness to them.

Charlestown, March 4, 1862.

The extent to which our regiment has followed the path of John Brown is somewhat curious. The last coincidence of occupation occurred on Sunday, when the men were assembled in the court-room of the court-house, and listened to our chaplain, who preached from the judges' bench! This morning Colonel Gordon and I went in to see the cell of Brown in the jail, and also went out in the open field, where, upon a knoll, can be seen the holes in which the gallows was set up. "This is a fine country," said Brown, as he came out into the field which commands a view of this grand country. "I have not had an opportunity of observing it before."

Charlestown, March 8, 1862.

I am writing in the Provost Marshal's office in the Charlestown jail. Colonel Andrews[5] is still Provost Marshal. John Brown's cell, on the opposite side of the entry, is full of contrabands, fugitives within our lines, most of them to be sent to work at Harper's Ferry. Again I give you an odd retribution from the whirligig of events.

Source: Life and Letters of Wilder Dwight (Boston: Ticknor and Fields, 1868), 63, 202, 204–205.

George Michael Neese, "Diary,"
January 3 and 26, 1862

As he camped near Harpers Ferry and then in Charlestown during January 1862, George Neese (1839–1921), a Confederate gunner, remembered Brown in his diary. Neese was from the northern Shenandoah Valley and had joined Captain R. P. Chew's Virginia Battery the previous month. The battery was eventually part of the Army of Northern Virginia, in which Neese was serving as chief of the artillery of the cavalry corps when he was captured in October 1864. He was held at Point Lookout Prison in Maryland until the end of the war.

January 3. This afternoon a company of our cavalry passed us, armed with lances, which consisted of a steel spear about ten inches long mounted on a wooden shaft about eight feet long. These were some of the identical weapons that the saintly martyr, John Brown, had at Harper's Ferry, to place in the hands of liberated slaves for the purpose of murdering men and women and perhaps children.

And yet, if all accounts be true, there are long-faced men and women in the North today who think that they are worshiping the great Jehovah by singing the praises of John Brown. O ye prejudiced, hypocritical souls, if you would have lived a little over eighteen hundred years ago you would have been in the crowd that shouted, "Crucify Him! Crucify Him!" especially if you would have had a lamb or two to sell.

January 26. This morning we received orders to go with Ashby's Cavalry on a scout. At nine o'clock we were on the march. We went up the Winchester pike ten miles to Bunker's Hill. There we left the pike and came by Smithfield to Charlestown, where we arrived after dark. We are quartered in the Court House. This is the town where the insurrectionist, John Brown, obtained a permit to paddle his canoe across the Styx.

Source: George Michael Neese, *Three Years in the Confederate Horse Artillery* (New York: Neale, 1911), 13–14, 20.

Nathaniel Hawthorne, "Chiefly about War Matters. By a Peaceable Man," July 1862

The Massachusetts writer Nathaniel Hawthorne (1804–1864) was no fan of abolitionists. He was dismissive of or hostile toward abolitionism when he mentioned it in letters, some of which he wrote while away in Europe during the 1850s. New England friends and acquaintances challenged his attitudes and also criticized his support for Democrat and Southern sympathizer Franklin Pierce, his close friend. Hawthorne wrote the campaign biography *Life of Franklin Pierce* (1852) and dedicated his book *Our Old Home* (1863) to Pierce. The war began soon after his return from Europe in June 1860, and Hawthorne maintained that the Confederacy should be released from the Union, so long as the border states remained. Then, in March 1862, he visited Washington, met Lincoln, and toured Union military installations. His essay about the trip, published in July 1862 under the byline "A Peaceable Man," includes a section about Brown and Harpers Ferry.

As we passed over, we looked towards the Virginia shore, and beheld the little town of Harper's Ferry, gathered about the base of a round hill and climbing up its steep acclivity; so that it somewhat resembled the Etruscan cities which I have seen among the Apennines, rushing, as it were, down an apparently breakneck height. About midway of the ascent stood a shabby brick church, towards which a difficult path went scrambling up the precipice, indicating, one would say, a very fervent aspiration on the part of the worshippers, unless there was some easier mode of access in another direction. Immediately on the shore of the Potomac, and extending back towards the town, lay the dismal ruins of the United States arsenal and armory, consisting of piles of broken bricks and a waste of shapeless demolition, amid which we saw gun-barrels in heaps of hundreds together. They were the relics of the conflagration, bent with the heat of the fire and rusted with the wintry rain to which they had since been exposed. The brightest sunshine could not have made the scene

cheerful, nor have taken away the gloom from the dilapidated town; for, besides the natural shabbiness, and decayed, unthrifty look of a Virginian village,
it has an inexpressible forlornness resulting from the devastations of war and
its occupation by both armies alternately. Yet there would be a less striking
contrast between Southern and New-England villages, if the former were as
much in the habit of using white paint as we are. It is prodigiously efficacious
in putting a bright face upon a bad matter.

There was one small shop, which appeared to have nothing for sale. A single
man and one or two boys were all the inhabitants in view, except the Yankee
sentinels and soldiers, belonging to Massachusetts regiments, who were scattered about pretty numerously. A guard-house stood on the slope of the hill;
and in the level street at its base were the offices of the Provost-Marshal and
other military authorities, to whom we forthwith reported ourselves. The
Provost-Marshal kindly sent a corporal to guide us to the little building which
John Brown seized upon as his fortress, and which, after it was stormed by the
United States marines, became his temporary prison. It is an old engine-house,
rusty and shabby, like every other work of man's hands in this God-forsaken
town, and stands fronting upon the river, only a short distance from the bank,
nearly at the point where the pontoon-bridge touches the Virginia shore. In its
front wall, on each side of the door, are two or three ragged loop-holes, which
John Brown perforated for his defence, knocking out merely a brick or two, so
as to give himself and his garrison a sight over their rifles. Through these ori-
fices the sturdy old man dealt a good deal of deadly mischief among his assailants, until they broke down the door by thrusting against it with a ladder, and
tumbled headlong in upon him. I shall not pretend to be an admirer of old
John Brown, any farther than sympathy with Whittier's excellent ballad about
him[6] may go; nor did I expect ever to shrink so unutterably from any apo-
phthegm of a sage, whose happy lips have uttered a hundred golden sentences,
as from that saying (perhaps falsely attributed to so honored a source), that
the death of this blood-stained fanatic has "made the Gallows as venerable as
the Cross!"[7] Nobody was ever more justly hanged. He won his martyrdom
fairly, and took it firmly. He himself, I am persuaded (such was his natural integrity), would have acknowledged that Virginia had a right to take the life
which he had staked and lost; although it would have been better for her, in
the hour that is fast coming, if she could generously have forgotten the criminality of his attempt in its enormous folly. On the other hand, any common-

sensible man, looking at the matter unsentimentally, must have felt a certain intellectual satisfaction in seeing him hanged, if it were only in requital of his preposterous miscalculation of possibilities.

But, coolly as I seem to say these things, my Yankee heart stirred triumphantly when I saw the use to which John Brown's fortress and prison-house has now been put. What right have I to complain of any other man's foolish impulses, when I cannot possibly control my own? The engine-house is now a place of confinement for Rebel prisoners.

Source: Atlantic Monthly, July 1862, 43–61 (53–54).

John Sherman, "To William Tecumseh Sherman," September 23, 1862

Writing to his older brother the day after President Lincoln's preliminary Emancipation Proclamation in September 1862, senator John Sherman (1823–1900) pointed to Brown as showing the kind of military leadership that might realize black emancipation. John Sherman had opposed the expansion of slavery as a U.S. representative from Ohio between 1855 and 1861. More sympathetic to abolitionism than his older brother, the famous Union general William Tecumseh Sherman, he continued to oppose slavery as a U.S. senator from 1861 onward. He sought the Republican nomination for the presidency in 1880, 1884, and 1888.

Mansfield, Ohio, Sept. 23rd, 1862

By the way, I received within a day or two a letter from a gentleman of the highest political status containing this passage: "Within the last few days I heard an officer say he heard your brother the General, abuse you roundly at Corinth as one of the *blank* abolitionists who had brought on the war, and that he was ashamed to own you as a brother." I have no doubt the officer said this but I knew you did not, and so contradicted it with decided emphasis. I only repeat it now to show you how persistently efforts are being made to separate the class of high regular officers to which you belong from civilians. Whenever that separation is effected all important commands will gradually be transferred to such officers as Banks, Sigel, Morgan, Nelson,[8] and to such regular officers as show a sympathy with the Radical faction as Hunter, Fremont and Doubleday.[9] I earnestly deprecate all such tendencies. I want the war conducted regularly according to the tenets of civilized warfare. I prefer regular officers and scarcely ever criticise them and never in public, but if the time shall come when emancipation of blacks and civilization of whites is necessary in order to preserve the unity of this country, then I would prefer a fanatic like John Brown to lead our armies and an abolitionist like Chase[10] with brains and energy to guide our counsels.

Affectionately yours, John Sherman

Source: The Sherman Letters: Correspondence between General and Senator Sherman from 1837 to 1891, ed. Rachel Sherman Thorndike (New York: Scribner's, 1894), 163–165 (164–165).

Charlotte Forten, "Diary" and "Letter," November 1862

It was not only Union soldiers who sang the John Brown song during the war. In a diary entry and a letter to William Lloyd Garrison, the African American writer and teacher Charlotte Forten (1837–1914) describes her black pupils singing the song on St. Helena's Island, South Carolina. Forten's entry of January 1, 1863, notes that the pupils sang it again to mark the Emancipation Proclamation. Forten was from a wealthy black abolitionist family in Philadelphia. In October 1862 she joined other Northern black and white women on the coastal Sea Islands of South Carolina. Occupied by the Union since November 1861, the islands were home to thousands of former slaves. In conjunction with the U.S. War Department, abolitionist groups sent teachers to educate the freedmen. Forten worked in South Carolina for two years and then returned to Philadelphia. She eventually married Francis J. Grimké, the nephew of the abolitionists Sarah and Angelina Grimké.

Nov. 10, 1862. We taught—or rather commenced teaching the children "John Brown," which they entered into eagerly. I felt to the full the significance of that song being sung here in SC by little negro children, by those whom he— the glorious old man—died to save. Miss T.[11] told them about him.

St. Helena's Island, Beaufort, S.C., Nov. 27, 1862.

Our school is kept in the Baptist church. There are two ladies teaching in it, beside myself. They are earnest workers, and have done and are constantly doing a great deal for the people here, old and young. One of them, Miss T., is physician as well as teacher. She has a very extensive medical practice, and carries about with her everywhere her box of homoeopathic medicines. The people welcome her as a ministering angel to their lowly cabins. Our school averages between eighty and ninety pupils, and later in the season we shall

probably have more. It is very pleasant to set how bright, how eager to learn
many of the children are. Some of them make wonderful improvement in a
short time. It is a great happiness, a great privilege to be allowed to teach them.
Every day I enjoy it more and more.

I cannot describe to you their singing. To me it seems wonderfully beautiful. We have just taught them the John Brown Song. I wish you could hear
them sing it; it does one's soul good. How often I wish their old "secesh" masters, powerless to harm them, could hear their former chattels singing the
praises of the brave old man who died for their sake! We are going to teach
them "The Song of the Negro Boatmen"[12] soon.

Source: Francis James Grimké Papers, 1833–1937, Manuscript Division, Moorland-Spingarn Research Center, Howard University; *The Liberator,* December 19, 1862.

Moncure Conway, *The Golden Hour,* 1862

After responding to Brown's raid and death in a sermon of December 1859, the Southern abolitionist Moncure Conway returned to Brown during the Civil War in his book *The Golden Hour.*
The book is a plea for emancipation. Often addressing Lincoln directly, it argues that emancipation will cripple the Confederate war effort and hasten peace. A few months after the book's
publication, in January 1863, Conway responded to the Emancipation Proclamation by remembering Brown again. He wrote a letter to his fellow abolitionist Mary Stearns that imagined
Brown could hear the sound of slaves' chains breaking. Later that year, in April, he traveled to
England on behalf of abolitionists in order to convince the British that the Civil War was about
slavery and abolition. Controversy erupted when he wrote to the Confederate envoy to Britain,
James Mason, on June 10, 1863, promising that abolitionists would oppose the North's prosecu-
tion of the war in exchange for the emancipation of all slaves in the Confederate states. The letter
claimed that Conway was authorized by America's leading abolitionists to make this offer. Mason
sent his correspondence with Conway to the London *Times,* which published it on June 19.
American abolitionists expressed anger, and William Lloyd Garrison repudiated Conway's claim
in a public letter of June 30, 1863, published in the *New York Tribune* and the *National Anti-
Slavery Standard.* Alienated, Conway lived in England and France for the rest of his life, except
for a period in New York between 1885 and 1893.

There is a point in the South by touching which the entire military power of
the South is paralyzed. Nat Turner touched that point, and with fifty negroes
behind him held the entire State of Virginia as if stricken by catalepsy for five
weeks. John Brown touched it, and with twenty-one men so held Virginia that,
had he had a fourth of McClellan's army,[13] he could in one month have occupied the entire State. It became a proverb, that John Brown had demonstrated
the weakness of Slavery. This huge machinery of armies and numbers is a
barbarism; it is as if we built great Roman aqueducts, ignoring the modern
discovery of the water-level, which makes a hydrant in one's yard answer the

same purpose, or a better. It is a rudeness far behind our civilization to think that numbers can conquer for us: numbers are as weak as they are strong. We are beyond that in our municipal governments. It is estimated that twenty policemen can conquer and disperse the largest riot or tumult that could occur in New York. Why? Because each policeman has the moral power of the nation at his back, whilst the rioters are mere bits of chaos. We do not have to set one half of a city to keep the other half in order. I have seen a half-dozen burly ruffians led to prison by a man weaker than either of them, but who had an *idea* symboled in the star on his breast, whilst the ruffians had none. When our country has an idea in this war, it need only send South a moderate police force. Nat Turner and John Brown, with stars out of heaven on their breasts, holding commissions from Almighty God to put down the organic disorder in the South, proved that Slavery cannot stir but as Freedom permits it; but McClellan, with seven hundred thousand men under him for six months, proved that men unarmed with ideas are as unable to cope with the kindled ferocity of wrong as they are without guns to cope with half their number of tigers. In a fearful sense our men are yet unarmed.

It is a common phrase with many of those who evidently think that the Union would be nothing without Slavery, that an edict of emancipation would not reach or free a single slave, and, to use a favorite phrase with certain journals, "would not be worth the paper upon which it should be written." I observe, however, that these always end their arguments by saying, For God's sake, do not try it! It is quite remarkable how nervous they are, lest an edict should be put forth which could have no effect whatever.

Have we considered well what would be the practical bearing if our government should declare every slave free? Slavery would by this stroke of the pen be exposed to the anti-slavery feeling of the world. If John Brown had a successor, he would march South under protection of the flag under which the old captain was hung. White and black crusaders would rise in Canada, Kansas, Ohio, Hayti, New England, following new hermit-leaders to rescue the holy places of humanity. Hayti would no longer need beg labourers to come to her shores, and pay them for coming: she need only send her ships to cruise near the inlets and creeks of the Southern coast, and pick them up as they should escape. . . .

The battle of Armageddon is one that never ceases. Let the Cabinets at Washington and Richmond join again around the communion-table, with the blood of the Christ crucified between them upon it—and the old siege of Liberty against the Union, which has been raised for a moment, begins again. Garrison, the old standard-bearer, will unfurl his banner of Disunion, which he keeps only tucked away in the *Liberator* room,[14] as Bennett of the *Herald* keeps the Confederate flag.[15] The clear bugle of Phillips[16] sounds the old martial call again. And all along the sky sleeping thunders will awaken, and ten thousand trumpets proclaim that the siege against the ancient wrong is renewed—the siege whose arrows are thoughts, whose shells are fiery inspirations of truth, whose sword is the Spirit of a just God. All this will go on until the ballot-box is conquered again, and some such man as Wendell Phillips is elected President. Then another Sumter gun will be heard. Then will come the war of which the present is but a picket skirmish. John Brown will be commanding general of all our forces then; and all will not be quiet on the Potomac. His soul will go marching on; 't is a way it has.

For I fear that over the eye of this nation Slavery has gradually formed a hard cataract, so that it cannot see the peace and glory which are an arm's-length before it—a cataract which only the painful surgery of the sword can remove. If it be so, we can only say—Bleed, poor country! Let thy young men be choked with their blood; let the pale horse trample loving hearts and fairest homes; if only thus thou canst learn that God also has his government, and that all injustice is secession from that government, which his arm of might will be sure to crush out!

Source: Moncure D. Conway, *The Golden Hour* (Boston: Ticknor and Fields, 1862), 43–45, 58–59.

Adalbert Volck, "Worship of the North" and "Writing the Emancipation Proclamation," 1863

Born in Germany, Adalbert Volck (1828–1912) immigrated to the United States in 1848 to avoid military service and settled in Baltimore as a dentist. Volck was proslavery and during the war served as a Confederate agent. He assisted those who wanted to go south and smuggled medicines and other contraband. He also offered himself as the Southern answer to the Northern caricaturist Thomas Nast. Under the pseudonym V. Blada, he published a limited-edition portfolio of etchings for two hundred Southern subscribers (and sold an edition with forty-five plates in London). The images caricature Lincoln, the Union Army, and abolitionists. In one, titled "Worship of the North," Northern leaders sacrifice a white man on a shrine. A black man sits on top of the shrine, Lincoln appears as a serpent carved into its base, and the central pillar is decorated with the words "Puritanism," "atheism," "rationalism," "witchburning," "spirit rapping," "free love," "negro worship," and "socialism." Charles Sumner holds a torch, Henry Ward Beecher wields a sacrificial knife, and Horace Greeley lifts an incense burner from which snakes sliver. On the right, Harriet Beecher Stowe kneels atop a copy of *Uncle Tom's Cabin*. At the center, General Benjamin Butler prays before the altar. Also present are Governor John Andrew of Massachusetts and Generals H. W. Halleck, Winfield Scott, and David Hunter. John Brown holds a pike and is raised above the rest as "St. Ossawatomie." In another image from the series, Lincoln writes the Emancipation Proclamation while the devil holds his inkstand. The back of his chair is an ass's head and the table legs are Satanic cloven feet. One painting on the wall shows a scene of black violence during the Haitian revolution, while the other shows a haloed Brown with a palm and a pike.

WORSHIP OF THE NORTH

WRITING THE EMANCIPATION PROCLAMATION

Source: V. Blada [pseud.], "Sketches from the Civil War in North America, 1861, '62, '63," *Magazine of History with Notes and Queries,* special no. 60 (New York: William Abbatt, 1917), frontispiece and 14.

John H. Surratt, "Diary," January 16 and 20, 1863

As Elizabeth Van Lew was spying for the Union in the South, John Surratt (1844–1916) was gathering information for the Confederacy about the North. Surratt began work as a postmaster in the Maryland town of Surrattsville in September 1862. There he passed dispatches to the Confederacy about Union troop movements in the area between Washington, D.C., and Richmond, Virginia. In a diary entry of January 1863 he compared Lincoln's "abolition policy" to Brown's raid. The following year he met John Wilkes Booth and helped him plan a kidnapping of Lincoln, which failed. Then, in April 1865, he was suspected of conspiracy in Lincoln's assassination. He fled to Canada, then traveled to England, Italy, and Egypt. He was caught and extradited in November 1866. His trial in Maryland ended in a mistrial in August 1867.

January 20, 1863.—Lincoln seems determined to carry out his Abolition policy. What was considered a crime in John Brown, and for which the old fanatic was hung with the calm approval of the North, is now being esteemed a rare virtue—why? Because he only attempted to free a few niggers, and Lincoln is making a wholesale job of the matter. Strange that vice should become a virtue, because more are engaged in it. But to kill a single man makes the doer of it a murderer; to kill thousands, a hero. But such it is, and ever will be.

Our order is getting less powerful throughout the North. Perhaps this arises from the number that have gone South to join the Confederate service; and perhaps it is caused by the recent exposures which have made some afraid. The northern spies have done us a great deal of mischief; but yet we are not quite broken up. There is yet work for the daring to perform.

Source: The Private Journal and Diary of John H. Surratt, the Conspirator, ed. Dion Haco (New York: F. A. Brady, 1866), 71.

Anonymous, "John Brown's Entrance into Hell," March 1863

While the John Brown song rang out in the North, Confederate troops sang patriotic songs of their own. Some were parodic adaptations of Union songs. Many identified with other revolutionary moments in history, including the French Revolution (with lyrics set to the "Marseillaise") and the American Revolution (urging the countrymen of Washington and Jefferson to live and die for liberty again). These Southern war songs frequently attacked abolitionists, and one imagines Brown entering hell to see places reserved for Lincoln, Charles Sumner, and Thaddeus Stevens. Brown also appeared in "Confederate Yankee Doodle," which castigates the "Priest of Harpers Ferry," and "Run Yanks or Die," where he is tied to an oak tree with Carolina cotton. Other songs were marching ballads; camp ditties; dramatic narratives about particular battles; odes to rebellion, freedom, the Confederate flag, and the glory of the South; ballads in praise of war heroes (especially Stonewall Jackson); and prisoner-of-war songs. Some appeared in newspapers and others were published as song sheets and broadsides, especially when Southern newspapers suspended publication during the later part of the war.

Come gentle muse and touch a strain,
'Twill echo back the sound again—
On scenes that pass'd we now must dwell,
When old John Brown arrived in Hell.

When Pluto[17] heard old Brown was hung
Old Tophet[18] with Hosannas rung;
For well they knew the lying thief,
Would make for them an honored chief.

Brown to receive they now prepare,
All eager in the joy to share;
Old Satan from his throne came down
And left his seat for Old John Brown

448

Not long, indeed, for him they wait,
For soon he thunder'd at the gate.
"Come in," says Pluto, "Quickly come,
You're welcome to your fiery home."

Three cheers roll'd forth in accents brief
To hail the Abolition chief—
Old John chim'd in, and thank the Fates—
He'd safely passed the pearly gates.

While Arnold[19] held him by the hand,
Old Satan took the Speaker's stand—
"Silence," cried he, "Now all sit down,
And hear me welcome brother Brown.

"You're welcome, John, to your reward,
You've cheated Riddle and the Lord—
Though pearly gates wide open flow,
They did not catch my servant true.

As oft you've murdered, lied and stole,
It did rejoice my burning soul;
You've run you length in earth's career,
And we are pleased to see you here.

You'll take your seat at my left hand,
Why I do this you'll understand;
Be not surprised, when I tell you,
Old Abraham[20] is coming too,

There on my right, that vacant chair,
Long since for him I did prepare—
And soon I know that he will come—
His earthly race is almost run.

John at my left, Abe at my right,
We'll give the heavenly hosts a fight;
A triune group we then shall be,
Yes, three in one and one in three.

Abe's Cabinet, 'tis very true,
Will soon knock here as loud as you—

In short, the negroizing clan,
Are traveling here unto a man.

I shall protest, most long and loud,
'Gainst taking in the motley crowd—
For well I know they'd me dethrone,
And swear that Tophet was their own.

Let Sumner, Stevens,[21] and their host,
When they on earth give up the ghost—
Unto a lower hell appear;
We have no room for them up here.

The Clergy, too, I much do fear.
Attraction's law will draw them here—
Their earthly teachings—though I tell,
Are doctrines long since preached in hell.

They, too, must find a lower home.
For hither sure they shall not come—
We are crowded now in every spot,
Save here and there a vacant lot.

These I've reserved through all our fights,
For those who have pre-emption rights;
That corner lot's for Backbone Tod,[22]
A renegade accursed of God.

The traitor here from his own place
Can view the scenes at Fortress Chase[23]—
Laugh at the woes of his old friends,
Till his curs'd life in horror ends.

There's other traitors I could tell,
They are too mean to come to hell—
So let each go and hunt his hold,
For green backs here won't pay their toll.

And now, O! John, on earth oppress'd,
You are with us a welcome guest;
On earth you played our part full well,
So now with us forever dwell."

Source: Song sheet, "John Brown's Entrance into Hell" (Baltimore: C.T.A., 1863).

J. Sella Martin, "Speech to the Emancipation Society," December 2, 1863

Four years to the day after his address at the Tremont Temple gathering on the evening that Brown was executed, the African American abolitionist John Sella Martin gave another speech about Brown. He spoke at a public meeting in London held by the London Emancipation Society to commemorate the fourth anniversary of Brown's execution. Martin had spent most of 1863 in England, giving numerous speeches and sermons about American slavery and the Civil War. In London, Oxford, and other British cities he explained that events such as the passage of the Fugitive Slave Act had caused the war and that only emancipation could end it. He asked the British government to refuse assistance to the Confederacy. Martin also visited England as an antislavery advocate in the winter of 1861, and he returned again in November 1865 to advocate and raise funds for Southern freedmen. In the United States after the war, he campaigned for the ratifications of the Thirteenth, Fourteenth, and Fifteenth Amendments and edited the *New Era* in Washington, D.C.

"John Brown was right," said a noble-hearted man, who, in uttering these words, was lifted as if by the breath of his own candour and the strength of the people's approval of it into the gubernatorial chair of Massachusetts.[24] Yes, John Brown was right; if not as to his method, at least as to his inspiration and his aim, and his righteousness produced two results. He touched and awakened the religious heart of the white Americans, and revived the dying hopes of the black race.

However ministers of the gospel may resent, and as I think justly, the infidel charge of priest-craft, it cannot be denied that the pecuniary interests involved in their support, the building of houses of worship, and therefore the retaining of wealthy members, have a powerful conservative influence in bringing them to agree with one another, and nearly all of them to agree with the powers that be. So that though the church is an ark containing at least pairs of all the truths worthy to be preserved, yet the doors are sealed so tightly to keep out the flood of iniquity, that the ministers can no more get out than those called the sinners can get in. *(Laughter)*. Well, for thirty years at least the American Ministers were just such prisoners, and they were glad for the church to rest at last on some political Ararat[25] like the fact of John Brown's martyrdom, that they might have the opportunity of bursting their prison doors, and touching the green earth of a common humanity once more. *(Applause)*. They had thought before that abolitionists were all infidels, but when they heard that an abolitionist was about to die with as sweet a resignation and as calm a faith as ever man died with; about to leave as broad a mantle of charity, and as noble a spirit of forgiveness, as ever covered or breathed upon the guilty, this side of Calvary; when they learned that this apostle of freedom had been thoroughly furnished for his work by passages from that Divine Book which they found "profitable for doctrine, reproof, and instruction in righteousness,"[26] and that he was scattering them through his wonderful letters, written in a prison where the angel came, not to break his chains, but to touch his lips with a live coal from God's altar; scattering them with a force of illustration, a depth of meaning, a power of pathos, and a wonder of application, which will consecrate them as part of the martyr literature of the age; when they heard and learned all this, why, they prayed for him—*(great applause)*—and for ministers to do such a thing for an abolitionist was as prophetic of a revolution as clouds are of a storm. *(Laughter)*. Why, sir, the abolitionists were as suspicious of a minister as the Christians were of Saul of Tarsus, and the watchword of confidence was "behold he prayeth"[27] for John Brown. The ministers were followed by their churches, and on the day of our martyr's death there were at least three prayer meetings in white churches where he was remembered. Thus began, sir, that religious awakening in the American Church which now makes every Sunday solemn with petitions for the overthrow of slavery; which flings open the pew door to the negro; which heaps eulogy upon the colored soldier; and, greatest proof of sincerity of all, which would welcome the presence of Garrison or Phillips.[28] *(Applause)*.

When the slaves learned that John Brown's murder was condemned by the North, and that many of their masters were as terribly frightened by northern condemnation of the deed, as they were grimly satisfied at the murder, their hope began to revive.

But they and their colored brethren in the north had to go through a few dark hours before they could see the coming dawn of that glorious proclamation which now lights them to the field of battle, and promises them a return of triumph with a future of glory. . . .

From the hour of John Brown's death, the negro has been led by his teachings in the pathway of social, political, and moral redemption. "John Brown's body lies mouldering in the grave, But his soul goes marching on," is not only a song; it is a creed as well, to the great majority of the slaves. In the South they seal the Bible to the slaves, they hide the form and scales of justice from the eyes, they keep the words of the declaration of independence from their ears; but the fact that John Brown died for *them,* that on the way to the scaffold he stooped to kiss a *coloured* child; that his dying testimony was, that he was of infinitely more use to the cause in giving his life for it, than he could be in any other way, has brought to their knowledge, by a living impersonation, God's great declaration, that he has made of one blood all nations of men to dwell on all the face of the earth.[29] *(Great applause.)*

Old Virginia, which put him to death, was the first among the slave states to realize, and no doubt will be the last to recover from, the devastation of war; but she has also been (unwillingly it may be) the first and largest contributor of coloured troops who are fighting to overthrow the system which John Brown gave his life to attack. Thus has it ever been, Mr. Chairman; lofty conviction in a pure soul has always been, and always will be, too powerful for the most gigantic wrong in the best wrought mail. Between slavery and freedom, the battle is the Lord's; and the youth who brings the sling of sincerity and the stone of truth, will be more than a match for the skilful warrior and his ponderous weapons.

Source: The Martyrdom of John Brown (London: Emancipation Society, 1864), 19–22.

William Henry Hall, "Oration on the Occasion of the Emancipation Celebration," January 1, 1864

During the Civil War, abolitionists marked the date of Brown's execution. After 1863 abolitionists also remembered Brown as they marked the Emancipation Proclamation. On the first anniversary of the proclamation, William Henry Hall (1823–1901) spoke at Platts Hall on Montgomery Street in San Francisco. He described the Civil War as punishment for the nation's sin of slavery, Brown's raid as a catalyst for the war, and his spirit as a presence hovering over the battlefields. Hall was a leader in San Francisco's black community. He was born in Washington, D.C., and moved to New York, where he campaigned for black suffrage in the 1840s. He settled in California in 1854 and worked as a barber. He chaired the California State Convention of Colored Citizens in 1857 and served on the convention's executive committee in 1865. He also was the first president of the San Francisco Literary Institute in 1861. After the war he campaigned for black suffrage and attended the National Labor Convention of Colored Men in 1869 as the California delegate.

The American people have committed a great national wrong, and, like other Nations and individuals, are now passing through a scourge, until the transgression is atoned for. They have departed from the maxims that made Plymouth Rock and the Pilgrims memorable; they have disregarded the deeds and ignored the spirit that made the men of '76[30] known and revered throughout the habitable globe; they invaded the scared ordinance of '87,[31] and with vandal ferocity mutilated the germs of peace, by endeavoring to blend freedom and slavery together, within the jurisdiction of one people, one language and one Christianity, until the element most despotic has nearly prostrated the vitality of all that was good and beneficial. So aggressive was this fiendish power upon the spirit and design that brought the republic into existence, that immense sacrifices were conceded to appease its anger. Reflective men beheld the danger of the encroachment, but sealed their mouths and remained dumb, in the anticipation that the impending peril would be overcome. . . . Two hundred and eighty thousand slaveholders began to see their darling scheme in danger of being circumscribed, and its demoralizing contagion no longer to infect the air, or corrupt the virgin soil of Kansas, Minnesota, Washington, or Nevada Territories. The decrees of the past had dedicated this immense area to progress and civilization, and it was futile for any earthly power to attempt to reverse the unalterable ends of destiny; but desperate men resort to furious measures. Not content with compromises and the power of the Government (against the public opinion of the world) to uphold their system, not content with the subversion of law, not content with the corruption and debasement of the great national heart, not content with the humiliating devotion of dough-faceism,[32] but it was impiously demanded that our country should perpetuate a dogma wrong in conception, false in fact and disastrous in circumstances; her refusal only revealed that the disguise of another Pisistratus[33] was about to be thrown aside. The contention was no longer the freedom of the white man and the slavery of the black, but it was capital against labor, from the humblest mechanic to the towering attitude of the senatorial incumbent. The machines of destruction and death were unerringly aimed. The massacre of John Brown, whose sainted soul is now hovering over every battlefield of victory, magnetized the senses of the laboring masses in their dream of security; the dignity of independence was yielded to the supposed blessings arising from a unity with antagonistic interests; the cohesion of party appellations destroyed all sympathy for the despised negro; every court was open to establish his vassalage; every arm was ready to extinguish the spontaneous gush of freedom, misnamed insurrection; but Harper's Ferry is the Bunker Hill of coming time. The spirit of Attucks[34] will linger around its incidents, and the blood of martyrdom will be purified in the earth by the prayers and deeds of those it was shed to save. A monument, imposing and grand, will yet be reared upon the same spot, at the same hour, and on the anniversary of the same day, to the renown of John Brown, whose immaculate intentions are cherished everywhere.

The great moral and physical revolution which is agitating the fibres of our political system, will accomplish a two-fold object, perhaps never conceived within the brain of man: the emancipation of the white race, from error and prejudice, and the regeneration and elevation of the black, from that debasement the want of intelligent contact has so long entailed. So grand an image could have emanated from no other source but that of a Creator, a God, a Ruler of the Universe.

Source: Pacific Appeal, January 9, 1864.

John Wilkes Booth, "Remarks on Lincoln and Brown," November 1864

Shortly before the presidential election of 1864, John Wilkes Booth visited his sister Asia in Phila-delphia. There he returned to a topic he had discussed in his speech of December 1860: Brown's superiority to politicians like Lincoln. His remarks to Asia also allege voting irregularities in the election of 1860. A few months later, on April 14, 1865, the day he murdered Lincoln, Booth sub-mitted a letter to the *National Intelligencer* that mentioned Brown again. In the letter, Booth pretended that he had helped to capture and execute Brown, observed that Brown "has since been made a God," and insisted that the Republican Party "deserved the same fate as poor old Brown."

That Sectional candidate [Lincoln] should never have been President, the votes were *doubled* to seat him. He was smuggled through Maryland to the White House. Maryland is true to the core—every mother's son. Look at the cannon on the heights of Baltimore. It needed just that to keep her quiet. This man's appearance, his pedigree, his coarse low jokes and anecdotes, his vulgar smiles, and his frivolity, are a disgrace to the seat he holds. Other brains run the country. *He* is made the tool of the North, to crush out, or try to crush out slavery, by robbery, rapine, slaughter and bought armies. He is walking in the footprints of old John Brown, but no more fit to stand with that rugged old hero—Great God! no. John Brown was a man inspired, the grandest char-acter of the century! *He* is Bonaparte[35] in one great move, that is, by overturn-ing this blind Republic and making himself a king. This man's re-election which will follow his success, I tell you—will be a reign! The subjects—bastard subjects—of other countries, apostates, are eager to overturn this government. You'll see—you'll see—that *re-election* means succession. His kin and friends are in every place of office already. Trust the songs of the people. They are the bards, the troubadours. Who makes these songs if not the people! "Vox populi"[36] forever! These false-hearted, unloyal foreigners it is, who would glory in the downfall of the Republic—and that by a half-breed too, a man springing from the ashes of old Assanonthime Brown, a false president yearning for kingly succession as hotly as ever did Ariston.[37]

Source: Asia Booth Clarke, *John Wilkes Booth: A Sister's Memoir,* ed. Terry Alford (Jackson: University Press of Mississippi, 1999), 88–89.

Walt Whitman, "Year of Meteors (1859–60)," 1865

On July 4, 1855, Walt Whitman (1819–1892) published the first edition of *Leaves of Grass*, a volume of poems that collapsed the boundaries between black and white and looked to an age of individual and national liberation. But Whitman's radical poetics did not translate into political action. He did not join the abolitionist movement, and in an article for the *Daily Times* published in 1857 he declared that slavery would probably disappear in a hundred years. He denounced the extremes of both proslavery advocates and abolitionists, once declared himself "afraid of agitators," and warned a friend: "Be not too damned radical." Then, although he knew Franklin Sanborn, Richard Hinton, and James Redpath, Brown's friends and co-conspirators, Whitman rejected Brown's militancy and observed that Brown lacked "evidence of great human quality," adding: "I am never convinced by the formal martyrdoms." Accordingly, his poem "Year of Meteors" does not celebrate Brown's martyrdom. Instead it fixes on Brown's humanity and vulnerability. The poem appeared in Whitman's volume *Drum-Taps*, published in May 1865. Whitman sent the volume to the printers before Lincoln's assassination on April 14, but in October 1865 he published *Sequel to Drum-Taps*, which included two laments for the dead president.

YEAR of meteors! brooding year!
I would bind in words retrospective, some of your deeds
    and signs;
I would sing your contest for the 19th Presidentiad;[38]
I would sing how an old man, tall, with white hair,
    mounted the scaffold in Virginia;
(I was at hand—silent I stood, with teeth shut close—I
    watch'd;
I stood very near you, old man, when cool and indifferent,
but trembling with age and your unheal'd
    wounds, you mounted the scaffold;)

I would sing in my copious song your census returns of
    The States,
The tables of population and products—I would sing of
    your ships and their cargoes,
The proud black ships of Manhattan, arriving, some
    fill'd with immigrants, some from the isthmus[39]
    with cargoes of gold;
Songs thereof would I sing—to all that hitherward
    comes would I welcome give;
And you would I sing, fair stripling! welcome to you
    from me, sweet boy of England![40]
Remember you surging Manhattan's crowds, as you
    passed with your cortege of nobles?
There in the crowds stood I, and singled you out with
    attachment;
I know not why, but I loved you . . . (and so go forth
    little song,
Far over sea speed like an arrow, carrying my love all
    folded,
And find in his palace the youth I love, and drop these
    lines at his feet;)
—Nor forget I to sing of the wonder, the ship as she
    swam up my bay,
Well-shaped and stately the Great Eastern[41] swam up my
    bay, she was 600 feet long,
Her moving swiftly, surrounded by myriads of small
    craft, I forget not to sing;
Nor the comet that came unannounced, out of the north,
    flaring in heaven,[42]
Nor the strange huge meteor procession, dazzling and
    clear, shooting over our heads,[43]
(A moment, a moment long, it sail'd its balls of unearthly
    light over our heads,
Then departed, dropt in the night, and was gone;)
—Of such, and fitful as they, I sing—with gleams from
    them would I gleam and patch these chants;
Your chants, O year all mottled with evil and good!
    year of forebodings! year of the youth I love!

Year of comets and meteors transient and strange!—lo!
    even here, one equally transient and strange!
As I flit through you hastily, soon to fall and be gone,
    what is this book,
What am I myself but one of your meteors?

Source: Drum-Taps (New York: William E. Chapin, 1865), 51–52.

Joseph G. Rosengarten, "John Brown's Raid: How I Got into It and How I Got Out of It," June 1865

As the war ended, commentators looked back and set Brown in the context of the war that followed his raid and death. Joseph George Rosengarten (1835–1921) from Philadelphia describes Brown's actions and death as grander than any during the four years of war and Brown himself as an "avenging spirit" that brought destruction on the South. Rosengarten was present at Harpers Ferry during Brown's raid. On October 17, 1859, he was traveling as a guest with the directors of the Pennsylvania Railroad on a tour of inspection between Cumberland and Baltimore. The train stopped at Martinsburg and Rosengarten heard about the raid. He made his way to Harpers Ferry but was taken into custody by local militia. Governor Wise ordered his release after he had spent a night in the Charles Town jail, and he went to see Brown in the engine house at the Ferry. When the war began, Rosengarten joined a company of volunteers with the Pennsylvania Artillery. He returned to Philadelphia after the war and worked as a lawyer.

In company with "Porte Crayon," Mr. Strothers,[44] a native of that part of Virginia, and well known by his sketches of Southern life in "Harper's Magazine," I went to the engine-house, and there saw the marks of the desperate defence and of the desperate bravery of John Brown and his men. I saw, too, John Brown himself. Wounded, bleeding, haggard, and defeated, and expecting death with more or less of agony as it was more or less near, John Brown was the finest specimen of a man I ever saw. His great, gaunt form, his noble head and face, his iron-gray hair and patriarchal beard, with the patient endurance of his own suffering, and his painful anxiety for the fate of his sons and the welfare of his men, his reticence when jeered at, his readiness to turn away wrath with a kind answer, his whole appearance and manner, what he looked, what he said—all impressed me with the deepest sense of reverence. If his being likened to anything in history could have made the scene more solemn, I should say that he was likest to the pictured or ideal representation of a Roundhead Puritan[45] dying for his faith, and silently glorying in the sacrifice not only of life, but of all that made life dearest to him. His wounded men showed in their patient endurance the influence of his example; while the vulgar herd of lookers-on, fair representatives of the cowardly militia-men who had waited for the little force of regulars to achieve the capture of the engine-house and its garrison, were ready to prove their further cowardice by maltreating the prisoners. The marines, who alone had sacrificed life in the attack, were sturdily bent on guarding them from any harsh handling. I turned away sadly from the old man's side, sought and got the information he wanted concerning "his people," as he called them, and was rewarded with his thanks in a few simple words, and in a voice that was as gentle as a woman's. The Governor, as soon as he was told of the condition of the prisoners, had them cared for, and, in all his bitterness at their doings, never spoke of them in terms other than honorable to himself and to them. He persistently praised John Brown for his bravery and his endurance;[46] and he was just as firm in declaring him a victim of shrewd and designing men, whose schemes he would yet fathom. . . .

In the morning I was glad to hear that my belated train had spent the last forty-eight hours at Martinsburg, and I did not a bit regret that my two days had been so full of adventure and incident. Waiting for its coming, I walked once more through the village, with one of the watchmen of the armory, who had been captured by John Brown and spent the night with him in the engine-house, and heard in all its freshness the story now so well known.

Then I bade Governor Wise good-bye, and was duly thanked for my gallant services to the noble Mother of States, and rewarded by being offered the honorary and honorable title of A.D.C. to the commander-in-chief of Virginia, both for past services and for the future tasks to be met, of beating off invading hosts from the North—all in the Governor's eye. Luckily for both sides, I declined the handsome offer; for my next visit to Virginia was as an A.D.C.[47] to a general commanding troops, not of the North, but of the United States, invading, not the Virginia of John Brown, but the Virginia of a wicked Southern Confederacy.

Not long after, I received a letter of thanks from Governor Wise, written at Richmond and with a good deal of official flattery. His son Jennings, an old acquaintance of mine in pleasant days in Germany, came to see me, too, with civil messages from his father. Poor fellow! he paid the forfeit of his rebellious treason with his life at Roanoke Island.[48] His father pays the heavier penalty of living to see the civil war fomented by him making its dreadful progress, and in its course crushing out all his ancient popularity and power.

In spite of many scenes of noble heroism and devoted bravery in legitimate warfare, and in the glorious campaigns of our own successful armies, I have never seen any life in death so grand as that of John Brown, and to me there is more than an idle refrain in the solemn chorus of our advancing hosts—

"John Brown's body lies mouldering in the ground,
As we go marching on!"

In the summer of 1862, I was brought again to Harper's Ferry, with my regiment, and the old familiar scenes were carefully revisited. The terrible destructions of public buildings, the wanton waste of private property, the deserted village instead of the thriving town, the utter ruin and wretchedness of the country all about, and the bleak waste of land from Harper's Ferry to Charlestown, are all set features in every picture of the war in Virginia. At my old head-quarters in Charlestown jail there was less change than I had expected; its sturdy walls had withstood attack and defence better than the newer and more showy structures; the few inhabitants left behind after the ebb and flow of so many army waves, Rebel and Union succeeding each other at pretty regular intervals, were the well-to-do of former days, looking after their household gods, sadly battered and the worse for wear, but still cherished very dearly. . . . The thousands who have come and gone through Harper's Ferry and past Bolivar Heights will recall the waste and desolation of what was once a blooming garden-spot, full of thrift and industry and comfort almost unknown elsewhere south of that fatal slave-line; thousands who are yet to pass that way will see in the ruins of the place traces of the avenging spirit that has marked forever the scene of *John Brown's Raid.*

Source: Atlantic Monthly, June 1865, 711–717 (715–717).

C. Chauncey Burr, "History of Old John Brown," July 1865

In the aftermath of the war, the Northerner and proslavery advocate C. Chauncey Burr (1817–1883) believed that slavery should be restored. He also believed that Brown was a thief who began a raid on the South that Lincoln finished. Together, Brown and Lincoln have ruined a civilization, Burr exclaims in an editorial of July 1865 for the Democratic journal *Old Guard*. Burr had published the magazine in New York since the summer of 1862. Yet as recently as the late 1840s he had edited a very different magazine: a Philadelphia-based reformist journal called *The Nineteenth Century* that denounced slavery and printed antislavery poetry by John Greenleaf Whittier. Originally from Maine, Burr had been an antislavery Universalist minister during the 1840s. After a tour of the South in 1849, he converted to a proslavery view and a belief in the inherent inequality of blacks and whites.

The pulpits generally, and a majority of Republican papers, now boastingly rejoice that *"the North has vindicated the cause of John Brown, and wiped out slavery."* Nor is this any foolish or unconsidered boast; it is strictly true. The policy of the Republican party, since it came into power, has been a faithful carrying out of the work begun by old John Brown. The administration of Abraham Lincoln was a John Brown raid on the grandest scale; and it was no more. That is the place it will occupy in history. The bloody business is done, and we do not write for the purpose of amending the great crime. We do not seek to raise the dead. We accept the *facts* as we find them; but it is our business to tell the truth about these facts. It is our business to strip off all these bandages of shams, hypocricies, and lies, and lay bare to the bone this monstrous carcass of frauds and despotism. The record of this party is in revolution and blood; in the revolution and blood inaugurated by John Brown. It has finished the raid which that prince of assassins and thieves, John Brown, began. . . .

It was the endorsement of the policy of this raider and murderer, by the North, that startled and aroused the South, and finally drove it into secession; for John Brown's raid *was* endorsed by the North. From almost every church and school-house, the voice of prayer and lamentation went up to Almighty God, canonizing his name, and endorsing his infamy. The whole Republican press lent its support to this abomination; and with entire consistency, when the New England soldiers marched through this city, they made it hideous as hell by singing and shouting *"John Brown's soul is marching on."* So it is, we have little doubt, *marching on,* through seas of fire, in company with fiends, thieves and assassins, such as were his companions and abettors in this life. So it is *marching on* to the music of despotism, ignorance, revenge and lust, that swells up like a gorgon from the bottomless pit, out of the brazen throats of the negro-worshipping mobs! *Marching on,* as a pestilence or contagion, or a thing of horror and death marches on! Behind its march are the wails of widows, the screams of children, the vain implorations of defenseless old men, and the humiliation of manhood. Before it, the insane gibberish and fantastic dance of negroes, of both the white and black complexion, making night and day hideous with infernal delight. Marching on!—alas, poor country! alas, human nature! Why do we write these things now? Because we love, and would save our country. Because we would bring our countrymen of the North to their senses, by holding up the John Brown raid as a glass for them to see their faces in. We would remind them that there is both a *God* and *history,* and that justice and truth, sooner or later, will whip all of the shams and lies out of the records of human events. If the South has *follies* to repent of, we have *crimes,* crimes which will roll out of their graves and hunt us like demons through the world. Vainly do we seek to assure ourselves, by shutting our eyes and saying, *verily, what a good people are we!* There is an eye that we cannot shut. There is an arm that we cannot stay. Time is an inexorable avenger of all men's wrongs; and time will strip us bare to the bone, and show what a carcass of frauds and shams we are. We repeat again, the last four years of Republican rule have been a stupendous John Brown raid. Logically, constitutionally, they have been just that, and nothing more. What we dare to say is this, that John Brown had as much Constitution and law for what he did, as the Republican administration had for what it has done. This is what we say, and no leading Republican dare attempt to debate the merits of the question with us before the people. They dare call names; but they dare not debate. We love truth and respect justice above all things. We hold no opinion which we will not gladly submit to the test of fair argument and debate; but these *traitors* of the John Brown school dare not argue. They carry all points by singing, shouting, and mobbing. Their throats are trumpets, and their brains gongs and sounding-boards. In a late speech, Senator Lowry, a prominent man in the Republican party of the State of Pennsylvania, said: "John Brown was the first martyr of this rebellion— Abraham Lincoln the last. The names of Abraham Lincoln and John Brown will go down in history together, as the first and lost martyr of this rebellion. The war could not be averted. God Almighty is fighting this war for the right. John Brown played his part, and Abraham Lincoln his."[49] Here the truth is owned. The Republican administration is simply a John Brown raid. The name of John Brown and of Abraham Lincoln will indeed *go down to posterity together;* and the name of Seward, and Sumner, and Garrison,[50] and such as they, will go with them—go with them into the abyss of infamy and eternal shame. Over the most prosperous land, over the fairest civilization in the world, they have brought ruin, barbarism, and woe. If the traitors of this school had never been born, the peace of our country had never been broken. That is a truth that will stand as firmly as the word of God, when the subterfuges and lies of this mad hour are swept away. The record President Johnson has given of John Brown's character and his raid[51] will stand the test of time. The historian will take it as the starting point of the policy which has ruled us of the North since the accession of the Abolition party to power. O, my countrymen! Have you abandoned yourselves permanently to the shame, to the eternal infamy, of this policy? The policy of a thief, a robber, and assassin! The name President Johnson has given him is the one he must wear in history; and you who follow John Brown's policy shall wear it also. Sing and shout, and dance while you may! Time will last longer than your songs, and justice will one day throw you under tie wheels of avenging retribution. If all history is not a liar, the day of your shame is sure to come. O, you sneer! So have hundreds of thousands of fools done before! If you did not sneer we should think we had done you injustice. Sneer and mock as you will, for this is *your day.* God's day, the day of justice, comes afterwards! It lasts forever!

Source: The Old Guard: A Monthly Journal Devoted to the Principles of 1776 and 1787, July 1865, 324–330 (324, 328–30).

Henry Ingersoll Bowditch, "Dear Mrs. H—," July 27, 1865

Americans not only remembered and recast Brown during the war's immediate aftermath, they also visited the sites where he lived and died. In late July 1865, the Boston abolitionist and physician Henry Ingersoll Bowditch (1808–1892), who had been active in the Anti-Man-Hunting League, which resisted the Fugitive Slave Act in Boston from 1854 onward, visited Brown's house and burial site near Lake Placid, New York. He wrote to one of his patients who had requested an account of the trip. The letter, which newspapers reprinted, describes Brown as the leader of the Union forces during the war. Bowditch went on to serve as the first chairman of the Massachusetts State Board of Health in 1869 and was a charter member and president of the American Medical Association. Other activists visited Brown's grave after Bowditch. The Niagara Movement, a black protest organization that became the NAACP, used the site for its annual meeting in 1908, and one of the NAACP's black activists, Jesse Max Barber, led an annual pilgrimage there from 1922 through the 1930s.

Saranac Lakes, July 27, 1865

Dear Mrs. H—

I promised to write to you from John Brown's grave. I thought while there of my promise; but as I had only a short time to stay, and many people were visiting the spot, I have postponed writing to you until now.

I am at Bartlett's[52]—the prince of hosts in these mountain regions—who, living here many years with his charming and energetic, warmhearted wife, makes a sort of paradise for lovers of angling and shooting, or still larger numbers of devotees to eating delicious trout or sweet, tender venison-steaks. In this little *bijou* of a hotel, and with the sound of rushing waterfalls in my ears, within close view of the eternal hills, and while breathing the clear, cool air of heaven, I redeem my pledge.

I stood by the side of John Brown's grave yesterday.

He was, or rather he is now, one of my God-sent heroes—a man specially allowed to appear at the appointed hour with a sort of John the Baptist mission, and who sealed that mission with his blood. I thought his design foolish and wrong; and how foolish was *my* thought as I consider subsequent events, which made him the leader of our hosts in the Civil War, during which "his soul was marching on," and compelled even his enemies to admire him even while they sought his life.

While I think now of his quiet self-possession in prison; his brave words to his companions just before his death; his admiration of the beauty of Nature while going toward the place of execution; his thanks to his jailer and others for acts of kindness; his walk, firm and elastic, up the scaffold-step; his gentleness and yet his perfect manliness even to the last—my reverence for him exceeds, far exceeds, the reverence I have for any other being save Christ, or Socrates while drinking the hemlock. And how ennobling is such an example as Brown's to all the race! Knowing him to be mortal like ourselves, we for a time at least understand the fine expression made use of by Dr. James Walker in one of his sermons: "There is the power of an archangel locked up in the breast of every man, and a sufficient motive only is needed to bring it forth."[53]

But a truce to all my musings! You want me to redeem my promise and to describe his tomb. . . . A finer spot for the tomb of a pious and brave man could not have been selected; and I could not help feeling how much the martyr must have gained in strength from his very residence. "I will lift up mine eyes unto the hills, whence cometh my strength."[54] I am sure that often to his genuinely pious soul, a lover of the Bible, the whole of this noble psalm must have suggested itself to him as he went forth in the morning to his daily toil, or returned from it at eventide.

John Brown's house is a prominent object, and the only one in sight—a simple, plain wooden structure, with a larger barn near by, in which I saw, as I passed by, a fine load of newly made hay. We entered the front door and met Mr. Hinckly, who married one of John Brown's daughters.[55]

He had a very intelligent countenance. He was one of the "chosen band" (in Kansas),[56] and had a sincere reverence for his great leader and for the objects he had in hand.

Mr. Hinckly regards Brown as the pioneer—as in fact the first martyr—in this war. I think he is right in his judgment of John Brown's position as history will put him.

I read to my boys and my brother the touching account of Brown's death, in order to impress upon my young companions the real nobleness of the soul whose body's resting place we were going to visit. Eight or ten rods from the door is seen a huge bowlder, rising about ten feet high, rugged and broad, and having a rather grand, irregular shape, making four massive sides. Directly in front of one of these, and facing, or nearly facing, the front door of the residence, lies John Brown, "alone in his glory."[57] A magnificently broad sodded tumulus alone marks the spot. I like its size. It was worthy in this respect to be placed over the remains of one of the old Scandinavian Vikings, huge and simple as his own great nature. It is surrounded by rosebushes, a little neglected. In front of it, and very awkwardly placed, is a tall, crumbling headstone, given originally to John Brown to mark the grave of his father, of the same name. Below the name of the father and time of his death appears, rudely cut and easily to be effaced, the statement that another John Brown was executed at Charlestown, Va., 1859. On the back of the slab were the names of the family; but it was all sad, as we thought, and my brother William and I almost vowed that we would send up a good stone-cutter, who, after removing the grotesque and inappropriate slab to another part of the lot, should be directed to cut *deeply* into one of the sides of the massive bowlder above mentioned, the simple words "John Brown," in large letters that could be seen at a glance from as great a distance as one could see the rock itself. This could be done, and the family would consent to it.[58]

It only remains for some of us who believe that such a man is worthy of such a memorial to make proper arrangements for so doing.

Respectfully yours, Henry I. Bowditch

Source: Hermann von Holst, *John Brown,* ed. Frank Preston Stearns (Boston: Cupples and Hurd, 1888), 197–203.

Charles Sumner, "The National Security and the National Faith," September 14, 1865

Speaking at the Republican state convention in Worcester after the end of the Civil War, Charles Sumner returned to the topic of Brown. He had met the abolitionist in early 1857 when Brown visited him in Boston and asked to see the bloodstained coat he was wearing during Brooks's attack. He had written about Brown in December 1859, calling him "courageous" and martyrlike. Now, in 1865, he describes Brown's mythical kiss of a slave child on his way to the gallows as a benediction and a legacy. Brown offered America a message of equality, Sumner explains, and Northern victory in the war meant the country could now embrace that message. Sumner went on to be a Radical Republican leader in the Senate during Reconstruction, where he fought for voting rights for the freedmen.

For myself, fellow-citizens, pardon me, if I say that my course is fixed. Many may hesitate; many may turn away from those great truths which make the far-reaching brightness of the Republic; many may seek a temporary favor by untimely surrender: I shall not. The victory of blood, which has been so painfully won, must be confirmed by a greater victory of ideas, so that the renowned words of Abraham Lincoln may be fulfilled, and "this nation, under God, shall have a new birth of Freedom; and government of the people, *by the people,* and for the people, shall not perish from the earth."[59] To this end I seek no merely formal Union, seething with smothered curses, but a practical, moral, and political Unity, founded on common rights, knit together by common interests, inspired by a common faith, and throbbing with a common love of country—where our Constitution, interpreted anew, shall be a covenant with Life and a league with Heaven, and Liberty shall be everywhere not only a right, but a duty. John Brown, on his way to the scaffold, stooped to take up a slave child. That closing example was the legacy of the dying man to his country. That benediction we must continue and fulfill. The last shall be first; and so, in this new order, Equality, long postponed, shall become the master principle of our system and the very frontispiece of our Constitution. The Rebellion was to beat down this principle, by founding a government on the alleged inferiority of a race. The attempt has failed, but not, alas! the insolent assumption of the conspirators. Pursuing our victory, I now insist that this assumption shall be trampled out. A righteous government cannot be founded on any exclusion of race. This is not the first time that I have battled with the barbarism of Slavery. I battle still, as the bloody monster retreats to its last citadel; and, God willing, I mean to hold on, if it takes what remains to me of life.

Source: Charles Sumner, *The National Security and the National Faith; Guarantees for the National Freedman and the National Creditor* (Boston: Rand & Avery, 1865).

James Buchanan, *Mr. Buchanan's Administration on the Eve of the Rebellion,* January 1866

As the U.S. president between 1857 and 1861, James Buchanan (1791–1868) was in office when Brown raided Harpers Ferry. He was a Northern Democrat with Southern sympathies, and while he viewed secession as unconstitutional, he did nothing to prevent it. He assured the South that the federal government had no right to use force, blamed secession on the antislavery movement, and urged a constitutional convention to create amendments that would protect slavery in the territories and states and prevent Northern states from interfering with the Fugitive Slave Act. After the war that he tried to prevent, Buchanan remembered Brown's raid in the first published presidential memoir. *Buchanan's Administration on the Eve of the Rebellion* appeared in January 1866 and explains that the Southern response to Brown was entirely justified.

John Brown was a man violent, lawless, and fanatical. Amid the troubles in Kansas he had distinguished himself, both by word and by deed, for boldness and cruelty. His ruling passion was to become the instrument of abolishing slavery, by the strong hand, throughout the slaveholding States. With him, this amounted almost to insanity. . . . In the already excited condition of public feeling throughout the South, this raid of John Brown made a deeper impression on the Southern mind against the Union than all former events. Considered merely as the isolated act of a desperate fanatic, it would have had no lasting effect. It was the enthusiastic and permanent approbation of the object of his expedition by the abolitionists of the North, which spread alarm and apprehension throughout the South. We are told by Fowler in his "Sectional Controversy,"[60] that on the day of Brown's execution bells were tolled in many places, cannon fired, and prayers offered up for him as if he were a martyr; he was placed in the same category with Paul and Silas, for whom prayers were made by the Church, and churches were draped in mourning. Nor were these

honors to his memory a mere transient burst of feeling. The Republican party
have ever since honored him as a saint or a martyr in a cause which they
deemed so holy. According to them, "whilst his body moulders in the dust his
spirit is still marching on" in the van to accomplish his bloody purposes. Even
blasphemy, which it would be improper to repeat, has been employed to consecrate his memory.

Fanaticism never stops to reason. Driven by honest impulse, it rushes on to
its object without regard to interposing obstacles. Acting on the principle
avowed in the Declaration of Independence, "that all men are created equal,"
and believing slavery to be sinful, it would not hesitate to pass from its own
State into other States, and emancipate their slaves by force of arms. We do not
stop to inquire whether slavery is sinful. We may observe, however, that under
the old and new dispensations, slaves were held both by Jews and Christians,
and rules were prescribed for their humane treatment. In the present state of
civilization, we are free to admit that slavery is a great political and social evil.
If left to the wise ordinances of a superintending Providence, which never acts
rashly, it would have been gradually extinguished in our country, peacefully
and without bloodshed, as has already been done throughout nearly the whole
of Christendom. It is true that other countries enjoyed facilities for emancipation which we do not possess. In them the slaves were of the same color and
race with the rest of the community, and in becoming freemen they soon mingled with the general mass on equal terms with their former masters.

But even admitting slavery to be a sin, have the adherents of John Brown
never reflected that the attempt by one people to pass beyond their own jurisdiction, and to extirpate by force of arms whatever they may deem sinful
among another people, would involve the nations of the earth in perpetual
hostilities? We Christians are thoroughly convinced that Mahomet was a false
prophet; shall we, therefore, make war upon the Turkish empire to destroy Is-
lamism? If we would preserve the peace of the world and avoid much greater
evils than we desire to destroy, we must act upon the wise principles of international law, and leave each people to decide domestic questions for themselves. Their sins are not our sins. We must intrust their punishment and reformation to their own authorities, and to the Supreme Governor of nations.
This spirit of interference with what we may choose to consider the domestic
evils of other nations, has in former periods covered the earth with blood. . . .
These days of darkness and delusion, of doing evil that good might come,

have, it is to be hoped, passed away for ever under the pure light of the Gospel. If all these acts were great wrongs in the intercourse between independent nations, if they violated the benign principles of Christianity, how much greater would the wrong have been had one portion of the sovereign States of a confederate union made war against the remainder to extirpate from them the sin of slavery! And this more especially when their common constitution, in its very terms, recognizes slavery, restores the runaway slave to his master, and even makes the institution a basis for the exercise of the elective franchise. With like reason might the State of Maine, whilst the delusion of the Maine liquor law prevailed,[61] have made war on her sister States to enforce its observance upon their people, because drunkenness is a grievous sin in the belief of all Christians. In justification of this, she might have alleged that the intemperance tolerated among her neighbors, and not her own spirit to intermeddle with their concerns, was the cause of the war, just as it has been asserted that slavery in the Southern States was the cause of the late war. We may believe and indeed know that the people of the North, however much they may have extolled the conduct of John Brown, would never in practice have carried out his teachings and his example; but justice requires that we should make a fair allowance for the apprehensions of the Southern people, who necessarily viewed the whole scene from an opposite standpoint.

Source: *Mr. Buchanan's Administration on the Eve of the Rebellion,* in *The Works of James Buchanan: Comprising His Speeches, State Papers, and Private Correspondence,* Vol. 12, ed. John Bassett Moore (Philadelphia: Lippincott, 1911), 1–261 (49–53).

Herman Melville, "The Portent (1859)," 1866

Herman Melville (1819–1891) never spoke out against slavery. But several of his works of fiction refute the racist framework that supported the slave system, including the novella *Benito Cereno* (1855), about a slave rebellion on board a merchant ship. Melville eventually responded to Brown in a poem published in August 1866 as part of his volume *Battle-Pieces*. Unlike Whitman's Brown, who is an old man trembling with age, Melville's Brown is more a symbol than a human being: his beard streaming like a meteor, his face hidden in a hood as if he were a blind Greek prophet, his very name concealed within parentheses like his hooded face. Melville did not list the poem in the book's table of contents. Instead it appears on what should be a blank page. Like Brown's death, the poem comes before the war as an omen of more battle pieces. Further emphasizing Brown's status as a portent or foreshadowing of the Civil War, Melville describes him as a "shadow" that falls across America's "green": a dark prophecy of America's end of innocence. Then, across the rest of *Battle-Pieces*, Melville continued to dwell upon the country's fall from grace during the war.

Hanging from the beam,
    Slowly swaying (such the law),
Gaunt the shadow on the green,
    Shenandoah![62]
The cut is on the crown
(Lo, John Brown),
And the stabs shall heal no more.

Hidden in the cap
    Is the anguish none can draw;
So your future veils its face,
    Shenandoah!

But the streaming beard is shown
(Weird John Brown),
The meteor of the war.

Source: Herman Melville, *Battle-Pieces and Aspects of the War* (New York: Harper and Brothers, 1866), unnumbered p. 12.

Gerrit Smith, "John Brown," August 15, 1867

The abolitionist and philanthropist Gerrit Smith (1797–1874) knew Brown from the 1840s onward. Over the course of his reform career, Smith spent $8 million on various causes, and between 1846 and 1850 he gave away 200,000 acres of land to poor blacks and whites. In 1846 he gave 120,000 acres of land in the Adirondacks to three thousand New York blacks and sold Brown 244 acres on extended credit in return for a promise to teach the black settlers about farming. As one of Brown's allies and funders, he faced questions about his involvement in the Harpers Ferry raid. On October 20, 1859, the *New York Herald* named Smith as the man who supplied Brown's "sinews of war." Although Governor Wise did not indict him, and although he had always been ambivalent about the use of violence—generally preferring not to know the precise details of Brown's plans—Smith felt guilty and suffered an emotional collapse after Brown's sentencing. His family committed him to the New York State Asylum for the Insane at Utica, from which he was released in early 1860. In August 1867 he wrote a public statement from his home in Peterboro, New York. The first half denied that he had funded Brown's raid, but the second half, below, imagines a future when Brown's friends might take pride in their connection to a great American hero.

I cast no blame on anyone for supposing that I had a full knowledge of Brown's plans and of his changes in them. That I had is, I admit, a not very unreasonable inference from the intimate relations both of business and friendship existing between us. Nevertheless, so it is, that I had but a partial knowledge of these plans and not the least knowledge of his exchanging them for others. Right here, too, let me say that I do not feel myself at all dishonored by the coupling of my name with any of Brown's endeavors for the liberation of the slave. Even where truth forbids the coupling, regard for my reputation does not forbid it. The more the public identifies me with John Brown, the more it honors me. As I knew Brown so well and loved him so well, it was not unreasonable to suppose that I, too, would give his character to the public. Thank

God! Brown did that himself. His life, crowned by his well-nigh matchless death, shows, unmistakably and fully, what was his character. His words, all the way from his capture to his death, sweeter or sublimer than which there have been none since Jesus walked the earth, leave no room for mistake or ignorance of his character. And, here let me say, that Jesus was in Brown's heart the Blessed and Loved One. Were I asked to say, in the fewest and plainest words, what Brown was, my answer would be that he was *a religious man*. He had ever a deep sense of the claims of God and man upon him, and his whole life was a prompt, practical recognition of them. Brown was entirely and, I might perhaps add, stiffly orthodox. I do not believe that he doubted the truth of one line of the Bible. Twice he attended the religious conversational meeting, which we hold in Peterboro; and, each time, he criticised remarks of mine, which he regarded as theologically unsound. His ever favorite hymn was that beginning: "Blow ye the trumpet, blow!"[63]

All the members of my family held Brown in high regard. Beneath that stern look beat one of the kindest hearts. He loved children; and they loved him. My little granddaughter was often in his lap.

A more scrupulously just man in matters of property I never knew. In 1858 he and a Mr. Thompson,[64] who was his neighbor in Essex County, came to my office. He had purchased Mr. Thompson's interest in a farm. Whilst I was making out the papers which they needed, Brown certainly twice and, I believe, three times, asked Thompson if the price were great enough:—telling him to make it greater if he thought proper. It occurred to me, at the moment, that Brown went beyond the Christian precept, and cared even more for his neighbor's rights than for his own. Let me add that Thompson beautifully declined to increase the price.

It is quite probable that John Brown will be the most admired person in American history. Washington worked well—but it was for his own race—only for his equals. William Lloyd Garrison has lived for a despised and outraged race. John Brown both lived and died for it: and few names, even in the *world's* history, will stand as high as his.

Men begin to ask why a monument to the memory of John Brown has not yet been built. The day for building John Brown's monument has not yet come. It will be built where stood his gallows; and it would, not yet, be welcome there. Its base will be broad and its shaft will pierce the skies. But the appreciation of his sublime character is, not yet, sufficiently just and widespread, to call for the rearing of such a structure. In executing this work of love and admiration, Southern hands will join with Northern hands. In rendering this tribute to the grandest man of the age, Southern zeal will not fall behind Northern zeal. Indeed, it may well be expected that the generous and ardent South will, ere the cool and calculating North is ready to do so, confess the enormous crime of the nation—of the whole nation—against the black man. Nay, it is just because the North is, not yet, ready to confess it, that there is, not yet, Peace between her and the South. That confession would, surely, bring the Peace. For it would involve the further confession of the common responsibility of North and South for the cause of the War: and it is the sense of that common responsibility, which would impel the North to afford such relief to the war-impoverished South, as would win her heart, and result in a true and enduring Peace.

But the North and South will both come right. They will both repent of having, for generations, trodden out the life of the black man. And, then, they will love each other. And, then, God will make them the happiest nation in all the earth. And, then, to have enjoyed the confidence of John Brown, as did Howe and Parker and Stearns and Douglass and Sanborn and Morton[65] and many others, will, no longer, be counted dishonor, but, on the contrary, high honor. Blessed, indeed, will be the day, which shall witness these things! Then John Brown's day will have come:—and then will John Brown's monument be built!

Source: Octavius Brooks Frothingham, *Gerrit Smith: A Biography* (New York: Putnam's, 1878), 257–259.

John Milton Hay, "Diary," September 10, 1867

John Milton Hay (1838–1905) of Indiana entered American politics soon after Brown's death. While working as a law clerk in Springfield, Illinois, in 1860, he helped with Lincoln's campaign for the presidency. Then he served as Lincoln's assistant private secretary from 1860 to 1864. After Lincoln's death he went to Europe as a diplomat. While serving as an envoy in Vienna in 1867, he made observations in his diary about Brown and the nature of revolution. Hay went on to work as an editor for the *New York Tribune* in the 1870s. In 1890 he published a ten-volume study of Lincoln, cowritten with John Nicolay, which belittled Brown. Between 1898 and 1905 he served as secretary of state under Presidents McKinley and Roosevelt.

Sept. 10, 1867. Garibaldi at the Geneva Peace Congress makes a war speech![66] This is bold and fine. The old man has not long to live and he will go up with a flash. He loved liberty and peace so well that he is willing to fight for them. He hates war—as a doctor hates drugs, but he uses it, for the good of the world. He ought to free Rome, if Rome is worth freeing? and then die. His short cuts, by the compass of abstract right, over the field of Government and law are too destructive to the Fetishes for him to lead a quiet life even in Italy free. John Brown is a saint now. Had he lived he would have been a malignant Rad,[67] and people would have tired of him. In America the current of national life is so healthy, that one man cannot disturb it. So that our revolutionists do not hurt anything. Error and truth, as we regard them, must never have full course. We must take both diluted.

Source: *Letters of John Hay and Extracts from Diary,* Vol I., ed. Clara Stone Hay and Henry Adams (Washington, D.C.: privately published, 1908), 330–331.

Richard Henry Dana, Jr., "How We Met John Brown," July 1871

Into the 1870s, friends and acquaintances continued to reminisce about Brown and set their memories in the context of the Civil War and the postwar period. In 1871, Richard Henry Dana (1815–1882) recounted his trip to the Adirondacks in the summer of 1849, when he and some companions came across Brown's home. Brown and his wife welcomed the travelers and gave them food and board. Dana was a Massachusetts lawyer and the author of *Two Years Before the Mast* (1840), a memoir about his voyage at sea. The year before his visit to Brown's cabin, he had helped to found the antislavery Free Soil Party. A few years later, in 1854, he represented the fugitive slave Anthony Burns in Boston. Dana served as a United States attorney during the Civil War and a U.S. counsel during the trial of Jefferson Davis in 1868. Remembering his encounter with a quiet farmer in 1871, he could hardly believe that Brown went on to change history.

We could not pass the Browns' house without stopping. I find this entry in my journal:—

"*June 29, Friday.*—After breakfast, started for home. We stopped at the Browns' cabin on our way, and took an affectionate leave of the family that had shown us so much kindness. We found them at breakfast, in the patriarchal style. Mr. and Mrs. Brown and their large family of children with the hired men and women, including three negroes, all at the table together. Their meal was neat, substantial, and wholesome."

How mysterious is the touch of Fate which gives a man immortality on earth! It would have been past belief, had we been told that this quiet frontier farmer, already at or beyond middle life, with no noticeable past, would, within ten years, be the central figure of a great tragic scene, gazed upon with wonder, pity, admiration, or execration by half a continent! That this man

should be thought to have imperiled the slave empire in America, and added a
new danger to the stability of the Union! That this almost undistinguishable
name of John Brown should be whispered among four millions of slaves, and
sung wherever the English tongue is spoken, and incorporated into an anthem
to whose solemn cadences men should march to battle by the tens of thousands! That he should have done something toward changing the face of civilization itself!

In 1859–60 my inveterate habit of overworking gave me, as you know, a va-
cation and the advantage of a voyage round the world. Somewhere at the an-
tipodes[68] I picked up, from time to time, in a disjointed way, out of all chrono-
logical order, reports of the expedition of one John Brown into Virginia,
his execution, and the political excitement attending it; but I learned little of
much value. That was the time when slavery ruled all. There was scarce an
American consul or political agent in any quarter of the globe, or on any island of the seas, who was not a supporter of the slave power. I saw a large portion of these national representatives in my circumnavigation of the globe,
and it was impossible to find at any office over which the American flag waved
a newspaper that was not in the interests of slavery. No copy of the *New York
Tribune* or *Evening Post*[69] was tolerated under an American official roof. Each
embassy and consulate, the world over, was a centre of influences for slavery
and against freedom. We ought to take this into account when we blame foreign nations for not accepting at once the United States as an antislavery
power, bent on the destruction of slavery, as soon as our civil war broke out.
For twenty years foreign merchants, shipmasters, or travelers had seen in
American officials only trained and devoted supporters of the slave power, and
the only evidences of public opinion at home to be found at those official
seats, so much resorted to and credited, were all of the same character. I returned home at the height of the Lincoln campaign of 1860, on which followed
secession and war; and it was not until after the war, when reading back into
its history, that I met with those unsurpassed narratives, by Mr. Wentworth
Higginson and Mr. Wendell Phillips, of their visits to the home of John Brown,
about the time of his execution, full of solemn touches, and marked by that
restraint which good taste and right feeling accept in the presence of a great
subject, itself so expressive of awe.[70] Reading on, it went through me with a
thrill—This is the man under whose roof I received shelter and kindness!

These were the mother and daughters and sons who have suffered or shed their blood! This was the family whose artless heroism, whose plain fidelity and fortitude, seem to have cast chivalry and romance into the shade!

It is no uncommon thing to visit spots long hallowed by great events or renowned persons. The course of emotions in such cases is almost stereotyped. But this retroactive effect is something strange and anomalous. It is one thing to go through a pass of fear, watching your steps as you go, conscious of all its grandeur and peril, but quite another sensation when a glare of light, thrown backwards, shows you a fearful passage through which you have just gone with careless steps and unheeding eyes. It seems as if those few days of ours in the Adirondacks, in 1849, had been passed under a spell which held my senses from knowing what we saw. All is now become a region of peculiar sacredness. That plain, bare farm, amid the blackened stumps, the attempts at scientific agriculture under such disadvantages, the simple dwelling, the surveyor's tools, the setting of the little scene amid grand, awful mountain ranges, the negro colony and inmates, the family bred to duty and principle, and held to them by a power recognized as being from above—all these now come back on my memory with a character nowise changed, indeed, in substance, but, as it were, illuminated. The widow bearing homeward the body from the Virginia scaffold, with the small company of stranger friends, crossed the lake, as we had done, to Westport; and thence, along that mountain road, but in midwinter, to Elizabethtown; and thence, the next day, to the door of that dwelling. The scene is often visited now by sympathy or curiosity, no doubt, and master pens have made it one of the most marked in our recent history.

In this narrative I have endeavored, my dear friend, to guard against the influence of intervening events, and to give all things I saw in the natural, transient way in which they struck me at the time. That is its only value. It is not owing to subsequent events, that John Brown and his family are so impressed on my mind. The impression was made at the time. The short extract from a journal which set down but little, and nothing that was not of a marked character, will, I trust, satisfy the most incredulous that I am not beating up memory for impressions. I have tried to recollect something more of John Brown's conversation, but in vain, nor can either of my companions help me in that. We cannot recollect that slavery was talked of at all. It seems strange it should not have been, as we were Free-Soilers, and I had been to the Buffalo Convention the year before;[71] but perhaps the presence of the negroes may have restrained us, as we did not see the master of the house alone. I notice that my journal speaks of him as "originally from Berkshire, Massachusetts." In examining his biography I think this must have been from his telling us that he had come from the western part of Massachusetts, when he found that we were Massachusetts men. I see no proof of his having lived in any other part of Massachusetts than Springfield. My journal speaks of the house as a "logcabin." I observe that Mr. Higginson and some of the biographers describe it as a frame building. Mr. Brown had been but a few months on the place when we were there, and he may have put up a frame house afterwards; or it is quite as likely that I was not careful to note the difference, and got that impression from its small size and plain surroundings.

Nearly all that the writers in December, 1859, have described lies clear in my memory. There can have been little change there in ten years. Ruth had become the wife of Henry Thompson, whose brother was killed at Harper's Ferry;[72] and the son I speak of as apparently the foreman of the farm was probably Owen, who was with his father at Ossawatomie and Harper's Ferry, and escaped. Frederick, who was killed at Ossawatomie, in 1856, was probably the lad whom we saw coming home with his father, bringing the negroes on the wagon. Among the small boys, playing and working about the house, were Watson and Oliver, who were killed at Harper's Ferry. I do not recollect seeing—perhaps it was not there then—the gravestone of his grandfather of the Revolutionary Army, which John Brown is said to have taken from Connecticut and placed against the side of the house; nor can I recall the great rock, near the door, by the side of which lies his body,

"mouldering in the ground,
While his soul is marching on."

What judgment soever political loyalty, social ethics, or military strategy may pronounce upon his expedition into Virginia, old John Brown has a grasp on the moral world.

Source: Atlantic Monthly, July 1871, 1–9 (7–9).

Henry S. Olcott, "How We Hung
John Brown," 1875

As acquaintances such as Dana remembered their preraid encounters with Brown, other commentators remembered the events of Brown's death. In 1875, Henry Steel Olcott (1832–1907) of
New Jersey told the story of how he witnessed Brown's execution by joining the Virginia military
recruits for the day. Between 1858 and 1860, Olcott was the associate agricultural editor of the
New York Tribune, an unpopular newspaper in Virginia because of the antislavery views of its
editor, Horace Greeley. Olcott therefore had to keep his professional identity hidden while visiting Charles Town. During the war he joined the Union Army, and then he worked as a lawyer
from 1868 to 1878. The same year that he wrote his article about Brown, Olcott cofounded the
Theosophical Society, which included the objective of a "universal brotherhood of humanity
without distinction of race, creed, sex, caste, or color." In 1878 he moved to India in order to develop the society and study Buddhism. He lived in India and Ceylon (Sri Lanka) for the rest of
his life.

It will be conceded that the first act in the bloody drama of the American Conflict had its climax on the 2d of December, 1859, when John Brown of Ossawatomie was hung at Charlestown, Virginia. Thirty years of agitation of the question of African slavery culminated in that direful event, which was at once the
prelude to one of the most terrible wars of modern times, and the harbinger
of a new era of equal rights and true republican government. Looking back
now over the intervening fourteen years, it seems incredible that so much
should have happened in so short a time. The rapid rush of events, the upheaval of our whole national system, the changed relations between the two
sections of country, and especially between the black and white races, make
the tragical end of John Brown appear as something that occurred at least a
generation ago; and the true story of his hanging, by an eye-witness, will perhaps be read with as much interest as any other thing I could contribute to the

present volume. It is time the story was told; for with negro ex-slaves sitting on the bench, in the gubernatorial chair, in legislatures, in Congress, serving as State treasurers, as cadets, as surgeons, as consuls, and as foreign ambassadors, it reads like fiction that the life of an editor should have been put in peril so recently, within the limits of this country, in the peaceful performance of his duty. And I am sure that if these lines should be read by any of the men whom I met at the exciting time of which I write, he will confess to mortification that such should have been the fact. . . .

When all was over, and the brave-souled Brown's spinal cord was broken, and we were all ready to turn homeward, and my fellow-guests refused to let me subscribe towards a service of silver for our hostess, merely because I was a Northern man—albeit, as they were so kind as to say, a deuced good fellow—I felt really hurt, and sorry enough to part with them. What made me feel worse than all was to go through the town, arm in arm with some of my new friends, cheek by jowl and all that sort of thing, and think how shameful, how pitiful and cowardly it was that, in this "land of the free and home of the brave," I was walking those streets with the specter of Death stalking lock-step behind me, never leaving me day or night, because I dared to write an honest letter to a great newspaper, and tell how a brave, if perhaps fanatical, man behaved and talked.

Source: Lotos Leaves, ed. John Brougham and John Elderkin (London: Chatto and Windus, 1875), 233–49 (233, 243–244).

Colored Citizen, "Wanted, a Few Black John Browns," January 4, 1879

The South's last Republican governments fell in 1877. Federal troops withdrew from the region, and redeemer governments began to roll back the gains of Reconstruction and reestablish white supremacist rule in the old Confederate states. Although the Ku Klux Klan had been suppressed in 1871, after attacking thousands of black Americans in the South during the immediate postwar years, other paramilitary groups continued to terrorize black Southerners. The Southern election campaigns of 1878 were marked by murder and repression. In response, thousands of black "Exodusters" left Louisiana, Mississippi, and Texas for Kansas in 1879 and 1880. A black magazine in Fort Scott, Kansas, reported on the terrors in early 1879. Observing that the same white Southerners who enslaved blacks were now murdering them, it calls for the same militant response now that met slavery in 1859: some black John Browns.

Brutal murders and barbarous outrages in the South are still continued. Almost every day a fresh outrage perpetrated by demons of some one of the same Southern States is reported. Such a thing as a black man finding any security for his life, provided he dares assert his manhood, in that devil-ridden country is out of the question.

There is no such thing as justice, none in all the South, that is, where there is a black man interested: if one works for a white man he is systematically swindled out of his wages, and if he protests, his life is taken from him, as ruthlessly, as if he were a brute. If he goes into the courts he finds judges, lawyers and juries all against him, and if he attempts to stand up like a man and demand a trial, that's fair an impartial, he is given quickly to understand that, in that country, that old demon Judge Taney's decision is in full force, that a "black man has no rights that a white man is bound to respect."[73] The fact is, the ex-rebels of the South never mean to permit the colored people to act in anything independent of their dictation, and it will yet be found out, that the loyal people of the North, who fought the late war to a successful termination, will have to say in language too thunderlike to be misunderstood, that they did not spend *billions of money, and shed rivers of blood for naught.* The war is not yet over, and if the American people imagine that the black people of this country will always submit patiently, and we came near saying, foolishly to the inhuman treatment that they have had to endure since the day they were first stolen from their native land and landed upon the shores of this cruel country, they will, the first thing they know, wake up and realize a state of affairs too horrible to contemplate. The South today is nursing a wind, that before they know it will turn upon them as the most terrific whirlwind that has ever been known in the history of the world. They will yet learn that "whatsoever a man soweth, that shall he also reap."[74] The civilized world has long since given the Black American credit for being the most docile, patient and forbearing human upon the Globe, but his long association with his white brethren is beginning to tell upon him, and he is fast coming to think and feel that he has suffered enough, and that it is about time that something of immunity from further persecution ought to be accorded him, and naturally enough he is looking to the people who broke his chains, and loosed his shackles, to see to it that he is made secure in his person and property, and as soon as it gets through his brain that he is always to suffer and never be protected by the strong arm of the Government he has always revered and for which he has always been ready to shed his blood, from the day that Crispus Attucks fell in defense of the flag of his country[75] down to the butchery at Fort Pillow,[76] and even on down to the successful termination of the late war for the Union; and that courts of justice are mere traps that serve to induce him to bring in his cause to the end, that he may be more easily and systematically murdered, he will then at last get the right conception of his duty, before his eyes, namely to bring about such a conflict as will *wake this country up,* from one end to the other. All that is needed is a few Black John Browns.

Source: Colored Citizen, January 4, 1879.

Eli Thayer, "To G. W. Brown," January 13, 1880

Although some of Brown's old allies celebrated his memory in the postwar period, Eli Thayer (1819–1899) condemned him in retrospect. In 1854, Thayer had organized the Massachusetts Emigrant Aid Company to send antislavery settlers to the Kansas Territory. The organization merged with its New York counterpart in 1855 to become the New England Emigrant Aid Company. Brown received arms from the organization to defend Free-Staters. He also visited Thayer in Worcester, Massachusetts, in 1857 and received help in procuring more arms. But by 1880 Thayer wanted to rewrite this history. Although he had been a Republican U.S. representative from Massachusetts between 1857 and 1861, he had lost the election to Congress in 1860 and again in 1872. Now marginalized, bitter, and hostile toward radicalism, Thayer virulently condemned Brown as a madman who had abused his trust. He offered this condemnation in a letter to George Washington Brown, who also had supported Brown in Kansas in 1856 and now condemned him in 1880. Thayer went on to publish *History of the Kansas Crusade* (1889), which attacked Brown further.

That a man so narrow and bigoted as he, so ignorant and deceptive, so ferocious and malignant, should have been puffed into the semblance of a moral hero, or inflated to the majestic stature of a god, is one of the greatest wonders of this wonderful century. . . .

The writer's confidence has been many times abused, but never in any other instance so grossly and wickedly abused as by John Brown. Not long before his attack on the United States arsenal he came to my house to ask for arms, with which, he said, he intended to protect some Free State settlements in Kansas, against an invasion of Border Ruffians, at that very time in process of preparation. He would not tell me how he had ascertained the fact of the intended raid, or what was the proof of it. He said he knew it and would like to be prepared to save our settlements. I gave him all the arms I had. I did not hear of him, or the arms in Kansas, or of any invasion of Border Ruffians, but I did hear of his attack *upon the United States' Arsenal, at Harper's Ferry, with these identical arms,* which were there captured. In this way he made my devotion to the free State settlements in Kansas, serve to aid and abet his own *Treason* in Virginia. Had he told me the TRUTH, effective measures would have been taken to prevent his suicidal and murderous work. When the end justifies the means *lying may be a holy vocation!*

So in all these transactions John Brown may have thought he was doing God's service. Ignorant, infatuated, intolerant—the ripest growth of Garrisonian disunionism[77]—he had the daring to do what the others of his school had only courage to resolve, to wit: that,

"The time has fully come for the people to practically assert their right of revolution."[78]

John Brown threw away his life in a futile effort to translate into heroic deeds the graceless gabble of a few Northern Secessionists. Stimulated by their sentiments, and exasperated almost to frenzy by his attempts and failures in Kansas to sustain them, he determined to rush, single-handed, against the power of the United States. Cervantes himself never wrote any thing one-half so Quixotic. If John Brown did not know that this was suicide he knew less than any other sane man in the country. But it was suicide, such as might be supposed to have attractions for a man of his obstinate ambition and adverse experience. It was suicide, to be justified by the teachings of disunion societies; to be sanctified by its simulation of martyrdom; to be glorified by all the abolition secessionists in the free States.

Some charitable people say that our "hero" was insane, but there seems to have been "too much method for madness." His disease appears to have been rather moral than mental, and of that kind that could not have been economically cured in any swine-producing country near the sea. But whether sane, or insane, he acted well the part of *heavy villain* in the Kansas drama. Now "his soul goes marching on!" Well, let it march—until it shall become infinitely remote!

Source: George Washington Brown, *The Truth at Last: History Corrected. Reminiscences of Old John Brown* (Rockford, IL: A. E. Smith, 1880), 78–80 (78, 80).

Frederick Douglass, "John Brown," May 30, 1881

After his defense of Brown's sanity in November 1859, Douglass celebrated and defended Brown several more times. In January 1860 he called Brown an "honest, truthful, earnest, God-fearing man" and "truly heroic." Although he was willing to admit that discussions with his friend sometimes "began to be something of a bore," he remarked on another occasion that Brown was the only white man he had ever met who was without racism. When the Civil War began, Douglass imagined that Brown looked down and saw his executioners suffering the "torments of their own kindling." Surrounded by an army of martyrs and saints, Brown saw "the faith for which he nobly died steadily becoming the saving faith of the nation," Douglass declared in January 1862. He returned to the topic of Brown's legacy in 1881, in an address at Harpers Ferry, at the historically black Storer College. Refuting the idea that his old friend's attempt was a failure, Douglass explains that Brown began the war that ended slavery.

It is not easy to reconcile human feeling to the shedding of blood for any purpose, unless indeed in the excitement which the shedding of blood itself occasions. The knife is to feeling always an offence. Even when in the hands of a skillful surgeon, it refuses consent to the operation long after reason has demonstrated its necessity. It even pleads the cause of the known murderer on the day of his execution, and calls society half criminal when, in cold blood, it takes life as a protection of itself from crime. Let no word be said against this holy feeling; more than to law and government are we indebted to this tender sentiment of regard for human life for the safety with which we walk the streets by day and sleep secure in our beds at night. It is nature's grand police, vigilant and faithful, sentineled in the soul, guarding against violence to peace and life. But whilst so much is freely accorded to feeling in the economy of human welfare, something more than feeling is necessary to grapple with a fact so grim and significant as was this raid. Viewed apart and alone, as a transaction separate and distinct from its antecedents and bearings, it takes rank with the most cold-blooded and atrocious wrongs ever perpetrated; but just here is the trouble—this raid on Harper's Ferry, no more than Sherman's march to the sea,[79] can consent to be thus viewed alone.

There is, in the world's government, a force which has in all ages been recognized, sometimes as Nemesis, sometimes as the judgment of God and sometimes as retributive justice; but under whatever name all history attests the wisdom and beneficence of its chastisements, and men become reconciled to the agents through whom it operates, and have extolled them as heroes, benefactors and demigods.

To the broad vision of a true philosophy, nothing in this world stands alone. Everything is a necessary part of everything else. The margin of chance is narrowed by every extension of reason and knowledge, and nothing comes unbidden to the feast of human experience. The universe, of which we are a part, is continually proving itself a stupendous whole, a system of law and order, eternal and perfect. Every seed bears fruit after its kind,[80] and nothing is reaped which was not sowed.[81] The distance between seed time and harvest, in the moral world, may not be quite so well defined or as clearly intelligible as in the physical, but there is a seed time, and there is a harvest time, and though ages may intervene,[82] and neither he who ploughed nor he who sowed may reap in person, yet the harvest nevertheless will surely come; and as in the physical world there are century plants, so it may be in the moral world, and their fruitage is as certain in the one as in the other. The bloody harvest of Harper's Ferry was ripened by the heat and moisture of merciless bondage of more than two hundred years. That startling cry of alarm on the banks of the Potomac was but the answering back of the avenging angel to the midnight invasions of Christian slave-traders on the sleeping hamlets of Africa. The history of the African slave-trade furnishes many illustrations far more cruel and bloody.

Viewed thus broadly our subject is worthy of thoughtful and dispassionate consideration. It invites the study of the poet, scholar, philosopher and statesman. What the masters in natural science have done for man in the physical world, the masters of social science may yet do for him in the moral world. Science now tells us when storms are in the sky, and when and where their violence will be most felt. Why may we not yet know with equal certainty when storms are in the moral sky, and how to avoid their desolating force? But I can invite you to no such profound discussions. I am not the man, nor is this the occasion for such philosophical enquiry. Mine is the word of grateful memory to an old friend; to tell you what I knew of him—what I knew of his inner life—of what he did and what he attempted, and thus if possible to make the mainspring of his actions manifest and thereby give you a clearer view of his character and services.

It is said that next in value to the performance of great deeds ourselves, is the capacity to appreciate such when performed by others; to more than this I do not presume. Allow me one other personal word before I proceed. In the minds of some of the American people I was myself credited with an important agency in the John Brown raid. Governor Henry A. Wise was manifestly of that opinion. He was at the pains of having Mr. Buchanan send his Marshals to Rochester to invite me to accompany them to Virginia. Fortunately I left town several hours previous to their arrival.

What ground there was for this distinguished consideration shall duly appear in the natural course of this lecture. I wish however to say just here that there was no foundation whatever for the charge that I in any wise urged or instigated John Brown to his dangerous work. I rejoice that it is my good fortune to have seen, not only the end of slavery, but to see the day when the whole truth can be told about this matter without prejudice to either the living or the dead. I shall however allow myself little prominence in these disclosures. Your interests, like mine, are in the all-commanding figure of the story, and to him I consecrate the hour. His zeal in the cause of my race was far greater than mine—it was as the burning sun to my taper light—mine was bounded by time, his stretched away to the boundless shores of eternity. I could live for the slave, but he could die for him. The crown of martyrdom is high, far beyond the reach of ordinary mortals, and yet happily no special greatness or superior moral excellence is necessary to discern and in some measure appreciate a truly great soul. Cold, calculating and unspiritual as most of us are, we are not wholly insensible to real greatness; and when we are brought in contact with a man of commanding mold, towering high and alone above the millions, free from all conventional fetters, true to his own moral convictions, a "law unto himself,"[83] ready to suffer misconstruction, ignoring torture and death for what he believes to be right, we are compelled to do him homage.

In the stately shadow, in the sublime presence of such a soul I find myself standing tonight; and how to do it reverence, how to do it justice, how to honor the dead with due regard to the living, has been a matter of most anxious solicitude.

Much has been said of John Brown, much that is wise and beautiful, but in looking over what may be called the John Brown literature, I have been little assisted with material, and even less encouraged with any hope of success in treating the subject. Scholarship, genius and devotion have hastened with poetry and eloquence, story and song to this simple altar of human virtue, and have retired dissatisfied and distressed with the thinness and poverty of their offerings, as I shall with mine.

The difficulty in doing justice to the life and character of such a man is not altogether due to the quality of the zeal, or of the ability brought to the work, nor yet to any imperfections in the qualities of the man himself; the state of the moral atmosphere about us has much to do with it. The fault is not in our eyes, nor yet in the object, if under a murky sky we fail to discover the object. Wonderfully tenacious is the taint of a great wrong. The evil, as well as "the good that men do, lives after them."[84] Slavery is indeed gone; but its long, black shadow yet falls broad and large over the face of the whole country. It is the old truth oft repeated, and never more fitly than now, "a prophet is without honor in his own country and among his own people."[85] Though more than twenty years have rolled between us and the Harper's Ferry raid, though since then the armies of the nation have found it necessary to do on a large scale what John Brown attempted to do on a small one, and the great captain who fought his way through slavery has filled with honor the Presidential chair, we yet stand too near the days of slavery, and the life and times of John Brown, to see clearly the true martyr and hero that he was and rightly to estimate the value of the man and his works. Like the great and good of all ages, the men born in advance of their times, the men whose bleeding footprints attest the immense cost of reform, and show us the long and dreary spaces, between the luminous points in the progress of mankind, this our noblest American hero must wait the polishing wheels of after-coming centuries to make his glory more manifest, and his worth more generally acknowledged. Such instances are abundant and familiar. If we go back four and twenty centuries, to the stately city of Athens, and search among her architectural splendor and her miracles of art for the Socrates of today, and as he stands in history, we shall find ourselves perplexed and disappointed. In Jerusalem Jesus himself was only the "carpenter's son," a young man wonderfully destitute of worldly prudence, a pestilent fellow, "inexcusably and perpetually interfering in the world's business," "upsetting the tables of the money-changers," preaching sedition, opposing the good old religion, "making himself greater than Abraham," and at the same time "keeping company" with very low people; but behold the change! He was a great miracle-worker, in his day, but time has worked for him a greater miracle than all his miracles, for now his name stands for all that is desirable in government, noble in life, orderly and beautiful in society. That which time has done for other great men of his class, that will time certainly do for John Brown. The brightest gems shine at first with subdued light, and the strongest characters are subject to the same limitations. Under the influence of adverse education and hereditary bias, few things are more difficult than to render impartial justice. Men hold up their hands to Heaven, and swear they will do justice, but what are oaths against prejudice and against inclination! In the face of high-sounding professions and affirmations we know well how hard it is for a Turk to do justice to a Christian, or for a Christian to do justice to a Jew. How hard for an Englishman to do justice to an Irishman, for an Irishman to do justice to an Englishman, harder still for an American tainted by slavery to do justice to the Negro or the Negro's friends. "John Brown," said the late Wm. H. Seward, "was justly hanged."[86] "John Brown," said the late John A. Andrew, "was right."[87] It is easy to perceive the sources of these two opposite judgments: the one was the verdict of slaveholding and panic-stricken Virginia, the other was the verdict of the best heart and brain of free old Massachusetts. One was the heated judgment of the passing and passionate hour, and the other was the calm, clear, unimpeachable judgment of the broad, illimitable future. . . .

Slavery was the idol of Virginia, and pardon and life to Brown meant condemnation and death to slavery. He had practically illustrated a truth stranger than fiction, a truth higher than Virginia had ever known, a truth more noble and beautiful than Jefferson ever wrote. He had evinced a conception of the sacredness and value of liberty which transcended in sublimity that of her own Patrick Henry and made even his fire-flashing sentiment of "Liberty or Death" seem dark and tame and selfish.[88] Henry loved liberty for himself, but this man loved liberty for all men, and for those most despised and scorned, as well as for those most esteemed and honored. Just here was the true glory of John Brown's mission. It was not for his own freedom that he was thus ready to lay down his life, for with Paul he could say, "I was born free."[89] No chain had bound his ankle, no yoke had galled his neck. History has no better illustration of pure, disinterested benevolence. It was not Caucasian for Caucasian—white man for white man; not rich man for rich man, but Caucasian for Ethiopian, white man for black man, rich man for poor man, the man admitted and respected for the man despised and rejected. "I want you to understand, gentlemen," he said to his persecutors, "that I respect the rights of the poorest and weakest of the colored people, oppressed by the slave system, as I do those of the most wealthy and powerful."[90] In this we have the key to the whole life and career of the man. Than in this sentiment humanity has nothing more touching, reason nothing more noble, imagination nothing more sublime; and if we could reduce all the religions of the world to one essence we could find in it nothing more divine. It is much to be regretted that some great artist, in sympathy with the spirit of the occasion, had not been present when these and similar words were spoken. The situation was thrilling. An old man in the center of an excited and angry crowd, far away from home, in an enemy's country, with no friend near, overpowered, defeated, wounded, bleeding, covered with reproaches, his brave companions nearly all dead, his two faithful sons stark and cold by his side—reading his death-warrant in his fast-oozing blood and increasing weakness as in the faces of all around him, yet calm, collected, brave, with a heart for any fate, using his supposed dying moments to explain his course and vindicate his cause: such a subject would have been at once an inspiration and a power for one of the grandest historical pictures ever painted.

With John Brown, as with every other man fit to die for a cause, the hour of his physical weakness was the hour of his moral strength, the hour of his defeat was the hour of his triumph, the moment of his capture was the crowning victory of his life. With the Alleghany mountains for his pulpit, the country for his church and the whole civilized world for his audience, he was a thousand times more effective as a preacher than as a warrior, and the consciousness of this fact was the secret of his amazing complacency. Mighty with the sword of steel, he was mightier with the sword of the truth, and with this sword he literally swept the horizon. He was more than a match for all the Wises, Masons, Vallandinghams and Washingtons[91] who could rise against him. They could kill him, but they could not answer him. . . .

An incident of his boyhood may explain, in some measure, the intense abhorrence he felt to slavery. He had for some reason been sent into the State of Kentucky, where he made the acquaintance of a slave boy, about his own age, of whom he became very fond. For some petty offense this boy was one day subjected to a brutal beating. The blows were dealt with an iron shovel and fell fast and furiously upon his slender body. Born in a free State and unaccustomed to such scenes of cruelty, young Brown's pure and sensitive soul revolted at the shocking spectacle and at that early age he swore eternal hatred to slavery.[92] After years never obliterated the impression, and he found in this early experience an argument against contempt for small things. It is true that the boy is the father of the man. From the acorn comes the oak. The impression of a horse's foot in the sand suggested the art of printing. The fall of an apple intimated the law of gravitation. A word dropped in the woods of Vincennes, by royal hunters, gave Europe and the world a "William the Silent," and a thirty years' war.[93] The beating of a Hebrew bondsman, by an Egyptian, created a Moses,[94] and the infliction of a similar outrage on a helpless slave boy in our own land may have caused, forty years afterwards, a John Brown and a Harper's Ferry Raid. . . .

He had been watching and waiting all that time for suitable heads to rise or "pop up"[95] as he said among the sable millions in whom he could confide; hence forty years had passed between his thought and his act. Forty years, though not a long time in the life of a nation, is a long time in the life of a man; and here forty long years, this man was struggling with this one idea; like Moses he was forty years in the wilderness. Youth, manhood, middle age had come and gone; two marriages had been consummated, twenty children had called him father; and through all the storms and vicissitudes of busy life, this one thought, like the angel in the burning bush, had confronted him with its blazing light, bidding him on to his work. Like Moses he had made excuses, and as with Moses his excuses were overruled. Nothing should postpone further what was to him a divine command, the performance of which seemed to him his only apology for existence. He often said to me, though life was sweet to him, he would willingly lay it down for the freedom of my people; and on one occasion he added, that he had already lived about as long as most men, since he had slept less, and if he should now lay down his life the loss would not be great, for in fact he knew no better use for it. . . .

But the question is, Did John Brown fail? He certainly did fail to get out of Harper's Ferry before being beaten down by United States soldiers; he did fail to save his own life, and to lead a liberating army into the mountains of Virginia. But he did not go to Harper's Ferry to save his life. The true question is, Did John Brown draw his sword against slavery and thereby lose his life in vain? and to this I answer ten thousand times, No! No man fails, or can fail who so grandly gives himself and all he has to a righteous cause. No man, who in his hour of extremest need, when on his way to meet an ignominious death, could so forget himself as to stop and kiss a little child, one of the hated race for whom he was about to die, could by any possibility fail. Did John Brown fail? Ask Henry A. Wise in whose house less than two years after, a school for the emancipated slaves was taught.[96] Did John Brown fail? Ask James M. Mason, the author of the inhuman fugitive slave bill, who was cooped up in Fort Warren as a traitor less than two years from the time that he stood over the prostrate body of John Brown.[97] Did John Brown fail? Ask Clement L. Vallandigham, one other of the inquisitorial party; for he too went down in the tremendous whirlpool created by the powerful hand of this bold invader.[98] If John Brown did not end the war that ended slavery, he did at least begin the war that ended slavery. If we look over the dates, places and men, for which this honor is claimed, we shall find that not Carolina, but Virginia—not Fort Sumter, but Harper's Ferry and the arsenal—not Col. Anderson,[99] but John Brown, began the war that ended American slavery and made this a free Republic. Until this blow was struck, the prospect for freedom was dim, shadowy and uncertain. The irrepressible conflict was one of words, votes and compromises. When John Brown stretched forth his arm the sky was cleared. The time for compromises was gone, the armed hosts of freedom stood face to face over the chasm of a broken Union, and the clash of arms was at hand. The South staked all upon getting possession of the Federal Government, and failing to do that, drew the sword of rebellion and thus made her own, and not Brown's, the lost cause of the century.

Source: *John Brown: An Address by Frederick Douglass at the Fourteenth Anniversary of Storer College, Harper's Ferry, West Virginia, May 30, 1881* (Dover: Morning Star, 1881), 7–12, 17–18, 20, 24–25, 27–28.

George Washington Williams, "John Brown—
Hero and Martyr," 1883

An African American from Pennsylvania and eventually one of the nineteenth century's most important black historians, George Washington Williams (1849–1891) enlisted with the Union Army at the age of fourteen. In the 1870s he became a Baptist minister and edited a short-lived journal called *The Commoner* in Washington, D.C., then moved to Cincinnati and studied law. In 1880 he became the first African American elected to the Ohio State Legislature. In early 1883 he published a history of black Americans and included a chapter on Brown. Calling him one of the world's greatest heroes, Williams explains that Brown gave slavery its death blow. He compares Brown to John the Baptist, Lincoln, Galileo, and others. But like Douglass, Williams also looks to posterity's tribunal—the future's "calmer judgments"—for a consensus on Brown's heroism. Six years later, Williams visited Central Africa and wrote a public letter protesting the treatment of the Congolese by Belgian colonizers. He died in England on his way back to the United States at the age of forty-one, his health broken by the tour of Africa.

On the 9th of May, 1800, at Torrington, Connecticut, was born a man who lived for two generations, but accomplished the work of two centuries. That man was John Brown, who ranks among the world's greatest heroes. Greater than Peter the Hermit,[100] who believed himself commissioned of God to redeem the Holy Sepulcher from the hands of infidels; greater than Joanna Southcote,[101] who deemed herself big with the promised Shiloh; greater than Ignatius Loyola,[102] who thought the Son of Man appeared to him, bearing His cross upon His shoulders, and bestowed upon him a Latin commission of wonderful significance; greater than Oliver Cromwell,[103] the great Republican Protector; and greater than John Hampden[104]—he deserves to rank with William of Orange.[105]

John Brown was nearly six feet high, slim, wiry, dark in complexion, sharp in feature, dark hair sprinkled with gray, eyes a dark gray and penetrating, with a countenance that betokened frankness, honesty, and firmness. His brow was prominent, the centre of the forehead flat, the upper part retreating, which, in conjunction with his slightly Roman nose, gave him an interesting appearance. The crown of his head was remarkably high, in the regions of the phrenological organs of firmness, conscientiousness, self-esteem, indicating a stern will, unswerving integrity, and marvelous self-possession. He walked rapidly with a firm and elastic tread. He was somewhat like John [the] Baptist, taciturn in habits, usually wrapped in meditation. He was rather meteoric in his movements, appearing suddenly and unexpectedly at this place, and then disappearing in the same mysterious manner.

When Kansas lay bleeding at the feet of border ruffians; when Congress gave the free-State settlers no protection, but was rather trying to drag the territory into the Union with a slave constitution—without noise or bluster John Brown dropped down into Osage County. He was not a member of the Republican party; but rather hated its reticency. When it cried Halt! he gave the command *Forward, march!* He was not in sympathy with any of the parties, political or anti-slavery. All were too conservative to suit him. So, as a political orphan he went into Kansas, organized and led a new party that swore eternal death to slavery. The first time he appeared in a political meeting in Kansas, at Osawatomie, the politicians were trimming their speeches and shaping their resolutions to please each political faction. John Brown took the floor and made a speech that threw the convention into consternation. He denounced slavery as the curse of the ages; affirmed the manhood of the slave; dealt "middle men" terrible blows; and said he could "see no use in talking." "Talk," he continued, "is a national institution; but it does no good for the slave."[106] He thought it an excuse very well adapted for weak men with tender consciences. Most men who were afraid to fight, and too honest to be silent, deceived themselves that they discharged their duties to the slave by denouncing in fiery words the oppressor. His ideas of duty were far different; the slaves, in his eyes, were prisoners of war; their tyrants, as he held, had taken up the sword, and must perish by it: This was his view of the great question of slavery. . . .

Distance lends enchantment to the view. What the world condemns today is applauded tomorrow.

We must have a "fair count" on the history of yesterday and last year. The events chronicled yesterday, when the imagination was wrought upon by exciting circumstances, need revision to-day.

The bitter words spoken this morning reproach at eventide the smarting conscience. And the judgments prematurely formed, and the conclusions rapidly reached, maybe rectified and repaired in the light of departed years and enlarged knowledge.

John Brown is rapidly settling down to his proper place in history, and "the madman" has been transformed into a "saint." When Brown struck his first blow for freedom, at the head of his little band of liberators, it was almost the universal judgment of both Americans and foreigners that he was a "fanatic." It seemed the very soul of weakness and arrogance for John Brown to attempt to do so great a work with so small a force. Men reached a decision with the outer and surface facts. But many of the most important and historically trustworthy truths bearing upon the motive, object, and import of that "bold move," have been hidden from the public view, either by prejudice or fear.

Some people have thought John Brown—"*The Hero of Harper's Ferry*"— a hot-headed, blood-thirsty brigand; they animadverted against the precipitancy of his measures, and the severity of his invectives; said that he was lacking in courage and deficient in judgment; that he retarded rather than accelerated the cause he championed. But this was the verdict of other times, not the judgment of today.

John Brown said to a personal friend during his stay in Kansas: "Young men must learn to wait. Patience is the hardest lesson to learn. I have waited for twenty years to accomplish my purpose."[107] These are not the words of a mere visionary idealist, but the mature language of a practical and judicious leader, a leader than whom the world has never seen a greater. By greatness is meant deep convictions of duty, a sense of the Infinite, "a strong hold on truth,"[108] a "conscience void of offence toward God and man,"[109] to which the appeals of the innocent and helpless are more potential than the voices of angry thunder or destructive artillery. Such a man was John Brown. He was strong in his moral and mental nature, as well as in his physical nature. He was born to lead; and he led, and made himself the pro-martyr of a cause rapidly perfecting. All through his boyhood days he felt himself lifted and quickened by great ideas and sublime purposes. He had flowing in his veins the blood of his great ancestor, Peter Brown, who came over in the "Mayflower"; and the following inscription appears upon a marble monument in the graveyard at Canton Centre, New York: "In memory of Captain John Brown, who died in the Revolutionary army, at New York, September 3, 1776. He was of the fourth generation, in regular descent, from Peter Brown, one of the Pilgrim Fathers, who landed from the 'Mayflower,' at Plymouth, Massachusetts, December 22, 1620." This is the best commentary on his inherent love of absolute liberty, his marvelous courage and transcendent military genius. For years he elaborated and perfected his plans, working upon the public sentiment of his day by the most praiseworthy means. He bent and bowed the most obdurate conservatism of his day, and rallied to his standards the most eminent men, the strongest intellects in the North. His ethics and religion were as broad as the universe, and beneficent in their wide ramification. And it was upon his "religion of humanity,"[110] that embraced our entire species, that he proceeded with his herculean task of striking off the chains of the enslaved. Few, very few of his most intimate friends knew his plans—the plan of freeing the slaves. Many knew his great faith, his exalted sentiments, his ideas of liberty, in their crudity; but to a faithful few only did he reveal his stupendous plans in their entirety.

Hon. Frederick Douglass and Colonel Richard J. Hinton[111] knew more of Brown's real purposes than any other persons, with the exception of J. H. Kagi, Osborne Anderson, Owen Brown, Richard Realf, and George B. Gill.[112]

"Of men born of woman,"[113] there is not a greater than John Brown. He was the forerunner of Lincoln, the great apostle of freedom. . . .

The man who hung him, Governor Wise, lived to see the plans of Brown completed and his most cherished hopes fulfilled. He heard the warning shot fired at Sumter, saw Richmond fall, the war end in victory to the party of John Brown; saw the slave-pen converted into the school-house, and the four millions Brown fought and died for, elevated to the honors of citizenship. And at last he has entered the grave, where his memory will perish with his body, while the soul and fame of John Brown go marching down the centuries!

Galileo, Copernicus, Newton,[114] and John Brown have to wait the calmer judgments of future generations. These men believed that God sent them to do a certain work—to reveal a hidden truth; to pour light into the minds of benighted and superstitious men. They completed their work; they did nobly and well, then bowed to rest—

"With patriarchs of the infant world—with kings,
The powerful of the earth,"[115]

while generation after generation studies their handwriting on the wall of time and interprets their thoughts. Despised, persecuted, and unappreciated while in the flesh, they are honored after death, and enrolled among earth's good and great, her wise and brave. The shock Brown gave the walls of the slave institution was felt from its centre to its utmost limits. It was the entering wedge; it laid bare the accursed institution, and taught good men everywhere to hate it with a perfect hatred. Slavery received its death wound at the hands of a "lonely old man." When he smote Virginia, the non-resistants, the anti-slavery men, learned a lesson. They saw what was necessary to the accomplishment of their work, and were now ready for the "worst." He rebuked the conservatism of the North, and gave an example of adherence to duty, devotion to truth, and fealty to God and man that make the mere "professor" to tremble with shame. "John Brown's body lies mouldering in the clay," but his immortal name will be pronounced with blessings in all lands and by all people till the end of time.

Source: George Washington Williams, *History of the Negro Race in America, 1619–1880*, Vol. 2 (New York: Putnam's, 1883), 214–15, 222–224, 227.

David N. Utter, "John Brown of Osawatomie," November 1883

The Chicago Unitarian minister David N. Utter (1844–1926) responded to positive postwar visions of Brown, like those of Douglass and Williams, by discrediting them as hero worship. His article for the *North American Review* focuses on the Pottawatomie murders and contends that the current generation will seek a factual—and unsympathetic—evaluation of Brown instead. Signaling that a struggle over Brown's legacy was under way, John Brown, Jr., the abolitionist Franklin Sanborn, and U.S. senator from Kansas John James Ingalls all responded publicly to Utter. For example, in February 1884 Ingalls published an article in the *North American Review* declaring that the nation had seized the flag of universal emancipation from Brown's hand on the scaffold and "bor[ne] it in triumph to Appomattox."

Whether John Brown was right in his invasion of Virginia, in 1859, is a question upon which good men may always differ. The movement was designed to excite insurrection among slaves, which in a legal sense may have been treason against the State. A number of men were killed, and a grand jury found the old commander guilty of murder. A rebellion that is successful is always washed clean of the stains of bloodshed and treason; but where the revolt is checked at its beginning, the leaders usually suffer immediately, and, for one reason or another, their names are seldom greatly honored. To John Brown the fates have been unusually kind. His story fell upon a time when the world was eager for a hero, and when the people of the northern United States must make one of whatever material must come to hand. It will be remembered that we were ready, early in the war of the great rebellion, to worship General Scott, or General McClellan, of Sigel, or Fremont, or Grant[116]—anybody who would show any activity or earnestness in fighting the South, or any real hatred of slavery. To hate slavery, and to be ready to fight, these were the virtues in those days that, especially in New England's eyes, covered a multitude of sins. Here was a man who had fought slavery for years, in Kansas, in Missouri, in Virginia, and had died a martyr to his principles. The very fact that he had fought unlawfully added to his glory. No doctrine has ever been dearer to New England than the doctrine of the "higher law." This is an invisible and unwritten law which each man must find for himself, read and interpret for himself, and obey in his own way. If it leads him to disobey certain human enactments, so much the better; if it even leads him to treason and rebellion against his country, he at least is right, however wrong his acts may seem in the eyes of men. The acts of John Brown fitted this doctrine admirably; indeed, he himself was no mean exponent of it, either with voice or pen. His defense of himself was on this line wholly. He had resisted "bogus" laws in Kansas; and the laws of Virginia sanctioning slavery were bogus also in his view. He was above all such laws; he had done right in breaking them, he had done no wrong even in killing men, because his motives were good. He scouted the idea of insanity, and he set his individual judgment against all the law books of Virginia, and staked his life on the issue.

The attitude was heroic. The man bore himself like a hero from the time his schemes failed till his death; and every work that he spoke was in such perfect accord with the doctrine of the higher law, that every sentence thrilled New England as though a prophet were speaking the very words of God. There arose in his defense, to sing his praises, a company of men and women whose peers did not exist in America. They have made our history and written it, and they have made our literature. They made the public sentiment that abolished slavery. They held the pen that awakened those who bore the sword that preserved the Union. When these men said, John Brown was a hero and a saint, the bravest and the cleanest of all the heroes of ancient or modern times, there was nothing for it but to accept the verdict.

It was not accepted hastily. Very many newspapers lamented the affair at Harper's Ferry as extremely unfortunate; and "fanatic" and "crazy old man" were the terms commonly applied to the old hero for fully a year after his death by all except those who were known to hold extreme antislavery views. But during the war all was changed: these extremists became our trusted leaders, and their version of the John Brown affair became accepted history, and, as such, it has been passed into encyclopedias and biographical dictionaries, not only in this country, but in England and Europe. The war has now been over nearly twenty years. A new generation is now upon the stage reading and thinking, and the deeds of old John Brown have a new interest as they pass again under review taking the form of final history. It is a time of revaluation of our war heroes, and some will gain in our estimation, and some, no doubt, will lose. This younger generation that is weighing, and sifting, and revaluing the deeds and characters of the men of twenty years ago may not love truth more than those who made the records that we read, but they probably need heroes less. The Zeitgeist has now more to say of science and fact, than of right or valor. Not that these latter terms are meaningless, nor that there is forgetfulness of what they signify, nor indifference toward such conceptions of ethics or qualities in men; but the keenness of interest now is all in the direction of getting at the exact facts in every case, let them be what they may.

Under the influence of this spirit there has been a growing impression that the deeds of John Brown do not warrant all the eulogies that have been pronounced upon him. Emerson spoke of him as the "saint whose martyrdom will make the gallows glorious like the cross."[117] Thoreau said, "He could not have been tried by his peers, for his peers did not exist"[118]. . . . These men were the radical abolitionists of the time, to be sure; but as has been already said, their words and sentiments were adopted during the war period by the entire North, and since then largely by the civilized world.

But to the average citizen of today such extravagant eulogy of a doubtful character is distasteful. The mention of the name of John Brown no longer brings down the house, and for two or three years a spirit of doubt has been slowly spreading eastward from Kansas whether the man deserves any eulogy whatever. . . .

At the time of Brown's execution in Virginia, which was called in Boston his public murder, while the deluded abolitionists were exalting to the skies a man they did not know, a Free-State paper, "The Herald of Freedom"[119] of Lawrence, was printing the plain unvarnished truth about him and begging the Republicans of America not to make a hero of him. Boston replied: "of course the small men in Kansas can see no greatness in Brown. Those who live near a hero never know him, he is often rejected by all of his generation. The distant view is the true view. Here we get the man in true perspective and his greatness is clear as sunlight."[120] Against these generalities we will not argue, for they doubtless contain a measure of truth; but as applied to Brown, they are fallacious wholly. Viewed in the largest possible way, there is little that is admirable in this man's character; and if our civilization is worth anything, his entire public or fighting career is to be utterly condemned. It was the right of Free-State citizens in Kansas to defend their homes, but old John Brown never had a home there to defend, and his influence led most of this sons to early graves. It may have been justifiable to steal slaves from their masters and free them; such is the writer's opinion; but in this sort of work Brown never acted with any discretion, not even with common good sense, if freeing the slaves had been his chief object. But his real object, from the fatal night on the Pottawatomie till his death was to provoke the South and to commit the North to violence and bring on a war. He did not do it; and, dispassionately weighed after twenty years, the verdict of thoughtful men must be that his influence in bringing on the war that afterward came was infinitesimal. The war was brought on by Northern votes and Southern secession. The war sentiment caught up the name of Brown and glorified it, but the man himself was all wrong in principle and practice.

His principles were those of Russian nihilists—first make a clean sweep of the present civilization, and let the future build what it can. Surely such a man is not a proper hero for the youth of our country to worship, and we believe that as his true history, too long concealed, becomes known, admiration for him will be changed to disgust, and disgust to anger, that we have been so long deceived.

Source: North American Review, November 1883, 435–446 (435–437, 445–446).

Mark Twain, "English as She is Taught," April 1887

The writer Mark Twain (1835–1910), born Samuel Langhorne Clemens in the slave state of Missouri, did not respond to Brown at length. But in 1887 he included Brown in his parody of taught history. Although Twain's account is deliberately and wildly inaccurate, his inclusion of Brown suggests that the abolitionist was starting to find a secure place in history as well as memory—like Christopher Columbus, George Washington, and other historical figures in the parody. Twain had recently written a short, highly fictionalized memoir called "The Private History of a Campaign That Failed" (1885), which described his two weeks in the pro-Confederate Missouri State Guard. But he eventually supported emancipation, observing that "Lincoln's Proclamation . . . not only set the black slaves free, but set the white man free also." He also campaigned for women's suffrage and was an anti-imperialist by the turn of the century.

I have just now fallen upon a darling literary curiosity. It is a little book, a manuscript compilation, and the compiler sent it to me with the request that I say whether I think it ought to be published or not. I said Yes; but as I slowly grow wise, I briskly grow cautious; and so, now that the publication is imminent, it has seemed to me that I should feel more comfortable if I could divide up this responsibility with the public by adding them to the court. Therefore I will print some extracts from the book, in the hope that they may make converts to my judgment that the volume has merit which entitles it to publication.

As to its character. Everyone has sampled "English as She is Spoke"[121] and "English as She is Wrote"; this little volume furnishes us an instructive array of examples of "English as She Is Taught"—in the public schools of—well, this country. The collection is made by a teacher in those schools, and all the examples in it are genuine; none of them have been tampered with, or doctored

in any way. From time to time, during several years, whenever a pupil has delivered himself of anything peculiarly quaint or toothsome in the course of his
recitations, this teacher and her associates have privately set that thing down
in a memorandum-book; strictly following the original, as to grammar, construction, spelling, and all; and the result is this literary curiosity. . . .

To proceed with "History":

Christopher Columbus was called the Father of his Country.

Queen Isabella of Spain sold her watch and chain and other millinery so
that Columbus could discover America.

The Indian wars were very desecrating to the country.

The Indians pursued their warfare by hiding in the bushes and then scalp-
ing them.

Captain John Smith has been styled the father of his country. His life was
saved by his daughter Pochahantas.

The Puritans found an insane asylum in the wilds of America.

The Stamp Act was to make everybody stamp all materials so they should
be null and void.

Washington died in Spain almost broken-hearted. His remains were taken
to the cathedral in Havana.

Gorilla warfare was where men rode on gorillas.

John Brown was a very good insane man who tried to get fugitives slaves
into Virginia. He captured all the inhabitants, but was finally conquered
and condemned to his death. The Confederasy was formed by the fugitive
slaves.

Source: Century Magazine, April 1887, 932–936 (932, 934).

Frank Preston Stearns, "Unfriendly Criticism of John Brown," 1888

As the thirty-year anniversary of Brown's raid and death approached, the Massachusetts writer Frank Preston Stearns (1846–1917) traced the progress of history's tribunal so far: Brown's contemporaries in the United States had responded, international figures had expressed their opinions, Brown had endured as a presence during the Civil War, and now different sides continued to wrestle with Brown's legacy. In his article, Stearns suggests that commentators should restore Brown's story to its antebellum context if they would understand him. But he also lifts Brown out of his context again to compare him to George Washington and William of Orange. He considers the new generation's perception of Brown and imagines how the whole antislavery struggle will be commemorated. Stearns himself represented a new generation of reformers, many of whom would use Brown as a symbol and find lessons in Brown's life and death: he was the son of the abolitionists Mary and George Luther Stearns, who were Brown's friends and supporters, and the younger brother of Harry Stearns, to whom Brown addressed his short autobiography of 1857.

At the time of John Brown's death, now nearly twenty-eight years ago, his praises were celebrated so eloquently by Emerson, Thoreau, Manning,[122] John A. Andrew, Wendell Phillips, and others, and were so well supported by public opinion, that it seemed as if his fame had been set on an enduring basis forever. Victor Hugo and the English anti-slavery people took up the refrain in Europe, and the reverberation of it had not died away on either side of the Atlantic, before the civil war began, and the John Brown song echoed throughout the land. In 1867, Phillips said of Emerson that after all his chief merit lay in the fact that having talked about heroism all his life, when the hero finally came he knew him.[123]

Now, however, as usually happens, we have an ebb tide again. The opposition, who were formerly constrained to silence by public opinion, come forward now to argue their views before a younger generation, in which there dwells a different spirit from that of the war period. Take any man out of his own time, and place him in another, and he will appear to great disadvantage. Imagine Socrates in the age of the Antonines,[124] or Martin Luther as a contemporary of Voltaire.[125] They would appear as violent or meddlesome persons. So if we take John Brown away from the fearful and exciting period of his career—a period of dark political intrigues and inhuman plots against the liberties of the people, while the first shocks of a gigantic revolution were agitating the most courageous minds—if we take him out of the element in which he lived, and study him with the peaceful and commonplace life of today as a background, his actions may appear monstrous, his character inhuman, his endeavor a failure. That, however, is not the way to study an historical character. We should either place ourselves in sympathy with the conditions of his life, or leave him alone, and interest ourselves in other subjects. . . . John Brown, moreover, was a unique character, so different from his cotemporaries that even among his admirers few can be said to have penetrated to the very heart of the man. No one should be blamed for not understanding him, or for misunderstanding him. There are excellent painters who do not appreciate the drawings of Da Vinci, and good composers who cannot realize the superiority of Bach's music. It is not any fault of theirs, but the accident of temperament, education, or mental capacity. What is difficult of comprehension attracts and interests the civilized man; but the pedant despises it, and the barbarian hates it. We should always endeavor to respect what we do not comprehend; for so only can we hope finally to comprehend it. . . .

The Harper's Ferry attack was not a success from a military point of view, or even from that of guerilla warfare; but to call John Brown an unsuccessful man is to deny history. It is difficult to understand how it could have been otherwise than unsuccessful, but those who have accomplished any great work by their own unaided exertions, and have not been mere flies on the wheel of prosperity—those know right well the narrow line that divides success from failure. John Brown, like Garibaldi, possessed a genius for irregular warfare, a very rare kind of genius. The methods of such men are a secret which, like that of Titian's coloring,[126] dies with them. How can any of us who are wholly incapable of such great actions pretend to judge them with exactness? Indeed, in a higher sense, as Lincoln said at Gettysburg, we have no right to judge them.[127] Not to be satisfied with their result would be ungenerous. The ignominy of failure fell at John Brown's feet like broken chains, and the moral grandeur of the man shone forth from the Charlestown jail with such a light that friends and foes bowed their heads in homage, and men of all nations rose to their feet with a shout of applause. It was like a bright meteor crossing the black sky of American politics and disappearing forever. He shook the South as Neptune was fabled to shake the nations with his trident, and Lincoln's army which invaded Virginia twenty months afterward was much less successful and produced less consternation.

"But John Brown was a rebel, and Lincoln the lawfully elected President," say alike the comfortable aristocrat depending on his traditions and the honest democrat holding fast to party principles. So was Henry Tudor a rebel when he fought against Richard III,[128] and William of Orange when he opposed the Spaniard,[129] and so were Washington and Mirabeau rebels.[130] Those men had law and authority pitched against them. They were the champions of a higher law and acted under it. When laws become unendurable, when, as Lowell says, "right is ever on the scaffold, wrong forever on the throne,"[131] then rebellion is a virtue and the higher law comes into play. Froude states it exactly when he says, "High treason is either the greatest of crimes or the noblest of virtues";[132] which it is depends upon the circumstances of the case. Webster wished to know where the higher law was to be found;[133] but when there is no such law in the hearts of men the laws in the statute-books have little force, as is the case in Mexico and portions of South America. On another occasion Webster also might have admitted this, for if he was not a man of keen moral sense, neither was he a narrow legal pedant. There is at least one form of higher law which even the most pedantic lawyers are compelled to recognize, and that is the right of revolution. The defeated party in a revolution rarely, if ever, justifies it, and the successful party invariably justifies it; but every one is sure to justify *some* revolution. Southerners might condemn the acts of John Brown, but the bombardment of Fort Sumter was just as illegal. Englishmen may think that we separated from the mother country without sufficient cause, but they all justify the glorious revolution of 1688.[134] The French jurists of the restoration were not so unwise as to attempt a return to the legal status of Louis XVI;[135] and when Charles X did so he was immediately dethroned.[136] It was the higher law which Jennie Geddes appealed to when she hurled her chair at the Scotch bishop and cried out, "Are you going to say mass in kirk?"[137] It was the higher law which our forefathers appealed to when they declared

"No taxation without representation." It was under authority of the higher law that Lincoln issued his proclamation of freedom to the slaves. So far as the practice of law is influenced by legal principles rather than the customs of mankind, and so far as legislators in framing the statutes are influenced by an idea of right and justice, just so far is the higher law recognized and accepted by the legal profession. Truly, it is this ideal of justice which constitutes the higher law. . . .

In a higher sense, as Lincoln would have said, it seems almost a pity that anything should have been written about John Brown. Almost immediately from the time of his death he became an ideal character in the thoughts of men. Probably he will remain so in spite of all that may be said about him; and in some future age, a more poetical and less critical one than the present, it is likely he will become the central figure in some epic commemorating the great anti-slavery struggle. Since Cromwell's time[138] there has been perhaps no other such grand personality.

Source: Hermann von Holst, *John Brown*, ed. Frank Preston Stearns (Boston: Cupples and Hurd, 1888), 204–232 (204–206, 217–218, 222–226, 228–229).

T. Thomas Fortune, "John Brown and Nat. Turner," January 12 and 29, 1889

In 1889 two more representatives of the new reform generation confronted Brown's legacy. Frederick Douglass, Jr., published an editorial in the *Washington National Leader* about the possibility of black Americans fund-raising for a monument to Brown. In response, the black journalist and activist Timothy Thomas Fortune (1856–1928) published an editorial in the *New York Age* on January 12. Brown's memory was secure, Fortune argued, and instead African Americans should raise a monument to the slave rebel Nat Turner, for whites cared nothing for Turner's memory. Replying in the *National Leader* on January 19, Frederick Douglass, Jr., said that Fortune had "drawn the color line" and insisted that Brown had brought black freedom. Fortune had the last word, in an editorial published on January 29. Neither memorial was ever produced. But in May 1935 the John Brown Memorial Association, which was founded and led by African Americans, did unveil a memorial at Brown's old home in Lake Placid, New York. The statue depicts Brown walking beside a black child. During the dedication, the association's leader, the black activist J. Max Barber, explained that Brown did not die in vain, for he showed the world that justice wins out. This time there was no struggle over the limited space of public memory: reporting on the memorial, one black newspaper, the *Pittsburgh Courier,* celebrated Brown's "militant spirit" and "holy resentment against wrong and oppression," called for "more John Browns," and added that there should be memorials to Turner, Denmark Vesey, Harriet Tubman, Sojourner Truth, and Frederick Douglass as well.

January 12, 1889

The *Washington National Leader,* of which Mr. Frederick Douglass, Jr., is associate editor, recently wanted to know if it was not almost time that the colored people were doing something to perpetuate the memory of John Brown.

We think not. We think John Brown's memory is strong enough to perpetuate itself even if all the Negroes in the universe were suddenly to become extinct. His memory is a part of the history of the government. It is embalmed in a thousand songs and stories. Your own father, Mr. Douglass, has written a lecture on the life of John Brown, which will help along the perpetuation of that great and good man.[139] A German scholar has just given a brochure to the world, which competent critics declare a most judicial and thorough study of the character of John Brown ever produced.[140] No; John Brown's memory stands no immediate prospect of vanishing into oblivion. But there is another, a forerunner of John Brown, if you please, who stands in more need of our copper pennies to be melted down into a monument to perpetuate his memory than John Brown. We refer of course to Nat Turner, who was executed at Jerusalem, Southampton County, Virginia, for inciting and leading his fellow slaves to insurrection long before John Brown invaded Kansas and planned an unfortunate raid on Harper's Ferry. Nat. Turner was a black hero. He preferred death to slavery. He ought to have a monument. White men care nothing for his memory. We should cherish it. It is quite remarkable that whenever colored men move that somebody's memory be perpetuated, that somebody's memory is always a white man's. Young Mr. Douglass should mend his ways in this matter. His great father will some day have a monument which he will have eminently deserved and it will have to be built by the pennies of colored people. White people build monuments to white people.

January 29, 1889

Fred Douglass, Jr., in the *National Leader,* exhibits too much temper in replying to our editorial suggesting a monument to Nat. Turner instead of one to John Brown. It indicates that we have touched the Achillean weak spot in his armor.

"That Nat. Turner has been dead many years" is almost equally true of John Brown. John Brown lost his life in urging and leading an insurrection of slaves. Nat. Turner at an earlier date did the same. The conduct of the one was no more heroic than that of the other. The whites have embalmed the memory of John Brown in marble and vellum, and Fred Douglass, Jr., now wants the colored people to embalm it in brass; while the memory of the black hero is preserved neither in marble, vellum nor brass.

What we protest against is Negro worship of white men and the memory of white men, to the utter exclusion of colored men equally patriotic and self-sacrificing. It is the absence of race pride and race unity which makes white men despise black men the world over.

We do not draw the color line. Fred Douglass, Jr., knows that his insinuation in this regard is a baseless invention. We simply insist that in theory "do unto others as you would have them do unto you" is splendid, but that in practice the philosophy of conduct is "do unto others as they do unto you," the sooner to make them understand that a dagger of the right sort has two edges, the one as sharp of blade as the other.

We yield to none in admiration of the character and sacrifices of John Brown. The character and sacrifices of Nat. Turner are dearer to us because he was of us and exhibited in the most abject condition the heroism and race devotion which have illustrated in all times the sort of men who are worthy to be free.

Source: New York Age, January 12 and 29, 1889.

Notes

Part I: In His Own Words

1. Brown's writing often includes misspellings, which have been retained for this volume.

2. The abolitionist William Lloyd Garrison and the abolitionist and women's rights advocate Abby Kelley.

3. Referring to the abolition of slavery in all French colonies in 1848.

4. Joseph Cinqué, who led a revolt on board the Spanish slave ship *Amistad* in 1839.

5. Referring to a provision of the Fugitive Slave Act of 1850.

6. In 1844, Captain Jonathan Walker attempted to help slaves escape from his ship. Found guilty of "negro stealing," he was branded with the letters *SS* (for slave stealer). Abolitionists published a sketch of Walker's branded hand.

7. In 1837, Elijah Lovejoy, an antislavery editor, was shot by a mob in Alton while defending his printing press. In 1844, Charles Torrey was accused of helping slaves to escape and was condemned to six years of hard labor. He died of tuberculosis in 1846, in Maryland state prison.

8. James Hamlet and Henry Long were arrested and remanded under the Fugitive Slave Act in September and December 1850, respectively.

9. Brown's brother-in-law, Orson Day.

10. Brown's eldest son, John Jr.

11. Brown's second son, Jason, who eventually refused to participate in the Harpers Ferry raid.

12. The First Kansas Territorial Legislature, meeting in 1855, was called the "Bogus Legislature" by its Free-State opponents.

13. Brown's third son, Owen, who accompanied Brown to Harpers Ferry and escaped from his assigned place at the Kennedy Farm toward the end of the raid.

14. Palmyra.

15. Samuel T. Shore of Prairie City, captain of a Free-State company.

16. Brown's fourth son, Frederick, who died on August 30, 1856, at Ossawatomie, Kansas.

17. H. Clay Pate, a proslavery captain of the Missouri militia.

18. Brown's son-in-law, husband of Ruth Brown.

19. Brown's sixth son, Salmon, who did not join the raid on Harpers Ferry.

20. Colonel E. V. Sumner, based at Fort Leavenworth, Kansas.

21. Free-Stater James B. Abbott of De Soto, Kansas.

22. The abolitionist and philanthropist Gerrit Smith was one of Brown's supporters.

23. Jason's wife, Ellen, and John Jr.'s wife, Wealthy.

24. Brown's eighth son, Oliver, who died fighting at Harpers Ferry on October 17, 1859.

25. Luke 10:15.

26. 2 Samuel 1:27.

27. Proverbs 30:31.

28. Brown quotes from the Dred Scott decision, handed down by the Supreme Court on March 6, 1857, and delivered by Chief Justice Roger Taney, which declared that no slave or descendant of a slave could be a U.S. citizen.

29. The editor of *Calendar of Virginia State Papers* notes that this version of the Provisional Constitution was copied from the original at Charles Town by order of the Executive Department of the State of Virginia on November 16, 1859. It has fewer obvious transcription errors than the version in *Executive Documents Printed by Order of the Senate of the United States: First Session of the Thirty-Sixth Congress, 1859–60*, Vol. 2 (Washington: George W. Bowman, 1860).

30. Quoting the opening of the Declaration of Independence.

31. Quoting and adapting the first paragraph of the Declaration.

32. Quoting the opening of the second paragraph of the Declaration.

33. Quoting and adapting the second paragraph of the Declaration.

34. Adapting material from the second paragraph of the Declaration, with the notable insertions of "most cruel bondage" and "Liberty."

35. Expanding on the end of the Declaration's second paragraph.

36. Quoting and adapting the third, fourth, and fifth grievances listed in the Declaration.

37. Referring to Chief Justice Roger Taney, who delivered the Dred Scott decision of 1857.

38. Quoting and adapting the ninth, tenth, and twelfth grievances of the Declaration, with the notable insertion of "Blood Suckers and Moths."

39. Quoting and adapting the fifteenth grievance of the Declaration.

40. Quoting and adapting the twenty-second and twenty-third grievances of the Declaration.

41. Adapting the twenty-fifth grievance of the Declaration.

42. Brown translates the Latin phrase *Salus populi suprema lex esto*, which is from Cicero's *De Legibus*, book 3, also quoted by John Locke in *On Civil Government* to describe the proper organization of government.

43. Matthew 7:2.

44. Quoting Cesare Beccaria's *On Crimes and Punishments* (1764).

45. In 1816 three hundred fugitive slaves and thirty Creek Indian allies held Fort Blount, an abandoned British fortress in Apalachicola Bay, Florida, for several days before being overcome by U.S. troops on July 27. Only forty fugitive slaves were still alive when the fort was surrendered.

46. Quoting from and adapting the third to last and penultimate paragraphs of the Declaration, with the notable additions of "Class of oppressors" and "cursed Institution."

47. Luke 10:7.

48. Quoting from the final paragraph of the Declaration.

49. Quoting from the final paragraph of the Declaration but omitting the original's "fortunes" ("we mutually pledge to each other our Lives, our Fortunes and our sacred Honor").

50. Quoting Thomas Jefferson's prediction of dire consequences for slavery in *Notes on the State of Virginia* (1781).

51. Possibly adapting the image of nature mourning Christ's execution from Matthew 27:45 ("There was darkness over all the land").

52. Adapting Joel 2:31 (repeated in Acts 2:20), a prophecy of the Apocalypse: "The sun shall be turned into darkness, and the moon into blood, before the great and terrible day of the Lord come."

53. The editor of *Calendar of Virginia State Papers* noted that he had transcribed the exact spelling, punctuation, and use of capitals found in the original, which he suspected to have been handwritten by Owen Brown (sometimes a copyist for his father). The original copy was pasted under white cloth, rolled up on a round stick, and tied with a string. This version in the *Calendar* has fewer obvious transcription errors than the version in *Governor's Message and Reports, Part 1* (Richmond: William F. Ritchie, 1859).

54. Three more men joined Brown shortly before his raid, to make twenty-one in his final band.

55. Brown is probably referring to Edwin Coppoc.

56. Brown refers to an incident of September 1858, when a group of Ohio residents rescued a fugitive slave from a U.S. marshal who was trying to return him to the South.

57. Aaron Dwight Stevens was a white raider from Connecticut. He met Brown in Kansas in 1856 and was executed on March 16, 1860.

58. Brown knew that the question was about Joshua Giddings, from Jefferson, Ohio.

59. Brown quotes Euripides's tragedy *Medea*.

60. Hebrews 13:3.

61. This volume retains the nineteenth-century spelling of the town, with an apostrophe, where sources use it. We use the current spelling (Harpers Ferry) in

selection introductions. The origins of the apostrophe stem from the original
purchase in the Colonial era: in 1751 Robert Harper acquired a patent for 125 acres on
the current site, and twelve years later the Virginia Assembly established the town of
"Shenandoah Falls at Mr. Harper's Ferry." Between 1794 and 1797 the federal government, under President Washington, purchased the land to create an arsenal. The
National Park Service officially (and correctly) spells it without the apostrophe.

62. Brown discusses his sons Oliver and Watson, and William and Dauphin
Thompson from North Elba, two brothers whose other siblings were married to
some of Brown's children. All four men died at Harpers Ferry.

63. Brown means Jeremiah Anderson, a white raider from Indiana who died at
Harpers Ferry.

64. Psalm 106:1.

65. Acts 27:23.

66. Deuteronomy 31:6.

67. Jeremiah 38:9–13.

68. Acts 8:27–39.

69. 2 Corinthians 4:17.

70. 2 Corinthians 7:4.

71. Psalm 72:12.

72. Ephesians 6:17.

73. 2 Corinthians 10:4.

74. 2 Corinthians 7:4.

75. Philippians 4:7.

76. Ecclesiastes 4:1.

77. Psalm 72:12.

78. Revelation 3:12.

79. 2 Corinthians 13:11.

80. Revelation 21:27.

81. Jeremiah Brown was Brown's younger half-brother.

82. Brown refers to his son-in-law Henry Thompson (the husband of his daughter
Ruth).

83. James 1:2.

84. 2 Timothy 4:7.

85. Harmon Vaill was Brown's former teacher at Morris Academy in Litchfield,
Connecticut, where he attended school between 1816 and 1817.

86. Psalm 57:4.

87. Psalm 56:9.

88. Hebrews 11:25.

89. Psalm 40:9.

90. Ephesians 6:17.

91. Joshua 3:15–17.

92. Brown cites John Bunyan's Christian allegory *The Pilgrim's Progress* (1678),
which quotes Joshua 3:17.

93. Luke 2:14.

94. Psalm 146:2.

95. Psalm 26:9.

96. Brown refers to the story of Judges 16. This was not the first time he had compared himself to Samson. In February 1858he wrote to Franklin Sanborn that he would effect "a mighty conquest even though it be like the last victory of Samson."

97. Matthew 6:10.

98. Hebrews 11:13.

99. Acts 27:22.

100. This was Mrs. Woodruff, at whose house Brown boarded during his time at Morris Academy.

101. Thomas Musgrave was the son of Brown's business friend, a Massachusetts wool merchant.

102. Brown quotes from the text of the Dred Scott decision of 1857.

103. 1 Corinthians 7:31.

104. Luther Humphrey was Brown's first cousin and a Presbyterian minister.

105. Brown refers to John Rogers, a Protestant martyr burned at the stake in London in 1555.

106. 1 Samuel 14:45.

107. Isaiah 58:5.

108. James McFarland was a minister in Ohio.

109. Philippians 1:18.

110. Brown borrows Christ's words on the cross, Luke 23:34.

111. Acts 4:19.

112. Hebrews 13:3.

113. Brown adapts Psalm 68:5.

114. Job 3:17.

115. Heman Humphrey was Brown's first cousin through his maternal grandmother and a president of Amherst College.

116. Humphrey had written to Brown on November 20, accusing him of an "amazing infatuation which was urging you on to certain destruction" and questioning whether Brown was in his "right mind."

117. Judges 13:5.

118. Brown compares himself to Samson again.

119. Hebrews 11:13.

120. Psalm 71:18.

121. Psalm 106:1.

122. This is a response to Humphrey's comment that even if Brown's was an "infinitely better cause" than Saul's, it was doomed.

123. See Brown's letter of November 19.

124. For example, the *Albany Evening Journal* had observed on October 19 that Brown had raided Harpers Ferry because he had a "thirst for revenge" after the proslavery violence in Kansas in 1856.

125. Daniel R. Tilden was a Republican and a judge in Cleveland, Ohio. As a young man he had known Brown and been employed in Brown's business.

126. 1 Corinthians 2:9.

127. Brown refers to Hiram Griswold of Cleveland, who appeared as additional counsel for Brown during his trial.

128. Tilden read this prison letter aloud at a public meeting in Cleveland, Ohio, on December 2, 1859, the day of Brown's execution.

129. Mary Stearns was a niece of Lydia Maria Child and the wife of Brown's benefactor George Stearns. She had been a supporter of Brown since 1857.

130. Though Brown was denied this request, he was spared the attentions of proslavery ministers.

131. Brown refers to John Rogers, the first Protestant martyr under Mary I of England. He quotes from Rogers's words of advice to his children, written a few days before his death in 1555.

Part II: Northern Responses

1. Greeley refers to Robert E. Lee, who led the militia and Marine force that overpowered Brown and went on to command the Confederate Army of Northern Virginia in the Civil War.

2. In fact, four of Brown's sons survived him: John Jr., Jason, Owen, and Salmon.

3. In fact, ten died in the battle or shortly afterward, four were captured, two escaped but were eventually caught and imprisoned, and five escaped and were never captured.

4. Greeley quotes a public letter of August 1856 by Rufus Choate to the Maine Whig Committee, in which Choate argues for the preservation of the Union and warns against organizing an antislavery Northern government around the "glittering and sounding generalities of natural right which make up the Declaration of Independence." Choate did not follow his fellow Whigs into the Republican Party but supported Democrat James Buchanan instead.

5. The plantation homes of Thomas Jefferson and George Washington, respectively, both in Virginia.

6. Like many responses to Brown, the article quotes William H. Seward's famous description of an "irrepressible conflict" between the forces of freedom and slavery, first offered during a speech of October 25, 1858.

7. The nickname "Osawatomie Brown" came from Brown's experiences in Kansas, especially the Battle of Osawatomie of August 30, 1856.

8. Seward.

9. Referring to the death of a deputy U.S. marshal in Boston during the attempt by an antislavery crowd to free the fugitive slave Anthony Burns and prevent his return to slavery in Virginia.

10. *New York Tribune* editor Horace Greeley, Ohio congressman Joshua Giddings, and Massachusetts governor Nathaniel Prentice Banks.

11. The abolitionists Theodore Parker and William Lloyd Garrison.

12. Referring to Lincoln's "House Divided" speech of June 16, 1858, which declared that the "government cannot endure, permanently half slave and half free."

13. Matthew 7:16.

14. Brown was hung at 11:15 A.M. and taken down thirty-five minutes later.

15. The abolitionist preacher Henry Ward Beecher observed in 1856 that rifles were more useful than Bibles to antislavery settlers in Kansas.

16. Referring to a letter that Gerrit Smith sent to Brown, dated June 4, 1859. Smith enclosed $200 so Brown could continue his "Kansas work"—a euphemism for the Harpers Ferry raid. The letter was reprinted in the *New York Herald* on October 21 and was read aloud at Brown's trial.

17. The letter arrived in an envelope that bore the inscription "God Hath Made Of One Blood All Nations Of Men" (from Acts 17:26).

18. Elizabeth Fry was an English prison reformer and Quaker, active in the first half of the nineteenth century.

19. In William Shakespeare's play *The Merchant of Venice*, Portia disguises herself as a male lawyer's apprentice in order to save the life of Antonio in court.

20. In *Notes on the State of Virginia* (1781).

21. Referring to a speech of 1844: the day of "redemption must come . . . whether in peace or in blood, let it come."

22. Riot (French).

23. Robert Ould, district attorney for Washington, D.C., was present in Harpers Ferry during the raid and took charge of the captured raiders after their defeat and arrest. He went on to serve as the Confederate agent for the exchange of prisoners during the Civil War.

24. John Floyd was the U.S. secretary of war at the time of Brown's raid, and communicated with General Robert E. Lee about Brown during and after the conflict between Lee's Marines and Brown's raiders at Harpers Ferry.

25. Senator James Mason, a proslavery Virginian, and congressman Clement Vallandigham, an Ohio Democrat and later a Copperhead (antiwar, pro–states' rights Northern Democrat), were part of the group that interviewed Brown immediately after his capture on October 18, 1859.

26. James Buchanan was U.S. president at the time of Brown's raid.

27. Henry Wise was governor of Virginia at the time of Brown's raid.

28. A daily newspaper out of Washington, D.C., the *Constitution* was published from April 1859 to January 1861 (and under the name the *Union* from 1845 to 1859). It was an administration organ, supporting the sitting administration and in receipt of subsidies and contracts for congressional printing. It condemned Brown and accused several leading Republicans (including William H. Seward) of complicity in the raid.

29. Launched in 1835, the *New York Herald* was a Democratic paper and strongly condemned Brown's raid.

30. Frederick Brown was killed in Kansas in 1856.

31. Beecher is incorrect that Brown had sixteen followers; he had twenty-one men at the Kennedy Farm and took eighteen with him to Harpers Ferry on the night of October 16.

32. This was the Concord postmaster.

33. Thoreau quotes Horace Greeley's editorial for the *New York Tribune*, October 19, 1859.

34. Most likely William Walker of Tennessee, who tried to conquer several Latin American countries in the mid-nineteenth century.

35. An allusion to Dante's *Inferno*, where the Minotaur lives among those damned for their violent natures, the "men of blood."

36. Between Brown's raid on October 16 and his execution on December 2, the Northeast witnessed a meteor shower on an unprecedented scale. Thoreau read about the meteors in newspapers and may have remembered them when he wrote this speech.

37. Marcus Porcius Cato, an opponent of Julius Caesar; William Tell, the fourteenth-century Swiss folk hero; and Arnold Winkelried, a Swiss hero of the Battle of Sempach (1386).

38. Walter Raleigh's *The History of the World* (1614).

39. Benjamin Franklin's *Poor Richard's Almanack* (1732–1758).

40. Washington Irving.

41. Thoreau cites Brown's purported remark from his jail cell, in response to the idea that his efforts had failed. Wendell Phillips quoted the remark in a speech of December 15, 1859, which was printed in the *New York Times*.

42. Thoreau alludes to the Franco-Austrian War of 1859.

43. From Andrew Marvell's "An Horatian Ode upon Cromwell's Return from Ireland" (1650).

44. Emerson excised this paragraph about Brown when he published the speech in *Society and Solitude* (1870).

45. Matthew 11:19.

46. Emerson refers to a comment that Brown made to Franklin Sanborn and others in 1857: "I believe in the Golden Rule and the Declaration of Independence. I think they both mean the same thing; and it is better that a whole generation should pass off the face of the earth—men, women, and children—by a violent death, than that one jot of either should fail in this country." The Golden Rule refers to Matthew 7:12: "Therefore all things whatsoever ye would that men should do to you, do ye even so to them."

47. Emerson quotes Brown's last speech to the court of November 2, 1859.

48. A logical but absurd consequence (Latin).

49. Gideon, of Judges 6–8, and Leonidas, the king of Sparta, both led their people against much larger armies.

50. The Battle of Thermopylae, 480 B.C., part of the Greco-Persian Wars, where a force of seven thousand Greeks led by King Leonidas I of Sparta held off a Persian army of several million men for seven days.

51. The legendary Roman general who led the city's soldiers against an enemy tribe, the Volscian.

52. William Wallace, who led a resistance during the wars of Scottish independence in the late thirteenth and early fourteenth centuries, and William Tell, the fourteenth-century Swiss folk hero.

53. Arnold Winkelried, a Swiss hero of the Battle of Sempach (1386).

54. From Antony's speech about Brutus's betrayal of Caesar in Shakespeare's *Julius Caesar*.

55. Jeremiah 21:12.

56. Stedman refers to the men who went with Brown to attack Harpers Ferry. Brown left three of his twenty-one men behind as sentinels at the Kennedy Farm.

57. Referring to the coup d'état on December 2, 1851, staged by Louis-Napoléon Bonaparte. At the time he was president of the French Second Republic, and after the coup he became Napoleon III, emperor of the French.

58. Joshua Giddings, Republican representative from Ohio; John Parker Hale, Republican senator from New Hampshire; Gerrit Smith, the abolitionist and philanthropist; and Ralph Plumb, Ohio attorney.

59. Matthew 7:12 and Exodus 21:16.

60. From the text of the Dred Scott decision.

61. Adapted from Thomas Paine's famous words in the opening of "The American Crisis," December 23, 1776.

62. Quoted from President Zachary Taylor's inaugural address of 1849.

63. In August 1831, Nat Turner led seventy other slaves in a rebellion in Southampton Country, Virginia.

64. Partisan investigation committees.

65. Acts 17:26.

66. Quoting and translating the Virginia state motto (Latin).

67. Describing the Great Seal of Virginia, which shows Virtue holding a spear with her foot on the prostrate figure of Tyranny.

68. Exodus 14:26–30.

69. In fact ten raiders died during the battle at Harpers Ferry and seven (including Brown) were hanged.

70. Quoting Henry Wadsworth Longfellow's poem "The Song of Hiawatha" (1855).

71. Stephen was tried for blasphemy and stoned to death in A.D. 34 (Acts 7:59).

72. Mary Dyer was a Quaker executed in Boston in 1660 because she had defied a law that banned Quakers from the colony.

73. Benjamin Franklin and Thomas Jefferson proposed this phrase as a motto for the Great Seal of the United States. Abolitionists used it frequently.

74. An allusion to the Virginia seal and motto: *Sic semper tyrannis* (thus always to tyrants).

75. Leviticus 25:10 (a passage on the jubilee year, used by Garrison as well as Wright).

76. Wright blends together 2 Timothy 4:8 and Luke 2:29–30, connected by his own addition, "when the last slave shall be free."

77. Wright echoes a famous sentence from Jefferson's *Notes on Virginia* about slavery: "The Almighty has no attribute which can take side with us in such a contest."

78. Isaiah 41:9–16.

79. Wright misquotes Henry Wise's comments about Brown, made on October 21. Wise called Brown "truthful," "of courage," a man of "integrity," and "humane," rather than true, brave, sincere, and noble.

80. Again Wright adapts Wise's comments that Brown was "truthful" and had "courage" and "integrity."

81. Wright describes the Great Seal of Virginia with the state motto (a Latin phrase meaning "Thus always to tyrants"). The seal shows Virtue holding a spear with her foot on the prostrate figure of Tyranny.

82. Heroes of the American Revolution.

83. Wright adapts 1 Peter 2:24.

84. 2 Corinthians 2:16.

85. Caiaphas was the Roman-appointed Jewish high priest involved in the trial of Jesus. He advised the Jews that it would be good if one man died for the people (John 18:14).

86. A famous phrase from Chapter 50 of Tertullian's *Apologeticus* (A.D. 197).

87. Daniel Webster was a U.S. senator who worked to quiet sectional conflict. He said of the Boston Massacre, in which Crispus Attucks, a black man, died in 1770: "From that moment we may date the severance of the British Empire."

88. Quoting Richard Hildreth's *Despotism in America* (1840), which claimed that the Southern "experiment of Despotism" made union between the North and South a "mockery" that was "inconsistent with humanity and with freedom."

89. Quoting John Wesley, the founder of Methodism, in 1772.

90. From Shakespeare's *Richard III*, Act V, Scene 3 (quoting King Richard, a humpback).

91. Only this resolution prompted some dissenting voices in the hall. It was carried nonetheless.

92. Deuteronomy 32:30.

93. Thus always to tyrants (Latin).

94. Fear is the proof of a degenerate mind (Latin).

95. Referring to the Democratic congressman Preston Brooks's attack on Republican senator Charles Sumner in May 1856.

96. Quoting Seward's "irrepressible conflict" speech of October 1858.

97. Song of Solomon 6:4.

98. Misquoting Governor Henry Wise's comments of October 21, 1859.

99. In fact Brown was fifty-nine years old when he died.

100. Turning Brown's execution into a crucifixion, Martin adapts Matthew 27 (especially verse 17: "Pilate said unto them, Whom will ye that I release unto you? Barabbas, or Jesus which is called Christ?").

101. Matthew 14:4.

102. Martin adapts the death of John the Baptist. After John was beheaded, Herod had his head presented on a platter (Matthew 14:10–11).

103. Martin may mean the *Boston Post*, which reported on November 4 that Thoreau's "Plea" had "blasphemously likened Brown to Christ."

104. Martin borrows from 1 Kings 19:18.

105. Last resort (French).

106. Martin refers to Henry Wadsworth Longfellow's poem "Excelsior" (1841).

107. The Reverend James Freeman Clarke opened the meeting and read from Judges 16, about Samson bringing down the temple.

108. Divine presence (Hebrew).

109. Martin quotes from a speech by the Irish politician John Philpot Curran, in 1794, that defends James Somersett, a Jamaican slave who declared his freedom upon being taken to Britain. Harriet Beecher Stowe also quoted the passage, as the epigraph to Chapter 37 of *Uncle Tom's Cabin* (1852).

110. Judges 7:20.

111. Most likely referring to an article published in the *New York Observer* on November 17, 1859, which describes the "demon of modern abolition infidelity" that is present in Brown, Frederick Douglass, and Gerrit Smith.

112. Garrison spoke after J. Sella Martin and the abolitionist Samuel Sewall. Garrison himself read Brown's last address to the court, before Martin spoke.

113. 1 John 2:4.

114. Heroes of the Revolution: George Washington, Joseph Warren, and John Hancock.

115. Marquis de Lafayette (France), Thaddeus Kosciusko (Poland), Kazimierz Pułaski (Poland), Baron von Steuben (Prussia), and Baron de Kalb (Germany) all fought with the Continental Army.

116. Scotsman Thomas Campbell's "Stanzas to the Memory of the Spanish Patriots" (1823).

117. 2 Thessalonians 2:12.

118. Garrison refers to the fugitive slave Anthony Burns, who was forcibly returned to slavery from Boston in 1854.

119. From Jefferson's letter to Jean Nicolas Demeunier, January 24, 1786.

120. Isaiah 16:3.

121. John Hampden, an English politician who by refusing to pay a new tax to King Charles I helped to precipitate the English Civil War of 1641–1651, in which he died fighting for the Parliamentarians; and Joseph Warren, the president of the Massachusetts Provincial Congress, who died at the Battle of Bunker Hill.

122. Acts 17:26.

123. Translated from Latin, a statement in 1778 about Franklin by the Frenchman Anne Robert Jacques Turgot.

124. The British poet Lord Byron took up arms and joined the revolutionaries in the Greek war of independence (1821–1829).

125. The Polish military leader Thaddeus Kosciusko and the Marquis de Lafayette of France fought in the American Revolutionary War with the Continental Army.

126. Matthew 25:21.

127. Under orders from Colonel Robert E. Lee, Lieutenant Israel Green and his U.S. Marines stormed the engine house at Harpers Ferry on the morning of October 18, 1859. Green wounded Brown with his sword.

128. Judges 16:30.

129. Newhall reworks Judges 16:23–30 to draw an extended parallel between Samson and Brown.

130. Mayor Fontaine Beckham was one of four men killed by Brown's raiders. On October 17, Christina Fouke, the sister of a hotel proprietor in Harpers Ferry, acted as a screen for the men who retrieved his body. Then she tried to intercede for William Thompson, one of Brown's white raiders, but a mob dragged him to the Potomac Bridge and shot him.

131. 2 Timothy 4:7.

132. Brown's men shot and killed Heyward Shepherd, an African American baggage handler on the Baltimore & Ohio train that had stopped in Harpers Ferry on the first evening of their raid. Two raiders confronted Shepherd near the Potomac River railroad bridge, where he was walking, and fired when he refused to halt.

133. In 1791 the slaves of St. Domingue rose in revolt, beginning a civil war in the French colony that led to the establishment of the free and independent nation of Haiti in 1804.

134. The 1860 United States Census counted approximately 4 million slaves and 8 million Southern whites.

135. Presidents George Washington, Thomas Jefferson, James Madison, and James Monroe and chief justice John Marshall were all Virginians.

136. Gerrit Smith, one of Brown's supporters and co-conspirators, suffered an emotional collapse after Brown's sentencing. His family committed him to the New York State Asylum for the Insane at Utica.

137. A British Catholic restorationist who failed to assassinate King James I of England and members of the Houses of Parliament in 1605.

138. François Ravaillac assassinated King Henry IV of France in 1610, and Jacques Clément assassinated King Henry III of France in 1589.

139. Italian revolutionaries assassinated Pellegrino Rossi, minister of the interior under Pius IX, in 1848.

140. Cushing means Count Latour (Theodor Franz), the minister of war who was killed by a mob in Vienna during the Austrian revolution of 1848.

141. Princess Windischgratz was shot during riots by radical Czech students during the June uprising in Prague in 1848.

142. Christian.

143. The committee published its congressional report about the raid in June 1860.

144. For this request, see Brown's letter of November 29, 1859.

145. Enoch and Elijah, of Genesis 5:24 and 2 Kings 2:11, respectively, are two men who do not die.

146. The English politician Algernon Sydney was executed for treason in 1683.

147. In fact these were the last words of the English politician Henry Vane, executed for treason in 1662.

148. Lincoln is quoting from a speech given by Stephen Douglas several months earlier.

149. The Gunpowder Plot of 1605, when a small group of English Catholics failed to blow up the House of Lords and kill King James I.

150. At an equal pace (Latin).

151. Lincoln quotes a draft fragment of Jefferson's autobiography from 1821.

152. Felice Orsini was an Italian revolutionary who tried to assassinate Napoleon III, emperor of the French, in Paris in 1858.

153. Orsini brought the bombs that he threw at the emperor's carriage from England.

154. Lincoln refers to Hinton Rowan Helper's widely read book *The Impending Crisis of the South* (1857), which argued that slavery hurt the Southern economy, most especially the economic interests of nonslaveholding Southern whites.

155. The Conspiracy of 1741, a rumored plot by slaves and poor whites in the colony of New York to revolt.

156. In 1820, Congress passed the Missouri Compromise, which admitted Missouri to the Union as a slave state and Maine as a free state and prohibited slavery in the former Louisiana Territory north of the parallel 36°30′ north. In 1854 the Missouri Compromise was repealed by the Kansas-Nebraska Act.

157. From Henry Highland Garnet's "An Address to the Slaves of the United States" (1843).

158. Brown in fact had twenty-one men.

159. The Battle of Austerlitz was one of Napoleon Bonaparte's greatest victories. On December 2, 1805, his French army defeated the Russo-Austrian army, which led to the end of the Holy Roman Empire.

160. Two of Brown's white raiders, Edwin Coppoc of Ohio and Aaron Stevens of Connecticut.

161. Referring to the 1861 Emancipation Reform, already in preparation in 1860, which freed all serfs in Russia.

162. The trade of African slaves was prohibited in the Ottoman Empire in 1858.

163. Quoting a speech by Henry Brougham, a British abolitionist and member of Parliament, to the House of Commons in 1830, during the struggle to pass the Slavery Abolition Act of 1833, which abolished slavery throughout the British Empire.

164. Referring to Brown and the six other raiders who were hanged near the Jefferson County Courthouse in Charles Town, West Virginia.

165. The 954 pikes that Brown ordered for his raid (and the anticipated slave uprising) from a Connecticut blacksmith each consisted of a 91/2- to 10-inch-long double-edged blade of forged cast steel and a 31/4-inch-long tapering ferrule, fitted onto 6-foot ash handles.

166. From Sir Walter Scott's poem "The Lay of the Last Minstrel" (1805).

167. Quoting Lincoln's "House Divided" speech of June 16, 1858, which expressed Lincoln's belief in the "ultimate extinction" of slavery.

168. Purvis was an African American abolitionist in Philadelphia who served as president of the Pennsylvania Anti-Slavery Society.

169. Governor Henry Wise; Andrew Hunter, the lawyer who prosecuted Brown; president James Buchanan; and senator James Mason.

170. Exodus 9:1 (the words that God gives Moses to speak to Pharaoh).

171. Lajos Kossuth, a mid-nineteenth-century Hungarian freedom fighter.

172. Gabriel, the slave of Thomas Prosser, planned a rebellion for August 1800 in Virginia; Denmark Vesey planned another slave rebellion, this time in South Carolina, for July 1822; Nat Turner led seventy other slaves in a rebellion in Virginia in August 1831; and Madison Washington led a slave revolt on board the U.S. brig *Creole* in 1841.

Part III: Southern Responses

1. Brown's raiders took Colonel Lewis Washington of Virginia hostage. He was a descendent of George Washington and a slaveholder.

2. Benjamin Mills had been master armorer at Harpers Ferry since 1858.

3. Brown was a member of the Richfield Congregational Church in Ohio until the mid-1840s but had no church ties in the last decade of his life.

4. This "safety fund" is described in Article XXIX of Brown's "Provisional Constitution."

5. At this point, accurate information about Brown's raiders (numbering twenty-one, not seventeen) had not reached every newspaper.

6. In fact Brown's band numbered twenty-one in addition to himself.

7. Riot (French).

8. Republican senators William H. Seward and John Parker Hale, Ohio congressman Joshua Giddings, philanthropist Gerrit Smith, and *New York Tribune* editor Horace Greeley.

9. Referring to Republican senator William H. Seward's "irrepressible conflict" speech of October 1858.

10. October 18, 1859.

11. Andrew Hunter was Strother's uncle and would later be the special prosecutor at Brown's trial.

12. Oliver Brown died on October 17, and Watson Brown died on October 19.

13. Aaron Stephens of Connecticut, one of Brown's white raiders, was wounded during the fighting but recovered and was tried and executed.

14. Heyward Shepherd was a free African American railroad worker killed by the raiders on the night of October 16.

15. Strother writes a fictional scene and uses the generic nineteenth-century term for an African American, Cuffee (or Cuffy).

16. Referring to Miguel de Cervantes's two-part novel *Don Quixote* (1605/1615).

17. Referring to Don Quixote de la Mancha (La Mancha being a region of Spain).

18. Anger is a brief madness (Latin).

19. Matthew 7:5.

20. Fontaine Beckham, the mayor of Harpers Ferry, and a local man named George Turner were killed during the fighting on October 17.

21. During the Indian rebellion of 1857, South Asian soldiers rose up against their colonial officers. A mutiny at Meerut, India, came after warnings by Indian soldiers to European officers. It was followed by a massacre of the British at Cawnpore and retributive violence against Indians in Delhi.

22. In 44 B.C. the Roman leader Julius Caesar was assassinated by a group of senators, led by Gaius Cassius Longinus and Marcus Junius Brutus, after warnings not to attend the Senate on that day.

23. The failed assassination attempt against King James I of England in 1605 was revealed in advance to the authorities in an anonymous letter sent to William Parker, Fourth Baron Monteagle.

24. Owen Brown remained behind at the Kennedy Farm to guard the arms during the Harpers Ferry raid. He escaped, served in the Union Army, and died in California in 1889.

25. Thomas Baltzell, chief justice of the Florida Supreme Court.

26. Susan's brother-in-law Junius Taylor.

27. Cornelia Platt, from Rhinebeck, New York.

28. Elias Edmonds.

29. Francis H. Smith, superintendent of the Virginia Military Institute.

30. Lewis B. Williams, Jr., commanded the Montpelier Guards, a volunteer company from Orange County, Virginia.

31. William Gilham was commandant of cadets at the VMI. He led the whole contingent of the cadet corps at the execution.

32. Daniel Trueheart was a lieutenant at the VMI.

33. Matthew 25:41.

34. Sheriff James W. Campbell of Jefferson County, Virginia, an undertaker named Mr. Saddler, and Brown's jailer, John Avis.

35. Lucius Sergius Catilina conspired to overthrown the Roman Republic in 63 B.C.

36. Exodus 20:13; Genesis 9:6.

37. Puritans and fanatics.

38. Conway quotes the famous confession of Frederick, explaining why he went to war with Maria Theresa of Austria in 1756.

39. Hebrews 13:3.

40. John Hampden, an English politician who in 1635 opposed a tax that King Charles I of England tried to levy without the consent of Parliament. The tax resistance was one cause of the English Civil War, in which Hampden was a leading Parliamentarian and which resulted in the execution of Charles I.

41. Socrates of Greece was a critic of democracy who was sentenced to death by a jury of Athenians in 399 B.C. Hypatia of Greece was a pagan, killed by a Christian mob in A.D. 415.

42. John 13:31.

43. Arnold von Winkelried was a legendary Swiss hero purportedly responsible for the confederation's victory against Leopold III of Austria at the Battle of Sempach in 1386.

44. King Leonidas of Sparta led the Greeks against the Persian Empire in 480 B.C.

45. Conway misquotes William Wordsworth's poem "The Church of San Salvador Seen from the Lake of Lugano" (1820); the line is "a sheaf of fatal Austrian spears."

46. From John Milton's *Paradise Lost* (1667), Book IV, 810–813. Satan is in Eden disguised as a toad. Ithuriel touches Satan with his spear, causing him to resume his proper likeness.

47. From the Irish poet Michael J. Barry's "The Place Where Man Should Die" (1843).

48. Republican senator from New York William H. Seward.

49. Davis quotes from Seward's speech of March 3, 1858, "Freedom in Kansas," throughout this address to Congress.

50. Davis is wrong: both Massachusetts and Vermont were free states.

51. John Cook of Connecticut tried to escape from Harpers Ferry but was captured, tried, and executed in 1860.

52. While Lecomptonite Democrats declared that Kansas must accept the proslavery constitution endorsed by President Buchanan for Kansas, anti-Lecomptonites

espoused the Stephen Douglas doctrine that the territory had the right to reject or accept slavery.

53. Stowe's father was the outspoken Presbyterian minister Lyman Beecher, and her brother was the abolitionist Congregationalist clergyman Henry Ward Beecher.

54. Here the writer refers to Lydia Maria Child.

55. Senator James Doolittle of Wisconsin.

56. Two of Brown's white raiders, John Cook of Connecticut and Edwin Coppoc (mistakenly called Coppie by reporters) of Ohio, were executed.

57. Eli Thayer, a Republican congressman from Massachusetts who aided antislavery settlers in Kansas.

58. The antislavery Republican senators Charles Sumner and William Seward, and William H. Leeman, who joined Brown in Kansas and at Harpers Ferry.

59. The New England Emigrant Aid Company (originally the Massachusetts Emigrant Aid Company), founded by Thayer after the Kansas-Nebraska Act of 1854, transported Free-Staters to Kansas Territory.

60. Hugh Forbes, a British soldier hired by Brown in 1857, betrayed the Virginia plans in advance to several political leaders, including Seward.

61. In 1555, Hugh Latimer and Nicholas Ridley were burned at the stake under Queen Mary of England, becoming martyrs of Anglicanism.

62. Referring to Caleb Cushing's speech at Faneuil Hall, Boston, on December 8, 1859.

63. Francis Merriam and Osborne Anderson escaped to Canada.

64. The date of Abraham Lincoln's inauguration as president.

65. Mason.

66. This was George W. Turner, a farmer and slaveholder who lived in the area and was one of the four men killed by Brown's raiders.

67. From Shakespeare's *Julius Caesar,* Act III, Scene 1, Mark Antony's lament over the body of Caesar.

68. In fact Owen Brown and Dangerfield Newby were born before 1830.

69. When New England patriots laid siege to British-occupied Boston in 1775, the Continental Congress requested that other colonies send men to aid in the effort. Virginia sent two rifle companies.

70. William Leeman, one of Brown's white raiders, was shot and killed on October 17, 1859, while swimming across the Potomac during the raid.

71. Daniel Morgan and Hugh Stephenson captained the Virginia rifle companies that marched to Boston to support the siege.

72. Quoting the Declaration of Independence (originally a grievance against the British for employing "merciless Indian savages").

73. General Fernando Álvarez de Toledo, the duke of Alva, led King Philip of Spain's army into the Netherlands in 1567 and then governed the Low Countries until 1573. His council tried and executed thousands of people as heretics and traitors.

74. The French conquest of Algeria began in 1830 with a bloody invasion of Algiers.

75. Massacres and atrocities took place during the Indian rebellion of 1857 and the repression of rebels by the British in 1858.

76. The Spanish conquistadores Hernán Cortés and Francisco Pizarro slaughtered thousands during their conquests of Mexico (1519) and Peru (1532), respectively.

77. The Nat Turner rebellion of 1831.

78. Meaning October 1859.

79. Hinton Rowan Helper's self-published book *The Impending Crisis of the South* (1857) was an attack on slavery aimed at nonslaveholding Southern whites. Nearly 150,000 copies were in circulation by 1861.

80. Sixty-eight Republican congressmen, including Giddings and Seward, endorsed a distribution campaign for the book in 1859.

81. The opponents blocked the election of Republican John Sherman as Speaker of the House because he had endorsed Helper's book.

82. Democrat Caleb Cushing of Massachusetts, former attorney general of the United States.

83. In July 1860, pro-Democratic newspapers charged abolitionists with setting fires that destroyed parts of Dallas, Denton, and other towns in north Texas. Slave insurrection would follow, alleged the sensational reports. From July until mid-September, vigilantes responded by hanging slaves and reputed abolitionists.

84. Quoting a campaign speech Andrew gave in Boston during the lead-up to his November election as governor of Massachusetts.

85. Simms refers to the slave insurrection panic in Texas in the summer of 1860, fueled by newspapers claiming that abolitionists had started fires in and around Dallas as the inauguration of a widespread slave uprising.

86. Quoting from Thomas A. Emmet's speech as the defense lawyer for William S. Smith during his trial of July 1806. Smith was charged with violating the Neutrality Act of 1794.

Part IV: International Responses

1. A direct assault that uses surprise to accomplish an objective with one swift blow.

2. Referring to the Gunpowder Plot of 1605, when a small group of English Catholics failed to blow up the House of Lords and kill King James I.

3. French lawyer Antoine Quentin Fouquier de Tinville successfully prosecuted the trials of royalists and other perceived enemies of the French Revolution during the Reign of Terror of 1793–1794.

4. In May 1859 peasants in the French town of Tarbes rioted in response to the introduction of a toll on livestock entering the market. Troops killed seven rioters.

5. Original in French; translated by the editors.

6. Norwid's "twelve stars" refer to the original colonies of America (although there were thirteen).

7. Thaddeus Kosciusko, a Polish national hero who fought in the American Revolutionary War, and George Washington.

8. The two ellipses in this epigraph are Norwid's.

9. Norwid means thirteen stars.

10. Both poems were written in Polish and translated into English by George Kliger and Robert C. Albrecht.

11. Andrew Hunter prosecuted Brown's case and Richard Parker sat as judge.

12. Hugo had received a false report of a stay of execution. He composed his appeal accordingly.

13. From the Latin word *fascis,* a bundle of rods tied together that symbolize strength through unity and appear in numerous national insignia, including the official seal of the U.S. Senate.

14. Original in French; this translation is by the American Anti-Slavery Society for its volume *Letters on American Slavery,* a collection of European texts that included writings by Alexis de Toqueville and Nikolai Ivanovich Turgenev.

15. Original in French; this translation was done for the U.S. edition of Hugo's letters, published in 1898.

16. The Franco-Prussian war of 1870–1871.

17. Original in French; translated for Sanborn's *Life and Letters.*

18. Original in German; translated by Christoph K. Lohmann.

19. Citing the Democratic *Times-Picayune* of New Orleans, Louisiana, which published numerous articles about Brown's raid between October 25 and December 2, 1859.

20. John A. Copeland and Shields Green, two black raiders, were hanged on December 16, 1859.

21. The writer misquotes John Dryden's poem "Absalom and Achitophel" (1681): "Great wits are sure to madness near allied / And thin partitions do their bounds divide."

22. This was reported in the *New York Times* on December 3, as part of an article on Brown's last meeting with his wife at the Charles Town jail during the evening before his execution: Brown wanted his body to be burned with the bodies of his sons and the Thompson brothers, who died at Harpers Ferry, observing that this would be less expensive.

23. Referring to Louis-Napoléon Bonaparte's coup d'état of December 2, 1851.

24. Referring to the bloody Irish uprising against British rule in the spring and summer of 1798.

25. Daniel O'Connell, an Irish political leader in the first half of the nineteenth century who campaigned for the repeal of the union between Ireland and Great Britain, and John Mitchell, a midcentury Irish nationalist activist.

26. James Radclyffe, 3rd Earl of Derwentwater, led a faction in a Jacobite rebellion of 1715, part of a series of uprisings between 1688 and 1746 that aimed at returning James II of England to the throne. Captured during battle, he was executed for treason on February 24, 1716. The aurora borealis appeared particularly bright on the night of his execution.

27. Referring to the myth that in 1521 the Protestant reformer Martin Luther threw an inkwell at the devil.

28. Referring to Phillips's funeral oration for Brown on December 8, 1859.

29. In Greek mythology, one of the five rivers in the regions of the underworld.

30. Matthew 19:14.

31. A British prison reformer active in the late eighteenth century.

32. Referring to the attempted black uprising in the town of Bolivar, Missouri, in December 1859.

33. Original in German; translated by the editors.

34. Referring to Victor Hugo, who lived in Guernsey, an island off the coast of France near Jersey.

35. Vincent Ogé and Jean-Baptiste Chavannes, free Haitian men of color, instigated a revolt against white colonial authorities in 1790 and were publicly tortured and hanged in 1791 as a warning to others.

36. Original in French; translated by the editors.

37. Referring to Brown's last address to the Virginia court, on November 2, 1859.

38. Original in French.

39. On April 17, 1861, the Virginia Convention voted to secede from the Union. On April 20, governor John Letcher of Virginia called for volunteers to assemble for the defense of the state.

40. Letters of marque and reprisal were given to private citizens by countries that could not afford large navies and were issued by the Confederate government in 1861. The recipients would use their privately owned ships to conduct raids on ports and ships and keep anything they took in the raids. This enabled a poor country to create an instant navy.

41. In an effort to prevent Confederates from seizing arsenal equipment, First Lieutenant Roger Jones set fire to the arsenal buildings on April 18, 1861, and then fled north to Carlisle, Pennsylvania.

42. John Anthony Copeland, Jr., reportedly made this statement on his way to the gallows at Charles Town on December 16, 1859.

43. Albert Hazlett escaped into Pennsylvania after the raid but was captured and taken back to Charles Town. He was executed on March 16, 1860. He made this comment in a letter of March 15, 1860, to Mrs. Rebecca Spring.

44. Quoting *The Anti-Slavery History of the John Brown Year,* the twenty-seventh annual report of the American Anti-Slavery Society, published in 1861.

45. Quoting Brown's "Provisional Constitution and Ordinances for the People of the United States" of May 8, 1858.

46. Original in French; translated by the editors.

47. Referring to the French intervention in Mexico of 1862–1867.

48. Original in Italian; translated by the editors.

49. Referring to the French coup d'état of December 2, 1851, staged by Louis-Napoléon Bonaparte.

50. 1 Chronicles 12:32.

51. Moncure Conway.

52. Adapting Hosea 9:16.

53. George McHenry's *The Position and Duty of Pennsylvania* (1863).

54. Forces occupying Mexico along the border with the United States during the Franco-Mexican War.

55. John Elliot, an English statesman who advocated the rights of Parliament and was imprisoned by King Charles I several times in the 1620s, and Oliver Cromwell,

one of the commanders of the New Model Army, which defeated the royalists in the English Civil War (1641–1651).

56. Giuseppe Mazzini and Giuseppe Garibaldi, mid-nineteenth-century heroes of Italian unification, and Lajos Kossuth, a mid-nineteenth-century Hungarian freedom fighter.

57. Richard Cobden and John Bright were British Liberal and Radical statesmen who helped achieve a free-trade treaty between the United Kingdom and France in 1860.

58. John Elliott Cairnes's *The Slave Power: Its Character, Career, and Probable Designs* (1862).

59. Judges 7:14.

60. Quoting Brown's comments to an old Pennsylvania neighbor, Mr. Lowry, from his jail cell.

61. The abolitionists Benjamin Lundy, William Lloyd Garrison, and Frederick Douglass.

62. The statesman Henry Clay gained congressional approval for the Missouri Compromise of 1820.

63. Original in German; translated by Philippe Marcou for *John Brown* (1888).

Part V: Civil War and U.S. Postwar Responses

1. From the French *impôt* (imposition or burden), possibly connoting an "iron hand."

2. All ellipses are in the original.

3. Quoting Samuel Johnson's *Rasselas* (1759).

4. The author Harriet Beecher Stowe, the *Tribune* editor Horace Greeley, the transcendentalists Henry David Thoreau and Ralph Waldo Emerson, and senator Charles Sumner.

5. George Leonard Andrews, colonel of the Second Massachusetts Infantry, detailed as provost marshal of Harpers Ferry in late February 1862.

6. Referring to John Greenleaf Whittier's poem "Brown of Ossawatomie" of December 22, 1859.

7. Misquoting Ralph Waldo Emerson's speech "Courage" of November 8, 1859 (Emerson said Brown "will make the gallows glorious like the cross").

8. The Union generals Nathaniel Prentiss Banks, Franz Sigel, George W. Morgan, and William "Bull" Nelson.

9. The Union generals David Hunter, John C. Frémont, and Abner Doubleday.

10. Salmon P. Chase, a former senator from Ohio who drafted the Free Soil platform and was currently serving as Lincoln's secretary of the treasury.

11. Laura Towne, a white abolitionist from Pennsylvania who remained as a teacher on St. Helena's Island until she died.

12. A section of John Greenleaf Whittier's poem "At Port Royal 1861," widely printed during the Civil War, written in the dialect of boatmen at Port Royal, South Carolina. The rest of the poem describes the experiences of Northern abolitionists like Charlotte Forten who arrived in areas near Port Royal to teach slaves.

13. General George B. McClellan, who served as general in chief of the Union Army from November 1861 to March 1862.

14. William Lloyd Garrison, the editor of the abolitionist *Liberator.*

15. James Gordon Bennett, the founder and editor of the Democratic *New York Herald.*

16. The abolitionist and orator Wendell Phillips.

17. The Roman god of the underworld.

18. A synonym for hell, Tophet is a location in Jerusalem where the Canaanites sacrificed children to the god Moloch (Jeremiah 7).

19. Benedict Arnold, a general during the American Revolutionary War who switched sides to join the British and whose name became a byword for treason.

20. President Lincoln.

21. The Radical Republicans Charles Sumner and Thaddeus Stevens.

22. The Democrat David Tod, governor of Ohio between 1862 and 1864, who supported the war effort.

23. The abolitionist Salmon P. Chase, Lincoln's secretary of the treasury.

24. Referring to John Andrew's comments in his speech at Tremont Temple on November 18, 1859, before he became governor of Massachusetts in January 1861.

25. The peak where, according to the book of Genesis, Noah's ark came to rest.

26. 2 Timothy 3:16.

27. Acts 9:11.

28. The abolitionists William Lloyd Garrison and Wendell Phillips.

29. Acts 17:26.

30. Invoking the Declaration of Independence.

31. Invoking the U.S. Constitution.

32. A term used to describe Northerners who were sympathetic to the Southern Slave Power.

33. A tyrant of Athens from 546 to 527 B.C.

34. The first of five men killed in the Boston Massacre of 1770, Crispus Attucks became an African American martyr of the American Revolution.

35. Napoleon Bonaparte, emperor of France from 1804 to 1815.

36. Voice of the people (Latin).

37. Aristion, a Greek philosopher who was tyrant of Athens from 88 to 86 B.C.

38. The Lincoln-Douglas contest of 1860.

39. The Isthmus of Panama, part of a route for the transportation of gold during the California Gold Rush of 1848–1859.

40. The Prince of Wales (Edward VII), who made a four-month tour throughout Canada and the United States in 1860. He reached New York on October 11.

41. A 19,000-ton steamship (six times larger than any ship ever built) that completed its successful maiden voyage from Southampton, England, to New York on June 28, 1860.

42. Likely referring to Donati's Comet, discovered in June 1858 and visible until March 1859.

43. Referring to a meteor shower of mid-December 1859 (and possibly recalling the great auroral storm of late August and early September 1859).

44. David Hunter Strother, who covered Brown's raid, trial, and execution for *Harper's Weekly.*

45. Referring to a supporter of Parliament (against King Charles I) during the English Civil War of 1641–1651.

46. See Henry Wise, "Comments in Richmond, Virginia," October 21, 1859.

47. Aide-de-camp, or camp assistant, a member of a general officer's personal staff.

48. Captain O. Jennings Wise died as a result of wounds on February 9, 1862, after a battle at Roanoke Island, North Carolina. His father, General Henry Wise (formerly the governor of Virginia) was the Confederate officer in command at the battle.

49. Quoting the abolitionist and Pennsylvania Republican state senator Morrow B. Lowry, who had visited Brown in prison in November 1859.

50. The Republican senators William H. Seward and Charles Sumner and the abolitionist William Lloyd Garrison.

51. See Andrew Johnson, "Remarks to the Senate," December 12, 1859.

52. A small inn midway between the Upper and Lower Saranac Lakes.

53. Quoting the Unitarian minister and religious philosopher James Walker of Massachusetts.

54. Psalm 121:1.

55. Bowditch means Alexis Hinckley, a neighbor of Brown's who rented the farm from 1863 and purchased it in 1866. His sister Abbie married Brown's son Salmon, but Bowditch is incorrect that Hinckley married one of Brown's daughters.

56. While Brown and his sons expressed hopes that Hinckley would join them in Kansas, there is no evidence that he did.

57. Quoting Charles Wolfe's poem "The Burial of Sir John Moore at Corunna" (1817), about the British general who achieved military success against Napoleon's forces in Spain.

58. This was done in 1886, by a stonecutter hired by Colonel Francis L. Lee of Boston.

59. Quoting Lincoln's Address at Gettysburg, November 19, 1863.

60. William Chauncey Fowler's book *The Sectional Controversy: or, Passages in the Political History of the United States, Including the Causes of the War between the Sections* (1863). For Fowler's discussion of Brown, see 200–201.

61. The Maine law, passed in 1851, prohibited the sale of all alcoholic beverages except for "medicinal, mechanical or manufacturing purposes" in the state. The law was repealed in 1856.

62. Melville might use this word because the Shenandoah River joins the Potomac River at Harpers Ferry. As well, the Shenandoah Valley, where Harpers Ferry is located, was the site of Civil War battles from 1862 to 1864.

63. Written by Charles Wesley in 1750, the hymn is based on Leviticus 25 and celebrates jubilee—the liberation of slaves at the fiftieth year.

64. Henry Thompson, who had married Brown's daughter Ruth in 1850.

65. Members of the "secret six" who funded Brown: Samuel Howe, Theodore Parker, George Luther Stearns, and Franklin Sanborn, plus the abolitionist Edwin Morton of Plymouth, Massachusetts, and the abolitionist and former slave Frederick Douglass.

66. The League of Peace and Freedom's Inaugural Congress ran in Geneva from September 9 to September 13, 1867. Garibaldi spoke on the first day, and the last of his program of twelve points declared that "the slave alone has the right to make war on tyrants."

67. An pejorative abbreviation of "radical," used after 1820.

68. A region that is on the diametrically opposite side of the earth, in this instance the Indian Ocean—the antipode of North America, where Dana traveled during his fourteen-month journey around the world in 1859 and 1860.

69. The *New York Tribune*, edited by the abolitionist Horace Greeley, and the *New York Evening Post*, edited by the abolitionist William Cullen Bryant.

70. Referring to Thomas Wentworth Higginson's article "A Visit to John Brown's Household in 1859," first published in James Redpath's *The Public Life of Capt. John Brown* (1860), and Wendell Phillips's funeral oration for Brown at North Elba, December 8, 1859.

71. Referring to the Free Soil movement's national convention in Buffalo, New York, in August 1848.

72. In fact, two of Henry's brothers, Dauphin and William Thompson, were killed during the Harpers Ferry raid.

73. Quoting the text of the Dred Scott decision.

74. Galatians 6:7.

75. Crispus Attucks was killed during the Boston Massacre of March 1770.

76. Referring to the massacre of black Union soldiers at the Battle of Fort Pillow in April 1864.

77. From 1842 onward, Garrison proposed disunionism. Arguing that the U.S. Constitution was proslavery and that abolition was impossible in the context of the Union, he explained that slavery would collapse if the North no longer protected slaveholders against slave insurrections.

78. Quoting a resolution offered by Henry Clarke Wright at a meeting of the American Anti-Slavery Society in May 1854.

79. Referring to the Savannah campaign, conducted across Georgia by the Union General William Tecumseh Sherman from November to December 1864.

80. Genesis 1:11 and Matthew 7:16–20.

81. Galatians 6:7.

82. Genesis 8:22.

83. Romans 2:14.

84. Adapting William Shakespeare's *Julius Caesar*, Act 3, Scene 2.

85. Matthew 13:57.

86. Douglass either refers to Seward's observation in his speech of February 29, 1860, that the deaths of the raiders were "necessary and just" or misattributes Hawthorne's comment in his article of July 1862 that Brown was "justly hanged."

87. Quoting John Andrew's "Speech at Tremont Temple," November 18, 1859.

88. Referring to a famous statement by Patrick Henry, a governor of Virginia and a prominent figure in the American Revolution, on March 23, 1775.

89. Acts 22:28.

90. Quoting Brown's "Interview with Senator Mason and Others," October 18, 1859.

91. Referring to Virginia governor Henry Wise, senator James M. Mason, and congressman Clement Laird Vallandigham, all present during Brown's interview at Harpers Ferry, and to Colonel Lewis W. Washington, one of Brown's hostages during the raid and then the chief prosecuting witness at his trial.

92. Drawing on Brown's autobiographical account, "To Mr. Henry L. Stearns," July 15, 1857.

93. Referring to the conversation between William the Silent (also called William of Orange) and King Henry of France during a hunt in France's Bois de Vincennes, when Henry unknowingly revealed French and Spanish plans to purge Protestants from the realm. William remained silent and went on to lead the Dutch revolt against the Spanish that began in 1568. The resumption of warfare in 1618 marked the beginning of the Thirty Years' War.

94. Exodus 2:11.

95. Remembering a conversation with Brown in late 1847, in Springfield, Massachusetts.

96. In 1865, the former governor of Virginia was denied permission to reclaim Rolleston Hall, his plantation outside Norfolk, which he had abandoned to Union troops in 1862. The Freedmen's Bureau used Rolleston as a school for freedmen.

97. A Virginian and former U.S. senator, Mason was confined in Fort Warren, Boston Harbor, between November 1861 and January 1862.

98. An antiwar, pro-Confederate Unionist, the former Ohio representative Vallandigham was arrested in May 1863 for violating General Order No. 38. Issued by Union general Ambrose Burnside, the order made it illegal to criticize the war. Vallandigham was tried and convicted by a military court and sentenced to two years' imprisonment.

99. Robert Anderson commanded Fort Sumter at the start of the Civil War.

100. A priest in Amiens, France, who helped instigate the First Crusade (1096–1099) against Islamic rule.

101. A late eighteenth- and early nineteenth-century self-proclaimed prophet from England who believed she would give birth to the new Messiah (Shiloh, of Genesis 49:10).

102. A Spanish knight and priest who founded the order of Jesuits (the Society of Jesus) in 1534.

103. One of the commanders of the New Model Army, which defeated the royalists in the English Civil War of 1641–1651.

104. An English politician who helped to precipitate the English Civil War.

105. King William III of England, who led the Glorious Revolution of 1688.

106. Paraphrasing a description of Brown's comments by James Redpath in *The Public Life of Capt. John Brown* (1860), 104.

107. Quoting an account by John Kagi (one of Brown's white raiders) of a conversation with Brown in Lawrence, Kansas, in June 1858.

108. 1 Timothy 3:9.

109. Acts 24:16.

110. Alluding to the book by the transcendentalist and abolitionist Octavius Brooks Frothingham, *The Religion of Humanity* (1873), which cites Brown as proof of the

existence of a "conscience of humanity" and as an example of "heroism that dies framing its indictment against tyrannies and wrongs."

111. A British-born abolitionist and journalist, Hinton met Brown in Kansas in 1856.

112. John Kagi, one of the white raiders; Osborne Anderson, one of the black raiders; Owen Brown, one of Brown's sons who joined him on the raid; Richard Realf, who was not at Harpers Ferry but attended Brown's constitutional convention of May 1858; and George B. Gill, who also was absent from the raid but who knew Brown in Kansas and attended the constitutional convention.

113. Job 14:1.

114. Galileo Galilei, the seventeenth-century Italian astronomer; Nicolaus Copernicus, the sixteenth-century Polish astronomer; Isaac Newton, the seventeenth-century English physicist. Williams is wrong that all three men were unappreciated while alive. Although Copernicus was not particularly famous before he died and Galileo was tried by the Inquisition and forced to recant his ideas, Newton was wealthy and celebrated in his own lifetime.

115. Quoting William Cullen Bryant's poem "Thanatopsis" (1817).

116. Winfield Scott, the Union general in chief at the start of the Civil War; George B. McClellan, the Union general in chief from November 1861 to March 1862; Franz Sigel, a Union general between 1861 and 1864; John C. Frémont, a Union general in 1861 and 1862; and Ulysses S. Grant, the Union general in chief from 1864 until the end of the war.

117. Quoting Ralph Waldo Emerson's speech "Courage," November 8, 1859.

118. Quoting Henry David Thoreau's speech "A Plea for Captain John Brown," October 30, 1859.

119. The *Herald of Freedom*, published in Lawrence, Kansas, was the first Free State newspaper in the territory and the organ of the New England Emigrant Aid Company. Its editor was George Washington Brown (who eventually wrote a hostile account of Brown in 1880), and it appeared from October 1854 until December 17, 1859.

120. Utter paraphrases a general New England response to Brown, thinking perhaps of the funeral oration by Wendell Phillips and the speeches by Emerson and Thoreau. But he also responds to Douglass's recent speech "John Brown," May 30, 1881, which explains: "We yet stand too near the days of slavery, and the life and times of John Brown, to see clearly the true martyr and hero that he was and rightly to estimate the value of the man and his works."

121. Referring to José da Fonseca and Pedro Carolino's Portuguese-English phrasebook *English as She is Spoke*, published in the United States in 1883, of which Twain observed: "Nobody can add to the absurdity of this book, nobody can imitate it successfully, nobody can hope to produce its fellow; it is perfect." A companion volume, *English as She is Wrote*, was published in the United States in 1883.

122. Jacob Merrill Manning, pastor of Old South Church, Boston, who spoke at a meeting in support of Brown on November 18 alongside Emerson, Phillips, and John Andrew.

123. Quoting a conversation between Phillips and George Luther Stearns on January 1, 1867.

124. Imagining the Greek philosopher (ca. 469–399 B.C.) living in the age of four Roman emperors who ruled between A.D. 138 and 192.

125. Imagining the sixteenth-century German Protestant reformer Martin Luther as a contemporary of the seventeenth-century French writer and philosopher Voltaire.

126. A sixteenth-century Italian painter whose use of color was influential.

127. Paraphrasing Lincoln's description of "our poor power to add or detract" in his "Address at Gettysburg" of November 19, 1863.

128. Henry VII of England seized the crown from Richard III on the field of battle in 1485.

129. William I, prince of Orange, led the Dutch revolt against the Spanish that began in 1568.

130. George Washington, commander of the Continental Army in the American Revolutionary War, and Honoré Gabriel Riqueti, comte de Mirabeau, a moderate leader during the French Revolution of 1789–1799.

131. Misquoting James Russell Lowell's poem "The Present Crisis" (1844). The lines should read: "Truth forever on the scaffold, / Wrong forever on the throne."

132. Misquoting a line from Vol. 3 of James Anthony Froude's *History of England* (1856): "High treason, if it be not a virtue, is the worst of crimes."

133. Referring to several speeches by U.S. secretary of state Daniel Webster between 1850 and 1852 that denounced William H. Seward's doctrine of the "higher law."

134. The overthrow of King James II of England by Parliamentarians and the Dutch head of state William of Orange.

135. Lawyers who may have attempted to restore the absolute monarchy of kings such as Louis XVI (executed in 1793 during the French Revolution) instead of the constitutional monarchy that lasted in France from 1814 to 1830.

136. Charles X was king of France from 1824 to 1830. His reactionary governance sparked a rebellion and his abdication.

137. A seventeenth-century Scottish market trader who threw a stool at a cathedral minister in protest against Scotland's first public use of the Anglican Book of Common Prayer. Stearns misquotes her exclamation, which was reportedly "Doest thou say mass in my lug [ear]?"

138. One of the commanders of the New Model Army, which defeated the royalists in the English Civil War of 1641–1651.

139. Referring to Frederick Douglass, "John Brown," May 30, 1881.

140. Referring to Hermann von Holst's *John Brown,* published in the United States the previous year.

Further Reading

Barry, Joseph. *The Strange Story of Harper's Ferry, With Legends of the Surrounding Country.* Martinsburg, WV: Thompson Brothers, 1903.

Beck, Janet Kemper. *Creating the John Brown Legend: Emerson, Thoreau, Douglass, Child and Higginson in Defense of the Raid on Harpers Ferry.* Jefferson, NC: McFarland, 2009.

Boyer, Richard O. *The Legend of John Brown: A Biography and a History.* New York: Knopf, 1973.

Carton, Evan. *Patriotic Treason: John Brown and the Soul of America.* New York: Free Press, 2006.

DeCaro, Louis A. *Fire from the Midst of You: A Religious Life of John Brown.* New York: New York University Press, 2002.

———. *John Brown: The Cost of Freedom.* New York: International, 2007.

Du Bois, W. E. B. *John Brown.* Philadelphia: G. W. Jacobs, 1909.

Ferguson, Robert A. *The Trial in American Life.* Chicago: University of Chicago Press, 2007.

Gilpin, R. Blakeslee. *John Brown Still Lives!: America's Long Reckoning with Violence, Equality, and Change.* Chapel Hill: University of North Carolina Press, 2011.

Hinton, Richard J. *John Brown and His Men.* London: Funk & Wagnalls, 1894.

Horwitz, Tony. *Midnight Rising: John Brown and the Raid That Sparked the Civil War.* New York: Holt, 2011.

McGinty, Brian. *John Brown's Trial.* Cambridge, MA: Harvard University Press, 2009.

McGlone, Robert E. *John Brown's War against Slavery.* New York: Cambridge University Press, 2009.

McKivigan, John R. *Forgotten Firebrand: James Redpath and the Making of Nineteenth-Century America.* Ithaca: Cornell University Press, 2008.

Nudelman, Franny. *John Brown's Body: Slavery, Violence, and the Culture of War.* Chapel Hill: University of North Carolina Press, 2004.

Oates, Stephen B. *To Purge This Land with Blood: A Biography of John Brown.* New York: Harper and Row, 1970.

Peterson, Merrill D. *John Brown: The Legend Revisited.* Charlottesville: University of Virginia Press, 2002.

Quarles, Benjamin. *Allies for Freedom (1974), Blacks on John Brown (1972).* New York: Da Capo, 2001.

Redpath, James. *Echoes of Harper's Ferry.* Boston: Thayer and Eldridge, 1860.

———. *The Public Life of Capt. John Brown.* Boston: Thayer and Eldridge, 1860.

Renehan, Edward J., Jr. *The Secret Six: The True Tale of the Men Who Conspired with John Brown.* New York: Crown, 1995.

Reynolds, David S. *John Brown, Abolitionist: The Man Who Killed Slavery, Sparked the Civil War, and Seeded Civil Rights.* New York: Knopf, 2005.

Ronda, Bruce A. *Reading the Old Man: John Brown in American Culture.* Knoxville: University of Tennessee Press, 2008.

Rossbach, Jeffery. *Ambivalent Conspirators: John Brown, the Secret Six, and a Theory of Slave Violence.* Philadelphia: University of Pennsylvania Press, 1982.

Russo, Peggy A., and Paul Finkelman, eds. *Terrible Swift Sword: The Legacy of John Brown.* Athens: Ohio University Press, 2005.

Sanborn, Franklin B. *The Life and Letters of John Brown, Liberator of Kansas and Martyr of Virginia.* Boston: Roberts Bros., 1885.

Scott, Otto. *The Secret Six: John Brown and the Abolitionist Movement.* New York: Times Books, 1979.

Stauffer, John. *The Black Hearts of Men: Radical Abolitionists and the Transformation of Race.* Cambridge, MA: Harvard University Press, 2002.

Stoneham, Michael. *John Brown and the Era of Literary Confrontation.* New York: Routledge, 2009.

Taylor, Andrew, and Eldrid Herrington, eds. *The Afterlife of John Brown.* New York: Palgrave Macmillan, 2005.

Villard, Oswald Garrison. *John Brown, 1800–1859: A Biography Fifty Years After.* Boston: Houghton Mifflin, 1910.

Von Holst, Hermann. *The Constitutional and Political History of the United States,* vol. 7: *1859–1861, Harper's Ferry—Lincoln's Inauguration.* Translated from the German by John J. Lalor. Chicago: Callaghan, 1892.

———. *John Brown.* Edited by Frank Preston Stearns. Boston: Cupples and Hurd, 1888.

Index

Note: *Throughout the index, "raid" refers to John Brown's raid at Harpers Ferry.*

Brown, John, Jr. (son): capture at Pottawatomie, 13; defense of father, 505; thank-you
letter to Haitian president, 400
Brown, Mary Day (wife): Brown's farewell
letter to, 70–73; during Brown's imprisonment, 60, 226; Brown's prison letters to,
56–58, 59–61; last visit with husband, 186;
letter to following Kansas battles, 12–16;
Louisa Alcott's comments on, 198;
marriages and children, xxiii; praise for, in
the *Aberdeen Herald*, 380–381. *See also*
fundraising for Brown family
Brown, Oliver (son), 56–57, 520n24
Brown, Owen (father), xxii, 61
Brown, Owen (son): appearance in Ruffin's
Anticipation of War, 262; escape by, 485,
520n13; ill health, 15; as imagined leader of
raid by blacks, 267–270; life after Harpers
Ferry, 532n24; during planning for raid, 503
Brown, Peter (ancestor), 64, 114, 389, 502
Brown, Salmon (son), 16, 520n19
Brown, William Wells, 7
"Brown of Ossawatomie" (Whittier), 190–191
Buchanan, James: attempts to arrest Douglass,
494; as Herod, in *Lloyd's Weekly*, 391; *Mr.
Buchanan's Administration on the Eve of the
Rebellion*, 473–475; as Northern Democrat,
473; presidential administration, 178, 335,
345; role during raid, xxx, 473
Bunker Hill monument, 136, 167
Burns, Anthony: Dana's representation of,
482; forcible return to slavery, 105; rescue
attempt, 164, 174, 524n9
Burr, C. Chauncey, 465–467
Butler, Andrew, 188
Butler, Benjamin, Volck caricature of, 445–446

Caledonian Mercury and Daily Express,
Edinburgh, 393–394
Calhoun, John C., xxxviii
California State Convention of Colored
Citizens, 454
Call, Richard K., 342
Calvinism, lii n15
Campbell, Elizabeth Georgiana (Duchess of
Argyll), 188–189
Campbell, James W., 533n34
Canada, abolitionist activity in, xxvi–xxvii;

xxx, 47, 50, 77, 94, 128, 375. *See also*
Anderson, Osborne Perry; Chatham,
Ontario, Canada
Cannibals All! (Fitzhugh), 316
capitalist exploitation: Fitzhugh's attacks on,
316; slavery and, Marx's view, 399
"Capt. John Brown Not Insane" (Douglass),
117–119
Carlyle, Thomas, defense of slavery, 415
Central Southern Rights Association, "Resolu-
tions," 262–264
Century magazine, 325
Chappelear, Armisted, 272
Charles I, king of England, 110, 533n40
Charleston, SC: Charleston New England
Society, xxxix; Democratic National
Convention, 1860, xliii–xliv; vandalism by
blacks following Harpers Ferry raid, 274.
See also Civil War; secession, dissolution
Charleston Mercury: Rhett article in, 237;
serializing of *Anticipations of War* in, 262;
Simms's letter in, 337
Charles Town Jail, Charles Town, VA (now
WV): Brown's imprisonment at, 1; Brown's
letters from, 19; Dwight's visits to during
the Civil War, 431–432; Rosengarten's
description of, 464; use of during war,
431–432, 464
Chase, Salmon P.: condemnation of raid, 99;
financial support for Brown's causes, xlv;
government service, 538n10; "To Joseph H.
Barrett," 99; political ambitions, xlv;
Sherman's praise for, 438–439
Chatham, Ontario, Canada: abolitionist work
in, 228; constitutional convention, xxx, 26;
Jackson in, 375
Chavannes, Jean-Baptiste, 401, 537n35
Cheever, George, 171
Chesson, F. W., 411
Chesnut, James, Jr., 429
Chesnut, Mary Boykin Miller, 429–430
Chew, R. P., 433
Chicago Defender, proposal of holiday on
Brown's birthday, xlviii
"Chiefly About War Matters. By a Peaceable
Man" (Hawthorne), 435
Child, Lydia Maria: antislavery writings and
poetry, 89; "Dear Captain Brown," 89–90;